NOTHING TOO DARING

D1563766

Nothing Too Daring

A BIOGRAPHY OF COMMODORE DAVID PORTER, 1780–1843

DAVID F. LONG

NAVAL INSTITUTE PRESS
ANNAPOLIS, MARYLAND

This book has been brought to publication with the generous assistance of Marguerite and Gerry Lenfest.

Naval Institute Press
291 Wood Road
Annapolis, MD 21402

First Naval Institute Press paperback edition published in 2014.
ISBN: 978-1-59114-430-4 (paperback)
ISBN: 978-1-61251-319-5 (ebook)

LIBRARY OF CONGRESS CATALOGUE CARD NO. 78–94781
ISBN 0–87021–494–2

♾ Print editions meet the requirements of ANSI/NISO z39.48-1992 (Permanence of Paper).
Printed in the United States of America.

22 21 20 19 18 17 16 15 14   9 8 7 6 5 4 3 2 1
First printing

TO MY CHILDREN, ELISABETH AND ROGER

I first became interested in Commodore David Porter, U.S. Navy, when, in connection with other work I was doing, I came upon the story of his abortive annexation to the United States of Nukahiva in the Marquesas Islands, an adventure that made him the first American imperialist. Research revealed that he also had fundamentally altered world economic patterns by crippling the British whaling industry in the Pacific during the War of 1812, thereby helping to give the United States what was, to all intents and purposes, a monopoly on that lucrative, if unpleasant, business until the time of the Civil War. As early as 1815 he suggested officially that the U.S. Navy force open Japan. First as a visitor to Chile in 1813–1814, then as a leading member of a cabal in Washington from 1816–1820, and finally as head of the Mexican Navy from 1826–1829, Porter greatly influenced the circumstances and directions of U.S. Latin-American policy. He seriously interfered with the quid pro quo of the Monroe Doctrine by invading Spanish Puerto Rico less than a year after the President had issued his famous policy statement. As the first U.S. chargé d'affaires in Constantinople and then as U.S. minister to the Ottoman Empire, he established direct diplomatic relations between the United States and the Middle East.

Porter was on terms of intimacy, either friendly or hostile, with Presidents James Madison, James Monroe, John Quincy Adams, and Andrew Jackson; with Henry Clay, Albert Gallatin, the Marquis de Lafayette, Washington Irving, Antonio López de Santa Anna, Sultan Mahmud II of the Ottoman Empire, Stephen Decatur, James Wilkinson, and a host of lesser lights. His foster-son, David Glasgow Farragut, and his own son, David Dixon Porter, were, respectively, the first and second admirals in the history of the U.S. Navy. His personal life was gaudy. His wife bore him ten children, but his relationship with her ended disastrously. Apparently, she was rather spectacularly unfaithful to him, helped ruin him financially, and refused to live with him during the final thirteen years of his life. Each tried to turn the children against the other, through mutual accusations of insanity; perhaps both were right. The eldest of Porter's seven sons was a liar, a cheat, an adulterer, and probably a thief; and all but one of them died under tragic circumstances.

Heretofore, only two biographies of David Porter have been written, and both are totally inadequate. The first, *Memoir of Commodore David Porter of the United States Navy,* was written in 1875 by his son, Admiral David Dixon Porter, whose exercise in filial devotion may be condoned, but not his astonishing mistakes and omissions. The second, *Commodore David Porter, 1780–1843,* was written in 1929 by Captain Archibald D. Turnbull, who managed to repeat almost all of David Dixon Porter's errors, while adding some of his own. Neither biographer bothered to check the records.

I owe many debts of gratitude for assistance in writing this biography. Individuals who have aided me either in personal interviews or by correspondence are: Abdul Aziz, Director of Antiquities, Tripoli, Libya; Marion V. Brewington, Peabody Museum, Salem, Massachusetts; Wendell Garrett, Associate Editor, The Adams Papers, Massachusetts Historical Society; Mrs. Marguerite Porter Glendinning, Annapolis, Maryland (David Porter's great-great-granddaughter); William F. Keller, Henry Marie Brackenridge's biographer; John D. Kilbourne, Librarian, Maryland Historical Society; Alberic G. Lightbourne, Postmaster, Fajardo, Puerto Rico; Robert B. Lyle, Executive Director, Columbia Historical Society; Jorge Ivan Rosa-Silva, Chairman of the History Department, University of Puerto Rico; Edouard A. Stackpole, whaling authority, Nantucket, Massachusetts; Mr. and Mrs. Carroll Van Ness, Owings Mills, Maryland (descendants of David Porter, who own some of his previously unused papers); Guy Weatherly, Archivist, Hall of Records, Annapolis, Maryland; the late Richard S. West, Jr., former Professor of History, U.S. Naval Academy, Annapolis, Maryland.

The staffs of the following libraries and archives have been most helpful: the Library of Congress, the National Archives, the Public Record Office (London), and the British Museum; the historical societies of Maryland, Massachusetts, New Hampshire, New Jersey, New York, and Pennsylvania, as well as the American Antiquarian Society, the Columbia Historical Society, and the Essex Institute (Salem, Massachusetts); the Boston Athenaeum; the state libraries of Massachusetts and New Hampshire; the city libraries of Atlantic City, Concord (New Hampshire), New York, and Portsmouth (New Hampshire); the Nantucket Whaling Museum, the Peabody Museum (Salem, Massachusetts), and the U.S. Naval Academy Museum; and the libraries of Bowdoin College, the

Catholic University, Columbia University, Dartmouth College, Harvard University, Makerere University College (Kampala, Uganda), the University of Michigan, the University of Pennsylvania, the University of Pittsburgh, Princeton University, the University of Puerto Rico, Trinity College, the U.S. Naval Academy, and especially the University of New Hampshire and its reference staff, headed by the tireless and perceptive Hugh Pritchard.

DAVID F. LONG

Durham, New Hampshire

TABLE OF CONTENTS

". . . I am getting old, have had many sorrows, much sickness and affliction. . . . I have never been elated with prosperity, and ought not, and I hope am not depressed at the loss of worldly goods. My country has thus far taken care of me, and I hope by good conduct to merit what she has done, by endeavoring to serve her to the utmost of my power. There was a time when there was nothing that I thought too daring to be attempted for her; but those times are past, and appear only as a confused and painful dream. A retrospect of the history of my life seems a highly-coloured romance, which I should be very loth to live over again. . . ."

DAVID PORTER TO DAVID GLASGOW FARRAGUT

20 JUNE 1835

ILLUSTRATIONS

Thomas Truxtun
Courtesy of Long Island Historical Society, New York

William Bainbridge
Courtesy of Mr. F. S. Hicks

The Stranding and Capture of the *Philadelphia* before Tripoli

Washington Irving

Samuel Hambleton
Office of Naval History

Evalina Anderson Porter and her Daughter, Evalina
Courtesy of Coward-McCann, Inc.

The Frigate *Essex*
From Painting by Joseph Howard in Peabody Museum

John Downes
U.S. Naval Academy Museum

James Biddle
U.S. Naval Academy Museum

William Gifford
Historical Pictures Service

Joel R. Poinsett
U.S. Naval Academy Museum

The *Essex* Capturing the Sloop *Alert*
Office of Naval History

Commodore Porter's Drawing of the *Essex* and Her Prizes Lying off
Nukahiva, with Madisonville in the Background

James Hillyar
Courtesy of Parker H. Kemble

Commodore Porter's Drawing of the Battle of Valparaiso

John Rodgers
U.S. Naval Academy Museum

Jesse D. Elliott
Office of Naval History

James Barron
Library of Congress

Stephen Decatur
Library of Congress

José Miguel Carrera
Library of Congress

José de San Martín

James Monroe

The Barges *Gallinipper* and *Musquito* off the Coast of Cuba
Office of Naval History

Samuel L. Southard
Office of Naval History

John Quincy Adams

The Waterfront at Constantinople

I

An older school of writing was apt to start the biography of a military or naval man with a lengthy perusal of his family background, and the more ancient and the more warlike, the better. Captain Archibald D. Turnbull, one of David Porter's biographers, went back to the Crusades, where he unearthed a forebear who held the gates of the king's palace so well that he was dubbed "Le Porteur." This discovery enabled Turnbull to accentuate the martial genes of the Porter germ plasm and to comment that "Good blood ran in their veins," since they all "had a nose for fighting."

In a handwritten account of his own ancestry, David Porter was content to begin with his paternal grandfather, Alexander, a captain in the merchant marine who was born in Massachusetts in 1727 and who took part in mid-century colonial wars. David Porter the elder,* born in 1754, was the first of Alexander's seven children. He commanded merchantmen and, in the American Revolution, served as a midshipman in the 32-gun frigate *Raleigh* under Captain John Barry. On 27 September 1778, the *Raleigh* was trapped off the coast of Maine by superior British forces and beached. Although Barry and some of the crew managed to escape, others were taken, among them David Porter. He was confined in the notorious British "hell-ship" *Jersey*, where he had to watch his brother and fellow-prisoner die.

According to family tradition, the affable David was so well liked by his British captors that he was smuggled to freedom in an empty water cask. In 1779 he participated in an expedition that tried to dislodge the British from the region of the Penobscot River in Maine. The American

---

* This designation is used to avoid confusion between the four members of the family who were named David: David Porter the elder; David Porter the younger, the subject of this biography; his son, David Dixon Porter, an admiral during the Civil War and his father's biographer; and his nephew, David H. Porter, who was killed in action in 1828 while serving under his uncle in Mexico.

fleet was cut off and almost all the ships were bagged, but most of the men made their way back by land to Massachusetts. Later in the Revolution, Porter commanded the privateers *Delight* and *Aurora*. About the time peace was concluded, David Porter moved from Boston to Baltimore, where he captained a revenue cutter and took charge of the signal station.[1]

Evidently, he disliked shore duty, for it seems that he took frequent leaves and spent them serving in merchantmen, but he always kept an eye out for a better job with the government. At least twice he tried to capitalize on his acquaintance with his former captain, John Barry. In 1793 he sought the appointment to the job of surveyor for Baltimore, but Barry would not recommend him. During the trouble with France in the late 1790s, he applied for command of a ship of war, but again Barry would do nothing; Captain Thomas Truxtun's assurance that he was "sober and attentive" was not enough to get him a command. Porter was apparently dropped from the federal payroll in 1799.[2]

On 13 February 1779 he married Rebecca Henry in Boston.* David Porter the younger, who was the oldest in their family of four daughters and two sons, was born in Boston on 1 February 1780, but he claimed little kinship with New England, since he was only three years old when his father moved the family to Baltimore. Save for the encomiums of her grandson, who describes her as "an excellent woman" of "strict integrity," "always guided by the principles of religion," little is known about Rebecca Porter. She seems to have been overly protective of her eldest child. Not only was her husband usually away at sea, leaving family responsibility to her, but young David was delicate—he was even described as a "puny stribling"—a condition sure to arouse the most aggressive maternal instincts. Nevertheless, she could never counteract the influence her husband had on their son. According to Washington Irving, when David Porter the elder was home he would pour out stories ". . . of peril and adventure and . . . the wonders and vicissitudes that chequer a seafaring life. Little David would sit for hours . . . and kindle at these marvelous tales."[3]

What documentation there is concerning David Porter the younger between 1796 and 1798 is fragmentary and confused. Most details of his activities during that period are based upon the undated and unsubstan-

---

* In a note published in *The New England Historical and Genealogical Register*, David Dixon Porter claimed that his grandmother's maiden name was Rebecca Gay. His memory must have failed him. A Rebecca Gay was born on 9 March 1756, but there is no record of the marriage of a person of that name in *Boston Marriages, 1752–1809*. The same source records for 13 February 1779, "David Porter married Rebecca Henry."

tiated material in his son's biography. One occurrence, however, was reported in detail by Baltimore's *Federal Gazette* during March 1796. Early that year, the sixteen-year-old boy was allowed to sail for the West Indies in the merchantman *Eliza,* commanded by his father, and it was a memorable first cruise. The *Eliza* put in at the port of Jérémie in the southwestern part of what is now Haiti. The crews of the sixteen American ships anchored there suffered from a fear that was common in that day—impressment. British warships habitually boarded neutral merchantmen to search for and remove ostensible deserters from the Royal Navy. If really shorthanded, they would kidnap American citizens or anyone else.

The arrival at Jérémie on 10 February of the British "private armed ship" *Harriet,* under a New Yorker named John Reynolds, created havoc. Although commanding only a privateer, Reynolds acted as if he trod the decks of an English ship of the line. He impressed several Americans, and returned for more. The beleaguered crews gathered in the *Eliza* and refused to allow him to board. They had no small arms, so they greeted him, reported the *Federal Gazette,* "with a warm salute of wood, stones, handspikes, and crow-bars, which obliged him to sheer off. In a short time he returned with his boat, and twenty men, armed with guns, swords, and cutlasses." Reynolds was quoted as shouting inelegantly, "Now you bugers * we will cool you!" but again he was beaten back. "Several men were killed and wounded on both sides, and one man was shot down by the side of the young Porter, who was lending his feeble aid to help drive the pressgang from the ship." The Americans then moved to a more defensible ship, and when Reynolds returned to the empty *Eliza,* he "cut her cables, sails and rigging, broke the cabin furniture, and destroyed every thing in a most outrageous manner." The Porters and their half-destroyed ship were back in Baltimore by 15 March, and when they told of their adventures, the local press was loud in its condemnation of this evidence of "British Amity!"

Whether David Porter the younger went along on the *Eliza's* next cruise is not known, but it too was an unhappy voyage. In a long and emotional letter published in the Baltimore papers, his father related that on 26 May, two days out from Jérémie, he had been stopped by two privateers flying the French colors, although their crews, totaling five whites and seventeen Negroes, were from the British Bahamas. Before the

---

* In view of the large amount of quoted material contained in this book, original spellings have been retained in order to avoid repetitious use of the word *sic.* Where misunderstanding might occur, the word intended has been inserted in brackets.

Eliza was permitted to continue on her way, her passengers had been robbed and her cargo looted.

According to the flimsy evidence furnished by his son, David Porter the younger had two other experiences during the years between 1796 and 1798. In the first, he shipped out once more for the Caribbean, this time without paternal protection. In one of the ports of "San Domingo," Porter's captain meekly acceded to a British search demand. The crew was imprisoned and given the alternative of enlisting in the Royal Navy or facing summary punishment by the cat-o'-nine-tails. Porter broke away and hid below—strangely enough the captain did not order any search for him—until friendly English sailors smuggled him ashore, in circumstances suspiciously like those of his father's escape eighteen years before. Having no funds, the only way he could get home was to take a Danish vessel to Copenhagen, and a second to the United States, working both passages as a common sailor.

In the second unsubstantiated account, Porter was taken off a merchant ship in the Caribbean and actually impressed into the Royal Navy, only to escape once more. Whether or not either of these episodes actually took place, it can at least be said that he suffered enough unpleasantness as an adolescent in the West Indies to give him an abiding detestation for Great Britain.[4]

With such a background, it was natural that David Porter the younger should turn to the U.S. Navy. That service, which had been moribund since the Revolution, was beginning to be rebuilt in the face of mounting hostility with France. In 1778, the United States and France had concluded a treaty but, by 1798, the United States had unilaterally terminated it and relations between the two countries had deteriorated to the point where shots were being exchanged. This state of affairs is called by the Navy "The Quasi-War with France," but is more generally known as "The Undeclared Naval War with France." When hostilities commenced, the only U.S. naval ships actually operative were the 44-gun *Constitution* and the 38-gun *Constellation,* but four other frigates and a number of smaller craft were under construction, and there was a corresponding need for men. Porter's commission as a midshipman, which was dated 16 April 1798, was the beginning of twenty-eight years of service in the Navy. In search of an appointment for himself, David Porter the elder wrote to John Barry and added a postscript to his letter: "I have put my son David on board the frigate *Constellation.* He is just entered his nineteenth year, he is active, and promising, and understands navigation well, a tolerable good scholer otherways; he has been several voyages to sea. . . ."

As sixth midshipman, Porter ranked twentieth in the *Constellation's* chain of command.* Captain Thomas Truxtun and First Lieutenant John Rodgers ranked first and second. That they ran a rough school on a taut ship is proven by the oddity that the only American to die during the engagement between the *Constellation* and the French frigate *L'Insurgente* was a sailor named Neale Harvey, and he was killed by Lieutenant Andrew Sterrett for panicking in action. In a widely published letter to his brother, Sterrett boasted of his deed: "One fellow I was obliged to run through the body with my sword, and so put an end to a coward. You must not think this strange, for we would put a man to death for even looking pale on board *this* ship."

Discipline in the *Constellation* was according to Truxtun's whim; no naval regulations had then been formulated. Midshipmen as well as ordinary sailors could be flogged or put in irons. Porter found these conditions almost unbearable, and is reported to have told the captain that he was considering resignation. Truxtun bellowed in reply:

> Why you young dog! If I can help it you shall never leave the navy! Swear at you? Damn it, sir—every time I do that you go a round on the ladder of promotion! As for the first lieutenant's blowing you up every day, why, sir, 'tis because he loves you and would not have you grow up a conceited young coxcomb. Go forward and let us have no more whining.

Moreover, on one occasion, when Porter found himself in a situation that could have been disastrous, Truxtun stood by him. Lieutenant Simon Gross, often drunk and always abusive, appears to have taken pleasure in baiting Porter, and once when the latter replied "disrespectfully," hit him in the face, knocking him down. Porter got up and felled the lieutenant with a single punch. Immediately arrested by Truxtun and charged with striking a superior officer, Porter was due to face a court-martial and, almost certainly, dismissal from the service. But after reviewing the evidence, Truxtun restored him to duty. Gross was soon ousted for drunkenness, and it is said that he returned to the Navy as a common seaman and served on Porter's barge during his attack off Tripoli in 1803.

Although Porter never forgot the humiliations of those first months in service, he maintained a lifelong friendship with Truxtun and is alleged to have congratulated himself on having been brought up "in such a thorough naval school." Forty years later, clearly with Truxtun in mind, he compared the Turkish Sultan to a captain in the U.S. Navy:

---

* At that time, naval officers were graded as follows: midshipman, lieutenant, master commandant (equivalent to lieutenant commander), and captain. "Commodore" was a courtesy title for a captain who commanded a squadron. The rank of admiral did not come into use until the time of the Civil War.

The Sultan Mahmoud [Sultan Mahmud II of the Ottoman Empire], the most absolute sovereign on earth, can afford to be kind and courteous to those around him, but the little tyrant, who struts his few fathoms of scoured plank, dare not unbend, lest he should lose that appearance of respect from his inferiors that their fears inspire. He has, therefore, no society, no smiles, no courtesies for or from anyone . . . a solitary being in the midst of the ocean. . . . A man of war is a petty kingdom, and is governed by a petty despot. . . ." [5]

The *Constellation*, under orders to attack any armed French ships, sailed for the West Indies on 20 August 1798 to protect American commerce. About noon on 9 February 1799 she was plying the waters off Nevis Island when a strange sail approached, soon identified as the French frigate *L'Insurgente* under Captain Barreault. *L'Insurgente* was known to be one of the fastest frigates afloat, and had recently enjoyed the triumph of retaking a captured French prize. Perhaps it was lucky for the *Constellation* that in a squall that morning her adversary had cracked her main topmast.* Nevertheless, Barreault was in a fighting mood.

So was Truxtun. As he later reported to the Secretary of the Navy, forcefully if ungrammatically, "the french Captain tell me, I have caused a War with France, if so I am glad of it, for I detest things being done by Halves." Indeed, Truxtun handled his encounter with Barreault by "Wholes." *L'Insurgente*'s fire power was concentrated in carronades, guns effective only at short range, and she carried about 400 men, to the *Constellation*'s 309. Truxtun, therefore, had to avoid closing with the crippled French vessel, so he sailed around her hammering her from afar with long guns. According to his son, Porter was responsible for saving the *Constellation* shortly after the battle commenced. As officer in charge of the fore-topmast, he noticed that it had been hit and was swinging loosely. In the din of combat, he could not attract the attention of his superiors for specific orders, so on his own initiative he climbed up to free and lower the damaged rigging before the weight of its hanging sails brought down the entire mast. An hour and a quarter later, *L'Insurgente* was wallowing helplessly, her masts in splinters and her sails in rags; more than seventy of her crew had been killed or wounded. Barreault surrendered.† Apart from the pallid sailor mentioned earlier who was unlucky enough to attract Lieutenant Andrew Sterrett's attention,

---

* A similar stroke of ill-luck crippled David Porter's *Essex* in her battle against the *Phoebe* and the *Cherub* off Valparaiso, Chile, in 1814. On large sailing ships of that day, the main topmast was essential for maneuvering.

† *L'Insurgente* could be called a Jonah. She was recommissioned as the USS *Insurgent* and during the summer of 1800 sailed on what was to have been an eight-week voyage. She vanished with all hands.

the only casualties in the *Constellation* were three wounded, one mortally.[6]

Truxtun dispatched Lieutenant John Rodgers, Midshipman Porter, and eleven sailors to take possession of the stricken enemy ship, whose decks were littered with bodies and gear. According to one account, the boarding party managed to transfer most of the prisoners to the *Constellation* during the remainder of the day, but after dark the two ships became separated. For the next three nights and two days, the thirteen Americans had the unenviable task of sailing a large, badly damaged frigate through heavy seas and, at the same time, controlling the 173 French captives still on board. Furthermore, by the time the Americans boarded her, the prisoners had thrown over the side all manacles, fetters, and iron hatchway grates. Rodgers and six or seven of the sailors operated the ship, while, by such means as a loaded cannon aimed at the main hatchway, ready to fire at the first hostile movement, Porter and the other sailors prevented her from being recaptured. Somehow, they managed to take *L'Insurgente* in to the harbor of St. Kitts, where she rejoined the *Constellation*.

It is quite a story, but its authenticity rests upon a single account not published until a quarter-century after the event: Charles Goldsborough's *United States Naval Chronicle*, 1824. Neither Truxtun, nor Rodgers, nor Porter mentioned the episode at the time. Truxtun's official report says only: "I immediately took possession of her, exchanged the Prisoners. . . . On the 13th [of February] after the greatest Exertions having been made, we gained these Roads [St. Kitts] with both ships. . . ." Rodgers said nothing about such an experience in a letter he wrote to a friend in Baltimore. Even more damaging to the creditability of the story is a letter David Porter wrote to his parents from St. Kitts on 16 February 1799: "I had the honor of being sent with Mr. Rogers to take possession of her." [7] It would be strange for an eighteen-year-old not to brag a little about such a memorable experience. On the other hand, Charles Goldsborough, who was appointed Navy Clerk in 1798 and spent most of his life in that service, on occasion as Acting Secretary, is considered reliable, and it is difficult to believe that he would have made up the episode. Furthermore, a year and a half after it is supposed to have taken place, Porter on his own accomplished very much the same thing on the *Deux Amis*. It is probably reasonable to conclude that, despite the lack of corroborating evidence, Rodgers and Porter did bring in *L'Insurgente* in the manner described by Goldsborough.

Before returning to the *Constellation*, Porter spent a couple of uneventful months in *L'Union*, a French prize, but by that time his career had been distinguished enough to attract the attention of his superiors.

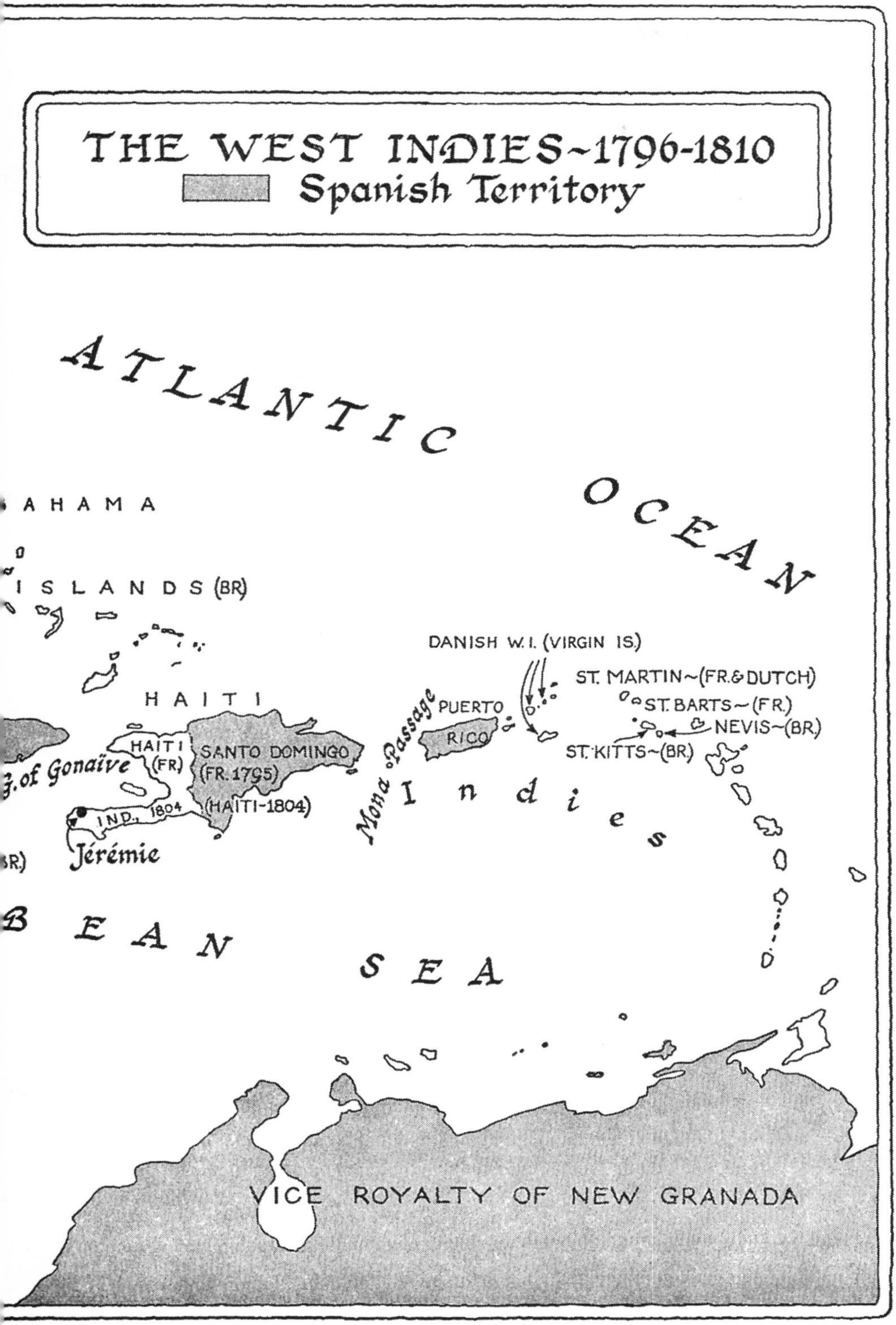

THE WEST INDIES ~ 1796-1810
Spanish Territory

ATLANTIC

OCEAN

AHAMA

ISLANDS (BR)

DANISH W.I. (VIRGIN IS.)

ST. MARTIN ~ (FR. & DUTCH)

ST. BARTS ~ (FR.)

NEVIS ~ (BR)

ST. KITTS ~ (BR)

HAITI

PUERTO

RICO

HAITI
(FR)

SANTO DOMINGO
(FR. 1795)

(HAITI-1804)

G. of Gonaïve

IND. 1804

Mona Passage

I n d i e s

Jérémie

BR)

B E A N

S E A

VICE ROYALTY OF NEW GRANADA

On 23 September 1799, Secretary of the Navy Benjamin Stoddert wrote to Samuel Barron, the new captain of the *Constellation,* to ask if Porter was qualified ". . . for a lieutenant of a Twenty-Gun ship or a 12-Gun Schooner. . . . But if he is not fit say nothing to him." He evidently was "fit": his commission as a lieutenant was dated 8 October 1799.

The nineteen-year-old Porter was assigned as Second Lieutenant in the *Experiment,* a 60-foot, shallow-draft, 20-gun schooner, designed for close offshore service in the West Indies. Although her name gives evidence that there was, at the outset, some doubt as to how useful she would be, the *Experiment* "turned out to be an ideal ship for Caribbean waters: fast as a streak, able to work windward far better than a square-rigger, and capable of ghosting along through the semi-calms of the islands." [8]

For almost forty years after 1790 the Caribbean was plagued by the disorders that attended, first, the French Revolution, then, the Napoleonic Wars, and, finally, the Spanish-American revolutions. During this period an assortment of ephemeral governments issued commissions to privateers, supposedly to assail enemy shipping only. But these privateers became afflicted with an opportunistic myopia which made it impossible for them to differentiate between friend and foe; they became neither more nor less than pirates.

In 1800 turbulence centered around the island of Haiti. Ever since the slave insurrection of 1791, there had been kaleidoscopic changes of power in the French western part of that island: Haitian whites, mulattoes, and Negroes; English, Spanish, and French invaders had all been involved. An able Negro, Toussaint L'Ouverture, finally emerged as the dominant personality on the island, although General André Rigaud, a mulatto and an enemy of L'Ouverture, still controlled western Haiti. Rigaud's pirates, the so-called "picaroons," swarming out from the coast in boats that carried a single gun and some forty men, harried the shipping of all nations.

When Porter joined the *Experiment,* her skipper was Lieutenant William Maley, an obvious misfit, who continuously quarreled with his officers, and his new lieutenant was soon numbered among the malcontents. To Maley's juniors, his unforgivable sin was the cowardice he exhibited on 1 January 1800 in Haiti's Bight of Leogane, now the Gulf of Gonaives. While convoying four American merchant ships along the coast, the *Experiment* was becalmed and soon about 400 of Rigaud's men in ten barges rowed toward the little flotilla. Maley studied this unpleasant scene and announced that resistance was hopeless; he would surrender. Backed by the other officers, Porter immediately shunted Maley aside and took command. The *Experiment* fired into the pirate barges effectively enough to compel them to withdraw. But, after gathering reinforcements, they returned and deployed so as to attack from several directions simultaneously. Maley took no part in the fighting, which continued for over three hours, and in the course of which the picaroons lost three barges and suffered heavy casualties.

Nevertheless, the Americans could not by any means claim total victory, for during the morning their assailants had temporarily occupied one merchantman, and during the afternoon they picked off two more before enough of a breeze came up to enable the *Experiment* and the two remaining vessels to escape. Porter was exposed throughout the engagement and received "a slight contusion" from a musket ball in his arm. Thirty-eight years later, however, when his friends were anxious to back his application for a disability pension from the Navy, it appeared that the "slight contusion" was close to a mortal wound.

Maley's official account of the action in the Bight of Leogane does not mention the fact that he was superseded by Porter, but there is no doubt that it was so. Although he managed to rid himself of his lieutenant, he never dared to prefer charges against him for assuming authority in battle, surely the most heinous of offenses against a commanding officer. However, the story leaked out, to be added to the complaints of Maley's juniors which had become too "numerous and complicated" for the Department to ignore. Maley was eventually investigated on eighteen specific counts, among them drunkenness, brutality, and—an unusually "complicated" complaint—his challenge to "all the officers of the *Experiment* cockpit to fight across the deck." The accused tried to explain to the Secretary of the Navy: "I was sitting in my cabin and heard Mr. Sheridan [Marine Lieutenant Nathan R. Sheridine] say that . . . I was a damn'd rascal for recommending the removal of Mr. Porter . . . alledging that I had done it out of enmity and ill will." Despite his protestations, he was dismissed from the Navy on 12 November 1800.[9]

Months before Maley's departure, Porter had been sent to the *Constitution,* commanded by Captain Silas Talbot, a tour of duty he looked upon with distaste. Not only did he revel in the comparative independence that serving in small craft allowed, but he had openly supported his old commander, Thomas Truxtun, against Talbot in a squabble about their relative seniority. However, Talbot showed no animosity. Instead, he delighted his new lieutenant by detaching him from the *Constitution* and awarding him his first command, that of the "armed tender" *Amphitheatre,** a small schooner that had been captured by the *Experiment.*

---

* Both primary and secondary sources occasionally use the classical name, *Amphitrite.* Fletcher Pratt is probably correct when he dismisses that practice as mere "prettying up," for there is no doubt that her name was *Amphitheatre.*

In March 1800 Porter was ordered to cruise off Haiti and to allow passage to vessels with "passports" signed by "General Toussant Louvertures." The exhilaration of giving, rather than taking, orders did not last long, and about the only excitement was an encounter with some pirate barges, during which the largest enemy boat was sunk and an American merchantman was recaptured. In July of that year, on orders from the Navy Department, Porter sailed the *Amphitheatre* to Philadelphia, where he sold her for an unimpressive $1,550.[10]

Porter was next assigned to the *Experiment,* not as commander but as First Lieutenant under Master Commandant Charles Stewart.* Despite his disappointment, he and Stewart co-operated perfectly, while forming a lasting friendship. One of their shared experiences was an act of mercy. Stewart spotted some white refugees crowded on a rock off Saona Island in the Mona Passage between Haiti and Puerto Rico, and sent Porter to investigate. It turned out that the shipwrecked group of sixty-odd, many of them women and children, had fled from a Negro uprising, and when the Danish ship in which they had taken passage ran aground two days before, they had been abandoned without food or water by captain and crew. The Spanish Governor of Puerto Rico conveyed to President Thomas Jefferson the profuse thanks of his government for the rescue.

Most of the *Experiment*'s work was, of course, belligerent. On 1 September 1800, in a short, spirited action, Stewart thrashed the French privateer *Deux Amis,* 8 guns and 40 men. Having sent Porter, as usual, to take possession, Stewart promptly dashed off after a strange sail, leaving his lieutenant and four seamen to deal with 40 pugnacious enemies. Porter was indeed "aukwardly situated." It is claimed that he acted in much the same way as Charles Goldsborough reported he had done under similar circumstances on board *L'Insurgente* some eighteen months earlier: drawing a line on the deck and announcing that the first prisoner who crossed it would be shot, he loaded one of his guns with canister and, over it, stationed a sailor with a lighted match. "For three nights and nearly four days Lieutenant Porter remained in this embarrassing situation, having to guard twelve times his own number, and navigate the vessel at the same time; he, however, conducted the *Deux Amis* safely to St. Kitts."

During the last months of the Undeclared War with France, Porter saw more action. In a sharp ten-minute engagement, the French armed ship of war *Diane* was taken. One night shortly thereafter, when an unidentified assailant fired on the *Experiment,* she replied so vigorously that

---

* Stewart's daughter, Delia, was the mother of the great Irish nationalist leader Charles Stewart Parnell, whose given names commemorated his maternal grandfather.

she left her adversary with four feet of water in her hold. The victim turned out to be the *Louisa Bridger,* an English privateer out of Bermuda, and since Britain and the United States were temporarily on good terms, Stewart apologized for his good shooting.[11]

Peace with France was concluded officially on 3 March 1801, accompanied by the swift reduction of the U.S. Navy. A standing army and a strong navy were anathema to the economy-conscious Democratic-Republicans of President Thomas Jefferson's day. In lieu of building expensive frigates and sloops of war, they launched scores of small vessels, each mounting a single gun. Most of the officers who served in these gunboats detested them, and Porter echoed their sentiments when he wrote later, "Burn the wretched gun boats and build some more useful vessels. . . ." The lessons of the Barbary Wars and growing hostility with Great Britain eventually brought about something of a naval renaissance, but until they did, American naval officers looked into a bleak future.

Even in the skeleton Navy, Porter's record was good enough for him to be selected as one of the thirty-six lieutenants retained. His old ship, the *Experiment,* had been sold at the end of the war, so he was sent as First Lieutenant to her sister, the *Enterprize* (spelled thus in contemporary documentation), under the command of Lieutenant Andrew Sterrett, the impromptu swordsman of the *Constellation.* The *Enterprize* was known as "the luckiest ship in the navy," but her scintillating record was based on more than luck. During the Undeclared Naval War with France, while commanded by Lieutenant John Shaw, she fought seven battles and captured nineteen enemy merchantmen.[12]

The *Enterprize* was ordered to join Commodore Richard Dale's squadron, which was readying for duty in the Mediterranean. The United States was finally striking back at the Barbary pirates. Morocco, Algiers, Tunis, and Tripoli tended to act as independent states, although they were all dependencies of, and usually paid tribute to, the Ottoman Empire. For many years they had lived mainly by operating a rather simple but effective protection racket: unless a Christian maritime nation paid regular tribute, its ships were attacked and its sailors imprisoned until ransomed. Every year, Great Britain, France, Spain, and such lesser powers as Venice, Denmark, the Netherlands, and Sweden appropriated sums ranging from a reported "three to five millions" of dollars by Spain, down to thirty thousand dollars by Denmark and the Netherlands. If the smaller tributaries were in arrears with their payments their ships were promptly assaulted, and even the most meticulous contributors were never really safe. The vessels of non-tributary nations were common prey. The Barbary states saw piracy as the only practicable buttress for their rickety economic structures. As the Dey of Algiers explained to an American diplomat: "If I were to make peace with every nation, what would I do with my corsairs? My soldiers cannot live on their miserable allowance."

A question that needs answering is why Great Britain, with its potent navy, not only permitted these pirate nations to exist but paid them $280,000 annually. It seems that Britain found their predatory activities highly beneficial, for Barbary corsairs understandably avoided British merchantmen and hounded the ships of its weaker maritime rivals, such as the United States. Prior to independence, American vessels had been under the umbrella of the Royal Navy, and the loss of this protection was one of the costs of freedom. As early as 1784 a policy-maker in London candidly observed: "It is not probable that the American States will have a very free trade in the Mediterranean. It will not be to the interest of any of the great maritime powers to protect them from the Barbary States. . . . That the Barbary States are advantageous to maritime powers is obvious."

Through the 1780s and 1790s the United States tried doggedly to arrange satisfactory terms with the four North African countries. Reasoning that tribute would be cheaper than war, the Americans were willing to pay, if the price were not too high. But only with Morocco were reasonably acceptable terms arranged and a treaty was signed in 1786. The pacts concluded with Algiers, Tunis, and Tripoli over the next decade were considerably less favorable for America. As a result of these agreements, each year the United States had to hand over stipulated amounts of money and to contribute specified presents, such as warships: during 1798 and 1799, one 36-gun frigate, one 22-gun brig, and three schooners —one of 20 guns, one of 18 guns, and one of 10 guns—were delivered to Algiers alone.*

Amid continuous demands from Dey, Bey, and Bashaw for additional money and ever more handsome presents, the capture of American ships and the enslavement of Americans went on. In May 1800, the United States was deeply humiliated when the able but unlucky Captain William Bainbridge sailed into Algiers Harbor in the 26-gun frigate *George Washington,* conveying tribute in cash and naval stores. Not until he had anchored under the guns of the Algerian forts was he told that he must perform an errand for the Dey: the *George Washington* was to carry an ambassador and gifts to the Turkish Sultan in Constantinople, and to fly the Algerian flag while doing so. Bainbridge expostulated in vain, for he would not have been able to slip anchor before being battered to pieces.

---

* It was at this time that Americans were thrilled by the slogan, "Millions for defence but not one cent for tribute!"

Off to Turkey he had to sail on his degrading mission. He released some of his frustration in an angry letter to the Secretary of the Navy: "The light that . . . [Algiers] looks on the United States is exactly this: you pay me tribute, by that you become my slaves, and then I have a right to order as I please. Did the United States know the easy access of this barbarous coast called Barbary, the weakness of their garrisons, and the effeminacy of their people, I am sure they would not be long tributary to so pitiful a race of infidels." [13]

By 1801 American relations with Morocco, Algiers, and Tunis were still in a state of semi-hostile peace, but with Tripoli there was war. Legally recognizing the suzerainty not only of Turkey but also of Algiers, Tripoli was the weakest of the Barbary states. However, it had established what amounted to independence under its Bashaw, Yusuf Karamanli. Yusuf's throne was shaky, as he had climbed upon it only after murdering his eldest brother, and usurping it from his next elder brother, Hamet, who was in exile in Egypt. A handsome, moody semi-paranoiac, Yusuf had smoldered ever since he found that the American-Tripolitan pact signed in 1797 was less generous than those that the United States had signed with Algiers and Tunis. When the United States refused to match for him the gifts of frigates it had made to the Dey and the Bey, he declared war on 14 May 1801 by the somewhat theatrical gesture of personally chopping down the flagpole of the American consulate.

On 2 June, long before word that Tripoli had decided on war reached the United States, Dale's squadron, consisting of the 44-gun flagship *President*, the 36-gun *Philadelphia*, the 32-gun *Essex*, and the 12-gun schooner *Enterprize*, sailed for the Mediterranean. The orders given to Dale were equivocal: if, when he reached the Mediterranean, peace still prevailed, he was to dispense tribute where required; if he found that a state of war existed, he was to defend himself, but he was to await further orders before attacking. In any case, he was to return before the winter.

When the American squadron dropped anchor at Gibraltar on 1 July, it found there two Tripolitan warships, the 28-gun *Meshouda* (formerly the American merchant ship *Betsey*), and a smaller vessel. By this time, Dale had heard of Tripoli's belligerency, but Tripolitan Admiral Murad Reis * asserted that the two countries were still at peace. Deciding to take no chances, Dale blockaded the two Tripolitan ships in Gibraltar

---

* Murad Reis was, in fact, Peter Lysle, a Scots sailor who had served in the *Betsey* where, apparently, he developed an abiding hatred of Americans. After the *Betsey*'s capture by the Tripolitans, he stayed with her, converted to Islam, adopted his new name, married the eldest daughter of the Bashaw, and was appointed Admiral of the Tripolitan Navy.

by assigning the *Philadelphia* to keep watch off the harbor. Thus, Tripoli immediately lost the services of the best ship in its navy, the *Meshouda*. Murad Reis and his men finally crossed over to North Africa, and the admiral made his way, mostly by water, back to Tripoli, but his men walked home.

After the departure of the Tripolitans from Gibraltar, the American squadron proceeded to Tripoli, where Dale, still unsure what he should do, contented himself with blockading the harbor. In this interim, he dispatched the *Enterprize* to Malta to replenish water supplies. On 1 August, when she was off that island, she came upon the 14-gun *Tripoli*, commanded by Rais Mahomet Rous and carrying a crew of eighty. Those odds were even enough for her to take on the *Enterprize*'s 12 guns and ninety-four men. Action commenced at close range and lasted for three hours. Thrice the Tripolitans attempted to board, and thrice they were beaten off; after each failure they struck their colors, only to run them up again and renew the fighting. When they did finally surrender, Porter and a boarding party found the *Tripoli* "shot to pieces. Of her eighty men thirty were dead and thirty wounded. . . . The deck was covered with bodies, splinters, blood, and wreckage." Here was a unique battle. Although the fighting had lasted for three hours and had been at point-blank range, not one American was even scratched. No wonder that a newspaper in Washington, D.C., mused, "We are lost in surprise."

Sterrett's orders were that while no enemy ships taken should be destroyed or made prizes, they could be rendered harmless, so the *Tripoli*'s masts were hacked down, and her cannon and small arms were thrown overboard. Carrying only a single spar with a tattered sail, the wrecked ship limped home. Considering his stout resistance, it seems unfair that the furious Bashaw had Rais Mahomet Rous mounted backwards on a donkey and carried around the city of Tripoli, then ordered that the soles of his feet be beaten 500 times with a bastinado. For their part in the battle, Sterrett, Porter, and everyone else in the *Enterprize* received a month's extra pay.

This spirited engagement evidently discouraged the Tripolitans, for there was no more fighting that year. By 17 November, Dale's squadron was back in the United States, having left the *Philadelphia* and the *Essex* to carry out convoy and blockade duties.[14]

When Porter joined the jinx ship of the early Navy, the frigate *Chesapeake*, he found himself under his old captain, Thomas Truxtun. He had not been in his new assignment very long when he was faced with the chilling possibility that he would be charged with murder. In March 1802 the Secretary of the Navy sent him to Baltimore to recruit 100 sailors for the *Chesapeake*. He was to receive two dollars for each man enlisted and to offer them twelve dollars a month, with two months' pay in advance. Some men accepted their advanced pay and promptly deserted, so Porter had to look for them through a district of Baltimore called Fell's Point. In the course of one of these searches, he stepped into a saloon run by a "McGlossin" or "McGlassin"—both spellings are used in the records and no first name is given—for "refreshment." McGlossin, who hated naval officers, was drunk and started reviling Porter. Finally, he knocked Porter down and started to "stomp" him. From the floor, Porter killed his assailant with a single sword thrust, then fled to his boat in order to evade an angry mob, whose stones "laid his cheek open." *

Having been notified by the Judge of the Baltimore criminal court that Porter had "stabbed a man at Fell's Point & in consequence the Man instantly died," Secretary of the Navy Robert Smith wrote immediately to Captain Richard V. Morris, who had replaced Truxtun in the *Chesapeake,* and told him to deliver Porter to the civil authorities in Baltimore. Three days later, however, on 30 March 1802, the Secretary notified Porter:

> I have received a communication from Baltimore which affords me the sincerest satisfaction because it goes to the extenuation if not the justification of the unfortunate act. I have in consequence of Col° Stricker's [Baltimore naval agent] letter . . . written to the Governor of the State requesting a *noli prosequi* in the case, & have no doubt but that all further proceedings on the subject will [be] thereby arrested.

The *nolle prosequi* was forthcoming, and Porter was ordered to rejoin the *Chesapeake* at Norfolk.

Somehow the incident was kept out of the press. A careful perusal of the Baltimore, Washington, and Philadelphia papers for March and April 1802 has not revealed a word about it: nor do there seem to be any pertinent court records. Porter's son claims that there was a coroner's inquest, at which McGlosssin's wife and two of his children testified that Porter had acted in self-defense. Furthermore, he tells of his father's remorse for his deed which, unavoidable though it was, became a "source of great grief to this high-minded man." According to his son, Porter later "provided for the daughters, obtained a situation for the son, and pensioned the wife as long as she lived . . . at his death the family mourned

---

* David Dixon Porter, A. D. Turnbull, and Fletcher Pratt all imply that this episode took place sometime between March and December 1799. Each places it immediately after his account of the battle between the *Constellation* and *L'Insurgente* and prior to his discussion of Porter's West Indian and Mediterranean service in the *Amphitheatre,* the *Experiment,* and the *Enterprize.* However, official records leave no room for doubt: Porter killed McGlossin late in March 1802, between his first and second tours in the Mediterranean.

him as their benefactor." [15] This may be so, but not a scrap of confirmatory evidence has been found in the Porter Papers or anywhere else.

On 27 April 1802, with this shadow removed, Porter sailed for the Mediterranean as First Lieutenant of the *Chesapeake,* and arrived at Gibraltar on 25 May. The squadron, under its new commander, Commodore Richard V. Morris, consisted of the flagship *Chesapeake,* the *Constellation,* and the *New York,* all of 36 guns, the 28-gun *Adams,* the 28-gun *John Adams,** and the *Enterprize.* On 6 February Congress had passed the equivalent of a declaration of war against the Bashaw of Tripoli, and there was reason to hope that this reinforced squadron would be strong enough to achieve a victorious peace. But events were to show that a few large frigates, armed with short-range cannon, could not accomplish the task. Moreover, Morris was hesitant and indolent, and what passion for violence he had was not enhanced by the presence during the entire campaign of his pregnant wife. One midshipman rather uncharitably remarked that Mrs. Morris looked "very well in a veil."

After a lengthy stay at Gibraltar, Porter's *Chesapeake* and the other warships spent most of the next year doing convoy duty and carrying messages, ranging back and forth from Malaga, Spain, to Syracuse, Sicily, and calling frequently at Ajaccio, Valetta, Tunis, and Palermo. Perhaps through ennui, young firebrands of the Navy turned to private combat. On 4 October 1802, in Leghorn, Italy, Porter took part in a duel for the first time. Subsequently, he did so often, but always as a second or a spectator. Considering his hot temper and touchy sense of personal honor that repeatedly immersed him in trouble, it is odd that he was never a principal. In the incident at Leghorn, two officers of the *Constellation,* Marine Captain James McKnight, seconded by Porter, and Navy Lieutenant Richard H. L. Lawson, seconded by Lieutenant Jacob Jones, dueled with pistols at only six paces, and McKnight was killed instantly.† The outraged captain of the *Constellation* arrested both Lawson and his second. It is difficult to understand why Porter was not charged, since his and Jones' guilt seem exactly the same. In any case, the affair blew over.

The boredom of convoy duty, which continued during the first five months of 1803, was broken by another duel, this one in Valetta, on 11 February 1803. Porter was not directly involved, but since the *Chesapeake* was in port at the time, he must have known about it. U.S. Navy Lieutenant Joseph Bainbridge, brother of Captain William Bainbridge,

---

* The Navy was not aiding clarity by designating two practically identical vessels with practically identical names.

† McKnight had married Stephen Decatur's sister. Their son, Stephen Decatur McKnight, served as a lieutenant under Porter in the *Essex* and went down in the *Wasp* in 1815.

was insulted by James Cochran, personal secretary to Sir Alexander Ball, British Governor of Malta. The flamboyant Stephen Decatur seconded Bainbridge and, aware of his principal's unfamiliarity with a dueling pistol, insisted on the murderous distance of four paces—twelve feet. Incredibly, both protagonists missed on the first exchange, although Bainbridge shot off the Englishman's hat. Decatur gave him the sensible advice, "Aim lower, if you wish to live." On the second exchange, Bainbridge's bullet went into Cochran's forehead. Sir Alexander threatened to prefer charges against all concerned, but the Americans were able to sail without further incident.

Sometime in April 1803, at Gibraltar, Porter transferred from the *Chesapeake* to the *New York*. He was not pleased by the assignment, as he had little respect for Commodore Morris, but his immediate superior was Lieutenant Isaac Chauncey, and the two hit it off famously. On 25 April, when the *New York* was near Malta, she was rocked by a tremendous explosion near her magazine, and fourteen of her crew were killed. Morris' panicky commands only added to the confusion, and the fire almost reached the powder supplies before Porter and Chauncey managed to douse the flames with "wet blankets and buckets of water." [16]

After repairs, the *New York* sailed on 22 May 1803 for Tripoli, where she participated in the first action for many months. On 2 June a number of Tripolitan coastal vessels laden with grain for the besieged city were hauled up on shore about 35 miles west of the capital; rude breastworks were made with sacks of wheat. Porter begged Morris to launch a night attack, but all he could get was permission to make a reconnaissance, an operation that did little more than excite the attention of the people on shore.

The next morning the Commodore allowed Porter to try an assault. Ably seconded by Lieutenant James Lawrence and Midshipman Henry Wadsworth, Porter led some boats towards the shore, but by this time the Tripolitans had been reinforced and the party met heavy fire from pistols and muskets at point-blank range. Porter was immediately hit twice, "a slight wound in the right thigh and a ball through the left," but, recorded Midshipman Wadsworth, all he did was to "set down in the Boat." Before they were beaten off, the attackers drew so close to shore that the Tripolitans "stepped from behind the breastworks and threw handfuls of pebbles and sand at the Americans, hoping that the wind would blow it in their faces and blind them. . . ." In spite of his severe wounds, Porter wanted to renew the attack, but Morris called it off, and the American squadron soon returned to Malta, where it resumed convoy duties.

Homeward bound in September 1803, the *New York* put in to Gibraltar, where she found a new squadron commander. Morris had been sharply censured for his "indolence and want of capacity," for had he ordered a night attack, "it would have resulted, without question, in the capture or destruction of the vessels with their valuable cargoes." [17] He was replaced by Captain Edward Preble, a hard-nosed Yankee whose harsh words, ruthless discipline, and exaggerated attention to picayune detail, aroused much resentment. But he was willing to fight and, eventually, he won the respect, if not the affection, of the young officers who soon became known as "Preble's Boys," and who were responsible for most of the brilliant naval exploits of the War of 1812. Although Porter was a prisoner of war in Tripoli during most of Preble's tenure, he too was one of the "Boys."

The new commander was impressed by Porter's qualities, and transferred him to the *Philadelphia* under Captain William Bainbridge, who was, apparently, equally impressed for he wrote, "Lieutenant Porter is fit for any command." Porter's service in the *Philadelphia* marked the beginning of a lifelong friendship between him and Bainbridge: "Bainbridge's culture and wide experience fascinated the younger man, who had been at sea so steadily since childhood as to have missed educational opportunities."

On 26 August 1803, shortly before Porter joined her, the *Philadelphia* was cruising off Cape Gata, in southeastern Spain, when she came upon a Barbary warship escorting a merchant vessel. Examination of her papers showed her to be the Moroccan *Mirboka* which had taken captive the American brig *Celia*. Since Morocco and the United States were presumably at peace, Bainbridge confided to the *Mirboka*'s captain that he would have to be hanged as a pirate. This resulted in the speedy display of a commission to prey upon American shipping, signed, not by the "Emperor of Morocco," but by his Governor of Tangier, who, there is every reason to believe, was simply a front for the "Emperor." In his uninhibited spelling and vocabulary, Preble called the Moroccans "a deep designing artfull treacherous sett of Villains," and flexed his maritime muscles by assembling part of his squadron at Tangier. After disavowing the actions of his governor and of his captain, and promising to punish them, the "Emperor," amid protestations of eternal affection, renewed the treaty of 1786.[18] The actions of Bainbridge and Preble may have prevented a war which, since Morocco faces the Atlantic as well as the Mediterranean, might have hamstrung American operations against Tripoli far to the east.

The *Philadelphia*'s next assignment resulted in her doom. Accompanied by the 12-gun sloop *Vixen*, she was sent to blockade Tripoli Harbor. When Tripolitan cruisers were reported near Tunis, Bainbridge made what turned out to be a serious error: he sent the shallow-draft *Vixen* to track them down. On 29 October, shortly after the *Vixen* left, the *Philadelphia* spotted an enemy warship making for the harbor and chased her through uncharted waters. The Tripolitan escaped, and as the *Philadelphia* turned toward open water, she ran upon a reef or, more accurately, a sand bar. There was a "harsh, grating noise . . . chilling the blood of every seaman aboard, and the next instant the bow shot five or six feet out of the water, the shock throwing many prostrate upon the deck." Just before the moment of impact, Porter had been "ordered into the mizen top to look into the harbor of Tripoli and observe if any cruisers were in port . . . about half way up . . . he felt the ship strike. . . ."

In spite of desperate efforts to refloat her, the *Philadelphia* lay helpless. Most of her guns and other heavy equipment were thrown overboard, and her masts were cut down, but to no avail. Tripolitan ships began gathering, cautiously at first, then more boldly after the *Philadelphia* heeled over so far that her remaining guns were inoperative. Had the Americans manned the boats and tried to pull her into deeper water astern, or tried to kedge her off with anchors and cables, they would have been shot to pieces by the Tripolitans. Only one thing might have saved the ship—the presence of the *Vixen*. She could at least have saved the crew and she might have been able to hold off the Tripolitans until a strong wind refloated the *Philadelphia* two days later. But there was no *Vixen*. As Porter later recounted, Bainbridge "coolly and prudently call'd a council of his officers who were unanimously of opinion that to save the lives of the Brave crew there was no alternative but to haul the colors down & with tears in his eyes did that truly brave man submit to the painful necessity."

A court of inquiry, headed by Captain James Barron,* convened on 29 June 1805 to investigate the loss of the ship, and concluded that Bainbridge had "acted with fortitude and conduct," and should have "no degree of censure." Some contemporary opinion was less gentle to Bainbridge. When the bellicose Preble received the news of the *Philadelphia*, he wrote the Secretary of the Navy the anguished comment, "Would to God, that the Officers and crew of the *Philadelphia*, had one and all, determined to prefer death to slavery; it is possible that such a determination might have saved them from either." [19]

The brief interlude between the decision to surrender and the arrival of the Tripolitans had been occupied in trying to make the ship use-

---

* James Barron was the brother of Samuel Barron, under whom Porter had served in the *Constellation*.

less to the enemy by drilling holes in her hull and trying to wreck her pumps. Wholesale looting started as soon as the boarding party arrived on deck and continued in the boats on the way to shore. Officers and men were stripped of "watches cravats money some of their coats—the Capᵗ treated no better than other officers." Bainbridge's epaulets were torn off, and only at the risk of his life did he manage to retain a locket with his wife's picture, while Porter lost his sword to the same assailant. According to Midshipman Henry Allen, when the Tripolitan ship *Mastico* was captured later, "the rascal" who had pulled the epaulets from Bainbridge's shoulders was found on board, and "he even had the impudence to wear . . . when he was taken the sword of the *Philadelphia*s 1st Leut. Porter."

The boatloads of prisoners were landed in front of the Bashaw's palace, and the crowds spat at them as they were marched between rows of soldiers into the sprawling edifice. They were ushered into the presence of Yusuf Karamanli, Bashaw of Tripoli. He was in a genial mood—and why not? His enemy had been deprived of a crack 36-gun frigate, and he had over 300 prisoners to hold for ransom.* The officers were given something to eat and sent "to a house where our Consul formerly liv'd . . . at present we are [treated] very well, much better than I expected . . . ," wrote Sailing Master William Knight,[20] but the sailors were thrown, supperless, into a warehouse so small that each man had only a couple of feet of floor space.

To add to the captives' unhappiness, their attempts to demolish the *Philadelphia* had failed utterly. Only two days after the surrender, a gale blew up and refloated her, and a little later the Tripolitans salvaged her guns. Thus, not only had the United States lost a frigate, but Tripoli had gained one, and that more powerful than any in Preble's squadron, save for the 44-gun *Constitution*.

Over a year and a half of captivity started for the *Philadelphia*'s complement. The sailors were worked hard, most of them on building new fortifications, but a few as cooks for the palace. Many of those who were skilled craftsmen, such as carpenters, were forced to refit Tripolitan ships, among them their own *Philadelphia*. Their diet consisted of barley *coos-coos,* small loaves of coarse bread, a little oil, on rare occasions some beef or pork, and sometimes camel meat. Discipline was harshly enforced with the whip and bastinado. Despite the harrowing conditions, only five of the crew became turncoats and adopted Islam. Considering that a high

---

* Reports on the number of captives taken from the *Philadelphia* vary between 303 and 315. A leading authority on the subject concludes that 309 is probably the correct total.

percentage of the sailors on the *Philadelphia*'s roster were British—some sources say one-third, while Bainbridge said "the greater part" *—the number of deserters is remarkably small.

Officers fared much better than the sailors. Their diet was adequate and, although the quarters assigned were unfurnished, they were considerably more spacious than those of the crew. Two men were instrumental in making conditions for the captive officers tolerable. The first was Sidi Mohammed D'Ghies, the Tripolitan equivalent of Secretary of State, who was more pessimistic, or at least more cautious, than was the Bashaw about the future of Tripoli, and he counselled his master to be moderate in his treatment of the *Philadelphia*'s officers. D'Ghies' attitude acted as a counterweight to that of Scots-born Admiral Murad Reis, who continued to manifest his dislike of Americans. The second man, Nicholas C. Nissen, the Danish Consul in Tripoli, was more important to the well-being of the prisoners. He did everything possible to lighten the burdens of captivity. He furnished the officers with bedding from his own house, arranged food supplies, sent and delivered mail, and most essential, provided books, first his own and then those from the *Philadelphia*'s library, which he bought at his own expense. Well deserved was the resolution passed by Congress on 10 April 1806: "That the President of the United States be requested to cause to be made known to Nicholas C. Nissen, esquire, his Danish majesty's consul residing at Tripoli, the high sense entertained by Congress of his disinterested and benevolent attentions manifested to Captain Bainbridge, his officers, and crew, during the time of their captivity in Tripoli."

Throughout the dreary months that followed, Bainbridge was sunk in gloom. As captain of the *George Washington,* he had suffered the degradation of being forced to perform an errand for the Dey of Algiers. In 1798 he had surrendered the *Retaliation* to the French. Now he had given up the *Philadelphia,* and had to live with the dismal knowledge that in all American naval history only two warships had struck their colors, and he had been in command of both. Understandably, he poured out his despair to his wife about his "apprehension which constantly haunts me, that I may be censured by my countrymen. These impressions . . . act as a corroding canker at my heart . . . it would have been a merciful dispensation of Providence if my head had been shot off by the enemy, while our vessel lay rolling on the rocks." [21]

With the captain usually in solitude, most of the day-by-day activi-

---

* Before the War of 1812, it was claimed in London that the American merchant marine and Navy were manned largely by British sailors, most of whom were deserters. Such a large percentage of Britons in the *Philadelphia* would seem to substantiate that assertion.

ties of the officers were directed by Porter and his fellow lieutenant, Jacob Jones. For the younger men, they set up a school whose curriculum paid some attention to culture but was directed primarily toward solving tactical problems in battles fought by wooden blocks pushed around the floor. According to the florid prose of Washington Irving, such activities robbed captivity "of its heaviest evils, that dull monotony that wearies the spirits, and that mental inactivity that engenders melancholy and hypochondria." Porter, whose formal education had been minimal, used his enforced leisure to advantage. He studied incessantly "history, drawing, the French language, mathematics, and the theory of his profession." He later made some history and, in his *Journal of a Cruise to the Pacific Ocean . . . during the War of 1812*, he wrote some. His drawings, especially those he did for his *Journal*, are first rate. He learned to speak and write French well enough to get along in that language, and he certainly mastered "the theory of his profession." If he acquired any mathematical knowledge, however, it does not seem to have helped him to keep either his personal or his official accounts in order: they were always chaotic.

Social diversions were few and far between, but at the end of the observance of Ramadan in February 1804 Bainbridge and Porter "were invited into the audience hall where the Bashaw . . . sprinkled the Americans with attar of roses and fumigated them with frankincense. . . ." On departure, he provided "sherbet and coffee," and allowed them to salute rather than kiss the royal hand.

Of course, mail was of primary importance, and poor Bainbridge's "apprehension" certainly did not ease when three months passed without a single line from Preble. Later it was discovered that there was nothing sinister about the silence: it was caused by the fact that the American consul at Malta did not speak English and he just hoarded all the letters. When the line of communication became two-way, Bainbridge began sending secret messages to Preble. He did this by writing between the lines of innocuous material with invisible "sympathetic" ink supplied by the ever-helpful Nissen. Two letters concerning Porter's captivity are extant. On 5 March 1804, he wrote Midshipman Henry Wadsworth about details of the loss of the *Philadelphia*, signing his letter "Your unfortunate but Affectionate Friend." During that summer, George Davis, the U.S. Chargé d'Affaires in Tunis, added a note for Porter in a letter to Bainbridge, assuring him that, "the only motive which can induce me to remain in Barbary, is the hope of unfettering your chains. . . . And place full confidence in the eternal tho' feeble exertions, of your friend." [22]

In December 1803, using his "sympathetic" ink, Bainbridge suggested to Preble that the *Philadelphia* be either recaptured or destroyed.

Preble had already decided to take such action, and when the same recommendation was made by Stephen Decatur, gave him the risky assignment but ordered him to destroy, rather than to recover, the frigate.

Decatur in the *Intrepid* and Porter's friend and former commander, Charles Stewart, in the schooner of war *Siren*, arrived off Tripoli on 7 February 1804, only to be immobilized for over a week by a raging storm. On the night of the 16th, while the *Siren* remained three miles out, the *Intrepid*, carrying Decatur and seventy-three men, crept into the harbor and moored alongside the lost frigate. The Americans boarded the *Philadelphia*, cleared her decks of Tripolitans, placed "combustibles" and ignited them, returned to the *Intrepid* and, joining the *Siren*'s crew, sailed away. Decatur had accomplished his mission flawlessly. The only American casualty was one man wounded.

"At ½ past 10," wrote Midshipman Robert T. Spence, "the Frigate *Philadelphia* was in a blaze fore and Aft . . . at 11 the Frigate's tops fell, and several of her Guns going off, the shot made considerable rattling in the town; shortly after her cables parted and she drifted under the Castle . . . at 6 the light could still be seen from the Deck, we being about 40 miles distant from her." *

Although the prisoners could not see what was going on, they were almost immediately aware of it. Their reaction was joy mixed with fear of Tripolitan retaliation, and the latter was soon forthcoming. According to one account, the officers were housed for a while in a cell with a single barred opening at the top. On 29 February Nissen wrote to the king of Denmark: "The Bashaw saw the whole business with his own Eyes. . . . The American Officers Prisonners of war here have been put under a strong guard since this event, it is not permitted to write them, etc." As was to be expected, the sailors were more severely punished: they were "put to work carrying stones on their heads and shoulders to repair the fortifications, and at this laborious employment they were kept from morning till night . . . with very insufficient rations."

Sometime during his imprisonment, Porter got into trouble on his own. On their way to work, the sailors passed the officers' quarters, and written communications were passed back and forth through a hole that

---

* Midshipman Spence is in error. The *Philadelphia* did not "drift under the Castle," which was at the extreme southeastern tip of the city. She burned off the "Lazaretto" and mole, well to the northeast. "Iron bolts, copper nails, and an eighteen pound cannon ball," discovered in the late nineteenth century proved the exact location. The Italians, who took over Libya in 1911, filled in the site and built a warehouse on it.[23]

Porter is said to have chopped in the wall. One day, someone was overheard as he conversed through the aperture, and general punishment was threatened. "I alone am responsible," Porter admitted, and he was taken away to face the Bashaw. What happened at that interview is not clear.

According to some accounts, he soon returned unpunished, and reported to his fellows that he had told the Bashaw that he was not sorry, and that Christians could show his pirates a thing or two about courage —or words to that effect. Other accounts say that Porter was temporarily put "in a filthy room in a distant part of the castle." The likelihood that he was punished is given added weight by a letter, written in invisible ink, in which Bainbridge notified George Davis at Tunis that Porter should be addressed as "Dʳ Ben Smith" because, "The chief Guard of the prisoners bears him malice and will not let his letters pass. . . . Give this information to Captain Porter of Baltimore." As the letter is dated 19 December 1804, ten months after Decatur's venture, it seems unlikely that the treatment of Porter referred to therein was a continuation of any general punishment emanating from the burning of the *Philadelphia*.

During the seemingly endless months of captivity, the United States made a number of attempts to come to terms with Tripoli about ransoming the crew of the *Philadelphia*. But the Bashaw's price was always too steep, and negotiations came to nought. Nor were efforts to enlist European diplomatic intervention on behalf of the prisoners successful, even though the French Minister of Foreign Affairs, the Marquis de Talleyrand, reported that Napoleon Bonaparte, eager for the Louisiana Purchase to be ratified, "was touched with the most lively commiseration" for the prisoners. During the summer of 1804, the disagreement on ransom between the United States and Tripoli was revealed. The Bashaw wanted $500 per man and, since Preble would give no more than $200, the war had to continue until Tripolitan defeat could lower the price.[24]

During his tenure as commander of the Mediterranean squadron, Preble prosecuted the war against Tripoli much more vigorously than did either his predecessors or his successors. Not only did he divest the enemy of the *Philadelphia*, but on 3 August 1804 he sent Stephen Decatur to use the newly purchased gunboats, with which his flotilla had been reinforced, against similar Tripolitan craft defending the city. The so-called "Battle of the Gunboats" that ensued involved perhaps the most spirited hand-to-hand fighting of the war. Decatur captured two Tripolitan craft and, in the process, had a number of narrow escapes. On one occasion, he was rolling around the deck grappling with one Tripolitan, when another, scimitar raised for striking, came up behind him. Decatur owed his life to sailor Daniel Frazier who, unable to use his already

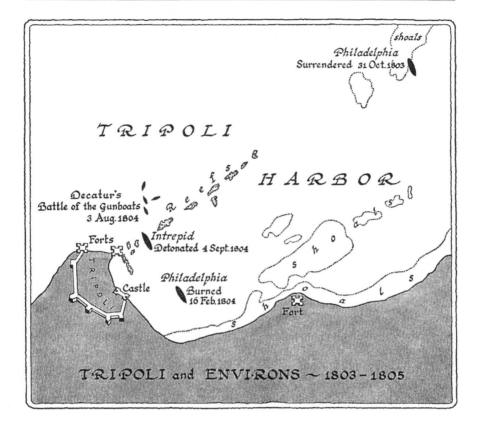

TRIPOLI and ENVIRONS ~ 1803–1805

slashed hands, put his head between Decatur and the descending blade.*

James Decatur, Stephen's brother, was not so lucky. He was preparing to take over a surrendered Tripolitan gunboat when her captain treacherously shot and killed him. Stephen hunted down the fleeing gunboat, stormed her, and exacted vengeance on the guilty man. According to Preble's Journal, at a cost of thirteen dead and four wounded, the Americans "captured 3 Gun Boats . . . 44 Tripolines were killed on board the 3 Boats and 52 made prisoners . . . the Enemy must have suffered very much in killed and wounded among their shipping and on shore. . . ." [25]

On 25 August Preble was ready again, and subjected the city of Tripoli to a night bombardment. It seems strange of Bainbridge to have reported that the American fire fell short, for one missile sailed into his room, ". . . and struck the wall opposite its point of entry, then, its force near spent, rebounded and hit Bainbridge's bed, carried off the bedclothes, but missed the body. The debris from the shattered wall . . . was scattered . . . over Bainbridge, who was found bruised and half-buried when his officers came running to his rescue."

The city was battered even more thoroughly on 28 and 29 August, when a second night attack brought the *Constitution* to hammer the Bashaw's castle at close range. During the afternoon of 3 September, an even less palatable dose wrought greater damage to Tripolitan fortifications, shipping, and morale, but the next night the Americans suffered a discouraging setback. Preble had decided to send a "fire boat" full of explosives in to the harbor and blow her up alongside the castle. This dangerous mission was entrusted to Master Commandant Richard Somers, one of the more able and popular of "Preble's Boys." †

---

* Frazier was cheated of deserved fame for this self-sacrifice by his shipmate, Reuben James. Decatur's chief biographer, Alexander S. Mackenzie, attributed the heroism to James, and years later when the latter was serving under Porter in the West Indies, he was still living off his unwarranted reputation. James is not mentioned in the medical report on the four Americans wounded in the Battle of the Gunboats, while there is mention of Frazier having suffered "two incised wounds on the head, one of them severe; one bad wound across the wrist & seven slightly about the hand." Charles L. Lewis, in an article in the *Maryland Historical Magazine* in 1924, was the first to correct the error.

† That Somers never lacked courage is proved by the almost unbelievable circumstances in which his duels were fought a few years before. Decatur and Somers were close friends and in relaxed banter between them, Decatur called him "a silly fool." Six of Somers' fellow officers refused to speak to him because he had accepted this "insult" from Decatur. Confusingly enough, the upshot was that Somers, seconded by Decatur, challenged all six men, one after another. Somers was slightly wounded by his first opponent, and badly hit by the second. Since he could not stand unaided, Decatur sat beside him, holding him up with

Decatur's old ship, the *Intrepid*, was given to Somers, Henry Wadsworth (now a Lieutenant), and ten volunteer sailors, who packed her with 150 shells and 100 barrels of gunpowder. As she entered Tripoli Harbor on the night of 4 September, the *Intrepid* detonated, killing all hands.* "In a few moments she went up—How awfully Grand!" wrote Midshipman Robert T. Spence, "Everything wrapp'd in Dead silence made the explosion loud, and terrible, the fuses of the shells, burning in the air, shone like so many planets, a vast stream of fire, which appeared ascending to heaven. . . ." Although the overwhelming weight of evidence shows that the *Intrepid* detonated accidentally, some contemporary opinion had it that she must have been boarded by the Tripolitans, and that Somers killed himself and his men with a heroism that had not been found in Bainbridge, Porter, and the complement of the *Philadelphia*.

Action off Tripoli during August and September 1804 was the last taken under Preble, and practically the last maritime fighting of the war. Preble, whose brilliant service was widely commended by his government and his fellow officers, returned to America that autumn and, three years later, died of tuberculosis.[26]

During 1804 and 1805 the Navy accomplished little, either to win the war or to free the crew of the *Philadelphia*. Commodore Samuel Barron, the onetime captain of the *Constellation* who succeeded Preble as commander of the Mediterranean squadron, kept away from Tripoli, preferring to nurse an ailing liver in other Mediterranean ports.

It was a quixotic military venture that helped to bring about the liberation of Porter and the others, if not to write a victorious peace for the United States. William Eaton, an aggressive soldier and tactless diplomat who was serving as Navy agent to the Barbary states, entered into a conspiracy with the rightful Bashaw of Tripoli, Hamet Karamanli, who had been in exile in Egypt since his throne had been usurped by his younger brother Yusuf. In order to place Hamet in power, Eaton had organized an invasion. In March 1805, in company with Hamet, a naval lieutenant, eight Marines, twenty-five cannoneers, thirty-eight Greek mercenaries, some Arab cavalry, and a host of camel drivers and footmen—about 400 in all—he started out from near Alexandria, Egypt, to cross the 500 miles of desert to the Tripolitan outpost of Derna, halfway to the capital.†

one arm, and helping him aim his pistol with the other. Collaborating thus, they managed to wound the third opponent, after which Somers fainted, and "honor" was declared satisfied. Such was the early Navy.

* Lieutenant Wadsworth was remembered by the two names given his nephew, Longfellow.

† This expedition is commemorated in the second line of The Marines' Hymn. "To the Shores of Tripoli."

Among the diversions experienced by the expedition were sandstorms, a chronic shortage of food and water, two mutinies among the camel drivers and three among the Arabs. But, as if to prove that nothing is certain, Eaton's implausible little army, with the aid of three American naval vessels that showed up in time to bombard the city's fortifications, not only proceeded to storm Derna on 25 April, but even to hold it against the counterattack of a newly arrived Tripolitan army. Then, just when it seemed probable that Yusuf could be replaced by Hamet, who might write a favorable treaty, news arrived at Derna that Tripoli and the United States were at peace.

The indolent and liver-conscious Captain Samuel Barron and the appeasement-minded U.S. Consul General at Algiers, Tobias Lear, had never entertained the slightest hope that Eaton's mad campaign could accomplish anything. On 3 June, Lear signed a treaty of peace, according to whose terms the United States was granted most-favored-nation status economically, and American ships were guaranteed freedom from attack. Since the treaty confirmed Yusuf as Bashaw and provided for the prisoners to be exchanged on payment of $60,000 ransom,[27] it made the accomplishments of Eaton and Hamet meaningless. The worst charge that can be leveled at the treaty is that it did not stop the troubles the United States had with the Barbary states: they continued until 1815, when Stephen Decatur led a powerful squadron to the Mediterranean and, at the cannon's mouth, wrote much more satisfactory new treaties.

The end of the Tripolitan War did, at least, mean freedom for the men of the *Philadelphia,* who had spent nineteen months and three days in captivity. Some of them, including Porter, were released quickly, but others had to wait a while because "the intoxication of Liberty & Liquor has deranged the faculties . . . of many of the Sailors." Bainbridge and many of the liberated men were sent home, but Porter remained in the Mediterranean for another two years. Captain John Rodgers, Porter's old mentor from the *Constellation,* had replaced Samuel Barron as commodore of the squadron on 22 May 1805. He appointed Porter acting captain of the famed *Constitution,* but shortly thereafter gave him an assignment much more to his liking, the command of his former ship, the *Enterprize.*[28]

Most of Porter's subsequent work consisted of dispatch-carrying throughout the western Mediterranean. He stopped in Marseille long enough to win accolades from the American consul there, who wrote to President Jefferson: "Mr. Porter is a very good and gallant officer, much esteemed here, where the good order, cleanliness of his ship, subordination and good health of his crew is admired, and we are intimate friends." During the winter of 1805–1806, Porter spent an exciting interlude of several weeks in Naples. That city was just being occupied by Joseph Bonaparte's French army, and Porter's letters are full of Neapolitan political news. Routine missions in the spring and summer of 1806 took him to Leghorn, Syracuse, Tunis, Gibraltar, Algiers, and Valetta, and it was in the course of these missions that he received a pleasant communication dated 28 April from Secretary of the Navy Robert Smith advising him that he had been promoted to "Master Commandant."

In the summer of 1806, he got into a jam serious enough to have ruined him professionally; it might even have started an Anglo-American war. Porter advised the Secretary of the Navy that on 5 August the *Enterprize* was in Valetta Harbor in Malta when a drunken English sailor rowed by and "was very insolent to one of my Officers." Porter ordered him to come on board and apologize to the officer concerned, but when the sailor continued his tirade, "I caused him to be punished with twelve lashes in the usual manner that Seamen are punished." The Royal Navy commander at Malta immediately demanded "particulars" of the incident, and Porter answered: "The indignity offered to the Flag under which I sail was of such a nature that I am convinced would not be overlooked under similar circumstances by one of His Britanic Majesties Officers. . . ."

A couple of hours later Sir Alexander Ball, Governor of Malta, sent an officer to inform Porter that the *Enterprize* would not be permitted to depart from the harbor until the flogging matter had been settled, and the following dialogue ensued:

I asked him if War had taken place between the United States & Great Britain, he said not that he had heard of, he believed my detention was owing to my having caused a British Seaman to be punished on board my Vessel, I then desired him to inform his Commander that I should sail that evening, he said the Forts were ordered to fire into my Vessel if I should attempt to leave the port, I replied I should attempt it, and if the Forts fired at me I should return the fire as long as resistance could avail, and when I could resist no longer should strike my colours, surrender my Vessel and consider myself a prisoner of War.

Messages went back and forth all day, with the British insisting that Porter must wait until Sir Alexander returned to town, since only he could rescind the order to fire, while Porter warned of the consequences of "detaining a public vessel of War sailing under the flag of a free and independant nation." Amid what must have been nerve-wracking tension, the *Enterprize* left on schedule, passed the silent forts, "and proceeded to Sea without molestation." [29]

Evidently, the flogging at Malta hung over Porter for many months. On his return to the United States more than a year later, he wrote his old commander, Thomas Truxtun, for confirmation and additional information about a case he hoped to cite as a precedent; this concerned a Captain Matson of HMS *Dolphin* who, under similar circumstances, had whipped an American sailor named "Giles." Truxtun replied with two long letters, recalling that the sailor was named "Childs," that the incident had occurred in 1799, and that since Matson was "right," he "was acquitted."

Porter passed on this information to the Secretary of the Navy, pointing out that he had whipped the Briton in "coolness and deliberation," while Matson had punished the American "in the heat of temper and haste." Porter revealed his apprehension by admitting to the Secretary that, "I may have exceeded the bounds of discretion," but he hoped that his "candid unextorted confession" would settle the matter satisfactorily. Apparently it did, for nothing more was said by the Navy Department. However, the episode was remembered in London. When news of Porter's depredations in the Pacific in 1813 reached England, *The Times* recalled that he was "the fellow who enticed a man on board his ship" at Malta in order to flog him, an act so despicable that, according to the newspaper, Porter had to run for his life.

This case was neither unimportant, nor, save for the flogging, was it typical of the impulsive behavior that caused Porter so much trouble during his life. As one commentator on American naval officers of the time shrewdly remarks:

> They were perfectly aware that the world was in flux, international law was being rewritten, and the men who plied words on sheets of foolscap in the chanceries were mainly occupied with rationalizing acts already performed; yet acts which, being established as precedent, would control the movements of generations unborn. If *Enterprize* submitted to being detained for this reason, there would be some other reason for holding the next American ship that came in; and presently the right of British port officers to grant or withhold exit passes would be established.[30]

On 15 August, only ten days after the incident at Malta and, naturally, long before it had been disposed of, the *Enterprize* was off Tarifa, near Gibraltar, when she was approached by seven Spanish gunboats, which for some unexplained reason started shooting, "a daring insult . . . to our Flag." Porter ran up his colors, repeatedly warned the Spaniards to desist, and finally returned the fire. His assailants fled, "oweing I suppose to the reception they had met with they did not seem disposed to renew the conflict." Captain Hugh Campbell of the *Constitution* was delighted that Porter had "behaved in a handsome and gallant manner." *

---

* In March 1807 Porter took Sidi Mohammed Mellimelli, former Tunisian envoy to the United States, to Gibraltar. This gentleman, known in contemporary documentation as "Mili Mili," had spent the winter of 1805 and 1806 in America trying to extract more tribute. If he failed in that endeavor, he was

Porter remained on routine duty in the Mediterranean until the autumn of 1807, and his last months there were spent in raising funds from his fellow officers for a memorial to six of their number "who fell in the different attacks that were made on the City of Tripoli in the Year of our Lord 1804." He drew up a scale of assessments, running from twenty dollars for captains to five dollars for midshipmen and, rather ungenerously, sent a list of those who contributed to the Secretary of the Navy, "in order that you may be able to ascertain who have not." An Italian sculptor in Leghorn was commissioned to design and execute the white marble structure, and when it had been completed, Porter was worried about its transportation in "Fifty one Cases," and its cost of "about Two Thousand Dollars," and begged Congress that he "may be relieved from paying a duty . . ."

The Tripoli Monument was dedicated to "Captain [actually Master Commandant] Richard Somers, Lieutenants James Caldwell, James Decatur, Henry Wadsworth, Joseph Israel, and John Dorsey [the two last named were Midshipmen] . . . The love of Glory inspired them. The Children of Columbia admire, and Commerce laments their fall." The monument arrived in Boston during the autumn of 1807 and was eventually carried to Washington, where it was assembled, not as had been hoped, at the Capitol, but in the Washington Navy Yard. Aesthetically, this allegorical statuary leaves much to be desired. If ever a man was guilty of damning a work of art with the faintest praise imaginable, Washington Irving is that man:

> The general style of the work is not of bad taste, and there are many points about it that are very excellent. Its execution is not of the first class, but it is not in any part bad, and for a work standing in our climate, in the open air, it is sufficient. The six figures . . . are very unequal in merit and execution. That of Commerce . . . is the best, the figure of America is the worst, and is unfortunately the most conspicuous . . . too much regard has been made to cheapness.

Along with many other public structures, the monument was mutilated when the British captured Washington in 1814: the pointing finger and thumb of the female figure representing the "Genius of America" were cut off; another female figure, representing "History," was robbed of her pen, and the hand was knocked off the figure of "Fame." Since 1861, it has had a permanent home at the U.S. Naval Academy in Annapolis.[32]

---

successful in another, his quest for girls, ". . . for whom he had a ravenous appetite. The prim little Secretary of State Madison had to have concubines supplied at public expense and wrote about it later, saying, 'Appropriations to foreign intercourse are terms of great latitude and may be drawn on by very urgent and unforeseen occurrences.' Madison never lacked the ability for choice expression."[31]

The busiest months of Porter's life were the six that elapsed between his return to the United States in the *Enterprize* in October 1807, after an absence of six years and four months, and his departure to command the naval station at New Orleans the following March. In that brief interval he managed to carouse with the literati of New York, sit for seven weeks on four successive courts-martial in Norfolk, Virginia, and get married in Chester, Pennsylvania.

In New York he became friendly with Washington Irving, a young author who was enjoying his first taste of national acclaim as a result of the publication of the *Salmagundi* essays. It is not known exactly how or where the two men met, but they were probably introduced by James K. Paulding, a mutual acquaintance, sometime after Porter's arrival in New York late in 1807. Their friendship seems to have been so close that Porter was for a while a "fellow-lodger" of Irving's. They shared an interest in alcohol: ". . . [Irving] was now prominent in New York literary societies; and he was also a leader among the wild, gossiping, bibulous 'Lads of Kilkenny.' These, all nicknamed, included besides William, Peter, Ebenezer, and Washington Irving, Peter and Gouverneur Kemble, Paulding, [Henry] Brevoort, Henry Ogden, David Porter, and Richard McCall."

For obvious reasons, Porter was dubbed "Sindbad," and joined his cronies in "homage to drinking" at various taverns in New York and Newark. At Gouverneur Kemble's mansion in New Jersey, "the members were free to jest, drink, play leapfrog, pelt Paulding in the top of a cherry tree, or fall asleep in miscellaneous groups." Porter's term of membership among the Kilkenny Lads was brief: in January 1808 he departed for Norfolk, Virginia. Nor was it long before the group was disbanded, for Irving soon tired of debauchery. However, the two must have seen one another on later occasions, and when Irving edited *The Analectic Maga-*

zine and Naval Chronicle during and after the War of 1812, he wrote a flattering personal sketch of that "second Sindbad, Capt. Porter." [1]

Porter was sent to Norfolk to sit as a judge on four courts-martial that arose from American outrage and humiliation over the *Chesapeake-Leopard* affair that had taken place on 22 June 1807. On that date, the 36-gun American frigate *Chesapeake,* under Captain James Barron, left Hampton Roads to sail for the Mediterranean. A peremptory order from the Secretary had led to her sailing before she was ready: her green crew was not trained for action, and her decks were covered with a jumble of naval stores destined for the ships of the Mediterranean squadron. Barron saw no cause for alarm when he was approached and hailed by 50-gun HMS *Leopard,* under Captain Salusbury P. Humphreys, which had been patrolling off the Virginia Capes. In that era of irregular mail deliveries, it was a common courtesy for warships of one nation to accept the dispatches of another bound for the same destination. Furthermore, although the Royal Navy regularly boarded and searched American merchantmen, it had never so acted against a U.S. ship of war.

To Barron's incredulous consternation, Humphreys, following specific orders from the commander of Britain's North American squadron, demanded the right to board the *Chesapeake* for the purpose of removing four deserters known to be among her crew. Barron tried to stall, but at point-blank range Humphreys fired a broadside into him and kept shooting. Amid the din and confusion of the one-sided battle, the *Chesapeake*'s rammers, matches, and gunlocks could not be extricated from the welter of other supplies that littered her decks. What national honor remained had to be satisfied with a single shot fired by a coal brought from below in an officer's bare hands just before the American colors were pulled down. By that time, three of the *Chesapeake*'s men had been killed and eighteen wounded, among them Barron, who was hit in the leg. Humphreys took the four deserters to the *Leopard* and, refusing to accept the *Chesapeake* as a captured prize of war, as Barron demanded, nonchalantly resumed his patrol. The battered *Chesapeake* put back into Hampton Roads.

Britain's eventual disavowal of this atrocity made little difference to Barron. The general public, and even his own junior officers, demanded that he be court-martialed. Barron made an ideal scapegoat; phlegmatic and morose, he was perhaps the most unpopular captain in the Navy. John Rodgers, Stephen Decatur, and David Porter, were among his judges, and having always disliked him, could not be expected to show him much sympathy for what they regarded as craven submission. Indeed, both Rodgers and Decatur were known to be his personal enemies. So heated had been their clashes in the Mediterranean that, in 1806, Rodgers, in effect, challenged Barron to a duel, and it was several months before intermediaries managed to have it called off. Decatur, who had detested Barron ever since serving under him as a midshipman, went aboard the *Chesapeake* the very afternoon she returned to port after the *Leopard's* mauling, and there received "first hand impressions that led him to believe that Barron had been grossly negligent of his duty. To this opinion he adhered ever afterwards." He even begged the Secretary of the Navy to excuse him from the court-martial on the grounds that he was prejudiced, but his request was refused. Porter, being a close friend and admirer of Rodgers and Decatur, would be apt to echo their sentiments.

Yet Barron refused to exercise his right to challenge any of the three, so convinced was he of his own innocence, in that he had acted in the only manner possible under the circumstances. On 8 January 1808 the court convened at Norfolk aboard the *Chesapeake,* a site that certainly could not help the defense. John Rodgers presided over the court, which was composed of four captains, three masters commandant, and four lieutenants. Master Commandant Porter attended the trial every day, and interrogated both defendants and witnesses more frequently than did any other member of the court. Barron's trial was the first of the four, and Porter, boring in on whether Barron's conduct during the battle had tended to "dispirit" either officers or crew, asked him and other witnesses more than sixty separate questions. The court rendered its decision on 8 February. Barron was cleared of such major charges as cowardice and unnecessary surrender of his ship, but was found guilty of " . . . neglecting, on the probability of an engagement, to clear his ship for action." He was suspended from the Navy for five years without pay. "It was a savage sentence and a terrible humiliation, the more terrible because Barron was convinced that it was undeserved." Indeed, from the vantage of historical hindsight, it is hard not to view Barron as the victim of wretched luck.

Porter remained on the court for the trials of the three other defendants. Navy Master Commandant Charles Gordon and Marine Captain John Hall were sentenced to be privately reprimanded by the Secretary of the Navy, but Gunner William Hook was dismissed from the service. One of the witnesses at Gordon's trial was Midshipman Jesse D. Elliott.[2] More than a decade later the repercussions of these sorry events brought together again in deadlier circumstances Barron, Decatur, Elliott, Rodgers, and Porter.

At the conclusion of the trials on 22 February, Porter hurried to Chester, Pennsylvania, to marry Evalina Anderson, the daughter of a tavern keeper who, later, became a U.S. congressman. According to family tradition, Porter first saw the fifteen-year-old Evalina playing with a doll when he visited the home of Commodore Thomas Tingey at the Washington Navy Yard. Dark-haired and blue-eyed, she was described as "a handsome young lady," and her portrait, although painted many years later, bears witness to this judgment. Understandably, Porter was attracted. Although he was far from being an Adonis—one nineteenth century historian described him as "a small, slight, and rather ill-favored New England man"—the dynamic Porter was draped in maritime glory, and he had little difficulty in winning his case. Commodore Tingey, unwilling to shoulder any personal responsibility for Evalina, quickly sent her back to Chester. Porter followed her there, and met the unbroken opposition of the Andersons, who found little to commend in a suitor whose prospects seemed to guarantee frequent absences rather than an adequate income. He is said to have been greeted first by Evalina's brother, Thomas, who insultingly ordered him out of the house. Porter countered with an offer to throw Thomas out of the window. Rather confusingly, this exchange somehow eroded Anderson resistance.

Although their son alleges that a long courtship ensued, they were married on 10 March 1808, only six months after Porter's return to America.[3] The father of the bride gave the couple a fine wedding present —"Green Bank," a large stone house on the Delaware River in Chester. Shortly before his marriage, Porter had been ordered by Secretary of the Navy Robert Smith to take command of the Naval Station at New Orleans and, since the couple left to take up that assignment less than a week after the wedding, two years passed before they were able to live in their new home. What happiness David and Evalina Porter may have enjoyed during their first years together proved ephemeral. Despite the birth of ten children, their marriage was always strained by financial troubles, and soon by rumors of Evalina's infidelities; it ended in years of total separation and mutual accusations of madness.

Porter's orders called for him to go to New Orleans "via the Western Country," which meant through Pennsylvania to Wheeling, in what is now West Virginia, then down the Ohio and Mississippi rivers to Louisiana. Along the way, he was to pick up gunboats to use on the trip downriver. Accompanied by his bride and a small retinue, he headed west from Chester on 16 March, leaving behind instructions to those of his officers who were to follow. At the behest of the Secretary, they were to occupy themselves en route with "Geographical, Historical, Philosophical, Topographical, Nautical, Thermometrical, Barometrical, Aquatical, Botanical, Mineralogical, and Astronomical Subjects," which presumably left little time for sightseeing and pleasure. When Porter reached the Ohio River and found the gunboats were not ready, he purchased "a galley" to transport his thirteen officers and servants plus, of course, his wife, on the long trip south. With lamentable timing, he also asked for a raise in salary as he had heard that New Orleans was "an extravagant place." His request infuriated the Secretary, who was already incensed by the extravagance of buying a ship without being authorized to do so. Here began the financial difficulties which, except for a couple of years immediately after the War of 1812, were to plague Porter for the rest of his life.

Porter reached New Orleans on 17 June to find trouble, both professional and personal. The naval station there was founded in 1806 by Captain John Shaw, who had scored so many triumphs in the *Enterprize,* but it had deteriorated badly since Shaw had traveled north to join Porter on the courts-martial emanating from the surrender of the *Chesapeake.* The base was furnished solely with Jeffersonian gunboats, vessels that were disliked by most officers anyway, but the ones at New Orleans were especially unpopular because the local builders had so thoroughly cheated the government that some of the boats rotted in less than two years. Theoretically, the base was manned by 400 sailors, but deaths, desertions, and terminations of enlistment had significantly reduced that number. The few who were left were racked by yellow fever and dysentery. Porter soon realized that in the prosecution of his duties he could expect little cooperation from either city or territorial authorities. His discomfiture was increased when he received the first of a series of nasty letters from Secretary Smith, who told him that the unauthorized expenses he had charged for the trip from Chester "give me great concern," and that, since his salary was fixed by law, he could not have a raise.[4]

The personal news that greeted him was even worse: his father was dying. On 4 August 1807 the old man had been given a warrant as a sailing master in the Navy and instructed to accompany his son to New Orleans, but this order was countermanded and he was assigned to gunboat service in Washington. There is no documentation that explains under what circumstances David Porter, the elder, made his way to New Orleans but, by the time his son arrived, he had been there several months. He had struck up a warm friendship with another sailing master, George Farragut, who was born in the Spanish Balearic Islands in 1755, and migrated to the United States twenty years later. Farragut served in several capacities during the American Revolution and, by the time it ended, had attained the rank of major in the cavalry. He spent some years in the merchant marine, then in 1790, moved to Knoxville, Tennessee, where he fought the Indians and acquired a farm. Five years later he married Elizabeth Shine, a thirty-year-old spinster. The second of Farragut's five children, David (originally James) Glasgow Farragut, destined to be the first admiral in the U.S. Navy, was born on 5 July 1801. Three years later, at the invitation of William C. C. Claiborne, Governor of the Territory of

Orleans, the family moved to New Orleans and subsequently met David Porter, the elder.

On an unusually hot day, probably in early June 1808, the elder Porter suffered a heat stroke while fishing on Lake Pontchartrain. Farragut, who lived beside the lake, saw his friend in distress and took him home to be nursed by his wife, Elizabeth. Early on 22 June, five days after his son arrived in New Orleans, the old man died. A few hours later, Elizabeth Farragut, perhaps exhausted from caring for the invalid, was suddenly felled by yellow fever and died. Both were buried two days later. Thus, before the younger Porter had been at his new post a week, double tragedy struck. Naturally, he felt "great shock" at his father's death and, according to his son, was soon prostrated by yellow fever himself, and required lengthy convalescence. Be that as it may, the unbroken frequency of his letters to the Secretary of the Navy indicates that he was not absent from duty for any extended period. He did what he could to assist Farragut. He informed the Secretary of the Navy that he considered "Mr. Farragut too old and infirm a man to perform the active duties required of the commander of a gun vessel," yet assigned him to just that service. Apparently, however, the old man did not have to spend much time at sea. Furthermore, Porter offered to care for two of Farragut's five motherless children. It must have been difficult for Farragut to agree to further breakup of his family, but he knew that Porter could provide for them better than he could, so he agreed to allow one of his daughters to live temporarily with Porter's sister, who had recently become the wife of Dr. Samuel D. Heap, the naval surgeon at New Orleans. David Glasgow Farragut, aged eight, was taken to Porter's own house. Young Glasgow (as he was called within the family) was never legally adopted by the Porters but he lived as one of their children, and his career was directed by his foster-father.[5]

It is widely believed in naval circles, and even by Porter's descendants, that David Farragut was David Porter's natural son. Charles Lewis, Farragut's chief biographer, offers the fact that, during "the year previous to young Farragut's birth David Porter was at sea," as proof that the story has no foundation. However, extant documentation neither proves nor disproves the allegation. Farragut, born on 5 July 1801, was conceived sometime during the autumn of 1800, and in August of that year Porter was in Philadelphia selling his little schooner *Amphitheatre*. There is no record of his whereabouts between that time and the following January, when he was in the West Indies aboard the *Experiment*. Hence, it is just possible that Porter met Elizabeth Shine Farragut and the result was David Glasgow.

But to accept Farragut as Porter's bastard, one would have to accept the following unlikely sequence: Porter went from the Atlantic coast to East Tennessee, had an affaire with a woman fifteen years his senior, kept in touch with her during his ensuing six years in the Mediterranean, and either was lucky enough to receive or managed to wangle an appointment to New Orleans so that he would be near Elizabeth and their son. There is not a scrap of evidence that Porter even saw Elizabeth Farragut prior to the last five days of her life. Certainly, the only acceptable conclusions are that Porter took in David Glasgow Farragut as an act of gratitude, and that Charles Lewis is right when he asserts that the rumor of an illicit blood tie between them has "not the slightest foundation in fact." [6]

Another man with whom Porter established a close personal association during his two years in New Orleans was Samuel Hambleton, Navy Purser, who remained his best friend for the rest of his life. Porter even named one of his sons "Hambleton," although the boy may occasionally have wished that his father had been content with "Samuel." Hambleton was a Marylander who seems to have been comfortably situated financially, either through inherited wealth or as a result of the few years he spent in business before he joined the Navy and was assigned to New Orleans. A lifelong bachelor, he was "one of those genial spirits one meets but rarely," [7] and he became closer to Porter than almost any relative, being used from time to time as a source of emergency income, and always as a confidant. Hambleton's letters show that he looked upon his friend with mingled affection and irritation; he appears to have been the one person who could give advice to Porter and expect it to be at least considered, if not followed.

There was little else pleasant for Porter in New Orleans. His monetary problems, both official and personal, remained unsolved. The first of a whole sequence of blows delivered by Secretary Robert Smith was his refusal to pay $500 or $600 (both figures are mentioned in the correspondence) for the "galley" Porter had ordered for his trip down the Ohio and Mississippi rivers, since the use of gunboats only had been permitted. Porter replied in cold fury, arguing that, when the gunboats promised were inoperable, he had no choice and that his galley "could be called a launch, barge, or anything else"; he demanded specific instructions in the future so that he could avoid "such truly humiliating reprimands [and] . . . censures. . . ." In a communication etched in acid, the Secretary informed Porter that, unless categorically authorized, he would not, under any circumstances, "accept any draft of yours, for money expended upon any object," and shortly afterward, called once more for economy, because "the constant enormous expenditures of the New Orleans Station exceed all calculations." Porter replied to these "mortifications" and "degradations" with defiance, and later suggested that the Secretary should appoint a professional committee composed of "three or five intelligent officers" to pass on essential expenses. Quarrels about his official accounts waxed and waned but never disappeared: according to his son, a final reckoning with the Department of the Navy was not reached until 1846, three years after Porter's death. Furthermore, the year 1808 which had opened so auspiciously for him closed with his personal finances in such disorder that he had to send a note to Hambleton asking him to "have the goodness to keep him from *starving* by sending him a little money by the bearer if he has any in the house." [8]

Some of the difficulties encountered by the commander of the New Orleans Station were routine in the Navy at almost any time or place: ship repairs, supplies, enlistments, desertions, and courts-martial. Others were peculiar to Louisiana during the early part of the nineteenth century. Relations with the Spaniards in their adjacent colony of West Florida were always touchy and, during his first month at New Orleans, Porter had to cope with a situation that could have set off international fireworks. Late in July, John Owings, one of Porter's lieutenants commanding a gunboat, landed, on his own initiative, at a plantation in West Florida to arrest and remove an American deserter. The Spanish governor immediately protested to William C. C. Claiborne. Porter acted with dispatch. He returned the deserter to West Florida, suspended Owings and later sent him back to Washington. In this instance, at least, he anticipated the wishes of Secretary Smith, who eventually told him to do just what he had done, because Owings had perpetrated "an outrage on the territorial jurisdiction of a friendly nation." [9]

Porter found that the most onerous of his duties was enforcing both President Jefferson's Embargo Act of 1807, which forbade the export of any American produce, and the recently introduced ban on international slave trade. The waters of Louisiana were filled with ships carrying cargoes of questionable origin and destination and sailing amid armed marauders, who ranged from legal privateers to outright pirates.* Within a week of assuming command, Porter notified Washington that he was busy dealing with "illicit trade." For the rest of the year, his gunboats plied river, lake, and bayou, picking up three slavers and seven merchantmen accused of breaking the Embargo.

Capturing a ship carrying contraband cargo proved to be only the first of the problems Porter faced in enforcing the Embargo. Once that

---

* Although the notorious pirates Jean and Pierre Lafitte were active in the area of New Orleans at this time, there is no evidence that Porter had any contact, hostile or otherwise, with them.

had been done, he ran into a variety of legal roadblocks thrown up by city and territorial officials, some of whom earned their livelihoods as fences for smuggled goods. The British schooner *Union*, which was nabbed in clear violation of the Embargo, provided a classic example of what Porter was up against. The New Orleans city attorney, probably in league with corrupt interests, told Porter that he knew the ship had broken the law, but since she had not really meant to, he was releasing both crew and cargo and permitting them to depart.

Similar harassments occupied the winter and early spring of 1809. In February, a Spanish schooner with the preposterous name of *Precious Ridicule,* bound from Spanish Baton Rouge to Pensacola with a cargo of wheat, cheese, oil, and clothing, was seized by one of Porter's gunboats. Porter had to determine what part, if any, of her cargo was of American origin and, therefore, contraband, and what part was of foreign origin and not subject to the Embargo. In this instance, he compromised, impounding the wheat as American, but releasing the other commodities.[10]

Knotty questions of maritime law enforcement were complicated by the ill-defended Spanish colony of West Florida, whose mere existence so close to American territory made execution of the Embargo practically impossible. Furthermore, it provided a haven for American deserters and other fugitives. Porter vented his frustration in a seven-page letter to the Secretary of the Navy, itemizing the legal violations committed by West Florida. American produce from many parts of the West went to Baton Rouge and, thence, through the bayous and along the coast to other Spanish ports, such as Mobile or Pensacola, finally reaching the open sea and world markets. To Porter, most West Floridians were renegade Americans who justified the betrayal of their own country by becoming super patriots of Spain, always crying "Viva el Rey Ferdinand VII." He was sure that Spain was plotting to "deliver the *disputed territory* to Great Britain," and concluded with the arguments, and even some of the exact language, of the Aix-la-Chapelle Dispatch (Ostend Manifesto) used in 1854 to advocate the forcible annexation of Cuba by the United States:

Has Spain the right to dispose of a Territory to another power without considering us when we have what we consider a just claim on that Territory? If she has not that right have we not the right of wresting from her by force that Territory when we see certain proofs of her intention to dispose of it?. . . . Batton Rouge could be taken now without spilling one drop of Blood . . . in a few months, perhaps in a few weeks, the British Troops from that Quarter may make the Blood of Americans flow in Torrents, lay this and the Western Country under contribution, destroy the object of those laws intended for the interest of our country, and execute the long vaunted threats of the Spaniards. The Public good requires that we should possess that Post—the perfidy of the present possessors requires that they should be deprived of it, Justice demands it, and the Spaniards have long expected it.

A month later, Porter was desperate enough to notify the Secretary that, somehow, he was going to stop *"an immense crop of cotton"* amounting to 6,000 bales from leaving West Florida, and the Secretary may have shuddered when he read that to do so Porter was willing "to make some encroachments on [the] National jurisdiction" of Spain. Smith must have been relieved when he heard that Porter had seen the Non-Intercourse Law and had "for the present" ceased to enforce the Embargo.

This shift in maritime law coincided with a brightening of diplomatic skies. In the spring of 1809, David M. Erskine, a representative of Great Britain, and Robert Smith, who had left the Navy Department to become Secretary of State—a change that must have made glorious news to Porter—signed an agreement that seemed to settle the outstanding differences between the two countries. During the brief period of sunshine that ensued, Porter was told by Charles Goldsborough, Acting Secretary of the Navy, that reinforcement of his gunboat squadron had been canceled because: "In consequence of the recent arrangement with . . . Great Britain there no longer exists a necessity for this increase." The decision not to reinforce the squadron was confirmed by Paul Hamilton, who replaced Smith as Secretary of the Navy. Hamilton wrote that the resources at the New Orleans Station should be "nursed" because "there no longer exists a probability of war" with England.[11] However, this spasm of international amity was brief. Erskine had exceeded his instructions, London failed to ratify the agreement, and within a few months Anglo-American relations had relapsed into their usual state of frigid semi-hostility.

In March 1809 Porter had to cope with a personal tragedy involving America's first medical family. Acting Lieutenant John Rush, eldest son of the eminent Dr. Benjamin Rush of Philadelphia, and brother of Richard Rush, later U.S. Minister to Great Britain, had a short and violent naval career. He had been dismissed from his first enlistment for threatening to beat with a "bludgeon cane" the ultra-Federalist editor, William Cobbett. He managed to rejoin the Navy and, sometime before Porter arrived, was assigned to New Orleans as a gunboat commander. Benjamin Rush reported to ex-President John Adams in September 1808, that once again his son was in trouble because of "a quarrel and gunplay aboard his vessel." John had quarreled with Lieutenant Benjamin Turner, his best friend, and was arrested for killing him in a duel. Although young Rush was released from custody, he went to pieces mentally. On 7 March Porter notified Secretary Hamilton that, during the previous December,

Rush had gone insane and, although he had been put under restraint to prevent him from harming himself or others, he had "found means to secrete a Razor with which he this morning cut his throat and it is with the utmost regret I am compelled to state that his life is despaired of." Unfortunately, Porter's prognosis was not right: Rush recovered, but only physically. He was sent back to Philadelphia in 1810, to be placed in the Pennsylvania Hospital, where, hopelessly insane, he lived until his death in 1837. His father was sure that the custom of dueling had ruined his son.[12]

At about the time Porter was occupied with the problem of John Rush, General James Wilkinson took over command of the Army in New Orleans. Wherever the General, a Marylander, born in 1757, appeared he was wrapped in a cloak of mystery and obscurantism, and his penchant for intrigue and peculation was noticeable from the first. During the American Revolution he belonged to the Conway Cabal and intrigued against General George Washington, rocketed from captain to brigadier general in a year and a half and, late in the war, attained the lucrative post of clothier-general, which he left amid accusations of personal corruption.

As a Western trader after the Revolution, he first went to New Orleans during 1787. There he started his lengthy intrigues with Spanish officialdom, becoming a paid agent of the Spanish crown at a salary of $2,000 a year. Still in the pay of Spain, he returned to the American Army in 1791 and, during the following decade, roamed the South and the West, always enveloped in mystery. When he was selected to assume military authority in New Orleans following the sale of Louisiana to the United States in 1803, he took the opportunity to negotiate with Vicente Folch, Governor of Spanish West Florida, about the failure of Madrid to pay his salary for the past ten years. Anticipating a satisfactory settlement, he offered Folch his *Reflections* on the situation in the West, which consisted of the warning that, if the United States took over the Floridas, Americans "like the ancient Goths and Vandals would precipitate themselves upon the weak defences of Mexico, [and] overturn everything in their path. . . ." Then, as the host of enemies that followed him like a retinue were closing in on him, he begged Folch, "For God's sake, help me out of the pool in which I am floundering." His combined stress on the obvious and the pitiful worked: he emerged from his "pool" only slightly damp, and Folch arranged to let him be dried with $12,000 of his $20,000 back salary.[13]

Wilkinson's next bizarre association was with Aaron Burr, a conspirator who was almost, but not quite, his equal. The General and Vice President Burr had their heads together in Washington during 1804 and

1805, and while the former served as temporary governor of Louisiana Territory, he acted as Burr's patron, welcoming him and writing letters of introduction for him, both in St. Louis and New Orleans.* There seems to be little doubt that Wilkinson was hand in glove with Burr in whatever arcane adventure the latter was planning—probably an invasion of Spanish Mexico. But the General, who had no peer in his uncanny ability to trim his sails to the prevailing breeze, changed his mind about Burr's plans when, during the summer of 1806, he was assigned to command of the Army in Orleans Territory. Enlisting the tacit support of Governor Claiborne, he proceeded to treat New Orleans as a conquered city. Ostensibly to protect it against Spanish invasion from the south and Burr's approach from the north, ". . . he declared martial law, rebuilt defences, embargoed vessels, and arrested and imprisoned . . . all whom he regarded as Burr's agents. He overrode the decrees of courts and spirited away those arrested by his arbitrary orders."

Wilkinson's timely defection foiled Burr's amorphous plot, whatever it was, and the latter came no closer to New Orleans (or Mexico) than Natchez, Mississippi, where he was arrested. Somehow, arch-intriguer Wilkinson not only managed to avoid being court-martailed for his participation in the plot, but he appeared as a prosecution witness in Jefferson's abortive attempt to have Burr convicted of treason in 1808. As Irving Brant, Madison's biographer, graphically put it: "In his dealings with Burr, Wilkinson was like a praying mantis devouring a wasp." But if the shifty General wriggled out of his association with Burr, his enemies managed to have him brought before a court of inquiry about his dealings with Spain. The court's ambiguous conclusions amounted to a whitewash: ". . . there is no Evidence of Brigadier General James Wilkinson having at any time received a Pension from the Government of Spain . . . for corrupt purposes." [14]

President Jefferson had a blind spot that prevented him from believing that there was any fire connected with the smoke that constantly attended Wilkinson. Not only did he approve the decision reached by the court of inquiry, but he reassigned the General to Army command in New Orleans. Although orders dated 2 December 1808 instructed him to proceed from Washington to Louisiana with all due speed, it took Wilkinson three months to get there, whereas dispatches could make the journey in three weeks. Chicanery was one reason for his tardiness; he left with a ship full of flour and apples, commodities whose export the Em-

---

* The Louisiana Purchase had been divided. Orleans Territory, with its capital at New Orleans, became the state of Louisiana in 1812. The ill-defined lands to the north, centered at St. Louis, were called Louisiana Territory until 1812, when the name was changed to Missouri Territory.

bargo Act strictly forbade. He wandered down the east coast and visited first Havana and then Pensacola, where, while plotting with Spanish officials, he apparently picked up some pocket money in return for part of his cargo. He arrived in April 1809 at New Orleans, where he was greeted with a signal lack of enthusiasm—he was remembered there—but perhaps he consoled himself by selling the rest of his produce.

Once ashore, Wilkinson plunged into what was evidently an attempt to promote rebellion throughout Spanish Latin America and, as head of the Army installation at New Orleans, he promptly got in touch with Porter; the Navy could be useful to him. Their association started on a jarring note: in trying to arrange a meeting, Wilkinson made the mistake of calling to Porter's attention, with lofty condescension, the difference in "our respective stations." Master Commandant Porter, already pushing for his captaincy, heatedly replied that although his *"rank* in the Navy" was inferior to that of a general in the Army, he was "Commander in Chief of Naval Forces," and he would meet him on terms of equality, and "on no other footing." Needing Porter's cooperation, Wilkinson began working on him through the agency of Purser Samuel Hambleton, and even offered "to wave punctilio" so that they could converse as equals.

Seldom was Porter more perceptive than in his dealings with the slippery General. His immediate suspicion that Wilkinson was "endeavouring to induce the Spanish Islands and Provinces to declare themselves Independent," was reinforced when Hambleton reported that the General claimed to have been sent to New Orleans "to meet an expected attack." According to Wilkinson, Mexico was "in a dreadful state," and he expected to get much information from an officer he had sent into the Mexican backcountry. He said he had already communicated with authorities in Mexico City and would soon meet with Governor Folch for a discussion on the situation. Hambleton warned Porter that Wilkinson was trying to get control of the Navy in order to carry out some kind of mischief in Mexico. Thoroughly alarmed, Porter mused about this "great and apparently unnecessary alarm; this strange mystery, obscurity, and ambiguity. . . . The character of General Wilkinson had long been considered doubtful by many. . . . What enemy is to attack us? Why the need of a private interview? Why is he trying to get my aid and counsel? Why is he willing 'to wave punctilio'?" [15]

Suspicion became certainty a day or two later when Porter attended a dinner at Governor Claiborne's house. Governor Folch, his Spanish officers, and Wilkinson were also present. The Spaniards "paid to, and received from, General Wilkinson great attention." Wilkinson proposed a toast that could have rocked Spanish-American relations, "Independence to the Mexican World and a close Union with the United States," then, turning to Folch, said, "Dam-me Governor we will soon see that country; I should not be surprised if we should shortly meet there." The Spanish Governor of West Florida nodded. This memorable evening ended with Porter being told by Wilkinson that he was "too damn'd stiff." The two met on the street the next day, and Wilkinson decided to backtrack: "Well, we got damn'd high last night . . . I believe on my Soul we got so far at last as to drink downfall to the Spanish Monarchy."

Porter lost no time in sending off a coded letter to the State Department, in which he made his suspicions known and asked if Wilkinson was acting on government orders. Several weeks later, he received a reply, also in cipher: ". . . I am authorized to assure you that no instructions have been given by the government [to] Gen'. Wilkinson to interfere in any manner with Spanish affairs and that the proceedings which appear to you to be in his contemplation are wholly unauthorized by the government. Shew this letter to the Governor [Claiborne] and have a frank [?] understanding with him [?] upon the subject." By that time it did not matter. Whatever Wilkinson had hoped to accomplish blurred into the fog of confusion that ever surrounded him. Porter attributed the collapse of his nebulous plot to the departure of Governor Folch for Pensacola, the onslaught of serious sickness in the Army, his own refusal to lend naval support, and the alarm of Spanish officers involved, following which, he "heard no more of revolutionary plans." [16]

But Wilkinson continued to make trouble for Porter. Although Wilkinson's *Memoirs* are otherwise untrustworthy, his recollection of the conditions he found when he arrived in New Orleans may be believed: "I found a body of two thousand undisciplined recruits, men and officers, with few exceptions, sunk in indolence and dissipation . . . and nearly a third sick . . . men deserting in squads; the military agent . . . without a cent in his chest . . . a great deficiency in camp equipage . . . medicines and hospital supplies. . . ." Unfortunately, the ameliorations he proposed only worsened matters.

He decided to move his ailing soldiers to a new camp and, in spite of warnings from the administration against choosing another site inside New Orleans, he chose Terre aux Boeufs, still in the environs of the city, where drainage and other facilities were totally inadequate. His enemies first whispered, then shouted, that personal financial considerations had influenced his selection. By the middle of the summer of 1809, 963 of the 1,574 soldiers were prostrated with " 'chills and fever,' dysentery and scurvey." Terre aux Boeufs became a charnel house. When news of these conditions reached Washington, Wilkinson was instructed to move his entire establishment north to the healthier terrain around Natchez. The

Navy was ordered to help in the move, but Porter told the Secretary of the Navy on 19 August that he could provide little assistance because there was so much sickness among his own men. He did eventually give Wilkinson some gunboats to accompany the Army barges and, amid clouds of mosquitoes, the combined operation inched upriver in appalling heat. Soldiers died by the score. Before colder weather ended most of the suffering, forty per cent of Wilkinson's total force was dead. The General attributed responsibility for the disaster to almost everything and everyone, himself excepted, but the Navy and Porter got the lion's share of the blame for failing to cooperate.

Wilkinson's tenure in New Orleans that began in 1809 ended in the same way as did almost all the other episodes of his tangled life. ". . . distrusted by his former Spanish friends, and pursued by vindictive enemies at New Orleans and elsewhere, he was forced to resign his depleted command and once more journey northward in a futile endeavor to clear his reputation from the weighty charges of inefficiency and personal corruption." In 1811, he finally faced a court-martial, whose verdict of acquittal was equivocal and "was so worded that the President [Madison] approved it 'with regret.'" Restored to command, Wilkinson's operations during the War of 1812 included the seizure of Mobile and a second part of Spanish West Florida,* and the mismanagement of a campaign against the British in Canada. After facing another court-martial and receiving another "not proven" acquittal, he was ousted from the Army, and eventually went to Mexico, where he dabbled in politics until his death in 1825. After his brief but memorable association with Wilkinson, Porter referred to him as "Gen¹. Puff . . . a man of duplicity [,] meanness and cowardice." [17]

Before, during, and after his connection with "Gen¹. Puff," money problems cast a pall over Porter. Before resigning as Secretary of the Navy, the antagonistic Robert Smith had turned down several additional bills submitted by Porter for his trip down the Mississippi to New Orleans. Threatening that if he were not permitted to argue his case in Washington, he would resign, Porter voiced his frustration to the new Secretary of the Navy: "Overwhelmed as I have been by censures undeserved, tortured as I have been in my mind and unjustly oppressed in my pecuniary concerns by having my Bills, to a considerable amount, drawn for the Public Service, returned to me protested [,] accompanied with expenses I have no longer the means to meet. . . ." Perhaps justifia-

* The United States acquired the Spanish Floridas in the following order: 1810—West Florida, from the Mississippi River to the Pearl River; 1813—West Florida, from the Pearl to the Perdido River; 1819—West Florida, from the Perdido to the Apalachicola River, and all of East Florida.

bly incensed by the tone of this letter, Hamilton replied so tartly that Porter apologized, and it is well that he did, for his relations with Hamilton were to be more cordial than they had been with the overbearing Smith.

At least Porter had the pleasure of enjoying fatherhood for the first time.* On 11 March 1809, Evalina gave what must have been premature birth to a son, named William, after Captain Bainbridge. David Dixon Porter writes that for many months the baby was so small that "he could sleep in a cigar box" and, because no clothing was small enough for him, he "had to be rolled in cotton." Dining with the Porters must have been a grisly experience, for the new father used to have the youngster "handed around the table lying on a napkin in a plate." Perhaps the frequent trips between cigar box and plate, while wrapped in cotton during a New Orleans summer, had a traumatic effect on the baby. As a grown man, William was, according to his father, an adulterer, a liar, a cheat, and a thief.

Domestic trouble of another variety roiled life at the New Orleans Station. While Porter was away from home during early June 1809, his slave Aaron was strongly suspected of having entered the bedroom of Mrs. Porter and Porter's sister about midnight "for some villainous purpose." Although Porter regarded Aaron as "a smart boy," he conceded that he had "his faults" (attempted rape might be characterized as a fault), and, hoping that his conduct would improve under a stricter master, decided to sell him.

Porter seems to have looked upon naval discipline in a different light. His letters to the Department are full of bickerings with his junior officers, especially a Marine captain whom Porter accused of refusing to obey orders. Toward his enlisted men, Porter was no Captain Bligh, but he was a strict disciplinarian: on one deserter he inflicted the unusually brutal punishment of "one hundred lashes on the bare back with a cat-of-nine-tails" and suspension of pay for nine months.

The cumulative effect of all he had gone through during his fourteen months in New Orleans—his father's death, financial difficulties, touchy relations with West Florida, troubles over enforcement of the maritime laws, suspicions about the activities of General Wilkinson, and personal clashes, both domestic and official—very likely caused Porter to yearn for greener and cooler pastures. In a fifteen-page letter addressed to the Secretary on 16 August 1809, he commented on the expedition of

---

* In order of their birth, the Porter children were William David, Elizabeth. David Dixon, Thomas, Theodoric, Hambleton, Evalina, Henry Ogden, Florence and Imogene. All, except Elizabeth and Florence who evidently died in infancy or childhood, are mentioned in the Porter correspondence.

Lewis and Clark, which had ended three years previously, displayed his geographical knowledge by itemizing earlier explorations, and asked for permission to lead another party into the Pacific Northwest. Seven months later, he returned to the subject, reminding Hamilton that he had already submitted "a manuscript" about his proposal that he lead an expedition to find the "nearest communications" from coast to coast. Knowing how economy-minded the Secretary was, he laid stress on the fact that the trip would not cost much: he pointed out that he already had available sufficient officers and men, and said they could travel in his "bomb brigs," the *Etna* and the *Vesuvius*. He should have been slightly embarrassed when, a few weeks later, he had to admit that these two ships were so "extremely rotten" that they would have to be torn down and rebuilt.[18]

Enforcement of the changing and ill-defined navigation laws continued to be a source of great difficulties for Porter. All three of the maritime powers of Europe were troublesome. British merchantmen and slavers, working with disloyal elements in New Orleans, gave rise to Porter's fear that he was menaced by a wholesale conspiracy—"a system of iniquity"—to break the "non intercourse laws and slave act." In a letter written to the Secretary in February 1810 he assailed the Spaniards, but remarked that "liberated as West Florida now is," he looked for amelioration in that quarter.* He hoped that he would now be able to enforce restrictions against Spanish trade there, but anticipated more trouble with Governor Folch, because of "the impertinence and obstinacy of that man."

It was the French who gave Porter his greatest anxiety, but they also provided him with an excellent opportunity to earn a personal fortune. For some months, three French privateers, *Le Duc de Montebello*, *L'Intrepide*, and *La Petite Chance*, which "took, plundered or burnt every American Spanish *or* English vessel" they met, had been interrupting trade in the Caribbean. During March 1810, Porter received word that the three corsairs were at Pilot Town, in the Mississippi Delta. He assembled what gunboats he had, sailed downriver to Pilot Town, anchored "where his guns would bear upon the privateers," and demanded their surrender. Luckily, the French decided not to fight, for Porter was outgunned, and his fragile boats might have been easily shot from the water. When the papers of the three captives were examined, it looked as though the case for their confiscation and sale was airtight. The *Montebello* had sailed from Baltimore as a legitimate merchantman bound for

---

* Porter was premature. The extreme western portion of Spanish West Florida was not annexed to the United States until 27 October 1810, following an uprising of Americans in Baton Rouge on 26 September of that year.

the West Indies, but had called at Charleston to pick up guns and a new crew for privateering ventures. *L'Intrepide* was carrying a French letter of marque from St. Martin Island in the West Indies. Neither, of course, had any legal right to attack neutral ships. The status of *La Petite Chance* was ludicrous: she was sailing under a letter of marque of a "pirogue"—or dugout canoe. In his report to the Department, Porter enclosed a protest from the *Montebello*'s crew, but said he was, nevertheless, sure he could get the ships "libelled and condemned." [19]

His optimism was soon dashed, as the civil authorities in New Orleans, headed by the city district attorney, openly supported by the mercantile community and, perhaps, with the clandestine backing of Governor Claiborne, proceeded to erect one legal barrier after another. It seemed that the laws Porter was trying to enforce could not possibly apply to these three ships. Hence, their crews must be released and allowed to roam New Orleans, free to whip up as much trouble as they could. Porter angrily avowed that the harassing tactics used by both city and territorial officials were causing him "many embarrassments." He especially resented the behavior of Governor Claiborne: more than a year later, he was still smoldering, as he told his friend, Hambleton, "I know not how to despise him enough." *

Claiborne did his best to dissociate himself from any involvement with Porter in the case of the three privateers. When he wrote to the Secretary of State on the subject on 30 March, he took care to enclose a petition, dated 26 March 1810, from the owners of the *Montebello* asking for the return of the ship and damages of $10,000 "for loss and injury." He told the French Consul in New Orleans that Porter was "entirely independent of my order or controul," and said he would be pleased to forward the Consul's protest to the President. He assured the Frenchman that the seizure was "alike opposed to the American Character, and to that correct Deportment which the President requires of all his officers . . . ," and gave it as his opinion that, if the facts were as reported, it would be disapproved by the U.S. government.[20]

When Porter was forced by the civil authorities to release the crews of the privateers from confinement, a Frenchman who verbally assailed him during a court session went unpunished, whereafter Porter had "to resort to military force for protection of myself and family." He vowed that, despite his "feeble means of personal protection," he would continue to do his duty, and said he thought the judge should make sure that

* Perhaps Porter was too harsh. Poor Claiborne, who could speak neither French nor Spanish (the languages of at least nine-tenths of the population of Louisiana), faced insuperable problems, and it is doubtful that any American governor of Orleans Territory at that time could have done much better.

criminals cannot offer "further insult and violence." Probably with the above incident in mind, he recommended to the Secretary of State that appointed officials in New Orleans, especially U.S. marshals, should be Americans, since the foreign elements were always prejudiced in favor of their fellow nationals. In the midst of all this confusion, one French captain reported that his "Christ" (crucifix) had been stolen, and before the matter was settled, Porter had written nine pages of correspondence about "the missing Christ."

Earlier, Secretary of the Navy Hamilton had ordered Porter to act with "caution and circumspection" in the disposition of captured ships, and to "take the opinion" of Claiborne and the city district attorney. But after the Secretary had read the details about the *Montebello*, *L'Intrepide*, and *La Petite Chance* and had heard from a private source that Porter had behaved impeccably, he ordered him to send any ships that he seized to either Savannah or Charleston for "adjudication," and told him that he should not, on any account, allow such cases to come up before the Louisiana courts. Hamilton undoubtedly had seen the analysis of the local situation which Thomas B. Robertson, district attorney of the Orleans Territory, had sent to the Secretary of State and which read, in part: "New Orleans is filled with desperadoes . . . accustomed to piracies and connected with the parties who furnish them with every facility to escape forfeitures or punishment . . . Commodore Porter . . . will doubtless communicate fully on these subjects. . . ." [21]

The *Montebello, L'Intrepide,* and *La Petite Chance* provided Porter with not one, but two, possibilities to make a fortune: first, prize money, namely his share of the proceeds from the sale of the three ships; and second, the handsome rewards that the *Consulado* of Havana, an association of Cuban merchants, offered for the capture of the ships. He lost no time in trying to collect the prize money. When he was in Washington in midsummer 1810, he discussed the matter with Paul Hamilton, but nothing was decided. He wrote Secretary of the Treasury Albert Gallatin asking for an opinion on his chances of collecting this fund, and the reply he received was a masterpiece of evasion: "The monies will, after a decision of the Supreme Court, be paid by the proper officer to the parties legally entitled to the same." In December, he petitioned Congress for "abandonment" of any financial penalties that the Louisiana courts might impose on him for having seized the vessels. At least one of his efforts to turn the capture of the privateers into personal gain materialized right away: he persuaded Samuel Hambleton to advance him $1,000 against future proceeds from the *Montebello*. Later, he appointed Hambleton his agent to press his claims before Congress, and eventually, Hambleton succeeded. In the summer of 1814 Congress passed an act giving Porter the right to distribute the prize money for the three ships condemned for violating U.S. laws and sold. No figure was mentioned, but his son says Porter's share was $25,000 but that, by the time he had paid legal fees and other expenses defending himself against a series of law suits by the ships' owners, "very little" of it was left.[22]

Porter's second opportunity appeared potentially even more lucrative. The *Consulado* of Havana had posted rewards totaling $60,000 for ending the careers of the three marauders that had so seriously harried Spanish commerce. On his way to Washington from New Orleans, late in June, Porter called at Havana to present his claims and pick up the money. His papers were in order, but the *Consulado* refused to pay without specific authorization from Madrid. A year later, traveling "incog" lest he be taken by "picaroons," Porter returned to Cuba on the same mission and, although he stayed in Havana from March until June, he accomplished nothing. Eventually, Spain offered him full settlement, but on conditions he could not accept, and he spent his latter years in fruitless quest of the $60,000 owed to him by the Havana *Consulado*.

The single-minded avidity with which he chased his potential fortune evoked so much criticism from his fellow Americans, that he complained to Hambleton that it was unjust: since he was prosecuting the cases for prize money and the reward at his own expense, he wrote, "where is the dishonor? Where is the impropriety?" Moreover, even before Porter seized the three privateers, France had protested officially about his activities against its shipping in Louisiana; and after that event the French Minister demanded his arrest and court-martial. Since the United States stood behind his actions, both domestic and foreign, in New Orleans, protests were useless, but Porter was annoyed enough to tell Hambleton that, "the Frenchman—may . . . go to the Devil for all I care."[23]

Despite his travails, Porter left "a well ordered naval command" to his successor, Captain Daniel T. Patterson,* who, four years later, ably assisted General Andrew Jackson in the Battle of New Orleans. When Porter returned to Washington, the administration congratulated him on a job well done in Louisiana. All in all, however, his two years in command of the Naval Station at New Orleans had not been pleasant; his duties there were certainly not congenial to what has been called his "martial disposition." For months he had been begging Secretary Hamilton for reassignment, and it must have been with vast relief that he and his family left New Orleans late in June 1810. His son made a strange error when he described the homeward journey: he said his father

---

* Patterson's daughter, George Ann, married David Dixon Porter in 1839.

traveled up the Mississippi in a gunboat, "seldom making more than thirty miles a day," and taking three months to get as far as Pittsburgh, where his arrival aroused much excitement. Documentation makes it clear that Porter left New Orleans on or around 21 June 1810 in the little *Vesuvius,* was in Havana on 1 July, in Washington around 23 July, and back in Chester no later than 3 August.[24]

Porter's return to Pennsylvania was not particularly happy, although it must have been pleasant to exchange Louisiana's heat and disease for life at Green Bank, the impressive stone "mansion" on the Delaware River given to him by his father-in-law as a wedding present. Porter considered renaming the house and, in one of his rare flashes of humor, wrote to Hambleton:

> I intend to call my new place "Montebello" so soon as I can get some of the *Montebello* . . . spoils. It happens to be nearer a bakery than a mountain but that makes no odds. . . . The Chester folk call me a Federalist and shun me as they would a rattlesnake because I wear imported cloth and gilt buttons. I am in hopes that the name will convince them to the contrary [,] it sounds so much like "Monticello."

But Porter's hopes that his monetary ills would soon be cured by the prize money and rewards due from the ships he had captured in Louisiana were not realized, and face-to-face discussions with the Secretary of the Navy Paul Hamilton and U.S. Treasury auditors helped little, if at all, in balancing his accounts with the Navy Department. Consequently, as he told his friend Samuel Hambleton, he felt "the hard hand of poverty." His wife was pregnant with their second child and, to the Secretary, he moaned that he had to worry about his "young and growing family." When health dictated a visit to a spa, he had to ask Hamilton for a $100 advance on his salary. Less than a month after his return from New Orleans, the financial burden was so oppressive that he submitted his resignation from the Navy, but when he received a very cordial reply from the Secretary, he withdrew it.[1]

Rank, title, and prestige were almost as essential to Porter as was money, and the requests for a captaincy with which he bombarded Hamilton came close to being ultimatums. When the year 1811 dawned and his commission still had not come through, he asked that he be given a captain's pay and granted the right to wear a captain's uniform, arguing that other officers awaiting promotion had been so accommodated. Although the Secretary answered courteously—it is not hard to imagine the brusque refusal Robert Smith would have sent—he could not stem the torrent of demands which crested shortly before the War of 1812. Porter finally became so incensed that he said he would refuse to command the frigate that Hamilton was trying to find for him, and asked that he be given command of a smaller warship, which would be a more fitting assignment for a mere master commandant. He bragged to Hambleton about his treatment of Hamilton, and added sneeringly: "The Secretary is unpopular here . . . from the *highest* to the lowest, he is disliked; it is supposed he has been too long in the habit of driving slaves [Hamilton was from South Carolina] to know how to regard the honorable feelings of gentlemen. . . ." * At this point, even the affable Hambleton lost patience with him and answered sharply that Porter's insistence on a lesser command was ridiculous. He told him that if he did not get his captaincy, he could charge it to the account of his "said letters in duplicate and triplicate." [2]

Sometime before the middle of 1812, still seeking escape from his financial difficulties, Porter made a second trip to Havana in the hopes of collecting the *Consulado*'s reward. Anticipating his immediate future, he requested that, in case of war, he be given command of a squadron in the Pacific with the mission of harrying British whalers and merchantmen. He also asked that he be appointed to fill the "vacancy in the consulate of Tripoli," because his long confinement there had given him an unusual knowledge of its people's habits and customs.[3]

Hamilton's search for a command to Porter's liking was complicated by the latter's insistence on promotion but, after a couple of offers and withdrawals, he presented the disgruntled master commandant with the 32-gun frigate *Essex*. This offer was gratefully accepted. The USS *Essex* was a small frigate of only some 860 tons, 140 feet in length, and 36½ feet beam,† and she carried a complement of around 300 men. When anti-French sentiment was at its height, President John Adams asked the government to "accept such vessels as might be built by the citizens for the national service, and to issue six per cent stock to indemnify the subscrib-

---

* Hamilton was in trouble, but it was due to alcohol. He could work only in the morning, for he was drunk every afternoon, once appearing "publicly intoxicated" at a naval ball in the *Constellation*. On 31 December 1812 he resigned under fire and was succeeded as Secretary of the Navy by William Jones.

† Authorities vary on her exact dimensions. The above figures are taken from the U.S. Navy, but a biographer of Admiral Farragut gives her length as 141 feet and her beam as 37 feet.

ers." Among the major coastal cities that answered the President's call was the thriving port of Salem, Massachusetts, where the *Essex* was built. At a public meeting there on 25 October 1798 "it was voted *unanimously* to build a frigate of thirty-two guns, and to loan the same to the government. . . ." The people of Salem and Essex County subscribed $74,700 for the ship herself, and the government provided $64,662 for her equipment, for a total cost of $139,362.[4]

Throughout the winter of 1798–99, the best white oak of surrounding Essex County was cut and hauled to an island in Salem Harbor, where the keel was laid in April 1799. A reporter for the *Independent Chronicle* of Boston wrote that when the *Essex* was launched on 30 September, she slid into the water "with the most easy and graceful motion . . . as fine a ship of her size as graces the American Navy. . . . She is well calculated to do essential service to her country." Porter was slow to agree with early accounts of the *Essex'* speed and, although he eventually did, Samuel Eliot Morison says, "a careful reading of Captain David Porter's log of her Pacific cruise proves her to have been an uncommonly slow sailer for an American frigate." According to naval records, she was designed to carry twenty-six 12-pound long guns and ten 6-pounders, but that armament was later changed, apparently making her somewhat top-heavy and, perhaps, causing her to lose her original speed.

The *Essex* was not ready for service until the Quasi-War with France was almost over, so she saw no action in the Caribbean. In June 1800, under the command of Captain Edward Preble, she was dispatched to accompany the 36-gun *Congress* to pick up American merchant ships in Dutch East Indian waters and escort them home. When the *Congress* proved unseaworthy, the *Essex* sailed on alone to Batavia and, after an eleven-month cruise, brought the convoy back to New York. On that voyage, the *Essex* became the first American warship to reach the Pacific by rounding the Cape of Good Hope: under the command of Porter, she became the first to reach that ocean via Cape Horn. During the ten years that followed her cruise under Captain Preble, she was commanded by such well-known officers as William Bainbridge, James Barron, and Charles Stewart. She went to the Mediterranean a few times, was out of commission between 1807 and 1809, and two years later brought back from England U.S. Minister William Pinkney—a severance of diplomatic relations with Britain that presaged the approaching war.[5]

During the summer of 1811, Porter assumed command of the ship with which his name became permanently associated. One of his many problems was finding a suitable crew. It was difficult to recruit sailors, and he protested to the Department that, those he did enlist were often snatched away from him by captains of higher rank. He had less trouble in getting the officers he wanted. He asked for John Downes, whom he had known since the Tripolitan War and whose "courage" he liked, as his First Lieutenant. His request was granted, and Downes brought an abundance of "courage," along with intelligence and loyalty, to Porter and to the *Essex*. Ever one to have an eye out for the benefit of his relatives, Porter placed his foster-son, David Glasgow Farragut, among his midshipmen. When the Porter family returned from New Orleans, young Farragut had been put in school and, one day, Porter took him to meet Secretary of the Navy Paul Hamilton, who promised to appoint him a midshipman when he reached the age of ten. Farragut's commission, signed 17 December 1810, arrived when he was only nine and half, so Hamilton did better than keep his pledge.* "Mr. Farragut" was a month over ten years old when, immaculate in his "short blue coat . . . with a button and a slip of lace on each side" of his high collar, he reported on board the *Essex*. He sailed on the shakedown cruise of the *Essex* during the late fall of 1811 and, on Christmas Day, experienced a tremendous storm that almost ran the ship aground.[6]

Porter's main concern during the months immediately preceding the war, was his ship's armament, for she was laden with carronades instead of the long guns with which she had been originally fitted. It is not known who made the switch, but one unreliable source suggests that Porter's predecessor, Captain John Smith, may have made it sometime in 1810. Lightweight and short-barreled, the carronade "could shoot only at short range, but weighed so much less than the normal long guns that greatly increased calibers, and a larger number of guns, could be used without straining the decks; and when carronades were used they gave a tremendous smashing effect at close quarters." Although they had been introduced more than a generation before, they were still controversial. On 12 October 1811, Porter asserted to the Secretary that carronades were still "an experiment in modern warfare," and continued: "I do not conceive it proper to trust the honor of the flag entirely to them. Was the ship to be disabled in her rigging in the early part of an engagement, a ship much inferior to her in sailing and in force, armed with long Guns, could take a position beyond the reach of our Carronades, and cut us to pieces without our being able to do her any injury." That is precisely what did happen to Porter in Valparaiso Bay more than two years later.

In a note jotted on the side of the above-mentioned letter, the Secre-

---

* Farragut was by no means the youngest midshipman commissioned in the U.S. Navy. The champion in that category was Samuel Barron, who was appointed at the commendable age of two years and one month, but had to suffer through almost all of a wasted decade before being taken on his first cruise when he reached the age of eleven.

tary wrote that Porter would be permitted to exchange defective carronades for good ones, but could have no more long guns. Within a week of
receiving this unwelcome information, Porter returned to the attack, asking for "a lesser ship with long guns," since he had "no confidence in Carronades alone." He set forth a compromise suggested by Lieutenant
Downes and the other officers: ". . . by taking four carronades and the
two long 12 pounders from the gun-deck and substituting, long 18 pounders she will be rendered as effective as is desired." Hamilton accepted
the suggestion, agreeing that the request to "substitute long 18-poun-
ders is unquestionably a good one . . . I therefore consent to your making the proposed change." [7] Even this minor alteration was not made.
The *Essex* sailed for the Pacific without the long guns that might have
saved her.

All this time, Porter and other aware Americans had been watching
clouds lower on international horizons. Remembering well his boyhood
experiences with Great Britain in the West Indies, Porter had always
blazed with resentment against that nation, and he had been outraged by
such later violations of American rights as British searches and seizures
that culminated in the *Chesapeake-Leopard* disgrace. On his way home
from New Orleans in 1810, he had spoken caustically about a British
warship firing on the USS *Vixen*. Presumably, he had exulted when his
old friend John Rodgers, while commanding the frigate *President,*
smashed the British sloop of war *Little Belt* in an accidental encounter on
16 March 1811. Questions of national honor arising from maritime
grievances would, naturally, have made a considerably greater impact on
Porter than would any possibilities of territorial conquest. Indeed, he
deplored plans to annex Canada as "the safest, but not the most noble
and dignified manner of retaliating."

Yet, his dislike of Britain by no means endowed him with any affection for France. He could recall personal encounters with that country
during the Quasi-War of 1798 to 1800, as well as the troubles he had with
French privateers in New Orleans. He saw through Napoleon's hood-
winking of the Madison administration in 1810 and 1811, and he described the French Emperor's ostensible revocation of his decrees against
the American carrying trade in Europe as "a sprat thrown out as bait to
catch a mackarel." A little later, he accurately characterized Napoleon as
one who "seems too loving to be sincere."

The Madison administration was trying to walk a tightrope between
involvement in a war for which the United States was quite unprepared,
and continued acceptance of national humiliations that evoked clamor
from bellicose Americans. The ambivalence of the government's attitude
can be seen in the communication the Secretary addressed to Porter on 9

June 1811: "You like every other patriotic American have . . . deeply felt the injuries and insults heaped on our country by the two great belligerents of Europe . . . [especially] the inhuman and dastardly attack on our frigate *Chesapeak.* . . . ." Then he instructed him to maintain strict neutrality, but "at any risk" to uphold the dignity of his flag, and to submit to no "unjust aggression." To such a well-known hothead as Porter, Hamilton's first instruction may have been necessary, but the latter was superfluous.[8]

Meanwhile, Porter was preparing for the onset of hostilities by molding officers and crew of the *Essex* into a fighting unit. Drill was incessant, with special emphasis on the rapidity with which the crew could be ready for action. At stipulated intervals during the day, and at any time of the night, the roll of drums would bring the men on the double, cutlasses in hand, to their posts. Many of the exercises were fire drills, fire being an ever-present hazard in those days of wooden ships. Gunnery was practised continually, often with live ammunition aimed at targets, while Marines sniped from the yards. Since his ship was overburdened with carronades, Porter had to plan on avoiding long-range encounters. Through superior seamanship, he would have to close on an adversary, deliver broadsides with his battering carronades, and then board. Particular attention had to be devoted to training for hand-to-hand combat. Late in life, Farragut reminisced that "never afterward on a ship where the crew of the *Essex* was represented but they were found the best swordsmen on board . . . every man with his cutlass as sharp as a razor. . . ."

Chief among the other matters that compelled attention from Porter was what he called "the health of my people." On the last day of 1811 he told Navy Surgeon P. L. Barton to be sure the *Essex* was well supplied with citrus juices for, he said, they were unexcelled in "removing scorbutic complaints." Even rhythm had to be considered. Just before the war, Porter stressed to the Secretary his urgent need for the additional "music" which he had ordered, "as it is indispensably necessary in getting the crew speedily to quarters." [9]

When war was finally declared on 18 June 1812, Porter and the rest of the American Navy faced almost insuperable odds in favor of Great Britain:

	Warships	Tonnage	Guns	Officers and Men
United States	17	15,300	442	5,025
Great Britain	1,048	860,990	27,800	151,572

It is true that Britain had worldwide commitments and the war against Napoleon was reaching a crescendo in Europe, but its superiority was, nonetheless, crushing. The three largest American warships were the

Constitution, the *President,* and the *United States,* all 44-gun frigates.[*] The Royal Navy possessed more than 250 vessels stronger than any that flew the American flag, for the United States had not a single ship of the line. How best to utilize its miniscule fleet caused argument in the administration. Some wanted it to be kept together and used primarily for coastal defense. Others argued that it should be dispersed and the vessels should sail against enemy commerce as if they were powerful privateers. A compromise was worked out, and the fleet was divided into squadrons of two or three ships, the *Essex* being assigned to the flotilla commanded by Commodore John Rodgers.

With all his efforts to have the *Essex* thoroughly prepared, Porter anticipated accompanying Rodgers from New York. But only a few days before the outbreak of war, it was discovered that the *Essex* had a rotting foremast and a badly fouled hull, which it would take four weeks to repair. Although Porter and his men accomplished their task in half that time, Rodgers' squadron had to leave on 21 June, well before the essential work on the *Essex* had been completed.

During the frustration of his enforced stay in New York, Porter became involved in two disputes. The first was with Lieutenant James Biddle, whom Porter had known in the Mediterranean. Biddle's assigned ship had sailed without him, and he was impatiently waiting in New York for new orders. He asked Porter if he might serve as a "volunteer" in the *Essex.* Porter agreed, but when his officers, led by First Lieutenant John Downes, protested against a newcomer who placed higher on the Navy list joining the ship at this late date and sharing any prize money that might be forthcoming, he reconsidered and withdrew his permission. Biddle "expressed much chagrin," argued with Porter, and even threatened him.[10] For the rest of their lives, the two men disliked one another.

If, as Washington Irving commented, Porter behaved "very properly" in the Biddle affair, it is difficult to condone his simultaneous action against one of the *Essex'* sailors. On three successive days during late June, Porter assembled his men, gave them a fighting speech, and concluded by asking if there were any among them who could not take an oath of allegiance to the United States. On 25 June, one John Ervin (Ervine, Erving, Irvin, Irvine and Irving are also used in contemporary documentation) replied that he could not take the oath because, although he had lived in the United States since 1800, he was still an English subject and if he were captured in battle, he would be hanged as a traitor. He said that shortly before joining the *Essex* in 1811 he had been in Nor-

---

[*] Most naval vessels carried guns in excess of their official listing. Certainly, American ships did.

folk where he met a sailor of like appearance, paid him "4 shillings 6 pence" for fake papers, and assumed a spurious identity. One of the other men shouted that Ervin was lying—he was not only an American, but a fellow townsman from Barnstable on Cape Cod. Whereupon the crew demanded that Ervin be whipped. Porter refused to allow that, but when the men asked for permission to tar and feather him, Porter consented. Accordingly, Ervin was covered "with a coat of old-fashioned Yankee manufacture, with appropriate labels," and put ashore, where he had to be taken into protective custody by the police.

It speaks well for both the New York press and the Navy Department that Porter was severely criticized for this "cruel and unwarrantable treatment of a foreigner for refusing to fight against his own country." Paul Hamilton was caustic: "It is indeed to be regretted that you did not suppress the proceeding . . . mobs should never be suffered to exist on board a man of war . . . I do exceedingly regret that an officer of your high rank and intelligence should have permitted the proceeding in question." Indeed, Porter was lucky that this action did not cost him his captaincy, but the Secretary was satisfied with issuing the above rebuke and, on 2 July, only two days later, signed his commission as captain.[11]

Shortly after Ervin had been put ashore, Augustus John Foster, British Minister to the United States, arrived in New York on his way home from Washington. Accompanied by the British consul, he visited Ervin in Bridewell Prison, praised him for his patriotism, and promised to take him back to England with him. Documentation does not reveal whether Ervin accompanied the British minister and consul when they sailed for England a few days later, but it seems likely that he did, even though Foster does not mention the episode in his narration of his American experience. Some accounts say that Ervin was an American who chose this dubious means of getting some shore leave. Others say that he later fought against the British on the Great Lakes, but there is no evidence to support such theories.

Englishmen were quite properly incensed over this disgraceful episode. William James, ultra-biased contemporary British naval historian, avowed that Ervin was from Newcastle upon Tyne, and castigated Porter for telling his officers to pour hot tar on him "in the petty launch." In circumstances to be recounted shortly, Porter heard more about the Ervin case when he returned from his first cruise in the *Essex*, but even that was not the end of it. In the summer of 1814, when the news of the *Essex'* capture at Valparaiso reached Britain, *The Times* of London referred to him as "Captain Porter (of tar and feathering memory)."[12]

So assiduously did all hands work on the damaged mast and hull that the *Essex* was able to lift anchor in New York on 3 July 1812 and head for open water. Porter's orders called for him to proceed as far south as St. Augustine, Florida, in search of a specie-carrying convoy protected by the British frigate *Thetis,* and advised him that, if he failed to find it, he could use his "sound judgment" in departing from the "letter of these instructions." His biggest disappointment was that he missed all that money floating off Florida, then sailed far to the north, only to miss it again off Newfoundland.

The rest of the voyage, which lasted more than two months, was more profitable. Near Bermuda on 11 July he approached seven British transports bound for Quebec and convoyed by the 32-gun frigate *Minerva.* Under cover of darkness, he cleverly cut out the *Samuel and Sarah,* carrying almost 200 soldiers, without her escort's knowledge. The next day, he challenged Captain Richard Hawkins of the *Minerva* to individual ship combat, but the Englishman, calculating that his first obligation was to protect the transports, showed more intelligence than valor and refused. One authority asserts that Hawkins "was never sure that the *Essex* was not one of the three big American frigates which could have shot him to pieces in ten minutes' firing." For some reason, Porter decided not to continue his attack on the convoy and, not wanting to take so many soldiers on board, permitted the *Samuel and Sarah* to depart after payment of $14,000 ransom. Two more prizes were taken that month: on the 13th the brig *Lamprey,* bound from Jamaica to Halifax, via Bermuda, carrying the pleasant cargo of rum, was sent into Baltimore as a prize; and on the 26th, the brig *Leander,* sailing from Liverpool to Newfoundland with salt and coal for that chilly fishery, was also dispatched as a prize.

The first two weeks of August were hectic. On the 2nd, the ship *Nancy,* Gibraltar to Newfoundland with the usual cargo of salt and coal, was captured and similarly disposed of. Later the same day, the brig *Hero,* Guernsey to Newfoundland in ballast, was, according to Porter's terse comment, "Burnt!" On the 3rd, the brig *Brothers* was seized, and since it would have been hazardous for the *Essex* to take in any more prisoners, Porter designated her a cartel ship * and sent her to St. John's. Five days later, the brig *King George,* carrying salt from Liverpool to Newfoundland, fell victim to the *Essex* and was dispatched to Boston as a prize. The next day, the brig *Mary,* in ballast between the same two ports, was burned.[13]

Nothing more than a shot across the bow had resulted in the prompt surrender of each of those vessels, but the calm was broken on the morning of 13 August. A ship, later identified as the 20-gun sloop of war **HMS**

---

* Under international law of that time, a "cartel ship" was used to exchange prisoners under a safe-conduct pass.

Alert, under Captain Thomas L. P. Laugharne, closed rapidly on the *Essex*. While on the prowl, Porter often followed a practice that was common in his day: altering the appearance of a fighting ship so that a frigate would seem to be no more than a disheveled merchantman. On this occasion, with gunports closed and British colors flying, Porter sent men aloft to shake out sails in simulation of a panicky flight. Laugharne was completely fooled. Washington Irving later wrote that the British captain thought the *Essex* was only "an English Indiaman, captured by the Americans." When his quarry came close enough, Porter hauled down the British flag and hoisted the American one, drawing a broadside from the *Alert* which did no more damage than to put "a few musket and grape shots in her hull and sails." The trap was sprung. The *Essex'* gunports were knocked out, and a single broadside was all that was necessary. Within eight minutes Laugharne struck his colors, although none of his men had been killed and only three had been wounded. The worst damage the *Essex* suffered was "having her cabin windows broke by the concussion of her own guns." Granting that the 20-gun *Alert* had no business tangling with a 32-gun frigate, she had fought shamefully. Morale among her men and officers alike seems to have collapsed. Porter asserted that he watched the men of the *Alert* loot their own vessel, causing pillage and destruction "that would have disgraced a corsair of Barbary." One naval historian says that several British sailors who demanded during the brief battle that their captain surrender, were later executed. Another account has it that the First Lieutenant of the *Alert* was "broke for cowardice," and that Captain Laugharne was "not again employed during the war." [14]

The result of what Porter admitted had been "so trifling a skirmish" was predictable. The *Alert* was the first British warship taken in the War of 1812, and both sides made out of it what they could. Americans naturally rejoiced, while Englishmen deprecated the affair. Tory historian James implied that the *Alert* was nothing but a barge "raised to the dignity of a sloop of war," and commented (James was no man for a cliché) that she had formerly "carried coals from Newcastle. . . ." In London, *The Times* produced a farrago of nonsense, reporting that the *Essex* was a 44-gun frigate, and that the "desperate action" had lasted for "thirty-five minutes." Beyond the ships' names, the only detail reported correctly was that when the *Alert* surrendered, she had *"seven feet of water in her hold."* [15]

The aftermath of the "skirmish" was almost fatal to the *Essex,* now crammed with eighty-six captives from the *Alert,* in addition to many from the merchantmen she had taken earlier. Midshipman David Glasgow Farragut, who had celebrated his birthday just after the *Essex* sailed, and was all of eleven years old, here proved his mettle. A couple of nights after the battle, he was in his hammock when he became aware that a pistol-carrying coxswain from the *Alert* was scrutinizing him. Had the boy moved, he probably would have been killed, but he maintained control enough to stay motionless, and after a moment the Englishman departed. Farragut then ran silently to tell the news, and Porter rolled out of bed shouting "Fire! Fire!" So well trained were the men of the *Essex* that:

> . . . they rushed to their stations without confusion, but the mutineering prisoners . . . became so confused that all their plans were foiled. Before they fully realized what was happening, they heard Captain Porter calling the boarders to the main hatch to secure them. This was Farragut's first real achievement in the United States Navy. Nor was it a little thing to thus save his ship from disaster.

After this narrow escape, Porter wanted to rid himself of the *Alert*'s complement, but not to lose the ship as a prize. He devised a clever ruse that accomplished both ends. He talked Captain Laugharne into accepting the *Alert* as a cartel to carry his eighty-six men to St. John's and promising to return her later to an American port. Lieutenant Stephen Decatur McKnight was the only American on board when the ship sailed for Newfoundland. Her arrival at St. John's caused much embarrassment to Admiral Sir John T. Duckworth, the naval commander there. Although he commended Porter on "the good disposition you have evinced to alleviate the distresses of war," it was only with the greatest reluctance that he accepted the terms agreed to by his subordinate. In a letter to Secretary Hamilton, Duckworth pointed out that to be a true cartel ship, a vessel must depart from a belligerent's home port. If prizes could be handled in Porter's manner, he continued, they would be "secure against the possibility of recapture; while the cruising ship would be able to keep at sea with an undiminished crew; the cartels always being navigable by the prisoners of war." Because of his "sacred obligation" as a British officer, he would acquiesce in Porter's conditions this time, but never again. Hamilton later agreed with Duckworth in objecting to the way in which Porter had used his own initiative in this matter.

The first cruise of the *Essex* concluded with another close call. On 4 September a British squadron loomed on the horizon and by shamming battle tried to draw Porter within range, but he first stood off, then fled. Three frigates pursued him, and one was gaining steadily until the *Essex* disappeared into the rainy night. Porter decided to switch from game to hunter. He doubled back, intending to surprise his pursuer, and in consideration of his carronades and his crew trained in hand-to-hand combat, he planned to board. This was the riskiest of maneuvers, with a strong possibility of a collision in the dark, but strained eyes were the only damage sustained. As Porter told the Secretary, "to the mortification of my officers and crew—the bird had flown!" Perhaps the *Essex* was lucky that the unidentified "bird" had flown: she was very likely the 38-gun frigate *Shannon,* under Captain Philip Bowes Vere Broke, whose crew "were better trained and understood gunnery better" than the crew of almost any other ship in the Royal Navy.[16] It was the *Shannon* that restored much lost British morale when she defeated the ill-fated *Chesapeake* on 1 June 1813.

In the months between the capture of the *Alert* and the *Shannon's* victory over the *Chesapeake,* the maritime war became no laughing matter in London. Steeped in centuries of naval superiority, Englishmen were accustomed to judge odds of two, or even three, to one against the Royal Navy as only making for a more interesting contest. But Porter's victory over the *Alert,* which it had been easy for the British to shrug off, was only the first of several losses. In 1812, three encounters between frigates ended in the same way: the *Constitution,* commanded by Captain Isaac Hull, defeated the *Guerrière* on 19 August, the *United States,* commanded by Stephen Decatur, defeated the *Macedonian* on 25 October, and the *Constitution,* under Hull's successor, William Bainbridge, defeated the *Java* on 29 December. Lesser vessels fought with the same outcome: the USS *Wasp* over HMS *Frolic* on 18 October 1812, and the *Hornet* over the *Peacock* on 24 February 1813. As one American exultantly put it, "Tell John Bull to his teeth, that Brother Jonathan had broken his nose and spilled his claret."

Of course, the Royal Navy was too strong to be withstood indefinitely. By the end of 1814, almost every American warship had either been taken or was bottled up in port. Nonetheless, the decline in English morale had been astonishing. *The Times,* which after the loss of the *Macedonian* wailed, "In the name of God, what was done with this immense superiority of force?", commented more philosophically on the news of the *Java's* defeat: "The Public will learn, with sentiments which we shall not presume to anticipate, that a third British frigate has struck her flag to an American . . . three frigates! Anyone who had predicted such a result of an American war this time last year would have been treated as a madman or a traitor." Whipping boys had to be found. An opposition journal, the *Morning Chronicle,* attributed the loss of the *Macedonian* to politics rather than her reported lack of manpower: "There, and only there, an Englishman has now to fear! for a Cabinet, like their frigate, may be scandalously *ill-manned. . . ."* Towards the end of the war, *The Times* pontificated on why the Americans had done so well in maritime action:

> We have suffered him to grow up to audacity, because we would not put out our strength and crush him to atoms, because we would not condescend to

examine . . . the superior strength of his vessels, their picked crews, their practised and murderous mode of firing, and the almost uniform advantage they possess in sailing. We may encounter them if we please, not merely on equal but on far superior terms; and it is our duty to do so, for the sake of humanity, as well as to re-assert our paramount naval reputation.[17]

On 7 September 1812, the *Essex* passed the Delaware Capes and a week later Porter and Farragut were back in Chester. During the month and a half before departing on his second and last wartime cruise, Porter was busy trying to compensate himself for the poverty-stricken years of peace by cashing in on the *Alert* and his other prizes. Congress had stipulated that one-half of a prize's sale price would go to the United States, and the remaining half would be divided into twenty equal shares, of which the captain would receive three. Porter appointed Hambleton prize agent for the *Essex* and itemized for him the accomplishments of the cruise just completed: "[I took] one sloop of war and one transport, burnt two merchantmen, liberated one, and sent in four. My prisoners amount to four hundred and twenty. . . ." Not satisfied with that tally, he added: "My next cruise I hope will prove more profitable to self and agents."

Porter notified the Department that, in the course of capturing prizes that he estimated to be worth $300,000 to the enemy, he had lost only one man, and he had died from natural causes. The Secretary congratulated him on his "successful cruise," and told him that the President would have to decide whether the *Alert* would be accepted into the U.S. Navy. However, he assured Porter that, at least, he could count on all her munitions being purchased by the government. After the *Alert* returned to New York with what the press described as "200 ransomed Americans," Porter renewed his queries to the Department about the disposition of this prize, stating that his men were concerned since, without shares, they lacked the "means" to provide for themselves, especially in anticipation of a second extended cruise. The Navy bought the *Alert,* and the prize money was paid. However, the ship proved useless for sea operations, and ended her days as a "block-ship" in New York Harbor, where she was "pointed out to the citizens as one of the national trophies of the war." [18]

On his return to Chester, Porter found the following challenge from Sir James L. Yeo, captain of the enemy frigate *Southampton,* published in a Philadelphia paper:

> . . . Sir James Yeo commander . . . [presents] his compliments to Captain Porter, commander of the American frigate *Essex*—would be glad to have a *tête à tête,* any where between the Capes of Delaware and the Havanna, where he would have the pleasure to break his own sword over his damned head, and put him down forward in irons.

Realizing that this remarkably insolent invitation to combat had been issued because he had allowed Ervin to be tarred and feathered, Porter replied:

> Captain Porter, of the United States frigate *Essex,* presents his compliments
> to Sir James Yeo, commanding H.M.S. frigate *Southampton,* and accepts
> with pleasure his polite invitation. If agreeable to Sir James, Captain Porter
> would prefer meeting near the Delaware, where Captain P. pledges his
> honor to Sir James, that no other American vessel shall interrupt their *tête
> à tête.* The *Essex* may be known by a flag bearing the motto, "Free trade
> and Sailors Rights;" and when that is struck to the *Southampton,* Captain
> P. will deserve the treatment promised by Sir James.

Understandably, there was some comment on the wording of Yeo's
challenge. William James doubted that Yeo would have couched it in
"vulgar terms," unless he intended to give Porter a chance to demonstrate typical American "blustering." A Baltimore journal remarked that
although the King had *"dubbed"* Yeo a knight, "we trust that Porter may
have the opportunity of drubbing him into a *gentleman."* Porter told
Secretary Hamilton about Yeo's challenge, and asked that no orders
might "deprive" him of the chance to meet it. Late in September he
sailed the *Essex* to the mouth of the Delaware River and hovered there
briefly, but Sir James did not appear, and their pleasant little *tête à tête*
never took place.*

During the weeks before he put to sea again, Porter hounded the Secretary for permission to exchange his command of the *Essex* for that of
the smaller, 28-gun corvette *Adams.* Only a fortnight before his departure, he became so vehement that he informed Hamilton that he must
have the *Adams* because of his "insuperable dislike to Carronades and
the bad sailing of the *Essex* that render her in my opinion the worst frigate in the service." [19] There was no time for such a switch, but Porter's
loss of the *Essex* would justify his forebodings.

---

* A short time later, in the Bahamas, Yeo managed to run aground both the
Southampton and her prize, the American sloop of war *Vixen,* for which he was
court-martialed but acquitted. He was then assigned to the Great Lakes, and his
repeated loss of nerve on Lake Ontario during 1813 was most helpful to the
American cause. Sir James appears to have talked to more effect than he fought.

IV

The most completely documented and best recorded episode of David Porter's life is his voyage to the Pacific from 28 October 1812 to 28 April 1814. He described it in an almost day-by-day, two-volume account, entitled *Journal of a Cruise made to the Pacific Ocean, by Captain David Porter, in the United States frigate Essex, in the years 1812, 1813, and 1814,* portions of which were first published by his old friend Washington Irving in the October and November 1814 issues of *Analectic Magazine.* When the whole *Journal* appeared in 1815, it was well received by most of Porter's fellow countrymen, and the modern maritime historian Samuel Eliot Morison describes it as a "salty narrative . . . the best bit of sea literature of the period."

British reaction to the work was as generally hostile as might have been expected. Naval historian William James shrugged it off as "that jumble of filth and falsehood," but William Gifford,* editor of the London *Quarterly Review* and renowned both for his merciless reviews and his animus toward Americans, delivered an unrestrained, thirty-one page attack upon the *Journal.* Robert Southey, the poet, mourned that Gifford looked upon authors as "worms—something beyond the pale of human sympathy." The *Quarterly Review,* founded by the Tories and still subsidized as their organ, exhibited the absolute detestation of liberalism, domestic, foreign, and especially American, that was typical of that wing of British opinion. As an author as well as an American, Porter felt the full brunt of this Tory vituperation. Gifford suggested that a more correct title for the *Journal* would have been "A History of the Pirates," except that such would be unfair to Henry Morgan and other bona fide freebooters who occasionally demonstrated "heroic courage and disinterested ingenu-

---

* Washington Irving met Gifford in 1820 and described him as "a small, shriveled, deformed man of about sixty, with something of a humped back, eyes that diverge, and a large mouth."

ity," but Porter showed himself to be "utterly destitute of both." This literary onslaught brought reaction even in England, where the eccentric editor, William Cobbett,* said that the explanation for Gifford's "very base attack" on Porter's character and conduct lay in the fact that he was "absolutely in the *pay* of the government." [1]

Americans rallied behind Porter. Washington Irving was outraged by the "spleen and spite," expressed in the *Quarterly Review,* William Bainbridge wrote Porter that he was indignant at the "scurrilous and wanton attack upon you," and an American historian of the time called attention to Gifford's "scandalous abuse." Porter's resentment may be imagined, but his duties as Navy Commissioner, protagonist of Latin-American independence, and gentleman farmer kept him so busy that it was several years before he replied. When a second edition of his *Journal of a Cruise made to the Pacific Ocean* was published in 1822, it carried a seventy-three-page preface which refuted and counterattacked Gifford's review. He sent a copy of the new edition to James Madison, and the ex-President replied that he considered the new preface "able and judicious. . . . The severity of its retaliations cannot be complained of by those who so wantonly provoked them." [2]

The three major sources of details concerning Porter's extensive trip to the Pacific from 1812 to 1814 form excellent counterweights to one another: Porter's original *Journal of a Cruise* published in 1815, the almost simultaneous attack on him in the *Quarterly Review,* and Porter's long retort contained in his second edition.

It may be said that the *Essex'* history-making voyage started on 6 October 1812, when orders were received from Bainbridge and, two days later, confirmed by the Secretary. The Navy had just been organized into three squadrons, each composed of two frigates and a sloop, under Rodgers, Decatur, and Bainbridge. The *Constitution,* the *Essex,* and the *Hornet* were assigned to Bainbridge and, sailing singly or together, were to proceed to the Cape Verde Islands, then back across the Atlantic to the island of Fernando de Noronha, and finally to work south along the coast of Brazil. Cape Frio, the island of San Sebastian (São Sebastião), and the island of St. Catherine (Santa Catarina) were designated as possible meeting places, in case the ships became separated. Depending upon circumstances, the squadron might either head for St. Helena and the South Atlantic, in order to plague enemy sea lanes to and from Asia, or round Cape Horn to seek British whalers in the Pacific. In his *Journal* Porter

---

* During the 1790s, William Cobbett had been the ultra-conservative Federalist editor of *Porcupine's Gazette* in the United States. He later returned to England and became, by contemporary standards, an extreme radical, both as editor of *Cobbett's Weekly Political Register* and as a member of Parliament.

boasted that he had planned the cruise before the war, and had received immediate approval from the Secretary, and later from Bainbridge.

He threw himself into the job of preparing the *Essex* for this voyage, which would certainly last months, and perhaps years: "I consequently directed the ship to be furnished with every requisite supply of stores, &c. &c; ordered for her a new suit of sails . . . taking in as much provision as she could stow, and providing ourselves with a double supply of clothing, and fruit, and vegetables, and lime juice as antiscorbutics. . . ." Morale was high, since prize money from the last cruise had been distributed, and the officers had been given three months' pay in advance. In the midst of his labors, Porter found time to brag a little to Hambleton: ". . . I sail on a long, a very long cruise; our destination and intended movements I am not at liberty to divulge, perhaps a more important cruise was never undertaken by the vessels of any nation, and I have vanity to believe that my plan for the 'first campaign' produced it . . . I join Bainbridge."

He bade farewell to Evalina, again pregnant, and to his two children, William and the baby Elizabeth, and on 28 October 1812, two days after the *Constitution* and the *Hornet* had left Boston, he and eleven-year-old Midshipman David Glasgow Farragut rowed from the lawn of Green Bank out to the *Essex*. Later that day, the frigate passed the Delaware Capes to open water. She was so laden with supplies that she wallowed in, rather than rode, the waves, and her seams opened during her second day. She was never in danger of foundering, but many supplies were ruined, and allotments of everything, except water and rum, had to be cut immediately. During the month's passage from the Delaware to the Cape Verde Islands, shipboard routine was established. Not only was the *Essex* packed with stores, but she was jammed with men. Claustrophobia might be expected on a vessel only 140 feet long and 36½ feet on beam which, according to Porter, carried a complement of 23 officers, 36 who might be designated as petty officers, 227 "seamen, ordinary seamen, landsmen, boys, and supernumeraries," a Marine complement of one officer, 6 non-commissioned officers, and 25 privates—for a total, including himself, of 319 men.[3]

Under such crowded conditions, discipline and cleanliness were essential. On departure Porter had pardoned those awaiting punishment so that all could start with a clean slate, but he warned that the first infractor would receive thirty-six lashes. Disciplinary problems were few and unimportant until he ordered his men to leave the sensual paradise of the Marquesas Islands in the South Pacific more than a year later. One of Porter's most attractive traits was his concern for his crew's comfort, which glows in the pages of his *Journal*. Each day was carefully organized with that end in mind. The men were to be kept busy "at the great guns" or on other duties from early morning to late afternoon, but the hours between 4:00 and 6:00 P.M. "should be allowed to them for amusement." Most frigate captains, afraid that hammocks might interfere with a speedy readying of the guns in an emergency, compelled their men to sleep below the guns on the berth deck, where there were no portholes or other adequate ventilation. Porter departed from this custom and waxed wroth at it:

> What can be more dreadful than for 300 men to be confined with their hammocks, being only 18 inches apart, on the birth-deck of a small frigate, a space of 70 feet long, 35 feet wide, and 5 feet high, in a hot climate, where the only aperture by which they can receive air are two hatchways about 6 feet square? The situation must be little superior to the wretches who perished in the black hole of Calcutta . . . the whole atmosphere of the ship becomes tainted . . . by the pernicious vapors arising from the birth-deck.

Arguing that hammocks could be cleared and the ship readied for action within fifteen minutes, more than enough time to meet any crisis, he allowed most of his sailors to sleep on the more commodious and airy gun deck.

Cleanliness was vital to health and morale, and Porter's officers were supposed to be paragons of immaculateness. He gave his crew the generous quota of a half-gallon of water a day, both for drinking and washing. All hands were told to bathe daily. At regular intervals, lime and sand were used to whitewash and dry-rub the decks. The ship was "fumigated in every part every morning, by pouring vinegar on a red-hot shot," which, of course, did no more than cover one stench with another. Despite this useless procedure, the pragmatic results of Porter's efforts to promote health were spectacular. When the *Essex* sailed, twenty-two men were ill (about one-third of them suffering from venereal diseases), but by the time she arrived in the Cape Verdes there were only three in sick bay. Health conditions during the remainder of the voyage were equally commendable.

During the first month at sea, sails were sighted or hailed six times, but, save for one spied at a distance and later correctly assumed by Porter to have been the USS *Wasp*, all proved to be Portuguese neutrals. Disappointment over the lack of prize money was somewhat mitigated by the debauch that attended crossing into the Tropic of Capricorn—today, the equivalent ceremony takes place at the Equator. Neophytes, among them David Farragut, who had never ventured so far south, were initiated at the court of "Neptune and his wife Amphitrite." Porter describes how, before the ceremony had long been under way, "their godships were unable to stand" because of "devotions so frequently to Bacchus," and their retinue had to complete the festivities: "First the unfortunates were daubed by the imps of Neptune with soap, tar, and any other disagreeable concoction that was available . . . they had the filth shaved from their faces by the official barbers armed with very dull wooden razors. Then they were ducked in the water. . . ." [4]

On 27 November, when the *Essex* was 3,500 miles from home, she entered the harbor of Porto Praya on the island of "St. Yago" (São Tiago) in the Portuguese Cape Verde Islands, off the westernmost extremity of Africa. Since Portugal had for centuries been loosely allied to Great Britain, Porter anticipated meeting cold neutrality, at best, and sent First Lieutenant John Downes ashore to gauge the prevailing political winds and to inquire about replenishing stores. Although, on that first afternoon, the Portuguese governor would not break his siesta, he made up for it later with cordiality, entertaining Porter and his officers at dinner, and accepting return honors on board the *Essex*.

During this five-day sojourn, Porter analyzed Porto Praya's economy and defense. He concluded that it could be a valuable adjunct to American commerce, as the only Englishmen who ever called there were from warships of "that imperious navy," and they engendered much resentment because of their high-handed and supercilious attitude. Although Porter itemized some of the products available there for American trade, he found it difficult to get supplies. Wells were located behind the town and, under a tropical sun, water had to be hauled to shore, then rowed through heavy surf to the ship. Meat was expensive and of poor quality, but he bought fruit in abundance, including 100,000 oranges. Sailors were allowed to go ashore in relays, but some returned drunk, laden with ferocious local rum which they smuggled onto the ship by a variety of devices. The number of pigs, goats, and monkeys brought back by the men caused the captain to complain that his ship "bore no slight resemblance . . . to Noah's ark."

As an outpost of empire, Porto Praya was ludicrous, and Porter was undoubtedly correct when he wrote that it "could be taken . . . by thirty men." Its garrison totaled some 400 soldiers, "destitute of clothing from the waist upwards," who lugged around miscellaneous hardware in lieu of arms, for "there are not five serviceable muskets" on the entire island. The "cavalry" waved broken swords from atop jackasses. Only one of the thirty guns was usable, and it could do no more than give salutes. The governor explained that these incredible conditions existed because his army had not received any pay, clothing, or arms for ten years.

The *Quarterly Review* sneered that the only response Porter, "this mirror of transatlantic politeness," made to Portuguese hospitality at Porto Praya was to "ridicule their whole establishment." Since Porter had given part of his *Journal* the subtitle, "Descriptions of the Cape de Verd

Islands," he was scoffed at for confining his remarks on the islands to "the price of fowls, and a few desultory remarks on bad rum, petmonkeys and baracouters. . . ." In 1822 Porter sarcastically congratulated the *Quarterly Review* on its "solicitude . . . for . . . the reputation of nations, and especially . . . [for] the honour of defending the chivalry of Port Praya." [5]

On 2 December the *Essex* stood out to the east of Porto Praya as if heading for Africa, but once out of sight, she swung southwest toward the Brazilian island of Fernando de Noronha, 1,400 miles away, where Bainbridge might be found. After a couple of days at sea, the assortment of animals that had joined the ship at Porto Praya created such a mess and made such inroads on essential water and food that Porter announced his intention of using them for an early Christmas dinner, and ignored petitions to save favorite pets. The pigs and goats were killed and eaten, leaving the *Essex* to men, monkeys, and rats. Save for the dispatch of the animals and the death of a sailor from "a paralytic affection," the first ten days' sailing out of Porto Praya passed without incident. On 12 December a small ship was sighted, approached, and hailed. When she tried to escape, Porter let her have one musket volley, and that was sufficient. To his delight, he found that he had nabbed the 10-gun British packet *Nocton,* carrying thirty-one men, one of whom was killed by the volley from the *Essex,* and a cargo of specie to the value of £11,000, or about $55,000. The bullion was taken on board the *Essex,* and later used to pay the crew and to buy supplies. It was not difficult for the captain of the *Essex* to persuade himself that the *Nocton* was "well calculated for the United States service," and he so notified the Secretary. The day after he took her he sent her off to the United States with fifteen Americans and seventeen Englishmen. Thirteen of the *Nocton*'s "strongest men" stayed behind and were, presumably, enlisted in the American Navy. Unfortunately, no prize money was ever realized from this catch. Near Bermuda the *Nocton* was recaptured by the British frigate *Belvidera.*

The *Quarterly Review* pounced upon Porter's fatuous remark that the men of the *Nocton* appeared "to consider their capture and trip to America more in the light of an agreeable adventure, and a party of pleasure, than a misfortune." Gifford quoted the following passage which, he said, Porter must have read: " 'How can you be so cruel,' said Beckford [probably the English novelist William Beckford] to a warrener, 'to sew up the mouths of your ferrets?' 'Lord, sir!' replied the fellow, 'they likes it.' " Perhaps Gifford's thrust wounded: instead of attempting to parry and riposte, Porter omitted his idiotic statement from his second edition.

On 14 December, some 300 miles off the eastern promontory of Brazil, Fernando de Noronha was sighted. Its central peak soared 1,094 feet, "a pointed shaft of stone symmetrical as a cathedral spire. . . . Sailing vessels steered by it. They called it the Mile Post." Only seven square miles in area, the little tract of real estate was a penal colony, populated by "a few miserable, naked, exiled Portuguese, and as miserable a guard. . . . There are no females on the island . . . from what motives I cannot conceive, except that it be to render the place of exile the more horrible."

Downes was sent ashore the following morning to tell the Portuguese governor that the *Essex* was the English merchantman *"Fanny"* from London to Rio de Janeiro, that she was suffering from shortages and scurvy, but could not anchor because her cables were bad. On his return he reported that only a few days previously, two British warships, the *"Acasta, of 44 guns"* and the *"Morgiana, of 20 guns,"* had departed, leaving a letter addressed to "sir James Yeo, of his majesty's frigate *Southampton.* to be sent to England by the first opportunity." Porter knew at once that he had just missed the *Constitution* and the *Hornet.* Downes went back to collect the letter in behalf of "a gentleman . . . intimately acquainted with sir James . . . ," who would be pleased to deliver it. Bainbridge's letter was not very subtle. It read:

> My dear Mediterranean Friend:
>   Probably you may stop here . . . I learnt before I left *England,* that you were bound for the Brazil coast; if so, perhaps we may meet at St. Salvadore or Rio Janeiro; I should be happy to meet and converse on our old affairs of captivity; recollect our secret in those times.
>   Your friend, of H.M.'s ship Acasta
>   KERR

Sure enough, in his invisible ink he had written between the lines: "I am bound off St. Salvadore, thence off Cape Frio, where I intend to cruise until the 1st of January. Go off Cape Frio, to the northward of Rio Janeiro, and keep a look out for me. Your friend."

Gifford in the *Quarterly Review* affected to be horrified that Porter "made no scruple to break open" a letter addressed to someone else. Porter easily demolished this silly charge. In his second edition, he explained that "Acasta" was a code word; the British frigate of that name was stationed off the U.S. coast, could not possibly have been in South American waters at the time, and everyone in the squadron knew it. Furthermore, he had instantly recognized Bainbridge's writing.[6]

Having no longer any reason to tarry at "this miserable Botany Bay of Portugal," the *Essex* left Fernando de Noronha the same day she arrived and, following Bainbridge's instructions, sailed southwest for Cape Frio. Offshore winds made the 1,400-mile passage hot and humid, and the only two vessels sighted were Portuguese. A British sloop of war was reported to be in the vicinity, and the possibility of chasing her was considered, but dropped. Christmas Day found the *Essex* hovering off Cape Frio to watch the sea lanes from Rio de Janeiro to Europe. All of 28 December was spent in pursuit of the British schooner *Elizabeth*, which had sprung leaks and had to drop out of a six-ship convoy under feeble naval escort. She was finally caught and a skeleton crew, with orders to go either to Rio de Janeiro or to the United States, depending on the vessel's seaworthiness, was sent to take her over.*

Despite heavy weather, the *Essex* crowded on sail and raced northeast after the rest of the convoy. By 12 January 1813 she had gone far to the east, faced steady contrary winds, and Porter had to conclude that further pursuit was useless. At one point, a lookout had excited hopes by mistaking an odd cloud formation for massed sails, but the convoy was never even sighted. In the course of the chase, the captain of a Portuguese merchantman told Porter that he had seen a frigate and a sloop near Bahia, hundreds of miles to the north, and Porter surmised that they were the *Constitution* and the *Hornet*. Hoping to fool the 74-gun ship of the line *Montague* and two other British warships known to be in the neighborhood, Porter told the Portuguese captain that the *Essex* was a British frigate engaged in chasing "a large American privateer." He contemplated sailing to San Sebastian, another prospective meeting place designated by Bainbridge, but thought better of it: San Sebastian was only a day's sail from Rio, where the *Montague* lurked, and that opponent was so formidable that she would be able either to blockade the *Essex* or turn her into kindling within a half hour.

Instead, Porter aimed for St. Catherine's, 500 miles south of the Brazilian capital, the final point of rendezvous agreed upon by the squadron. The next week's sailing was enlivened only by the sudden need to reduce the ration of alcohol and to control gambling. Porter discovered that the rum supply was running low; grog would have to be cut by one-third. The men courteously suggested an alternative: they would continue on full rations until the rum was gone, then they would cheerfully do without. Porter felt, however, that total abstinence would make them "dejected," so he told them that the tub would be put out two-thirds full, and overturned fifteen minutes later. Apparently, the men agreed, and they observed the strictest punctuality at grog time. The cash from the *Nocton* had been distributed, and to scotch any temptation to gamble, the captain proclaimed that, ". . . he who asked for, or paid a gambling debt, should be punished; and that all monies, staked in gambling, should be forfeited to the informer, whose name should remain secret."

---

* Unfortunately, the *Elizabeth* continued to leak, Brazil refused to allow sanctuary, and she had to be burned. The crew returned to Newport, Rhode Island, a year later.

The *Essex* arrived at St. Catherine's on the night of 19 January, and anchored the next morning. The six days she spent in that port were taken up with watering and efforts to provision. After the Brazilians tried to profiteer in foodstuffs, and Porter had chastised a sailor for "paying a dollar for a dozen of rotten eggs," he put into effect a spur-of-the-moment fair trade act that shattered the artificial price structure. Some of the beef purchased was so putrid that it had to be thrown overboard, where it attracted the attention of "an enormous shark—at least twenty-five feet in length . . . with a quarter of a bullock in his mouth. . . . A man would scarcely have been a mouthful for him." Most of the officers and some of the crew had been swimming alongside the ship the evening before and were, understandably, horrified. More excitement was provided when a boat carrying provisions capsized during a squall, and the men had to ride her bottom for four hours before they managed to right her. However, no one was lost, and most of the buoyant articles were recovered the next day. Porter judged that St. Catherine's, whose fort and army were reminiscent of those at Porto Praya, was indefensible. The island's population of 10,000 was composed of "handsome, graceful women," and men "extremely jealous of them, and I believe they have sufficient reason to be so." With his usual solicitude for the possibilities of American commercial expansion, he commented favorably on St. Catherine's flourishing trade and the existence of a whale-oil fishery run by the Portuguese government.

On 26 January a Portuguese ship only four days out of Rio de Janeiro arrived, and furnished Porter with an abundance of the latest news, some of it true. When he was told that an American frigate had beaten her British equivalent, he promptly surmised that the American must have been the *Constitution*. That both the information and his surmise were correct was proven by later tidings that Bainbridge had avenged his many earlier humiliations by shattering HMS *Java* off Bahia on 29 December 1812. Porter was told also by the Portuguese that the *Montague* had taken the *Hornet*, and that a British flotilla of one frigate and two brigs of war had arrived in Brazilian waters and would soon be reinforced by ships from South Africa and England.[7] These last two pieces of information turned out to be nonsense.

Porter had called at four stipulated rendezvous without finding Bainbridge and was in a dilemma about what he should do next. He proceeded to winnow the likelihoods from the harvest of conflicting information available to him. He must assume that the *Essex* was alone, since he had been told that the *Hornet* was lost and since, even though the *Constitution* had been victorious over the *Java*, she probably would have been sufficiently mauled to necessitate repairs at home. He had also been notified of British warships in Brazilian waters, which meant that, at any moment, he could be bottled up at St. Catherine's. The last place specifically mentioned in his orders was St. Helena in the South Atlantic, but he could not anticipate getting supplies at that remote island, and it was unlikely that he would find prizes there. If he returned to America, he might run into British cruisers off the coast, in which case, even if he made port safely, he could be blockaded there for the duration of the war. His orders permitted him considerable leeway if it became impossible to adhere to the original schedule. A voyage to the Pacific had long been under consideration, and the possibility that the whole squadron might go there had been discussed. But Porter knew that if he departed from the letter of his instructions and sailed south instead of going to St. Helena, he might later be censured by the Department. Furthermore, passage to the Pacific involved sailing through the fearful seas off Cape Horn, with no chance to take on supplies until he reached Chile, which would take at least two and a half months. Nevertheless, a balancing of the pros and cons convinced him that he should go to the Pacific.

In arriving at this decision, Porter's motives were partly altruistic and partly selfish. There were solid strategic grounds upon which, as a patriotic American, he could justify his forthcoming voyage. C. S. Forester wrote:

> . . . he could count on the news of his arrival in the Pacific forcing the British into a disposition of force which could be inconvenient at least. The real justification of the enterprise lies in the fact that it would excite apprehension in the minds of the British authorities as to where American activity could be looked for next; well executed, it could be counted on to have moral effect which was the objective in going to war, and its nuisance value would be magnified in the imagination of the enemy.

James Fenimore Cooper went even further when he said that Porter's decision was "as much characterized by wisdom and prudence as it was by enterprise and spirit." [8]

Nevertheless, profit and glory probably were the chief reasons why Porter embarked on his dangerous cruise. He longed to emulate Lord George Anson's exploits against the Spaniards in the Pacific from 1741 to 1744. Anson's fleet headed for Cape Horn, while a powerful Spanish expedition was simultaneously hurrying south to intercept him. Although they never saw one another, both fleets fell victim to the same tremendous storm near the Cape. The Spanish squadron was practically wiped out by the loss of four huge ships and 3,000 men. Anson's fleet was dreadfully battered also, but what was left of it managed to proceed up the west coast of South America to sack the city of Paita in Peru. In 1742

Anson crossed the Pacific where he earned his fortune by seizing the Spanish ship that plied annually between Manila and Acapulco, Mexico. In 1744 the *Centurion,* Anson's flagship and the only remaining vessel of his squadron, arrived back in England with a treasure amounting to £500,000, so bulky that it required thirty-two oxcarts to transport it to the Tower of London. Porter admitted that he hoped to give back to Anson's "haughty government, some of the evils to which he had subjected the pusillanimous and unprepared Spaniards"; and to make the *Essex* as well known in the Pacific Ocean as the *Centurion* had once been. He may have thought also of the four British frigates that had captured two Spanish treasure ships in the Bay of Biscay during October 1799: each of the four captains concerned received more than £40,780 as his personal share of that treasure.[9] Finally, even if such fortune escaped him, he knew that the well-equipped British whalers in the Pacific would be valuable prizes.

On the afternoon of 26 January 1813, the *Essex* sailed for Cape Horn. The first week at sea was spent preparing the ship for the cold and stormy weather that surely lay ahead: winter clothing was distributed, sails useful only for the tropics, and all heavy articles, save the guns, were stored below; the ineffective fumigating was stopped so that the vinegar could be issued as rations. On 3 February a notice, well calculated to elevate his crew's morale, was issued by Porter:

> Sailors and Marines:
> A large increase of the enemy's forces compels us to abandon a coast that will neither afford us security nor supplies. . . . We will, therefore, proceed to annoy them, where we are least expected. What was never performed, we will attempt. The Pacific Ocean affords us many friendly ports. The unprotected British commerce, on the coast of Chili, Peru, and Mexico, will give you an abundant supply of wealth; and the girls of the Sandwich Islands, shall reward you for your sufferings during the passage around Cape Horn.

> [signed] D. Porter

Admitting that the notice must have kept the crew "in good humour," the *Quarterly Review* commented that it was "couched in the meanest buccaneer-style." Porter defended himself as best he could by contrasting his proclamation with that issued by British General Sir Edward Pakenham at New Orleans in January 1815. Sir Edward was reported to have signaled the attack with the slogan "booty and beauty." Porter said that "to ravish and pollute by force a civilized matron, is not altogether analogous to the acceptance of favors willingly offered by savages. . . ."

For the next several days the *Essex* worked south toward the Horn. Ships of that day often avoided the Strait of Magellan in favor of Le

CRUISE OF THE FRIGATE ESSEX

TROPIC   OF   CANCER

E Q U A T O R

Galápagos Is. 4/17-6/8
& 7/22 – 10/3/1813

Nukahiva~10/25-12/13
1813
Marquesas Is.

TROPIC   OF   CAPRICORN

12/13/1813 – 1/

S O U T H   P A C I F I C   O C E A N

0   3000
Miles

160°   140°   120°   100°

Delaware Bay, 10/28/1812
11/1
11/10
11/20

Azores
Madeira Is.
Canary Is.

20°

Cape Verde Is.
P.Praya~11/27

12/8
12/11
0°

Fernando de Noronha
12/14

Guayaquil~6/19-30
Tumbes

Callao~3/29

Bahia

Rio de Janeiro

C.Frio~12/25 → 1/12/1813

Coquimbo

St.Catherine's~1/20-26

Valparaiso~3/15-22/1813;
2/3-3/28/1814; captured
Concepcion

...ha I.
...1813

2/3

20°

40°

...29

S O U T H

A T L A N T I C

O C E A N

Le Maire Str.~2/13
C.Horn~2/14

...24

0°   60°   40°   20°   0°

Maire Strait between the eastern promontory of Tierra del Fuego and Staten Island. Porter hoped to bypass any inland passage by staying well to the east of Staten, but high winds, "a tremendous sea," and "dreadful breakers" forced the *Essex* westward and, on the foggy, rainy night of 13 February, he was left with no choice but to hazard Le Maire passage. When the murk lifted next morning, to the "unspeakable joy" of the captain and his crew, the ship was riding in the more placid waters of the strait, and by noon she was sailing southwest to pass between Cape Horn and Diego Ramirez Island. As captain of the first American warship ever to round Cape Horn,* Porter allowed himself some chest-thumping over his accomplishment in comparison to that of Anson:

> But how different was the situation of my lord Anson! . . . he sailed through the Streights of Le Maire with a fleet of six stout ships of war, well equipped and well manned; mounting 236 guns and carrying 1510 men . . . all of which were near a year in preparing for this expedition into the Pacific. This powerful fleet . . . was reduced in its passage around Cape Horn, to three miserable hulks, having, altogether, only 355 men and boys alive on board, and of this number, only one ship arrived in England. . . .†

On the afternoon the *Essex* traversed Le Maire Strait, a bad storm drove her off course, where she remained until 18 February, when she reached the southwesternmost point of her voyage—latitude 60°7′, and longitude 76°20′. A spell of good weather raised spirits, and Porter hoped to start working north. However, he was disappointed again, for the respite was of brief duration. On 18 February the *Essex* was hit by a storm "which, for its violence, equalled any. . . . The squalls came at intervals of from 15 to 20 minutes, with so little warning, and with such tremendous blasts, that it was impossible to shorten sail . . . I, therefore, saw no alternative but running before the wind. . . ." When the storm abated three days later, Porter calculated by dead reckoning that he was far enough away from the west coast of Tierra del Fuego to proceed north in safety, but when clouds lifted and he could take "a lunar observation," he discovered that the *Essex* was still too far to the east, and had to stand out to sea. By this time, supplies were alarmingly depleted: "the bread . . . had been attacked by worms and weavils . . . our peas and beans . . . we found only a mass of chaff and worms." Fresh meat was particularly desired, and the pet monkeys from Porto Praya were finally

---

* In 1800, under the command of Captain Edward Preble, the *Essex* had become the first U.S. warship to pass the Cape of Good Hope.

† According to Anson's biographer, only one ship was lost, for two turned back. There were 636 casualties,[10] which was bad enough, but not 1,155, as Porter implies. Porter does not mention this comparison to Anson in his second edition.

killed, while "a rat was esteemed a dainty." The water, at least, was not contaminated, and Porter marveled to find a tiny fish from the Delaware River still alive in one of the casks.

By 24 February, it seemed that the rigorous passage around Cape Horn had been completed and, with a brisk wind blowing steadily from the south, the *Essex*, now "fairly in the Pacific Ocean," made excellent progress up the coast of Chile. But a few days later, when she was at the 50th latitude and the worst danger should have been over, there came from the west a storm whose fury, Porter was sure, "was rarely equalled, and . . . never exceeded":

> From the excessive violence with which the wind blew, we had strong hopes that it would be of short continuance; until, worn out with fatigue and anxiety, greatly alarmed with the terrors of a lee-shore, and in momentary expectation of the loss of our masts and bowsprit, we almost considered our situation hopeless; and to add to our distress, our pumps had become choaked . . . the ship made a great deal of water, and the sea had increased to such a height, as to threaten to swallow us at every instant; the whole ocean was one continued foam of breakers, and the heaviest squall I had ever before experienced, had not equalled in violence the most moderate intervals of this tremendous hurricane.

It blew for three days. The pumps were cleared in time to save the wallowing vessel, but "violent jerks of the ship" buffeted her men unmercifully. After he had been thrown for the third time, Porter had to take to his cabin.

At three o'clock on the morning of 3 March, a gigantic sea swept over the *Essex*, smashing in her gunports, wrecking her boats, and leaving her "perfectly deluged and water-logged." Midshipman Farragut recalled late in life that this was the only time he ever saw experienced sailors completely panicked by the elements: some were on their knees praying, while a petty officer from the *Nocton* was shouting that the ship was sinking, and it was not hard for men who had just been inundated in their hammocks in the middle of the night to believe that he was right. According to Farragut, Boatswain's Mate William Kingsbury, a physical giant who had acted the role of Neptune when the *Essex* crossed into the tropics, restored the crew's courage when he roared, "Damn your eyes, put your best foot forward, there is one side of her left yet!" The deck watch kept their heads during the emergency, and the officers managed to bring the ship around, but perhaps the return of good weather was all that saved the *Essex*.[11]

Porter's "boisterous and unpleasant passage" around Cape Horn impelled him to add a few pages to his original *Journal* warning others who

considered taking that route that it was "the most dangerous, most difficult, and attended with more hardships, than that of the same distance,
in any part of the world. . . ." Avoid it, he recommended, especially in
February, and he advised "those bound into the Pacific, never to attempt
the passage of Cape Horn if they can get there by any other route . . . ,"
a rather clumsy way of saying, go via the Cape of Good Hope.

Both contemporary and modern authorities have challenged Porter's
analysis of the perils involved in rounding Cape Horn. Gifford said
that the American captain had overlooked the simple fact that "no less
than forty or fifty whalers have, for the past twenty or thirty years, annually doubled Cape Horn at all seasons of the year, and, we believe,
without the loss of a single ship in that part of their voyage. . . ." Furthermore, he added, February is not the worst, but "the best month . . .
in the year . . ." for making that passage. Gifford gave it as his opinion
that Porter's exaggerations were only excuses for the later loss of the
Essex to the *Phoebe* and the *Cherub*. A modern challenge comes from
Samuel Eliot Morison who writes, in connection with Boston ships bound
for the Pacific Northwest, "Yet so far as I have learned, not one of these
. . . failed to round the Horn in safety." Porter's later defense is uncon-
vincing.*

A reasonable conclusion to the controversy might be that, while the
westward passage of Cape Horn in a sailing vessel could never be described as recreational, Porter had exceptionally bad luck and took advantage of it to beat his own drum.

During the days following the storm, the *Essex* proceeded up the
coast "to look into Mocha, a small uninhabited island," where British
whalers were known to "resort." She arrived there on the morning of 6
March and found no ships, but Porter and some of the officers who
landed to procure fresh meat for the crew, popped away at random at the
wild horses and hogs that abounded. As dusk fell, the nearsighted Lieutenant Stephen Decatur McKnight, not seeing that Gunner's Mate James
Spafford was standing directly behind a horse he was aiming at, fired.
The bullet passed through the animal and hit Spafford in the chest.
McKnight shouted, "I have killed him!" and the stricken man replied,
"Sir, you have shot me! I am a dying man; take me to the boat." The re-
morseful McKnight did all that he could to comfort his victim, but to no

---

* On HMS *Bounty*'s famous cruise in the late 1780s, Captain William Bligh
reported that for a solid month he had attempted to round Cape Horn, only to
give up, and sail to the Pacific via the Cape of Good Hope. As late as 1939, sixty
Germans died when the Hamburg-America Line's training ship *Admiral Karp-
fanger* disappeared, apparently foundering somewhere in the vicinity of Cape
Horn during a voyage from Australia to Europe.[12]

avail. Spafford was taken on board the *Essex,* where he lingered almost a month. He died on 4 April.*

With only an inadequate chart to guide him, Porter spent the next week inching gingerly along "the dreary, barren, and iron-bound coast of Chili, at the back of which the eternally snow-capped mountains of the Andes reared their lofty heads, and altogether presented us a scene of gloomy solitude. . . ." Plagued by gales, the *Essex* stood off the harbor of Concepción waiting for British whalers, but the sea remained empty. Then, after three days of heavy fog which obscured visibility, the frigate sailed north to Valparaiso, and on 14 March she looked into the harbor there. Among the vessels swinging at anchor were several Spanish merchantmen preparing to depart, in all likelihood for Lima to warn of the *Essex'* unexpected arrival. When Porter discerned that one of the ships in port was a British whaler, he went offshore to wait for her, but returned to Valparaiso the next day. In both editions of his *Journal,* the captain slides over his reason for this abrupt change of mind, but Farragut avers that he called the men together and told them "in his usual animated and enthusiastic style" that, at this point, they should abstain from "the pleasures of being in port, that they might enjoy them the more in the future," to which the crew responded with "a burst of applause and a determination to abide by his will." This vote of confidence from men who had been shipbound for seven weeks is alleged to have made Porter realize that his sailors had "suffered too much already; it would be tasking them ungenerously; I shall go in, if only to give them a run on shore." [13]

Porter had to expect hostility at Valparaiso, for relations between the United States and Spain had long been unfriendly, and an Anglo-Spanish alliance that was battling Napoleon had done nothing to improve them. But Valparaiso gave the *Essex* a cordial welcome during her sojourn there from 15 through 23 March. Since Porter had last heard news of Chile, that country had been caught up in the Latin-American revolutions which erupted spasmodically, and there had been a political overturn. When Porter arrived at Valparaiso, Chile was under "patriot" control, and the loyalists had been driven into hiding. Power lay with the Carrera brothers, Juan José, José Miguel, and Luis, who controlled the armed forces of the revolutionary *junta,* although the patriot governor, Francisco Lastra, was an opponent of theirs. The dashing José

---

* Farragut was an eyewitness to this episode, and his account of it differs slightly from Porter's. For instance, he has Spafford crying, "Yes, and you have killed me too. Please have me put into the boat and carried on board that I may die under my country's flag." One of Farragut's biographers says that Porter omitted McKnight's name from his account because McKnight was the nephew of his friend Decatur, and he is probably correct.

Miguel Carrera, just back from the Peninsular War, was de facto dictator.

The driving force behind the Chilean revolution in general and the Carreras in particular was a remarkable South Carolinian, Joel R. Poinsett, world traveler, linguist, and intriguer. At one time or another, he supported uprisings in Greece, Argentina, Chile, and Mexico. Although he later served as a congressman and was Secretary of War in the administration of Martin Van Buren, he is remembered for having introduced from Mexico to the United States the flashy red flower that bears his name. In 1811 President Madison sent him to South America on "a Quixotic odyssey to save the continent" for antimonarchical liberalism. Specifically, he was Madison's "personal agent to Buenos Aires and Chile, who was to inform the President of conditions there." He was instructed that, if rebels were in the saddle at either place, he should negotiate commercial pacts with them.[14]

After writing a favorable commercial treaty between Chile and the revolutionary authorities in Argentina, despite strong British pressure exercised against him, Poinsett crossed the Andes, arriving in Santiago, the capital of Chile, on 14 February 1812. His orders were "to take all measures possible for aiding Chile that would not be incompatible with the position of neutrality, but the latitude which he gave to the interpretation of these instructions was nothing short of astonishing." He promptly became an open advocate of the Carrera dictatorship, started the first Chilean newspaper to spread revolutionary principles, helped to write a constitution for the new country, and took command of "a division," although there was certainly nothing in his orders to justify such a flagrant breach of American neutrality. He even led his troops into battle. Shortly after the *Essex* departed Valparaiso for the Galápagos Islands on 23 March 1813, Poinsett learned that 1,500 Peruvian royalists in two warships had seized twelve American whaling vessels at Talcahuano, near Concepción, and, with only 400 men, he marched to their rescue. The American captains were surprised and gratified when they found their liberator was one of their own countrymen "exercising his functions as Chargé d'Affaires in this novel and efficient way." It is difficult to disagree with the statement: "In the whole of diplomatic history there can hardly be a case to parallel Poinsett's. After drafting a constitution for a country in whose internal affairs he had no right to interfere, he took up arms in behalf of one group in a civil war in which his country was neutral."[15]

In order to bolster the spirits of the Chilean rebels Poinsett promised them American aid. He is reported to have requested Washington to send a frigate to the Pacific, both to protect American commerce, and to "show our flag in these seas." The *Essex'* voyage which, as has been narrated, was undertaken for other reasons, was not in any way connected with

Poinsett's appeal, but he took advantage of Porter's fortuitous arrival to prove "that the United States desired an alliance and was ready to support the Chilean cause by force of arms." News that there was a U.S. frigate at Valparaiso was received with enthusiasm in Santiago, where bells rang the whole day and there were "illuminations" in the evening. Poinsett and Luis Carrera soon left the capital for Valparaiso, where they arrived on 21 March to find that Porter, who had been there only six days, had already shrewdly sized up local sentiments. After the *Essex* had anchored on 15 March and the proper salutes had been exchanged, Governor Lastra took a party on board and the *Chileños* expressed surprise that the United States could build a ship so large. From the tenor of their remarks, Porter gathered what Poinsett had led them to expect, and he was not the man to disabuse them: "I had prepared my officers and crew to secresy," he wrote in his *Journal,* in order that "the good people of this place should put the most favorable construction on our arrival among them. . . ."

He concluded that Governor Lastra's revolutionary zeal was "lukewarm and cautious," and that he was still looking for a "creep-hole" in case the royalists came back into power. But he found Luis Carrera "a spirited youth," and became an ardent supporter of the Carreras. On Sunday, the 22nd, while he was preparing to take a party of Chileans out to the *Essex,* Porter was dismayed to see a strange frigate enter the harbor. The ladies in his party were unceremoniously left on the beach while he, Poinsett, and Carrera rapidly made for the *Essex.* Luis Carrera longed to take part in a naval battle, and was very disappointed when the visitor proved to be a Portuguese frigate out of Rio de Janeiro bound for Lima. Equally unhappy were the castaway ladies and the other inhabitants of Valparaiso who had climbed to the rooftops hoping to see some action. When the excitement was over, the *Essex* stood out to sea, where she stayed overnight. Poor Carrera was so seasick that he probably hoped that any belligerent enterprise in which he was involved in the future would be exclusively military.[16]

Replenishing the *Essex'* supplies took up much of Porter's nine-day visit at Valparaiso. Provisions "of excellent quantity, and at a more moderate price than in any part of the United States" were stowed away, and fresh-water tanks were filled. In spite of his preoccupation with supplying the ship, the pages of Porter's *Journal* pertaining to Valparaiso are primarily concerned with amusement. He was introduced to Chilean society when the governor invited him and his officers to a ball. With his typical appreciation of femininity, the captain at first deemed the 200 women present "very handsome," with "agreeable features," and "large dark eyes . . . remarkably brilliant and expressive." His enthusiasm lessened when he became aware of their "rotten teeth and unsavory breaths," caused by addiction to the variety of tea called "matti [maté]." He enjoyed the minuets, but found the local folk dances "lascivious," and ungallantly mentions that, at their conclusion, a girl would have "large drops of sweat running down her neck and breast."

Other social customs that fascinated or repelled Porter were the twenty-course dinners that crammed the guest "with a part of everything before him," the distressing communal use of knives, forks, and silver tubes for drinking maté—they have "a peculiar relish for the taste of each others dirty mouths"—and the oddity that a "Chilean lady would sooner be caught in bed with a gentleman than be seen walking arm in arm with him. . . ." He thoroughly approved of the Valparaiso Sunday, which was spent in feasting and dancing, for the Catholic "is above the vulgar protestant prejudice of devoting one day in each week to the worship of the Almighty, when he has it in his power to spend it so much more agreeably in amusement."

Porter's forthright and indelicate commentary did not escape the notice of the *Quarterly Review*, which ironically congratulated him on "his choice phraseology" in "the taste of each others dirty mouths," then blasted him for the "perverted ideas" in his "lively sally against the pigheaded *protestants,* who prefer *prayers* on a Sunday to debauchery and rebellion." Gifford noted that on the ship's roster was "David Adams, *chaplain,*" a fact that engendered utter astonishment, since "we could not perceive the slightest indication that any one on board the *Essex* had any better notion or knowledge of a God, or anything connected with religion, than the inhabitants of Tierra del Fuego." Porter made about the only retort he could: he voiced objection to "the facility with which an exemplary regard to religion may be coupled with grossest ribaldry," and defended Chaplain Adams for "his pure morals, his amiable manners, his great scientific attainments, and his indefatigable activity in the discharge of every duty." He left his remark about a Sunday passed in religious devotion being "a vulgar protestant prejudice" in his second edition, but omitted his comments on "sweat" and "dirty mouths," and modified his statement that Chilean girls would sooner be "caught in bed" to an immeasurably more genteel "would consider it a high indecorum."[17]

On 23 March, the *Essex,* fully provisioned, put out to sea. Porter was in a hurry to leave because he was sure that the Spanish merchantmen he had seen preparing to sail when he arrived in Valparaiso had carried news of his arrival to Lima, and he must strike before British vessels became aware of his presence. Prior to Porter's departure from Chile, Captain Benjamin Worth of the Nantucket whaler *George* told him the whereabouts of several British ships, and recommended that the *Essex* steer, first, for Paita on the coast of Peru, then for the Galápagos Islands, where the enemy tended to congregate. E. A. Stackpole, an authority on whaling, comments: "The information which Worth gave Porter was such as to determine his whole course of action, and by the same token, change the course of whaling history as well." Porter knew that English whalers sometimes mounted as many as 20 guns and that, since their voyages often lasted as long as three years, they were well stocked with provisions and naval stores. Less powerful American whalers might not yet know that war had broken out, and even if they did, they would be helpless against their adversaries. Furthermore, he was aware that privateers, or more properly "picaroons," still loyal to the Spanish crown, were operating from Peru against American shipping.

At daybreak on 25 March, the *Essex* hailed the Nantucket whaleship *Charles,* and heard that two other American whalers had recently been taken by a Peruvian and a British privateer working together. A short while later, with his frigate disguised as a merchantman under English colors "as a little artifice," Porter approached what turned out to be the 15-gun Peruvian privateer *Nereyda.* Completely fooled, the *Nereyda's* lieutenant came on board the *Essex* and complained that his two American prize whalers had been snatched from him by the British privateer *Nimrod.* The captain of the *Nimrod,* he said, had argued that, since the American vessels had broken no Peruvian law, Spanish courts in Lima would liberate them, but that he, a belligerent, could keep them. The crews of the whalers were, however, being held on board the *Nereyda.* Still playing his part, Porter had the twenty-three American prisoners brought to him, revealed to them in private his real identity, and learned that the *Nereyda* was attacking American whalers solely on the ground of their national origin. The American captives did their best to enumerate the whalers, both British and American, that were in the eastern Pacific at that time: they thought there were about twenty of the former, and knew there were twenty-three of the latter.

After conversing with the Americans, Porter raised the U.S. flag, and the frightened Peruvians handed over a privateering commission signed by the Spanish governor of Peru. When the *Nereyda* had been stripped of her "guns, ammunition, small arms . . . and light sails," she was allowed to depart, carrying a letter addressed to "His Excellency the viceroy of Peru":

I have this day met with the ship *Nereyda,* mounting fifteen guns, bearing your excellency's patent, and sailing under the Spanish flag. On examination . . . I found on board her, as prisoners, the officers and crew of two vessels belonging to the United States of America, employed solely in the whale-fishery of those seas, and sent for Lima, after being plundered of boats, cordage, provisions, clothing. . . . I have therefore to preserve the good understanding [between our two governments] . . . deprived the *Nereyda* of the means of doing the American commerce any further injury . . . and have sent her to Lima, in order that her commander may meet with any punishment from your excellency as his offense may deserve. . . .

Porter was, of course, using the same tactics as he and Andrew Sterrett had used in the Mediterranean against the *Tripoli* more than ten years previously: it is to be doubted, however, that the captain of the *Nereyda* was bastinadoed.

While he was at Valparaiso Porter was given more detail about the *Constitution*'s victory over the *Java* on 29 December, and heard for the first time about the *Wasp*'s victory over HMS *Frolic* on the preceding 18 October. Significantly, he had commented that the news "makes us pant for an opportunity of doing something ourselves." But information travels both ways, and Porter realized that if the British did not already know that the *Essex* was loose in the Pacific, it would not be long before they did, and sooner or later strong detachments would be sent around the Horn. He must use to best advantage what time he had before that happened. Never underestimating his financial potentialities, he calculated the value of the English whaling fleet at some $4,000,000, and prize money from even a small percentage of that sum would be adequate recompense for the alternately dangerous and boring days of his lengthy cruise. Furthermore, his mere presence would save American whalers from British or Spanish privateers, and, even if he did not take any prizes, he would thus have done his country "an essential service."

Accompanied by the whaler *Charles,* the *Essex* raced after the *Nimrod* and her two captive Americans. At Coquimbo, Chile, those of the prisoners who so desired were sent ashore in the *Charles.* On 28 March, when the *Essex* was off Callao, three sails were sighted, and while one was being overtaken, the other two made their escape. The recaptured vessel was the whaler *Barclay* under Captain Gideon Randall. Manned by some of her original crew liberated from the Peruvians and a few men from the *Essex,* the whaler went northward with Porter toward Paita. Only minor events enlivened the tranquillity of the next few days: myriads of tiny crayfish temporarily turned the ocean blood red; the disturbing discovery was made that the water taken on at Valparaiso had "a disagreeable brackish taste," producing "costiveness"; and an inquiry held over the death of James Spafford completely exonerated Lieutenant McKnight.

On 6 April when Porter was sailing, as usual, under false colors, officers from a Spanish merchantman babbled to him that Peru held Great Britain "in high repute," the United States in "very little estimation," and that war between Spain and the latter "was momentarily expected." Also, they confirmed what Porter had been told ever since he had been in the Pacific—the place to find British whalers was the Galápagos Islands. After his chatty Spanish guests, still ignorant of the *Essex'* identity, had departed, Porter made one final effort to track down the *Nimrod*. He sailed for Paita, the town that Anson had pillaged three-quarters of a century before. When he arrived off Paita Harbor and was told by the crew of a Peruvian catamaran (log raft) that there were no sizable vessels in port, he gave up the chase, and on 11 April the *Essex* and the *Barclay* stood out to sea and headed for the Galápagos.[18]

The 500-mile passage to that archipelago was uneventful. In preparation for action against British whalers, Lieutenant John Downes was assigned to prepare to attack with squadrons of small boats because frequent calms had to be expected in the waters of the archipelago. The two vessels arrived on the 17th, and spent two days moving about among the southernmost islands, from Chatham (San Cristobal), to Hood (Española), and, finally, to Charles (Santa Maria). On the last-named island, there was a box known as "Hathaway's Post-office," where whalers left messages for one another and, even though the letters found there were months old, they proved that British whalers did assemble in the area. But the first week and a half in the Galápagos was a time of utter frustration. Not a single vessel was seen in a region supposedly aswarm with enemy whalers. A couple of mistaken "sail ho's" only served to deepen the disappointment.

Porter devoted five pages of his *Journal* to recapitulating a story told him by Captain Randall of the *Barclay*. For several years the only inhabitant of Charles Island was Patrick Watkins, an Irish refugee from a British ship who, for some reason, called himself "Fatherless Oberlus." After learning how to distill alcohol from the vegetables he grew, he became his own best customer, although he sold his surplus to those who called at the island. On one occasion, he was robbed of what little money he had, and in revenge managed to collect four or five deserters, steal a boat, and make it all the way to Guayaquil in modern Ecuador. He arrived there alone, having in all probability murdered his fellows to save water for himself. He managed to persuade an Indian girl to accompany him back to Charles Island, but instead of returning to the Galápagos, he ended in Paita's jail. Porter wondered whether, had the two gone to Charles Island, a different race would have developed from "the issue which might be produced from the union of a red-haired wild Irishman, and a copper-colored, mixt-blood squaw."

The most likely place for British whalers to be was Elizabeth Bay, between Albemarle (Isabela) Island, by far the largest of the group, and Narborough (Fernandina) Island to the west, for not only was it well

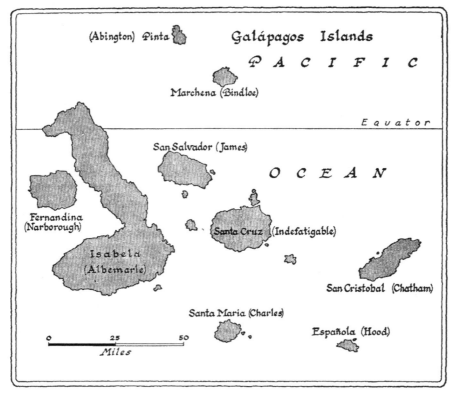

Names in parentheses are those used in Commodore Porter's time.

protected, but it teemed with squid, a favorite food for whales. Consequently, the *Essex* and the *Barclay* worked their way west, but a thorough
four-day reconnaissance turned up nothing. The atmosphere on board
the ships was described by Porter:

> The spirits of the crew had been highly excited by the prospect of making
> prizes, and the disappointment had occasioned no trifling degree of dejec-
> tion and despondency among them. . . . There were few on board the ship
> who did not now despair of making any captures about the Gallapagos
> Islands . . . many began to think that the information we had received . . .
> [of] British vessels frequenting these islands . . . had been altogether
> deception; but I could not so lightly lay down my opinions . . . and I
> determined not to leave the Gallapagos so long as there remained a hope of
> finding a British vessel. . . .

Porter worried constantly about the scarcity of water, since the islands were almost entirely bereft of that essential. He thought the reason
for this lack was that the "light and spongy" soil of the Galápagos could
not retain moisture. Water might have been in short supply, but there
was exotic fauna to marvel at, and Porter's *Journal* is full of zoological
observations. On landing at Albemarle, to their "great surprise and no
little alarm," the men were confronted with "myriads of [i]guanas, of
enormous size and the most hideous appearance imaginable," but the
creatures proved to be so timid that the men "knocked down" hundreds
of them with clubs and found them "excellent eating." During a trip
down the island's coast in a ship's boat, "a multitude of enormous
sharks" caused no little uneasiness, for they snapped at the oars and had
to be repulsed with boarding pikes, since "a gripe" from one of them
would have torn the fragile boat to pieces. Sea lions, seals, and fish were
caught in quantity.

Naturally, the captain was most impressed by the turtles, especially
the giant variety peculiar to the Galápagos. Several times he wrote about
the "elephant tortoise," weighing up to 300 pounds, which could be kept
in the hold for eighteen months without loss of weight, and carried about
"two gallons" of their own "perfectly sweet" water. To men who, with
the exception of a few days in port, had been subsisting on the dull, taste-
less, and often nauseating, seagoing fare of that era, the giant tortoise
must have been exquisite, for, as Porter wrote, it made "wholesome, lus-
cious, and delicate food . . . the finest green turtle is no more to be compared to them . . . than the coarsest beef to the finest veal . . . every
other animal food fell greatly in our estimation." [19]

On 28 April, Porter was so discouraged that he abandoned Elizabeth
Bay, and wandered north around the tip of Albemarle, then south towards James (San Salvador) Island. His luck improved abruptly. The

next morning, one sail was sighted, then two more. The English ship *Montezuma*, 2 guns and 270 tons, carrying 1,400 barrels of whale oil, was quickly taken,* and as soon as a prize crew had been sent to her, the *Essex* hurried off after the others. When she got within eight miles of them, the wind died away, a situation that had been anticipated, so Downes' small boats rowed to attack the similarly becalmed Englishmen, and after some harmless shooting, both surrendered. They were the *Georgiana* and the *Policy*, six 18-pound and ten 6-pound guns, 280 and 275 tons, respectively. Porter commented: "The ease with which the last vessels were taken by our open boats, gave us but a poor opinion of British valour," but this is an extremely unfair presentation of the facts. According to Farragut, who was in the leading boat, as Downes approached the Englishmen, he waved an American flag, at the sight of which the crews of the *Georgiana* and the *Policy*, many of whom were impressed sailors, cheered and shouted, "We are all Americans!" No wonder little "valour" was shown. Gifford of the *Quarterly Review* must have been unaware of the facts, for his only comment was, "surrounded by six or eight boats full of armed men, with a fifty gun frigate within hail, we really do not see what resistance a couple of fishing vessels could properly offer."

The satisfaction of the *Essex'* men may be imagined, for in one day they had inflicted more direct damage on the enemy than they had during the previous six months. The captain took the opportunity to deliver another of his pronouncements to his "Sailors and Marines":

> Fortune has at length smiled on us, because we deserved her smiles, and the first time she enabled us to display *free trade and sailors' rights,* assisted by your good conduct, she put in our possession near half a million of the enemy's property. Continue to be zealous, enterprizing, and patient, and we will yet render the name of the *Essex* as terrible to the enemy as that of any other vessel, before we return to the United States. My plans shall be known to you at a suitable period.
> April 30, 1813
>
> [signed]   D. Porter

Furthermore, the three prizes solved all the supply problems save that of water, for they were laden with "cordage, canvas, paints, tars . . . and

---

* American whalemen from Nantucket were lured by London's bounties and other compensations to establish an English "whale fishery" in the Pacific. In 1786, about 120 such men went to Dartmouth, Nova Scotia, for that purpose, and in 1793 many of them crossed the Atlantic, some going to Milford Haven in Wales, others to London. As late as the War of 1812, most whaleships flying British colors in the Pacific were manned by these Nantucket expatriates, as was the *Montezuma*. Porter does not explain why, although of about average tonnage for a British whaler of that time, the *Montezuma* carried only two guns. Certainly, she must have been by far the weakest British vessel in the Pacific.

. . . a stock of provisions." During their flight, the British whalers had thrown overboard all their giant tortoises, but fifty of them were later recovered.

Judging by the pages of Porter's *Journal* that pertain to it, the month following that excitement was probably among the most tedious of the entire voyage. Much time and effort had to be expended on reorganizing the squadron, for, by then, Porter's command had grown sufficiently to justify that lofty status. The abundance of naval stores taken from the captives was used to repair the flagship, especially her guns' frayed breech ropes, the breaking of which in a battle would have been calamitous. Before her first whaling voyage, the *Georgiana* had been a British East India Company "packet," so Porter decided to place the *Policy*'s guns on board her and make her his armed consort. Her heavy whaling equipment, such as the huge iron blubber boilers, was removed, but her external appearance as a whaler was carefully retained. The invaluable Downes was placed in command, and her crew was composed of forty-one men from the *Essex* and five from her own original crew who volunteered to serve. On 8 May, the refitted *Georgiana* ran up the "American ensign and pendant," then gave and received cheers and salutes.[20]

At this point in his account of his father's cruise, David Dixon Porter sums up what he had already accomplished:

> The *Essex* had now been at sea upward of six months, and since leaving the United States, had not drawn on the government for a dollar, having depended on the amount furnished by the purser when the ship sailed, to pay for the outfit in Valparaiso. The $50,000 captured in the *Nocton* had given the sailors plenty of cash; and now the frigate was once more filled with provisions and stores at the enemy's expense. Better than all, the government was provided with a new cruiser, of whose existence it was not aware, and whose equipment had not drawn a cent from the public exchequer. Half a million dollars worth of property had been captured, and a smart brig of war [the *Nocton*] had been sent in to add to our naval force; and the colonial governments had been taught to respect our flag, by the summary treatment of the Peruvian privateer *Nereyda*.

Obviously, there is some truth in the above, but it is exaggerated. The *Essex*, one of the very few U.S. frigates, had been at sea for nearly six months and had taken only four prizes. This should be contrasted to the nine ships she had captured, including the *Alert*, in only five weeks during her first cruise.

The *Essex* and the *Georgiana* parted company on 9 May, and Downes was given elaborate instructions about where to go in the archipelago, what to do, and how to rendezvous with the *Essex*. Accompanied by his two prizes and the *Barclay*, Porter continued sailing among the central Galápagos, looking more for water than for the enemy. On Charles Island there was a spring three miles inland and, by dint of exhausting effort, the men loaded 2,000 gallons of water, which proved to be "of a filthy appearance, having a bad taste and smell, and filled abundantly with slime and insects." At one point, the *Georgiana* rejoined the *Essex* but was promptly sent out again. On 21 May, the *Essex* and her little convoy put in at several islands, at some of which messages were left for Downes. At about this time, the flagship's doctor and one of the sailors died, but the rest of the men, both crews and prisoners, remained in excellent health.

Boredom ended on the afternoon of 28 May, when a strange sail was sighted. She was chased, but after nightfall she vanished. Porter dispersed his vessels in as wide an arc as possible, and the next morning the *Barclay* signaled that she had found the stranger. Weather played into Porter's hands, for a sudden breeze enabled him to draw up on his becalmed prey, which turned out to be the *Atlantic,* mounting six 18-pound guns and weighing 351 tons. Had it not been for the freakish wind, it is unlikely that the *Essex* could have caught the *Atlantic,* for she was the swiftest English vessel west of Cape Horn. No sooner had Porter closed on the *Atlantic* then he heard the welcome "sail ho!" Forthwith, McKnight and a prize crew transferred to the *Atlantic,* and both ships raced off in pursuit of the new quarry, leaving the slower *Barclay* and the crawling *Montezuma* to tag along as best they could. After the sun went down, Porter's night glasses enabled him to follow the fleeing vessel's attempts to escape. Thus, he was able to catch up with her and, after a brief show of resistance, the whaler *Greenwich,* 10 guns and 338 tons, carrying a British letter of marque, struck her colors. She and the *Atlantic* were particularly valuable prizes. Not only did they carry the plethora of naval stores common to British whalers, but the *Atlantic* alone carried 100 tons of fresh water and 800 large tortoises.

When Obediah Wyer (Porter calls him "Wier" and "Weir"), commander of the *Atlantic,* came on board what he thought was a British frigate, he was happy to confide to Porter that although an American, whose wife and family lived in Nantucket, he was still an Englishman at heart.* His ship, he said, had sailed from Britain to Porto Praya under the *Java*'s protection, but had proceeded alone into the Pacific. Wyer ended his revealing confidences by telling Porter that Concepción, Chile, was the place to nab American whalers, for he had recently seen nine of them there, all "unprotected and defenceless." At this juncture, Porter let

---

* Although Porter does not mention it, Wyer was undoubtedly one of the Nantucket expatriates described in the note on page 96.

him know to which navy the *Essex* belonged. If Wyer felt any embarrassment, it was evidently only momentary, for he soon joined Captain John Shuttleworth of the *Greenwich,* who "had taken in a good stock of Dutch courage," in "the most abusive language against our government, the ship and her officers, lavishing upon me in particular the most scurrilous epithets . . . that would have suited a buccanier." By the next day Porter had taken enough from this duo and determined "to make them sensible of the impropriety of their conduct, and did so without violating the principles of humanity or the rule of war." He does not mention what magical tour de force he used, but it seems to have been effective, for he complacently writes that after he was through, "they would have licked the dust from my feet. . . ."

The six-ship flotilla (the *Georgiana* was still absent) spent the next few days nosing around the Galápagos, plagued by the frequent calms which Porter thought must be the reason why the Spaniards called them "the Enchanted Islands." Two days after a spectacular volcanic eruption had enlivened the night of 6 June, Porter decided to move on to the coast of what is now Ecuador, both to seek more prizes and to find Downes in the *Georgiana.* In his *Journal* he ends his narration of this first foray in the Galápagos with some nine pages on the whaling industry in general and Britain's in particular.[21]

On 14 June, the *Essex* arrived off the mainland of South America, and a couple of days were spent in an unsuccessful search for water on an uninhabited island. In case Downes should put in there later, Porter left a letter for him near a rock, on which he painted the large capitals "S.X.". With confidence little short of touching, he was sure that Downes would understand the message, but that it would be incomprehensible to anyone else. On the 19th the *Essex* anchored off Tumbes, Peru, almost on the Ecuadorian border, and Porter welcomed on board the governor of that town and his entourage, but their appearance was so "contemptible," that it "excited the risibility" of his crew, a situation which, the captain wrote, made him blush for his guests. Uncertain of the political reliability of the Peruvians, Porter was on his guard when he returned the honors ashore the next day. Tumbes was a miserable little town, sprawling over swampy lowlands that reminded Porter of some of the less attractive portions of the Mississippi. The "numerous" and "enormous" alligators could be avoided by living in houses built on stilts, but there was no way to avoid the vicious attacks of fleas and "musquetoes." If Porter found the men of Tumbes unworthy of notice, he judged the women "of fine forms, animated, cheerful, and handsome," but wanting in the utmost delicacy. To prove his point, he told how the governor's wife, who prided herself on having "plenty of milk," took out one of her breasts and "spirted the milk to a considerable distance," in order to demonstrate her capacity. He omitted this little gem from his second edition.

When Porter returned to his ship, he found trouble. James Wilson, Third Lieutenant, identified by the captain as "Lieutenant W., the (then) second lieutenant," * was an alcoholic, and several times had been "violent and offensive," but had been kept on duty when he promised to "abstain from ardent liquors." Nevertheless, during Porter's absence at Tumbes, Wilson had imbibed steadily, and when the captain ordered him to appear, remained drunk in his cabin. Porter went below and found him collapsed in his bunk. When told he was under arrest, Wilson grabbed a pistol and tried to load it. Porter wrenched it away, but the persistent lieutenant found another and the scene was repeated. Wilson sobbed that he had not meant to shoot the captain, but to commit suicide. After a few days of confinement under the guard of two "centinels," Wilson was released by Porter and temporarily restored to duty.

Back in the Galápagos, Downes had met with success. He arrived at Tumbes in the *Georgiana* to report that on 24 June, near James (San Salvador) Island, he had taken the British whalers *Catherine, Rose,* and *Hector.* His first two victims, the *Catherine* and the *Rose,* 270 and 220 tons respectively, and each mounting 8 guns, had suspected nothing until they were helpless under Downes' cannon. Leaving them with prize crews, Downes chased and finally caught the 11-gun *Hector,* 270 tons. Such as it was, this was the most concerted action that took place in the Galápagos, for the *Hector* resisted. However, five broadsides, which caused several casualties and did much damage to the ship, brought down the English colors. After placing a prize crew on board his third captive, Downes found himself in the impossible position of having only ten men to guard seventy-five prisoners. Sensibly, he turned the *Rose,* most sluggish of the three, into a cartel under her captain, and sent her off to St. Helena with all his prisoners, then caught up with Porter. The *Catherine* and the *Hector* brought the American flotilla to nine vessels.

The next couple of weeks were spent in still another reorganization of the fleet. The *Atlantic* was larger and faster than the *Georgiana,* so

---

* Fletcher Pratt incorrectly identifies the drunken officer as Second Lieutenant James P. Wilmer (who could, of course, be "Lieutenant W."). When First Lieutenant Downes became acting captain of the *Georgiana,* all the other officers moved up a grade. Hence, Third Lieutenant James Wilson was "the (then) second lieutenant," as Porter calls him. Final proof is that it was Wilson who sailed for America in the prize *Georgiana,* whereas Wilmer died in battle at Valparaiso.

Porter refitted her under the name of *Essex Junior* and made her his chief auxiliary. Naturally, Downes was appointed captain and Porter assigned him sixty men, a few of them volunteers from the British whalers. Most of the prisoners were put ashore at Tumbes under promises not to fight against the United States unless formally exchanged. With the carpenters still hammering away at the *Essex Junior,* the fleet left the coast of Peru on 1 July. Independence Day was "spent in the utmost conviviality": salutes were exchanged and rum, seized from the prizes, was distributed to the parched crews and "double relished from their having for some time been entirely destitute of it." On 9 July the squadron separated. The *Essex,* the *Georgiana,* and the *Greenwich* were assigned to keep up the search through the Galápagos. Downes in the *Essex Junior* was ordered to accompany the prizes *Hector, Catherine, Montezuma,* and *Policy,* and the American whaler *Barclay,* to Valparaiso, and to sell at least four of them for the best prices he could get; the *Policy,* laden with valuable whale oil, might be sent to the United States. Having completed that mission, Downes was to look for Porter in the Galápagos, and if he missed connection there, proceed to the Marquesas Islands in the South Pacific.[22]

By this time, so many of the officers had had to be assigned to prizes that the only one left to command the *Barclay* was twelve-year-old Midshipman David Glasgow Farragut. Her navigator was the aged and choleric Gideon Randall, who commanded her when she was a whaler and whose outbursts were so abusive that almost everyone feared him. Randall wanted to continue whaling, not to go to Valparaiso and give up his vessel, so when Downes' squadron lifted anchors, he tried to take command, storming at Farragut, "You'll find yourself off New Zealand in the morning," which would have found them only 6,000 miles off course. David Glasgow decided that the time had come for him "at least to play the man," and he ordered the *Barclay* to follow Downes. The enraged Randall disappeared below to get his pistols, but the crew promptly obeyed Farragut's command. Encouraged by the sailors' compliance with his order, Farragut sent word to Randall that if he showed up armed he would be put overboard. That ended the tiny mutiny. The old man feebly tried to explain away his insubordination by insisting to Downes, "I was only trying to frighten the lad," to which Farragut answered, "Captain Downes, ask him if he thinks he succeeded; to show him that I do not fear him I am ready to go . . . with him to Valparaiso." Downes replied, "Well done, Glasgow," and the remainder of the voyage passed without incident.

At Valparaiso, Downes was greeted cordially enough, but the war between the Peruvian royalists and the Chilean rebels had intensified and all economic activity was at a standstill. He could not sell the ships at any price, so he sent the oil-laden *Policy* off to the United States, and simply moored the others in the harbor. Meanwhile, the American consul in Buenos Aires had given him the unpleasant news that a British squadron composed of the frigate *Phoebe,* the sloops of war *Cherub* and *Raccoon,* and a store ship, had departed for the Pacific to find and destroy the *Essex.* As soon as he could get away, Downes hurried off to warn his captain.

Porter, in search of three enemy whalers that had touched at Tumbes shortly before he called there, reached the Galápagos Islands on 12 July. Two days later, three sails were spotted, and the *Essex,* the *Greenwich,* and the *Georgiana* went after them, although the last seems to have taken no part in the subsequent action. The *Charlton,* 10 guns and 274 tons, was taken easily, but the *Essex* had to delay her pursuit of the others until a prize crew had been sent on board her captive. Meanwhile, the *Greenwich* proceeded alone to close on the second stranger. Shots were exchanged, and the English vessel *Seringapatam* was disabled. She appeared to surrender, only to try once more to escape, but the *Essex* soon arrived and completed the victory. Leaving the *Greenwich* in charge of the second prize, the flagship easily overhauled the third vessel, the *New Zealander,* 10 guns and 259 tons. Porter was particularly exultant over the taking of the *Seringapatam,* 14 guns and 357 tons, originally built for Tippoo Sahib and named after his capital in Mysore, the state in southern India over which he ruled. Not only was she "the finest British ship in those seas" but, shortly before her seizure, she had captured an American whaler out of Nantucket. When Porter asked to see the letters of marque that granted him privateering rights, William Stavers, captain of the *Seringapatam,* "with the utmost terror in his countenance," had to confess that he had none but said he was sure that they were on their way to him and must have already reached Lima. Porter called him a pirate and put him in irons.

The sudden acquisition of three more ships necessitated still another fleet reorganization. The *Seringapatam* was turned into a 22-gun auxiliary cruiser for the *Essex.* The *Charlton,* "an old ship and a dull sailor," was made into a cartel to carry the new prisoners to Rio de Janeiro. Frightened that, once out in the Atlantic, they might be impressed into the Royal Navy, the captives begged to be allowed either to stay in the *Essex* or be put into small boats. Porter dared not carry so many in his flagship, and feared that, if he acceded to the latter request, he might later be accused of marooning them. So, on 19 July he forced them to go to Rio in the *Charlton.* Six days later, the *Georgiana* was sent to the United States. Since she should arrive in midwinter, the best time to avoid British blockaders, she was to carry whale oil worth $100,000, as well as the *Seringapatam*'s piratical captain and the few sailors whose enlistments were up and who opted for discharge. Most important, her departure provided a tactful way to get rid of Lieutenant James Wilson, who had to some extent redeemed himself during the fight between the *Greenwich* and the *Seringapatam,* and for whom the other officers were constantly interceding. Nevertheless, a man who had pulled a pistol on his captain had no business on board the flagship, and Porter, apparently shrugging off the possibility that, on his own, the lieutenant might settle down to really serious drinking, put him in command of the *Georgiana.* Wilson almost succeeded in getting his ship to America, but she was apprehended by HMS *Barossa.*

If 14 July was one of the squadron's most successful days, the 29th and 30th were among the most ill-starred. The *Essex* was becalmed as she drew near an enemy vessel. Boats had to be lowered to tow the heavy frigate, but as the stranger was using the same means to escape, no headway was made. Finally, when the *Essex'* men began collapsing from fatigue, Porter ordered Lieutenant McKnight to cut loose his boats and row on ahead, not to attack, but to make it impossible for the Englishman to continue towing operations. Taking advantage of slight gusts, the *Essex* crept up on her immobilized prey, but at the instant British colors were being lowered, an errant breeze filled the enemy's sails and allowed her to escape, while the *Essex* languished in the doldrums.[23]

Nothing much happened during the next six weeks, and Porter's *Journal* is largely confined to navigational directives and haphazard remarks about the topography, geology, botany, and zoology of the Galápagos Archipelago. The time was spent making the small repairs that were constantly needed to keep the *Essex* operational, laying in new supplies of turtles, roaming the waters between the several islands, and making frequent landings. Sometime in mid-August, a duel was fought without the knowledge of the captain—he described dueling as "a practice which disgraces nature"—and it ended in such tragedy that he felt obliged to "throw a veil over the whole . . . proceedings." On the third exchange in the encounter, Lieutenant John S. Cowan was killed by a fellow officer whose name Porter never revealed, and the secret has since been kept. The inscription over the slain officer's grave reads:

Sacred to the memory,
Of Lieut. John S. Cowan,
Of the U.S. Frigate Essex,
Who died here anno 1813,
Aged 21 years.
His loss is ever to be regretted
By his country;
And mourned by his friends
And Brother officers.

Ennui terminated on 15 September when a ship was sighted and her crew could be seen cutting up whales. So well had Porter disguised his frigate that he drew within three miles of the stranger before a warning was sounded. After a few shots had been exchanged, the whaler-privateer *Sir Andrew Hammond*, 10 guns and 301 tons, gave up. To the vast satisfaction of the men in the *Essex*, their new prize proved to be the ship that had been snatched away from them two months earlier by what Porter had called a freakish wind. Porter waited while David Adams, ubiquitous chaplain of all trades, directed the unsavory task of rendering the blubber from the *Hammond*'s whales into oil. Then, the *Essex* and her prize rejoined the *Greenwich*, the *Seringapatam*, and the *New Zealander*, which had been left in the Galápagos to endure the "irksome monotony," broken only, if at all, by "the screaching of sea-fowls and the melancholy howling of the seals."

The *Sir Andrew Hammond* carried all sorts of precious articles, including "two puncheons [169 gallons in all] of choice Jamaica spirits." Porter could not say whether "the great strength" of the rum, or the length of the time his men had been without any, was responsible for the fact that almost everybody got drunk and stayed that way even after he had the liquor considerably diluted. Taking into account how little his men had complained throughout their long drought, the captain decided that "no evil was likely to result from a little inebriety, provided that they conducted themselves in other respects with propriety." His admirable tolerance seems to have worked well, except that the drunkenness of one of the quartermasters, who always headed the crew's grievance committees and had been marked as a malcontent, led to insubordination. Porter threw him in irons, and decided to drop him off at the first port. However, he later changed his mind, broke the offending quartermaster to seaman, and put him in the *Seringapatam*.

Two weeks dragged by before the *Essex Junior* appeared on 30 September, bringing the news that HMS *Phoebe* and her consorts were under way. Porter had reasons other than this to sail as quickly as possible to the safety of the Marquesas Islands, which American whalers had described in rhapsodic terms. His tense and frustrated crew deserved some relaxation, and before any battle could be dared, the *Essex* would have to be beached, scoured, repaired, refitted, and thoroughly fumigated. Porter rather slides over the need for fumigation, a condition repugnant to more squeamish modern taste:

> . . . the rats . . . had increased so fast as to become a most dreadful annoyance to us, by destroying our provisions, eating through our water-casks, thereby occasioning a great waste of our water, getting into our magazine and destroying our cartridges, eating through every part of the

ship, and occasioning considerable destruction of our provisions, clothing, flags, sails, &c. &c.

Perhaps the graphic statistic is that on a sailing vessel only 140 feet long and 36½ feet wide, rats outnumbered men by between four and five to one.

With his cruise through the Galápagos concluded, Porter summed up the results of his work. Proclaiming that "we have completely broken up that important branch of British navigation, the whale-fishery of the coast of Chili and Peru" by taking almost every whaler, Porter engaged in some arithmetical legerdemain. He asserted that the total worth of the ten prizes he had taken was $2,500,000, and observed that a second $2,500,000 should be added, since he had saved a like number of American ships, which, had he not done so, would in all probability have been captured. Another quarter-million dollars was assessed against the British government for "outfitting the *Phoebe*'s expedition of one frigate, two sloops of war, and a store-ship" for an entire year. He relented enough to subtract $80,000 for the annual value of the *Essex*' service, and arrived at a net balance of $5,170,000. He ended his summary by comparing, greatly to his own advantage, his accomplishments to those of Lord Anson.

Porter's cruise to the Pacific did not end when he left the Galápagos Islands, but his constructive contribution to the U.S. war effort did. Consequently, it seems reasonable to follow his own summary of his achievements with an account of the repercussions that it produced, even though to do so entails touching upon events that had not taken place at this date.

It is impossible to know exactly how much Porter earned personally from his cruise to the Pacific; he never mentioned any precise figure. His two biggest windfalls were his shares of the $55,000 taken from the *Nocton* and of the $25,000, for which the *Essex Junior* was sold to the U.S. Navy. He told the Department that all the prize money for captain, officers, and crew had been divided into two equal parts, one for immediate distribution and the other for the establishment of a pension fund which he managed, charging a commission of five per cent for the extra labor involved.[24]

As might be expected, British and American opinion about Porter's analysis of his cruise tended to divide along national lines. To be sure, a Canadian paper grieved that the *Essex* had "annihilated our commerce in the South Seas," and caused more injury to the British Empire "than all the rest of the American Navy." In London *The Times* grumbled that the enemy voyage had been "tolerably successful." A Canadian account written during the 1920s waved the Union Jack and compared the *Essex*' work in the Pacific with that of the German cruiser *Emden* in the same general vicinity in World War I. The *Quarterly Review* spoke for most Englishmen when it sawed away on its usual chord, in this case emphasizing two strings: Porter's cruise had been a failure, and it could not rival Anson's. Pertaining to the first, Gifford wrote: ". . . none of his prizes, NO NOT ONE, ever reached America, and his own ship (a circumstance which unfortunately slipped his memory) ought to have been carried on the *contra* side of the account." With the exception of the *Essex Junior*, which was used as a cartel to transport Porter and the other survivors of the *Essex* from Valparaiso back to the United States and was sold to the American government, Gifford was right about none of the prizes reaching America. William James itemized the ships that fell captive to the Americans and what happened to each: the *Georgiana*, the *Policy*, and the *New Zealander* were recaptured off the coast of the United States by the British frigates *Barossa*, *Loire*, and *Belvidera*, respectively; the *Rose* and the *Charlton* were sent off as cartels; the *Greenwich*, the *Hector*, and the *Catherine* were burned at sea; the *Montezuma* was sold at Valparaiso; the *Sir Andrew Hammond* was recaptured in Hawaii by HM sloop of war *Cherub;* the *Seringapatam* was seized by mutineers in the Marquesas, sailed to New South Wales in Australia and eventually returned to her English owners; the *Essex* and the *Essex Junior* became victims of the *Phoebe* and the *Cherub* at Valparaiso, with the former ending up in the Royal Navy and the latter as the aforementioned cartel for Porter.

Gifford was both infuriated and amused by the American captain's denigration of Anson:

> Lord Anson was not sent to make war on whalers; his expedition defeated the vast designs of Spain, and ultimately led to the ruin of a mighty armament [the Spanish fleet sent after him that was smashed trying to round the Horn]. He captured, too, a vessel as powerful as his own, and having rounded the world, returned in safety, and *in his own ship,* with all his treasure. Captain Porter, on the contrary, after losing half his crew, was taken by a ship of inferior force, and . . . [was] sent home in a *cartel!* It is impossible to pass such ridiculous vanity without a smile.[25]

While scoring heavily in the above, the *Quarterly Review* loses points in claiming that Porter lost to a lesser ship. As shall be seen, the Americans were heavily outgunned and outmanned by the British at Valparaiso.

The first news of Porter's voyage reached the United States in the summer of 1813, when a Baltimore publication quoted an item from Brazil stating that the *Essex* had left for Cape Horn. A month later, the same source reprinted a letter, dated 8 May, from the U.S. vice consul in Buenos Aires, announcing that Porter had been at Valparaiso. From then on, stories about the *Essex* in the Pacific appeared regularly. One American commented in his diary: "Captain Porter in *Essex* frigate successful in South seas; many good prizes of whalemen, so that he has acquired a fleet of 8 or 9 sail of armed vessels from Britons', with all accommodations! His letters to Secretary of Navy, elegant." * Some of the accounts published were either misleading or incorrect. Early in 1814, *Niles National Register* stated that two British frigates arrived in Barbados on 1 December after "a fruitless search of *six* months for our little frigate," while a small weekly paper in Maine had Porter capturing "altogether twenty two sail (ships and brigs) . . . ," and reported three weeks later that the *Essex* was in "Pernambuca," Brazil. An account written after the cruise mentioned that ". . . numerous ships were sent out to the Pacifick in pursuit of him; others were ordered to cruise in the China Seas, off New Zealand, Timor, and New Holland, and a frigate was sent to the river La Plata." [26]

Even when the war was over Americans continued to uphold the value of Porter's accomplishment on the other side of the Horn. Washington Irving was effusive:

> It occasioned great uneasiness in Great Britain. The merchants who had any property afloat in this quarter, trembled with apprehension for its fate; the underwriters groaned at the catalogue of captures brought by every advice, while the pride of the nation was sorely incensed at beholding a single frigate lording it over the Pacific . . . in saucy defiance of their thousand ships; revelling in the spoils of boundless wealth, and almost banishing the British flag from those regions where it had so long waved proudly predominant.

Another commentator stressed that ". . . he was at this time completely master of the Pacific Ocean. This may be regarded as a novelty in naval incidents, and there is no doubt, had it been performed by an English naval commander, it would have been applauded to the skies, but in an American it was the deportment of a buccanier." Several pages of Senator Thomas Hart Benton's *Thirty Years' View* were devoted to the voyage of the *Essex* and described how it had resulted in the destruction of the British whaling industry. This meant, said Benton, that "the supply of oil was stopped . . . and a member of Parliament declared that the city [London] had burnt dark for a year."

The ebullient and bellicose Theodore Roosevelt praised Porter for qualities he liked to apply to himself—audacity and skill: "It was an unprecedented thing for a small frigate to cruise for a year and a half in enemy's waters, and to supply herself . . . purely from captured vessels,

---

* The reference is to two letters, both dated 2 July 1813, that had arrived in the United States giving a précis of Porter's accomplishments.

with everything. . . . Porter's cruise was the very model of what an expedition should be, harassing the enemy most effectively at no cost whatever." Still another maritime authority comments that "as a raid there was nothing to match this cruise until the *Alabama* ran amuk . . . half a century later," a comparison that might better have been applied to the *Alabama*'s fellow raider, the *Shenandoah*. In circumstances closely akin to those that attended Porter's ravages of the British "whale-fishery," the *Shenandoah* helped to write "finis" to American whaling by cutting to pieces much of New Bedford's fleet in the Bering Sea at the end of the Civil War. This point is emphasized by Fletcher Pratt, who writes that the *Essex'* voyage "destroyed an industry and raised one up; for after her cruise the whale fishery remained almost exclusively American until the coming of coal-oil and the Civil War put an end to it." * C. S. Forester was not impressed by the fact that Porter took twelve prizes in five months, contrasting the feat to that of the USS *Argus,* which took nineteen in one month. He did, however, laud Porter's remarkable accomplishment in staying at sea for eighteen months with practically no loss of life, and having more men under his command at the end than at the beginning of his cruise, "something unique in the naval history of the period." [27]

Even allowing for Porter's conceited overestimation of what he had done, the *Essex'* voyage from the Virginia Capes through the Galápagos Islands may be judged successful. He argued and with justification that, although he had not been able to contribute to the U.S. war effort by bringing his prizes home, he had hurt the British war economy by destroying them. Unquestionably, this was the most praiseworthy phase of his entire wartime effort. His ensuing sojourn in the Marquesas Islands brought him some merited criticism. The final phase of his cruise was determined by his quest for glory, which impelled him to return to Valparaiso and a defeat that cost him not only his frigate but also a top rating in American naval history.

---

* Pratt exaggerates. After the War of 1812, Great Britain made a major effort to rebuild its whaling fleet with Nantucket Islanders. According to Edouard A. Stackpole, by 1822 Britain possessed 132 whalers and had spent $200,000 on bounties. But twenty years later, whaling was again practically an American monopoly. Porter's termination of London's first effort interrupted momentum, and aided to ensure that its second would also fail.

On 2 October 1813 Porter's ships headed for the Marquesas Islands, the easternmost archipelago of Oceania, located some 2,500 miles southeast of Hawaii and 850 miles northeast of Tahiti in the Society Islands. A few of the southern Marquesas had been discovered in 1596 by the Spanish captain, Álvaro de Mendaña y Castro. He grandiloquently named them for the wife of the then viceroy of Peru, "Las Islas Marquesas de Don Garcia Hurtado de Mendoza de Cañate," now mercifully shortened to the French "Les Iles Marquises." Mendaña observed the sexual habits of the Marquesans and was, perhaps, exhibiting a sense of humor when he named one harbor, "Bay of the Virgins." Mendaña found no gold, and not only quarreled with the islanders, but even fired at them. This first contact with Europe, which introduced violence to the islands, was evidently totally forgotten, for, by Porter's time, there seems to have been not even the faintest recollection of Mendaña.

The Marquesas' long and happy isolation from the West lasted until Captain James Cook touched there on 8 April 1774. Other Englishmen visited the archipelago.[1] American claims there date from the time Captain Joseph Ingraham made a voyage from Boston to China in the small brigantine *Hope*. On 14 April 1791, he came upon the islands visited by Mendaña and Cook. Five days later, he discovered to the north some others that were not marked on Spanish or English charts. Unable to find suitable anchorage, he sailed among them, patriotically naming the group "the Washington Islands," and commemorating John Adams, Benjamin Lincoln, John Hancock, and Henry Knox by giving their surnames to individual islands. Nukahiva, where Porter later resided, was named "Federal Island." Ingraham was greeted with cheers when he announced that these discoveries henceforth belonged to the United States. Since this visit was made a year before that of the Englishman, Hergest, Porter was sure that history and geography would "do justice to the discovery of Mr. Ingraham," and soon tried to make the latter's un-official annexation official. Only three weeks after the *Hope* had departed, the Marquesan group Ingraham had found was "discovered" again, this time by Captain Etienne Marchant in the *Solide,* and if Mendaña's violence was one aspect of Western impact on the Marquesas, the Frenchman's interest in sex was another. One authority on Polynesia says that the *Solide* was turned "into a floating bagnio."

In 1792 Captain Josiah Roberts of the American ship *Jefferson* dallied in the Marquesas, unaware that his countryman Ingraham had been there a year before. He went ashore frequently and, on one island, ran into trouble: the theft of some ship's tools led to a general melee, in the course of which stones were rolled on the Americans, a local chief was wounded, and his brother was killed. As that decade wore on, U.S. whalers frequented the islands more and more and, in 1798, the crew of one ship wounded another Marquesan. In 1803, members of a Russian expedition led by Captain Ivan Federovich Krusenstern drew pictures of the islands and their people, and observed native customs.[2] By this time, Great Britain, the United States, France, and Russia, the nations which led in opening East Asia and the Pacific to Western influence during the nineteenth century, had presented in this miniscule archipelago a preview of the development of part of a continent and most of an island world.

Porter's passage from the Galápagos to the Marquesas Islands was enlivened only by Downes being sent ahead in the *Essex Junior* to search for a British whaler which might stop off in the Marquesas on her way to China, and by the captain's speech to his men on the reasons for their voyage to the South Seas:

> We are bound to the Western Islands, with two objects in view: Firstly, that we may put the ship in a suitable condition . . . for our return home; Secondly, I am desirous that you should have some relaxation and amusement after being so long at sea, as from your late good conduct you deserve it. We are going among a people much addicted to thieving, treacherous in their proceedings, whose conduct is governed only by fear. . . . We must . . . be ever on our guard . . . we must treat them with kindness, but never trust them, and be most vigilant when there is the greatest appearance of friendship. Let the fate of many who have been cut off by the savages of the South Sea islands be a useful warning to us. . . . It will require much discretion and good management to keep up a friendly intercourse with them. . . .

The message had a predictable effect on the sailors: "For the remainder of our passage they could talk and think of nothing but the beauties of the islands . . . every one imagined them Venus's, and amply indulged themselves in fancied bliss. . . ."

The little fleet reached the Marquesas on 24 October 1813, and the following day put in to Ruahuga (Adams) Island. Americans and Ruahugans were mutually suspicious. Canoes hesitantly put out from the shore, and it took all Porter's persuasive powers, exerted through Tamaha, a Tahitian interpreter he had recruited on one of the captured British whalers, to reach an agreement. While some Marquesans were enticed on board to become unwitting hostages, Porter dared row ashore, where the heavily armed Americans swapped iron hoops and fishhooks for foodstuffs. Here, the captain recorded the only instance of "dishonesty" during his entire stay in the islands. For a breadfruit apiece, three Marquesans were given two fishhooks, "to be divided among them." Porter fails to explain how this arithmetical miracle might have been accomplished, but one of the Marquesans solved the problem by reneging on the bargain and swimming off with his breadfruit.

When that transaction had been completed, the Americans rowed a couple of miles to a small cove where about fifty men and a few girls awaited them. The latter tried to inveigle Porter ashore "with gestures which we could not misunderstand; and the girls themselves showed no disinclination to grant every favor." However, the wary visitors stayed out, and when the nude girls swam toward the boats, the sailors "threw them handkerchiefs for a covering, with which they concealed those parts which modesty teaches should not be exposed," behavior which soon became utterly atypical of the men. Porter soon returned to the *Essex,* released the hostages and sailed off to the northwest. His visit to Ruahuga had lasted but a few hours.

The captain had never before met any Marquesans and his comments on the Ruahugans and their customs in the first edition of his *Journal* deserve attention. He described the men, some of them dressed in black plumes, collars, and tapa-cloth robes, as "remarkably handsome; of large stature and well proportioned . . . [with] a great difference in the color of the skin. . . ." He observed that this last feature pertained particularly to the chiefs but, on close examination, found that their darkness was caused by intricate tattooing, which left the skin like "a highly wrought piece of old mahogany." To his surprise, he found that the "foreskin of their privates was drawn so close over and tied with a strip of bark as to force that member entirely into their bodies, and gave them a strange and unnatural appearance."

According to Herman Melville, the Spaniard Mendaña found the girls of the islands almost unbelievably beautiful and, at least until the degeneracy of the late nineteenth century set in, every subsequent Western visitor concurred in his judgment. Porter was no exception:

> The young girls . . . were . . . handsome and well formed; their skins were remarkably soft and smooth, and their complexions no darker than many brunetts in America. . . . Nakedness they cannot consider offensive to modesty . . . and there is but one part which they seem to think it necessary to hide . . . hands are employed when no other covering can be obtained . . . they have a high sense of shame and pride . . . [yet] intercourse with strangers is not considered by them criminal; but on the contrary, attaches to them respect and consideration . . . if there was any crime, the offense was ours, not theirs; they acted in compliance with the customs of their ancestors; we departed from the principles of virtue and morality which are so lightly esteemed in civilization.

That passage was almost perfect grist for the mill of the *Quarterly Review:* "We cannot pollute our pages with the description which Captain Porter gives of his transactions with these people. His language and ideas are so gross and indelicate, so utterly unfit for this hemisphere, that we must leave the undivided enjoyment of this part of his book to his own countrymen. We are at a loss to determine which is the most disgusting and offensive—his nauseous ribaldry, or his impudent disavowal of his improper conduct . . . but more than enough of this profligate, this pernicious trash." [3] Yet, it was by no means "enough" for Gifford; when Porter described in similar vein what happened on Nukahiva Island, he returned to the offensive. Since the captain replied to both attacks with a single defense in his *Journal* of 1822, it shall be narrated later.

It was still 25 October when Porter's fleet entered Taiohae Bay on the southern coast of Nukahiva. To men who, for many months, had viewed nothing but the emptiness of sea and sky, the scene must have been literally paradisiacal. A long stretch of white beach fronted on a valley covered with lush grass, hundreds of fruit-laden trees, and yellow-thatched dwellings. Inland, the valley divided into several glens, ending below a massive escarpment that soared to over 3,000 feet, from which waterfalls danced in the sun. The valley was inhabited by the Taii tribe ("Taeehs" to Porter).

As the Americans entered the harbor, to their amazement, they were hailed by three white men in a canoe. Porter thought they were deserters from ships that had called there earlier, and so firmly was his mind "prejudiced against them" that, at first, he would not even talk to them. A few hours later, however, contact was made and they proved to be an American naval officer, an American sailor, and an English beachcomber. The officer was Midshipman John Minor Maury,* who had been given a

---

* John Minor Maury was the elder brother of Matthew Fontaine Maury, the famous American navigator and oceanographer, who visited the Marquesas in the USS *Vincennes* in 1829.

long furlough so that he could sail in the merchantman *Pennsylvania Packet* to collect sandalwood in the Marquesas for the Chinese market. His laden ship had departed for Canton, leaving him and five sailors to amass another load of wood. But the War of 1812 broke out, the ship did not return, and the six men were marooned. Four of the sailors had since died. Maury requested and received permission to serve with Porter, and was assigned as Downes' executive officer in the *Essex Junior*. After the defeat at Valparaiso, he returned with Porter on that ship, and died in 1823 while serving under him in the West Indies.

The beachcomber, the third white man on Nukahiva, was named Wilson, but no source provides his first name. He had lived on the island for several years, and tanning and tattooing had made him quite indistinguishable from the Nukahivans. Porter bypassed the Tahitian Tamaha and appointed Wilson his chief interpreter, calling him "an inoffensive, honest, good-natured fellow, well disposed to render every service in his power, and whose only failing was a strong attachment to rum." Actually, the Englishman was a marplot who, as long as it was necessary to do so, hid the hatred he felt for the Americans, but later roused the Nukahivans against the small party left behind when Porter sailed for Valparaiso. In the second edition of his *Journal*, the captain reassessed his conclusions about Wilson: "I have since had occasion to be satisfied that he was a consummate hypocrite and villain." [4]

Porter describes his stay at Nukahiva almost in diary form. This part of his *Journal* is hard to follow as it jumps from subject to subject on a strictly chronological basis. It may be easier to assimilate his material when it is presented by topics: outfitting the fleet; observing and often participating in local sexual and other customs; engaging in two local wars, and using the interim between them to annex Nukahiva Island to the United States.

With perfect timing, Downes, having found no trace of the British whaler he sought, brought the *Essex Junior* in to Taiohae Bay the very afternoon Porter arrived there. Almost at once, the flotilla's crews began laboring on the *Essex*, which after so many months at sea and so many buffetings from storms around the Horn, was in dire need of "general caulking of leaky seams and extensive repairs to her bottom from which the copper was coming off." The flagship was careened on the beach and stripped of everything. Carpenters were kept busy making her watertight, while coopers constructed new barrels. Her mainmast had to be rebuilt, the exterior oiled, and the "injured copper" repaired. A ropewalk was established for making new cables. Nukahivans were assigned to remove the barnacles from her fouled hull by scraping it with coconut shells. Charcoal fires were lit to fumigate the ship, and the captain asserted that, exclusive of the young who died in hidden nests, the smoke killed "from twelve to fifteen hundred" rats. However, one species of vermin seems to have been replaced by another. Nukahiva teemed with cockroaches, and the ship was soon infested with them: "they were taken on board in the sails, the wood, and in the seamen's clothing; for every night when they came on shore on liberty, their blankets, and frequently their mattresses were brought with them, which were generally well stocked by those animals on their return. . . ."

For the first week or so of their stay at Nukahiva, the Americans lived in tents, but early on the morning of 3 November some 4,000 Nukahivans from several tribes appeared on the scene and, before dark, had built them a village. Porter wrote that the new community consisted of "a dwelling place for myself and another for the officers, a sail loft, a cooper's shop, and a place for our sick, a bake house, a guard house, and a shed for the centinels to walk under. . . ." He rewarded the local laborers with several harpoons and old iron hoops, which made all "perfectly happy and content." [5]

Routine was quickly set. All hands worked until 4:00 P.M. and thereafter were at liberty until the next morning. One-quarter of the ships' companies was given shore leave each night. These weeks in the Marquesas were idyllic to those for whom seafaring usually added up to no more than hard work, brutal discipline, miserable food, and sexual starvation. The younger midshipmen, among them David Glasgow Farragut, were kept under the watchful eye of Chaplain Adams, both to further their education and to keep their presumably innocent minds from the contamination that would inevitably result from exposure to the antics of the sailors and their girls. At least, the midshipmen were often allowed ashore during the day, so that they could swim, fish, and roam about with Marquesan boys of their own ages.

For the older Americans, life at Nukahiva seems to have been a total holiday from puritanical repressions. While Porter is relatively discreet about his own activities, he gives abundant hints that he felt no inclination to pursue celibacy "when a handsome and sprightly young girl of sixteen, whose almost every charm [is] exposed to view, invites to follow her." He records one incident where he was rebuffed "with a sternness which astonished me": the girl in question, an 18-year-old granddaughter of the Taii chief, was "neet, sleek, and comely," but she received his advances "with a coldness and hauteur which would have suited a princess, and repelled everything like familiarity. . . . [and] formed a connection with one of my own officers." But the captain had his revenge, for she showed "little fidelity" to her lover and, in a classic exercise in sour grapes, he wrote in his *Journal* that she had proved to all—especially to himself—that her reputation as "a notorious jilt" was justified.

Porter's wounded pride did not prevent him from congratulating his officers on their self-control: "none indulged in that indiscriminate intercourse . . . each confined himself to one object, and she of the best family and rank. This was as much perhaps, as the most zealous celibiate would have required from men all healthy, youthful and amorous, who had scarcely seen a female for more than a year." On the other hand, with the common sailors and their girls, "all was helter-skelter, and promiscuous intercourse, every girl the wife of every man. . . . it was astonishing to see with what indifference fathers, husbands, and brothers would see their daughters, wives, and sisters fly from the embrace of one lover to that of another, and change from man to man according as they could find purchasers." Perhaps nothing in the original edition of his *Journal* earned for Porter greater condemnation than his philosophical observations on the interpersonal relations between Americans and Nukahivans late in 1813:

> Let the philosopher mourn over the depravity, as he may call it of human nature; let him express his horror, that civilized man can, for a moment, be lured by the charms of a savage; let the moralist, from his closet, preach the charms of virtue and the deformity of vice; still I shall not let fall the curtain; the veil shall be raised and nature exposed; I shall exhibit her deformities, when I meet them; but shall also display her beauties. The charms of wild uncultivated nature are not the less admired, and the rose of the wilderness is not the less beautiful than that of the parterre.[6]

Some Americans reacted with asperity to the candor with which Porter described the sexual freedom in which his men indulged in the Marquesas. One historian says that the "Government" suppressed the edition of his *Journal* that was published in 1815 because of "its too familiar and detailed description of some unlicensed portion of a sailor's life in the Pacific Isles." During Porter's court-martial in 1825 an inimical newspaper remembered his "revolting narrative" about his exploits on Nukahiva and, in later times, an anthropologist accused the expedition of having spread venereal disease among the islanders. Perhaps so, but Porter, who listed cases of the malady among his crew when he left the United States, says that when he left Nukahiva, "I had no sick on board my ship."

Gifford in the *Quarterly Review* was unsparing: "And all this, a débauchée of fifty (if we may form a judgment from the forbidding portrait stuck as a frontispiece to these volumes) tells us 'is written chiefly for the *improvement* and information of his son'. . . ." He concluded that Porter's description of his activities on Nukahiva makes up "a most nauseous and indelicate account of the bestial amours of himself and his ship's company, affording an exhibition of moral depravity which any man of sense and proper feeling would be ashamed to avow."

In the second edition of his *Journal*, Porter replied to his critics by suggesting that since he had been in "new and untried situations," the fairest moral yardstick was a comparison between his conduct and that of others who are upheld as paragons of correct deportment. In much the same manner as he had used Lord Anson to justify what he had done in the Galápagos, he proceeded to use Captain James Cook as his whipping boy for his actions on Nukahiva by quoting from the *Journal of Cook's Voyages:*

> During our stay in the Island [Tahiti], we had hardly a sailor who had not made a very near connexion with one or the other of the female inhabitants; *nor, indeed, many officers who were proof against the allurements of the better sort*—who were no less amorous and artful . . . than those of the inferior orders. . . . The officers began to be punctilious, and our seamen to be licentious. Several of the latter were punished severely for indecency surpassing even the natives. . . .

Porter angrily defied his critics to produce any passage in his own *Journal* that conveyed such "a picture of voluptuous sensuality, and indiscriminate, vulgar licentiousness." He admitted that he had deleted from his second edition "a few passages that might possibly admit of some objections, and which he can only apologize for, on the ground of having been led astray by the example of so many British navigators." [7] Indeed, some dozen detailed accounts of sexual interest that appeared in 1815 were excised from his edition of 1822.

The captain commented on other aspects of Nukahivan morality. He judged it a crime-free society, for its members "live like affectionate brethren of one family . . . I saw no punishment inflicted, nor did I ever hear that there was any cause." Considering that South Sea Islanders had a reputation for thievery, Porter was pleasantly surprised to find that, despite abundant opportunity to steal tools and clothing, "no article, of the most trifling nature, was ever missed by any person, except the small articles which were pilfered from the sailors by their girls, and this was in all probability in retaliation for the tricks which had been played upon them." Presents and other property were divided amicably "without riot, without confusion, without disputes," and without authoritative pressure. He paid his hosts extravagant compliments:

> They have been stigmatized by the name of savages; it is a term wrongly applied; they rank high in the scale of human beings, whether we consider them morally or physically. We find them brave, generous, honest and

benevolent, acute, ingenious, and intelligent, and their beauty and regular proportions of their bodies, correspond with the perfection of their minds.

The *Quarterly Review* admitted that Porter was correct in describing the people of Nukahiva as a "fine race of men," but wondered how, for the favors received, he could be so ungrateful as to war on them.

Porter's *Journal* abounds with evidence of his avid interest in all aspects of Nukahivan life. Economically, the island was practically self-sufficient. Some items of Western manufacture, especially clothing; iron articles such as harpoons, knives, scissors, and tools; beads, "junk bottles," and other glass objects, were desired but money was contemptuously refused. At the apex of Marquesan economic wants were whale teeth to be worn as necklaces or as ear ornaments. Porter asserted that "no jewel, however valuable, is half so esteemed in Europe or America," and, to prove his point, added that for ten large whale teeth the Nukahivans would cut, carry to the beach, and stow on board enough sandalwood to fill a 300-ton ship, a cargo sure to command "near a million of dollars" in the market of Canton, China.

Several pages of the *Journal* were devoted to Marquesan agriculture. Following some commonplace remarks about coconut trees, the "twenty different varieties of bananas," "highly esteemed" poi paste from the "tarra [taro] root," and miscellaneous fruits, Porter goes into detail on the kava root and breadfruit. He had the usual Western abhorrence for the former, which the natives turned into a semi-intoxicant by chewing, spitting the saliva into a bowl, and allowing time for it to ferment. According to the captain, kava addiction resulted in what amounted to a one-product plague: "it renders them very stupid . . . making their skin fall off in white scales; affects their nerves, and no doubt brings on premature old age." His enthusiasm for breadfruit was wholehearted. This marvelous, all-purpose commodity not only provided the basic food for the islanders and their pigs, but, "the trees afford them an agreeable and refreshing shade; the leaves are an excellent covering for their houses; of the inner bark of the small branches they make cloth; the juice, which exudes, enables them to destroy the rats which infest them; and of the trunk of the tree they form their canoes, many parts of their houses, and even their gods."

In order to aid their agriculture, Porter furnished seeds of "mellons, pumpkins, peas, beans, oranges, limes, &c. together with peach stones, wheat and indian corn," and promised to pay a whale's tooth for every melon and pumpkin brought to him on his next visit to the islands. He also gave them English hogs, goats, and Galápagos turtles. He admired the islanders' ingenious two-part fishhooks made from mother-of-pearl, but their bone and wooden harpoons were obviously much inferior to his iron ones. The waters of the Marquesas abounded with fish but, except when a school was trapped in shallow water and driven toward the shore, relatively few were caught.[8]

The best adjective that Porter could find to apply to the Nukahivan social organization was "patriarchal." He was wrong, but should not be blamed, for this aspect of Marquesan culture was remarkably complex. Actually, the society was neither patriarchal nor matriarchal, but primogenital—status was determined by how far back ancestry could be traced from the eldest child, either male or female. Landholding had some influence on social status, but real prestige was hereditary. Gattenewa, chief of the Taiis, with whom Porter had a close association, was said to be able to rattle off the names of eighty-eight generations of his ancestors. Perhaps because of this sequoia of a family tree, he was protected by several taboos: the top of his head was sacred and nothing must be placed over it, no gate could be closed against him, and no female dared touch his sleeping mat. Yet, as was true of the other chiefs, he had no more direct authority than "that of fathers among their children"; he had to fish, paddle his own canoe, and work on communal chores, as did his fellows of lesser status.

Porter wrote that the religion of the Nukahivans "not only perplexed Captain Cook, but all the learned men that accompanied him to find out, and as may be naturally supposed has greatly perplexed me." Nevertheless, he valiantly tried to explain it to readers of his *Journal.* Although the scores of taboos on persons, things, or areas that, for the most part, governed behavior, were strictly obeyed, on one occasion the Taiis broke one of them for him, an honor that was not accorded even to Wilson, who had lived there so long: they took him to their chief place of worship, located in a beautiful grove high in the mountains. In his opinion, the life-sized stone image was poorly done, but he was complimentary about the thirty-five-foot bamboo "obelisks" on each side of it. He was nauseated by the unbearable stench that came from "four splendid war canoes," each of which contained a dead priest; one canoe was filled with partially decomposed bodies of eight prisoners of war. When two more bodies were added, the captain thought it was done to provide enough oarsmen to paddle the canoe to heaven, but he misunderstood. The ten dead required for this ceremony symbolized ten parts of the body. Gattenewa brought out a Nukahivan god which Porter shrugged off as "a parcel of paper cloth," like "a child in swaddling clothes." In fact, he wrote, "In religion these people are mere children . . . and their gods are their dolls." Although the Taiis danced and sang around their idols, the captain judged their attitude toward their deities was amused contempt.

Porter's comments on the local reaction toward Christianity explain the failure of much of the missionary activity that has been carried out among the Polynesians. He told of describing to the Nukahivans "the nature of the Christian religion, in a manner to suit their ideas." His hosts agreed politely that his God must be greater than theirs, because white men themselves were superior to Nukahivans. But he proselyted with no more success than had a British missionary who, a few years before, had tried to convert Gattenewa's wife. After listening to his attacks on her religion, she remonstrated that it was wrong for him to ridicule her gods since she did not ridicule his. "Our gods," she reasoned, "supply us with bread-fruit and cocoa-nuts, bananas and tarra in abundance; we are perfectly contented and we feel satisfied . . . you who reside in the moon [the Nukahivans thought that only this origin could explain the color of their Western intruders] come to get the produce of our island; why would you visit us, if your own gods and your own island could supply all your wants [?]" [9]

All the early European and American visitors to the South Seas speculated about the prevalence of cannibalism, and Porter was no exception. After one local battle, the captain found the Taiis gathering around the bodies of their enemies, and "my blood recoiled with horror at the spectacle I was on the point of witnessing." His allies persuaded him that they had no intention of partaking of a meal immediately, that all they wanted to do was to "sing and perform ceremonies" over the bodies. Porter mistakenly concluded that "these people were not cannibals . . . although they did not deny that they sometimes ate their enemies, at least so we understood them, but it is possible we may have misunderstood." They did not misunderstand. Not only did the Marquesans practise cannibalism, but in all Polynesia they were probably the most enthusiastic consumers of human flesh, which they graphically called "long pig." Herman Melville lived in the Marquesas during the early 1840s, and the characters in his book *Typee* were constantly afraid that they might furnish the entrée for a Nukahivan banquet, and their apprehension was no more than a sensible cognizance of a possibility all too real.

Much of Porter's difficulty in comprehending the people among whom he lived hinged upon linguistics. Even when aided by the most adroit interpreter, he and other Westerners found the transmission of complex ideas between two such fundamentally different cultures to be almost impossible. The Marquesan languages could convey with perfect clarity their interfamilial relationships and system of taboos, which, to alien mentalities, were incredibly complex. Porter, however, concluded that his difficulty in communicating arose from his hosts' lack of vocabulary. He complained that on Nukahiva, one word had to do the work of many: *motee* meant "I thank you, I have enough, I do not want it, I do not like it, keep it yourself, take it away, &c. &c."; the meanings of *mattee* ranged from receiving a pinprick to being killed; and *kava* applied to "every thing we eat or drink of a heating or pungent nature . . . rum or wine . . . pepper, mustard, and even salt . . . also our spittle."

Other aspects of the local culture that earned Porter's approbation or special attention were the well-built and airy houses, with their floors made from large stones, mat walls, and thatched roofs; the daring with which the inhabitants made the long and perilous journeys from island to island in canoes which seemed far too frail for such enterprise; the intricate feather headdresses; the tapa-cloth costumes worn by both sexes; and the masterful workmanship in their elaborate fans. The captain furnished some details about their outré methods of shaving, tattooing, and circumcision. Prior to Porter's arrival in the islands, beards and other hair had to be either shaved with sharks' teeth or plucked out with shells, but with his advent the ubiquitous iron hoops, ground to an edge, became the vogue. Considering the prevalence of tattooing and circumcision, it is unfortunate that less agonizing methods could not have been developed. According to Porter, tattooing was done with bone tips rubbed with the residue from burned coconut shells, set as comb teeth, then hammered "into the flesh by means of a heavy piece of wood . . . the operation is extremely painful and streams of blood follow every blow." He noticed that a few Nukahivans had even the insides of their lips tattooed. Circumcision appeared equally gruesome: the foreskin "was slit . . . [with] a shark's tooth," and later a "ligature" was tied "around the extremity of a certain part of the body," an oddly reticent way for the candid Porter to describe the process.[10]

Not all of the captain's time on Nukahiva was taken up with amatory dalliance and rapt absorption in anthropological curiosa. He found it impossible to avoid involvement in local wars. Mountains running to the sea divided Nukahiva into several valleys; other ranges crisscrossed the island laterally and diagonally. Consequently, the topography was ideal for the creation and continuation of tribal disunity and hostility among the 40,000-odd who lived on the island.*

---

* It is obviously impossible to report the exact population of Nukahiva in 1813. Citing as his source Porter's *Journal*, Charles L. Lewis gives the figure of "about 20,000," but the former's precise enumeration of 19,500 applied only to the warriors that the island's thirty-one tribes had available for battle. That number might have been in the neighborhood of a third of the total population, which would have included women and those too young and too old to fight. On the other hand, although the Marquesans vehemently denied that female infanticide was practised, Ralph Linton, the anthropologist most conversant with the subject, writes that in the Marquesas during modern times, "the ratio of males to

The Americans resided among the Taii tribe, whose enemies were the Happahs, a tribe that lived inland. Wars were constant between them, and if deaths were never numerous, since Marquesan weapons tended to wound rather than kill, Happah attacks had destroyed many Taii breadfruit trees. Porter's immediate neighbors naturally appealed to him for help. At first, he tried to weaken Happah intransigency and stiffen Taii resistance by frequent demonstrations of his fire power, both with cannon and musket. After extracting a promise from the Taiis that if he gave them a cannon they would carry it high into the mountains in order to control the path leading between the two tribes, he was amazed when they finally managed to push and pull "their darling gun" into place.

Porter described the psychological warfare he tried to wage against the Happahs: he told them that he had come "with a force sufficiently strong to drive them from the island, and if they presumed to enter the valley [of the Taiis] . . . I should send a body of men to chastise them . . . they should cease all hostilities as long as I remained among them; that if they had hogs or fruit to dispose of, they might come and trade freely with us, as I should not permit the natives of the valley to injure or molest them." The Happahs answered courageously by notifying the captain that they were going to fight him, since they were sure the Americans "were afraid to attack them, as we had threatened so much without attempting any thing."

Late in October, in order to convince the Happahs that Porter meant what he said, John Downes led an expedition of sailors and Marines, accompanied by a large party of Taiis under their war chief, Moina, against the recalcitrant Happahs. Porter stayed behind with Gattenewa, retaining the chief as a hostage to ensure the good behavior of his people.* At first, it was easy for those left in the valley to follow the progress of the expedition, for one Taii carried an American flag. As the in-

---

females was about two and a half males to one female." If this ratio is correct, Porter's enumeration of 19,500 warriors could indicate a total population of only 40,000 or less. We do not know, of course, whether the ratio of $2\frac{1}{2}$ to 1 pertained in Porter's day or whether it was the result of later Marquesan social deterioration. Another expert calculates that, before the arrival of Captain James Cook, the entire Marquesan archipelago contained a "possible 100,000 to 120,000." Anthropologist H. L. Shapiro gives an approximation of 100,000 for all the islands when Porter was there.[11] As Nukahiva is the largest, a population of 40,000 in 1813 would seem to be as reasonable a guess as any.

* Gattenewa would not have taken part in the expedition under any circumstances. The capture or death of a chief meant absolute social disgrace for a Marquesan tribe, so during a battle he was always kept far away under heavy guard.

vaders advanced, the Happahs retreated to a fortified crest, from which they let fly a volley of spears and sling-cast stones. Downes was hit in the stomach with a rock which "laid him breathless on the ground," while another American was "pierced with a spear through the neck." To add insult, the Happahs "scoffed at our men, and exposed their posteriors to them." When Downes recovered, he led a charge that stormed the hill, killing five of the enemy and driving the rest in rout. The fact that the resistance of some 3,000 to 4,000 Happahs collapsed after sustaining such a miniscule number of casualties, proves that Nukahivan warfare was not supposed to be deadly. A couple of days later, a Happah envoy came to confess that his tribe was "in the utmost dismay, and desired nothing more ardently than peace." Later, when a delegation of Happahs arrived, Porter "gently expostulated with them on their imprudence," and levied an indemnity of hogs and fruit. Even though later events showed that the Happahs secretly hated their conquerors, they led almost all the other tribes in helping to build the village for the Americans and, at that time, in sending produce.[12]

No sooner had the Happah war been concluded than a more dangerous conflict loomed in prospect. When one of the tribes failed to deliver promised foodstuffs, Porter questioned them and found that they were closely allied to the Taipis (Typees, to Porter and Melville), the strongest and most belligerent tribe on the island. He used the same tactics with the Taipis as with the Happahs, but the result was equally negative. He paraphrased the Taipis' masterful answer to his boast of American strength: ". . . why should they desire friendship with us? why should they bring us hogs and fruit? that if I was strong enough they knew I would come and taken them; and that my not doing so was an acknowledgement of my weakness. . . ." When Porter made another attempt at conciliation, the Taipis' response was even more aggressive. According to the captain, it ran:

> . . . all the people of the valley [Taiis and Happahs] were cowards; that as to myself and my people, we were white lizards, mere dirt; and as the most contemptible epithet which they could apply, said we were the posteriors and privates of the Taeehs. We were, said they, incapable of standing fatigue, overcome by the slightest heat and want of water . . . and yet we talked of chastising the Typees, a tribe which had never before been driven by an enemy. . . .

Moina, the Taii war chief, who had "frothed with rage" at the first reply, was so furious about the second that he told Porter to his face that he was "a great coward," upon which the captain chased him with a loaded musket to force an apology from him.

Hoping that he might be able to avoid combat, Porter continued to work for time. He quieted the impatient Taiis, who demanded an immediate attack, by promising that he would invade the Taipi Valley, but not until he had planned his strategy and amassed supplies. By these tactics, he gained almost a month, during which he had a fort built on the plateau above the American settlement: water casks filled with dirt formed a breastwork, with apertures for sixteen guns, although only four were mounted. Coincidentally, a mate from the prize ship *Sir Andrew Hammond* was plotting to immobilize the crew of the *Essex Junior* with rum and laudanum so that all the English prisoners could seize that vessel and sail past the careened *Essex* to freedom. Information about the plot was relayed to Porter before the conspirators had done much more than collect alcohol. Rather sadistically, the captain played with them, contenting himself for the moment with secretly punishing the Marine guards for having stood by while the rum was stolen, and announcing that a general tightening of security was essential. The next night, a Marine was reported to be asleep on duty, and the captain's punishment was, to put it mildly, summary. He claimed not to want the trouble of a court-martial and the possible infliction of a mandatory death sentence, so instead he crept up on the sleeping sentry and shot him "through the fleshy part of the thigh." There seems no doubt that Porter was correct when he smugly stated that his action made "every person more vigilant, particularly the marines."

At just the wrong moment, so far as the British prisoners were concerned, the *Albatross,* an American ship from Astoria, John Jacob Astor's trading post at the mouth of the Columbia River in the Oregon Country, arrived off the island, and the *Essex Junior,* their prospective means of escape, dashed off to investigate. Wilson Hunt Price, Astor's agent, had come to Nukahiva in an attempt to talk Porter into dispatching one of his armed prizes to the Columbia for the purpose of evacuating the Americans there. The captain quite properly refused, but it would have made no difference had he acceded to Price's request. A couple of weeks after the *Albatross* came in to Nukahiva, the British sloop of war *Raccoon* arrived at Astoria, and no lesser ship than the *Essex* herself would have been strong enough to meet the English fire power.

Porter suddenly dropped his cat-and-mouse game with the conspirators: he slapped them into irons, and sentenced them to the hard labor of building a wall around the American settlement. The attempted uprising of the British prisoners set in motion a sequence of disciplinary problems which, by and large, Porter had escaped since the *Essex* had left the United States over a year before. No sooner had the mutiny been aborted than a malcontent quartermaster on the flagship, who had committed an infraction, said that if he were whipped he would do no more work, because his enlistment had expired. Since most of the crew were in the same status, Porter struck hard. He told the quartermaster that he would be whipped anyway and then marooned ashore, and he gave the others three choices: first, re-enlist with full perquisites of pay, prize shares, and shore leave; second, refuse to re-enlist but work, in which case they would be given neither pay nor shares, but would be fed until they were put ashore at the first civilized port; and third, neither re-enlist nor work, in which case they would be abandoned on Nukahiva. Practically every one of them chose re-enlistment, even the original culprit who was forgiven by the captain after the officers interceded for him and he tendered a craven apology.[13]

On 19 November 1813 Porter performed one of the most extraordinary acts of his extraordinary life. He annexed Nukahiva Island to the United States, thereby earning title as the first American imperialist.* He had prepared for his spate of expansionism by providing a brand-new nomenclature: he christened Nukahiva "Madison's Island," the American settlement "Madisonville," his defensive position there "Fort Madison," and, afraid perhaps of too much of a good thing, contented himself with calling Taiohae Bay "Massachusetts Bay." Having assembled his men, the English prisoners of war, visitors from the *Albatross*, and a large crowd of presumably bewildered Marquesans, he proceeded to read the following declaration:

> It is hereby made known to the world that I, David Porter, a captain in the navy of the United States of America and now in command of the United States frigate the *Essex*, have on the part of the said United States, taken possession of the island called by the natives Nooaheevah . . . but now called Madison's Island. . . .

> Our rights to this island being founded on priority of discovery, conquest, and possession, cannot be disputed; but the natives . . . have requested to be admitted into the great American family, whose pure republican policy approaches so near their own; and in order to encourage these views to their own interest and happiness . . . I have taken on myself to promise them they shall be so adopted; that our chief shall be their chief. . . .

> [Porter then lists the thirty-one tribes of Nukahiva, among them such syllabic monstrosities as the "Tomavaheenahs," the "Tickeymahues," the "Attestapwyunahs," and the "Attakakahaneuahs."]

> Influenced by considerations of humanity, which promises speedy civili-

---

* Imperialism is defined here as the taking of distant territory already heavily populated by an alien people, in contrast to expansion into nearby, scarcely populated areas which would be populated with Americans bringing with them American institutions.

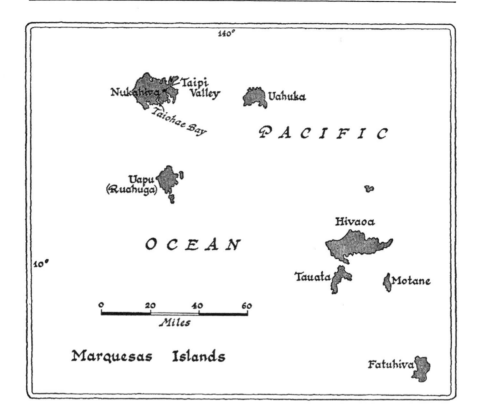

zation to a race of men who enjoy every mental and bodily endowment which nature can bestow, and which requires only art to perfect, as well as by views of policy, which secures to my country a fruitful and populous island . . . And that our claim to this island may not be hereafter disputed, I have buried in a bottle at the foot of the flag staff in Fort Madison, a copy of this instrument, together with several pieces of money, the coin of the United States. . . .

[*Signed*] David Porter.

Among the official witnesses to the document were naval officers Downes, Wilmer, McKnight, and Maury, Chaplain Adams, Marine Lieutenant John Gamble, and from the *Albatross* the captain, some officers, and an "agent for the American North Pacific fur company [Wilson Hunt Price]."

Porter dispatched to America on one of his returning prizes the news that the United States had become an imperialistic power, but President Madison did absolutely nothing about it. To be sure, the captain was not censured for exceeding instructions, even though the administration must have been startled by his pushing the boundaries of the United States several thousand miles to the southwest. The main reason for executive inaction was that the intelligence of Nukahiva's entry into the Union arrived just about the time the British were invading Chesapeake Bay, burning public buildings in Washington, and driving the President into humiliating flight. Irving Brant, Madison's biographer, remarks: "Having trouble nearer at home, Chief Madison of the Attakakahaneuahs and thirty other tribes did not ask Congress to accept the island. . . ."

Although Porter kept pushing the issue, nothing more happened about Nukahiva's annexation. Just after the war, Porter wrote Secretary of State James Monroe:

> Sir.—I have the honor to enclose you the original declaration of taking possession of Madison's Island . . . situated in the South Pacific Ocean.
> The climate, fertility, local situation, friendly disposition of the natives, and convenience of this island promise to make it at some future day of great importance to the vessels of the United States navigating the Pacific . . . I consider it a duty I owed my country to use every effort in my power, to secure to her an indisputable title to it.[14]

Monroe's inertia equalled that of Madison. The letter was neither answered nor even acknowledged.

Although, both at the time and later, there was some comment about the captain's spasm of imperialism, there was rather less of it than might have been expected. One contemporary newspaper did lose itself in admiration for his taking possession "of a territory, making himself at once an admiral and a governor. Who has equalled it? . . . Porter . . . is the

Leonidas of naval annals—his men are Spartans. . . ." As late as 1819, the *Providence* (Rhode Island) *Chronicle* was still taking the annexation seriously. Reporting the arrival at Providence of three young Nukahivans, it commented: "They appear to be inoffensive youths, and as they are American citizens, having been adopted into the great American family, we think they will be treated with kindness and hospitality." *

Late nineteenth and early twentieth century imperialists praised most extravagantly the attempt to add Nukahiva to the United States. David Dixon Porter commented that his father was "only following the custom of all civilized nations." He pointed out that owning the islands gave the United States advantages that were not as evident in his father's time as they were in his own day, "but Captain Porter fully appreciated their value *then*. . . ." He concluded that it was not in the best interest of the United States for the Marquesas to be in the possession of the French, as they had been since 1842, and forecast that, once a Panama canal had been built, Nukahiva would become the principal port on the route between Britain and Australia.

In 1908 an article written by a naval officer and entitled "The Pioneer of America's Pacific Empire: David Porter" appeared in a professional journal. The author claimed that "Porter's mind was imperial in its conception. He had the prescience to see that American control of the Pacific was essential to the national stability, and this in 1814, when the United States extended theoretically but little west of the Mississippi." Had Porter's work been followed through, continued the author, America would possess Nukahiva as well as Hawaii, and its relationship to the South Pacific would be the same as that of Hawaii to the North Pacific. He castigated James Monroe for being "so blind to the Pacific which Porter had swept of the foe and delivered to his native land as a solemn possession," especially since he was the President who had "blazed with the inspired vision of an America from Baffin's Bay to the Horn . . . ," where the Atlantic was concerned. The writer mourned that, as an American, Porter was "almost forgotten," whereas, had he been English, he would have "ranked with Drake." Then he spoiled his comparison by telling of an English captain who, in 1816, urged his government to annex Hawaii, only to be ignored as completely as was Porter.[15]

---

* These may have been the Nukahivans who were the subject of a story mentioned in a French newspaper and reprinted in a Baltimore journal in 1817. Three Nukahivans had been held as hostages while some men from an American ship went ashore, and had been carried off when the merchantman fled after discovering that "these insular Anthropophagi" had killed and eaten two of the Americans. On the voyage to America via Europe the three were said to be good sailors, but "afraid the captain intended to eat them."

Some of the comment was highly unfavorable. The *Quarterly Review* restricted itself to observing that it would "pass over the farcical ceremony of taking possession," but the anti-administration press in the United States was not so reticent. The addition of Nukahiva was called "foolery," and renaming Taiohae Bay was described as the "prostitution" of the noble title of Massachusetts: "Let it be called Virginia Bay, or Kentucky Bay, Tippecanoe Bay, Gerrymander Bay, or Tar-and-Feather Bay if you please," wrote the *Salem Gazette*, "but no improper liberties with 'Massachusetts Bay,' we say. . . ." Four days later, the *Gazette* rejoiced in the possibility that if "the feeble and pusillanimous" Madison actually went to Nukahiva to become chief of its thirty-one tribes, the United States would be rid of him. A contemporary historian, who was otherwise pro-Porter, disapproved of his annexation, even if the natives had requested it: the European nations, he said, "have uniformly possessed themselves by violence of such portions as they wanted, whereas the United States have uniformly obtained them by purchase." J. C. Furnas, a popular modern writer, has given a breezy finale to Porter's annexation of Nukahiva: "Little came of this gesture, except some colorful chapters in his journal and, when he saw fit to interfere in local feuds, some dead Marquesans . . . though Madisonville was allowed to decay as if it had never been built, the U.S. Navy had a Pacific squadron operating out of South American ports within twelve years." [16]

Meanwhile time was running out as far as Porter's attempts to avoid war with the Taipis were concerned. Not only did his potential enemies refuse to be conciliated, but pressures from his Nukahivan allies steadily intensified. The Happahs were close to outright rebellion, and even the more loyal Taiis, demonstrating strong displeasure, told the Americans, "you have long threatened them; their insults have been great; you have promised to protect us against them, and yet permit them to offer violence to us; and while you have rendered every other tribe tributary to you, you permit them to triumph with impunity." Porter finally gave in, announcing that he personally would lead an expedition against the Taipis.

His first attack could well have cost him his life, so slipshod was his planning. He erred in two most important strategic fundamentals, underestimating both the difficulties of the terrain to be covered, and the numbers and defensive strength of the enemies to be overcome. He later admitted that the force he took with him was "very inadequate," for it consisted of only thirty-five Americans and about 5,000 Taiis and Happahs, who would be sure to run at any critical moment. On 28 November his boats, accompanied by a number of large Taii war canoes and the *Essex Junior*, rowed northeast along the coast to the bay in front of the

Taipi Valley, and the next morning he and his men started inland. He led them along a narrow path into a "high and almost impenetrable swampy thicket," which he mistakenly assumed was not extensive.

While he and his men were still making their way through the swamp, the Taipis, who had offered only brief resistance at the beach, suddenly launched a full-fledged attack with "spears and stones, which came from different parties of the enemy in ambuscade. We could hear the snapping of the slings, the whistling of the stones; the spears came quivering by us, but we could not perceive from whom they came; no enemy could be seen, not a whisper was to be heard among them." Aware of his peril, but convinced that a retreat might shatter the morale of his allies, Porter ordered the advance to continue. He reached a small but rapid, deep, and steeply banked river, where a stone felled Downes and broke his leg. The captain dared not send his lieutenant back in the company of Marquesans alone, since Taipis lurked along the path to the rear, so he was forced to reduce his already tiny band of Americans by dispatching five men on that errand. At this point, his situation was desperate; except for Moina and "two or three" others, all his allies had disappeared, as they had been expected to do if the situation became critical. Nevertheless, following the river, he pushed on until he came to a ford and, commanding that a volley be fired to provide cover, he and his men splashed across. On the other side of the river, there was a quarter-mile of boggy undergrowth, through which the Americans had to inch their way, before emerging to face a most disheartening sight: "a strong and extensive wall of seven feet in height, raised on an eminence crossing our road, and flanked on each side by an impenetrable thicket."

Porter was about to lead a charge against the fortification, which he later found would have been sure to fail, when he discovered that he had very little ammunition left, and he had to send Marine Lieutenant John Gamble and four others to get more cartridges. This left him with an "army" of only nineteen able-bodied Americans and, on second thoughts, he concluded that he must withdraw or die. In order to lure the Taipis from their stronghold, he started a sham retreat and after a couple of those who rushed out had been killed, the others fled back into the fort. The ruse gave the harassed Americans an opportunity to recross the river and fight their way back to safety. When he reached the beach, Porter tried one more bluff: he sent an emissary to the Taipis with a surrender demand couched in "the air of a conqueror (although I must confess I felt little like one) ." When he pointed out that with a small force he had driven them back to their fort and inflicted casualties, and vowed that he would return with a strong army unless they gave up, the Taipis replied with contempt. Not only did they have abundant manpower, but they despised the American muskets which often missed fire, rarely killed, and caused wounds less painful than those inflicted by spears and stones. Porter, "perfectly sick of bush fighting," did the only thing he could; he rowed back to the Taii village to the constant refrain from his Nukahivan allies, "The Typees have driven the white men. . . ." [17]

He spent the next day in making more adequate preparations for his task. He collected 200 of his best men and, recalling his recent travails, determined to climb over the mountains and descend into Taipi Valley well behind the fortification that had so baffled him, rather than attack from the beach. That decision caused young Farragut, who had missed the first attack, intense disappointment for it barred him from the second. He later reflected that he had not been allowed to go because his "legs were too short" for such uphill work.

Although Porter and his expeditionary force began climbing the steep incline early in the evening, they did not reach the crest until after midnight, and he sensibly decided that his exhausted sailors could stand no more exertion. What remained of the night was almost intolerably uncomfortable: a continuous downpour and a "cold and piercing wind" were made worse by the apprehension that water-soaked powder would make their muskets useless. When dawn broke and Porter could see the height to which they had ascended, he was astonished and so alarmed by the almost perpendicular, rain-slicked precipice they would have to descend that he ordered a retreat to a nearby Happah village where his men could rest and dry out. Before leaving his position, he had a volley fired with what muskets were still operational, both to overawe the untrustworthy Happahs, and to warn the Taipis that he was coming so that "they might remove their women and children, their hogs, and most valuable effects . . . from the pillage and destruction" of his Nukahivan allies. The shots caused a tremendous uproar among the Taipis; they "shouted, beat their drums, and blew their war conches from one end of the valley to the other; and what with the squealing of the hogs . . . the screaming of the women and children, and the yelling of the men, the din was horrible."

At the Happah settlement, whose inhabitants were about to conclude that the withdrawal presaged inevitable defeat for the Americans, the atmosphere was tense. Porter's wet, hungry, and tired men were given nothing to eat, while armed Happahs gathered menacingly and the women kept out of sight. Porter told the chief to surrender the weapons of his people, and threatened that if food and dry clothing for his men were not immediately forthcoming, he would take them. The threat worked, and the Americans, full of the baked pig supplied by their reluctant but disarmed and cowed hosts, spent a relatively comfortable night.

Returning to the ridge the next morning, Porter surveyed the lovely scenery he was about to defile:

> The valley was about nine miles in length, and three or four in breadth, surrounded on every part, except the beach . . . by lofty mountains: the upper part was bounded by a precipice of many hundred feet in height, from the top of which a handsome sheet of water was precipitated, and formed a beautiful river, which ran meandering through the valley and discharged itself at the beach. Villages were scattered here and there, the bread-fruit and cocoa-nut trees flourished luxuriantly and in abundance; plantations laid out in good order . . . and every thing bespoke industry, abundance, and happiness—never in my life did I witness a more delightful scene, or experience more repugnancy than I now felt for the necessity which compelled me to punish a happy and heroic people.

The risky descent into the valley was made amid clouds of Taipi stones and spears. A fortified village was taken, and the expeditionary force split into small bands to attack different strongholds. Porter fought his way to the largest town, set it afire, and then spread havoc to the farthest extremity of the valley. With his Marquesan fair-weather friends laden with booty, he returned to the foot of the cliff he had come down that morning but, deciding that it would be impossible to scale it, he marched instead toward the beach. On the way, he came to the massive stone wall that had checked his advance two days before and was doubly impressed. It was "built of large stones, six feet thick at the bottom, and gradually narrowing at the top to give it strength and durability." He tried to tear it down, but came to the conclusion that "time alone can destroy it," and contented himself with widening a breach that was already there. He continued to the sea but, without boats, had to make his way through the hills to Madisonville. At the apex, Porter halted to cast a final look back into the valley which, when he had seen it that morning, had been all "abundance and beauty"; but "a long line of smoking ruins now marked our traces from one end to the other; the opposite hills were covered with the unhappy fugitives, and the whole presented a scene of desolation and horror. Unhappy and heroic people!" *

The three-day, sixty-mile march had so exhausted Porter's company that two days after its return to the American village, one Marine corporal died. A Taipi delegation soon sued for peace, which was granted on terms of a 400-hog indemnity. All the other tribes joined with offerings of swine and fruit, and for the first time Porter was plagued by abundance.

---

* A traveler who visited the Taipi Valley during the 1930s found it "a lovely valley with bitter memories," whose total population consisted of seven or eight persons.

Not having enough salt to cure the meat, he had to notch his pigs' ears for later identification, and turn them loose.

The captain tried to console himself for the ruin he had wrought by reflecting that he had brought peace to the entire island, not only between the Americans and Nukahivans, but among the tribes themselves. Fearing that his conduct might be censured as "wanton and unjust," he included in his original narrative a lengthy apologia for his assault upon the Taipis:

> But let us reflect a moment on our peculiar situation—a handful of men among numerous warlike tribes, liable every moment to be attacked by them and cut off; our only hope of safety was in convincing them of our great superiority over them. . . . I had received many wanton provocations from them . . . and repeated complaints were made to me on the subject. I had borne with their reproaches, and my moderation was called cowardice. I offered them friendship, and my offers were rejected with insulting scorn . . . a mere thread connected us with the other tribes; that once broken our destruction was almost inevitable . . . had they been convinced that the Typees could keep us at bay, they must have felt satisfied that their united forces were capable of destroying us; a coalition would have been fatal to us—it was my duty to prevent it . . . by reducing the Typees before they could come to an understanding with the other tribes . . . I hoped to bring about a general peace and secure the future tranquility of the Island.

Porter went on to boast that many of the old men of the island had told him that, until the advent of the general serenity he had created, they had never been out of the valley in which they were born, but thereafter they could go anywhere. To ensure the continuation of amity even after his departure, he lied that he would eventually return to punish any who resorted to belligerency. To prove that he had almost miraculously established good-fellowship, he mentioned the name-swapping—a sign of the greatest respect in Marquesan society—that followed his victory over the Taipis. So many, he said, insisted on adopting the name "Apotee" (the closest the Nukahivans could come to saying Porter), that late-comers had to be satisfied with the name of his relatives: "The name of my son, however, was more desired than any other, and many old men . . . were known by the name of Pickineenee Apotee. . . ." *

Porter's wars on Nukahiva, especially the one against the Taipis, aroused a chorus of condemnation, broken in only a few instances. The

---

* Porter did not know that the Nukahivans were undoubtedly vying with one another for the name of his son rather than his own. In the Marquesan culture, the father was "socially outranked by his eldest son from birth." [18]

USS *Vincennes* under Captain William C. Finch * arrived at Nukahiva in 1829, and the official account of her voyage says that not only did the Taii chief, Gattenewa, remember Porter, but that all American vessels were still called "Porter's ships." The account went on, "Commodore Porter appears to be held in very high general and kind remembrance . . . the elder chiefs and people often inquiring where and how he is, and whether he will ever return to see them—and the younger asking, in reference to the captain of the *Vincennes* 'whether this chief is Pota?' " Finch is said to have agreed with Porter that Nukahiva should be taken by the United States, as it would be the best port in the Pacific to serve American interests, at least until a canal through the isthmus of Central America was constructed. In one respect, however, Finch's actions could not have diverged more widely from Porter's, for the *Vincennes* was made "*tabu,* forbidden to the native women, and the sailors were ordered to behave in a way that would convince the Polynesians 'of the moral worth of Americans.' "

Historian Henry Marie Brackenridge, who had objected to Porter's annexation of Nukahiva, came to his rescue on the question of whether he should have participated in local battles:

> The destruction of the Typee villages has given rise, on the part of the British writers, to the most scandalous abuse of commodore Porter and the American people, by which means they have endeavored to bring the acts of the Americans to a level with their own. The destruction of a few wigwams . . . effected by an American officer in self-defence, and for the sake of peace, is to be viewed with horrour; while the conduct of the British government in India, in America, and throughout the world, without another motive than base rapacity, is to be passed over unnoticed.

Among the British writers to whom Brackenridge referred was Gifford of the *Quarterly Review.* Vitriol had poured from his pen:

> It is impossible to read without the strongest feeling of indignation the feats of destruction committed by this execrable marauder on the property of these innocent people. . . . Well may your conscience suggest to you, Mr. Porter, 'that your conduct *may* be censured as wanton and unjust'—it *must* . . . their blood is on yours—and all the efforts of your supporters will be found insufficient to wash out the stain. The mark of Cain is upon you! . . . . And when he had finished his work of destruction, with a feeling of diabolical delight . . . he thus affects to wail over the fate of the unfortu-

---

* Finch had been the Fourth Lieutenant in the *Essex* when she began her cruise to the Pacific, but had been detached just after leaving the Cape Verde Islands to command the prize crew of the *Nocton.* He later changed his name to Bolton and rose to fleet command in the Navy.

nate valley. . . . And what were the tears of pity shed by this accursed 'instrument of their fate?'—an extortion from these ruined people of four hundred hogs. . . !

Gifford ended his long review of Porter's *Journal* with a ten-page comparison between the unfortunate conditions of the Taipis and those in which the descendants of the *Bounty*'s mutineers lived on Pitcairn Island: "O happy people! happy in their sequestered state! and doubly happy to have escaped a visit from 'Captain Porter of the United States Frigate *Essex!*' May no civilized barbarian lay waste your peaceful abodes; no hoary proficient in swinish sensualism rob you of that innocence and simplicity which is peculiarly your present lot to enjoy!"

Porter replied to Gifford's onslaught with anger equally unrestrained. He devoted seventeen pages in the preface of his second edition to contrasting his actions in the Marquesas with those of Captain James Cook throughout the Pacific. He summarized what the latter had done:

> . . . in almost every instance . . . the severities of Captain Cook originated on the most trifling offenses, and were prosecuted for the most insignificant purposes. The loss of a sextant is punished by cutting off a man's ears . . . ; the theft of a boat-hook is punished with death on the spot; and the loss of a single goat revenged by the burning of two hundred houses; the destruction of fruit-trees, the desolation of plantations, and the conflagration of war canoes. Captain Cook nowhere attempted or effected a permanent settlement; his objectives were all temporary. . . .

He objected vehemently to being "singled out to be stigmatized as a monster, because he adopted the measures necessary to his security," and he wrapped up his defense with a strong personal offensive against Gifford. He vowed that he would not be "the silent sacrifice of a literary bravo, whose ignorance is equal to his arrogance, and whose wilful perversion of the truth exceed[s] either or both." [19]

Unfortunately, some of Porter's compatriots reacted to his intervention in Nukahivan tribal quarrels with almost as much antagonism as had the *Quarterly Review*. Hostile newspapers in New England wrote of his "bloody and exterminating war" in the Marquesas, and asserted that he should have been court-martialed "for landing at Nooaheevah, marching into the country, laying it waste by fire and sword, and slaughtering the natives, with whom we were at peace." Some years later, a missionary publication in Hawaii wrote that Porter's attacks "reflect but little honor upon the commander . . . humanity must weep to know that on so many of the early visits of civilized man to these savage shores, the painful anticipations of Captain Cook have been so often realized, and thousands have regretted that their Islands have been discovered."

Herman Melville admits that Porter was "a brave and accomplished officer," but speaks of his men as "invaders" who left the Taipi Valley "a long line of smoking ruins," which "defaced the once-smiling bosom of the valley, and proclaimed to its pagan inhabitants the spirit that reigned in the breasts of Christian soldiers. Who can wonder at the deadly hatred of the Typees to all foreigners after such unprovoked atrocities?" * An authority on the whaling industry pointed out that since "the ill-advised actions of Commodore Porter in the U.S. frigate *Essex* . . . the natives had often fiercely resisted the efforts to trade by the white men, and there were instances of boats being cut off and their crews massacred." He goes on to mention specific attacks on American ships in 1828, 1832, 1836, and 1839.[20]

These polarized opinions would appear to have some justification. Given the circumstances under which he had to operate on Nukahiva, Porter could not have avoided clashing, first, with the Happahs, then, with the Taipis, if he were to live in safety among the Taiis. His total force amounted to only some 350 men and he was engulfed by, perhaps, 40,000 Nukahivans. It would seem that division, conquest, and even annexation were the only policies which would allow him to exist on the island. But the crucial word is "circumstances." Only his own convenience had taken him to the Marquesas: he wanted to repair his frigate and provide amusement for his crew. He was an intruder on other people's possessions, and his presence made inevitable the tragedy that unfolded. No matter how altruistic his motives in annexing the island, no matter how plausible the excuses he offered for his warfare, no matter that the subsequent history of the Marquesas would probably have been the same in any case, his influence was baleful and it formed part of one of the great horror stories of modern times: the decimation of the Polynesians and the eradication of their native culture.

By early December the expedition was readying for departure from the archipelago. Aware that he must anticipate difficulty in tearing his sailors away from their paradise, Porter started to tighten discipline. Overnight shore leave was canceled, and when three adventurers sneaked ashore anyway, they were caught and brought back for "the most exemplary punishment." This action may have stopped absences without leave, but it caused increased mutterings of discontent at the prospect of relatively unpleasant sea duty. The Nukahivan girls helped not at all,

---

* Nukahiva is the scene for Melville's book *Typee,* and he claimed that Porter's *Journal* was a work he "never happened to meet with." Yet, some of the details he records seem to have come directly from the *Journal,* and one of his biographers is probably correct when he writes that Melville must have read it because "none of the other secondary accounts of Porter's activities in the Marquesas are so specific as his."

begging the captain to lift his restrictions on their "restless, discontented, and unhappy" lovers. They lined the beach "from morning until night . . . [they] laughingly expressed their grief by dipping their fingers into the sea and touching their eyes. . . . Others would seize a chip . . . [to] cut themselves to pieces in despair; some threatened to beat their brains out with a spear of grass."

Just prior to departure, matters reached the point of mutiny. On Sunday, 12 December, Robert White, a sailor in the *Essex Junior,* who must have enlisted during the cruise since he was not on the *Essex'* original muster roll, told several of the latter's crew that he was sure they would either refuse to leave Nukahiva or, if they did, would soon mutiny in order to return. As usual, Porter found out what was going on. The next day he assembled the men and explained to them that his new rules had been issued in preparation for sea duty, not as punishment. Then, trembling with rage (and perhaps fear), he told them he did not believe the stories of possible mutiny, but if true, "I should without hesitation put a match to the magazine and blow them all to eternity." When he commanded that those who would obey his orders without question step to one side of the ship, all complied, even White. The captain advanced upon White and accused him of fomenting mutiny the night before. The culprit tried to deny the charge, but when the *Essex'* sailors who had heard him joined in the accusation, he jumped overboard, swam to a passing canoe, and went ashore.*

Final sailing preparations were hurried through that same day. After his seven-week sojourn in the islands, Porter was going back to South America with the *Essex* and the *Essex Junior,* but he wanted to retain a Marquesan base where he would be able to make any repairs that might be necessary after the action he anticipated against the British. The *New Zealander,* the *Seringapatam,* the *Sir Andrew Hammond,* and the *Greenwich* were left behind with Marine Lieutenant Gamble, twenty-two volunteers, and six prisoners of war. This small detachment was ordered to spend the next five and a half months keeping the peace on Nukahiva and growing vegetables. Gamble's instructions were that if no word from Porter had arrived by 1 May, he would be at liberty to depart for Valparaiso as best and with what ships he could.

There is no entry in the captain's *Journal* about the leave-taking on

---

* According to Farragut, the captain told the crew that he "would blow them all to hell before they should succeed in a mutiny," and a lengthy dialogue between Porter and White ended with the former shouting, "Run, you scoundrel, for your life," whereupon the frightened sailor went over the side.

Monday, 13 December 1813.* Farragut says that while the anchor was being lifted, the musicians played what must have been a poignant and applicable melody, "The Girl I Left Behind Me." Many years later, Farragut recalled the sailing of the frigate and her escort out of Taiohae Bay as "one of the most exciting scenes I ever witnessed, and made such an impression on my young mind that the circumstance is as fresh as if it had happened yesterday." †

Following a long account of his own travails at the Battle of Valparaiso Bay and after, Porter concluded the second volume of his 1822 edition with fifty-three pages devoted to the unhappy history of Lieutenant John Gamble and his volunteers on Nukahiva. For a while, Gamble prospered. On 28 December he loaded the *New Zealander* with whale oil, and, as Porter had recommended, sent her off to the United States, only to have her captured by HM frigate *Belvidera* when she was one day out of New York. For a while, the lieutenant was able to trick the Taiis and other tribes into thinking that the number of men of his command ashore at any one time was but a fraction of his total force. He prevented the Nukahivans from slaughtering Porter's hogs and, on more than one occasion, successfully intervened to quell tribal warfare.

In reality, he had woefully few men, and to make matters worse, those from the British prizes became steadily more insolent and insubordinate, eventually reaching the point of desertion and open mutiny. In order to keep the Nukahivans from learning how few were the Americans, he forbade any Marquesans aboard ship. In early January 1814, when a few girls were found in the *Seringapatam,* he had the guilty sailors whipped. The rainy season was miserable, the grog ran out, and supplies were so low that for a week and a half the *Sir Andrew Hammond*

---

* In his first edition, Porter did not specify the date but, in the second, gave it as 12 December. The *Journal* of Midshipman William Feltus says 13 December, as does Farragut, who notes that it was a Monday and, since Sunday was the 12th, Porter's memory clearly erred.

† In connection with the departure of the *Essex,* Porter tells a story that is little short of incredible. For some minor infraction, Tamaha, the Tahitian interpreter, was struck in the face by a petty officer and was so overcome with humiliation that he tried to commit suicide by jumping overboard more than twenty miles out from Nukahiva. Porter regretfully narrates this story in 1815, but in the second edition of his *Journal,* he provides a happy ending. Although drawn under the *Essex* and severely bruised, Tamaha somehow managed to stay afloat for a day and two nights while he swam back to Nukahiva. He then sailed for the United States in the *New Zealander,* but when that ship was intercepted off New York, the presumably bewildered Tahitian found himself impressed into the Royal Navy.[21]

toured among the other islands looking for food, but got little because the Americans were unwilling to pay by participating in intertribal squabbles. Early in March a sailor who had deserted was found ashore and given the brutal sentence of "5 dozen lashes." A few days later four men, among them the sixty-stripe deserter, stole a boat and rowed away, taking with them much ammunition, clothing, and such essentials as a compass, sextant, telescope, and "all the carpenter's tools." * By early spring the formerly loyal Taiis were rapidly hardening against the Americans. Gamble was sure that Wilson was responsible for the change, because he had told the Nukahivans that *"Opotee* would not return." The lieutenant decided that he must leave at the first possible moment, but he was so shorthanded that it was weeks before he could do so.

On 7 May full-fledged mutiny broke out in the *Seringapatam*. An order of Gamble's had been ignored, and when he tried to assert his authority, the crew rose against him and his two midshipmen, William Feltus and Benjamin Clapp,† tied up all three of them, and put them below. Others who stayed loyal to Gamble were bullied into submission. The mutineers, among them Robert White who had tried to raise a mutiny against Porter, elevated the English colors and sailed out of the harbor.‡ They decided to abandon their American prisoners in a small boat without weapons, and while the transfer was taking place, either deliberately or accidentally, they shot Gamble through the left heel. Although weak from pain and loss of blood, the lieutenant managed to persuade his assailants to turn over a couple of muskets and with at least that

---

* A story that appeared in a Boston paper three years later would seem to refer to these deserters. They were reported to have stopped at an uninhabited island some twenty miles from Nukahiva, where a squall destroyed their boat. Three of them died, and the survivor, who drank "out of the skull of one of his deceased comrades," existed for eighteen months before being rescued. Although he had no better explanation than that he and his fellows had left Gamble to seek bird feathers valued by the Nukahivans, he was not punished for his desertion. The Englishman, Wilson, nursed him back to health, and he shipped for Canton on a New Bedford brig later reported lost at sea. Porter's account of the episode is entirely different. He says that all the deserters survived, and while one of them enlisted on HM frigate *Briton* at an island "about three day's sail" from Nukahiva, the others refused to join.[22]

† The daily journal of the cruise kept by Midshipman Feltus is dull and uninformative, save for the chronology, but he may be forgiven, since he was only sixteen years old when he died. Clapp was not a member of the *Essex'* original crew. He may have been from the merchantman *Albatross*, being listed only as one of two "Citizens of the U. States" when he witnessed the annexation of Nukahiva on 18 November 1813.

‡ The *Seringapatam* sailed all the way to New Zealand and was eventually returned to her English owners.[23]

much protection, he, in company with his two midshipmen and two seamen, managed to reach the *Greenwich.*

A week later, the Taiis rose against the twelve Americans still on Nukahiva.* Four of the six who had gone ashore were soon butchered, among them the youthful Midshipman Feltus. The two survivors, chased by Taii boats, splashed back to the *Sir Andrew Hammond,* where the wounded and fever-stricken Gamble had to hop from gun to gun before beating off the attacks. That afternoon the *Greenwich* was set on fire, and the eight men still alive (Gamble, the two survivors of the massacre, and five others who had been on the *Sir Andrew Hammond*) sailed away.

Since only two of her crew were without wounds, illness, or long-standing debilities, the *Sir Andrew Hammond* needed perfect weather to reach Hawaii. But there her luck ran out, for she was snapped up by HMS *Cherub,* which had arrived from Valparaiso after helping to defeat the *Essex.* Porter angrily accused Captain Thomas Tudor Tucker of the *Cherub* of brutality toward his unfortunate lieutenant, for he kept Gamble under close confinement while the *Cherub* meandered through the Hawaiian Islands and went on to Tahiti in the Society Islands before she sailed back to Valparaiso in late September. It took Gamble two months to get from that port to Rio de Janeiro, where he had to wait until February 1815 before tidings of peace between Britain and the United States arrived. Thereafter, he shipped for Europe amid weather so foul that a week out of Rio he found himself 300 miles farther away than when he started. By the time he arrived home, on 27 August, more than a year after his captain's return, he had been absent for thirty-four months. It would seem that Porter was entirely justified in describing Marine Lieutenant John Gamble as "an officer and a gentleman . . . distinguished by his coolness and bravery." [24] Perhaps few men have had greater opportunity to demonstrate those qualities in so short a time.

Porter's immediate impact on the Marquesas was ephemeral. His physical establishment at Nukahiva fell to pieces within months. When the frigates *Briton* and *Tagus,* which had been sent to the Pacific to take the *Essex,* should the *Phoebe* and *Cherub* fail to do so, stopped at Taiohae Bay in 1814, Wilson told the Taiis that the ships were British, not American. According to the biased *Quarterly Review,* the Nukahivans, "delighted beyond measure" at the news, tore down the flagpole and dug up and destroyed the declaration of American annexation. Porter confirms the story, but, naturally, without the anti-American overtones. Nor

---

* Porter gives the date as 9 May, but he is wrong. The last item in Feltus' *Journal* is dated 14 May and reads in toto: "Shifted the Sir A—out in the Bay—."

did the vaunted accomplishment of creating Marquesan good will for the United States fare any better, in view of the Taiis' prompt attempt to wipe out Gamble's entire command. If the official report made after the USS *Vincennes* visited Nukahiva in 1829 offers evidence of continued friendship, the explanation may lie in an intelligent Nukahivan recognition that they might as well tell heavily armed Americans what they wanted to hear.[25] Moreover, the tribal peace that Porter was so proud of having achieved soon fell apart, and hostility between the tribes returned. By the 1830s any American influence that existed in the archipelago had been replaced by that of French missionaries and soldiers.

There was relatively little comment when, in 1842, Captain Abel Dupetit-Thouars officially annexed the Marquesas Islands to France. Herman Melville was there at the time and reported that the French carefully avoided the Taipi Valley, "from a recollection of the warlike reception given . . . to the forces of Captain Porter. . . ." An English newspaper wondered whether French occupation would void the rights of American sailors and missionaries in the Marquesas, but made no mention of Porter. A couple of American papers harked back to the captain's venture into imperialism. A missionary organ noted that the advent of France to the Marquesas clashed with Porter's claim of U.S. sovereignty there: "It will probably be a question of some importance whether the claims of France will receive a ready acceptance on the part of our government," but hoped that neither country would take away the islanders' independence. A New York journal, anticipating that the French would establish a penal colony there,* commented that, thanks to Porter, "We have as much right in the Marquesas as the French, and we had hoped to see them occupied by our government as a penal colony." [26] Nevertheless, annexation by the French drew no protest from the U.S. government.

The later history of the Marquesas is tragic. French administration only hastened the destruction of the population and local culture. Catholic missionaries insisted on smashing the indigenous religion, but Christianity was never able to fill the void. During the 1860s, refugees from a Chilean "blackbirder"—a ship that kidnapped Pacific islanders and forced them into semislavery—introduced smallpox, and the resultant epidemic wiped out more than half the population of the islands. Measles, tuberculosis, and venereal diseases contributed to the process of decimation. Programs such as the planting of cotton, which were intended to improve the economy, failed, and by the 1890s France had more or less written off the entire archipelago and its authority there was little more than

---

* Actually, New Caledonia in the southwest Pacific was later selected, and served this dismal purpose until the late nineteenth century.

titular. The collapse of morale implicit in cultural ruin led to the only "dignified and effective resistance that was open to them; they ceased to breed." In short, "Marquesan society died a horrible, wasting death. By the early 1920s, only 1,500 confused, hostile, and apathetic survivors remained of the possible 100,000 to 120,000 that had inhabited the islands in 1767."

Today, no air or shipping line has regularly scheduled service to the Marquesas, and they are among the most remote areas of the globe. A modern encyclopedia puts the population at just under 4,000,[27] a figure that shows a modest recovery, but certainly does nothing to counter the assertion that no people of the Pacific suffered more from what Alan Moorehead calls "The Fatal Impact" of the West than did the Marquesans, and David Porter's visit in 1813 paced off an important step along the road to their doom.

VI

Porter's reasons for sailing back to the mainland of South America when he left Nukahiva may be summed up in the phrase "the search for glory." He had been aware for several weeks that the British had dispatched the 36-gun frigate *Phoebe* and two sloops of war, the 28-gun *Cherub* and the 22-gun *Raccoon,* to destroy the *Essex.** He was explicit about his intentions to seek combat with this stronger force and, since Valparaiso would be the enemy's natural destination, the *Essex* and the *Essex Junior* headed for that port. On 4 April 1814, he admitted to William Jones, who had succeeded Hamilton as Secretary of the Navy, that "agreeable" to his expectations, the *Phoebe* had sought him at the port where he was waiting for her. Three months later, he said he had hoped to cap his voyage "by something more splendid" than he had accomplished up to that time.

Such attitude and behavior were consistent with the character and personality of David Porter. The premium he placed on physical courage and his keen ambition to rise in his profession glow through all his correspondence. He realized that the single-ship victories won by his colleagues, Hull, Decatur, and Bainbridge, would lastingly eclipse his meager accomplishment—the capture of fifteen merchantmen, an armed packet, and a small sloop of war—unless he could score a resounding triumph. His preoccupation with personal fame did not escape the notice of contemporary observers: "Glutted with spoil and havock, and sated with the easy and inglorious captures of merchantmen, captain Porter now felt eager for an opportunity to meet the enemy on equal terms, and to signalize his cruise by some brilliant achievement." Indeed, he did not seek "equal terms"; he went "in quest of a frigate of superior force, for the glory of fighting her."

---

* In the early nineteenth century, some British warships had names that were distressingly unmartial. Not only were the *Phoebe* and the *Cherub* in commission at that time, but so was the 18-gun "brig-sloop" *Fairy.*

It may not be difficult to understand Porter's desire for self-aggrandizement, but it is hard to condone it. He had no business whatever to engage in such quixotic behavior. His cruise had already contributed to the American war effort, and its continuation could have been valuable. His depredations in the Pacific had caused much alarm in Great Britain, far more in fact than was warranted by his actual accomplishments. One American frigate on the loose somewhere between Capes Horn and Good Hope was worth more than any conceivable number of British frigates captured. Porter was cognizant that London was making almost frantic efforts to hunt him down: ". . . besides those ships which had arrived in the Pacific in pursuit of me [the *Phoebe*'s squadron], and those still expected [the frigates *Tagus* and *Briton*], others were sent to cruize for me in the China seas, off New Zealand, Timor, and New Holland, and . . . another frigate was sent to the river La Plata."

Had he not been blinded by his quest for personal fame, he must have perceived his mandatory responsibility: to avoid anything like equal combat unless he was cornered. There were alternatives since, by his own admission, he was fully equipped for many months of cruising. He could have rounded Cape Horn and tried his luck against British commerce in the South Atlantic by lying in wait either near St. Helena, as suggested in his original instructions, or off the Cape of Good Hope. His most attractive opportunity was spotlighted by the historian, Henry Adams: "Porter would have done better to sail for the China Seas or the Indian Ocean." [1] Of these two, Chinese waters would have been preferable, for he could have used the neutral harbor of Portuguese Macau for refitting, recuperation, and selling his prizes. But he shrugged off these more sensible options and returned to South America to seek a fight and, despite his misfortune and heroism, to find the disaster that he deserved.

The uneventful passage of the *Essex* and the *Essex Junior* from the Marquesas to Chile took about a month. As the ships approached the mainland of South America, Porter gave Downes specific instructions for the battle he knew would be forthcoming: if the *Phoebe* were accompanied by both her sloops of war, combat should be avoided, if possible; but if only one sloop were with the frigate, Downes should try to draw her off so that Porter could fight his more powerful antagonist, ship to ship. After touching at Mocha Island, off the coast of Chile, on 12 January 1814, the *Essex* and her consort edged up the coast, examining a few ports on the way, and stayed outside Valparaiso for a time before entering that harbor on 3 February. On arrival, Porter was told that the *Phoebe*'s squadron had not been heard of for months and was presumed lost while trying to pass Cape Horn, but he did not believe it. During the first four days at Valparaiso, minor repairs were made, the men were given shore liberty, and the *Essex Junior* was sent to patrol off the entrance to the harbor.

Although the people of Valparaiso were more hospitable than they had been on his first visit, the captain reported that Chilean officialdom had cooled noticeably. The first dictatorship of José Miguel Carrera and his brothers was in the process of falling before a cabal in Santiago which favored the pro-British Peruvian royalists. Joel R. Poinsett, U.S. Envoy, had openly backed the Carreras, and the hostile Governor Lastra had decided to get rid of him as soon as he could. But U.S. naval strength still predominated in Chilean waters, so Lastra remained outwardly affable. On the evening of 7 February, Porter gave a ball on board the *Essex* for the governor and his entourage; Poinsett, Downes, and the other officers were on hand. Dancing continued until midnight, when the guests went ashore and Downes returned to his watchdog duties in the *Essex Junior*. Early the next morning, he sighted two warships approaching the harbor, and forthwith notified his captain. A sizable number of the crew were still ashore, so Porter fired a gun to recall them, then went out with the *Essex Junior* to take a closer look. As expected, the ships were the frigate *Phoebe* under Captain James Hillyar and the sloop of war *Cherub* under Captain Thomas Tudor Tucker. Porter hurried back to the *Essex* and was delighted to find her completely prepared for action, with every man at his post.[2]

Fifty years old and gray-haired, Captain Hillyar had already written a commendable record. He first attracted attention in 1800 when, in Barcelona Harbor, he used a neutral Swedish merchantman to screen his ship's boats so that he could creep up on and destroy two unsuspecting Spanish corvettes. During the following year he fought against Napoleon in Egypt, and then served in the Mediterranean throughout most of that decade, usually being stationed at Gibraltar. The *Phoebe*, whose command he was given in 1810, was built in 1795 and had been victor over a French frigate in 1801 as well as a participant in the Battle of Trafalgar in 1805. In 1811 Hillyar took her to attack the island of Mauritius in the Indian Ocean, then cruised through the Netherlands East Indies.

Alfred T. Mahan, America's leading naval strategist, described Hillyar as "an old disciple of Nelson, fully imbued with the teaching that achievement of success, not personal glory, must dictate action." Furthermore, the Englishman already had "a well established reputation for courage," and obviously felt no need to prove himself further in that particular.

In 1807, when both Hillyar and Porter were in the Mediterranean, they had become close friends. According to Porter: "While his family resided at Gibraltar, I was in the habit of visiting them frequently, and had spent many pleasant hours in their company. For Captain Hillyar and his family I entertained the greatest respect; and among the American officers generally, no officer of the British navy was so great a favorite as Captain Hillyar." When Hillyar's wife and children needed passage from Malta to join him at Gibraltar, they traveled in Commodore John Rodger's flagship.[3]

Three specific assignments had been given to Hillyar: to end American influence in the Oregon Country; to terminate the *Essex'* cruise in the Pacific and her career as a commerce destroyer; and to restore rebellious Chile to Spain and, thereby, promote British interests in lower South America.* In order to fulfill his first mission, he ordered the sloop *Raccoon* to proceed to the Columbia River and seize Astoria, but her mission proved unnecessary. Not only was she almost wrecked on the great sandbar stretching across the river's mouth, but upon arrival on 30 November 1813, found that the Americans there had already been told that a British warship was en route, and had sold their entire establishment to the Hudson's Bay Company, the great private spearhead of British expansionism in the Northwest. It has been said that Astoria was lost for want of a single frigate. If that is correct, the *Essex* might have saved Astoria but, as has been seen, Porter had business to execute in Nukahiva.

The second of Hillyar's missions was his paramount responsibility: to stop the *Essex'* career as a commerce destroyer. According to a contemporary American journal, while en route to the Pacific, he was instructed not to respect the neutrality of any port in which he found the enemy. The English captain's actions at Valparaiso demonstrated that he would let nothing—the rights of nonbelligerents, lust for personal fame, his "honour" as an officer and a gentleman—interfere with the successful completion of his assignment. As Mahan commented, a man who had deliberately violated Swedish neutrality at Barcelona would not be overly concerned about Chile's neutral rights. After the battle, Porter reproached Hillyar for violating both international law and his pledged word, and reported that "tears came into his eyes, and, grasping my hand, he replied, 'My dear Porter, you know not the responsibility that hung over me with respect to your ship. Perhaps my life depended on taking her.' " †[4]

---

* Hillyar's work in Latin-American politics was accomplished well after the completion of his first two assignments, and shall be discussed in chronological context.

† Hillyar may have recalled that Admiral Sir John Byng was shot by a firing squad for failure to engage a French fleet off Port Mahon in the Balearic Islands during 1756. Voltaire sardonically remarked that this stiff penalty was imposed "to encourage the others."

On 25 March 1813 the *Phoebe* had departed from England and, after dropping off the convoy she was escorting, proceeded to Rio de Janeiro, where she picked up the sloops *Cherub* and *Raccoon*. In all likelihood, this rendezvous had been planned in London, although an American historian, citing conversations with Joel R. Poinsett, at that time Special Agent to Chile, flatly asserted that "the *Phoebe* sailed alone; her consorting with the *Cherub* was accidental." Although they did not leave Rio de Janeiro together, all three ships headed south and all ran into navigational problems, since the Admiralty had neglected to furnish them with charts of the waters off lower South America. By the end of August, they had passed the Horn and the *Raccoon* had gone on to Oregon. Somewhere in the South Pacific the *Phoebe* and the *Cherub* were reunited and sailed north together, putting in at Juan Fernández Island, 400 miles west of Valparaiso, where Hillyar picked up news of Porter's recent activities. During the next weeks, as he nosed along the mainland coast, he received many reports on his enemy's whereabouts, but they were always a month or more old.[5]

At one point, the Spaniards in Valparaiso told Hillyar that Porter had gone back, via Cape Horn, to the Atlantic and that a British fleet was blockading him somewhere on the coast of Brazil. Had he accepted that information as true, his career might have been ruined, but the astute Englishman was "not quite satisfied of the final departure of the American Frigate and her little Squadron." Still in search of Porter, the *Phoebe* and the *Cherub* sailed to the Galápagos Islands, where they stayed until the end of October. Then, having found no trace of the enemy, they resumed their quest along the coast of South America, putting in to Lima from time to time, before arriving at Valparaiso on the morning of 8 February 1814.[6]

Porter knew enough about Hillyar to realize that when he met the Englishman in combat his own ship would have to be in fighting trim. Consequently, the *Essex* was well prepared for action when the enemy vessels sailed into the harbor. It is not clear whether Hillyar planned to attack at once. Farragut, who reported that an English merchantman had put out from Valparaiso and had told Hillyar that most of the *Essex'* crew were ashore and the ship would be helpless, had no doubt that Hillyar had gone in to Valparaiso Harbor with every intention of immediately opening fire. Yet, Hillyar must have known that the *Essex* had an unusual concentration of short-range carronades, and he may have been aware that her men had been specially trained for hand-to-hand combat. Under anything like normal conditions, he would not have come to close quarters with a ship possessed of those advantages. But, probably intending to reconnoiter and to attack only if he found the situation advantageous, he did approach the *Essex*.

Overconfidence and a tricky wind almost ruined the Englishman. Porter says that when the *Phoebe* came within hail, Hillyar "very politely inquired after my health; to which inquiry I returned the usual compliment." Then, as the enemy remained on course, Porter warned Hillyar that he was prepared to fight, and would, if attacked. In what Porter describes as "a careless and indifferent manner," Hillyar replied, "O, Sir, I have no intention of getting on board of you." By this time, intermittent gusts had brought the *Phoebe* to within fifteen feet of the *Essex*, and her jib boom swung across the American frigate. Porter shouted to his men to board the moment contact was made between the two ships, and Hillyar awoke to the realization of his peril. He could see the matches glowing above the *Essex'* guns, and her crew, cutlasses and pistols in hand, tensed to leap. Porter contends that, at that instant, "not a gun from the *Phoebe* could be brought to bear on either the *Essex* or the *Essex Junior*," while the *Cherub,* a half-mile away, was in no position to assist. No wonder Hillyar raised his arms and "exclaimed with great agitation: 'I had no intention of getting on board you—I had no intention of coming so near you.'" Provided the vessels did not come into actual contact with one another, Porter was willing to accept Hillyar's frantic assurances of peaceful intent, so he replied, "You have no business where you are. If you touch a rope yard of this ship, I shall board instantly." * Amid tension that must have been almost intolerable, the *Phoebe* pulled slowly by, her yards just missing the *Essex'* rigging. The *Cherub* soon joined her at anchor near the port, which was some distance away.[7]

Both Porter and Farragut were positive that they had had the *Phoebe* completely at their mercy. The captain states, "I could have destroyed her in fifteen minutes," and most accounts, at the time and later, agree with him. To be sure, Hillyar's correspondence ignores the episode, as does the British naval historian William James. A Canadian historian writing in the 1920s demonstrates a bias that would have been forgivable a century before, when he tries to make out that Porter "blustered," and that "his voice had rather the ring of a man who would fight if only he could get someone to hold his coat." None of the evidence gives him the slightest basis for such statements.

C. S. Forester hedges on what might have been the outcome had a battle been fought that morning: he says only that Porter had a "likeli-

---

* Farragut says that the battle was almost joined at this moment. One of the *Essex'* men had returned from shore still drunk and, as he tried to focus his eyes on the enemy directly across from him, imagined that a British sailor was smirking at him. Shouting, "Damn you, my fine fellow, I'll stop your making faces," he raised his musket to fire but, with one blow, Lieutenant Stephen Decatur McKnight "sprawled him on the deck." Porter does not mention the incident.

hood of an immediate close engagement and a fair chance of victory." All the other standard accounts of that morning's events conclude that, had the shooting started then, the *Phoebe* would, inevitably, have met her doom, and it is difficult to disagree. The intense shattering effect of a single volley from the *Essex'* massed carronades would have caved in the English frigate. The Americans were primed and could have boarded at a moment's notice, and the *Cherub* would have been helpless to assist. Porter boasted that his forbearance was motivated only by a desire to respect Chilean neutrality, and after his defeat, he vowed that if similar circumstances arose again, honor would compel him to act in the same way.[8] Noble sentiments, certainly, but they cost him his ship. He had been given one chance to acquire glory, but let it go. He was to have no other.

The relative strength of the rival forces at Valparaiso may now be particularized, although Porter and British authorities differ in minor details about men and armament. Porter says the *Essex* had a complement of 255 men and was armed with 46 guns, 40 of which were 32-pound carronades and six were 12-pound long guns. A British source described his long guns as 9-pounders, but Porter should have known what he carried in his own ship. There is slightly greater variance concerning the details of the *Phoebe*. Porter gives her a crew of 320; the English, only 300. All agree she carried 30 long guns (26 18-pounders and four 9-pounders), 16 carronades (14 32-pounders, an 18-pounder, and a 12-pounder), and from two to seven miscellaneous small guns. As for the *Cherub,* Porter numbers her crew at 180, as opposed to a mere 121 assigned by British commentators. All sources say she had only two long guns, either 6-pounders or 9-pounders, and 25 or 26 carronades of different weights. The uncertainty about the number of carronades she carried explains why the Americans give her 28 guns, the British 27.[9]

In short, the *Essex* had 46 guns throwing some 1,350 pounds of metal as against some 1,700 pounds that the 70 guns of the two British ships could throw—certainly not hopeless odds against the Americans. It must be emphasized, however, that the above comparison would have meaning only in an encounter that took place at a range short enough for Porter to use his 40 carronades. Almost all of the battle that did take place was fought at such long range that Porter's six long guns and 72 pounds of metal were hopelessly outclassed by the 32 guns and approximately 520 pounds of metal that Hillyar had at his disposal. In fact, during much of the fight, only three American long guns could be fired.

The day after his arrival in the port of Valparaiso, Hillyar, his confidence restored, called upon Porter at the home of the American consul. Asked by Porter whether he intended to respect the neutrality of the port, Hillyar answered emphatically, "You have paid so much respect to the neutrality of the port, that I feel bound in honour to respect it." The key word here is "port." Hillyar's correspondence reveals that, in his opinion, he had pledged only to avoid battle directly in front of the city, so as to protect Chilean persons and property. Porter talked as though he had received unconditional assurance that, so long as he remained anywhere inside the three-mile limit of Chilean territorial sovereignty, he would be immune from attack—quite an assumption when it is considered that Chile stretched 2,620 miles along a coast that was largely uninhabited. It is hard to believe that Porter was sincere. Then, as well as later, infringements of nonbelligerent rights were frequent. Porter himself had already breached Chilean neutrality by keeping his warships for many days at Valparaiso without the justification of an emergency. Furthermore, as will be seen, he tried to launch a surprise attack on the *Phoebe,* burned British prizes in the harbor, and, according to Hillyar, fired at his British frigate.[10] Finally, his constant readiness for battle demonstrated that he never thought legal niceties would deter the British captain from seizing any opportunity that might suddenly arise.

For several days the British ships remained in port to lay in supplies and permit their men some relaxation ashore. At first, the Americans and the English practically fraternized, with the rival crews competing in songs and slogans. The *Cherub* was moored close to the *Essex,* so melodic battle was especially keen between them. The Englishmen selected words to fit a tune that is not exactly a smash hit today—"the sweet little cherub that sits up aloft"—while the Americans were content to use the more prosaic "Yankee Doodle." Porter conceded that the songs of the *Cherub*'s crew may have been "better sung," but considered those of his men "were more witty and more to the point."

Slogans were bandied about in a manner worthy of modern Madison Avenue. For a long time, the *Essex* had flown a banner proclaiming "Free Trade and Sailors' Rights." When the *Phoebe* ran up the insulting retort, "God and country; British sailors' best rights; traitors offend both," Porter responded by running up a new flag, "God, our Country, and Liberty; tyrants offend them." Hillyar expressed his pleasure at the "temper and forebearance" of his crews when boats full of Americans on liberty passed by the British ships, "the parties carrying small Flags with inscriptions on them, Such as Sons of Commerce, Free Trade, &c. &c., who after landing paraded on the Hills and before the Ships; Shouting very insultingly. . . ."

In a message sent to the *Phoebe,* the men of the *Essex* challenged:

The sons of liberty and commerce, on board the saucy *Essex,* whose motto is "free Trade and Sailors' rights," present their compliments to their oppressed brother tars, on board the ship whose motto is too tedious to mention, and hope they will put an end to all this nonsense of singing, sporting, hunting, and writing, which we know less about than the use of our guns—Send the *Cherub* away, we will meet your frigate and fight you. . . .

[signed]   From the Sons of Liberty.

"With the approbation of com. Hillyar," a midshipman in the *Phoebe* replied in poetry of a sort:

> Your vile letter which on board was brought,
> We scorn to answer, tho' with malice fraught;
> But if, by such foul means, you think to make
> Dissensions rise our loyalty to shake,
> Know that we are Britons all, both stout and true,
> We love our king, our country, captain too;
> When honor calls, we'll glory in his name,
> Acquit like men and hope you'll do the same.[11]

One dark night during the first week that the adversaries were at Valparaiso, Farragut says that Porter tried to make a surprise attack on the English frigate. The *Essex'* boats rowed with muffled oars toward the *Phoebe* and drew so close that snatches of conversation on board the enemy ship could be heard. The tenor of these remarks convinced Porter, who was in one of the boats, that the *Phoebe*'s men were crouched in readiness for just such an attempt, and he silently returned to his ship. Although Porter does not record the episode in his *Journal*—possibly because it shows that he was guilty of violating Chilean neutrality—Hillyar did report it to the Admiralty.

From that night on, there was a tone of asperity in the correspondence between the two captains. When a British prisoner jumped overboard from the *Essex Junior,* and was picked up by the *Cherub,* Hillyar refused to surrender him, and accused Porter of cruelty for keeping some of his captives in chains. The American retorted that the prisoners in question were being punished for flagrant violations of parole while at Nukahiva, and said they would remain in irons until exchanged. He then offered to do just that. At first, Hillyar turned him down, but later relented, telling the Admiralty that, as a result of correspondence and "interviews" he had had with Porter, some British seamen who were Porter's prisoners had been freed, and added: "I have pledged myself that they shall not serve on board any Ship under my Orders, and that the British Government will immediately . . . restore an equal number of Americans to their Country." [12]

Having spent a week in the harbor of Valparaiso, the *Phoebe* and the *Cherub* sailed out to commence blockading in earnest. In the course of the month that followed, Porter made many attempts to maneuver

Hillyar into accepting his invitation to fight the *Essex* with the *Phoebe* alone. He argued that his "32-gun" frigate (actually mounting 46 guns) was weaker than the "36-gun" *Phoebe* (carrying between 48 and 53 guns), a difference which gave him the right to challenge. Even though Porter was sure the *Essex* had the heels on the *Phoebe*,* and he could have escaped any time, his undimmed desire for personal glory made him stay: "I did not like, however, to abandon the hope of bringing the *Phoebe* to action; and . . . I endeavoured to provoke my adversary to combat." The cautious Hillyar refused to fall into Porter's snare. Unconsciously foretelling what happened in the coming battle, he replied to one of Porter's challenges: "the results of naval actions are very uncertain; . . . and the loss of a mast or a spar, often turned the fate of the day." He would not "yield the advantage of superior force," and contented himself with blockading Porter while he awaited the arrival of reinforcements which he anticipated. He was ready to fight, but would do so only if compelled, notifying his superiors, "I expect an awful Combat if the two ships meet, but humbly wish to repose my trust in God's goodness for a favorable result." [13]

On 25 February, while he was on his long patrol off the harbor, Hillyar had occasion to demonstrate iron self-control. That day, Porter towed his British prizes, the *Hector* and the *Catherine*, out into the harbor, burned them, and hurried back to anchor. Later, when Hillyar was defending himself against Porter's charge that he had broken Chile's neutrality, he enclosed in his report to the Admiralty a letter written by six British merchants in Valparaiso who protested that the burning of the *Hector* "within musket shot of the shipping . . . most grossly and shamefully violated the neutrality of the port." †

If Porter is correct about what happened two days later, Hillyar may have been retaliating for the American arson, but British sources ascribe a different motivation for it. According to Porter, the *Phoebe* slipped her cables, sailed straight for the *Essex*, and fired a single shot at her. He and his officers took this as an unmistakable challenge. As the *Essex* cleared for action and got under way, the British frigate turned and raced back to the *Cherub*, which had remained on station. American scorn and anger were unrestrained. Porter told his men that the enemy's behavior was "cowardly and dishonorable." Hillyar reports that the episode was simply another of Porter's attempts to bring him to combat. He

---

* Porter was correct. When the two frigates sailed back to England together late in 1814, the *Essex* proved the faster ship.

† For some reason, the *Catherine* is not mentioned in any of the British protests about the burning of the *Hector*, yet there is conclusive evidence that both prizes were destroyed in Valparaiso Harbor on 25 February 1814.

says that the *Essex* and the *Essex Junior* approached his ships, whereupon he ordered them cleared for action and advised his crew "to be calm & steady, which was received with three cheers. . . ." He claims, furthermore, that it was the *Essex* which fired, and not a single shot, but three, then, in company with her escort, hurried back to anchor.

Side by side with his consort, Hillyar maintained patrol for another month. The conditions under which he had to operate were anything but favorable, and C. S. Forester paid tribute to the seamanship he exhibited: "Hillyar kept the roadstead closely blockaded—no easy feat on that precipitous coast with the treacherous winds blowing down savagely over the hills above the town. To have maintained station . . . without once being taken unawares was a remarkable achievement on Hillyar's part." [14]

In late March, Porter came to a number of belated conclusions: the *Phoebe* would never fight without the *Cherub;* the sloop *Raccoon* would return any day from her mission to Oregon; and the *Tagus,* the *Briton,* and, perhaps, other frigates, might arrive at any moment. He decided that he had better make his break at the first opportunity. Events soon proved that his judgment was correct. Had he waited another fifteen days, he would have been trapped and surrender would have been his only course. On 13 April, HMS *Tagus* came in to Valparaiso, and it would have been suicidal for Porter to attempt combat with Hillyar's squadron reinforced by a powerful frigate. And even had the *Tagus* not come in, he would have had a reprieve of only five weeks, for on 21 May, the frigate *Briton* arrived.* [15]

Although Porter had decided to make his break as soon as an opportunity arose, it was freakish weather that precipitated him into action. Valparaiso is situated on an open roadstead, a mere indentation in the coast, rather than an enclosed harbor. To the south, the bluffs that rise to 1,500 feet usually protect shipping from the prevailing winds, but offer no haven from the erratic gusts that blow now and then. While the *Essex* was riding at anchor on the afternoon of 28 March, a strong wind snapped her port anchor cable and tore out her starboard anchor. As his ship began to drift, Porter saw a chance to escape to windward of the *Phoebe* and the *Cherub* which lay nearby. He crowded on sail and

---

* The *Briton* added her footnote to history when, in combing the South Pacific in search of the *Essex,* she put in at Pitcairn Island, where, for a quarter of a century, the mutineers from the *Bounty* had found sanctuary. Although the last survivor and his descendants had been discovered by the American ship *Topaz* in 1808, the island had been mislocated on the *Topaz'* charts. The *Briton* rectified the error and brought Pitcairn Island into regular contact with the outside world.

dashed for open water. As the *Essex* rounded a promontory, the weather betrayed him again. A vicious squall ripped off her main-topmast, and the four or five men aloft were thrown into the water and drowned. Perhaps no other single mishap could hamper so effectively the maneuverability of a large sailing vessel.* As the *Phoebe* and the *Cherub* moved up to capitalize on their good fortune, Porter saw that he could neither stand out to sea nor return to his anchorage in front of Valparaiso. He ran into a small bay several miles from the city and, by his own admission, dropped his anchor "within a pistol shot of the shore."

Since much of the controversy that followed the action hinged on the question of whether the British ships had violated Chilean neutrality, it should be pointed out that, during the entire battle, Porter was well inside the three-mile territorial limit. Hillyar proved it when he reported that the *Essex* was "so near the shore as to preclude the possibility of passing ahead of her without risk to His Majesty's ships." But he claimed that he himself was "more than five miles" from Valparaiso proper, and was, therefore, at liberty to act as he pleased. As mentioned above, Porter professed to believe that the *Essex* had been guaranteed safety from attack anywhere inside Chile's territorial limits.[16]

On the very day of the battle, Joel R. Poinsett used the same reasoning. He was on board the *Essex* when she tried to escape from Valparaiso, but disembarked after the loss of the main-topmast had driven the ship back toward shore. Although the American frigate was well away from Valparaiso's main fortifications, she was within range of a single Chilean battery about a half-mile distant from her. Poinsett hastened to urge local authorities to fire on Hillyar if he broke Chilean neutrality, but his appeals were ignored. Chile's amity for the United States varied in direct proportion to the fluctuations of American power. At this time, British strength predominated, and official opinion switched accordingly. Hillyar wrote that from the moment of his arrival in Chile his reception had been "friendly," and that the government was "favorable to England." The people of Valparaiso, however, seem to have been stoutly pro-American, and they gathered on rooftops to watch the battle. Poinsett reported to the Secretary of State that every point scored by the *Essex* was hailed with "bursts of delight," and her failures with "groans of sympathy." [17]

When the British ships came within range of the stricken *Essex*, the *Phoebe* took position off her stern, and the *Cherub* off her bow. According to Porter, they opened fire at 3:45 P.M., while Hillyar put the time at

---

* A similar mishap befell the French frigate *L'Insurgente* shortly before she met the *Constellation* in February 1799.

"a little past 4." * As the enemy approached, Porter spent his time doing whatever he could to compensate for the all but irreparable damage already suffered by his ship. Three times during the first half-hour he attached springs to his anchor cables in order to swing the *Essex* into broadside position, but each time they were shot away.[18] After the first few minutes, the *Cherub,* finding her position off the *Essex'* bow "a hot one," moved around to join the *Phoebe* off the stern. Since both the English ships stayed beyond the range of the *Essex'* carronades, Porter ran three of his long guns out of the stern gunports. This meant that the Essex had to fight most of the battle with only three of her six long guns, while the British used a total of 32 long guns; 36 pounds of metal thrown as opposed to more than 500. Yet, with this pitifully small offensive power Porter did well enough to evoke Hillyar into admitting that after thirty minutes of fighting "appearances were a little inauspicious"; the *Phoebe* and the *Cherub* had to draw away for makeshift repairs.

At 5:35 when he was ready to re-engage, Hillyar moved his ships off the *Essex'* starboard bow, still out of reach of her carronades, and now safe from the long guns at her stern. What Porter called "a most galling fire," which he was unable to return, began taking a heavy toll of the *Essex'* men, and her ropes, spars, and masts were being cut to pieces. On examining his rigging, Porter found that the flying jib was the only important sail still operational; the others hung limp, their lines shot away. He calculated that he had one slim chance left. Cutting his one remaining cable, he made for the *Phoebe* with the intention of boarding her. On the way, his battered ship drew so close to the *Cherub* that, for a moment, he was able to use his carronades and drive the enemy escort off, but the *Phoebe,* dancing just beyond range, kept up her remorseless fire. Fifteen men died at one of the *Essex'* guns, and as the captain later lamented, "our decks were now strewed with dead, and our cockpit filled with wounded . . . our ship had been several times on fire, and was rendered a perfect wreck."

Unable to catch the *Phoebe,* Porter headed back to the shore, planning to beach his ship, allow time for his men to escape, and then blow her up. Just when success seemed within reach, the weather turned pro-English for the third time that afternoon. A stiff offshore wind came up and drove the *Essex* back toward the enemy's implacable guns. Again, Porter decided to try to board. Again, he was frustrated by Hillyar's nautical skill. At this juncture, Downes pulled over from the *Essex Junior*—his ship not having taken any part in the battle—but there was nothing

---

* William James, apologist for the British Navy, erroneously stated that Porter had fired first while trying to escape from the harbor.

he could do to help, and Porter soon sent him off with some of the *Essex'* wounded.*

As a last resort, Porter directed "a hawser to be bent to the sheet anchor," and let go the anchor in order to bring the *Essex* around and keep her from moving. The sheet anchor being in the waist, this maneuver enabled him to use his carronades until, a little while later, the hawser parted, leaving the *Essex* helpless. By this time, "flames were bursting up each hatchway," and while they were being extinguished, the captain announced that those who wished to jump overboard were free to do so, but not all of the men who jumped were able to swim the three-quarters of a mile to shore. The British cannonading, if less concentrated, became more accurate; Hillyar was aiming as though he were practicing firing at a stationary target: "his shot never missed our hull," recorded Porter, "and my ship was cut up in a manner which was, perhaps, never before witnessed." According to James Fenimore Cooper, the enemy must have thrown "not less than 700 eighteen pound shot, at the *Essex.*" So many men had been taken below for treatment that the surgeons announced that there was room for no more. Porter faced the inevitable truth—failure to surrender would mean death for all on board. At 6:20 P.M., about two and a half hours after the fight had been joined, the *Essex'* colors were hauled down. Ten minutes later, enemy shot was still pouring into the floating wreck and Porter, convinced that Hillyar had decided on "no quarter," was ordering his colors run up again, when the guns on the *Phoebe* and the *Cherub* fell silent.[19] Amid the confusion of battle, Hillyar had not seen the *Essex'* standard lowered.

One contemporary American source described the scene on the *Essex* shortly after the surrender: "She was completely cut to pieces, and so covered with the dead and dying, with mangled limbs, with brains and blood, and all the ghastly images of pain and death that the officer who came on board to take possession of her, although accustomed to scenes of slaughter, was struck with a sickening horror, and fainted at the shocking spectacle." Washington Irving also tells of the swooning English lieutenant, but he is not mentioned by Porter, Farragut, or Hillyar.

---

* The *Essex Junior* was so lightly armed, mounting 10 "short 6-pounders" and 10 18-pounder carronades, and so flimsily built that she would have been useless in close action against a sloop of war, to say nothing of a frigate. It is difficult to understand, however, why nuisance value alone did not bring her in against the *Cherub.* Such intervention might, at least, have slackened enemy fire sufficiently for anchor ropes to remain intact just long enough to draw the *Essex* into broadside position. A lucky shot or two might have reduced the *Phoebe's* maneuverability and allowed Porter to board. Instead, the *Essex Junior* lay idle while the slaughter on the flagship continued to its inevitable conclusion.

Acts of heroism were commonplace on board the *Essex* on that dreadful afternoon, and Porter did praise some of his men by name but, for the most part, he used generalities in reporting the engagement. Fortunately, Farragut, that precocious twelve-year-old who spent the battle dashing around the ship on a host of errands for the captain, records considerable detail. He never forgot how he felt when he saw the body of a boatswain's mate whose abdomen had been "entirely taken out." That was the first death in combat he saw, but the incessant butchery soon put him into a merciful daze. One of his most unpleasant assignments resulted from the only recorded act of cowardice: Porter, having learned that Quarter Gunner Adam Roach (or Roche) had panicked and fled from his assigned station, handed Farragut a pistol and said, "Do your duty, sir." The midshipman searched for Roach, but he had gone over the side.* Late in the battle, Farragut had a lucky escape from serious injury. He was climbing a ladder onto the deck when a 200-pound sailor was hit in the face with a cannon ball and fell back on him. He managed to squeeze out from under the body with only minor damage.

Farragut tells what happened to several of his shipmates. His close friend Lieutenant John G. Cowell had a leg severed just below the knee, and cried to the midshipman, "O Gatty [one of Farragut's nicknames], I fear it is all up with me." Cowell probably would have been saved if he had received medical attention immediately, but he refused to claim an officer's priority, and bled to death before the surgeons could attend to him. Lieutenant James Wilmer was knocked overboard and drowned; his little Negro servant is said to have committed suicide by jumping in after him. A Scottish-born sailor, whose leg had been shot off at the groin, announced that since he could no longer be of use to his adopted country, he would not be a burden to it. He pulled himself up to a gun port and went overboard. Another sailor, shot through the body, was evidently trying to recite the ship's slogan "Free Trade and Sailors' Rights" when he died with the word "rights" quivering on his lips. After the surrender, a sailor drowned himself rather than become a prisoner of war. William Kingsbury, the boatswain's mate who had helped restore morale when the *Essex* came close to foundering after passing Cape Horn, was burned "in almost every inch of his body." Somehow, he managed to swim

---

* When the *Phoebe* and the *Cherub* first entered Valparaiso Harbor on 8 February, Roach stood out in front of all the others, eager to be the first to board. But under adverse conditions, his nerve collapsed. He was lucky to escape that afternoon, for Farragut was not the only one hunting him: a sailor with a leg shot off was stumping about trying to get a shot at him. Roach managed to reach shore and presumably hid until Porter and the rest of the crew left for the United States.

ashore, and was in such agony for several days that he was "deranged." However, he recovered and served under Porter in the West Indies a decade later.[20]

In his first account of the battle, Porter told the Navy Department that he could not ascertain exactly what losses he had suffered, but he did know that they were "dreadfully severe." Indeed, they amounted to a startling 60 per cent of the *Essex'* complement of 255 men. His final accounting, in which he named each man, showed 58 killed, 65 wounded (broken into two categories of 39 "severely wounded" and 26 "slightly wounded"), and 31 missing. Although he had suffered a minor head bruise during the battle, he did not bother to list himself among the "slightly wounded." Hillyar counted the *Essex'* losses at only 111. The way in which the wounded were listed is partly responsible for this discrepancy: Porter's list included those temporarily incapacitated, while Hillyar's must have contained only those with permanent injuries. So strong was William James' anti-American bias that he would not credit even Hillyar's total: he manufactured his own figures of 24 killed and 45 wounded, and sneered that Porter had exaggerated "to prop up his fame." [21]

Porter may be believed concerning his own casualties, but he was wrong when, in his first report to the Secretary, he said "the loss in killed and wounded has been great with the enemy." About the only correct information he conveyed on that subject was that Captain Tucker of the *Cherub* had been wounded and First Lieutenant William Ingraham of the *Phoebe* killed.* In fact, British casualties amounted to a mere fifteen men—five dead and ten wounded. Porter also overestimated the damage wrought to the *Essex* and to the *Phoebe*. He asserted that both "were left in a sinking state," and were afloat only because the water was unusually calm. He forecast incorrectly that neither ship could be repaired sufficiently to sail round the Horn for England. In midsummer the two frigates left together and, after an uneventful voyage, arrived in Britain on 13 November 1814. The *Essex* served in the Royal Navy until 1833, when

---

* Ingraham was a favorite of the Americans, all of whom attended his funeral at Valparaiso. Farragut learned that at the height of the battle, Ingraham tried to persuade Hillyar to board the *Essex*. It was, he told his captain, "deliberate murder to lie off at long range and fire at that ship as though she was a target." Characteristically, Hillyar retorted, "I have gained my reputation by several single-ship combats, and I expect to retain it on this present occasion only by an implicit obedience to orders, viz., to capture the *Essex* with the least possible risk to my vessel and crew. As I have a superior force, I have determined not to leave anything to chance, as I believe that any other course would call down upon me the disapprobation of the government."

she was decommissioned. The last year of her memorable career was spent in service as a prison ship in Jamaica, a sorry anticlimax. After being sold at public auction at Kingston in 1837, she disappeared from sight.[22]

Porter, Farragut, and Hillyar all analyzed the Battle of Valparaiso Harbor and left eyewitness accounts of it. Porter was suffering from the tremendous shock of having had to strike his colors, and his analysis shows that he was looking for scapegoats. He found them in the persons of Hillyar and Paul Hamilton, the former Secretary of the Navy. To William Jones, Hamilton's successor at the Navy Department, he wrote:

> . . . I now consider my situation less unpleasant than that of Captain Hillyar, who, in violation of every principle of honor and generosity, and regardless of the rights of nations, has attacked the *Essex* in her crippled state within pistol shot of a neutral shore, when for the last six weeks I have daily offered him fair and honorable combat on terms greatly to his advantage, the blood of the slain must be on his head, and he has yet to reconcile his conduct to heaven, to his conscience, and to the world.

In the same communication, he let fly at Hamilton:

> I must in justice to myself observe that if the *Essex* has been lost for want of suitable armament, I am not to blame, myself and officers applied to Paul Hamilton Esq[r]. for a greater proportion of long guns which were refused us; and I now venture to declare that if she had been armed in the manner I wished, she would not have been taken by the *Phoebe* and *Cherub;* with our six twelve pounders only we fought this action, our Carronades were useless, what might we not have done had we been permitted to take on board a few long eighteens?

Years after the battle, Farragut praised his captain's courage and perseverance at Valparaiso Harbor, but criticized his professional competence. He accused Porter of making two fundamental errors, one at the start of the battle, the other while it was being fought. He was of the opinion that, when the squall ripped off the *Essex'* main-topmast, Porter should have run out of the harbor, suffering the *Phoebe*'s fire on the way, and, depending on circumstances, either boarded the English frigate or bypassed her to reach the open sea. Having done that, he could have taken the time to make emergency repairs. The second mistake was that he waited too long before running the *Essex* aground. Had he done so earlier, he could have moved her into broadside position, fought as long as possible, and then set her on fire.*

---

* Farragut fails to explain how a frigate without her main-topmast could have either eluded or outrun an undamaged adversary of equivalent qualities. As to the second recommendation, when Porter first tried to run his ship aground, he was foiled by shifting winds. Had he done so at the start of the battle, he might justifiably have been accused of cowardice.

Hillyar's official report on the action at Valparaiso abounds in modesty and generosity:

> The defence of the *Essex*, taking into account our superiority of force, the very discouraging circumstances of her having lost her main top-mast and being twice on fire, did honour to her brave defenders, and most fully evinced the courage of Captain Porter and those under his command. Her colours were not struck until the loss in killed and wounded was so awfully great, and her shattered condition so seriously bad, as to render further resistance unavailing.

When Hillyar became aware that Porter was making a major issue of British violation of Chilean neutrality, he indicted Porter on the same charge. In a letter to the Admiralty, he pointed out that Porter's actions before the battle had so shattered Chile's sovereignty that he had forfeited any right to consideration on that score. Specifically, he charged that his enemy had burned a British prize in the harbor of Valparaiso, tried to attack the *Phoebe* with ship's boats, and fired at the *Phoebe* when she was much closer to the port of Valparaiso than the *Essex* had been when the British squadron attacked her on 28 March.[23]

In England, comment on Hillyar's victory was abundant. Although a Baltimore periodical wrote that the news gave great joy in England, a perusal of contemporary British papers shows otherwise. When Hillyar's first report was published, most newspapers admitted that, under the conditions in which the *Essex* had had to fight, she faced hopeless odds, and they applauded the courage of her captain and crew. But when Porter's lengthy apologia for his loss was published in London, Britons contrasted his "ostentatious and evidently partial manner" with the "plain narrative" of Hillyar. Particularly resented was his harping on the fact that Hillyar had refused to fight alone. The British *Naval Chronicle* expressed the wish that the *Cherub* had not been present so that the *Phoebe*, by herself, could have had the pleasure of whipping the *Essex*. A leading English naval expert of that day dwelt on the same point: "We can only express regret," he said, "that the *Essex Junior* did not venture out of port, in which case the *Cherub* would have been detached in pursuit of that ship, and the *Phoebe* no doubt [would] have given an equally good account of her immediate opponent." *The Times* accused Porter of breaking faith with Hillyar by permitting some of his men to escape after the surrender, a deed which clearly showed that "his sentiments of honour are but American." Gifford's article in the *Quarterly Review* pretended to take no notice of Porter's "garbled account of the capture of the *Essex*," but did call attention to his "base and malign aspersions cast on the conduct of Captain Hillyar . . . charging him with cowardice, treachery, and falsehood." [24]

Anti-American venom courses through all three accounts of the battle written by William James. To him, simple drunkenness was responsible for the courage with which the men of the *Essex* fought: "buckets of spirits were found in all parts of the main-deck; and most of the prisoners were in a state of intoxication." * James described as cowards those Americans who jumped overboard, said that no trace could be found of the devastating fires referred to by Porter, and he was so skeptical of the *Essex'* casualty figures that he made up his own. He assessed the damage done to the *Phoebe* as "trifling," and regretted that Porter had not come up against a British officer more ruthless than "the meek and gentlemanly" Hillyar, whose literary transactions made him "the dupe of that finished hypocrite, his prisoner," a man "of whom few in his own country will venture to speak well." Porter proved himself to be no more than the "slanderer of a gallant British officer." 25

In America, the results of the battle aroused greater interest than they did in England. Most newspapers rallied to Porter and characterized his behavior as "brave," "persevering," "determined," and "gallant." More often than not, the outbursts of applause for Porter were coupled with condemnations of Hillyar. Especially vindictive was *Niles National Register,* which referred to the British captain's "arrogance" and "cowardice." It even compared, much to Hillyar's disadvantage, his "unmanly" and "unlawful" violation of Chilean neutrality with Napoleon's seizure and judicial murder of the Duc d'Enghien on German soil a few years before. The *Independent Chronicle* of Boston said Hillyar's deeds at Valparaiso were "ferocious, cruel, and unjust," and wailed that it was only by "keeping a respectful sneaking distance" from his disabled antagonist that he had been able to win. Another paper tried to excuse the defeat on the grounds that the *Essex* had been on such a long cruise that she was not "in good condition for hammering." 26

To commemorate the loss of the *Essex,* that ardent patriot, Philip Freneau, ground out one of his topical poems. Its last few stanzas are enough to demonstrate its tone and literary merit:

> With every shot they raked the deck,
> Till mingled ruin seized the wreck:
> No valor could the ardor check
>   Of England's martial tars!
> One hundred men the *Essex* lost:
> But *Phoebe* found, and to her cost,

---

* Another source, probably plagiarizing James, says: "Brandy by the bucketful stood between the guns, and added to the chaos below decks. Men who were not crazed by burns and wounds were fighting drunk." No other narratives mention alcohol.

> That Porter made them many a ghost
> To serve in Satan's wars.
> Oh, clouded scene!—yet must I tell
> Columbia's flag, indignant fell—
> To *Essex,* now, we bid farewell;
> She wears the english flag!
> But Yankees she has none on board
> To point the gun or wield the sword;
> And though commanded by a lord
> They'll have no cause to brag.

The accolades conferred by the President of the United States must have been most valued by Porter. In his Message to Congress in 1814, Madison said:

> On the ocean . . . a second frigate has fallen into the hands of the enemy: [the taking of the *Chesapeake* by the *Shannon* is the other] but the loss is hidden in the blaze of heroism with which she was defended. Captain Porter . . . whose previous career had been distinguished by daring enterprize, and by the fertility of genius, maintained a sanguinary contest against two ships, one of them superior to his own . . . until humanity tore down the colors, which valor had nailed to the mast. This officer and his comrades have added much to the rising glory of the American flag; and have merited all the effusions of gratitude, which their country is ever ready to bestow on the champions of its rights, and of its safety.

Nevertheless, American opinion concerning Porter was not unanimous. A long letter signed "Camillus" that appeared in a Boston periodical denied that Hillyar had violated neutral rights, or had been "perfidious, cowardly, cruel," and it called upon Porter to match the gallantry he had shown in the past with present generosity. The ultra-Federalist *Salem Gazette,* which evidently considered Porter some kind of an opposition pet and regularly belabored him, upheld Hillyar on the question of neutral rights, and went on to deliver the unkindest cut of all. If Porter ever read the *Gazette*'s comparison between what Oliver Hazard Perry wrote after his victory at Lake Erie and his own literary explanation of what happened at Valparaiso, he must have writhed: Perry had written "nine words" about his victory—"We have met the enemy and they are ours;" Porter "nine long columns" about his defeat.[27]

Many years passed before American historians were able to shrug off wartime animosities and equalize Hillyar's masterful seamanship and single-minded devotion to duty with Porter's desperate courage. Immediate postwar commentary is typified by the following: "Perhaps a more dreadful example of determined, unconquerable courage was never exhibited than in the defeat of the *Essex:* to an American, no victory can afford more pleasing and proud recollection; to the enemy it cannot be remembered without shame, as gained by unmanliness in the first place, and in the next by violating neutral rights." A half-century later, Henry Adams could coldly describe the battle as "frightful and useless carnage," which only resulted in an unnecessarily "bloody defeat." This conclusion is denied by a modern naval expert who commends Porter for fighting on so long, since many naval engagements, apparently hopelessly lost, have swung the other way in the end. In judging Hillyar's behavior at Valparaiso, Theodore Roosevelt emphasized the most delicate and abstruse points of personal honor. He chided the Briton for being "over-cautious" in refusing to meet Porter without the *Cherub*. He excused him for violating a meaningless Chilean neutrality, admitting that the United States had acted in precisely the same manner when a Union warship seized the Confederate raider *Florida* at Bahia, well inside Brazilian territorial limits. Roosevelt ended by reproving Hillyar for breaking, not neutrality, but his personal word of honor as a gentleman by pledging not to attack Porter, and then doing so, a "deliberate and treacherous breach of faith."

To summarize the actions of Porter and Hillyar at Valparaiso: Porter's luck could not have been worse, and under the most impossible conditions he fought skillfully and courageously; Hillyar had the best of fortune, but he deserved it. Porter had no right to fight any battle at all: he should have continued as a commerce destroyer and naval irritant. Hillyar could not match his fiery antagonist in glamor and derring-do, but he was not that type of man and that was not his job. As one commentator puts it, "Captain Hillyar's tactics may not have been heroic, but they were professional, level-headed, and strictly adapted to the problem confronting him." A Canadian source that is usually unfair, for once made a remark that it is possible to accept without qualification: "Hard work, not heroics, a policeman's arrest of a burglar, was the task of the *Phoebe* and *Cherub*." [28]

After the battle, Porter and the *Essex'* other survivors spent much of their time in caring for the wounded, a task made easier by the sympathetic assistance of the women of Valparaiso and by the cooperation of Captain Hillyar. Despite his resentment at what his adversary had done before and during the battle, Porter notified the Department that, since the surrender, Hillyar had demonstrated "the greatest humanity to my wounded, and has endeavoured as much as lays in his power to alleviate the distresses of war by the most generous and delicate deportment toward myself, my officers, and crew."

During his brief sojourn in Latin America, Hillyar busied himself with the third of the assignments that had been given him in London: to restore rebellious Chile to the jurisdiction of the Peruvian royalists and, thus, promote British interests. Internal dissensions in that country aided him. According to Porter, the pro-American Carrera brothers were "being stripped of power and being thrown into prison, the government of Chili being usurped by their most inveterate enemies." Hillyar completed his political duties with the same sober aplomb with which he had terminated the cruise of the *Essex*. He journeyed to Santiago and then to the spot where the opposing royalist and revolutionary armies were preparing for battle. After spending several days trotting back and forth between the two camps, he engineered the signing of the Treaty of Lircay on 3 May.* He wrote that his "Happy labours [had been] terminated by restoring Peace to two Countries which ought ever to be United in the Strictest Bonds of Friendship," and described his successful efforts at Lircay as "the most heart-elating I ever experienced." Porter says: "For this service, Captain Hillyar was made a Hidalgo, and honoured with a conspicuous place in a religious procession, commemorative of the occasion, where he wore the habit of a friar, and bore in his hand a waxen candle." [29] This form of honor might have been painfully embarrassing to a very proper English naval officer, but Hillyar obviously enjoyed it.

Special Agent Joel R. Poinsett, who, for some time, had been marked for removal, was a casualty of Hillyar's successful diplomacy. A British captain in Santiago had notified his government that "a Mr. Poinsett, who is styled the Consul-General of the United States . . . [is] particularly diligent and active in propagating doctrines and opinions prejudicial to the British government and subjects." Porter was worried about Poinsett, and advised him to leave Chile immediately: "Let the fate of your friends [the Carreras] be a warning to you," he wrote to Poinsett on 13 April, "time is too precious to be wasted." Poinsett was desperate and asked for permission to accompany Porter back to the United States, but Hillyar refused to allow this "arch enemy of England to return to America while the two countries were at war." In the middle of June 1814 Poinsett informed Secretary of State James Monroe that he had been officially ousted from Chile. He spent eleven dreary months getting home by way of Buenos Aires, Bahia, and the Madeira Islands. In Washington he was publicly congratulated by President Madison "for the skill and zeal he had shown in his mission," [30] but his career as a diplomat in Latin America, both at this time in Chile and later in Mexico, indicates that he exercised more zeal than skill.

In Valparaiso, Hillyar and Porter made arrangements for the disposition of the captive Americans. Hillyar designated the *Essex Junior*

---

* The rapprochement between the royalists and patriots in lower South America lasted only a short time. After Hillyar's departure, the Carreras returned to power in Chile, but, as will be seen later in this narrative, were soon ousted once more by their domestic enemies.

as a cartel ship, provided her with a safe-conduct pass, and on 27 April Porter and 130 of his crew * sailed for the United States. However, a few of the American prisoners had been exchanged on the spot for some Englishmen from the *Sir Andrew Hammond,* and were required to wait until 31 May when they left with Hillyar in the *Phoebe,* escorted by the *Essex.* On his way home, the English captain put in at Rio de Janeiro,† and it was not until 13 November that he announced his arrival in England with both ships and "£20,000 of specie." ‡

The uneventful passage of the *Essex Junior* from Valparaiso to New York occupied almost two and a half months. On 5 July she was hailed off Sandy Hook, New Jersey, by the razee § HMS *Saturn.* The British captain acted with "great civility" as he examined the papers of the *Essex Junior.* He gave Porter "late newspapers" and "some oranges," then allowed him to proceed. The safe conduct Hillyar had issued could not have been more specific: "Captain Porter, his officers and crew . . . will remain on board on parole, not to take arms against Great Britain until regularly exchanged . . . I therefore request, that the said ship the *Essex Junior,* may be permitted to pass freely to the United States, without any impediment—and that the officers commanding his majesty's ships of war . . . will give . . . every aid and assistance. . . ." [32] Nevertheless, within two hours, the captain of the *Saturn* changed his mind and halted the *Essex Junior.* Understandably furious, Porter stormed

---

* Porter says 132 of his men sailed with him, but Farragut provides proof that two of the men had to be left behind because their wounds had not healed sufficiently to allow them to travel.

† Among the Americans involved in the exchange were Lieutenant Stephen Decatur McKnight and Midshipman James Lyman. At Rio, Hillyar gave them permission to leave for England right away, and they sailed in a Swedish merchantman. In midpassage, they were intercepted by the American sloop of war *Wasp,* under Master Commandant Johnston Blakely. McKnight and Lyman naturally boarded the *Wasp,* and were never heard of again, the ship foundering somewhere with all hands. It is ironic that McKnight, who showed much of the elan possessed by his uncle and namesake, Stephen Decatur, should have fought through the carnage at Valparaiso without a scratch, and then die because of a chance meeting at sea.

‡ Hillyar was eventually knighted and promoted to admiral. Evidence that American naval officers did not hold him reprehensible for his actions at Valparaiso may be seen in Captain John Rodgers' visit to "Admiral Sir James and Lady Hillyar" at Plymouth, England, in 1837.[31]

§ When a ship had her original upper deck removed and was thereby reduced to the next lower classification, she was described as a razee. Apparently, the *Saturn* had been built as a ship of the line and had later been cut down to the size of a frigate. Mahan says the British used this means of hurriedly creating vessels that could match American 44-gun frigates without having to provide the large crews required by ships of the line.

that this breach of contract made him consider himself a prisoner of war and, since he was no longer bound by his parole, he would escape, if possible. Later that night he gave Downes a letter to deliver to the captain of the *Saturn* saying that "Captain Porter was now satisfied, that most British officers were not only destitute of honour, but regardless of the honour of each other."

At seven o'clock the next morning, a fast whale boat was lowered, and Porter and some of his men started for Long Island, some forty miles away. For a while, the *Essex Junior* served as a screen between his boat and the *Saturn,* but his escape was soon discovered and the enemy went after him.* For once, Porter was favored by the weather: "fortunately it grew very foggy and by changing my course I was enabled to shake them . . . , he wrote to the Secretary. After rowing about sixty miles, Porter and his men landed at Babylon, Long Island. At first, the suspicious townsmen thought he was a British spy, but when he produced his commission, the atmosphere changed to one of "the most liberal hospitality." [33]

In New York, Porter was given a hero's welcome. In reporting the event, the *American Advocate* of Hallowell, Maine, commented: "It was really pleasant to see the joy which animated the AMERICAN citizens of New-York where he was received with six hearty cheers. . . . This is the way Americans receive their heroes, tho' they may have been unfortunate." The *Essex'* crew "rendezvoused at the Battery," then "with colors flying, accompanied by Com. Decatur's band of music," they proceeded to Tammany Hall, where they were served "an elegant dinner." Their reception in Philadelphia was even more enthusiastic. Porter and the mayor passed along streets "hung with stripes and stars," while huge crowds cheered. Some of the sailors unharnessed the horses from Porter's carriage and pulled it themselves. When they reached the Mansion House Hotel, they hoisted Porter on their shoulders, and "carried him in with huzzas." The same day, he went to Chester for a reunion with his family, after an absence of eighteen months, three weeks, and five days. Evalina introduced him to his second son and future biographer, David Dixon, born some eight and a half months after his father had departed for the Pacific.

After a short respite at home, Porter proceeded to Washington. Secretary of the Navy William Jones took him to dinner at the White

---

* The *Essex Junior* had a miserable time getting in to Sandy Hook: twice more she was stopped for British examination, and when she got inside the harbor, two separate American batteries fired on her. Luckily, the aim of the gunners was as lax as their nerves were tense. The *Essex Junior* was bought by the Navy for $25,000, and his captain's share made a pleasant financial boon for Porter.

House, where he regaled President Madison with stories about his cruise. It may be that early in August he made a quick trip to Boston, for on 28 July William Bainbridge wrote that he was looking forward to seeing Porter, his wife, and his eldest son William, "my little namesake," at the Charlestown Navy Yard. Bainbridge promised Porter to "drown you in lieu of hanging but not in *pure* water. Bacchus . . . shall overflow you." Records do not show whether this alcoholic reunion took place: when next they refer to Porter, he was in New York on 22 August.[34]

When Porter caught up with the war news, he found little in it to comfort him. Since he had left home in October 1812, the U.S. Navy had done poorly, except on inland waters. Not only had the *Essex* and the *Chesapeake* been taken, but there was a period of fifteen months during which the United States gained not a single major victory at sea. By late 1814, the five remaining frigates were all blockaded: the *President* at Sandy Hook, the *United States* and the *Macedonian* at New London, the *Constellation* at Norfolk, and the *Constitution* at Boston.* Along the Canadian border matters had gone somewhat better for the United States. Captain Oliver Hazard Perry's triumph on Lake Erie in September 1813 had compensated for some of the disgraceful American losses in the northwest during 1812.†

American campaigns against Canada resulted in victories mingled with defeats. One so-called American triumph was a hit-and-run attack across Lake Ontario which temporarily captured York, the capital of Upper Canada, in the spring of 1813. Public buildings there were burned, but the United States paid for that destruction with heavy interest a year later, when the British attacked Washington, D.C.

By the summer of 1814, the war was approaching its crescendo. The abdication of Napoleon in April had, for the first time, enabled London to focus attention on the American war, theretofore a sideshow in comparison to the main tent in Europe. Some 14,000 crack troops who had

---

* The *President* and the *Constitution* were the only frigates that went out again. In January 1815, Decatur managed to sneak the *President* past the enemy blockade, but soon was trapped by a much stronger force and compelled to surrender. Certainly, his resistance was less spirited than Porter's had been in somewhat similar circumstances. In view of her scintillating record, it was fitting that the *Constitution* should score the final victories, defeating the frigate *Cyane* and the sloop of war *Levant* off the Madeiras in February 1815, well after the end of the war.

† Even though the casualty rate on Perry's flagship, the *Lawrence,* was higher than it was on the *Essex*—66 per cent as opposed to 60 per cent—he fought on and eventually won. Those who described Porter's desperate defense of his ship as useless carnage should have kept in mind the value of Perry's continued resistance.[35]

served in the Duke of Wellington's Peninsular Campaign became available for service across the Atlantic. The British planned to use them in a three-pronged assault on the United States, which, if successfully completed, should enable London to dictate a victor's peace. The first prong was an overland expedition from Canada toward Albany; the second, a strike in the region of the Chesapeake Bay, namely, Washington, Alexandria, and Baltimore; and the third, an invasion of the South, pointed especially at New Orleans. In the first, General Sir George Prevost marched south along a route that, for a century or more, had been well traversed by British, French, and American armies, but his lines of communication and supply were shattered by the spectacular naval triumph of Captain Thomas Macdonough on Lake Champlain in September, and he was forced to retreat to Canada.

Admiral Sir Alexander Cochrane's invasion of the Chesapeake Bay was well planned and daring. Although he had only 5,000 of Wellington's veterans under the command of General Robert Ross, they were escorted by Admiral Sir George Cockburn's armada of over fifty vessels, including six ships of the line and twenty-one frigates. Few episodes in American history are more appalling than the national capital's "defence" between 19 and 27 August 1814. Almost 10,000,000 citizens of the United States had been at war for more than two years, yet no more than 7,000 could be mustered to defend Washington. Save for a detachment of 500 sailors and Marines under Captain Joshua Barney, a sprightly naval veteran of the Revolution, the defenders were untrained Maryland and Virginia militia under the command of the incompetent General William H. Winder. On 19 August Ross landed 3,500 soldiers north of the Potomac River, where the Patuxent enters the Chesapeake Bay. Accompanied by Cochrane, Ross set out on a march toward Washington and met no opposition, other than the ferocious 98-degree heat, until he reached Bladensburg, Maryland, a few miles northeast of the capital. There, he came up against the militia who, proving themselves better sprinters than pugilists, fled at the first fire. For a while, Barney's 500 provided some staunch opposition to Ross' 3,500, but they were soon overwhelmed, and their captain received a wound that eventually proved mortal.

As military and civilian officials, among them President and Mrs. Madison, were fleeing into Virginia, Ross, Cochrane, and only 1,500 troops entered the deserted capital on the evening of 24 August. During that night and the next day, the British set fire to the Capitol, the White House, and almost all other public buildings in Washington. Among the victims was the Tripoli Monument that Porter had sponsored, and he later posted a notice on it, reading "Mutilated by Britons, 1814." The

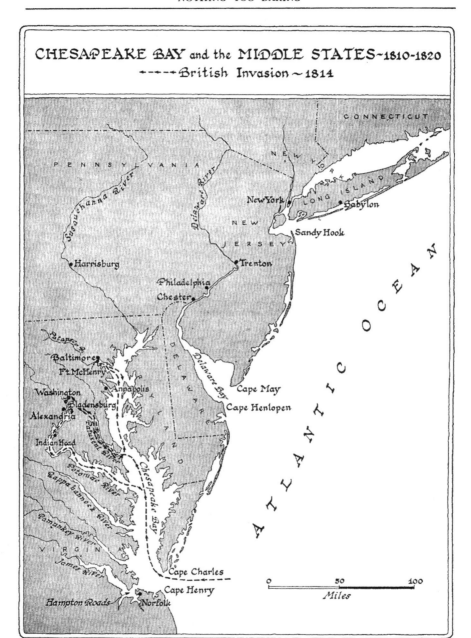

CHESAPEAKE BAY and the MIDDLE STATES~1810-1820
----British Invasion~1814

U.S. government ordered the Navy Yard at Washington destroyed and two warships that were nearing completion were lost in the flames: they were the sloop *Argus* and the 44-gun frigate *Essex,* originally called *Columbia* but, after being promised to Porter, renamed in honor of his old ship. One private dwelling in the city was burned, but the incident caused little comment since snipers had fired from it as the British approached. The havoc wrought in Washington evoked an explosion of American condemnation, and was criticized even in England. One British publication, while delighted that only public buildings had been damaged, admitted that the deed had brought "censure" from Europe as well as from the United States. It concluded: ". . . the destruction of edifices consecrated to the purpose of civil government, and affording specimens of the advance of the fine arts among a rising people, was thought an indulgence of animosity more suited to the time of barbarism than to . . . civilized policy." [36]

Porter was in New York when news of the British attack in the area of the Chesapeake Bay reached Washington, and the Secretary of the Navy promptly ordered him to report for the capital's defense. On 22 August he posted the following notice in the New York newspapers:

> Free Trade and Sailors' Rights
> To the crew of the old *Essex:* Sailors, the enemy is about attempting the destruction of your new ship at Washington, and I am ordered there to defend her. I shall proceed immediately, and all disposed to accompany me will meet me at three o'clock this afternoon, at the navy agent's office.

A few of his former shipmates joined him and he hastened south. When he passed through Chester, Farragut, then a schoolboy, begged permission to go with him but, as he later wrote, "Captain Porter was inexorable; he said I was too young for land fighting. I therefore missed the engagement. . . ." Granting the probability that Porter felt guilty about the many dangers to which the boy had already been exposed and what he had experienced on the decks of the *Essex,* it seems that he was over-solicitous in denying Farragut another chance for glory.

On 27 August, Porter got as far as Baltimore only to learn of the capture of Washington and the destruction of his new frigate. He notified the Secretary that he was placing himself under the command of Captain John Rodgers to save Baltimore "from the ravages of the enemy," and later the same day reported that, since the citizens of that city had recovered from their panic, prospects were more encouraging. Rodgers had assembled "upwards of a thousand sailors and marines" and divided them into two regiments, one under Porter, and the other under Captain Oliver Hazard Perry.[37]

As part of the original British master plan, Captain James A. Gordon had been instructed to sail his two frigates and five smaller craft up the Potomac River while Ross and Cochrane were advancing overland on Washington. It had been anticipated that the two forces would meet at the capital, but by the time Gordon reached Alexandria, Virginia, Washington had already fallen, and he contented himself with levying tribute on the terrified city, "which made a shameful capitulation" to save itself from destruction. Gordon began stowing aboard his ships "a large amount of flour, tobacco, cotton, sugar, coffee, and many other articles." When the tidings from Alexandria reached Rodgers, he changed his mind about defending Baltimore and sent his two regiments overland to cut off Gordon's escape down the Potomac.

At Alexandria, Porter decided to make a personal reconnaissance of conditions, so he and his subordinate, Captain John Orde Creighton, slipped away from their companions. Creighton was skipper of the *Argus,* the sloop that had been burned at Washington along with Porter's new *Essex,* a fact that led an English source to attribute his and Porter's escapade to personal grievance, the loss of their ships having "thrown them out of employment." Porter's behavior during the hour that the venture lasted seems to have been little short of lunatic. Not only was he, in the eyes of the British, a parole violator for skipping away from the *Essex Junior* off Long Island,* but he and Creighton were wearing civilian clothes when they entered the enemy-controlled city. On either of those counts, he could justifiably have been shot. Yet, according to English accounts, corroborated by his son, he and Creighton rode up to the docks at Alexandria and watched teen-aged Midshipman John W. Fraser of HMS *Euryalus* direct the loading of tribute. The two captains made an impromptu decision to kidnap Fraser, and galloped down upon him. Creighton reached out and, grabbing him around the neck, lifted him into the air, but the boy's overstrained "cravat" broke, and the frustrated Americans rode away.[38]

Porter then returned to his command at a place called the White House on a bend in the Potomac, some thirty miles below Washington. By this time, Captain Gordon had finished collecting his loot from Alexandria and was sailing down the river. From the 1st until the 6th of September, Porter's sailors and Marines, aided by local militia, who fought much more bravely than they had done at Bladensburg, disputed Gordon's passage. They manned land batteries, dueled with British bomb

---

* There was Anglo-American bickering as to whether or not Porter had broken his parole. The U.S. government accepted his argument that he had been automatically released when the British violated Hillyar's safe-conduct pass, but even after the war was over Sir Alexander Cochrane insisted that Porter had never been legally discharged from his obligation.

brigs, and might have stopped the enemy had they been able to use their 32-pound cannon, but the guns were useless, since their carriages never arrived. By the time Gordon finally made good his escape, eleven Americans had been killed and nineteen wounded, in exchange for the five killed and twelve wounded reported by a British deserter. The English flotilla had less difficulty getting past Captain Perry's batteries at Indian Head, farther downstream.

There is nothing in the official records to show where Porter spent the rest of September. A British authority claims that he participated in the defense of Baltimore, which lasted from 12 to 14 September. It is true that Rodgers' command was helping to defend the overland approaches to that city,[39] but no specific mention is made of Porter, nor did he communicate with the Secretary of the Navy during that time. With or without his assistance, the defenses of Baltimore held firm. When General Ross was killed by a sniper's bullet, much of the spirit was drained from the British Army, and failure to quiet Fort McHenry discouraged the English Navy. The attack was called off, and within a month Cochrane's forces had abandoned the Chesapeake Bay. After resting briefly, the British proceeded to the third phase of their over-all strategy: an attack on New Orleans. Although the Treaty of Ghent had been signed the previous 24 December, news of it did not reach New Orleans until well after Andrew Jackson's forces had torn the British to shreds on 8 January 1815, exchanging 2,036 British casualties for 21 Americans.

After the enemy withdrawal from the Chesapeake, Porter must have been able to spend some time in Chester, but by 5 October 1814 he was in New York. He had not languished for long without an assignment; the Navy had awarded him command of the *Fulton,* a large steam frigate under construction in New York. Initially, Porter was somewhat distrustful of such mechanical intrusion into his world of wood and canvas, but he changed his mind when he watched the launching of his new ship. Exuberantly he wrote to the Secretary that "she promises to meet our most sanguine expectations," proving to be "buoyant, shallow drafted, and easily maneuverable." It was probably during this sojourn in New York that he lived with his old friend, Washington Irving, for he was listed as one of the inmates of Irving's house in 1814.

It would obviously be many months before the *Fulton* would be ready to go into service (she was not completed until well after the war ended), so Porter looked around for other ways to occupy his time. No one knew better than he the value of commerce raiding, so in mid-October he asked the Department for permission to assemble a squadron of small, fast schooners to operate out of southern U.S. ports against British trade in the Caribbean. Permission was granted, and he busied himself trying to collect the ships and men he would need. In December he was able to report that he had bought three "fine vessels." After that, his progress slowed, and early in February 1815 he despondently notified the Secretary that his mission had been plagued by lack of public confidence in the government's fiscal soundness, cold weather, high wages in New York, and better enlistment terms for prospective sailors on the Great Lakes.

Furthermore, the War of 1812 was coming to its conclusion. The United States had been attempting to get out of the war almost from the moment it had been declared. By late 1814 the British wanted peace for a number of reasons: their attacks against Albany and Baltimore had failed, the Duke of Wellington refused to assume command in America, the anti-French alliance in Europe was disintegrating, there were premature rumors that Napoleon had escaped from Elba, and, after fighting the French for some twenty years, England was war-weary. Another important factor was the cumulative effect of the depredations of American privateers. In 1814 these raiders discovered that the waters around the British Isles formed an excellent hunting preserve. So many prizes were taken, even in the Irish Sea and off the mouth of the Thames, that London's maritime insurance rates soared almost out of sight. More than 500 American privateers seized some 1,000 British merchantmen during the course of the war. A British publication expressed the gratification of both sides at the signing of the Treaty of Ghent: it described the war with the United States as unhappy, an epithet, the publication remarked, that it peculiarly deserved, because neither side had an objective whose attainment could in any way compensate for the evils of the conflict.[40]

When the news of Ghent reached the United States in February 1815, Porter turned his fertile mind to finding an alternative to unemployment. He hoped he had found it in the Mediterranean. Algiers had taken advantage of the United States' preoccupation with the War of 1812 to open hostilities, and was seizing American ships and imprisoning American sailors. Since the squadron Porter wanted to use against the British in the Caribbean was, at last, ready for service, he wrote to the Secretary of the Navy, Benjamin W. Crowninshield, that if his ships had to remain idle they would be "a dead loss to the government. . . . Allow me, Sir, to suggest to you the propriety and advantages which would result by pushing up the Mediterranean and intercepting the commerce and cruisers of Algiers." In forty days, he said, he could be at work there. But Porter was bypassed in favor of Stephen Decatur who, later in the year, forced the Algerians to come to terms. The concomitant decision of Britain to end once and for all the nuisance of the Barbary pirates wrote finis to the depredations they had practised for several centuries. Downcast over his lost opportunity for glory and apprehensive about his financial prospects, Porter notified the Department in late February that he was returning to Chester as he saw "no immediate or very urgent" call for his services.

Porter's itch for activity did not subside when he was passed over as commander of the squadron that sailed against the Barbary corsairs. In April he commenced his duties as one of the three captains on the newly established Board of Navy Commissioners, and a few months later was attempting to get permission to lead an expedition to the Pacific. On 31 October 1815,* describing himself as "a solitary individual," he addressed a letter to President Madison recommending that his naval forces explore the waters of the North Pacific, then join an overland expedition to the Oregon Country which would seek transcontinental routes other than those traversed by Lewis and Clark. But he reserved his greatest enthusiasm for another aim of his proposed expedition: the opening of Japan. After giving the President a brief geography lesson, which accentuated the honors won for other nations by their globe-trotting officers, he set forth his plan:

> The important trade of Japan has been shut against every nation except the Dutch. . . . Great changes have since taken place in the world—changes which may have affected even Japan; the time may be favorable, and it would be a glory . . . for us, a nation of only forty years standing to beat down their rooted prejudices—secure to ourselves a valuable trade, and make that people known to the world. . . . My views are general: the whole world is embraced in them. Let us visit those parts that have been perfectly explored; search out those of which we have only traditional accounts, and traverse those parts of ocean over which a ship has never passed. . . . Everything now favors the object. . . .

The letter closed with a brief plea on behalf of himself and other naval officers: "The world is at peace. . . . We have ships . . . [and] officers who will require employment." [41]

If Madison ever replied to Porter's suggestions, no copy of his letter appears to have survived, but there is abundant evidence that the prospect of combining explorations in the Pacific with those in the continental Northwest so intrigued the administration that it went beyond mere verbal support. Secretary of the Navy Crowninshield tentatively assigned vessels and men for the expedition. Porter was to have the *Java* as his flagship, and Captains Oliver Hazard Perry and Charles Morris were to command frigates under him. Since the *Java* had been Perry's ship, he was understandably "wounded by the proposition," and announced that he would be subordinate to no one. The "proposition" did not, however, spoil his friendship with Porter, which continued with "the liveliest senti-

---

* Samuel Flagg Bemis gives the date as October 1818, but that is not correct.

ments of admiration and regard." In June 1816 Captain Charles Morris was ordered "to prepare for a cruise to the Pacific," evidently as part of the administration's response to Porter's suggestion. He reported that his mission was to occupy the mouth of the Columbia River and to rearm the fort there, but later orders shifted him to the Gulf of Mexico, because of a minor squabble with Spain.[42]

About a month after Morris received his first set of orders, Porter was writing to warn Joel R. Poinsett that he should keep secret what he knew about the expedition to the Pacific, since it was still in prospect, but that he, Porter, having "yielded to the importunities" of his family and friends, had decided not to go. A week later, he told Poinsett he had reconsidered his decision to refuse "a command of so much importance and so flattering to me." However, it did not matter what he decided for the expedition was canceled. It has been suggested that the niggardliness of peacetime naval appropriations caused the cancelation, but the concurrent eruption of difficulty with Spain and rumors of a possible Spanish attack on New Orleans were more likely the reasons. The Secretary of the Navy ordered all ships to be ready for service in the Caribbean.[43]

Nevertheless, Porter's recommendation that Japan be opened by the United States was not forgotten. The captain himself, bored with shore duty and with his personal finances in dishevelment, resurrected his proposal for such an expedition by publishing in 1821 the letter he had written to President Madison six years before. Although his suggestion brewed enough enthusiasm to inspire 300 citizens to endorse it to President Monroe's attention, nothing was done about it at that time. During the early 1850s, a decade after Porter's death, the feasibility of sending an expedition to Japan was the subject of national discussion, and Matthew C. Perry made his famous and successful voyage to the Orient. In order to show when American interest in Japan was first aroused, the influential Southern magazine *DeBow's Review* reprinted the letter Porter wrote in 1815, but indicated that he had addressed it to Secretary of State James Monroe, rather than to President Madison. That error caused confusion among some later historians.* A leading modern student of American influence on the Far East has made the comment that Porter's "proposal to open Japan may be said to have marked the high tide of American interest in the Pacific until 1830." Another authority states that subsequent American explorations in the Pacific, including Perry's well-publicized opening of Japan, "all developed from the idea which the proposal of 1815 initiated." [44]

* One such historian is C. O. Paullin. In 1940, A. B. Cole rectified the mistake by reprinting the letter with its correct addressee, James Madison.

From the spring of 1815 until the end of 1822 David Porter's life was crowded with diverse activities. In addition to writing the 1815 and 1822 editions of his *Journal of a Cruise to the Pacific Ocean*, and his abortive planning to lead an expedition to the Pacific, he busied himself as one of the three Navy Commissioners, man-about-Washington-society, gentleman farmer, close observer of a famous duel, and a leading protagonist of Latin-American independence.

The Board of Navy Commissioners had been established in response to the sentiment, widespread among naval officers, that control of the Navy should not be, as it had theretofore been, almost entirely in the hands of civilians. Porter certainly deemed that some of the trouble into which he had run resulted from amateur ignorance. He could recall vividly the unpleasant arguments with the Department over expenses while commanding at New Orleans; and he was unlikely to forget his desperate and futile remonstrances against the inadequate armament of the *Essex*. Most officers had suffered similar frustrations. Late in the War of 1812, Porter had joined his colleagues Stephen Decatur, Oliver Hazard Perry, and Lewis Warrington in recommending that three senior naval captains be appointed to a "board of inspectors" for the Navy, with the Secretary as presiding officer, a proposal supported by the Navy Department itself. During the early part of the war, Secretary William Jones had complained that the supply problem occupied so much of his time that his operational planning suffered, and the situation did not improve even when he delegated much of his paper work to his clerks. He passed on this complaint to his successor, Benjamin W. Crowninshield.

With praiseworthy speed, Congress responded to both service and civilian pressure and, on 7 February 1815, passed a law establishing a "Board of Navy Commissioners," to be composed of three senior captains. Although the Secretary of the Navy was to be in "superintendence" of the

Board, he was not to be a member of it. Porter had the signal honor of being selected as one of the first three commissioners, and joined his fellows, John Rodgers and Isaac Hull, at the Board's first meeting on 25 April 1815. As senior captain, John Rodgers was the presiding officer. "Secretary for the Commissioners" was James K. Paulding, who had been a friend of Porter's since the days of the Kilkenny Lads in 1808, and who later became Secretary of the Navy. One of the clerks on the Board was Charles Goldsborough, who, almost without interruption, served the Navy in one capacity or another from its founding in 1798 to his death in 1843. Until 1820 the Board met at remote and unsatisfactory quarters; thereafter, it met in the navy building, just west of the White House.* [1]

Within a month of the founding of the Board, Porter and the other commissioners were involved in a jurisdictional dispute with Navy Secretary Crowninshield. Congress had stipulated that the Board was to discharge "ministerial duties" concerning naval stores and supplies, ships' matters, and estimation of responsibilities. The looseness of that language made controversy almost inevitable. As the commissioners saw it, their duty was to ensure that the Navy would no longer be completely in the hands of men who were amateurs in maritime affairs: hence, they should have primary control over naval personnel and material, and should leave to the Secretary the provision of necessary funds. Finally, they argued that their authority bypassed the Secretary and ran directly to the President. Crowninshield held that, while the commissioners might advise him, they could not take over his "direction of naval forces," and he insisted that policy-making must remain where the Constitution had placed it—in civilian hands.

The controversy ended up in the White House. While President Madison mulled over the opposing arguments, William Bainbridge, reflecting the general feeling in the Navy, wrote Porter that he hoped Crowninshield would be defeated and added that, if he were not, the commissioners might well be "in the honorable Status of Clerks to the Secretary's Clerks." It did not, however, take Madison long to decide that if the Board were independent of the Secretary of the Navy, it would be "independent of the President also, thus destroying the unity, efficiency, and responsibility of the Executive." Consequently, he ruled against the Board. Although neither Porter nor Rodgers enjoyed being overruled, they accepted the decision but, according to one authority, Isaac Hull did not.

* John Rodgers served on the Board of Navy Commissioners for a total of nineteen years: from 1815 to 1824, and from 1827 to 1837. David Porter served from 1815 until the end of 1822, and was succeeded by Charles Morris.

He resigned to take over the Boston Navy Yard, and was replaced on the Board by Stephen Decatur.[2]

Besides this clash with Madison, Commissioners Rodgers and Porter had a confrontation with the succeeding administration. Following the resignation of Crowninshield in 1818, President James Monroe offered Rodgers the job of Secretary of the Navy. After some hesitation, Rodgers turned down the appointment, preferring to retain the security represented by his status as senior captain in the Navy and as President of the Board of Navy Commissioners. Later, in an article that appeared in the *National Intelligencer* Rodgers denied that he had ever been offered the position. According to Secretary of State John Quincy Adams, this stand angered President Monroe, and Adams himself, who soon learned that Rodgers and Porter, for some inexplicable reason, had planted the article, wrote testily: "How, then, can Porter or Rodgers justify themselves for passing this deliberate falsehood upon the public?"[3] Although the spat was minor and quickly passed, it may have had significance in that it left Adams with an abiding distrust of Porter.

As a Navy Commissioner, Porter worked with Rodgers and Decatur on a wide variety of problems. They investigated the need for and the location of Navy yards and dry docks; drew up specific rules of conduct for officers and men; procured and stockpiled supplies; decided upon proper armament for ships; and recommended such reforms as regulated systems for the appointment, promotion, and dismissal of officers, the founding of a naval academy, and the creation of high ranks.

The three commissioners made a lengthy investigation of Navy yards and stations. They found that much of the land that earlier administrations had bought for naval installations had been little developed, and that many of the existing yards were either badly situated or inefficiently managed. They recommended that two new yards, one in Narragansett Bay and the other in Chesapeake Bay, shoud be built, and that those at Norfork, Washington, Philadelphia, New York, and Portsmouth, N.H., should be abandoned: the Boston yard was the only one they considered efficient enough to be retained. But they soon found, as others have since, that when local interests are threatened with the loss of such handy recipients of pork-barrel legislation, they can evoke potent support from their congressmen and senators. The Board's efforts to produce greater competence at less cost were thwarted: it was unable to reduce the number of yards or to promote greater efficiency.

Initially, the situation concerning dry docks was even worse. Prior to the War of 1812, there was not a single dock in the whole country that could handle large ships. In 1811, Secretary of the Navy Paul Hamilton had reported to the Speaker of the House of Representatives that the only way to repair frigates was to dismantle and then reassemble them. The Speaker introduced a bill advocating the construction of adequate docks, but it was thoroughly emasculated, and the best that Congress would do in this essential matter was to appropriate $100,000, but even that sum was not used. In 1821, after prolonged effort, the Board of Navy Commissioners opened in Washington the first modern dry dock in America.[4]

Naval regulations were especially in need of reform. American naval codes, established during the Revolution and based upon British precedents, were loosely worded and prolix enough to spawn endless confusion. Rodgers, Porter, and Decatur spent considerable time reforming them and, by 1818, had promulgated extensive and detailed rules that ". . . contained instructions respecting naval discipline, the duties of officers and the equipment of ships, and regulations for the government of the navy-yards. They prescribed the navy ration, allotting for each day of the week fixed quantities of . . . suet, cheese, beef, pork, flour, bread, butter, peas, rice, sugar, tea, molasses, vinegar, and spirits. The daily allowance of spirits, that is of rum or whiskey, was fixed at half a pint."

Recalling his anguished correspondence with Secretary of the Navy Robert Smith while he was in New Orleans, Porter must have thrown himself into supply problems with special zest. To avert emergency shortages, a system of stockpiling vital commodities was inaugurated. Regular, streamlined procedures were instituted to provide in quantity at standardized prices the myriad items needed by a wood and canvas navy and its men: "live oak and yellow pine beams, long guns and carronades, beef and pork, kentledge [pig-iron ballast], juniper shingles, ship chandlery and paints, slop clothing, canvas, patent cordage, anchor iron, masts and spars, stone, coal, gunner's stores, groceries . . . whiskey, and tobacco." Spiritual fare of another sort was not forgotten; bibles were allocated on the basis of thirty for a ship of the line, twenty for a frigate, twelve for a sloop, and six for a schooner.

The commissioners would naturally have much to say and do about improving ordnance for the U.S. Navy. Having the wrong guns had wrecked Porter's chances in the *Essex*, and, at one time or another, both Rodgers and Decatur had suffered casualties from exploding cannon in their ships. Long guns and carronades continued to be furnished, but the 12- and 18-pound long guns of only a few years before were replaced by 42-pounders. Under careful government inspection, ordnance contracts were awarded to three factories: at West Point, Georgetown, and Richmond.

In spite of the care with which the commissioners handled ordnance matters, they could not devise a scheme that would prevent accidents from defective guns. Porter himself was victimized in 1822. An inventor was demonstrating a new gunlock when the entire device exploded, hurling a piece of metal into Porter's hand and inflicting so severe a fracture that he never recovered its full use. It is ironic that after the Board had devoted twenty-seven years to efforts to improve gunnery and make it safer, the United States should lose a Secretary of State as well as a Secretary of the Navy, when a gun on board the *Princeton* exploded in 1844.

The commissioners were moderately successful in categorizing procedures for the appointment of officers, but failed in their efforts to regularize promotions and dismissals. Previously, appointment to the Navy was often the result of political pressure, but by 1819 the Board had managed to establish regular examinations for young men seeking appointments as midshipmen. Efforts to found a naval academy, however, did not succeed until 1845, three years after the Board was dissolved. Promotion continued to be based on such unpredictable factors as the whims of superiors. Equally frustrating were attempts to weed unwanted officers out of the Navy. Rodgers, Porter, and Decatur were aware that many of the incompetents who had been enticed into the Navy during its rapid expansion in the War of 1812, still clogged service rolls, but they were powerless to remove them. Unless they committed offenses that made them subject to courts-martial, there was no way in which the Navy could scrape off those barnacles who were willing to cling to the same grade year after year. Finally, the commissioners urged that ranks higher than those of captain or commodore be established, but the Navy had to wait until the Civil War for its first admirals.[5]

Despite many disappointments and failures during Porter's tenure, the Board of Navy Commissioners furnished real service to the government. Its work was highly praised by a visiting British officer: ". . . the organization of the American naval department, or for practical work, [seems] to be the best system extant. Their ships are the best built, and their timber is unsurpassed. Their frigates are competent to cope with ships of the line . . . the whole administration of the navy is conducted with comparatively little expense."

Perhaps the best proof of the Board's value to the Navy was that it succeeded in averting anything like the drastic cutbacks in appropriations that had followed the ending of hostilities with both France and Tripoli. The United States came out of the War of 1812 with a relatively large fleet, which was not dismantled after the Treaty of Ghent. Although naval officers could never be happy about peacetime financial support, Congress did provide regular additions to the fleet. The commissioners rightly considered that one of their primary functions was to feed, wine, and amuse the congressmen upon whose votes the fate of the Navy depended, and the private, as well as the public, efforts of Rodgers, Porter, and Decatur played no small part in acquiring favorable votes. All three men were solidly in the capital's social swim, providing open-handed hospitality and, when occasion permitted, embellishing it with all the nautical pageantry they could. A case in point was the launching of the *Columbus* on 1 March 1819:

> . . . yesterday the noble ship of the line "Columbus" glided from its bed at the navy-yard in the city in the most majestic style in the presence of thousands of spectators, who, in spite of the unfavorable weather, had assembled to witness this interesting scene. The occasion was robbed of much of its brilliance by the state of the weather; but it lost none of its intrinsic grandeur. The vessel was greeted on its descent by a national salute from the artillery, by patriotic airs from the band of the marine corps, and by the shouts of thousands of Columbians gathered together from every quarter of the Union. . . . It is a very general impression that a more beautiful launch was never witnessed in any country.

Porter and his family arrived at the navy yard in their carriage, were saluted by sentries at the gates, then followed the Marine band toward the ship. A holiday atmosphere prevailed as Porter joined the official party, headed by President Monroe and Secretary of the Navy Smith Thompson. To their total delight ten-year-old William and six-year-old David Dixon Porter were allowed to board the *Columbus* and accompany her down the ways and into the water.[6]

Having decided that he should live in a setting commensurate with his social position, Porter collected what was left of his prize money from the war, stretched his credit to the limit, and on 18 March 1816 paid $13,000 for 110 acres of the former Peters Estate, situated on Meridian Hill, the highest point in the District of Columbia.* When he took possession of his new property, he "patriotically" suggested to the government that, since it was not proper that American time should be based on Greenwich, England, Washington, D.C. should become "a first meredian for the United States." [7]

To build his new home, Porter selected George Hadfield, a top-flight architect who had designed Washington City Hall and the Custis-Lee Mansion on the grounds of the present national shrine at Arlington, Virginia. Although Porter was residing at Meridian Hill at least as early as the autumn of 1817—he used the address in a letter written late that

---

* David Dixon Porter claimed that his father bought 157 acres. The tract lies about a mile north of the White House, running from Florida Avenue to Columbia Road, east of 16th Street. In Porter's day it was well out of town.

October—another two years passed before Hadfield completed what James K. Paulding, a sometime boarder there, referred to as the "stately mansion." Evalina and the children did not move down from Chester to occupy their new home until 1819. Unfortunately, the purchase of the land and the cost of building and maintaining not so much a single residence as an entire village, left Porter seriously overextended. "There were many servants about the house, nursemaids, kitchenmaids, dairymaids, boys to cut wood, stable boys to groom the horses and keep the mud washed off the carriage . . . There was the English gardener who did nothing but cultivate the five-acre kitchen garden and take care of the fancy cattle. . . . There were families who worked in the grain fields." [8]

Porter became a one-man laboratory for the latest agricultural fads, often following the advice of his friend, John Stuart Skinner,* publisher of a farm magazine, postmaster of Baltimore, privateer-owner, and fellow-enthusiast for Latin-American independence. After commenting that the soil at Meridian Hill was so poor that crops did not seem to flourish there, David Dixon Porter went on to recall that his father:

> . . . supplied his acquaintances with the best of vegetables for nothing. He had a . . . garden of five acres and had to buy vegetables for winter; he had a hundred acres in corn, oats, wheat, &c., and was obliged to purchase grain for his stock. He imported English bulls at twelve hundred dollars [more than one-third of his annual salary as a Navy Commissioner] apiece . . . people would not patronize them. He had the finest piggery in the country, but alas, it did not pay. Thousands of cartloads of manure were hauled upon the farm, only to be washed away by the spring rains; the place was in beautiful order, highly satisfactory to the casual observers, but it yielded absolutely nothing.

The picture of Captain David Porter, U.S. Navy, in the guise of a gentleman farmer lent itself to farce. Paulding wrote a satire in which he characterized Porter as an Englishman who, attempting to risk American husbandry, bought "an English bull, English cows, English sheep, English hogs, an English dairy-woman, an English ploughman, English plows," but the dairymaid ran off to get married; the ploughman learned that the only sensible way to ward off the chronic fevers of Washington was by drinking whiskey and, thereafter, lay around stupified; and it cost so much and took so long to erect the huge barns for the bumper harvests anticipated that the crops never got planted.

David Dixon Porter says that, during these years, his father and some

---

* As a Navy purser during the War of 1812, Skinner had been beside Francis Scott Key during the British bombardment of Fort McHenry, and was personally responsible for urging him to publish his famous poem.

of his friends financed a joint-stock company to run a horse-drawn boat between Washington and Alexandria, at the time connected only by a slow stagecoach. Unfortunately, the boat proved even slower than the coach, and any slight chance of profits was dissolved by the captain's affable distribution of free passes to all his acquaintances.

Porter's growing family contributed to his mounting financial difficulties. By 1819 there were five children: William, Elizabeth, David Dixon, Thomas, and the helpless baby afflicted with the name Theodoric.* As might have been expected, David Dixon supplied an abundance of anecdotes concerning life with father. On one occasion, he took advantage of the captain's absence to steal a shotgun, climb a tree, and kill some of his father's tame pigeons. Porter returned earlier than expected and caught him in the act. Ordering his son down from the tree, he went after him, slashing with a whip, but the youngster outdistanced his winded father. The incident ended with Porter convulsed with laughter at the taunt the boy shouted back at him: "Pop if you didn't chase the British better than that, no wonder you made so little prize money." Other stories in the same style told how Porter brought to an abrupt halt an English servant girl's terrorizing of the Negro help by out-ghosting her ghost act; of a controversy with neighborhood students about stolen apples; and of the so-called gallantry Porter displayed toward a lady of questionable reputation, by loudly insisting that she be treated with proper respect at a Washington ball.

A constant stream of visitors rode out to Meridian Hill to be entertained as overnight guests or to attend the expensive dances and dinners that Porter regularly provided. Naval colleagues William Bainbridge, Oliver Hazard Perry, and many others gathered to reminisce. David Farragut, home after years of service in the Mediterranean, was a welcome visitor in 1820,† and four years later spent several days of his honeymoon at Meridian Hill.[9]

Expenses connected with his property, the failure of his efforts at farming, the collapse of his Washington-Alexandria boat franchise, the

* Elizabeth must have died shortly thereafter, for she is not again mentioned in Porter family documentation. Despite the difference in spelling, evidently Theodoric was named for Judge Theodorick Bland, who worked closely with Porter for the cause of José Miguel Carrera and Chilean independence.
† Farragut had not seen his "friend Commodore Porter" since May of 1816, when Porter and Rodgers had boarded the ship of the line in which Farragut was serving as a midshipman. Incidentally, the fact that Farragut regularly referred to himself as Porter's friend, rather than as his son, tends to prove that he was never legally adopted by Porter.

support of his large family and a host of servants, and his incessant lavish entertaining quickly brought Porter to the edge of financial disaster. As early as 1817, he had spent his prize money from the war, and the salary of $3,500 a year that he received as a Navy Commissioner proved totally inadequate. In desperation, he expanded his credit as much as possible, borrowing from friends and banks alike. As usual, Samuel Hambleton bore the brunt of his friend's financial woes. The captain's poverty, that had been the mournful theme of the letters between the two men when Porter was in New Orleans a decade before, again characterized their correspondence between 1817 and 1820. Sometime in 1817 Porter wrote to ask Hambleton for $200 or $300, but added that if that was too large an amount, "any sum however small would be an accomadation to me." When President Monroe told Porter that Spain would soon cede East Florida to the United States "on certain conditions which would be accepted," the captain announced that he was considering speculating in Florida land, but he never had funds available for investment. In the spring of 1818 he borrowed money from John Skinner, but still had to tell Hambleton that he was "rather short of cash," and needed him to cosign a note for $1,000. Within six months, he was reduced to begging Hambleton for a pittance of $20 and, a couple of weeks later, confessed that he had been forced to sell stock and some of his estate merely to cover current expenses. By this time, the banks were closing in on Porter, and he frantically notified his ever-patient friend that there was "something wrong in my affairs at the US Bank—you alone can arrange them." A tightening of credit that resulted from the financial panic of 1819 worsened Porter's already precarious situation, and in July he asked Hambleton to co-sign two notes, one for $1,250 and the other for $1,500, owed to the Farmers and Mechanics Bank.[10] He also borrowed heavily from John Downes, who had been his lieutenant in the *Essex*. Although he managed to ride out this storm, the relief he so ardently craved never came, and most of the subsequent turns and twists of his career were caused by his consuming need for money.

During his tenure on the Board, Porter was intimately associated with his fellow commissioners, Rodgers and Decatur. At this time, his relationship with his old superior in the *Constellation* was still amicable, and Rodgers called him "a man of far more than ordinary natural talents, indefatigable in whatever he undertakes; and added to these, his acquirements, professional as well as . . . scientific are respectable." Between the two younger men, however, there was some acerbity. On occasion, Porter flared up at Decatur for usurping his administrative duties, and Rodgers would separate them "as if they were mere boys." Yet, the two men not only respected each other, but were in debt to one another professionally. Decatur had presided at the court of inquiry which exonerated Porter from any censure for the loss of the *Essex,* and, when the former was absolved from blame for surrendering the *President,* he acknowledged Porter's backing: "I have received your friendly letter and thank you. . . . You can judge a man's feelings who has lost a ship even although he has the proud consciousness of having discharged his duty well." [11]

Porter's association with Decatur involved him in an ancillary role in the duel between Decatur and James Barron that took place in 1820. This encounter was the delayed, but nonetheless direct, outgrowth of Barron's surrender of the *Chesapeake* to the *Leopard* twelve years before. Rodgers, Porter, and Decatur had sat on the court-martial that tried him in 1808, and participated in the infliction of his severe punishment —suspension from the Navy for five years without pay. Shortly thereafter, Barron, lacking private funds, left the United States and for the next decade earned a living of sorts in the European carrying trade. When his suspension ended in 1813, he was placed on half-pay and could have come back for reassignment as a captain in the Navy during the latter part of the war. But, possibly because he was ashamed of his lowly status or simply because he could not pay his passage, he stayed abroad. When he did return in 1818, he applied for reappointment to active service, pleading that it was poverty that had kept him away so long. If granted, he would stand next to John Rodgers in naval seniority, since his commission dated back to 1799.

When Barron's request was considered, it was unsuccessfully opposed not only by the three commissioners but by all the captains in the Navy, except Richard Dale and Jesse D. Elliott. During his early years in the Navy, Decatur had repeatedly clashed with Barron and had made no attempt to hide his abhorrence of him for surrendering to the *Leopard.* Now his open opposition to Barron's reinstatement was "marked by scorn and contempt." Barron retaliated with "resentment, bitterness, and a strong sense of injustice." He had earned harsh punishment and continued unpopularity for giving up the *Chesapeake* in peacetime under circumstances that he felt could not have been anticipated, whereas Decatur was the darling of the government and of the public, even after his questionable surrender of the *President* under conditions of war. [12]

Some curiously stilted and deadly correspondence concerning a duel passed between the two men and, late in the winter of 1820, Barron issued a formal challenge. In view of his reputation, Decatur might well have considered that there was no need for him to demonstrate further his physical courage, but he decided to accept.* He asked Captain Charles Morris to be his second; Morris declined on the grounds that he was about to embark on a tour of sea duty. Then Decatur approached John Rodgers, who not only refused his request, but warmly advised Decatur to drop the whole matter forthwith. Whether Porter was the third man asked by Decatur to stand with him is a moot question. In view of the relationship between the two, it would seem likely that he was, but Porter's letters do not mention the subject, and authorities differ.† William Bainbridge finally accepted, which would prove that the bad blood there had been between them had disappeared. Bainbridge had deeply resented Decatur's successful conclusion of the Algerian campaign in 1815; he felt that he had been elbowed out of the public recognition he merited, and his letters of that time are full of his anger and hurt. The two "did not speak to each other for several years afterwards." Perhaps Bainbridge's acceptance was in belated gratitude for the time in Malta eighteen years before when Decatur had stood beside his brother Joseph.‡ Decatur appointed, as another second, Porter's friend and financial backer, Samuel Hambleton.[13]

Barron was seconded by Captain Jesse D. Elliott, and that fomenter of dissension proceeded to pour on the fire all the kerosene he could. Like Barron, he was a controversial figure. He had served under Barron in the *Chesapeake,* and had appeared as a witness in one of the courts-martial that followed the surrender of that ship. As Oliver Hazard Perry's second-in-command at the Battle of Lake Erie in 1813 he had carefully kept his ship, the *Niagara,* out of action for the first two hours while Perry's *Lawrence* was being hammered to pieces. Alexander Mackenzie, Perry's biographer, charged that he had held aloof in hopes that his commander would be killed. Only when the *Lawrence* seemed hopelessly wrecked, did Elliott join the battle. In his official report, Perry praised him, and re-

---

* Decatur had a lengthy acquaintance with dueling. In 1799 at Newcastle, Delaware, he had shot in the hip an officer of a merchantman. A little later he had seconded in two duels, the first for Joseph Bainbridge in Malta, and the second in the round-robin fracas of Richard Somers. In 1818 he had been Oliver Hazard Perry's second in the latter's harmless encounter with Marine Captain John Heath. Evidently, Barron had never participated in a duel, although he had come close to fighting John Rodgers in the Mediterranean in 1806 and 1807.
† Hamilton Cochran does not mention Porter, but C. S. Forester says that he was approached by Decatur.
‡ Cochran is wrong when he says that Decatur "had acted for him [Bainbridge] when he was a midshipman." He is obviously confusing Joseph with William Bainbridge.

marked to Samuel Hambleton, a participant in the battle, that it was "better to screen a coward than to let the enemy know there is one in the fleet."

In spite of the fact that Perry had officially commended Elliott, he later blasted him, and there was considerable controversy about what did happen. The argument lived on a good many years. James Fenimore Cooper spoke for Elliott, while Mackenzie's defense of Perry was later picked up by Mahan and others. Elliott, who has been accurately described as "a man of violent likes and dislikes. . . . erratic, suspicious, jealous, and voluble," spent several years trying to provoke Perry into a duel.* After Perry died in 1819, Elliott's venom sought and found a new objective—Decatur, who had sided with Perry in the controversy over responsibility on Lake Erie. The row between Barron and Decatur was made-to-order for Elliott's talents, and he labored "to bring about a meeting with pistols between the two commodores." [14] Elliott, more than anyone else, must bear the onus for the tragedy that ensued.

Details for the duel were quickly arranged. Barron and Decatur were to meet at Bladensburg, Maryland, on the morning of 22 March 1820, with pistols at eight paces. It was a damp, cold, thoroughly unpleasant day when the group assembled. Three of the five men—Barron, Decatur, and Elliott—who had been intimately connected with Barron's court-martial twelve years before, were directly involved in the duel; the other two—David Porter and John Rodgers—were so consumed with worry and curiosity that they could not stay away. Although they kept out of sight until after the shooting ended, they were close at hand throughout the proceedings.† It is said that while the principals were waiting for their seconds to complete last-minute details, Barron called out: "Now, Decatur, if we meet in another world, let us hope that we will be better friends," to which Decatur answered, "I was never your enemy." At that moment the whole silly and murderous affair could have been terminated, but for some unaccountable reason, Bainbridge said nothing, and mischief-maker Elliott hurriedly shouted, "Gentlemen, to your places!"

As the antagonists stood sideways, separated from one another by

---

* Although Elliott could not bring Perry to fight him, he did help to get him involved with another. In 1816, while commanding the *Java*, Perry quarreled with Marine Captain John Heath, called him derelict in duty, and, losing control of himself, struck him in the face. Perry and Heath filed countercharges against each other, and courts-martial resulted in each being privately reprimanded. Many concluded that Perry had been whitewashed, among them Elliott, who picked away at Heath until the latter challenged. Elliott was probably much disappointed when Heath shot and missed, while Perry refused to shoot back.

† Porter and Rodgers deserve condemnation for having done nothing to prevent an encounter about which they knew everything, as their presence proves.

only twenty-four feet, they formed a sharp contrast: Decatur, medium-sized, slender, dark, handsome, vibrant; Barron, tall, paunchy, florid, swollen-featured, phlegmatic. According to agreed terms, they were to aim at the first command and fire between the second and third. At the second word, both men fired, both staggered, and both fell. Each bullet smashed into the other's hip; the one fired by Decatur glanced off Barron's femur, and inflicted a painful, but not mortal, wound in his thigh. Barron's bullet, however, ricocheted into Decatur's groin—a fatal blow. According to some accounts, Decatur said, "Oh, Lord, I am a dead man"; others, less credible, quote him as saying, "I am mortally wounded. At least I believe so and wish I had fallen in defence of my country." There is general agreement that the prostrate Barron called out, "Decatur, I forgive you from the bottom of my heart."

At this point, Porter galloped up from his hiding place. Much as he despised Barron, he gaped to see Elliott leave his principal stretched alone on the rain-soaked ground, jump into the carriage that had brought them there, and dash away towards Washington. It is undoubtedly correct to ascribe Elliott's incredible behavior to sheer panic: he had been the prime instigator of the sorry business, and feared chastisement from legal authorities or from a lynch mob. After attending briefly to Barron, Porter hurried after Elliott, and overtook him within a mile. According to David Dixon Porter, Elliott "asked in a trembling voice, how things fared on the ground." Porter, white with rage, answered, "They fare so badly, sir, that you left your friend weltering in his blood upon the bare earth; go back and do what you can to lessen the mischief you have aided in committing; go back and do your duty to your wounded friend." [15]

When Porter got back to the dueling site, he found that Rodgers had made his appearance. The two wounded men still lay on the ground, Decatur surrounded by friends, Barron alone. According to the latter, the two argued about why, when his suspension from the Navy ended, Barron did not immediately return to the United States. The surgeons probing for bullets, however, soon short-circuited conversation. Since Elliott had not returned by the time Decatur's friends were ready to remove him, Decatur offered to take Barron in his carriage, but there was not room. As the entourage departed, Barron called, "God bless you, Decatur." The only response the dying man could make was a faint, "Farewell, farewell, Barron."

While Barron, covered with the overcoats of the men still on the scene—he is said to have given his to Decatur—lay trembling with cold and shock on the dank grass, minute after minute dragged by and Elliott did not return. In desperation, Porter commandeered a private carriage that was passing by, and Barron was gingerly lifted into it. As the party proceeded towards the District of Columbia, it met Elliott inching toward the dueling ground, obviously hoping that he would not get there until all had left. When the two carriages came together, Porter dismounted, and reaching into Elliott's, shouted, "Your place is here, sir, alongside your wounded friend. I insist upon your getting in!" He literally pulled Elliott out of one carriage and pushed him into the other, and the entire party proceeded into town.

Barron was taken to a friend's home, where he remained in strict seclusion until he had recovered. There was no official investigation of the duel and the circumstances surrounding it. Barron was not only reinstated on active duty but, after the death of John Rodgers in 1838, became senior officer of the U.S. Navy. He never again served at sea, but commanded Navy yards until his death in 1851. Decatur was taken home and, that night, died in agony so great that at one point he cried, "I did not know that any man could suffer such pain!" Porter served as a pallbearer at his funeral, which was attended by President Monroe, the Cabinet, the diplomatic corps, the military establishment, and thousands of spectators.*

Porter's contempt for Elliott's craven flight from the scene of the duel was enhanced when the latter tried to shift onto Bainbridge his own responsibility for the tragedy. On the very day of the duel, Elliott remarked to Porter how unfortunate it was that Bainbridge had not called off the encounter when Decatur made what amounted to an apology. Porter was so overcome with disgust at Elliott's attempt to exonerate himself by making Bainbridge the scapegoat, that he did not deign to reply. Nevertheless, Elliott continued to protest his own innocence and Bainbridge's guilt in the matter. In a long letter to Hambleton, written only a month after the happenings that so intimately concerned them both, Porter quoted Elliott as writing that Bainbridge "did not encourage a reconciliation when the conversation took place between Com". D and B before firing," and went on to castigate him: "he fled from the ground taking with him the only means of conveyance for his wounded friend, that he left him for an hour in a helpless state on the wet ground. . . . Self, self, self was his only consideration." A couple of years later, John Rodgers accused Elliott of trying to foment trouble between Porter and himself, and wrote to his fellow commissioner about "that rascal Elliot[t] whose scurvey paper I send you." [17] Relations between Porter and Elliott remained unfriendly for the rest of their lives.

* Decatur's wife, nearly insane with grief, eventually closed their palatial home and, many years later, died in a convent in Georgetown.[16]

During his tenure on the Board of Navy Commissioners, Porter devoted much attention to the cause of Latin-American independence.* Between 1816 and 1820 he worked, not so much to liberate most of a hemisphere from European overlords, as to promote the interests of a minority faction in a single country of South America—the Carrera brothers in Chile. He had met Chilean dictator José Miguel Carrera and been treated most cordially by him during his first visit to Valparaiso in 1813. But by the time he returned to Chile a few months later, Carrera had been ousted by the opposing faction, whose titular head was Governor Lastra. The latter had voiced no objection to British violation of Chilean neutrality when Captain James Hillyar captured Porter's *Essex*. Shortly thereafter, Hillyar had easily persuaded the Lastra administration to sign the Treaty of Lircay with the Peruvian royalists which restored Spanish authority in Chile, in circumstances already described. The contrast in the behavior of the two Chilean factions toward him permanently solidified Porter's outlook on that country's politics: the *Carreristas* were pro-American, independence-minded, and democratic; their opponents were pro-British, pro-Spanish, and monarchical.

Hillyar's diplomatic triumph was only temporary. On 22 July 1814, less than two months after his departure from Chile, a coup d'etat brought José Miguel Carrera back to power for the second and last time, and the Treaty of Lircay was nullified. Within ten weeks, three factors ruined Carrera: increased factionalism in Chile, intervention by Argentina, and invasion from Peru. First, Lastra was being elbowed aside as leader of the anti-*Carreristas* in Chile by Bernardo O'Higgins, illegitimate son of Ambrosio O'Higgins, an Irishman who had risen from humble origins to Spanish Viceroy of Peru. The younger O'Higgins saw that he might be permanently eclipsed by José Miguel Carrera, and knew that his future depended on dislodging his rival. Second, either directly or indirectly, power in Argentina was being assumed by José de San Martín, the man who eventually liberated lower South America. San Martín interested himself in Chilean internal politics, and his antipathy toward Carrera steadily increased. Third, late in September 1814 a royalist army from Peru marched into Chile.

In the face of invasion, Carrera and O'Higgins put aside their differences, and their combined armies met the Peruvians at Rancagua. After two days of battle, 1 and 2 October, the *Chileños* were routed, and with only a remnant of their forces, Carrera and O'Higgins fled across the

---

* For some inexplicable and inexcusable reason, David Dixon Porter's *Memoir* omits this important aspect of his father's life.

The Winning of Chilean
Independence~1812-1825
X~Battles

SOUTHERN and WESTERN SOUTH AMERICA: 1812~1825

Andes into Argentina.* O'Higgins had little trouble in persuading San Martín that the disaster at Rancagua had been Carrera's fault.

With doors locked and bolted against him in Chile and Argentina, the defeated and discredited José Miguel Carrera decided that the best way for him to recoup his political fortunes was to go to the United States, enlist men, borrow money, and gain the support of the American government. So destitute that he had to pawn his wife's jewels to pay for his passage, he sailed from Buenos Aires on 9 November 1815, arriving at Baltimore on 17 January 1816.[18] He anticipated unrestrained support from the two influential Americans who had collaborated with him so closely in Chile: Joel R. Poinsett and David Porter. But Poinsett, who had commanded a detachment of Carrera's troops while officially representing the United States, now refused to commit himself. Apparently he had become so discouraged by the factionalism in Chilean politics that he washed his hands of the whole business and would neither sponsor Carrera nor provide him with urgently needed funds. He did no more than offer occasional advice, and keep closely in touch with developments through his correspondence with Porter. The reluctance of the influential South Carolinian to act in his favor was a crushing blow to Carrera.

Porter, on the other hand, devoted considerable time and effort toward advancing the cause of his Chilean acquaintance. There seems no reason to doubt that Porter really liked Carrera, and was sincerely interested in promoting the latter's brand of Latin-American independence. But, by now, he was feeling the financial pinch that eventually became so painful. He could advance no funds, and probably used Carrera in hopes of making his fortune. Avid for another chance at prize money, he even considered offering his services to Carrera's navy, but sensibly held back. The collapse of *Carrerista* prospects in 1817 and 1818 ended any such speculation.

Whether for selfish or altruistic reasons, and probably a combination of the two, Porter lent significant aid to the *Chileño*. Always ready with counsel, he impressed upon Carrera the importance of swinging American public opinion to his side, and emphasized the desirability of his learning English. Carrera followed Porter's advice about the language so assiduously that after five months in the United States he was writing his own articles for the press. More important than the advice he gave was the fact that, as a Navy Commissioner, Porter had entry to the highest

---

* The action at Rancagua was part of the temporary Spanish reconquest of rebellious Latin America during 1814 and 1815 which restored the authority of King Ferdinand VII almost everywhere except in Buenos Aires.

places in government. Within a month of Carrera's arrival, Porter had introduced him to Secretary of State James Monroe and taken him to meet informally with President Madison at the White House. The President greeted Carrera so cordially and listened to him so attentively that José Miguel wrote his brother Luis, "I was received as a man working for the same cause as they." Madison was only being polite: he had no intention of intervening in Latin America at a time when Spain appeared to be reestablishing its rule there, and he certainly had no inclination to meddle in any Chilean factional dispute. Porter may have been responsible for Carrera's subsequent trip to Lexington, Kentucky, to visit Henry Clay, champion of U.S. recognition of Latin-American rebel governments. Clay was affable, but refused to commit himself any more than the President had done. Eventually he would opt for Carrera's enemies.[19]

Besides providing Carrera with top-level introductions, Porter formed a triumvirate to assist him. For the first year of its existence, the group, which consisted of Porter, John Skinner of Baltimore, and Baptis Irvine of New York, operated on a loose and informal basis, but by 1817 it had tightened its organization and decided upon specific objectives. The cabal always centered its efforts in Baltimore, many of whose most prominent citizens had a personal financial stake in the maintenance of disorder in the Caribbean and farther south, because it enabled them to continue their profitable and quasi-legal privateering activities. All three members of the cabal had Baltimore affiliations. Porter had spent much of his early life there, Skinner was a longtime resident, and Irvine had previously published a newspaper in that city. Only Skinner still lived in Baltimore, but daily mail service kept him in easy and rapid communication with Irvine in New York and Porter in Washington.

Among Carrera's American supporters, John Skinner was particularly important. He did what Porter could not do at all, and what Irvine could do to only a limited extent: he provided most of the financial backing with which Carrera could sign on volunteers and buy ships, guns, and ammunition—without which his attempted comeback in South America was hopeless. Skinner appears to have combined the hard-headed ruthlessness of a mid-nineteenth-century entrepreneur with an ultra-idealism characteristic of the revolutionary epoch. The first of those aspects was illustrated by his flagrant privateering in Latin America which compromised American neutrality so thoroughly that he was indicted in Baltimore for piracy. His acquittal was not entirely unanticipated after he maneuvered the appointment of his father-in-law, Judge Theodorick Bland, to preside over the trial. His idealistic side might seem to be illustrated by his loaning Carrera $4,000, but the image fades when the terms of the loan are examined: repayment in specie twelve months later at one hundred per cent interest.[20]

Nevertheless, Skinner was unquestionably a real liberal in his advocacy of Latin-American independence. "It is . . . well known that it is enough for a man to go into Mr. Skinner's house and call himself a Latin American Patriot to find welcome and assistance. . . ." Except for a couple of others who made small loans, only Skinner provided Carrera with a large amount of cash, exorbitant though his conditions might have been. Like Porter, he could and did introduce the *Chileño* to luminaries —John Jacob Astor, Eli Whitney, Edmond Charles "Citizen" Genet, and Aaron Burr.* It was primarily the avenues opened by Skinner that gave Carrera access to the foreign soldiers of fortune who accompanied him to South America. Some West Point cadets offered him their services, but he wisely ignored their juvenile ardor. John Quincy Adams described John Skinner:

> He is a man of mingled character, of daring and pernicious principles, of restless and rash temper, and yet of useful and honorable enterprise. Ruffian, patriot and philanthropist are so blended in him that I cannot appreciate him without a mingled sentiment of detestation and esteem. I consider him as the originator and cause of all the Baltimore piracies which have injured and still dishonor this nation. He has infected not only that city, but the moral feelings of the whole community. . . .[21]

Irish-born Baptis Irvine, who rounded off the pro-Carrera circle, was thoroughly radical in his advocacy of contemporary issues. He took Carrera to many meetings where the Chilean aroused enthusiasm among reformers by pledging, with the aid of a few private citizens from the United States, to remake Latin-American society. Irvine's most important contribution to Carrera's cause was that he provided him entry to American newspapers. Porter and Skinner also helped him in that respect, and it may have been as a result of the former's ministrations that, a few days after his arrival in the United States, Carrera was interviewed by Hezekiah Niles, publisher of the influential *Niles National Register*. Not long after that interview, however, Niles swung behind Henry Clay in support of the O'Higgins faction and closed his columns to Carrera. But Irvine allowed Carrera to write at will for the New York *Columbian,* of which he was part owner, as well as for both the journals with which he had formerly been associated, the Baltimore *Whig* and the Washington *Gazette*.

---

* Burr and Carrera fascinated one another, but nothing came of Burr's offer to accompany Carrera back to Chile.

In the articles he wrote, Carrera naturally laid the responsibility for his ouster and exile at the feet of Bernardo O'Higgins and his Argentine supporters, and he cloaked his obvious bias by using such signatures as an Argentine "gentleman of the first consideration," or a "South American gentleman of the first respectability." [22]

By loaning Carrera $500, apparently on non-usurious terms, Irvine proved himself more altruistic than either Porter or Skinner, but he too had selfish motives. He asked that, in the event Carrera returned to power in Chile, he be given a monopoly on that country's exports, and also aspired to a diplomatic appointment in Latin America.* The judicious John Quincy Adams, whose evaluation of Skinner is quoted above, wrote of Irvine: ". . . one of the men with whom this age abounds—a fanatic of liberty for the whole human race—honest, but with a brain always in a snarl—with learning just enough to be pedantic, and temper just enough to be indiscreet; bitter in his dislikes and unmeasured in his resentments —but withal indefatigable, industrious and persevering. . . ." [23]

With the aid of Porter, Skinner, and Irvine, Carrera was able to stay in the United States for eleven months. Although he never satisfactorily solved his financial dilemma, sometimes being reduced to borrowing from one creditor to pay another, he finally scraped together enough money to buy a 28-gun frigate, a schooner, and two brigantines. Accompanied by some seventy soldiers of fortune and "a dozen venturesome teachers, artists, and mechanics," Carrera sailed on 5 December 1816 and arrived in Buenos Aires on the following 9 February.

His timing could not have been worse. Juan Martín Pueyrredón, backed by Carrera's enemies San Martín and O'Higgins, had just seized control in Argentina. During his tenure in office from 1816 to 1819, Pueyrredón viewed Carrera as a troublemaker, and brusquely turned down his suggestion that an all-water expedition sail around Cape Horn to attack Valparaiso. Indeed, Carrera landed in Buenos Aires just as the armies of San Martín and O'Higgins were crossing the Andes into Chile. On 12 February 1817, the combined rebel forces thrashed the Peruvian royalists at Chacabuco, thereby establishing de facto Chilean independence, although it was not officially proclaimed until the next February. Carrera, of course, played no part in this triumph; in fact, Pueyrredón confiscated his ships, recruited his men, and finally ordered the arrest of all three Carrera brothers. Luis got away, but the other two were taken. José Miguel, however, soon managed to escape into Montevideo, Uru-

---

* During 1818–1819 Irvine was U.S. Special Agent to Venezuela, but John Quincy Adams sourly commented that he had accomplished his mission "assuredly without having done any good."

guay, but Juan José was held for a while. Pueyrredón then sent a two-man mission, headed by Manuel de Aguirre, to the United States to counter any lingering effects of Carrera's sojourn there, and to seek active support for his regime in Buenos Aires.[24]

When Porter, Skinner, Irvine, and other pro-*Carreristas* learned of these dismal events, they were shocked into more concentrated and unified action, and in 1817 formed "the first pressure group in the United States for the support of a South American state." Porter redoubled his efforts among Washington officials, and in getting favorable publicity for Carrera. He wrote Poinsett that he had free access to the columns of John Skinner's *Maryland Gazette* which "teem with S[outh] A[merican] affairs, and the Editor is devoted to the Patriotic cause." Irvine laid down a propaganda barrage in his New York organ. It was John Skinner, however, who assumed the main burden of whipping up opinion against the "persecution of the gallant Carrera." Under the non de plume "Lautaro," * he wrote a series of seven letters which appeared in the Richmond *Whig* and the Baltimore *Patriot* without arousing much attention. It was not until they were reprinted during 1817 and 1818 in the *National Intelligencer* and the Buenos Aires *El Censor,* that they drew national and international comment. Porter settled the identity of "Lautaro" by jotting a note in the margin of a letter to Poinsett, "Confidentially: Mr. J. Skinner postmaster of Baltimore is the author of Lautaro. . . ."[25]

The Lautaro Letters combined far-sighted internationalism with intense parochialism. Skinner's world outlook might be seen in an idea incorporated in the Monroe Doctrine: that between all parts of the American hemisphere, under the leadership of the United States, there exists a natural affinity of interest which must exclude European concepts. He was sure that the chief foreign threat to the Western Hemisphere came from the "arts, intrigues, and corruptions of the British Government." Skinner exhibited parochialism in his contention that only one regime, Carrera's, in one country, Chile, was worthy of American recognition and support. The government at Buenos Aires and its Chilean adherents were presented throughout the letters as monarchical, pro-Spanish, and pro-British. In a couple of the letters Skinner shrugged off the question of foreign intervention: he maintained that Britain, recalling its difficulties during the recent War of 1812, would abstain from such action, and that if Spain intervened, so much the better, as that would give the United States an opportunity to adjudicate by force its Spanish frontiers.

---

* Lautaro was a Chilean Indian who led a rebellion against the Spaniards in the middle of the sixteenth century.

In a long communication to Poinsett, Porter summed up what the American *Carreristas* hoped to accomplish by this barrage of publicity:

> I had intended to have written you fully agreeable to promise on S[outh] A[merican] affairs, but the plot thickened so rapidly that I knew not where to begin. . . . I take on myself to say that I first started this host of writers in favor of our taking a decided stand in the affairs of S America. The pieces in defense of Carrera . . . were written [some] by myself . . . some by a friend of mine—and that same friend is the author of Lautaro. . . . We want to make it appear that the interests of the U.S. are jeopardized by the machinations of England through their agents, that we are the *natural* allies of S America [,] that unless we aid them they will throw themselves into the arms of our worst enemy. . . . That no time is to be lost—that England has been so long at work to effect her object &c. &c. &c.—with these views we have taken some pains to heat the public mind as well as to enlighten it, and by so doing we hoped to produce some effect on both Congress and Govt [the Monroe administration]. The views of the latter I believe to be in some degree (to a great degree) in conformity to our own. . . .[26]

When Porter used the term "Govt" in the letter quoted above, he was probably thinking not only of President Monroe, but also of Henry Clay, to whom Skinner dedicated the Lautaro Letters. But Clay remained aloof. He had become a whole-hearted supporter of Pueyrredón, San Martín, and O'Higgins, and was working closely with Manuel de Aguirre, envoy from Buenos Aires. He later announced in Congress that Carrera, far from being a martyr, was personally responsible for the debacle at Rancagua and the ensuing reconquest of Chile by the royalists. He characterized the Carreras as "hostile" to the Buenos Aires government, and declared that their "power of doing mischief" had had to be curtailed. He became especially indignant in the spring of 1818 when his enemies in Congress quoted Lautaro on the subject of dictatorial tendencies in Buenos Aires and lack of popular support for the government there, and thus helped defeat his bill to recognize Argentine independence.[27]

The two antagonistic factions were splitting U.S. supporters of Latin-American revolutions. Porter and the other *Carreristas* were arrayed against Henry Clay and his followers, who backed O'Higgins and his Argentine allies. Both factions saw opportunity for profit when the Monroe administration announced in mid-1817 that a fact-finding mission was to be sent to South America. It seems clear that Monroe hoped this group would not only clarify the confused situation there, but would help quiet temporarily the public clamor over the question of Latin-American recognition, and thus allow Secretary of State John Quincy Adams to complete his delicate negotiations with Spain over the Floridas and the Spanish-American boundaries to the west.

Joel R. Poinsett was the President's first choice for the mission.

Claiming prior responsibilities in his home state, the South Carolinian refused to accept, but promptly notified Porter that the mission was being planned, for which he was later thanked. The announcement that Caesar A. Rodney and John Graham had been selected as members of the mission gave the *Carreristas* little reason to applaud. Rodney, who had served as Attorney General of the United States from 1807 to 1811, was a prominent administration supporter from Delaware, and a suspicion that he agreed with Clay's pro-Argentine policy was soon proven correct. John Graham was a close friend of Madison and he spoke Spanish fluently. He had been Chief Clerk of the State Department from 1807 to 1817 and, during the few days' interval between the Madison and Monroe administrations, he had been honored with the appointment of Acting Secretary of State. His opinions about Latin America were not known. Nor were the Secretary of State's original instructions to the mission comforting to Porter and his cronies. Rodney and Graham were ordered to go "with impartial neutrality" to Buenos Aires and Montevideo to learn all they could: they might acquire "useful information" about Chile, but were not to visit there.[28]

Henry M. Brackenridge, who had defended Porter's participation in local battles on Nukahiva Island in 1813, was selected as the mission's Secretary. He had just published a lengthy pamphlet, *South America: A Letter on the Present State of that Country, to James Monroe.** Only a few of the points made therein were likely to be acceptable to Porter, Skinner, and Irvine. They would concur with Brackenridge's argument that the United States, as the natural leader of the Western Hemisphere, must champion the Americas against Europe, especially Great Britain. They would find less palatable his conclusion that the United States should not intervene in Latin America, for that might trigger European counterintervention. And, since, at that time, O'Higgins was in control of Chile, they would not agree with his recommendation that the United States should immediately recognize the independence of that country. Brackenridge's opinions on South American political organization would be equally obnoxious to them, for he judged it inconsequential which form of government these new Latin-American countries adopted: republics might be preferable, but the United States could live with monarchies or dictatorships, provided they were independent of European control.

---

* This pamphlet was reprinted in Brackenridge's definitive work on the subject. A. P. Whitaker states incorrectly that Brackenridge was "connected with the David Porter–Joseph Skinner propaganda machine." He calls John Stuart Skinner "Joseph H." throughout.

Nevertheless, Porter was confident that Brackenridge could be swung to his side and he greeted the appearance of the latter's pamphlet with a trick play. He wrote him an affable letter and, after claiming to have become a better "patriot" since reading his tract, continued:

> . . . I thank you most sincerely for the treat you have afforded me—my ideas accord precisely with yours on the subject of S[outh] American affairs, and as to the conduct this Government should adopt in regard to the independents—the conclusions you draw from facts, and your reasonings, are so just that I have no doubt that your production will attract, not only the attention of "the wise and upright Statesman" [Monroe] to whom it is addressed but that of the people of the United States generally. . . .

He ended with an invitation to Brackenridge to come to dinner immediately and "unceremoniously": "I have sent my carriage in the hope that you might favor me with your company today." Brackenridge must have known that, basically, Porter disagreed with him, and he was understandably wary. There is no evidence that they met. It seems obvious that Porter was trying to draw Brackenridge into the Carrera fold prior to his departure for South America as Secretary of Monroe's mission. His attempt failed, to be sure, but at the time Porter could still afford to be sanguine about his influence, not only on Brackenridge, but on the Monroe administration: "Being near the govt., and obtaining a knowledge of its views and having some knowledge of the situation in Chili . . . I have an opportunity of biasing to some degree measures respecting that country and S[outh] A[merican] affairs generally." [29]

To what extent Porter was directly responsible for the change is not clear, but late in 1817 the complexion of the Monroe mission became more favorable to Carrera, both in its composition and in the instructions it was given. Judge Theodorick Bland, Skinner's father-in-law, was appointed the third member of the mission. His opinion on South American politics had already been formed: he looked upon "Carrera and his followers as martyrs, the O'Higgins faction as despots, and the Buenos Aires government as robbers." New instructions from Secretary of State John Quincy Adams allowed the inclusion of Chile in the mission's itinerary, and any member who so desired could go there "over land." *

Rodney, Graham, Bland, and Brackenridge sailed from the United States during December 1817, and late the next February arrived in Montevideo, where José Miguel Carrera still chafed in exile. Porter had ar-

---

* Practically simultaneously with the departure of the mission, Monroe dispatched John B. Prevost as U.S. Special Agent to Buenos Aires, Chile, and Peru. Prevost eventually sided with Henry Clay and others who backed O'Higgins and the Buenos Aires regime.[30]

ranged to have the mission meet him, and notified Carrera to that effect. About all that was learned from the Chilean was that Pueyrredón, San Martín, O'Higgins, and their followers were a "pack of scoundrels." By the time the mission reached Buenos Aires on 3 March 1818, it was already hopelessly divided; Bland and Brackenridge were barely speaking to one another. For the next couple of months the four men went their separate ways on interviews and research. Bland spent some of his time in Argentina trying to collect from the Pueyrredón government the $4,000 that his son-in-law, John Skinner, had loaned Carrera. He argued that Buenos Aires was responsible since it had seized Carrera's ships, but received no satisfaction.[31]

These were exciting times in which to be in lower South America. On 19 March, a little more than a fortnight after the mission arrived, the Peruvian royalists routed O'Higgins' army at Cancha Rayada near Talca in Chile, and panic swept through both Chile and Argentina. Then, only a few weeks later, on 5 April, at Maipú, near Santiago, San Martín thrashed the Peruvians in what proved to be the decisive battle for the permanent liberation of Chile.*

On 24 April, amid the celebrations attending the news from Maipú, Rodney, Graham, and Brackenridge sailed from Buenos Aires for the United States. At the same time, Bland crossed the Andes into Chile, where he approached Bernardo O'Higgins about the loan that Skinner had extended to Carrera, and had better luck than he did in Buenos Aires. Apparently, O'Higgins, then dictator of Chile, forced Ignacio Carrera, José Miguel's father, to pay the debt, but whether the principal alone was repaid or the principal with one hundred per cent interest cannot be ascertained from available documentation. With his mission in Chile completed, Bland left on 6 May for Argentina, where he stayed until sailing for home on 15 July.[32]

The Monroe mission cannot have been of much assistance in the formulation of U.S. policy toward South America. Disagreement about both the situation there and recommendations for future action was practically total among its members, as is proven by the production of four separate reports and a two-volume book. Rodney, Graham, and Bland filed reports, as did Joel R. Poinsett, who was not a member of the mission and had not even been in South America for four years; Brackenridge wrote the two volumes. John Quincy Adams observed that the only point upon which all were agreed was that Spain could not reconquer

---

* Between 1820 and the end of 1822 San Martín invaded Peru, took Lima, and proclaimed Peruvian independence, although years passed before royalist power there was completely eradicated.

Buenos Aires, and with delightful understatement remarked, "Of their internal conditions the aspect is more equivocal."

"More equivocal," indeed. In his long report, Rodney gave solid support to Pueyrredón and San Martín in Argentina and O'Higgins in Chile; President Monroe suspected that his description of the Buenos Aires regime had been painted in "coleur de rose." Graham found hardly anything to admire in either Argentina or Chile, and wrote only a brief summary. The 55,000 words penned by Bland added up to a relatively mild defense of Carrera and a rather restrained attack on O'Higgins. Even so, the latter complained to U.S. Special Agent John B. Prevost that Bland's conclusions were based upon "a mass of incidents loosely brought together and frequently collected from doubtful sources." Poinsett reported on conditions generally, and gave it as his opinion that U.S. recognition of any South American government would be premature.

In 1819 Brackenridge published his *Voyage to South America, Performed by Order of the American Government in the Years 1817 and 1818, in the Frigate Congress.* He enthusiastically backed the Buenos Aires government and emphatically denied that in Chile ". . . the Carrera party was friendly to the United States, while that of O'Higgins is inclined to the British." With Brackenridge publicly on the side of Clay's pro-Buenos Aires faction, Porter and his colleagues moved against him. Baptis Irvine, just back from Venezuela, where he had served as U.S. Special Agent, led the assault by anonymously publishing a tract with the agonizing title: *Strictures on a Voyage to South America as Indited by the "Secretary to the (Late) Mission to the La Plata." By a Friend of Truth and Sound Policy.* He described Brackenridge's volumes as "destitute of order, void of perspicacity, wanting in veracity, discolored with gall," and charged that "the spirit of intelligence has never breathed" on them.[33]

While his supporters and opponents in the United States were belaboring one another in print, the cause of José Miguel Carrera in South America was falling from the disastrous to the catastrophic. When he was in exile in Uruguay, his brothers Juan José and Luis, acting on their own, planned to leave Argentina for Chile in order to "kill the bastard" O'Higgins. They were still at Mendoza in Argentina when their plot was discovered. The government at Buenos Aires ordered their arrest and had them shot on 8 April 1818, just three days after Chilean independence had been assured at Maipú. O'Higgins struck hard at prominent *Carreristas* in Chile, executing some and imprisoning others. In an act of consummate meanness, San Martín forced the elderly and dying Ignacio Carrera to pay the costs of killing and burying his two sons.[34]

These events soon became known in the United States, yet more than six months later, Porter acted in a manner that can be described only as fatuous. He wrote to President Monroe: "A great revolution is about taking place and ere this Chilli with Carrera at the head . . . may be free and independent. I know the love the people bear to him, and that Chilli is better prepared for a republican form of government than any of the Provinces of South America." One of the last literary efforts made by the *Carreristas* in the United States was Irvine's protest about the "Robespierrean executions" perpetrated by the regimes of Pueyrredón and O'Higgins. He made the protest in his *Strictures* against Brackenridge's *Voyage:* ripping into "the despotic government" of Buenos Aires, he lamented that it had "become worse (if possible) than that of Spain: *because Buenos Ayres tyrannizes in the name of independence. . . .*"

Meanwhile, the frantic José Miguel Carrera had left Uruguay and plunged into an Argentine civil war, seeing there his only chance to recoup his political fortunes and avenge his brothers. He terrorized the Argentine backcountry with irregular troops, some of them Indians, and committed atrocities which form a dishonorable anticlimax to his generally honorable career. He was finally taken at Mendoza, the same city in which his brothers had been captured and executed, and on 4 September 1821, he was shot by an Argentine firing squad. His body was dismembered, and parts of it were nailed to trees in the city's streets.[35]

Well before "the gallant Carrera" fell, Porter and others of his faction turned away from the crusade for Latin-American independence. To some degree, Porter's labors as part of the pro-Carrera bloc had worked against this movement. His group fell into dispute with those in the United States who backed the Pueyrredón, San Martín, and O'Higgins *juntas.* American policy in behalf of the liberation of the continent might have been unified, had it not been immobilized by partisanship. Each bloc devoted most of its efforts toward downgrading the heroes and denigrating the work of the other. Four or five years of factional charges and countercharges blunted American enthusiasm for the Latin-American rebels, and so confused the issues that most people in the United States adopted a "wait and see" attitude that allowed Britain to lay the groundwork for its eventual economic supremacy in South America. Specifically, the partly altruistic, partly selfish insistence of Porter and his confreres, that in all Latin America the defeated leader of a minority in a small and remote country was the only rightful recipient of U.S. recognition and support, made it difficult for the Monroe administration to give even moral support to other, more populous, more important areas of South America, such, for example, as Argentina.

But from another point of view, Porter's labors may have served his country well. His efforts as part of the pro-Carrera cabal from 1816 to

1820 neutralized the attempts of Clay and his colleagues to have the government at Buenos Aires immediately recognized by the United States, a move that might have required intervention in Argentina. The slackening in the momentum of American public demand to recognize rebel governments gave John Quincy Adams time to complete successfully his negotiations with Luis de Onís, Spanish Minister to the United States, which resulted in the Transcontinental Treaty of 1819, giving the American republic clear title to all the Floridas and an acceptable western boundary. A more vigorous U.S. policy in support of Latin-American revolutionaries could well have meant war with Spain and that, in turn, might have had ramifications such as embroilment with Great Britain and, perhaps, even the intervention of the powerful nations in the reactionary Concert of Europe. Even if, as a protagonist of Carrera, Porter helped to cloud issues, he kept alive U.S. interest in Latin America. Finally, his emphasis on the potential danger to the United States arising from the machinations of Britain and the continental European powers in South America may have contributed significantly to the concepts of intercontinental solidarity and to the special hemispheric ideology spelled out by the Monroe Doctrine in December 1823.

None of his efforts to supplement his naval pay having succeeded, by late 1822 David Porter had come to the conclusion that the best way to escape financial embarrassment was to return to sea duty. Apparently, the Navy Department permitted him to resign from the Board of Navy Commissioners and appointed him to command the West India Squadron, effective 31 December 1822. Announcement of his new job aroused considerable comment in the press, and *Niles National Register* spoke for the majority when it hailed "the gallant commodore" who had given up a sinecure at home to accept a dangerous and unhealthy task afloat. Once again, it said, he had proven his devotion to his country, and "if the measure of his success equals that of his zeal . . . [it] will do honors to the American name."[1]

The setting and circumstances of his assignment must have seemed familiar to him. Ever since the outbreak of the Wars of the French Revolution, the Gulf of Mexico and the Caribbean had been as disorderly as any areas in the world. So Porter had found them around the turn of the nineteenth century when he had first shipped there, and from 1808 to 1810 when he had commanded the naval station at New Orleans. If anything, the West Indies had become even more chaotic since the Napoleonic Wars ended in 1815. The catalyst was the interminable, if intermittent, warfare between Spain and its former dependencies of Mexico, Colombia, and Venezuela. The Spaniards tried to eke out their naval resources by commissioning privateers to harry all trade with their erstwhile colonies. Even worse, they imposed some of the most patently illegal blockades in history. When they announced the blockade of more than 1,200 miles of coastline in northern South America, John Quincy Adams, noting that the force available to execute this ambitious project totaled one frigate, one sloop of war, and one brig, quite justifiably commented that it was no blockade at all, but "a war of extermination against all neutral commerce."

Spanish activity was only part of the problem faced by nonbelligerent traders in the West Indies: Spain's rebellious colonies were striking back at their former masters, and both Mexico and Colombia planned to build regular navies. In the early 1820s, however, privateering was the only means by which they could possibly cripple Spanish maritime power. Yet, as had been the case since the 1790s, the term "privateering" was meaningless, since most of those who practised that occupation were pirates, whose letters of marque were either not recognized or illegal, and who were quite incapable of differentiating between the inimical red and gold standard of Spain and the neutral red, white, and blue of Britain's Union Jack; the white and gold of Bourbon France's fleur-de-lis; or the red, white, and blue of the United States. Furthermore, the tactics used by these privateers, pirates, freebooters, corsairs, buccaneers, or picaroons were similar to those used in the same waters a century or two before by L'Ollonais, Morgan, or "Blackbeard" Teach. David Dixon Porter described these activities as:

> . . . piracy of the worst kind, filling the West Indian annals with accounts of horrors . . . the coasts of Cuba, Porto Rico, St. Domingo, and the Spanish main, were the resorts of merciless freebooters who plundered and burned vessels with impunity, and frequently murdered their passengers and crews, after inflicting upon them the most shocking brutalities. Families bound for the West Indies, in merchant vessels, disappeared from the face of the earth, and often the only clue to the fate of passengers and crew, would be the charred hulk of their vessels drifting about the gulf of Mexico.

Accounts of piratical attacks filled the pages of the newspapers of the time. The following account is typical: on 15 May 1822, the American brig *Aurilla Howland* was boarded by eighty to a hundred men from two schooners. ". . . the passengers and crew were cruelly treated, beat with swords and pistols, and one of the former was hung up at the yard arm, and then dropped into the water, apparently lifeless. The vessel was plundered of every thing of the least value. . . . The women were brutally ravished, and the most shocking excesses inflicted on their bodies. After committing the most wasteful and indiscriminate plunder, and . . . acts of the most barbarous enormity and shameful indulgences, they ordered the captain to cut his cable at 10, next morning and be off." A statistically-minded Philadelphian, who is reported to have kept a careful count of "piratical acts" committed in the West Indies during the eight years from 1815 to 1822, stated that they numbered precisely "three thousand and two." [2]

As long as Spain and its former colonies persisted in using such illegal measures against each other's commerce, normal trade in the Caribbean and the Gulf of Mexico was almost impossible. Even before 1820, both Britain and France had found it imperative to dispatch squadrons to the West Indies for the protection of their merchantmen. By the time the American West India Squadron was established in 1822, the French had withdrawn, but the British were still there and cooperated with the Americans.

When the navies of London and Paris moved against the pirates, the latter turned more and more of their attention to unprotected American vessels. Especially hard hit was the shipping of New Orleans, for that port was enjoying a tremendous boom, and was well on its way toward becoming the second export city of the nation. The merchants of New Orleans and of other American ports petitioned for relief from the depredations, and before long American naval officers were complaining about their impotency to act against the pirates. These combined appeals called upon the government to protect American shipping from illegal seizures, whether by pirates or by warships patrolling in paper blockades, and to safeguard the transportation of specie from the mines of Latin America, either from one port to another in that area, or from there to the United States. Since gold and silver were the products most hotly coveted by pirates, ships carrying such cargoes were the most vulnerable to attack and only the Navy was strong enough to afford them protection. Although naval officers were not authorized to perform this service, they frequently did so and were paid a small percentage of the value of any specie carried safely to its destination. Consequently, naval officers were among the loudest advocates of legalized specie-carrying.

On 26 February 1819, after little debate, Congress responded to these pressures and passed a bill entitled, "An Act to protect the commerce of the United States, and to punish the crime of piracy." On the following 3 March President Monroe signed it into law. This action permitted the Navy to convoy American merchantmen, including those carrying specie, and to recapture American citizens and vessels "unlawfully" taken "upon the high seas." [3]

A direct consequence of this legislation was the establishment of a permanent U.S. West India Squadron. Its first commodore was Captain James Biddle, Porter's old acquaintance, if not his old friend. Biddle's orders, dated 26 March 1822, called for him to protect American trade by assailing pirates off the coasts of Cuba and Puerto Rico, as well as along the mainland from Veracruz, Mexico, to La Guaira, near Caracas, Venezuela. To carry out his mission, he was given a sizable squadron, consisting of two frigates, two sloops, and four schooners, mounting in all 178 guns and carrying 1,330 officers and men.

Even though Biddle captured some thirty pirate vessels, his ten-month tenure as Commodore of the West India fleet has to be character-ized as a failure. First, he suffered a humiliating loss when his schooner *Alligator* was attacked by pirates; Lieutenant William H. Allen and four sailors were killed. Second, his ships drew too much water to operate im-mediately offshore, the only way in which they could have coped with the small, swift, shallow-draft enemy vessels. Third, the Spaniards would not give him permission to go ashore. He recognized that, so long as his crews chased pirates onto the beach, only to watch them dash into the bush with impunity, he could accomplish nothing of real importance. Biddle tried to cajole the Spanish Governor of Cuba into allowing Americans to terminate the hunt ashore, but did not succeed: "I . . . propose that your excellency should . . . sanction the landing upon the coast of Cuba of our boats and men, when in pursuit of pirates," he wrote. "This measure is indispensable to the entire suppression of piracy, and is not intended in any manner to infringe upon the territorial rights of your excellency." The governor replied by pledging full cooperation against the pirates in various other ways, but as to U.S. armed forces landing on Cuban soil for whatever purpose, "I cannot and must not consent to it." [4]

Biddle's request and the Spanish governor's answer highlighted a continuing controversy between Spain and the United States during these years. The Spaniards took the position that no nation able to prevent it, could allow the soldiers and sailors of another country to invade its terri-tory without specific request and permission. Even if any Spanish officials had been inclined to grant such a liberty, they probably would have been first overruled and then punished by Madrid. The American stand was well delineated in 1818, when John Quincy Adams called attention to the fact that Spain's unwillingness or inability to meet its international obli-gation to preserve law and order in West and East Florida had justified Andrew Jackson's invasion of those Spanish colonies. This no-man's-land between Spanish insistence on the rights of national sovereignty and American stress upon meeting international responsibility constituted an impasse for both Biddle and Porter. As the former saw clearly the unlike-lihood that the pirates could be defeated if they could not be followed ashore, he probably did not regret relinquishing his command to Porter less than a year after he had assumed it.

Porter was plagued not only by the same troubles that had frustrated Biddle, but by new complexities that arose out of the changed interna-tional situation at the time of and immediately after pronouncement of the Monroe Doctrine. Guided by the reactionary Quadruple Alliance, post-Napoleonic Europe maintained "legitimacy" as one of its major standards: the "legitimate" ruler must be restored to and kept on his ancestral throne. Obviously, revolutions in Spanish America were a direct challenge to this concept, and the situation worsened in 1823 when they were duplicated inside Spain itself. When Ferdinand VII, who had been restored to the Spanish throne after the defeat of Napoleon's forces in Spain, was ousted by his long-suffering subjects, France sent its armies across the Pyrenees in support of his rule. French forces were everywhere victorious, and their capture of Cadiz in October 1823 virtually ended revolutionary opposition in Spain.[5] Now that one of the reactionary great powers of Europe had shown itself willing and able to restore Bourbon rule in Spain, might it not try to restore Bourbon rule from Mexico to Argentina, and perhaps take a West Indian island or two as the commission due the friendly broker?

Few prospects could be more repugnant to the administration in Washington. Casting about for the best means to avert any such occurrence, President Monroe and several members of his Cabinet at first harkened to British Foreign Secretary George Canning's proposal that England and America issue a joint statement against any European intervention aimed at restoring Spanish rule over its former dependencies in America. But Secretary of State John Quincy Adams viewed Canning's suggestion with cold suspicion, and recommended that the United States should act unilaterally. His proposal was soon accepted, and on 2 December 1823 the Monroe Doctrine was proclaimed. In that message, the United States announced that it would permit no further European colonization in the Western Hemisphere, but pledged itself neither to interfere with already established European possessions in the Americas nor to meddle in Europe's internal affairs.

Only in areas where the Latin-American revolutions were continuing was there any reasonable likelihood of a clash between the United States and the European powers. There, the delicate international equilibrium could be upset in a number of ways, one of which would be the invasion of any European colony by U.S. armed forces, no matter how valid the reasons for such action. Yet, piracy in those waters had to be terminated. Porter was in a difficult position. On the one hand, his refusal to act against the pirates with sufficient firmness and dispatch might be construed as dereliction of duty, and, on the other, his pursuit of them ashore might bring the United States into an undesired and unnecessary confrontation with one of the great powers of Europe. To maneuver himself successfully along this tightrope, he would have to apply calm judgment to each case and proceed with caution. Heretofore, those traits had not characterized his behavior.

Secretary of the Navy Smith Thompson's instructions to Porter, dated 1 February 1823, show two primary concerns: a recognition that the new commodore's responsibilities were conflicting, and an uneasy apprehension that he might be unable to handle them. Thompson's directive may be studied with admiration as a masterpiece of bureaucratic ambivalence which would make the Navy Department right and Porter wrong, should anything go amiss. The Secretary commenced by telling his Commodore that he was being sent to the West Indies "for the purpose of suppressing piracy and affording effectual protection for the citizens and commerce of the United States," then went on to warn him that he must always "observe the utmost caution not to encroach upon the rights of others." If he should be brought into "collision with any foreign power in relation to such rights," the Commodore was told, he must act "with as much moderation and forebearance as is consistent with the honor of your country and the just claims of its citizens."

The Secretary next issued some straightforward orders: Porter was to cooperate fully with foreign naval forces engaged in the same work as his American squadron; to establish his West Indian "depot" at Thompson's Island (Key West), unless he found a better location; and he was to notify Spanish authorities of his arrival off their coasts, assure them that he was only chasing pirates, and seek their "favorable and friendly support." The Secretary was sure that the Spaniards would cooperate, since "Pirates are considered, by the law of nations, the enemies of the human race."

Thompson then returned to ambivalences. He tried to draw a sharp differentiation between the privileges and responsibilities Porter had in pursuit of pirates in the settled areas of Spanish America and those he had in unsettled areas. Concerning the first, which the Secretary defined as occupied localities under Spanish jurisdiction where "a Government exists and is felt," Porter must never land unless he did so "in aid of and co-operation with" local officials. As to the second, he pointed out that the "banditti" often retreated to "uninhabited parts, to which they carry their plunder," and in such cases Porter was "at liberty to pursue them," but he should never go ashore, even on an empty coast, if that privilege had been denied him "by the competent authority of the local government."

Other points dealt with by the Secretary concerned prisoners, privateers, and convoys. Porter was to turn over to the Spaniards any prisoners taken, unless he had bona fide reasons to suspect that the local authorities would not "receive and prosecute" them. In such instance, he should keep his captives on board his ships, while he notified the Department of what he had done. He was ordered to procure from Madrid's authorities a list of all privateers sailing under Spanish commissions, so that he could ascertain the nature of their instructions in respect to American trade with "Mexico and the Colombian Republic." He must always remember that the United States refused to countenance paper blockades, that is to say, those not actually enforced by a superior force. Finally, Porter was to protect American merchantmen, and to convoy specie from Mexico to the United States.[6]

In sum, Thompson directed Porter to annihilate piracy and protect American commerce in the West Indies by utilizing every means at his disposal, except, of course, those which he should not. In the controversy over Porter's landing at Fajardo, Puerto Rico, almost two years later, Porter quoted Thompson's instructions to prove his commendable fidelity to orders, and the Navy Department quoted them to prove that he was guilty of a flagrant violation of orders.

Porter provided himself with the men and ships needed for his West Indian assignment. Two of the 1,150 officers and men he would command were particularly close to him, a foster son and a brother. Midshipman David Glasgow Farragut had asked to go along as Acting Lieutenant. Porter complied with the request and his young friend was shipping with him for the first time since he had left the blood-soaked boards of the *Essex* nine years before.

Also accompanying Porter was his younger brother, John, who is something of a mystery. He is almost never mentioned in David's voluminous correspondence * but, since David Glasgow Farragut served under him in the schooner *Greyhound*, Farragut's biographers are the chief sources of information about him. Evidently, he was often drunk and, when in that condition, he acted with a rash bravado. En route to the West Indies, the *Greyhound* ran into a savage storm, and John, well in his cups, refused to shorten sail. Farragut had to wait for him to disappear below before he could make the necessary adjustment to the rigging and thus save the ship. Off Puerto Rico, a couple of weeks later, John Porter manifested equal irrationality when a Royal Navy brig—much more powerful than the tiny *Greyhound*—sent a couple of shots across his bow, and he fired back. He may have been saved from immediate destruction solely by English unwillingness to create an incident. John Porter was sent home from the West Indies, evidently for drunkenness. Somehow he managed to get promoted to Master Commandant, but soon resigned, probably under duress. He lived in Watertown, Massachusetts, and when he died there in October 1831, he rated a one-line obituary in a Boston newspaper.[7]

---

* In a letter David Porter wrote to Evalina three years later, when he was in Mexico, he made one of his rare references to John: "I note what you say respecting my unfortunate brother and his family. It is a cause of great regret to me that he does not mend his ways, but what can I do?"

Biddle had discovered that trying to end West Indian piracy with deep-draft frigates was akin to swatting flies with a sixteen-pound sledge-hammer, so David Porter began reorganizing the squadron. He retired the heavy ships and kept three of Biddle's sloops, the *John Adams,* the *Hornet,* and the *Peacock,* flying his commodore's pennant from the *Peacock.* The schooners *Spark, Grampus,* and *Shark* were already in the West Indies waiting for him. In order to have enough vessels suitable for scouting the fleeing pirates in the swamps and estuaries along the Cuban and Puerto Rican coasts, he bought eight more schooners and ordered the construction of five special barges. He purchased the schooners in Baltimore for a total of $10,190: known as "bay boats," these small vessels averaged a little more than 50 tons and each one mounted three guns and carried thirty-one men. Their predatory responsibilities were emphasized by their names: *Fox, Greyhound, Jackall, Beagle, Terrier, Weasel, Wild Cat,* and *Ferret.* The barges he ordered were 20-oared, and with a gloomy, if unconscious, prescience of things to come during the next summer, he dubbed them *Musquito, Gnat, Midge, Sandfly,* and *Gallinipper.*[8]

In New York, he bought the *Decoy* and the *Sea Gull,* and these acquisitions completed his squadron. He fitted the *Decoy* with six guns, and earmarked her as his storeship. The miniscule steamer *Sea Gull,* a converted Hudson River ferryboat, has been described as having "high sides to keep the waves from washing over her decks and quenching her fires. Her side wheels, located amidships, were of a dimension equal to a third of her length. She had a stump of a mast forward and two tall funnels." She proved to be surprisingly fast, once making the voyage from Matanzas, Cuba, to Washington in nine days. Furthermore, she rendered invaluable service against the pirates, for she could be used when Porter's sailers were becalmed or when it was necessary to dispatch a vessel on a mission that involved too great a distance for oarsmen on the barges to row. The tiny *Sea Gull* deserves a place in history, for she was the first steam warship to engage in actual hostilities.*[9]

Porter's West India Squadron sailed from New York on 14 February 1823, and on 3 March arrived at St. Thomas Island, in what were then the Danish West Indies, now the Virgin Islands. The *Sea Gull* made a tremendous impression on the people of St. Thomas, the local paper marveling that she could traverse "almost the whole extent of the harbor . . . propelled by her machinery alone."[10]

---

* It will be recalled that in 1814 Porter had been assigned the steam frigate *Fulton,* but she never saw action. He seems to have been destined, one way or another, to command the first belligerent steamship.

The squadron then proceeded the short distance to Puerto Rico. On 4 March Lieutenant John Porter's *Greyhound* was sent into San Juan Harbor to ask Miguel de la Torre, Spanish Governor of Puerto Rico, for a list of all privateers operating under his letter of marque, and to await his answer. Two days later, the *Greyhound* having failed to return, the *Fox*, under Lieutenant William H. Cocke, was dispatched to put a little more pressure on Torre and, as she entered the harbor, a battery of San Juan's great fort opened up on her. The first shot missed its mark, but the second shattered Cocke's shoulder—a mortal wound. Four more shots were fired before the *Fox* managed to find safety under the guns of the fort. Although Porter quite justifiably called the killing of Cocke the act of a "dastard," he managed to control his temper, and contented himself with writing Governor Torre that he had been "much surprised to observe that six guns were fired," especially since "the character of the vessels could not have been misunderstood, as my squadron at the time of the departure of the *Fox* was lying in full view of the castle, with colors flying."

Torre replied that he was absent when the unfortunate episode took place, and that the officer who had been left in charge had orders not to allow any foreign ships to enter the harbor. The Governor explained that, during the previous year, an expedition against Spanish Puerto Rico had come in to St. Bartholomew Island under the American flag, and since then the Spaniards had become naturally suspicious of the approach of any armed vessels, no matter what their colors. Even so, Torre continued, there had been no intention of firing any but warning shots: either "the trembling of the sea [!], or some bad pointing," he said, must have been responsible for "depriving the United States of a citizen, your Excellency of an officer, and of filling Porto Rico with mourning, and myself with inexpressible sorrow." [11]

After ordering his officers to commemorate their fallen comrade by wearing "crape on the left arm and swords for one month," Porter sent the melancholy news to Washington. Secretary of State Adams called the Spanish action "utterly wanton and inexcusable," and demanded that Madrid arrange the "trial and punishment" of the officer responsible. Yet, almost nine months passed before the American Minister presented the Spanish government with an official protest against the "flagrant, wanton, and unprovoked" murder of Cocke. Apparently, Madrid took no action and Washington did not press the matter. Nevertheless, Cocke's death seems to have worked to his country's advantage in that Torre's harassment of American commerce became less severe. The Governor soon notified Porter that he was lifting the blockade—only a paper one, anyway—which he had maintained against neutral trade with the rebellious portions of former Spanish America, and was offering a pledge that he would not grant any more letters of marque to privateers.[12]

Long before these diplomatic exchanges were completed, Porter left San Juan and went with his fleet to Matanzas, in western Cuba. There, he divided the squadron into two flotillas and sent one to patrol the northern coasts and the other the southern coasts of Cuba and Haiti, while he went to Key West and implemented his instructions to establish a base there by building storehouses and a hospital.

Early spring in the Caribbean was delightful, but by June duty afloat was anything but pleasant. Porter's schooners, barges, and boats were fully occupied against the pirates, but his sailing vessels were frequently becalmed, and the humid heat made long-distance rowing almost impossible. Close to shore, there were worse aggravations. Clouds of mosquitoes and other insects delivered agonizing, infuriating, and continuous punishment that soon became lethal. Ashore, conditions were equally uncomfortable. Farragut later reminisced that, on one occasion, when he sallied into Cuba after escaping pirates, he had to cope with "the thick and almost impenetrable chaparral . . . ; marsh and bramble . . . ; the country very rocky . . . with sharp edges . . . ; thorns . . . ; the heat became so intense that Lieutenant Somerville . . . fainted . . . ; my pantaloons were glued to my legs, my jacket torn to shreds, and I was loaded with mud."

Amid a host of minor victories, the fleet scored a major success by capturing the pirate, Domingo, off Havana on 8 April 1823. Only eight days before, Domingo had seized a ship carrying mail addressed to the officers and men of Porter's squadron. He forwarded the letters with an accompanying note:

> You are a gallant set of fellows, and I have no wish to keep your letters from you but I will retain the miniature of Lieutenant G[ardner]'s wife, in case I shall meet the original. I think, if she looks like the picture, I will make love to her.

Perhaps it is fitting that Domingo, "the notorious head of this horde of desperadoes," was one of only two who escaped from the American trap with his life.[13]

Available evidence is conflicting, but it was probably during August 1823 that the barges *Gallinipper* and *Musquito* closed on a 60-ton schooner which proved to be the flagship of Diablito, the notorious pirate whose well-advertised atrocities had earned him his nickname.* After

---

* There is much confusion about when this episode took place, and an outside possibility that two, not one, pirates were involved. One naval historian places

brief and spiritless resistance, the pirates went over the side. One of the barges went after the swimming pirates, while the crew of the other boarded the schooner. As Diablito struggled in the water, he was recognized and shot, and all eighty-odd of his men were either killed or captured.[14]

Despite their triumphs, pirate-hunting was hard service for the commander as well as for his men. Porter lamented that his work was hampered not only by climate, terrain, and piratical opposition, but by the American press and Spanish officials. When an article that was published in New York criticized him for failing to end piracy, he replied that his problem lay in his inability to get Spanish permission to go ashore. In prose that soared like his "sea-birds," he observed that he and his men had to seek the "freebooters and murderers . . . not among civilized authority," but "among barren and desolate secret and retired places . . . among the roaring of the breakers and the screams of sea-birds." He also protested that advance notice of his operations printed in the American press gave the pirates ample opportunity to escape. *Niles National Register* gently corrected him in this stand, pointing out that the public's right to be informed must come first; then it sugar-coated its criticism with a paean stating that all Americans were grateful to the Commodore for his efforts, since no new successes in the West Indies or elsewhere "could add anything to his renown as a seaman or a soldier." [15]

Porter's argument that, for the most part, he accomplished what he did in spite of, not because of, Spanish assistance, was certainly valid. Not only were local Spanish authorities concerned about what would happen to their careers if they permitted American armed forces to invade territory under their jurisdiction, but many of them shared in piratical profits. Hence, one impediment after another was placed in Porter's way, and he mourned: "Our enemy is an invisible one; he has only to throw on the fairy mantle of a Spanish passport with which they all go furnished. . . ."

Governor Torre at Puerto Rico was especially adamant in his refusal

the death of Diablito in April 1823, about the time Domingo's forces were defeated, but a year later, one of Porter's officers mentioned that Diablito was still alive. His ship, which bore his name, was reported a member of the American flotilla during the summer of 1824, which would imply that the action took place between April and August of that year. Yet, Diablito's vessel was a schooner, and the craft mentioned above was a barge. Sometimes the boat is called *Diablito,* and sometimes *Diabolita,* so there is a possibility that there were two actions. In May 1825, at Porter's Court of Inquiry, the victory of "Lt. [William] Watson" at Singualpa Bay in August 1823 was described as "a gallant action peculiarly destructive to the pirates," and this might have been when Diablito's force was overwhelmed.

to permit armed Americans ashore. Governor Dionisio Vives of Cuba was considerably more cooperative, but still, he could only go so far. He permitted Porter's ships to "shelter themselves on the uninhabited coast," but added the proviso that such must be "compatible with the territorial privileges conformable to the laws of nations"—a plus and a minus which added to zero. Nevertheless, when Porter ended his assignment, he thanked Vives for his "good understanding and cooperation."

The Spaniards did more than impede Porter's efforts: they assumed the offensive in the form of spirited protests about his activities, as, for instance, when men from the *Peacock* chased some pirates ashore in Cuba. Although their quarry escaped, the Americans recovered much stolen property and seized some enemy craft. When Madrid filed a complaint, John Quincy Adams was outraged, and declared that the Spaniards could see nothing in the situation "but a *violation of his Catholic Majesty's territory;* a sentiment on such an occasion, which would be more suitable for an accessory to the pirates than for the officer of a Government deeply and earnestly intent upon their suppression." [16]

If Porter was hindered rather than helped by the Spaniards, he found the British considerably easier to work with. During his tenure in the West Indies, a Royal Navy squadron was assigned to that area and it assisted its American counterpart "in every way." When Porter was undecided about what to do with forty-two pirates captured off Cuba, since the Spaniards would claim no jurisdiction over them, the British solved his problem nicely by taking the captives to Jamaica where they were tried, convicted, and hanged.* According to Porter, he was equally cooperative, and his letters to Sir Edward Owen, commanding the British West Indian Squadron, and to other English officers, were affable, except for the time when an American merchantman fouled the rigging of a British sloop, an incident that will be described later.

With the pirates caught between the jaws of the British and American navies, attacks on shipping in the West Indies dropped off sharply. As early as May, Porter was able to notify the Navy Department that his "arduous and fatiguing" cruise had already resulted in "the complete dispersal of piratical gangs" along a large section of the Cuban coast. By midsummer, the energetic operations against the pirates had driven most of them "off the water, with their lurking places invaded, their plunder seized, their occupation afloat gone. . . ."

Pirates who survived the onslaught at sea had little alternative but to become land-based bandits. If this move protected them from the Ameri-

---

* The men in question were probably from Diablito's schooner, for roughly half of his complement of eighty was captured.

can and British navies, it added new enemies in the form of Spanish ground forces. Porter wrote to the Department:

> When I left Matanzas, the country was alarmed by large bands of robbers who had plundered several estates, and committed some murders. . . . Bodies of horsemen were sent in pursuit of them, and the militia were all under arms . . . it was said that these bands were composed of freebooters which lately infested the coast, who having been impelled to abandon the ocean had taken up this new line of business.[17]

Because of these new circumstances, local Spanish authorities, many of whom had watched assaults on the shipping of detested foreigners with either detachment or avaricious anticipation, were forced to take action against the pirate-bandits. No other course was open to them so long as Spanish citizens were being killed and Spanish property destroyed. In consequence, the outlaws were struck from both sea and land.

From the beginning, Porter had found fault with the "pestilential" climate of Key West and recommended that it not be made a permanent naval base, "for it is occupation enough here to keep one's self free from Musquitoes and Sand Flies." Unfortunately, his men, who had accomplished so much against human enemies in the spring, were unable to "keep free" from the attacks of aedes mosquitoes in the summer and, by August, a virulent epidemic of yellow fever had erupted. Scores of men were prostrated, and of the twenty-five officers stricken, twenty-three died. The Commodore was among those felled, but after lingering several days on the verge of death, he managed to pull through. Details of his illness did not become known until he applied for a naval disability pension fifteen years later. At that time, a naval surgeon testifying in support of his application told the Navy Department: "During his illness, the left clavicle which had years before been wounded,* began to separate and pieces of bone exfoliate . . . I have no doubt the fever was the cause of the exfoliation." One of the officers who was serving with Porter at the time of the epidemic attested that Porter never recovered from the fever, and added that "the pestilential exhilation of the climate" resulted in the American Navy losing "more officers and men, in proportion, than in any service in which they were ever engaged."

As soon as he had recovered from the fever enough to be moved, Porter was advised to go home, and in the autumn of 1823, he sailed north in the *Sea Gull*, taking Farragut with him. In a voyage broken by brief stops at St. Marks and Savannah, the *Sea Gull* pitched and tossed for twenty-three days before she arrived in Washington on 26 October with the Commodore "weak and disabled in one arm." [18]

---

* The reference is to the wound Porter received while on board the *Experiment* off Haiti on 1 January 1800.

Unfairly, one of Porter's biographers blames the disastrous epidemic at Key West on governmental incompetence, because the Commodore's "many letters asking for medical officers and medicines went practically unnoticed." Medical knowledge of that day was totally unable to control yellow fever and, under the circumstances, the Department appears to have done about all it could. Well before Porter arrived back in the States, Samuel L. Southard, the new Secretary of the Navy,* was expressing his "uncertainty and anxiety" about the health of Porter and his men, and he sent Captain John Rodgers, senior naval officer, hastening south with three navy doctors. Rodgers sailed on 6 October, and a little over a fortnight later reached the charnel house called Key West to find that Porter had just departed. He sent home the fifty-nine men who were still prostrated by the fever, did what he could to improve conditions, gave the squadron interim orders, and was back in Washington by late November.[19]

Although the ravages of disease brought 1823 to a discouraging conclusion, Porter had done well during his first year in command of the West India Squadron, and Secretary Southard wrote him a most enthusiastic testimonial: "You have displayed . . . intelligence, promptitude and vigor . . . [which] justly entitle you to the unqualified approbation of this Department, and to the thanks of your Country." The President of the United States agreed: five long paragraphs of his message to Congress on 2 December 1823—which, among other things, enunciated the Monroe Doctrine—were devoted to Porter's activities in the Caribbean:

> In the West Indies and the Gulf of Mexico our naval force . . . has been eminently successful in the accomplishment of its object. The piracies by which our commerce in the neighborhood of the island of Cuba had been afflicted have been repressed and the confidence of our merchants in great measure restored. The patriotic zeal and enterprise of Commodore Porter to whom the command of the expedition was confined, has been fully seconded by the officers and men under his command. And in reflecting with high satisfaction on the honorable manner in which they have sustained the

---

* On 31 August 1823 Smith Thompson resigned as Secretary of the Navy to accept appointment as an Associate Justice of the Supreme Court. Captain John Rodgers served as *ad interim* Secretary until October, when he was succeeded by another temporary appointee, Captain Isaac Chauncey. According to Samuel L. Southard's biographer, President Monroe did not appoint him Secretary of the Navy until 9 December 1823, but a Massachusetts paper announced his selection early in September, and he was signing Departmental correspondence throughout most of that month. Southard, a New Jersey lawyer and former U.S. Senator, served for the remainder of Monroe's term as President and throughout that of his close personal friend, John Quincy Adams. He was an effective administrator, and under his direction the Navy expanded. But he was irritable, thin-skinned, and utterly tactless with subordinates.

reputation of their country and its Navy, the sentiment is alloyed only by a concern that in the fulfillment of that arduous service the diseases incident to the season and to the climate . . . have deprived the nation of many useful lives, and among them several officers of great promise.

After mentioning Porter's attack of yellow fever and Rodgers' mission to Key West, the President concluded the subject by contrasting the squadron's success in terminating piracy off Cuba with its relative failure to do the same in Puerto Rican waters, a failure which he blamed on the uncooperative attitude of Spanish officials in San Juan.* Porter's subsequent aggression at Fajardo may have been based in some small measure on Monroe's implication that he had accomplished his tasks better in Cuba than in Puerto Rico.

In the cool weather at home, Porter recovered rapidly from his yellow fever. He looked with anticipation toward renewing his campaign in the West Indies, and was heartened by the Department's permission to take his family with him. On 10 December 1823, with his wife, their five youngest children, and a retinue of servants, he sailed in the *John Adams* for Norfolk. He was scheduled to spend a few weeks there to allow repairs to be made to some of the squadron's ships but, as will be seen, the stay lengthened into more than two months.

During his enforced sojourn at Norfolk, Porter had ample time to pore over four pages of detailed new instructions sent by Secretary of the Navy Southard to "Capt. David Porter, Com'g U.S. Naval Force, West Indies, Gulf of Mexico and Coast of Africa." As indicated by this new form of address, the instructions widened Porter's command by several thousand miles to the east, and ordered him to send "one of the large Schooners" to West Africa, "ministering to the wants of the African Agency, and thence returning in the usual tract of the Slave Ships." † On 24 January 1824 Porter assured the Secretary that he was sending the *Grampus* to carry correspondence to the U.S. "colony on the West Coast of Africa," and added that, if he had a bigger force, he could send a ship to Africa every six weeks.

Southard next discussed the practice of American naval vessels trans-

---

* Monroe's distinction between the squadron's achievements in Cuba and those in Puerto Rico was contradicted during November 1823, when two letters written by the U.S. Consul in San Juan to the Secretary of State complimented Porter for having practically ended piracy in Puerto Rico.[20]

† The American Colonization Society was, at this time, making its first attempts to place freed slaves on land bought from West African tribal chiefs in what is now Liberia. American warships were supposed to participate in enforcing the ban on the international slave trade, but did little until the Civil War, thanks to opposition from the southern slave states.

porting specie, and told Porter that he was permitted to carry specie from one port to another in his command area, or from there to the United States, provided that it was the property of American citizens and that his engaging in this traffic neither interfered with his other duties nor transgressed local laws. Under no circumstances, continued Southard, should he resort to "public advertisements" to attract specie-carrying assignments, and, "from time to time," he must make full reports on his activities in that connection. The following October, Porter notified the Department that during the previous ten months, ships in his squadron had carried specie worth $399,000, and charged 1¼ per cent for the service.

Southard's third directive pertained to tightening disciplinary controls over officers. Perturbed about the rising number of courts-martial in recent years, the Secretary wrote: "By a course of rigid discipline and attention to language and conduct of Officers, it is hoped that there will be less call for public trials which have heretofore been so numerous and lessened the warm attachment of the Nation to the Navy." Despite the Secretary's hopes, Porter was soon deeply involved with courts-martial, but these will be discussed later. The Secretary's lengthy instructions concluded with calls for more impartial treatment of midshipmen, sharp restrictions upon "Acting Appointment of any description," and encouragement of American commerce and agriculture,[21] matters which apparently never needed elaboration by the Commodore.

On 18 February Porter and his family sailed in the *John Adams* with the little steamer *Sea Gull* as consort. When he first reached the West Indies, he spent some time cruising about the islands, looking for pirates off St. Bartholomew, St. Kitts, Puerto Rico, Haiti, and Jamaica. All was quiet. He then split the squadron into small flotillas which he dispatched to various parts of his extensive command. While his crews were busy on the same kind of work that had occupied them the year before, Porter exerted himself to elaborate the shore facilities at Key West which he had started before he went home to convalesce. He worried constantly about yellow fever, and early in May wrote the Department: "I beg leave to observe that the medical department of the squadron under my command never has been in a worse condition. . . . The sickly season is fast approaching . . . should desease rage this year as much as the last, our situation would be truly deplorable." His apprehension was thoroughly and quickly justified. Later that same month he was struck down again by yellow fever, and since the post's only doctor was similarly afflicted, Evalina Porter was left to her own devices for nursing her husband. When his crisis was safely passed, she evidently had little trouble in persuading him to recuperate in the United States. The family and servants crowded into the *Sea Gull,* which immediately proceeded to Matanzas, Cuba. There, coal was loaded, instructions were left for the squadron, and, especially important, arrangements were made to send ahead the *Wild Cat* with a dispatch advising the Navy Department that compelling reasons of health necessitated the prompt return of the Commodore.

It was on this occasion that the *Sea Gull* made the voyage from Matanzas to Washington in the remarkably short time of nine days; she left on 15 June and arrived in Washington on the 24th. The Porter entourage must have suffered considerable discomfort during the voyage, for the steamer's "cumbersome machinery and her coal took up practically the whole of her buoyancy, [and] she had little space for bunking her crew."

This rapid trip from the West Indies did nothing to improve Porter's relations with President Monroe, Secretary of the Navy Southard, and, probably, Secretary of State John Quincy Adams. As the *Sea Gull* steamed up the Potomac, she passed the *Wild Cat* and arrived in the capital "some hours" before the latter delivered the dispatch explaining why the Commodore had abandoned his post.[22]

When Monroe learned that the commander of his West India Squadron was strolling the streets of Washington, he asked Southard whether orders had been given for Porter's recall. On receiving a negative answer, the President was outraged, and concluded that the Commodore's unauthorized return meant that he felt free to come and go as he pleased. He discussed the situation with Captains Rodgers and Chauncey, as well as the Secretary, and pondered what course to follow. While he was doing so, he heard that Porter was planning to visit him in the White House, so he sent Chauncey to tell him "in the most delicate manner" that he would not be welcome while his case was under advisement. After much reflection, Monroe decided "to pass the affair over without further notice, & of which I requested them [Rodgers and Chauncey] to inform him. He accordingly called afterwards & was received with kindness." Nevertheless, there is no question but that the President's initial outrage left its mark, and Porter was never able to erase it.

When Southard heard that Porter was home, he "expressed great surprise," and later told the Commodore, "Your return to this place without permission was unexpected; but no complaint has heretofore been made. . . ."[23] It seems obvious that this episode formed a watershed in his relations with his commander in the West Indies. From the moment of his unauthorized return until his naval career ended, Porter found Southard's hostility toward him virulent and unrestrained. As for Secretary of State Adams, he tended to think along lines similar to those taken by his close friends and administrative colleagues, Monroe and Southard.

Furthermore, it would seem only natural that members of the Monroe administration would discuss among themselves two recent incidents which cast the gravest doubts on Porter's discretion: a clash with the British in the West Indies, and the Kennon court-martial. Only a few weeks before the Commodore suddenly showed up in Washington, the government had received a British protest about Porter having condoned a duel between an American and a British officer. The situation arose out of an incident that took place on 27 June 1823, when an American merchantman, the *Hiram*, under Captain Sylvester Allen, came so clumsily to anchor in Havana Harbor that she fouled the rigging of the British sloop of war *Eden*, commanded by Captain John Lawrence. In retaliation Lawrence ordered his first lieutenant * and some sailors to hack away the *Hiram*'s rigging. Allen protested, and then apologized, recognizing that the first wrong had been his. In return, the British captain made a tacit apology by sending over to the American ship "about fourteen fathoms" of new rope to repair the damage, and "two bottles of old Port wine" for "medicinal purposes."

One might suppose that the most tremulous sense of honor would have been satisfied, but not that of Lieutenant Francis A. Gregory, commanding Porter's schooner *Grampus*, who was in Havana at the time. When he learned that the British had boarded the *Hiram*, he immediately sent a challenge to the *Eden*'s first lieutenant. Captain Lawrence forwarded a copy of Gregory's "extraordinary letter" to Porter at Key West and suggested that a stop be put to such nonsense, as a duel "might have a tendency to destroy that harmony which thank God exists between the officers of the two nations."

Porter's reply defies understanding. He deemed the *Eden*'s behavior toward the *Hiram* "wanton and unjustifiable," and expressed the opinion that, since Gregory had orders that compelled him to leave Havana almost at once, his method of settling the issue would be quicker and easier than the time-consuming process of referring it to Spanish port authorities: Gregory, he said, was correct in asking for "a personal encounter." Porter did express his regret that his lieutenant had "permitted his feelings to master him so far," but concluded: "I can see nothing that requires as official interference on my part; there is no insult offered or intended to the British officers or the British flag . . . I view it, therefore, as a personal affair. . . ."

Lawrence dispatched this bizarre communication to Sir Edward Owen, commanding the Royal Navy squadron in the West Indies. Owen, in turn, wrote to Porter saying he feared that a single encounter could

---

* In none of the correspondence examined was the *Eden*'s first lieutenant referred to by name.

lead to a "general massacre," which could not fail to weaken Anglo-American friendship. He found it incredible that an officer of Porter's stature would support Gregory's behavior. Porter defended himself stoutly: he denied that he was "an advocate of duelling," but said he could not forgive Lawrence's "act of wanton, violent and unprovoked aggression on an unoffending merchant vessel," especially in a Spanish port. He promised to continue to do all in his power to "preserve harmony" with Great Britain, but if anyone hoped that he would "permit violence to be offered . . . to the persons and property of my fellow-citizens or an insult to our flag with impunity, too much is expected of me." [24] Owen bundled up all the correspondence and fired it off to London.

In the spring of 1824, the British Chargé d'Affaires in Washington lodged an official protest about Gregory's "extraordinary conduct . . . in making a complaint of a public nature an excuse for attempting to provoke a private quarrel with a British officer," and expressed his great regret that Porter had been "induced to sanction a proceeding of so intemperate a character." His Majesty's Government hoped that the United States would express its "displeasure" to both Gregory and Porter in order to prevent anything similar from happening in the future.

Three days after receipt of that note, Monroe's Cabinet met, talked it over, and accepted the protest. John Quincy Adams spoke for all when he concluded that "Porter and Gregory were wrong." According to his *Memoirs,* the only thing that stopped him from personally delivering "a strong censure" was that he was engaged in a struggle with Andrew Jackson, Henry Clay, and William H. Crawford for the National Republican Party's nomination as candidate for the presidency, and he might have been accused of electioneering. It was left to the Secretary of the Navy to chastise Porter. In a cold, cutting rebuke, Southard quoted verbatim some of the British accusations against the Commodore and his bellicose lieutenant, and stating that the President wished "an early explanation of his motives," he insisted that Porter recognize the special responsibility that he and other naval officers had to keep peace with Great Britain and, by implication, with all other nations.

Porter affected astonishment that he could be charged with backing Gregory, because he had disapproved of the challenge and had said so. Also, he knew of his duty to maintain the best relations with Great Britain, and his correspondence with Owen showed such an awareness. But, he said, "I did not & could not approve the shameful, wanton & disgraceful conduct of capt. Lawrence. . . ." He complained that Owen should not have behaved in such a righteous manner, since he had promised to investigate the entire affair thoroughly and had not done so.[25] This appears to have ended correspondence on the matter, both between Southard and Porter and between London and Washington. But the administration had been given prima facie evidence that, in questions of international relations, the Commodore's judgment was, at best, erratic.

In another incident, occurring about the same time, Porter once again proved himself anathema to Monroe, Adams, and Southard, when he involved himself in a head-on clash with Lieutenant Beverly Kennon, commanding the *Weasel* in his squadron. During the summer of 1823 Kennon had seized a Spanish ship after she had fired on him, and taken her in to Key West for adjudication. Porter and Governor Vives of Cuba disposed of the subject to their mutual satisfaction, and eventually the vessel was returned to her Spanish owners. Kennon apparently cast some kind of vague aspersions on the propriety of his superior's decision, and Porter was furious, expressing his displeasure in a letter to his subordinate. Kennon replied in similar vein, and before long, the correspondence between the two men appeared in newspapers in Virginia and Georgia. Late in December, Porter demanded the court-martial of his lieutenant.*

When the Commodore drew up his indictment, the weakness of his case against Kennon became obvious: he accused the lieutenant of defaming his character by such "base means" as wrongfully ascribing to him a letter published in the Norfolk and Portsmouth *Herald;* going back on an apology that Porter had "extracted" from him; and describing him "in public print [with] a term which is seldom applied to other than pick pockets, rogues, gamblers, etc." The "term" Kennon had used was "noted," and the nature of Porter's vindictiveness may be seen in that he chose to misinterpret it as "notorious." Kennon fought back with all his resources. Even before Southard officially notified him that he would be tried, he had called for the arrest of the Commodore. The Secretary refused to comply with that demand, and wrote both Porter and Kennon setting the date of the latter's court-martial.[26]

Porter had a miserable time during Kennon's trial which lasted from 28 January to 20 February 1824. Not only was he being kept from the work he wanted to do in the West Indies, but his lieutenant launched a strong counterattack. As evidence of his superior's malice, Kennon introduced a letter which Porter had written against him and had had published anonymously in the Savannah *Georgian.* In his closing statement to the court, Kennon let his anger burst forth:

---

* Simultaneously, Porter was preferring charges against another of his officers, Master Commandant Sidney Smith of the *Hornet,* whom he accused of taking cochineal dye on board his vessel for his own profit. The court-martial's decision was odd. Smith was found guilty and cashiered "forever" from the Navy. Yet, on the advice of the court, President Monroe restored him to full rank.

A Captain in the Navy, throwing off all the insignia of his rank, and contemning all the regulations of the Service, has put on the mask of the anonymous libeller, and wantonly, grossly, unjustly assailed the character of his inferior. When convinced of the injustice, he has aggravated the wrong by contumelious temper; which deemed the injured party too low for reparation, too humble for redress.

On 24 February 1824, the court found that Porter's charges had not been proved, and that Kennon was "fully acquitted."

It was a humiliating and deserved defeat for Porter. Referring to the orders he had earlier given Porter about courts-martial, Southard wrote him an I-told-you-so letter during late March. He said the trial had "excited" the country and expressed the hope that all officers would "perceive the necessity of avoiding in future, whatever will have a tendency" to end in court action. He enclosed a copy of a letter to Kennon, dated 16 March, authorizing him to publish details of his acquittal. It is doubtful if Porter was much comforted by being told that the Secretary had once again refused to order his arrest "on the charges prefered by Lieutenant Kennon."

The Commodore answered Southard as best he could, asserting that he was delighted at the decision to print the court-martial testimony, since this would give him, "a perjured man," a chance to clear himself with the public. Further, he disclaimed responsibility for causing any national "excitement," and, in words he should have found embarrassing a few months later, took issue with the Secretary's directive about avoiding situations which might end in public trials:

Courts Martial are at all times inconvenient, and occasion more or less "public excitement." Yet they are a necessary evil, are provided for by the Laws of the Government of the Navy, are the only proper appeal of those in the Navy who believe themselves injured, [and] it is made the duty of every Officer to prevent a violation of the Laws which regulate them, and this duty I felt myself in the performance of when I arrested and brought to trial Liet. Kennon.

He ended his letter with the request that the Secretary "make allowance for any warmth of expression which may have escaped me in this letter. . . ." Undoubtedly, Southard mentally filed it away as yet another indication that, basically, Porter was an insubordinate troublemaker.

Another sad byproduct of the Kennon case was that it spoiled the relationship between Porter and John Rodgers, an association that dated back to the decks of the *Constellation* in 1799. Even before the court-martial convened Rodgers showed his bias by writing Porter a far from cordial letter, in which he stated flatly that he could say nothing "that would be gratifying to you." He added that Kennon "will do everything in his power to injure you," because he believed that "you have persecuted him," and concluded with harsh remarks about Porter having taken a service dispute to the newspapers.[27] It is significant that more than ten years later, Rodgers refused to endorse Porter's application for a retroactive disability pension.

While events leading to the destruction of his career in the U.S. Navy were piling up, Porter settled down in the capital, which seemed to him not only healthier than Key West, but just as good a place from which to direct his command, now that West Africa had been added to it. However, while he was passing the summer in pleasant relaxation, attending, among other social functions, a banquet given by the President for the venerable Marquis de Lafayette, who spent the greater part of 1824 and 1825 on a fiftieth-anniversary visit to the United States, complaints that his absence coincided with an upsurge of piracy started coming in from the West Indies. Late in July, Southard protested about this matter, but Porter took a leisurely two weeks to reply. He defended his squadron's work and bemoaned the difficulties under which he had to work. The next day he wrote again to the Secretary demanding that he be given for his flagship one of the heavy, deep-draft frigates that he had rejected when he took over the squadron from Biddle, because his quarters in the *John Adams* were too cramped.[28]

Fuel in the form of dispatches from two American officials in the West Indies was added to the fire of the Secretary's mounting wrath. John Mountain, Acting U.S. Consul in Havana, reported that, because the American squadron was conspicuous by its absence, the coast of Cuba was "entirely neglected," and Americans citizens were "at the mercy of a set of cut-throats." Early in September, Thomas Randall, "United States Agent of Commerce and Seamen at Porto Rico and Cuba," wrote from Havana to advise the State Department that if the fleet had been withdrawn from Cuban waters in the belief that piracy had been suppressed, "the opinion was erroneous and its consequence deplorable." Six weeks later Randall returned to the assault, itemizing recent piratical atrocities and blasting the Navy for its failure to protect American trade, a failure which, he said, was caused not by "want of zeal, enterprise, or courage," but by the preoccupation of the officers with more profitable duties, such as carrying specie.[29] Mountain's and Randall's accusations claimed the attention not only of the administration, but of Congress as well, and they played no small part in compounding the difficulties that lay ahead for the Commodore.

Early in October, seemingly aware of the pressures building against him, Porter wrote a long letter to the Department giving the location of each ship in his squadron, and explaining that most of them were stationed where they were "for the protection of our commerce between St. Barts and the east end of Cuba." He assured Southard that all was well with the fleet. The Secretary ignored the letter and, implying that the protests of Mountain, Randall, and others were based upon fact, told Porter that the administration was tired of his directing the activities of the West India Squadron from his home in Washington: "It is deemed expedient by the Executive, that you proceed as speedily as possible to your station . . . that by your presence there the most effective protection may be afforded our commerce, and you will be able to meet any contingencies that may occur. . . ."

Southard added a note of mystery to his letter when he promised that the frigate *Constellation* would soon be sent to Porter, both to provide him with a more spacious flagship, and to carry him directions "to proceed to the island of Haiti, there to accomplish certain objects, which will be particularly explained to you, and instructions given." What Southard had in mind is not clear to this day. A leading authority on Haitian-American relations points out that, at the time, Haiti feared that a French expedition was preparing to sail against it for the purpose of reconquest. Southard's comment to Porter is the single indication that the United States took seriously such a possibility. But by the time Porter was recalled from the West Indies, it had become apparent that the French had no intention of attacking Haiti, and the matter was relegated to limbo.[30]

Porter reacted to Southard's letter with choler and insubordination. He objected vehemently to returning to a "most arduous" service that had caused him "expense, exposure, and fatigue:" he could not understand why he was not permitted to wait until the *Constellation* was ready, in fact, he did not know why he had to return to the West Indies at all, since Washington was closer than Key West to the center of a command area stretching from Mexico to West Africa. He had had enough of the assignment, anyway. He said that when he was first sent to the West Indies he felt he enjoyed the administration's confidence, but that confidence had been replaced by a "dissatisfaction" which manifested itself in demands for explanations "at every step" which were "almost handed daily to me." He asked to be relieved of command.

Southard's answer is a superb example of his ability to write an infuriating communication:

> Your letter dated 19th inst. has created surprise. . . . The command which was given to you, at your earnest request on the 1st February 1823, was a highly important one, and your conduct in discharge of its duties, satisfactory to the President. The interval since you left that station, has been interesting, and it is understood that piracy has revived, and is making

extensive ravages on our commerce. . . . The presence there of an Officer of rank and experience is, of course, necessary. The size of the vessel in which he sails is matter of small moment. . . . You are aware of the intention to send the *Constellation* . . . as soon as she can conveniently be prepared . . . had you earlier apprized the Department, that you considered this place within the limits of your station, that the command has ceased to be pleasant to you, and you were apprehensive of the climate, you would have been relieved, and a successor appointed. But having failed to give this information and the presence of a commander on the Station being indispensable, you will proceed to it. When it is convenient to the Department, your wish to be relieved shall be gratified. . . .

The Secretary gave warning when he concluded: "I purposely abstain from comment upon certain matters in your letter,—You will hereafter hear from the Department on the subject."

Southard must have been enraged, not so much by Porter's reply that Smith Thompson's orders had permitted him to use his discretion as to how he would execute his assignment, or by his repeated demand to be relieved if he had to go to the West Indies during "the sickly season," as by his writing to President Monroe in an attempt to bypass the chain of command and go over his head. Porter complained to the President that the Secretary's "conduct toward me . . . [is] unexampled I believe in the Annals of our Navy. I hope that such will never be repeated." He wailed that "mortification after mortification have been heaped upon me," especially since he had asked for reassignment, with the result that "My convenience, my comfort, my feelings, nay my life are therefore entirely held at his mercy!" Porter told Monroe that he went to the West Indies "with the strongest and most anxious apprehension for the future." Considering what lay in wait for him, never was he more prophetic. Naturally the President "deemed it improper to reply" to such a communication, and Porter later admitted that he "most sincerely" regretted having written it.[31]

Although Southard must have ached for revenge, when he reported to the President on naval affairs in 1824, he spoke in a complimentary manner about his man in the Caribbean:

> The activity, zeal and enterprise of our officers [in the West Indies] have continued to command approbations. All the vessels have been kept uniformly and busily employed where the danger was believed to be the greatest, except for short periods when the commander supposed it necessary that they should return to the United States to receive provisions, repairs, and men, and for other objects essential to their health, comfort and efficiency.

He went on to aver that privateering was a thing of the past in the West Indies, and that if "some piratical depredations" still took place on occasion, it was hardly the fault of the Navy, as the squadron was too small "to watch every part of the coast."

Monroe's annual message to Congress, 7 December 1824, was considerably less optimistic about the West Indies than had been the case a year before. He spoke of the atrocities still being committed by the pirates, and ascribed this unhappy situation to the "relaxed and feeble state of local government." He said he did not hold the Spanish authority in Cuba responsible, since he knew that if the Governor "had the power . . . [he] would promptly suppress" the pirates.

Shortly before the President's message, the Cabinet met to discuss Cuban pirates, in general, and Porter's specific privileges to land in pursuit of them, in particular. John Quincy Adams later recalled: "I remarked that Commodore Porter was already authorized by his instructions to land, in cases of necessity, in fresh pursuit of pirates. The President, Mr. Calhoun, and Mr. Southard contested this fact. . . ." To prove the point, Southard then read to the Cabinet Smith Thompson's orders of 1 February 1823, which showed that if the Secretary of State had been generally correct in his assumption, Porter's permission to land in Spain's American possessions was strictly "limited to the unsettled parts of the island." [32] It was bad luck for Porter that his instructions about going ashore were thrashed out so thoroughly by the Cabinet barely a fortnight before Washington learned that he had landed on occupied soil in Spanish Puerto Rico.

Late the previous October, Porter had sailed in the *John Adams*— this time without his family—to carry out the Secretary's peremptory orders that he assume closer personal supervision over his squadron. On 12 November he put in to St. Thomas, where Lieutenant Charles T. Platt, commanding the bay schooner *Beagle,* recounted an incident that had taken place during the Commodore's absence. He listened with growing fury as Platt told him that when he made a routine call at St. Thomas on 26 October he was informed by Stephen Cabot, partner in the mercantile firm of Cabot, Bailey, & Company, that the concern's store had been broken into the night before, and goods, primarily handkerchiefs and other textiles, valued at $5,000, were missing. Cabot believed that his property had been carried to Fajardo (Foxardo, and even Faxyardo, in contemporary documentation) on the eastern tip of Puerto Rico, only about forty miles away. On previous occasions, missing property had been traced to Fajardo, whose *alcalde,* or mayor, and other local officials were purported to work in league with pirates. Since Cabot was U.S. Consul in St. Thomas, Platt agreed to investigate personally.[33]

Leaving St. Thomas on the same day, the lieutenant headed the *Beagle* for Fajardo and, en route, boarded an abandoned vessel which he concluded had been the carrier of the purloined goods. He spent the night off Fajardo beach, and on the morning of 27 October went ashore, accompanied by Lieutenant Robert Ritchie and one of Cabot's clerks. In his report of the incident, Platt explained that, because he deemed his mission nonmilitary, he and Ritchie, for their "better success," went ashore "in the character of civilians," a line of asinine reasoning that landed him in trouble. On the beach, the Americans were met by "a parcel of Ragamuffins" who, at first, would not let them proceed, but finally relented, and even provided horses for the trip to the town, which was a half hour's uphill walk from the shore. When Platt reached Fajardo he was met by the "Captain of the Port," who pronounced himself satisfied with Platt's identification—a letter from Cabot. When the *alcalde* showed up, he was equally affable and, reported Platt, "approved very much of my having come on Shore in Citizens dress."

When the *alcalde* stated that he thought he could find the stolen goods, Platt and Ritchie left Cabot's clerk to assist him, and breakfasted in a restaurant. Two soldiers soon appeared and hauled the American officers back before the captain of the port who, this time, behaved in a "most insulting, most provoking, and most aggravating manner." He demanded to see the *Beagle*'s register, not the easiest request to meet since ships of war carried none. After some expostulation, Platt walked away, but had gone no more than "about five rods" when he was arrested and placed under guard. Only after two more hours of argument was he permitted to send the clerk out to his ship to fetch his uniform and commission. It must have been a furious and sweat-drenched Platt—even in October the midday temperature in Fajardo usually stands in the humid eighties—who struggled into his uniform and presented his credentials. The captain of the port examined the papers, and announced Platt's "commission a forgery and me and my officers a damned pack of pirates." He ordered Platt and Ritchie detained in the *alcalde*'s office. After another hour of waiting had passed, the clerk once more went out to the *Beagle*, this time to bring back Porter's orders to Platt. It was late afternoon when the Americans were suddenly released, and, according to Platt, "we left the village mortified very properly, hissed at by the ruff scuff of the place. . . ."[34]

In sharp contrast to the control he had exercised when Lieutenant Cocke was killed in San Juan Harbor in March 1823, Porter was boiling by the time Platt had concluded his story. Within hours he boarded the *John Adams* and set out for Fajardo, accompanied by the *Beagle* and the *Grampus*. On the way, his ships were becalmed and he was forced to chafe through the night. On the morning of 14 November, he and 200 armed men rowed ashore in boats from the *John Adams*. Observing that a handful of Spanish soldiers were manning a two-gun battery a short distance inland, Porter sent some sailors and Marines toward them. At the approach of the Americans, the Spaniards fled, leaving the guns to be spiked. Under a flag of truce, a lieutenant bearing an ultimatum from Porter was sent ahead to Fajardo. The language of the Commodore's message was explicit: if the local officials who had "shamefully insulted and abused" Lieutenant Platt refused to apologize, he wrote, "I shall take with me an armed force competent to punish the aggressors, and if any resistance is made, the total destruction of Foxardo will be the certain and immediate consequence."

When the lieutenant had departed, Porter and his men began toiling slowly uphill toward Fajardo. Although they were enervated by the heat, they found energy enough to spike a few more guns along the way. They arrived on the outskirts of town to find some 400 to 500 militia milling about, and Porter drew his 200 men to attention facing them. When the *alcalde* and the captain of the port appeared, Porter demanded a reply to his ultimatum, and the officials were delighted to apologize to the outraged lieutenant. Platt listened to them, and announced that his honor was satisfied. After refusing an invitation to enjoy the hospitality of Fajardo and declining to accept a peace offering of "some bullocks and a number of horses" delivered on the beach by Spaniards "bearing a white flag," Porter and his force returned to their ships. The episode had lasted about three hours.*

The next day Porter sent the details of his Fajardo landing and his explanation of it to the Navy Department:

> Indignant at the outrages which have so repeatedly been heaped on us by the authorities of Porto Rico . . . [I went to Fajardo and] found them prepared for defence, as they had received information from St. Thomas's of my intention of visiting the place. I . . . sent in a flag requiring . . . the principal offenders to come to me to make atonement for the outrage. They appeared accordingly and after begging pardon (in the presence of all the officers) of the officer who had been insulted, I permitted them to return to the town, on their promising to respect all American officers who may visit them hereafter.

He then settled down to await the commendation he expected the government to extend for his willingness to uphold "national honor" at Fajardo. He later avowed that the only thing that made him uneasy was fear that he might be chided officially for "not having seized and garrisoned, or destroyed the village at the harbor, and even the town of Foxardo, as pernicious pirate nests." [35]

---

* Platt says that they "partook of refreshment" on the beach.

IX

The Commodore's first intimation that the Navy Department might view with hostility his landing at Fajardo came in January 1825 when he was visiting Havana and read in the local press that he was being recalled. He hastened back to Key West where "nothing could exceed the astonishment" with which he read a communication Southard had addressed to him on 27 December 1824:

> Your letter, of the 15th of November last, relating to the extraordinary transactions at Foxardo . . . has been received and considered. It is not intended, at this time, to pronounce an opinion on the propriety of these transactions, on your part, but their importance demands of them a full investigation, and you will proceed without unnecessary delay to this place, to furnish such explanations as may be required.

The Secretary told Porter to bring along with him Lieutenant Platt and other officers connected with the Fajardo landing and, in language that did not make it clear whether Porter was permanently or only temporarily suspended, ordered him to turn over command of the West India Squadron to Captain Lewis Warrington.*

Porter's account of his actions at Fajardo had reached Washington in mid-December, and first became a subject for Cabinet discussion on the 16th, but apparently nothing definite was done. On the 24th, it was the subject of much wrangling among the members of the Cabinet. From the beginning, President Monroe, Secretary of State Adams, and Secretary of the Navy Southard condemned Porter's actions and pressed for his immediate arrest and trial. Secretary of the Treasury William H. Crawford, Porter's only advocate, argued "with strong excitement" that General An-

---

* The suspension was permanent. On the same day that he wrote to Porter, Southard appointed Warrington, whom he regarded as "an active, systematic, and enterprising officer," to succeed him.[1]

drew Jackson's behavior in the Floridas had been "ten times worse" than anything Porter had done at Fajardo; he favored no punishment at all for the Commodore.* The other Cabinet members were undecided. After several hours of discussion, a compromise was reached: Porter was to be recalled to explain his actions.

In some jottings made a few months later, Monroe claimed that his sentiments toward Porter had been motivated solely by a "high respect for his services and merits," but he had been forced to conclude that at Fajardo the Commodore had been "making war," not working "on the side of peace." When the President was questioned by the court-martial that tried Porter, he stressed the international issues involved:

> This command was deemed a very important one, . . . [and] I knew that it would attract the attention, not of Spain alone . . . but of the new governments, our neighbors, to the south, & in certain respects, of several of the powers of Europe . . . [Porter's orders were] dictated by a desire rather to err . . . on the side of moderation, than to risk a varience [?], with any of the nations concerned. . . . My intention was that the Commander of the Squadron, & all actions under him, should take nothing on themselves, but confine themselves to the duty especially injoined on them. . . .

Monroe's position was summed up admirably by a Massachusetts paper: Porter had been instructed to act with "cool deliberation . . . to avoid giving any cause of alarm . . . to any of the European nations." American armed intervention in the West Indies could be considered permissible "by treaty alone . . . with any of these powers." Since Porter enjoyed no such right, he had clearly violated his orders.[2]

John Quincy Adams, who had long distrusted Porter, was unsparing in his denunciation of what happened at Fajardo. "Porter's descent on Porto Rico was a direct, hostile invasion of the island, utterly unjustifiable," he wrote in his *Memoirs,* in short, it was "one of the most high-handed acts I have ever heard of."

Three factors were probably responsible for Samuel L. Southard's animus against Porter: first, the Secretary was a close friend of both Monroe and Adams, and would be likely to echo their sentiments; second, he knew Porter hated him and, the previous October, had gone over his head to the President; third, his own unpleasant personality, for while his associations with his superiors and equals were affable enough, his correspondence shows that he was one of those impossible individuals who demonstrate that they have the most delicate regard for their own sensi-

---

* Crawford had been a leading candidate for the presidency in the recently concluded election of 1824, and he may have been taking this opportunity to strike simultaneously at his two more successful rivals, Adams and Jackson.

tivities, but are totally oblivious of the possibility that their inferiors might be similarly endowed.

The news of Porter's landing at Fajardo and the administration's handling of it had immediate repercussions in Congress. On 27 December the House of Representatives passed a resolution asking the President for "information explanatory of the character and objects of the visit . . . to the town of Faxyardo." Monroe answered the next day: "I hereby transmit a report of the Secretary of the Navy, with a letter of Commodore Porter. . . . Deeming the transaction adverted to of high importance, an order has been sent to Commodore Porter to repair hither without delay, that all circumstances connected therewith may be fully investigated." [3]

Among the reasons why the Monroe administration took such prompt and vehement exception to Porter's landing at Fajardo were, of course, the international situation and Porter's recent delinquencies. Just a year had elapsed since the pronouncement of the Monroe Doctrine, to which some of the European nations had reacted with anger and contempt. No direct challenge had been made, but the memory of French intervention in Spain was still fresh. Then arrived the intelligence that Porter had led 200 armed men ashore at Fajardo, not to chase pirates, but to browbeat Spanish officials into making an apology for insults allegedly offered an American lieutenant who, at the time, had been little more than a mufti-clad, quasi-official searcher for stolen goods. The landing had taken place in settled territory clearly under direct Spanish administration, sans treaty right or special invitation. It might be just the excuse that the European powers were looking for to justify intervention in the Americas. "The Government could not overlook this highhanded demonstration, committed by its officer, in the territory of a foreign and friendly state. . . ."

As already narrated, the Commodore had long been suspect to certain members of the administration. He had incurred the distrust of Monroe, as well as of Adams, in 1818 when he joined John Rodgers in a denial that they had planted a false story in the press. Within the past year, two American officials, John Mountain and Thomas Randall, had accused Porter of dereliction of duty in carrying specie rather than fighting the pirates. He had left his command in the West Indies without authorization, shown a distressing lack of judgment in condoning Lieutenant Gregory's belligerency and in bringing Lieutenant Kennon to trial, and been thoroughly resentful and insubordinate toward Secretary Southard.

Nevertheless, it is difficult to understand why the administration was so eager to stir up the controversy sure to come with the humiliating recall of so famous an officer. And the mystery is compounded by one of the greatest oddities in the affair: the Spaniards apparently never made a protest of any kind about Porter's landing at Fajardo. Madrid seems to have ignored it completely. In San Juan a blanket of silence was spread over the incident; the official Puerto Rican government bulletin never even mentioned it. Porter and the Spanish governor of Cuba, Dionisio Vives, were exchanging sentiments of mutual admiration long after the news of Fajardo had been circulated. Before departing from the West Indies, the Commodore thanked the Governor for "the many facilities and accommodation, the good understanding and cooperation I have found." Not to be outdone in amicable courtesy, Vives congratulated Porter for "the able manner" in which he had executed his West Indian assignment, and specifically mentioned his appreciation that the Commodore had always respected "the territorial rights of the island of Cuba."

David Dixon Porter avows that during the summer of 1825, just when the Commodore was being tried by court-martial, Governor Torre of Puerto Rico, who had dismissed the *alcalde* of Fajardo, pronounced a new policy "for the extermination of the vile rabble which disgraces humanity," and stated: "American officers, in pursuit of pirates, shall be privileged to all ports, harbors, anchorages, etc., which they may think proper to enter; and that all authorities will give them necessary aid and notification for discovering them, and . . . the civil and military authorities will join themselves with the said American officers, to pursue the pirates by land and sea." [4]

True, Torres' statement did not constitute carte blanche for actions such as Porter's landing at Fajardo, but it did seem to be tacit approval of what he had done. In view of that attitude, to say nothing of the absence of any goad in the form of a Spanish protest, the vigorous buffeting to which the Monroe and Adams administrations subjected Porter remains perplexing. It might be argued that Spain had no need to object since Washington struck so quickly against the Commodore. But diplomats usually delight in furnishing their home office with written proof of their zealous guardianship of the national interest. Indeed, Spain's seeming acquiescence to a violation of its territorial rights must have been disappointing to the American government. An official protest from Madrid would certainly have strengthened its case against Porter.

While Washington was commencing to dig a pit in which to bury Porter, he was reaching for a shovel. To be sure, his attitude toward Captain Lewis Warrington, his successor as Commodore of the West India Squadron, was totally cooperative: he wrote Warrington full details about location of ships and problems of the command. It may have hurt Porter's ego that the new commodore, enjoying almost perfect cooperation from the Spaniards and the British, had practically eradicated piracy from the West Indies by the end of 1826. But Porter's policy toward the administration was not one of compliance and apology, but of massive resistance from the moment he read the Secretary's letter of recall. On 30 January 1825, he defiantly told Southard that he would justify his conduct at Fajardo "in every particular, not only by the laws of nations and of nature, and highly approved precedents, but, if necessary, by the orders of the Secretary of the Navy." A few weeks later, he wrote to the Department in such an intemperate vein that Southard told Rodgers: "I have rec'd a letter from Porter—He is still turbulent & I fear will destroy himself." The Secretary's "fear" that Porter might "destroy himself" was patent hypocrisy, for he was doing everything in his power to accomplish precisely that end.

Meanwhile the administration was amassing evidence against the Commodore. Early in January, Thomas Randall met Adams in Washington. He had with him a letter from John Mountain, once more castigating Porter for his work in the West Indies, and he verbally filled in details for Adams. Toward the end of the month, Platt's written account of what happened at Fajardo reached the capital, and after reading it Adams had no difficulty in concluding that the case "appears very disadvantageously to Porter." [5]

The infuriated Commodore took his time in complying with Southard's order to come home, although he could argue with justification that the details of a two-year command could not be wrapped up in a few days. It was not until 1 March that he notified the Department that he had arrived in Washington, and was awaiting further instructions. Unfortunately for him, his return coincided with the ceremonies attending the inauguration of John Quincy Adams as President, and for two weeks he was compelled to bide his time, while his temper smoldered.

Not that he was idle during that fortnight; partly because of his anger about the "foul charges" of Randall and Mountain, he opened a tremendous campaign for his vindication. The "charges" had been picked up in Congress during debates on a bill for the suppression of piracy introduced by John Forsyth of Georgia, Chairman of the House Committee on Foreign Relations. During February and March there was considerable implied criticism of Porter's command in the West Indies, and the carrying of specie was mentioned. But what must have hurt Porter the most was a speech made by his old friend Joel R. Poinsett, now a Representative from South Carolina, with whom he had shared such exciting times in Chile. Porter had just spent two years trying to eradicate piracy from the West Indies and it should have been humiliating for him to read what Poinsett had to say on conditions there:

From long impunity, the pirates have become very numerous—not less . . . than 60 or 70,000 persons being engaged in that nefarious trade. They have organized themselves into a society under the name of *Muselmanes* (Muselmen), known to each other by signs, as Free Masons are, and governed by rules and regulations . . . they are protected by magistrates and officials of government, who profit by their plunder, and they are encouraged by merchants, who purchase their goods at a low price . . . they are to be seen walking the streets of Havana and Matanzas—nay, the entire population of Regla, a town in the Bay of Havana, is composed of pirates.

Stung by these criticisms, outright or implied, and convinced of the rectitude of his behavior, Porter spent much of early March trying to get appointments with former President Monroe and the newly inaugurated Adams. On 10 March he wrote Monroe requesting an audience for the purpose of "explaining his conduct." Two days later, the former President replied that although he held "in high esteem your gallantry and patriotism," he could not receive him. Furthermore, Monroe accepted full responsibility for what had happened. All Southard's orders, including the one recalling Porter, had been "given under my inspection. They were dictated by a sense of duty to my Country, and with no unkind feelings toward you." Since he was now a private citizen, he considered it incorrect to impinge upon the authority of his successor. Putting on the best face he could under the circumstances, Porter replied to Monroe's letter the same day he received it; he thanked the former President for his compliments, protested that he only wished to see him for "pure personal respect," and expressed the hope that Monroe was not suffering from "wrong impressions" about him.[6]

He had only slightly better luck with John Quincy Adams. He wrote the new President on both 10 and 11 March, and finally managed to arrange an interview with him on the 12th. Apparently nothing much happened when the two men met, certainly not to the Commodore's advantage. Adams mentioned the audience in his terse *Diary*, but omitted it from his lengthy *Memoirs*. Three days after the interview, in a letter to his close friend Samuel Hambleton, Porter insisted that he had been "very well received by the government [Adams]," but had been unable to see Southard. He cast about optimistically, being sure his actions at Fajardo would be completely vindicated, and that Randall, Mountain, and their Congressional allies would "soon be ashamed of themselves."

On 17 March Porter's dwindling reservoir of patience ran dry. He wrote Southard a letter so impertinent that it was specified in the later court-martial charge of insubordination. He began by paying lip service to a recognition that the installation of a new administration had to take precedence over anything else, but went on to complain that he had waited two weeks without further information or new instructions. He asked that "there may be as little delay in the investigation of his conduct . . . as is consistent with the public interest," and expressed the hope that the government would end his "ignorance and uncertainty," by granting him a quick opportunity to "vindicate" himself from "a species of suspension, and supposed condemnation." He ended by asking whether or not he was still in command of the West India Squadron.

That letter must have crossed one in which Southard told him: "It has become my duty to apprise you of the determination of the Executive that a Court of Inquiry be formed . . . to examine into the occurrence at Foxardo. . . . It was the intention of the Department, in ordering Captain Warrington to the West Indies, to relieve you of the command of the squadron there." Porter responded by demanding that the court of inquiry also investigate Randall's charge that, through carrying specie, he had been remiss in his duties.[7]

During the month and a half before the court of inquiry convened, Porter turned once more to the task of trying to change John Quincy Adams' opinion of him and his recent action in Puerto Rico. A few days in mid-April swarmed with activity. On the 10th, he wrote again to the President who, being a Sabbatarian, resented the letter "because it was written and sent and received by me on a Sunday." Five days later, Adams unbent enough to grant an appointment, but evidently Porter gained nothing from it, since the President spent the next day attending to details connected with the forthcoming court of inquiry.

Porter's flurry of useless effort ended with his writing yet another missive to the embattled President, who was so enraged by what he termed its "impertinent and angry" tone that he had it cited in Porter's court-martial as evidence of "insubordinate conduct." [8]

The Commodore did not forget Southard. In a letter dated 13 April he aired two major complaints: first, the Department's "positive injunction" that he come home immediately had deprived him "of the opportunity . . . of obtaining, by personal application, the written testimony necessary in the case"; second, the administration was using his perfectly justifiable action at Fajardo as "the occasion of my recall . . . of my being displaced from my Command; it is that affair which now keeps me suspended from the exercise of my Official functions."

A week later Southard replied and, after expressing his "surprise" about the tenor and contents of the above letter—the Secretary seems to have used "surprise" to mean "infuriated incredulity"—pointed out that Porter had been ordered to bring along Platt and other officers whose testimony would be necessary for his defense. Certainly, he said, it was known to the Commodore that the Department had been seeking an officer to replace him at the earliest opportunity. Southard ended with the ominous statement: "No further notice of the style and manner of your letter is deemed necessary at this time, than to remind you of the relation which subsists between you and the Department." [9] Indeed, this letter of 13 April was another that the Secretary would use against Porter in his court-martial.

On 2 May, the "Court of Inquiry directed to investigate the conduct of David Porter" sat, with Captain Isaac Chauncey presiding.* Captains William M. Crane and George C. Read were members of the court, and Richard S. Coxe was Judge Advocate (government-appointed prosecutor). The court was asked to investigate two particular matters: the rectitude of Porter's landing at Fajardo, and whether he had neglected his duties as Commodore of the West India Squadron in order to carry specie.

Porter spent the first three days of the inquiry listening to Lieutenant Platt, who had come from the West Indies to testify. Then, on 5 May, he committed a series of major blunders. He objected to the competency of the court, on the grounds that two of the three officers serving on it were junior to him on the Navy list.† Next, he commenced reading aloud from a batch of correspondence that he had brought with him. When he began making nasty remarks about Southard, he was stopped, and, after some discussion, the court decided that it would accept evidence from Porter only if it were in writing and were delivered through the medium of the judge advocate. Upon hearing this decision, Porter walked out. He later claimed that he had done so to avoid "a very useless sacrifice of my feelings as . . . it could do me neither good nor harm. A court more powerless and yet more calculated to harm the accused was perhaps never formed. . . ." He did not attend any more of the sessions, a course of action which only deprived him of the opportunity to interrogate witnesses, and aroused more sentiment against him in administrative circles. Bereft of a chance to present his evidence in his own way, Porter dispatched a number of documents to Southard, who hurried to consult Adams on how they should be handled. Even though the papers had not been presented through the prescribed channel, the two men decided to send them along to the prosecution, rather than return them to the Commodore.[10]

---

* Captain William Bainbridge was appointed to preside, and although his request to be excused on the grounds of his long friendship with Porter was turned down by the President, he somehow managed to wriggle out of this unpleasant duty.
† This argument would seem weak. If followed to its logical conclusion, the senior officer of the Navy would be exempted automatically from any trial by his peers.

The findings of the court, which were rendered on 9 May, were in many ways complimentary to Porter. He was fully acquitted of the charge of dereliction of duty through carrying specie, because the evidence of Randall and Mountain had been "derived from the representations of others." Any transgressions he may have committed were due solely to his "indiscreet zeal" in executing his orders, and his campaigns in the West Indies were summed up as "highly honorable . . . effective . . . in conformity with the orders and instructions" of the Navy Department. But because he "did not communicate with the constituted authorities of Porto Rico," he was censured for his landing at Fajardo, "a hostile invasion of a peaceful territory," and a court-martial on that charge was recommended.[11]

The Adams Cabinet assembled on 12 May to discuss the findings of the court of inquiry, and all agreed that Porter should be punished: the only controversy hinged on what means should be used to accomplish that end. Exhibiting his malice, Southard opposed a court-martial, favoring instead a direct Executive censure. Why? The Secretary admitted that he was "distrustful of . . . naval officers" (an interesting and revealing remark for the Secretary of the Navy to make), and feared that they would acquit Porter. Adams, whose opinion was shared by Secretary of State Henry Clay and Secretary of War James Barbour, was sure that officers would "do their duty, however unpleasant," and decided to hold a court-martial. Southard remained unconvinced and, a couple of days after his objection had been overridden, remarked to the President that he still believed "Porter will come out clear. . . ." On 28 May, the Secretary notified Porter that he would be arrested and tried. Then, after almost a month had passed, he informed Porter that receipt of the notification had actually constituted arrest, and that he need not surrender his sword or have "limits" assigned to his freedom of movement.[12]

During May the President held several meetings connected with the Porter case. On the 17th, he was closeted with Randall and Mountain, and it must be assumed that nothing good for the Commodore came of their conversations. Late in the month, he had a number of sessions with Comptroller of the Treasury Joseph Anderson, who had served as a senator from Pennsylvania and was related to Porter by marriage. Anderson took upon himself the impossible task of changing the Executive mind about Porter. In his *Memoirs,* Adams noted three conversations with Anderson jammed into three days, and then a long meeting on the 30th, to which he devoted more than two pages.

This interview is important, for it provides a keen insight into the President's sentiments concerning Porter. Anderson began the conversation by "intimating a suspicion" that Adams had been "influenced" against the Commodore by his Secretary of the Navy. This, the President denied, as he did the allegation that Southard was "hostile" to Porter; indeed, he said, the decision to hold a court-martial had been made "against the advice and opinion of Mr. Southard." * Adams went on to state that the only charge against Porter would be that he had made an unauthorized landing at Fajardo, "unless," he added, "I should direct an additional charge [which he soon did] for his insubordinate and insulting letters to the Department, to Mr. Monroe, and to me."

Anderson next cast doubt on the ability of a naval court-martial to judge matters concerned with abstruse details of international law. Adams thought it would be competent to do so, but if not, he as the President could make any necessary rectifications. In his opinion, a court-martial would be the fairest method of handling Porter. Finally, Anderson asked what the President would do if Porter should "acknowledge that he had been wrong." Adams replied: "That would change the whole aspect of the affair. In that view of things, there might be room for considerations of indulgence; but Porter himself had shut the door upon them by the tone of defiance and insult which he had hitherto maintained—claiming honor and reward for that which demanded reprobation." †

While the President was telling Anderson that a contrite attitude by Porter would be advisable, Porter, with an execrable sense of timing, was publishing a pamphlet entitled: *An Exposition of the Facts and Circumstances which Justified the Expedition to Foxardo*. Although the pamphlet contained defiance of the administration of John Quincy Adams, Porter had the effrontery to dedicate it to the President personally. He explained that, since he had not been permitted to give his evidence orally to the court of inquiry, he had to use this means of bringing it directly to the Executive attention.

After calling upon "the laws of nations and of nature, highly approved precedents, and the orders of the secretary of the Navy" to support the righteousness of his conduct at Fajardo, Porter's pamphlet quoted John Quincy Adams: "I subscribe to the yet stronger measures which have been recently recommended by the executive, to wit, 'nothing short of authority to land, pursue them, and hold the authorities of

---

* John Quincy Adams was being jesuitical. To be sure, Southard had opposed a court-martial for Porter but, as recorded above, only because he wanted to obviate what he thought was the likelihood that the Commodore's fellow officers would acquit him.

† Anderson was persistent. Adams mentions two more appointments with him early in July, and another during the first part of August. It seems likely that the Porter case would have been mentioned at those meetings, although the President furnished no details.[13]

places answerable for the pirates who issue from and resort there . . .' can put down this disgraceful system." Porter also agreed with the President's observation that "neither the government of Spain . . . [nor its colonies] could reasonably complain" about any measures taken against piracy. In words that shouted defiance, the Commodore wrote that the American government should *"protect, countenance, and support"* any officer engaged in the unsavory business of tracking down pirates, and not have him "degraded by punishment before complaint, or removed from his command without being allowed the opportunity to explain the reasons for his conduct." He tossed off the remark that by dismissing him, the administration had encouraged West Indian piracy, and concluded with the statement that any errors—if such there were—that he might have committed were due to the complexities of his position, poised between "nice and intricate questions of national rights" and his "zealous desire to act fully up to the wishes of the government." Tacked on as the finale to so ill-tempered a tirade, this attempt at conciliation was meaningless.

If any pro-Porter sentiments still lingered in Adams and Southard, the *Exposition* eradicated them, and it was probably the deciding factor in the administration's conclusion that Porter must be charged with insubordination as well as with disregard of orders in landing at Fajardo. Adams spent an entire day reading the pamphlet, and complained that Porter talked as if his landing in Puerto Rico had been "in fresh pursuit of pirates." As usual, Southard was even more hostile than the President. He wrote one of his icy letters to acknowledge receipt of Porter's *Exposition,* and once again said he was "surprised," this time that the Commodore had "considered it proper," to issue a "publication" while his case was pending. Furthermore, he found the contents of the pamphlet "deficient" and "inaccurate." The letter in which Porter replied the next day was unpleasant enough to become the fourth and final missive cited in his court-martial as contemptuous of the Secretary.[14]

So direct a confrontation between an American administration and a famous American naval officer could not, and did not, go unnoticed. Most newspapers carried running accounts of the combatants' latest moves and countermoves. Journalistic comment was, however, somewhat noncommittal, at least until after the court-martial had delivered its verdict. Typical was an editorial that appeared in *Niles National Register* in mid-June: it conceded that Porter's *Exposition* had been "prematurely published," and that the government certainly possessed "the right of inquiry." On the other hand, the paper contended, ". . . much irritation exists as to his recall . . . and great allowances should be made on account of the feelings which an honorable officer must necessarily have on such an occasion."

While Porter was waiting for his court-martial to sit, he might have reflected—but undoubtedly did not—that there was an element of justice in his having to face the same ordeal as those he had hounded in the past. Throughout his career in the Navy, he had been one of the most voluble and implacable of court-martial judges. His relentless questioning of the accused in Barron's court-martial in 1808, and his vindictive attempts to have Lieutenant Beverly Kennon cashiered were described earlier, but the recounting of one other case will, perhaps, give credence to the above generalization. In 1822 Lieutenant Joel Abbot made vague accusations of peculation against Captain Isaac Hull, commanding the Navy yard at Charlestown, Massachusetts, and Navy Commissioner Porter was sent to Boston to investigate the charges. Porter came to the conclusion that his close friend Hull was being persecuted by his underling. A court-martial, in which Porter acted as main prosecutor, found the lieutenant guilty of trying "to injure and defame the character of a superior officer . . . ," and of "scandalous conduct." Abbot was suspended from the Navy for two years without pay or allowances.[15]

Captain David Porter's own court-martial convened on 7 July with Captain James Barron presiding. Members were Captains Thomas Tingey, James Biddle, Charles Ridgely, Robert Spence, John Downes, John Henley, Jesse D. Elliott, James Renshaw, Thomas Brown, Charles Thompson, Alexander Wadsworth, and George Rodgers. As at the court of inquiry, the Judge Advocate was Richard S. Coxe. Six of the names on the panel stand out: two as friends of the accused, and four as his enemies. Tingey and Downes might both have been designated as Porter champions, although only the latter may be marked as a certainty. Tingey might remember that Porter had long admired and supported him, and that as a young lieutenant he had met his future wife at Tingey's house. Downes and Porter liked and respected one another both during and since their service together in the *Essex*.* Downes, however, had no right to act as Porter's judge, not because he was Porter's good friend, for such could be considered only fair, since four of the Commodore's enemies were acting in the proceedings against him, but because Porter owed Downes the sizable amount of $4,500. In 1822 he had borrowed $3,000 from his former lieutenant, and when, on 1 January 1825,

* Downes returned to the Pacific in 1831 when he commanded the USS *Potomac* in successful action against pirates at Qualla Battou, in what is now Indonesia. This was the first major engagement of an American warship in Asian waters.

he asked for and received a second loan from Downes, this for "$1,500 at six per cent interest per annum," he had not repaid one penny in principal or interest on the first loan.[16] Had the court known of this intimate financial relationship, Downes would certainly have been excused, but obviously neither party concerned said anything.

Biddle, Barron, Elliott, and Coxe were Porter's enemies. Biddle, to be sure, was in a category somewhat different from the others. Although he and Porter disliked one another, Biddle's character and reputation seemed to guarantee that he would be able to rise above his personal predilections and render a fair verdict. The same compliment cannot be paid to James Barron or Jesse D. Elliott: their careers proved that they were grudge-carriers of the first water, and both had excellent reasons to hate Porter. Barron could recall that Porter had needled him throughout his court-martial for the loss of the *Chesapeake*, had publicly opposed his reinstatement in the Navy after the War of 1812, and had backed Decatur during the preliminaries to the tragic duel in 1820. Ever since Elliott had panicked while seconding Barron against Decatur, he had been openly called a coward and cut socially by the man he was now asked to judge. It is not as easy to discern why Richard S. Coxe should have been so implacably anti-Porter, unless it was simply because, as the Commodore himself observed, the "Judge Advocate . . . received his appointment from the Secretary [Southard], and is his warm friend and protégé."

The court-martial was asked to deliver verdicts on two charges against Porter, the first backed by one specification, and the second by five. Charge number 1 was "Disobedience of orders, and conduct unbecoming an officer," in that

> [Porter had landed] . . . on the island of Porto Rico, in the dominions of his Catholic Majesty the King of Spain, then and still at amity and peace with the United States, in a forcible and hostile manner, and in military array and did then and there commit divers acts of hostility against the subjects and property of the said King of Spain, in contravention of the constitution of the United States and in violation of the instructions from the government of the United States to him, the said David Porter.

Charge number 2 was "Insubordinate conduct and conduct unbecoming an officer." The five specifications in this charge were, in order, that Porter had written on 17 April a letter of "an insubordinate and disrespectful character" to President John Quincy Adams; sent similar letters dated 30 January, 17 March, 13 April, and 14 June, to Samuel L. Southard, Secretary of the Navy; published a pamphlet concerning the court of inquiry before the latter could print its official findings; issued in it statements that were not only incorrect, but "highly disrespectful of both the secretary and the court"; and had "made public official communications" to and from the government without permission.[17]

When the court-martial opened on 7 July Porter announced his acceptance of all his judges, including Biddle, Barron, and Elliott, saying that he believed too much in "the known character of my brethren in arms, to think of scrutinizing the motives of any." But he challenged Coxe as judge advocate, charging that when acting in a similar capacity on the court of inquiry, he had been unfair. Moreover, declared Porter, Coxe had since written and published "at least one anonymous article, distinctly asserting the truth of the specifications now exhibited against me," and had already prepared for publication a pamphlet answering the Commodore's *Exposition* about Fajardo.* Presiding officer Barron took Porter's exception under advisement but, under the law, the only person who could disqualify Coxe was Coxe himself. To the astonishment of no one, he refused to do so, and continued to play a key role in the drama of Porter's fall. About all that Porter accomplished on the first day of his trial was to ask for and receive permission to appoint Walter Jones, an able attorney, as his counsel. The next day he pleaded not guilty to both charges.

Testimony and argument lasted for five weeks, making it one of the longest courts-martial in naval history. One of Porter's biographers aptly commented: "Everyone concerned gave evidence at the greatest possible length. The prosecution dragged in everything it could think of, relevant or irrelevant, while Porter on the defence wandered far afield." [18]

A parade of prosecution witnesses, among them Lieutenant Platt and Consul Cabot, established the admitted facts in the first charge: Cabot's goods had been stolen at St. Thomas, Platt had gone to Fajardo in a semi-official capacity to search for them and had been insulted there. In retaliation, Porter had landed armed forces on Spanish soil and, at bayonet's point, had dictated apologies from Fajardo's local officials. It was no more difficult for the prosecution to prove on the second charge that Porter had written the specified letters to the President and the Secretary of the Navy, that he had published a pamphlet about the proceedings of his court of inquiry and the Secretary's part therein, and that he had made public official correspondence. In reality, the case was occupied not at all with facts, but with interpretations alone: Had Porter's landing at Fajardo been in contravention of his orders? Had his literary output been sufficiently disrespectful of his superiors to warrant condemnation?

---

* Porter's allegations were true. Coxe's article had appeared anonymously in the *National Intelligencer,* and his anti-Porter pamphlet was published so soon after the court-martial issued its verdict, that it must have been written previously.

Porter's almost interminable defense, presented orally by Counsel Jones, ran to some 50,000 words. It commenced by emphasizing the difference between the two charges the court was called upon to decide: one, he thought, was fundamental, the other picayune. He described the first charge as dealing with the "most important and vital principles of the high and awful sanctions, by which national sovereignty is to be maintained, and vindicated by arms." In elegant language, he shrugged off the second as concerning no more than "the minute punctilios of ceremonious respect."

To defend himself against the charge of disobeying instructions when he occupied Fajardo, Porter flitted from authority to authority, all the way from "the venerable and illustrious Grotius" to the presumably less venerable and less illustrious John Quincy Adams. He wondered how he could be accused of disobeying orders, arguing that such could apply only to a refusal to carry out directives given by a commanding or superior officer in the field, not to "general *instructions* from the *government*." After making a few more verbose observations on the principles of international law, he arrived at a major item in his defense: the similarity between what he had done at Fajardo in 1824 and what Andrew Jackson had done in the Floridas seven years before, and the utter contrast in how the government had treated him and the General. He stressed the wording of the orders Secretary Thompson had addressed to him on 1 February 1823—"Pirates are considered, by the law of nations, enemies of the human race"—then called President Monroe to stand beside Jackson as a defense witness in absentia:

> We find that the president [Monroe] in his message to congress, explaining and justifying the conduct of General Jackson towards the Spanish authorities in Florida, enumerates . . . their encouragement of buccaneering, as one of the enormities which had forfeited their neutral character. General Jackson himself . . . justifying his apparent severity against persons claiming Spanish protection, can find no more emphatic reprobation of their character . . . than to denounce them as land pirates.

The Commodore pounced upon one word in Smith Thompson's instructions. He had been ordered to cooperate fully with local officialdom when its rule not only existed theoretically, but was "felt." He denied that the Spanish government at Fajardo could have been "felt" while local authorities were either criminals themselves or were cowed into compliance by the pirates who were their fellow townsmen. He was sure the Spanish sovereignty that Jackson had disregarded in the Floridas was more in evidence than was the Spanish authority at Fajardo. He closed his defense on the first charge by arguing that he could be found guilty only if he had been "positively ordered to do something that I omitted, or positively forbidden to do something that I did," but since government orders were merely "discretionary," neither could have been the case, and he was therefore innocent.

When he answered the charge of "insubordinate conduct" toward members of the administration, Porter bristled and made no effort to rein his bitterness:

> The manner of my recall, so incommensurate as I then knew and still know, with the merits of my conduct . . . the inequality of the treatment I received and that extended to others under like circumstances; the continuing to hold me up as an ambiguous object of denunciation and calumny, or of indefinite suspension . . . were all circumstances that bore heavily on my thoughts.

During the course of this onslaught, he paused to declare that he was not "capable of an insult or rudeness" to the President or the Secretary of the Navy, but that when he had pondered the treatment extended to him and that given to General Jackson, he had no choice but to express his objections to his superiors. If such right of appeal were denied, he said, he and other officers would be condemned to "the basest servility," to "pusillanimous silence under the strongest sense of injury," or to "cringe at the doors of departments and bureaus for justice." [19]

As the court-martial dragged through the rigors of Washington's summer heat, public opinion tended to divide along political lines—pro-administration journals being automatically anti-Porter, and vice versa. Yet, a trend against the Commodore is discernible in the nation's press. A week or so after the trial opened, *Niles National Register* wrote: "Every body is deeply interested in the fate of com. Porter—but all are more interested in preserving the law, and maintaining that degree of discipline without which the navy must fall to pieces like a rope of sand." The *New-York Spectator* castigated the Washington *Gazette,* the New York *Advocate,* and other organs with similar views, for their angry attacks on the administration: it admitted that the charge of insubordination was "frivolous," but declared that no man could be deemed to be above the law. Furthermore, asked the paper, had not Porter persecuted Lieutenants Abbot and "McKennon"? Obviously, the *Spectator* considered that one good persecution deserved another. The same journal commented a week later that the "Commodore's defence has weakened his case where it has been read."

The Salem paper that had belabored Porter in 1814 was plowing the same field a decade later. It agreed with a Boston periodical that, although Porter fought "obstinately" for himself, President Adams was correct in his dedication to the thesis that the military must remain under civilian control. "If," wrote the *Salem Gazette,* "it is the fate of Capt.

Porter by his own imprudence to be . . . a . . . victim" of that Executive determination, such a verdict could be accepted with equanimity. Sniping at the Commodore continued from the same source: "Our officers have heretofore proved that they are fit to command, they must now shew that they are fit to obey. If . . . the laws are too slender a net to hold them, the navy will be scuttled and sunk. . . ." The same issue of the *Gazette* quoted an article protesting that "distinguished" was not a correct adjective with which to describe Porter, since throughout his career he had been "distinguished" only for "his unauthorized acts." [20]

While testimony continued, governmental circles remained active against Porter. In his *Memoirs,* the President noted that Southard was "much worried by the offensive defence" of the Commodore, and dreaded the possibility that he might be compelled to testify before the court-martial. However, when the trial was little more than two weeks old, a naval colleague wrote John Rodgers that "Comm. P—— is thought to have been very indiscreet toward the Department, & for this he has lost friends." Years later, Thomas Hart Benton, anti-administration senator from Missouri, recalled that he had been "a close observer" of Porter's trial, and had had no trouble in deciding that, from beginning to end, the Commodore's chances of acquittal were nil. Courts-martial, he believed, were solely for the purpose of convicting or acquitting by a priori agreements, "as the court is appointed by the government, dependent on it for future honor and favor, acts in secret, and [its conclusions are] subject to the approval of the Executive." *

The court-martial finally drew to an end when the defense rested on 6 August. On the 9th, the court was still waiting for a transcript of it and Barron, after criticizing the defendant for not having it ready, announced that the decision would be delivered the next day without his written defense, and so it was. On the first charge, Porter was found guilty of "Disobedience of orders, and conduct unbecoming an officer" for his unauthorized landing at Fajardo. On the second charge, he was found guilty of "Insubordinate conduct and conduct unbecoming an officer" toward the President and the Secretary of the Navy, although the court decided that his letter of 17 March to Southard had not been

---

* Commenting on courts-martial procedure, Porter's biographer, Turnbull, states that acquittals "are nowadays [the 1920s] about as common as dust-storms in mid-Atlantic," and he says there is no reason to suppose that they were any more common a hundred years earlier.[21] Between the two, Benton makes the better point. It was not so much that convictions were preordained as that the results tended to be. For instance, Lieutenant Beverly Kennon was acquitted of Porter's charges, and it is likely that the bad relations between the accuser and the Navy Department were a factor in that verdict.

proven insubordinate. Conviction on two such heinous charges could have been sufficient cause for instant dismissal from the Navy.* Instead, Porter's sentence was remarkably lenient. He was given a six-month suspension from the Navy, but allowed to retain full pay and allowances. Furthermore, the court made a strange addendum to its verdict: Porter's conduct, censurable though it was, had been caused by "an anxious disposition, on his part, to maintain the honor and advance the interest of the nation and the service." [22]

The Commodore's defense, which ran to more than 230 handwritten pages, was presented a few days later, and, after commenting that it varied in certain details from the oral presentation made by Walter Jones, and denying that Judge Advocate Coxe had been biased against the defendant, the court reaffirmed its decision of the 10th.

The findings of the court-martial were sent to President Adams on 13 August and, in the course of the next few days, he and Southard read the entire proceedings. Adams concentrated on Walter Jones's presentation of Porter's defense, which, he said, contained "some severe insinuations" against Judge Advocate Coxe. The total entry in his diary for 16 August 1825 reads: "Swam 30 minutes. Southard finished Porter's trial." On the 17th, Adams officially approved the decisions of the court-martial, "according to the precedent in the case of Captain Barron." † [23]

The verdict, with the President's signature, was sent to Porter on the same day. He immediately acknowledged its receipt, and at the same time asked for a leave of absence during his suspension. On the 19th Southard called on the President to advise him of the Commodore's request, which was granted.

Despite this accommodation, the administration slackened its hostility toward Porter not a whit. It is hard to forgive John Quincy Adams for the social boorishness he displayed in a situation involving Porter and the Marquis de Lafayette which arose shortly after the court-martial had ended. That eminent Frenchman was still on his anniversary tour of the United States, and periodically during 1824 and 1825 appeared in

---

* A short time before, John Quincy Adams had written about one ill-starred midshipman who had been court-martialed for no more than "writing a letter" to the Secretary of the Navy asking for reassignment. Even though it had not been proven that he had actually mailed the letter, he was found guilty, and, according to the President, dismissed from the Navy. Adams' memory failed him. The court ruled that Alexander Van Dyke, the midshipman in question, should be "severely reproved" for the letter, but not dismissed, and the President had approved the verdict.

† The cases of Barron and Porter were so different, both as to circumstances and results, that this seems a murky analogy to come from the usually precise Adams.

Washington, both to recuperate from his travels round the country and to take part in festivities in his honor.[24] There are two versions of what happened between Adams, Lafayette, and Porter. According to David Dixon Porter's ever-suspect biography of his father, it was during the late spring of 1825 that Lafayette, who knew and liked the Commodore, accompanied him to the White House in the hope of bringing about a reconciliation between him and Adams. When the two arrived, the President, who was awaiting the carriage, shook hands with Lafayette, and linking arms with him, drew him away, leaving the offended Porter standing alone. When Lafayette later heard the full details of the controversy, it "deepened his feelings of esteem" for the "slighted commodore."

David Dixon Porter is wrong in at least two major particulars—timing and motive. He says the confrontation took place in the late spring, presumably meaning in May or June, which would place it between the sessions of the court of inquiry and the convening of the court-martial. It actually occurred on 3 September, three weeks after Porter had been convicted by the court-martial. And, it was not Lafayette, but "Mr. Du Pont," * who arranged the meeting. The most reliable information on the subject is contained in an eight-page, undated, unsigned letter in the David Porter Papers in the Library of Congress. Through matching handwriting samples, I am convinced that this letter came from the office of Richard S. Coxe and was written either by the Judge Advocate himself or by his secretary. How the letter ended up among the Porter papers, I do not know. Anything that Coxe said about the Commodore should be used with the utmost circumspection, but in this instance his evidence is, at least partially, corroborated.

According to Coxe, the meeting of 3 September was held at the behest of "Mr. Du Pont, a warm friend" of Porter's, who took him to meet Lafayette at "the President's House." Adams confirms Coxe's account; his diary entry on that date reads, "With Lafayette . . . met Du Pont and Porter." Both the President and Lafayette were waiting for the carriage. When it arrived, Adams shook hands with du Pont and, while he was doing so, saw Porter emerging from the carriage, whereupon he pushed past Porter "without speaking to him," and climbed into the carriage. Lafayette got in and the two men were driven away. The French visitor asked the President why he had behaved so oddly, and was told

---

* Which du Pont this was is a matter of conjecture. It could have been either Eleuthère Irénée du Pont or his brother, Victor Marie. Both were friends of Lafayette and Adams, both took part in celebrations honoring the Frenchman, and both were in the vicinity at the time. John Quincy Adams, Judge Advocate Richard S. Coxe, and the biographers of the du Ponts all fail to make the identification.

that there were "abundant reasons why . . . either in his private character, the friend of Mr. Monroe, or in his official character as the President of the United States, [he] should decline to recognize in Com. Porter an individual entitled to receive from him any marks of courtesy or civility." Later, he showed Lafayette an anti-Monroe article published in a Washington newspaper and written by Porter at the very time he declined to attend a dinner given by the President in his honor. After reading the article, the Frenchman concluded that Adams had every right to act as he did.[25]

A letter written by Captain Charles Morris to John Rodgers confirms one part of Coxe's story: "I regret that P—— does not seem disposed to allow any branch of the Executive to be on good terms with him—a letter of his in reply to some of the citizens who invited him to a public dinner gave great offense to the President and Sec'y [of the Navy] from the manner in which he expressed himself of Mr. Monroe."

Adams may have felt some twinge of remorse for his behavior toward Porter. Some months later, when the Commodore's suspension was nearing its end, and the President knew that he planned to join the Mexican Navy, he wrote rather defensively, "all the steps taken against Porter had been reluctant, and after full warnings, and that so long as he persevered in his course he would find himself wading deeper into difficulties." [26]

When Porter was first quoted on his reaction to the verdict of the court-martial, he put his best foot forward. He said he was delighted that he had received a "full acquittal of every *moral* offense . . . ," and continued, "I have been tried and judged by my peers . . . I trust that I can bear my punishment without repining. No one has yet heard me murmur at my sentence . . . I do not *express* a doubt that strict justice has been dispensed to me."

He did not mean a word of it. He was thoroughly and lastingly convinced that he had been shabbily treated by the administration, and was filled with contempt for his naval colleagues who had served on the court-martial. He believed that the latter had manifested a two-fold cowardice, daring neither to acquit him (as they should have done) nor to dismiss him from the service (as they were almost obliged to do after convicting him on such serious charges). Instead, they had found him guilty, and then tried to placate him with soft words about "his anxious disposition . . . to maintain the honor and advance the interest" of his country and its Navy. He announced that he could never again "associate with those who were led by men in power to inflict an unrighteous sentence."

The wound inflicted on Porter by the verdict never healed. A year and a half later, when he was in Mexico, he wrote his wife of his love for the United States, and of how willingly he would die for it, but he said he could no longer live there, since to do so he would have to "cringe and bow and be a sycophant." At about the same time, Evalina Porter wrote a letter for newspaper publication, in which she spoke for her husband:

> Why is Porter in Mexico? . . . . Does a man leave country, family, friends voluntarily? Are ties so sacred so loosely twined around the heart as to [be] broken for a song? . . . . Did Com. Porter obtain fair and candid trial? The voice of the people . . . say no! . . . he was condemned!—for what? To appease it appears the wounded pride of those in power over him. . . . Look at the sentence of the court . . . and it plainly shows he was to be whipped like a boy for a fault and chuckled into good humor by a sugar plumb. . . .*

In 1832 when Porter was U.S. Chargé d'Affaires in the Ottoman Empire, his censure over Fajardo still rankled. From Constantinople he wrote Hezekiah Niles, publisher of *Niles National Register,* asking him to print any additional material he had about "Foxardo," since he feared "posterity" would deem his landing there "ill-judged, rash, unjustifiable, and unnecessary." He recalled that he had not been able to get "oral" testimony from Puerto Rico in time for his trial, and that the written evidence he had was not admitted. He went on to cite a letter, dated 5 June 1831, that he had addressed to the former French Consul at "St. John, Porto Rico" asking him to confirm a report that twelve men had been hanged at Fajardo for piracy.[27] No action of any kind seems to have resulted from this correspondence.

The case stirred up and retained so much interest that there was, of course, abundant comment on it, both at the time of the trial and later. Porter's two previous biographers assert that opinion in the contemporary press was heavily in favor of the Commodore and correspondingly against the administration. Random sampling of the newspapers of the time shows that, while reaction was mixed, it was rather more against Porter than for him. About the only unqualified defense of the Commodore was unearthed from a Philadelphia daily: "three-fourths of the people of Pennsylvania disapprove of the . . . sentence . . . the attempted disgrace of Com. Porter, is a disgrace to the country." Apart from that wholehearted defense, ostensibly pro-Porter newspaper commentary was always hedged, as in the following grammatical monstrosity:

> The American people will learn with grief and astonishment that the gallant Porter . . . has been pronounced guilty of all charges alleged against him . . . that he would have received some censure on the second charge [insubordination] we were prepared to hear, if his quick and sensitive feelings had led him into error, it was in that he had offended against propriety, but that, for humbling a nest of piratical banditti, and resenting

---

* This is the only item written by Evalina Porter that I have been able to find.

with spirit, yet with moderation, and not excess, an insult offered to his country, he should be punished—this, we confess, we were not prepared to see.

An editorial in *Niles National Register,* though generally sympathetic to Porter in tone, concluded that the court had had no option but to declare him guilty on both counts. In the first, commented the paper, "he did not affect to deny the facts," and in the second, "he himself will frankly admit that he suffered his feelings to overcome his judgment." The *American Annual Register* discerned a silver lining in the cloud of conviction which overhung Porter: "It afforded no small gratification to the friends of the Navy, that . . . captain Porter's conduct . . . was not tainted with peculation, and that he was actuated with the most earnest desire to promote the interest and honor of his country." A Richmond paper agreed with Porter's contention that he and Jackson had behaved in much the same manner: "The cases are not exactly parallel. But the conduct of General Jackson does not differ so widely from Com. Porter but that both may be brought to test on the same general principles." [28]

Press opposition to Porter was intense. One journal rejoiced to see that "governmental indulgence" had proven superior to Porter's "ill-natured quibbling," and saw no connection between the actions of the General and those of the Commodore, for Jackson had been "in fresh pursuit" of his enemies; Porter had not. Another editorialized that Porter's conviction had been "ratified by public opinion," because he had lost popularity through his "captiousness, which he unfortunately took for independence." He never should have counted on the support of the anti-administration "Kennel press," for it was motivated not by love of the Commodore but by "hatred to the administration."

Porter's journalistic bête noire, the *Salem Gazette,* was as unsparing as ever, delving back more than a decade for anti-Porter ammunition:

> The Court Martial on Porter has done its duty to the nation, and at the same time, shewn nothing but mercy to him. The *lenity* of the sentence is all that excites surprise. . . . He and his sycophants will probably pay as little respect to this judgment of his peers, as he has been accustomed to shew to the laws of his country. He ought to have been tried ten years ago for landing at Nooaheevah, marching into the country, laying it waste with fire and sword, and slaughtering the natives, with whom we were at peace.

Perhaps the best commentary upon the case was written in an obscure Massachusetts weekly: "Upon the escutcheon of a brave man, of an ardent supporter of his country's, a stain has been discerned and laid bare to the malicious gaze of an envious world. The brilliancy of our maritime fame is eclipsed. A pall is thrown over those heroic achievements which have hitherto shone with unrivalled splendour on the pages of our naval history. . . ." Nevertheless, the paper considered Porter's sentence just: "Once introduce negligence and licentiousness among subordinates, or allow to commanders, the indulgence of discretion without limits, and you may as well spike every gun, or fasten a torpedo at the bottom of every vessel in our navy." [29]

Contemporary non-journalistic opinion was also mixed. Thomas H. Benton concluded that Porter had been "hardly dealt by." A prominent Bostonian, Edward Everett, wrote his son Alexander, soon to be appointed Minister to Spain, that the Porter court-martial was a major topic of the town: ". . . the suspension of 6 months being so slight a punishment gives the whole thing a *pro forma* air which without appeasing Porter, perplexes those who thought his conduct exceedingly censurable. A division of opinion exists . . . I heard Geo. Blake declare he would never be found guilty . . . speaking of him as a much injured man." *

If newspaper editors and political commentators tended either to waver in their support or to oppose the discredited Commodore, one judicial group in his home state came out foursquare on his side. Members of the Grand Jury of Bradford County, Pennsylvania, declared on 15 September that they had heard "with astonishment and regret" of the court-martial's findings. They were convinced that Porter had been punished, not for anything he had done at Fajardo, but because Southard was hostile to him, and Porter had failed in only one particular: "complaisance to the noble Secretary." *Niles National Register* aptly called this judicial opinion "an incomparable curiosity." [30]

Later comment also varied, but there was a much greater tendency to back Porter. One historian, writing only five years after the trial, emphasized the sharp cleavage between the justice of the government's case against the Commodore, and the injustice of the way in which it had handled the case. He ripped to pieces Porter's apologia for his landing at Fajardo, especially his contention that he had done no worse than Jackson: ". . . one bad precedent should not be made use of to justify another; and if the government had been too remiss in the first instance, there was the more necessity for an example in the second." But the same author concluded in a pro-Porter vein: "For a single error in judgment . . . which had been attended with no evil, and which fell far short of cases which had been overlooked, he had been taken from his command, ordered home, arrested, tried by a court-martial, and suspended."

David Dixon Porter devoted almost fifty pages of his father's biography to the landing at Fajardo and its consequences. To his own satisfac-

* George Blake was a U.S. Attorney who had worked closely with Porter in the court-martial of Lieutenant Joel Abbot in 1822.

tion, at least, he vindicated his parent on every charge and specification. To him, it was crystal clear that the government had worked with a single malicious end in mind—to "degrade a faithful officer" who had been only "doing his duty":

> The whole affair looks as if the object had been to find an excuse to deprive Commodore Porter of his command . . . [he] was really tried by a judge advocate, whose competency he denied, and tried; not as an officer . . . who might at worst be guilty of an error in judgment, but as a criminal upon whom it was necessary to cast the greatest obloquy. Many years have passed since these events occurred, but their evil effects are felt to this day; in the destruction of a handsome competency and a happy home; and in the scattering of a large and dependent family, who were called upon to give up a parent who had become an alien in foreign lands, to enable him to provide for their support.*

It would be too much to expect David Dixon Porter to be unbiased about Fajardo and its aftermath. As his own biographer judiciously puts it, the son had always idealized his father as "his one great hero. His hero had now been publicly stricken from the pedestal. But the faith of the worshipper was not disturbed. . . . His father's enemies became his enemies." Indeed they did. David Porter never forgave his colleagues who had found him guilty, and neither did David Dixon Porter, even though, at one time or another during his long career in the Navy, he served under several of his father's judges. The younger Porter inherited from his father a dislike for both politicians and appointees, such as Secretaries of the Navy, and "it is not strange that he was to be caught in many a squall and many a difficult seaway." [31]

Showing almost as much sympathy for David Porter as did his son, a more modern historian wrote that the Commodore "was not always, or even usually, conciliatory and tactful, and doubtless caused irritation. But this could have influenced only men of small stature. His great services to his country, and his value to the navy should have outweighed his offenses. . . . Every true American, from that day to this, knowing the facts, has rejoiced in his landing at Foxardo."

Porter's biographer Turnbull contrasted the treatment accorded to Porter after Fajardo, not with that given to Jackson in the Floridas, but with that meted out to Admiral Henry T. Mayo: in April 1914, some American sailors were arrested in Tampico, Mexico, and although they were released within a few hours, Mayo demanded that the local officials

---

* In a letter to his publisher, fifty years after his father's conviction, David Dixon Porter claimed that he had rewritten the account of the trial in order to "soften down some of the very sharp things I said . . . [to] smooth it over with a flat-iron." He seems to have blunted his statements little, if at all, in the final result.

apologize and salute the American flag. To be sure, Mayo did not land at Tampico, but perhaps only because the episode took place at about the time U.S. armed forces were storming Veracruz. Washington backed Mayo all the way and, far from court-martialing him, promoted him. "History, it appears, would be justified in giving Porter the benefit of comparison," comments Turnbull.

Fletcher Pratt spoke severely against the government's behavior toward Porter: "To Porter (and to many people since his time) this seemed the most appalling mistreatment for an act which merited reward instead of punishment." Pratt saw Southard, "one of the most tactlessly irritable individuals who ever sat in the Cabinet," as the culprit, and described the appointments of Barron and Elliott to the court-martial as outrageous.[32]

Looking at the Fajardo incident and its aftermath from the vantage point of almost a century and a half, it does not appear that anyone connected with them emerged with laurels. As for Porter, he had no right to go ashore at Fajardo. He acted to heal Platt's wounded honor, but the lieutenant had landed, not as an officer chasing pirates, but as little more than a plainclothesman in search of stolen goods. Platt had no proof that those who had taken the missing property were residents of Fajardo, or that it was sequestered there. Porter, with no more evidence than Platt had, and obviously not in "fresh pursuit" of pirates, invaded an inhabited area under direct Spanish control, and bullied Spanish subjects into apologizing under the threat that refusal to do so would mean the destruction of Fajardo. All this had been done without permission from any higher authority, Spanish or American. Given the diplomatic situation of the time, the government had no choice but to dissociate itself from the actions of its rash and impulsive Commodore, and the charge that he had flouted orders seems thoroughly justifiable. As to the second charge, Porter's conduct toward two Presidents and one Secretary of the Navy had, to say the least, fallen far short of courtesy.

Nevertheless, it appears that the Monroe and Adams administrations treated Porter much more harshly than was necessary. Perusal of the documentation involved leaves the reader with the unmistakable impression that President Monroe, President Adams, Secretary Southard, and Judge Advocate Coxe labored singly and collectively in a prearranged agreement to accomplish Porter's humiliation and punishment, while piously disclaiming that they had any animus whatever. First, he was suspended from duty without being given an opportunity to explain his actions; then, he was immobilized while rumors and articles planted in the press excited public sentiment against him. When he reacted with understandable anger, he was chastised for that, too. Neither the Monroe nor the Adams administration ever made the slightest allowance for Porter's sensitivity at having his proud reputation impugned, or for the fact that the original instructions given him were highly ambiguous, or for the possibility that he was not aware that the international situation had changed drastically since Jackson's action in the Floridas.

On the last point, Porter's avowal that he and the General had acted in the same way but were dealt with differently was true. Two wrongs may not make a right, but perhaps they should be dealt with in roughly the same manner. John Quincy Adams was intimately involved both in Jackson's unauthorized invasion of East and West Florida, and in Porter's unauthorized invasion of Puerto Rico, but his reactions were totally disparate. In 1818 when Adams was asked whether, by irrupting into the Floridas, Jackson had exceeded his instructions, he answered with a ringing defense: "If the question is dubious, it is better to err on the side of vigor than of weakness—on the side of our own officer, who has rendered the most eminent services to the nation, than on the side of our bitterest enemies, and against him." This was the same John Quincy Adams who, some seven years later, said that Porter's landing at Fajardo was "a direct, hostile invasion . . . utterly unjustifiable . . . one of the most high-handed acts I have ever heard of," [33] and who, by using all the power and authority available to a President, engineered the Commodore's conviction.

Admittedly, the international situation had changed since 1817. Jackson's deeds were tailor-made for Adams' purposes, and Adams used them most effectively to help him expel Spain forever from the Floridas. Porter's expedition to Fajardo, made only a year after the promulgation of the Monroe Doctrine, tended to compromise seriously the position of the United States vis-à-vis the European powers. But if anyone should have been able to comprehend that a mere naval officer might not realize that decisive and extralegal action which at one time might be useful to his country and merit applause, might at another time have to be condemned, that individual was John Quincy Adams.

Porter deserved no accolades for his temporary occupation of Spanish territory. Perhaps a reprimand was necessary, and Porter, being the man he was, would probably have been aggrieved by any treatment short of public congratulations. But the court-martial, especially on the charge of insubordination, seems to have been only vindictive. As evidence of administrative mercy, Adams' supporters have stressed the unusually mild sentence. That, however, was the doing of the court-martial, not of the President, and, even there, his judges' kind words about patriotism and service had little effect other than to drip acid into Porter's already lacerated pride, and help send him into what turned out to be lifelong exile.

Sometime before the court-martial delivered its decision, Porter had decided that, if convicted, he would enter the naval service of Mexico. Only a few days after his recall to Washington from the West Indies, he wrote John Rodgers that he considered his prospects in the U.S. Navy were hopeless, but that he was "prety confident" that he could carve out a new career in Latin America.

He had long been attracted by the experiences of foreign officers in the service of fledgling Latin-American republics. In 1817, envious of the success of the Irishman William ("Admiral Guillermo") Brown, who was operating in the Pacific under the aegis of the revolutionary government in Buenos Aires, he gave some consideration to joining José Miguel Carrera in Chile, but had wisely decided to stay in Washington.[1]

A few years later, Thomas Cochrane excited Porter's jealousy. Cochrane had been a highly esteemed British naval officer and a prominent radical member of Parliament, but in 1814 his career seemed irretrievably shattered when he was accused of complicity in a swindling case, convicted, and dismissed from the Royal Navy. In 1815 he accepted appointment as an admiral in the Chilean Navy, and the ensuing five years were triumphant for him. With daring artifice, he captured the city of Valdivia, and his dispersal of Spanish sea power in the Pacific aided San Martín and O'Higgins in the liberation of Peru. But the irascible Englishman soon quarreled with San Martín, and in 1822 resigned his Chilean commission.[2] He was offered command of the Mexican Navy—an offer accepted by Porter a few years later—but instead served the Brazilians against the Portuguese from 1822 to 1825.* In 1826, he took

---

* In Brazil, Cochrane seized an entire province near the mouth of the Amazon by resorting to trickery. So completely did he break up a Portuguese convoy sailing out of Bahia that only thirteen of sixty ships managed to reach Lisbon.

command of the Greek Navy and fought against the Turks until 1828: that was the only assignment in which he accomplished nothing. He eventually proved himself innocent of the charge on which he had been convicted in 1814, and in 1832 was reinstated in the Royal Navy.[3]

In view of the dismal financial situation that lay ahead for Porter in Mexico, it is unfortunate that he knew all about Cochrane's glory and presumed riches, and nothing about his impressive monetary troubles. At the time of his resignation from the Chilean Navy, Cochrane wrote: ". . . even the pay so often promised was withheld, and food itself was denied, so that we were reduced to a state of the greatest privation and suffering . . . and the seamen . . . were in a state of open mutiny. . . ." Moreover, the Englishman passed the rest of his life trying, through litigation, to collect the fortunes which he claimed Chile and Brazil owed him. In 1845, *"twenty-three years after* the liberation of Peru and the annihilation of Spanish power in the Pacific," Chile paid him £6,000 but, he complained, his legal expenses amounted to £25,000, hence the transaction "cost me £19,000 out of my own pocket." As late as 1859, the year before he died, Cochrane was still trying to pry £100,000 out of Brazil; his estate was eventually reimbursed by £40,000.[4]

Of course, even if Porter had known about them, he could not have foreseen that Cochrane's difficulties would soon be his own. All that rose before his eyes were visions of the fortune that had so far evaded him and of a refurbished reputation. With such thoughts in mind, his decision to serve Mexico was reinforced when the court-martial found him guilty. His suspension from the Navy ran from 9 August 1825 to 9 February 1826, and while he waited for it to expire, he worked with his old friend from Chile, Joel R. Poinsett, who had recently been appointed U.S. Minister to Mexico. As early as 21 August, Porter wrote Poinsett that he saw "a bright field" for himself in Mexico.

He also established contact with Pablo Obregón, Mexican Minister to the United States, to see on what terms he might serve in the Mexican Navy, and wrote Poinsett that he had asked the Minister for the same title as "Lord Cochran had, or at least nothing inferior to it." When Obregón expressed pleasure about Porter's "desire to enter the Mexican Navy," Porter answered, "rank is the most important consideration with me." A month later, still strumming the same theme, he wrote to Obregón: "the tender of my services was on condition that I should be placed on the same footing as Lord Cochran in the Chillean navy, and if such is the intention of the Mexican government, there will not be a moment's hesitation on my part to resign my commission." On this issue

Porter met the first of his many defeats in Mexico. In spite of his repeated requests for promotion to admiral, and even for a brigadier general's commission,[5] the highest rank he ever attained was *Capitán de Navio* (captain of a ship-of-the-line squadron) .

The fact that before two months of his suspension had elapsed, the influential *National Intelligencer* was musing, "the invitation from Mexico must be very gratifying to Com. Porter's feelings. . . ." proves that Porter made no effort to keep his negotiations with Mexico City secret. To the contrary, he apparently wanted the news bruited about, for if one nation desired to have his services, others, namely, Spain and the United States, might be enticed into making him a better offer. Spain is said to have tried to bribe Porter into rejecting Mexican service by promising to pay the $60,000, plus accumulated interest, that the Havana *consulado* had owed him since his capture of the privateers *Le Duc de Montebello, L'Intrepide,* and *La Petite Chance* in 1810. His son says that because the circumstances and timing of the offer made it so obviously a bribe, Porter indignantly refused it.[6] However, the Commodore may have been aided in reaching that decision by the realization that Madrid probably had no intention of paying it anyway.

Porter was simultaneously using newspaper publicity in the United States to accomplish two purposes: to entice from Washington a counter-offer attractive enough to keep him home, and to aid him in recruitment. While negotiating with Mexico, he was trying to persuade other American officers to accompany him south. He notified Poinsett, "Every mail brings me fresh applications from officers wishing to enter the Mexican service." In a letter written a few years later to Senator Mahlon Dickerson, Porter suggested that his tactics had worked: "Mr. Adams offered me the best command in the navy if I would not go to Mexico." There is at least some evidence that, as the Commodore's suspension neared its end in February 1826, the Adams administration commenced behaving in a more conciliatory manner toward him. At almost the moment of his reinstatement, Porter requested a six-month furlough, which Adams granted although he knew that Porter would use the privilege to make a trip to Mexico and that, if he found conditions there favorable, not only would he resign his U.S. commission and accept a Mexican one, but he might take with him many other officers. This possibility worried the President and, according to his *Memoirs*, when Captain William B. Finch asked for permission to go with Porter to Mexico, he "advised Mr. Southard not to allow in any instances a furlough to an officer upon the known intention upon his part to accompany Captain Porter. It is in truth an enticement of officers from our service, and the object is to attempt an invasion of the island of Cuba. This is a project which we ought by no means to encourage or countenance." *

Adams' reference to an impending invasion of Cuba alluded to widespread rumors of a forthcoming alliance of Latin-American countries against Spain. This anticipated coalition was to be made up of Mexico, Colombia, and the "Confederation of Central America." Hearsay became fact a few months later when the delegates to the Pan-American Conference at Panama drew up plans for a unified American fleet, to be furnished by a ratio of two Mexican ships for one Colombian, and supplied from Central America, as well as from the larger nations. This fleet was to protect the coastline of Latin America and liberate Cuba by smashing the Spanish Navy and merchant marine. The plans were apparently nearing completion at the time Porter was mulling over the pros and cons of accepting the Mexican assignment, and the prospect of commanding a combined Mexican-Colombian armada was undoubtedly an added inducement for the Commodore.

But no sooner had he irrevocably committed himself to Mexico than the grand alliance collapsed. Not only had Great Britain and the United States made known their opposition to a coalition that had such potential to disrupt the status quo in Latin America, but a quarrel between Mexico and Colombia dealt an even worse blow: the latter pulled out of the alliance. Porter, after his return from Mexico, demonstrated considerable bitterness about the refusal of Colombia to cooperate with him. Colombians, he said, were characterized by "a disregard to the national faith and honor . . . want of intelligence and chivalrous feeling." The alliance had fallen apart only through "some trifling and puerile remarks" in the press of both countries. In short, "There would be no invasion of Cuba, no unified American fleet to blockade Havana, and no League of American States to which Mexico would contribute the ships so laboriously figured out at Panama." For the next couple of years, rumors periodically resurrected the Mexican-Colombian alliance, but it remained comatose.

No matter how strong his predilection for Mexican service, Porter would not sever all ties by resigning his American commission until he had investigated the circumstances of his prospective assignment. Consequently, when his suspension ended on 9 February 1826 he was ready to sail for Veracruz. However, he decided to delay his departure until a new

---

* Actually, Southard treated Finch's application with the utmost delicacy. Amid assurances of the Department's "high estimation . . . of your character and conduct," he told Finch that his furlough could not be granted *if* such were for Porter's "gratification and convenience," but that if the trip were for his "own purposes," he would be permitted to go. Finch remained in the U.S. Navy.[7]

ship being built in New York for the Mexican Navy was completed. Probably designed and constructed by the well-known ship builder Henry Eckford, the vessel in question was a handsome, 22-gun brig, named originally *America,* later *Tancitaro,* and finally *Guerrero.* It was late April—probably the 22nd—when Porter and his entourage were able to depart. There was nothing approximating the exodus feared by President Adams. In fact, only three American naval officers sailed with Porter: two midshipmen and Porter's twenty-one-year-old nephew, Lieutenant David H. Porter from Pennsylvania.* Two of his sons were taken along, ten-year-old Thomas, his favorite, and twelve-year-old David Dixon. His physician, Dr. Daniel Boardman, and his secretary, Edmund Law—an Englishman known at one time or another in Mexican documentation as "Low," "Lau," and even "Laure"—also accompanied him. The monotony of the voyage was broken only when a Spanish warship appeared off the coast of Mexico and gave chase. Her pursuit, however, was reluctant and short-lived, and Porter entered Veracruz Harbor on 16 May 1826.[8]

Although by late 1821, Spain had been expelled from the mainland of Mexico and that country had managed to achieve de facto independence, Madrid tenaciously held on to San Juan d'Ulua for four more years. This fortress stands on a reef dominating Veracruz Harbor, and Spain kept it to maintain a measure of direct rule, and to provide a springboard for eventual reconquest. Spanish possession of San Juan d'Ulua was an intolerable threat to Mexican national security, and was directly responsible for the creation of a Mexican Navy. During the early 1820s Mexico assembled a small fleet, most of whose ships had been bought in Great Britain; many of its officers were English, but a sizable number of them were Spanish. In October 1825, the Mexican Navy scored the greatest victory in its history by first outmaneuvering, and then driving off, a Spanish fleet attempting to reinforce San Juan d'Ulua. The fortress was compelled to surrender on 16 November. Unfortunately for Porter, this impressive triumph was followed by a decided slackening in Mexican naval morale, and although he had some success in reversing the trend, the fleet never again reached the heights it achieved at San Juan d'Ulua.

Furthermore, at the time of Porter's arrival, Mexico was being riven by the opposing forces that kept it in a state of turbulence for many years. During the 1820s the basic division was between the conservative, autocratic, clerical-minded, British-oriented Mexicans and their somewhat more liberal, democratic, federalistic, anti-clerical, pro-American

---

* He was the son of Porter's sister, Ann, who had married a cousin named Alexander Porter.

opponents. Although they fought their battles on Masonic grounds—the conservatives tending to cluster in the Scottish Rite Masonic lodges (*Escoces*) and the liberals in the York Rite lodges (*Yorkino*) —the observation that they were no more than "revolutionary and conspiratorial groups using the forms of Masonic orders," is undoubtedly correct. For once, David Dixon Porter may be taken literally when he says that the result was "for political intrigue Mexico compared to Washington . . . as Mount Orizaba to a level plain." [9]

Since the *Yorkinos* naturally gravitated toward the United States, American Minister Joel R. Poinsett sided with them. He had carried with him from the United States the charters for five already existing *Yorkino* lodges, and was soon active in founding new ones. This brought him into political conflict with the newly appointed British Chargé in Mexico, Henry George Ward, who backed the more anglophilic *Escoceses*. The *Yorkinos* won the elections of 1826, and for a while, the Americans seemed to have the better of the contest. In the long run, however, Poinsett's meddling in the internal affairs of Mexico proved harmful both to himself and to his protégé, Porter.[10]

Almost immediately after his arrival in Veracruz, the Commodore, deeming it essential that he argue his case for rank and salary with top Mexican officials, went on to Mexico City. Accompanied by Boardman, Law, and his two sons, he traveled on horseback, and arrived there on 5 June. During the month he spent in the capital, he stayed with Poinsett, and met President Guadalupe Victoria, Vice President Nicolás Bravo, and Minister of War and Marine, Manuel Gomez Pedrasa.*

The tone of many of the letters Porter wrote from Mexico gave the impression that they had been written for publication in American newspapers. Consequently, he must have taken great pleasure in sending home news of how he had been received. According to the *National Intelligencer,* he wrote to a friend "that nothing could be more delightful than his accommodations . . . every provision having been made for the comfort of himself and his party by the Mexican government."

Despite the warmth of Mexico's official greeting, he was by no means able to write his own ticket as to his terms of employment. As usual, David Dixon Porter's account occupies a position between fact and fancy: he says that all his father's demands were met by the Mexican government—appointment as "General of Marine" (Admiral) ; a salary of $12,000 a year, "plus perquisites"; command of the fortress of San Juan d'Ulua; and the right to appoint officers. He implies that his father was

---

* Victoria was thirty-seven years old, yet with characteristic inaccuracy, David Dixon Porter described him as "the honest old President."

given a huge land grant in recompense for his having surrendered his claims against Spain.[11] In fact, Porter's title was never more than *Capitán de Navio;* his salary, most of which was never paid anyway, was in pesos, not dollars; he soon lost command of San Juan d'Ulua; he so abused his power of appointment that it was taken away; and he was never able to collect on his land grant.

By the time the conditions of his assignment were made known to him, Porter had so thoroughly committed himself to Mexico that he had to accept them, no matter how keen his disappointment. In a terse note to Southard, dated 1 July 1826, he closed twenty-eight years of service in the U.S. Navy by resigning his commission, effective the following 18 August. His intention to resign had been so obvious that on 8 July, long before the resignation took effect, Poinsett wrote Secretary of State Henry Clay that, "contrary to my expectations," * Porter had accepted appointment as "Capitán de Navio" in the Mexican Navy. He said that Porter anticipated commanding a joint Mexican-Colombian fleet against Spain, but that he, Poinsett, doubted that such a force would come into being. He warned Clay to ready himself for difficulties in store, since the Mexican government had prepared blank letters of marque to be issued to American and English privateers.† [12]

After placing his two little boys in a Mexico City school, probably to study Spanish—a language he never learned to speak—Porter left the capital for Veracruz on 6 July. On his arrival in Mexico, he wrote Poinsett, "I find Naval affairs in a most wretched condition," a first sign of the discouragement which later became total. He found them no better when he returned to Veracruz, and admitted despondently that he was "heartily sick" of that city and it was "heartily sick" of him. He complained that his quarters at San Juan d'Ulua were "a dungeon," and said he had been more comfortably housed when he was a prisoner of the Bashaw of Tripoli.

Nonetheless, with characteristic energy, he threw himself into the task of bringing the Mexican Navy to fighting trim. He was constantly faced with problems concerning both ships and men. The 22-gun brig *Guerrero,* in which he had sailed from New York, was the only effective

---

* It seems odd that Porter's resignation should have been "contrary" to Poinsett's "expectations." For the past year, all the correspondence between them had been based upon just that assumption.
† Poinsett's letters to Washington during Porter's tenure in the Mexican Navy indicate that the former was playing a double game: encouraging Porter to use whatever means were necessary to accomplish his objectives in Mexico, while wording his dispatches to Secretary of State Clay in such a way as to protect himself against any charges of complicity.

vessel he had. Apart from her, the fleet consisted of the 32-gun frigate *Libertad;* two brigs, the 18-gun *Victoria* and the 14-gun *Bravo;* and some smaller craft. In dealing with matters of supply and ordnance, Porter was in his natural realm. He specialized on the *Libertad,* hoping that if he turned that dilapidated hulk into a crack fighting ship, his captains would be spurred to emulation. His tactics worked, and in a surprisingly short time he had a fleet ready to take the offensive.[13]

But his efforts to make sailors out of his men had a much rockier course to follow, and skirted the edge of disaster. Between the sixteenth and nineteenth centuries, most of the great oceanic powers had well-organized merchant marines which they could tap for naval manpower. In Mexico, however, those were the years of colonial subservience, when the imperial merchant marine and Navy were manned almost exclusively by Spaniards. In 1826, with independence barely achieved, Mexico had not had time to develop interest in maritime affairs or to acquire experience afloat. Most of its naval officers had been recruited in Europe, primarily England and Spain, and local Indian boys had to serve as crews. The Mexican armed forces were used as depositories for criminals, the relative status of the Navy being revealed by the fact that, while minor offenders were sent to the Army, real felons were sent to the Navy.

When Porter, with his "abysmal ignorance of the Spanish language and the Mexican temperament," assumed command, he was appalled at the human resources with which he had to deal. Having spent his life in the U.S. Navy, he was used to a clearly defined chain of command, stressing automatic compliance with orders, crisp discipline, and an immaculate appearance of both ships and men. Right away, he introduced rules similar to those of the American and English navies, and the sailors promptly learned that the new regime meant whippings "unsparingly dealt out" as a matter of course.[14]

He was as hard on his officers, whose casual attitude toward their profession enraged him, as he was on his men. David Dixon Porter recalled that Mexican officers of that day were accustomed to "playing monte on the quarter deck, or smoking in all parts of the ship, wearing their dressing gowns on duty, or sitting . . . in their shirt sleeves." It would have been fun to stand beside David Porter on the *Libertad* and watch his reaction the first time he saw a bathrobed, cigar-puffing subordinate hurrying on his way to a card game. Porter concluded that if "they make officers of Mexicans, they must make them of the next generation, not of this."

In many ways, he asked for trouble from his officers. He was, after all, a foreigner, and, sans explanation, he was barking out a barrage of new orders and regulations through the medium of his ever-present interpreter. Many Mexican officers had been opposed to having an American placed over them and, at the time of Porter's arrival, his appointment had caused a brief newspaper skirmish. Spanish officers resented Porter's unconcern about their naval records, many of which were lengthy and commendable. British officers detested him, a sentiment cordially returned by the anglophobic Commodore. A stream of resignations, some voluntary, some forced, began pouring into Mexican naval headquarters, and Porter had to depend more and more on the officers he had brought with him. His high-handed behavior was not well received in Mexico City, and he complained that his efforts to bring "quarrelsome" subordinates to heel were receiving no encouragement from Gomez Pedrasa, Minister of War and Marine.[15]

As a result of Porter's harsh punishment of the sailors and his harrying of the officers, mutiny broke out at Veracruz during August 1826. Details of that uprising are scanty and confusing. It seems to have been started when Porter cashiered a junior Mexican officer, one of those "idle young men of influential families . . . with no intention of following the sea as a profession," who joined the Navy only to "wear a gaudy uniform and draw pay from the government." * The Mexican government rushed reinforcements to Veracruz, and the trouble was rapidly quelled. By September the situation within the fleet was again quiet.[16]

Back in the United States, Porter's well-oiled publicity machine was grinding out complimentary stories, regardless of his failures. The *National Intelligencer,* quoting a Mexican source, waxed lyrical over what he had accomplished in Veracruz: "The discipline of the crews, the cleanliness of the vessels, their order and government, the cheerfulness of the address with which the maneuvers were performed in the presence of their worthy commander-in-chief General Porter, attest . . . [to his] indefatigable exertions. . . ." Another paper saw a glittering future ahead of him: "Do not be surprised that com. Porter . . . should at the head of the allied navies of Mexico and Colombia become the terror of the Spanish coast . . . it is his destiny to exact from the mother country, by the brilliance of his achievement, an acknowledgement of the independence of the southern republics."

By late autumn Porter deemed his progress noteworthy enough to tell his wife with disarming modesty, "I have accomplished wonders." A few weeks later, his self-satisfaction must have been even more inflated by the receipt of a most complimentary letter from the Mexican govern-

---

* The officer concerned may have been one "Landara," with whom Porter admitted he had quarreled.

ment, congratulating him for the improvements he had brought to the "national marine." [17]

It is difficult to know how much the above encomiums were padded, but one thing at least is clear: by December 1826, he had done enough to be able to lead the Mexican Navy, for the only time in its history, into offensive action against the Spanish fleet. He had finally achieved something like esprit de corps among his men and had managed to "transform a company of scrawny, ill-fed Mexican soldiers with balls and chains on their legs into hard, husky, moderately dependable seamen." Unfortunately, he had not been given any more ships, and his squadron was much less potent than the one in Havana that the Spanish Vice Admiral Angel Laborde could throw against him. Since the *Guerrero* was still awaiting some guns, the 32-gun frigate *Libertad,* the 18-gun brig *Victoria,* the 14-gun brig *Bravo,* and the tiny, 5-gun hermaphrodite schooner *Hermón,* were all he had available.*

Cognizant that it would be foolhardy for him to meet the entire Spanish squadron in action, Porter planned his campaign of 1826–1827 as an adventure in economics and politics rather than an exercise in naval tactics. He hoped to wound the Spanish economy by slashing at its Caribbean sea lanes, and to reward his new country by using prizes to replenish his own stores from enemy stockpiles, as he had done in the Pacific. Needless to say, he expected simultaneously to help himself with personal profits from his captives. He saw political advantage in operating off Cuba as long as he could, not so much to conquer that island or to spark an uprising there—although he did have hopes along those lines—as to attract and hold Laborde's attention, for if the Spaniards were occupied in either chasing or watching the Mexican flotilla, they would have neither the strength nor the time for other errands—the reconquest of Mexico or Colombia, for instance.

He recognized that he might not be able to stay for long off the Cuban coast and intended, if superior enemy forces drove him away, to proceed to Key West for the purpose of seeking asylum in U.S. territorial waters. His experience as commander of the West India Squadron had made him as familiar with the environs of Key West as he was with those of Chester or Meridian Hill, and a more comfortable and useful haven for him would be hard to imagine. Partly on his own recommendation, Key West had been abandoned in favor of Pensacola as the American

---

* In his *Mexican Navy,* R. L. Bidwell lists the guns of the *Libertad,* the *Victoria,* and the *Bravo* as 40, 20, and 18, respectively, when Porter sailed on his cruise. Apparently the extra guns were added during the autumn of 1826.

Caribbean base. "The presence heretofore of a military force had been a check on the turbulent and refractory part of the inhabitants" of Key West, but the departure of the Navy had meant the departure of organized government and that political vacuum had not been filled. The only authority that existed was civilian, embodied in the person of William Pinkney, Collector of the Port of Key West. Pinkney was a nephew of Captain John Rodgers, and Porter probably already knew him, but even if not, he soon proved himself a true friend of the Commodore.[18]

On 5 December 1826 Porter notified Poinsett that he was leaving Veracruz, adding that the latter could undoubtedly "make a reasonable guess" as to his "eventual destination," and the Mexican fleet headed out to sea. It soon reached the northern coast of Cuba, and remained near Matanzas for the next three weeks. Shortly before Christmas, Porter's raiders took their first two prizes. News of the captures was immediately relayed to Havana and, on 23 December, the energetic and able Laborde closed that port and prepared to move against Porter. Knowing that if he needed reinforcement, he could call on Spanish ships already at sea, Laborde sailed with only two powerful frigates. On Christmas Day the Mexicans sighted the approaching Spaniards, and Porter, deciding not to hazard a head-on encounter, fled north under cover of a storm that arose fortuitously. He entered Key West on board the *Libertad*, accompanied by the *Bravo*. A couple of days later, the squadron was reunited by the arrival of the *Victoria* and the *Hermón*. Porter stayed at Key West for several months, while Laborde stood offshore with a force that varied between two or three frigates and three or four brigs. Whether Porter was blockaded or not is a moot point. His own testimony is conflicting. In mid-January 1827 he admitted to Poinsett that he was blockaded, and told him the same thing again in early March. On 13 February he tried to come out against the Spaniards, but had to hasten back to sanctuary when reinforcements for Laborde showed up. On the other hand, he boasted to Samuel Hambleton that it was "preposterous" to say that he was blockaded, since his brigs and prizes "come in as they please in open day." Furthermore, according to *Niles National Register*, he had no trouble sending his first two captured ships back to Veracruz for sale.[19]

Meanwhile his economic war with Spain went well. During his entire tenure at Key West, he kept picking off Spanish merchantmen, retaining some to replenish his supplies, selling others at Key West, and sinking those that were of no use to him. He claimed that during the first few weeks of his cruise his raiders had taken ships and cargoes valued at $150,000. In June 1827, an American newspaper named the ships and itemized the cargoes captured by Porter's squadron during the first six months of its operation, and gave the total of vessels as twenty-one: four brigs, sixteen schooners, and one sloop. The Commodore bragged, "with my beggarly little force I have made the war with Spain my own." [20]

Nevertheless, Porter's difficulties were mounting. One of his prizes was refitted as a cruiser and sent out under the command of Mexican Lieutenant Alexander Thompson, formerly a midshipman in the U.S. Navy. Off the Cuban coast, six Spanish ships were seized, but the enemy crews rose against their captors, and sailed into Havana with Thompson and the other Mexican-Americans as prisoners. Although they were released after officers of the American West India Squadron had interceded for them, it was a humiliating reverse for the new Mexican Navy.

Finances presented a worse problem. Early in the cruise, lack of funds temporarily dumped Porter into despondency. In January he wrote to Poinsett that, since his departure, Mexico City had given him "not a cent of money," and that if this niggardliness typified the Victoria administration's attitude toward him, he would resign. Mourning that his life consisted only of "toil and travail," he begged Poinsett, *do for Gods sake* open their eyes to their true interest." But his low spirits were soon raised by the arrival of new prizes with which he was able to provision and supply his squadron so well that "Their ration . . . gave them an abundance of food, such as they had never before dreamed of possessing."

During the spring of 1827, Porter easily eluded Laborde's blockaders and returned to Mexico. He reached Veracruz on 20 May, and stayed either there or in Mexico City for a couple of weeks. He spent some time readying the *Guerrero* for fleet service, and some in trying to get his hands on the money that he should have received from the two prizes he had sent back to Veracruz. However, by that time, whatever proceeds had been realized from that source had already disappeared into the bottomless pit that was the Mexican treasury, and Porter was able later to disavow any responsibility for them: "As for funds of the prizes, it is quite evident that neither their disposal nor disposition depends on me. . . ." He made up his mind that he would not send any more prizes to Veracruz. He left Mexico early in June, and after a "tedious" voyage of more than three weeks, put in to Key West on the 23rd.[21]

His activities at Key West during 1827 involved himself and his new country in three disputes with the United States, all of which dragged on for many months after the termination of his cruise. First, he violated U.S. territorial rights by his presence at Key West; second, he threatened American commerce by announcing the issuance of letters of marque for Mexican privateers, and granting at least one; and third, he recruited sailors for Mexico on U.S. soil.

There could be no doubt that he was guilty on the first count. He clutched at what technicalities he could to justify his stay at Key West, but for several months his Mexican squadron based itself on and fought from that port. It was not long before Washington showed concern about the behavior of its unwanted guests. In February, the U.S. Consul in Havana warned the Secretary of State that Admiral Laborde was considering attacking Porter inside American territorial waters. Upon receipt of this information, John Quincy Adams called a Cabinet meeting, and the administration agreed that any such Spanish attack would have to be resisted by the Navy. Although the President declared that Porter must not "be permitted to make our territory his lair for sallying forth against the enemy," he took no steps to compel Porter to abandon his base. Evidently, Adams was wary of Porter's continuing personal popularity, the adulatory reports about him in the anti-administration press, and an instinctive American sympathy for the underdog—in this case, Mexico.

Officers of the West India Squadron were unhappy about Porter's de facto possession of Key West. A naval captain in Pensacola advised the administration that, in his opinion, Porter was using Key West "as a station of annoyance to the Spanish commerce, and abusing its neutrality, obviously for the purpose of making misunderstanding between the United States and Spain." By spring, similar protests were appearing in American journals. At the end of March, *Niles National Register* objected to Porter's long residence at Key West, and demanded that the situation be "corrected" by the administration.[22]

Early in June, *Niles* returned to the attack. In a blistering editorial, it stated that Key West was now no more than

> . . . a place of rendezvous for carrying on a predatory and inglorious war against the commerce of Cuba. This must not be permitted . . . we cannot allow any foreigner to involve us in his quarrel. . . . We are at peace with the people of Cuba, and they are among our best customers . . . the captain-general [might] shut his ports in retaliation of these aggressions. . . . It would be better for us that Key West be shovelled into the sea. Let com. Porter seek the open ocean, and there do what the law of nations permits to his enemy—but not to shelter himself under the flag which he has abandoned, to depredate on the property of the Spanish subjects.

Anticipating protests from Madrid, Secretary of State Clay wrote to Pablo Obregón, Mexican Minister in Washington, and called to his attention the fact that Porter had originally been given permission to enter Key West only "for the purposes of hospitality, which the United States are ever ready to dispense alike to the public Vessels of all friendly foreign Countries"; then, when a superior Spanish fleet had blockaded him there, he had been allowed to continue his asylum. Porter, he said, had used this privilege "to increase his force, and to send out cruizers to annoy the Spanish Commerce." Clay asked the Mexican government to take such steps as would lead to a prompt cessation of this "violation of the neutrality of the United States." Within a week of receiving Clay's communication, Obregón replied with a promise that his government would act upon the matter.

As expected, Spain lodged a strong protest about Porter's occupation of Key West. The message arrived in the first week of June, and on the 7th the Adams Cabinet met to discuss for the second and last time the question of Mexico's violation of U.S. territorial rights. It would be kind to say that the conclusion of that discussion was equivocal. To be sure, it was decided that no Mexican prizes would be granted entry into Key West and no privateers would be dispatched therefrom, and Charles Ridgely, Commodore of the West India Squadron, was told to check periodically on conditions in that area. However, the U.S. Navy was not given direct orders either to compel the Mexican fleet to respect American rights or to oust it by force. Those responsibilities were placed on William Pinkney. No outcome could have been more to Porter's liking. Pinkney might issue orders, but he was powerless to make them effective and, by that time, he was practically a colleague of Porter's. During the following months, Pinkney's reports to Washington consisted of not much more than repeated assurances that Porter was not in any way violating American rights. In short, the Cabinet meeting of 7 June did little more than hamstring any possibility of effective naval action, and Captain Charles Ridgely was justifiably furious.[23]

Thanks to action taken, not in Washington, but in Mexico City, the squabble over Porter's illegal use of American territory to carry on his war against Spain died down. Obregón had followed through on his promise to Clay. He wrote Porter that he must behave with propriety in regard to American neutrality, and a little later called the attention of the Mexican government to the potentially dangerous issues involved. By October, the Mexican government was able to notify Washington that Porter had left Key West. At the end of that month, the captain admitted to Poinsett that he had abandoned his Florida base primarily "to avoid giving cause for complaint" to the United States.[24]

The second dispute between Mexico and the United States sparked by Porter's activities concerned his granting letters of marque to privateers. It will be recalled that, even before Porter officially joined the Mexican service, Poinsett had warned Clay to expect the issuance of such letters. Furthermore, during the Mexican fleet's residence at Key West, Captain Charles Ridgely notified the Secretary of the Navy that Porter carried with him "forty blank commissions for Privateers to be fitted out by him and to be fitted out anywhere and to be manned by anybody[.] I much fear our commerce will be much molested. . . ."

This problem was mainly academic. According to the leading authority on the first Mexican Navy, Porter may have granted several letters of marque, but only one instance of his doing so can be substantiated: that was in the summer of 1827, when the privateer *Carabobo* came in to Key West with her original Colombian commission about to expire. In order to give the captain of the *Carabobo* his Mexican letter of marque, Porter sailed more than three miles beyond the harbor, thereby technically avoiding any compromise of American neutrality.

There the situation rested until late 1827, when Porter announced from Mexico that he was introducing a policy to promote privateering, and would issue numerous letters of marque. Then the Spanish foreign office protested to the American Minister in Madrid that "David Porter styling himself Commander of the Squadron belonging to the pretended Republic of Mexico" was offering "to grant letters of Marque and ordering the Inspection and detention of all vessels having Spanish property on board or articles contraband of war destined for His Majesty's service." The note forecast that American shipping would "be the first to feel the effects of the wrong," and asked that the United States refuse to accede to such illegality.

The American Minister replied that his government had not officially informed him of this development, nor had it instructed him how to deal with it, but he would immediately forward the Spanish note to Washington. He was sure that his government would, as it always did, put "the most liberal construction" on neutral trading rights.[25] Correspondence on the subject apparently ended there, for the Mexican Navy soon collapsed and Porter returned to the United States.

The third Spanish-American dispute arose over Porter's recruitment of sailors on U.S. soil. In mid-July 1827, shortly after he returned to Key West from his visit to Mexico, Porter went to New Orleans to try to enlist men for his fleet and to replenish supplies, both of which he expected to be able to finance with Mexican funds that were to be awaiting him. En route, he paused at Pensacola to assure his former naval colleague, Charles Ridgely, that he was doing nothing that would embarrass the United States. He remained in Louisiana a little more than a month, and spent at least some of the $10,000 in cash sent to him by Mexico on recruitment: the pay he offered prospective enlistees was $14 a month, $2 higher than that of the U.S. Navy, and comparable to that of the American merchant marine. Although he boasted, "my lodgings have been swarming with volunteers," he suffered one defeat. Seventy sailors were enrolled and sent down the Mississippi to board the *Guerrero*, which was hovering off the mouth of the river. Unfortunately, all of them were arrested by American officers and returned to New Orleans in chains, and only a few of the seventy were released. Better luck attended one hundred other sailors who were sent down the river shortly thereafter and reached the *Guerrero* safely.[26]

The most pleasant aspects of Porter's sojourn in New Orleans were social. His family traveled all the way from Washington to be with him, and he renewed friendships made a decade and a half before, when he commanded the New Orleans Naval Station. He was received by the Governor of Louisiana, and several dinners were given in his honor, including a testimonial banquet held on 26 July by the Mayor of New Orleans: he told Hambleton that "Adamites, Clayites, and Jacksonites" attended the banquet and greeted him with an "ovation."

In early September, his work in Louisiana concluded, Porter journeyed overland to Mobile, where he waited in vain for a ship to pick him up. When none appeared, he took a carriage and drove to Pensacola, where some of his squadron were waiting for him, and he sent word to those still at Key West to join him. His reassembled fleet sailed for Veracruz in late October, thereby terminating the Commodore's only cruise with the Mexican Navy.

Porter's expedition to Cuba and Key West had its failures as well as its successes. On the debit side, Spain had not been forced to recognize Mexican independence. None of the other Latin-American republics in revolt against Madrid, not even Colombia, had done anything to help Mexico. Laborde's fleet was still supreme in West Indian waters. Porter's violations of American neutrality had strained relations between the United States and Mexico, and the Mexican government had given him little, if any, support. Conversely, with a tiny Mexican squadron he had maintained sufficient sea power to harass the enemy, seriously harmed Spanish commerce in the Caribbean, taken enough prizes to keep his own flotilla supplied, and prevented the Spaniards from mounting an offensive elsewhere in Latin America by forcing Laborde to pay close attention to him at Key West.

Never one to hide his accomplishments under a blanket of diffidence, he summed up his achievements. A leading expert on relations between the United States and Latin America paraphrased the Commodore's own summary:

> He had saved Colombia from a counter-revolution by immobilizing in the west the fleet which was to have aided the counter-revolutionaries . . . he had compelled Spain to reinforce Cuba "at enormous expense," had paralyzed its commerce and caused great discontent among the inhabitants of Cuba and had "established a character of activity for the Mexican Marine, which if the gov[ernment] thought proper to take advantage of would be highly injurious to the interests of Spain." [27]

Porter's popularity in Mexico was at its height when he returned from Key West in October 1827, but a series of events starting in that year reduced the Mexican economy to a state of chronic insolvency and its political structure to rubble. Two European investment houses crashed, carrying with them a fortune in Mexican cash and credits. On 20 December 1827, the government ordered the expulsion of all Spanish subjects resident in the country, but allowed them to export their assets. "The Spaniards left by the hundreds, and their gold and silver by the millions of pesos." The departure of this wealthy and influential class had a ruinous effect upon the Mexican economy, and nowhere was the damage greater than in the state and city of Veracruz, where Porter was based.

In politics, this dismal year was punctuated by an *Escoces* uprising, spearheaded by Vice President Nicolás Bravo. The Victoria administration sent General Vicente Guerrero to quell the rebellion, which he did so successfully that the power of Scottish Rite Masonry was virtually eradicated. In the long run, the uprising had an equally devastating effect on the presumably victorious, pro-American *Yorkinos*, for ". . . instead of trying to heal the wounds afflicted during the past troubles, they opened new ones. Dissension soon broke out against them, which paved the way for the overthrow and extinction of the party."

Porter was caught up in the debacle and soon felt the brunt of these changes. For a time the *Escoceses* maintained their hold on Veracruz, and Porter found that during their tenure he had been removed from command of San Juan d'Ulua, beneath whose guns his fleet had to anchor. Economic deterioration was tragic for the future of the Mexican Navy. Even the trickle of funds that had previously been available for the service dried up completely, and it became impossible for the fleet to make a second cruise. At the end of November 1827, the American Consul in Veracruz notified the State Department that although Porter's squadron had returned safely from Key West, it would not sail again because the government was not in a position to supply its needs.[28]

All that Porter could do was send out his ships as commerce-raiding cruisers, and the *Bravo* and the *Hermón* were reasonably successful in taking prizes in 1828 and 1829. In spite of his proclamation about commissioning many new privateers, he did not dare grant any more letters of marque because, if he did, he would surely stir up resentment and, possibly, counteraction in the United States and elsewhere.

Either in late January or early February 1828, the *Guerrero,* manned largely by foreign officers and a crew picked from other ships in the fleet, sailed from Veracruz under the command of Lieutenant David H. Porter, the Commodore's nephew. Although courageous and able, David H. was perhaps the most feared and hated officer in the Mexican Navy. Even his young cousin, Midshipman David Dixon Porter, who went on the cruise, described him as "a strict disciplinarian . . . more addicted to the cat and colt * than to moral suasion. He was not over twenty-one years of age, and had not learned the art of governing men by kindness. He punished for every offense. . . ." †

On 10 February, while the *Guerrero* was operating off the coast of Cuba not far from Havana, she came upon a large convoy of merchantmen guarded by two armed Spanish brigs. David H. Porter promptly attacked, and the ensuing fire was sustained and intense. Considerable damage was done to the *Guerrero*'s rigging before the heavier Mexican cannon began to take effect. Just when triumph seemed assured, the 64-gun Spanish frigate, *Lealtad,* sent out from Havana as soon as the cannonading was heard, bore down on her smaller adversary. Sensibly, the *Guerrero* spent the rest of that day and all that night fleeing from her foe, and it seemed that she had made good her escape. However, through his night glasses, the Spanish captain had been able to track every move she made, and when the 11th dawned, the *Lealtad* was close enough to open fire, concentrating on the *Guerrero*'s masts and spars.‡ The Mexicans shot back effectively enough to keep the outcome in doubt for a couple of hours, but eventually the Spaniard immobilized the smaller vessel, then stood off out of range, and hammered her at will. After conferring with his officers, David H. Porter decided to surrender his ship, and ordered her colors struck. But the flag had been shot away twice, and when it came down once more, the Spanish captain assumed that the same thing had happened again. He moved in and ended the battle with a point-blank broadside that swept the decks of the *Guerrero*. David H. Porter was "cut in two." [29]

Sixty years later, David Dixon Porter compared the encounter between the *Guerrero* and the *Lealtad* with the many engagements he fought during the Civil War, and remarked: "I don't know any battle on record that will beat it." There is some confusion about both the number

---

* The "cat" was, of course, the well-known cat-o'-nine-tails. The "colt" was a short, knotted rope used by boatswain's mates to punish infractors on the spot.

† On an earlier cruise David H. Porter's merciless discipline on board the prize ship *Esmeralda* generated outright mutiny. With difficulty, the mutineers were overcome and later "punished through the fleet"—whipped on board every vessel —before serving terms at hard labor on the fortress of San Juan d'Ulua.

‡ Bidwell and David Dixon Porter give different accounts of the details. The latter states that the two Spanish brigs were escorting forty-two vessels; the former mentions no convoy. David Dixon Porter says the *Guerrero* fell victim to the *Lealtad* only because David H. Porter, after escaping, doubled back to try to pick off the convoy in the dark, and had the bad luck to stumble into the Spaniard.

of casualties and the treatment accorded to prisoners. A Spanish source estimates that 40 men were killed or wounded in the *Guerrero*, while David Dixon Porter puts the number at 80 out of the 186 men on board. The captain of the *Lealtad* claimed that only one of his men was killed and two or three were wounded, which is ridiculous, but not as ridiculous as the account that appeared in an American newspaper estimating Spanish casualties at 200. David Dixon Porter, who was an eyewitness, takes strong exception to a report that the Spanish captain treated his prisoners well, and that he buried David H. Porter "with high military honors." He says that the wrecked *Guerrero* was left to wallow untended for four hours, while the enemy was throwing overboard his dead and making emergency repairs to his frigate in order to hide battle damage; that the prisoners were shamefully plundered; and that, far from being given a military burial, the remains of David H. Porter were simply tossed over the side.[30]

News of the battle between the *Guerrero* and the *Lealtad* evoked international comment. *Niles* spoke for most of the U.S. press when it hailed the gallantry of a 22-gun brig fighting a 64-gun frigate. The American Consul in Veracruz reported that the fight aroused "some excitement" in Mexico, and temporarily united all factions in acclaiming the heroism of David H. Porter and his men. There was a flurry of support for the Navy, and even private citizens made contributions to keep the sea arm operating; the barbers of Mexico City came through with five pesos. This unanimity was short-lived, however. Mexicans soon began asking why the *Guerrero* had fought at all: she was supposed to be a commerce raider, wounding Spain and helping Mexico by taking prizes. The fight with the *Lealtad,* they complained, had resulted in the loss of the nation's best warship—and for nothing. Interest in the *Guerrero* soon waned, and with it went interest in the Navy: before long, the Mexican press dropped all mention of maritime matters.[31]

The abrupt decline in the prestige of the Mexican Navy was reflected in a lowering of the status of *Capitán de Navio* David Porter. His fortune, his mental stability, and his health steadily eroded during the year and a half that elapsed before he returned to the United States. All through his Mexican assignment he "relied upon the influence of Mr. Poinsett to clear away all difficulties." After the loss of the *Guerrero,* he sent him such a stream of anguish-filled letters that the American Minister must have winced when he saw the Commodore's easily identifiable scrawl on yet another envelope.

Underlying much of Porter's distress was his chronic homesickness. Late in 1826 he confided to his wife that he yearned to spend the last years of his life at Meridian Hill, "that most beloved of all spots on the earth."

He hoped one day to show her Mexico, but only as tourists, for they would never reside there permanently, he told her, adding, "the U.S. is my country still, and however zealously and faithfully I may fullfill my obligations as to this Gov⁺ nothing can ever mar [?] my affections for the land of my birth." A few months later he wrote to Hambleton that he was in Mexico for one reason only—to earn enough money so that he could retire at home, "to vegetate,—to be fix't like a plant to its peculiar spot, 'to draw nutrition propagate and rot.' " [32]

His hopes of fulfilling that purpose soon faded. Instead of allowing him to amass a retirement fund, his Mexican assignment took him to the brink of bankruptcy. Save for unhappiness about the distribution of prize money, he was fairly well satisfied with his financial condition during 1826 and 1827. He was able to make arrangements with the Mexican Minister in Washington to have $300 a month paid through the Bank of the United States to his wife. This amount appears to have been dispensed regularly for some time; how long is uncertain. In February 1828 Porter told Poinsett that his wife had just notified him that she had received nothing since the previous May; but the Mexican Minister wrote Evalina Porter that he had paid her $300 for September and a like sum for October 1827. Be that as it may, it is certain that no more funds came from Mexico after that autumn. Evalina Porter's financial difficulties became so great that, late in 1828, an official of the Bank of the United States extended her a loan of $200, payable by her husband on his return from Mexico, and expressed his sympathy about her "embarrassing situation, in consequence of the failures of the Mexican monies . . . to pay your allowance." [33]

Naturally, Evalina kept her husband informed about her descent into poverty, and his letters to Poinsett became ever more frantic. In January 1828, he wrote that he and his family were "suffering the every extremity of want and misery. I am living from day to day on the bounty of friends." Four months later he pleaded: "If my family is to be brought to distress by my joining this service I shall be distracted. For Gods sake do not let this happen." The only change was from bad to worse, and by summer he was wailing that he had never imagined "such a set of Devils" as the Mexicans existed. He must find release: "I will tender my resignation . . . if they will not accept my resignation, I will desert; if I cannot desert, I will die. . . ."

Porter's professional life had become as frustrating as his financial one. Not only was his fleet rotting in Veracruz Harbor, but his pride as a commanding officer was wounded by his inability to aid the Mexican sailors whom he had taken such pains to turn into able seamen. A few months after the battle between the *Guerrero* and the *Lealtad* he angrily reported that the "poor fellows who fought the *Guerrero* so gallantly are starving on the streets of Vera Cruz," and he complained that Mexico had "driven allmost every man out of the Navy." He interceded with the government in behalf of his men, but that move backfired, for instead of assisting him in his commendable task, the Ministry of War and Marine took the opportunity to chide him for commissioning new officers without official permission.[34]

One personal disaster after another befell him. Within a single year, one of his nephews died, one of his sons was imprisoned by the Spaniards, another of his sons died, he was bitten by a poisonous spider, and he received word that his wife had been somewhat spectacularly unfaithful. This miserable sequence was set in train by the loss of the *Guerrero*. The resultant death of David H. Porter and the capture of David Dixon Porter impelled him to write: "I have lost a nephew whom I love dearly, my son David on whom I doate is a prisoner." * Presumably he felt better when his son, who claims to have refused a Spanish parole because of his resentment about the treatment of the *Guerrero*'s crew, was nonetheless sent back to Veracruz on 30 March for a brief reunion with his father before leaving Mexico permanently for the United States.[35]

Porter's relief over David Dixon's safety was shattered a few months later, when his son, Thomas, died of yellow fever. Prostrated by the blow, he wrote Poinsett a moving, if hysterical, letter:

> . . . the death of my adored Thomas—He perished the day before yesterday with the terrible disease so fatal in this climate . . . he was my favorite child, I loved him to a degree that was unpardonable, and I am punished for it . . . I feel my heart breaking, my brain bursting. I cannot bring tears to my relief, grief hangs heavy on me.

Probably, at least in partial consequence of his sorrow, his health deteriorated and, in July, he admitted he had been "a good deal sick, and suffered very much from the bite of a tarantula which kept me confined to my cabin about a month." All through that autumn he remained in "abject misery, bodily and mentally," immersed in a hopeless situation caused by such political "corruption, intrigue & imbecility" that he was sorry he "ever planted my foot on Mexican soil." [36]

The calamitous year 1828 ended on an even lower note with the ar-

---

* An unfortunate error in connection with David H. Porter's death plagued his uncle. The Mexican government voted pensions to the families of those who died in the *Guerrero*. Porter's unfamiliarity with the Spanish language led him to err in having the pension of David H. Porter allocated to a nonexistent wife, rather than to his mother. Considerable correspondence was necessary before the mistake could be corrected. The anti-American *Escoces* faction attacked Porter for attempting to perpetrate a fraud upon the Mexican government.

rival of letters from the United States telling Porter of his wife's alleged infidelity.* When he read that "Mrs. Porter the wife of Com' Porter of the Mexican Navy has eloped with her own nephew disguised as a negro!" he wrote Evalina that he thought her "incapable of the horrid crimes" imputed to her, and said that if he did not believe her "honor unsullied," she would be "no more than worthless." He told her he had long feared that her "conduct might give rise to suspicions in others," and wound up his letter with the hope that "my dear Evalina" would henceforth "pay some attention to appearances." If she did, he said, together they might yet defeat "the malice of this dirty world."

Porter referred to this mysterious episode a month later. His wife must have judged his faith in her somewhat halfhearted, for in January 1829, he wrote: "I . . . assure you of my entire belief in your perfect innocence, but, indeed, Evalina, it is a wonder from the letters I had received that my confidence in you was not shaken . . . there are some that I can never let you see or know the contents of." It is to be doubted that after reading the above, Evalina Porter was able to follow her husband's final directive: "Banish the matter from your mind and be once more happy."

Nothing more is known about the incident to which Porter alluded. In the first letter he wrote to his wife on the matter, after quoting the report that she had eloped with her nephew "disguised as a negro," and without making a new paragraph to indicate any change of subject, he made a cryptic remark:

John Q. Adams has been thus far my ruin and the ruin of my family. I shall have my satisfaction, I hope, on the 4th of March next about 10 o'clock in the morning to be on the steps of the North door of the White House to make *another* bow to him as he leaves it.[37]

What did Porter mean? He could well blame the manner in which the President had handled the Fajardo incident for the "ruin" of his career, but why, in the context of his wife's alleged infidelity, did he blame him for the "ruin" of his family? Did he simply mean that because John Q. Adams had driven him into self-imposed exile in Mexico, his wife had been left unprotected from either her own folly or from vicious gossip misinterpreting her innocent actions? Had Adams made remarks about the unsavory incident? Was there some connection between Porter's charge and his leasing Meridian Hill to Adams about a month later, in that serious inconvenience was brought upon his family, or that the price Adams paid was so low as to cause "ruin?" The records supply no answers,

---

* These letters have not survived, nor have Evalina Porter's replies to the letters of her husband.

and discussions with the editors of the Adams Papers at the Massachusetts Historical Society revealed that they are as mystified as I am by Porter's strange allusion.

During the period when Porter's personal life was descending into purgatory, Mexico was sliding into the political anarchy that allowed General Antonio López de Santa Anna to come into and go out of power on eleven separate occasions during the next quarter-century. It will be recalled that the abortive Bravo uprising, which took place at the end of 1827, set in motion ominously divisive tendencies. In mid-1828 a presidential election to choose a successor to Guadalupe Victoria was fought between two *Yorkinos,* Manuel Gomez Pedrasa, former Minister of War and Marine, and Vicente Guerrero, who had smashed Bravo's rebellion. Gomez Pedrasa won, but the followers of Guerrero refused to accept the decision, and late in the year launched a revolt, which succeeded in overthrowing Gomez Pedrasa, and Guerrero was declared president on 1 January 1829.

As naval commander at Veracruz, Porter was caught in the middle of these political upheavals. After hesitating about which faction to support, he finally opted for Guerrero and, when he so notified the new government, he was thanked. Porter, briefly at the top of one of his oscillations between optimism and pessimism, told his wife that Guerrero was his "warm friend," from whose government he anticipated receiving better treatment. By this time, however, his Mexican tenure was approaching its end. Although details of how his fall came about are unclear, it is likely that a leading factor was the enmity of Antonio López de Santa Anna.

Porter and Santa Anna met in 1827—if, indeed, they had not met before—when the latter was the Vice-Governor of the State of Veracruz. During the disorders attending the Bravo rebellion and the simultaneous ouster of the Spaniards, some priests, who were attempting to pass through Veracruz to waiting ships, were attacked by a mob. While Santa Anna's troops stood by, Porter sent some Marines to the rescue, and it is said that the flamboyant Mexican was so embarrassed that he never forgave Porter.[38]

In the aftermath of Guerrero's victory over Gomez Pedrasa, Santa Anna was appointed Governor of the State of Veracruz. He treated the Commodore with courtesy, but both Porter and his son accused him of having plotted against the former and marked him for death. According to David Dixon Porter, Santa Anna notified his father of orders calling him to Mexico City at once. Accompanied only by Dr. Daniel Boardman and a Mexican servant, Porter set out for the capital. En route, the party was attacked by four armed horsemen. Porter managed to kill two of them, and the others fled. Boardman was seriously wounded, and when Porter took him back to Veracruz for treatment, he found that no orders had been received from Mexico City. Porter himself later charged that the men who assailed him on the road to the Mexican capital were "robbers and assassins," sent out by Santa Anna, "the chief Bandit of Mexico." * Bidwell, however, says there were orders dated "April 1829" calling Porter to the capital, and is satisfied that the attack on him was typical of the outrages committed by the highwaymen who infested all Mexican roads at the time.[39]

Porter returned to Mexico City and spent the spring and summer of 1829 there. His status during that period is uncertain. An American newspaper reported that he was under arrest, but that does not seem to be true, although he may have been in some kind of protective custody that restricted him to the capital. Everything he tried to accomplish there failed, primarily because other, more important events were taking place. Besides dealing with their perennial difficulties in achieving financial solvency and political stability, Mexican officials were preoccupied with a Spanish invasion during that summer. A few thousand troops were landed on the Mexican coast, but shortly after they had disembarked, storms drove away the fleet, lowland fevers riddled their ranks, and a hurricane completed the havoc. Santa Anna, who led Mexican forces against the invaders and accepted their surrender, became a national hero.[40] The fact that neither Porter nor the Mexican Navy took any part in repelling the Spanish attack speaks volumes about the influence of the one and the efficacy of the other by this time.

Indeed, the Mexican Navy was in the process of disappearing. By mid-1829 the American press reported that the "Mexican men-of-war at Vera Cruz were all stripped," and there was only "a guard of two men" on board each. The British Chargé in Mexico scoffed at the idea of a nation with neither maritime tradition nor a merchant marine attempting to start a navy, and said that the hiring of Porter had been a mistake from the beginning. The Mexican government that took office in 1830 agreed that frigates and brigs were luxuries too rich for such a poor country, and decided that gunboats alone would have to suffice in the future. By that time, two ships were still in commission at Veracruz, only one of which was considered seaworthy. When that vessel left the harbor and tried to come about, she foundered.[41] Such was the dismal anticlimax to almost a decade of effort to create and operate a Mexican Navy.

---

* The younger Porter records a second attempt on his father's life. This one, he says, was made in Veracruz, when two assassins crept into Porter's bedroom. The Commodore killed one of them with a sword thrust, but the other escaped.

Meanwhile, the *Capitán* of a *Navio* rapidly becoming extinct was exerting himself in Mexico City in efforts to collect something from either his unpaid salary or his unconfirmed land grant. As to the first, he besieged the Treasury Department, only to be told every time *"no hay dinero."* Pointing out, "I am entirely destitute of funds and were it not for the charity of my friends should absolutely perish of want," he pleaded in vain with the Secretary for some recompense.

No better luck attended his attempt to profit from the land grant bestowed on him by the government. He wrote that upon his arrival in Mexico he was given, in lieu of the Spanish treasure he had forfeited by joining the Mexican Navy, "a large tract of land in Texas." Evidently, that grant was later exchanged for an even more extensive one on the Isthmus of Tehuantepec, a site which Porter viewed as perfect for an interoceanic canal, because it lay much closer to the United States than Nicaragua or Panama, both of which were under consideration. He found it impossible to clear his title in 1829, but, undaunted, he, and after his death, his son, dogged the Mexican government for the next half-century in trying to turn this amorphous grant into a negotiable asset.

Bidwell sums up neatly the reasons for Porter's failure to achieve any of his objectives in Mexico City during 1829: "In a capital torn by party strife and suspicion, with a Spanish invasion during his stay, and . . . the headlong course of the government into bankruptcy, it is not to be expected that much attention was given to Porter, or to the navy if Porter ever took his mind off his personal problems."[42]

Other matters that must have caused apprehension in Porter were the deteriorating position of his mentor, Joel R. Poinsett, and the general lessening of American influence in Mexico. Poinsett's five-year tenure as U.S. Minister has to be judged a failure. Although it is unlikely that any other American could have done much better under the circumstances, part of the responsibility for his lack of success was his own. Just as he did in Chile, he constantly dabbled in the internal politics of the nation to which he was accredited. By such action, he may have won some friends for the United States, but he made potent enemies as well. Significantly, one of the major planks in Bravo's platform when he ran for president in 1827 called for the dismissal of Poinsett.

But forces beyond the control of the American Minister also contributed to his failure. An ill-timed offer by the Adams administration to buy Texas aroused deserved suspicion about the disinterested friendship of Mexico's northern neighbor, and fear of its expansionist appetite. Furthermore, Poinsett proved no match for His Majesty's Chargé d'Affaires in Mexico, Henry George Ward, "the imperial bagman of the British foreign office." The two diplomats dueled for controlling influence over the

Guadalupe Victoria administration, and the Englishman won. Ward, his energetic and fecund wife, and his brood of children served Great Britain's Latin-American policy by, among other things, showing the most marked courtesy to the Mexican President's mistress. It might be thought that Ward and Poinsett would suffer equally when both the pro-British *Escoceses* and the pro-American *Yorkinos* fell to pieces, but the American was hurt the more, as Mexico City swung toward London. Considering Ward's relatively impregnable position because of his country's prestige, military power, and economic strength, perhaps nothing could have prevented Mexico from gravitating into Great Britain's orbit. Poinsett soon gave up the unequal struggle and sailed for home on 3 January 1830.*

As for Porter, the pronounced drift toward anti-Americanism, reinforced by his own experiences, filled him with an ardent desire to quit Mexico. He had wanted to leave for many months, but considered it useless to return to the United States while the hostile John Quincy Adams still resided in the White House. Porter's despondency was slightly alleviated by regular correspondence with Jacksonites, especially Senator Mahlon Dickerson of New Jersey.† In April 1827, the Senator assured the Commodore that his persecutors would "find themselves out of power in less than two years." The election of 1828 proved entirely to Porter's liking, for it was won by Andrew Jackson. Just prior to the inauguration of the new president, Dickerson wrote a letter that must have been pure oxygen to Porter, suffocating in despair. He said that Jackson had:

> . . . expressed the highest respect for your character and services, and his utter detestation of the persecution that drove you into exile, he authorized me to say to you, that it would afford him the highest satisfaction to see you again in this country, and that . . . he would . . . provide for you in some way agreeable to yourself. . . . of the Cabinet Eaton you know is your devoted friend, Van Buren is equally attached to you, and Ingham, Branch, and Berrian are friendly to you; but none of them more attached to you than the president himself.‡

---

* Porter's urgings may have had something to do with Poinsett's departure from Mexico. The Commodore expressed great concern for Poinsett's safety, writing from Chester, Pennsylvania, that he "would pray most fervently for your escape from that den of devils, free from harm." Porter told Senator Mahlon Dickerson of New Jersey that Poinsett's life was "not safe from the dagger of the assassin." 43 Since Poinsett was home before Porter left for the Mediterranean, the two men may have met again, but there is no proof that they did.

† Mahlon Dickerson, lawyer and businessman, had already been a Justice of the New Jersey Supreme Court, Governor of that State, and U.S. Senator since 1817. From 1834 to 1838, he served as Secretary of the Navy under Jackson and Van Buren.

‡ In Jackson's first Cabinet, John H. Eaton was Secretary of War; Martin Van Buren, Secretary of State; Samuel D. Ingham, Secretary of the Treasury; John

In answering that letter Porter prophesied an early meeting with Dickerson, for he was positive that the Mexican government would send him "on a commission to the U.S. on affairs interesting to this Republic." [44]

Nothing about Porter's Mexican assignment proved simple, not even the act of leaving that country. Poinsett had warned him to flee before his enemies killed him. He resigned his commission on 20 September 1829, and shortly thereafter sneaked from the capital to Veracruz and, in secret, boarded the first ship sailing for the United States. He later asserted that so intense was the opposition to him from Santa Anna's henchmen that President Guerrero had not dared give him a passport.

Shortly before his departure, Guerrero wrote him a politely reserved testimonial, dated 14 August:

> I give you thanks, in the name of my country, for the very important services you have rendered it during your command in our marine; and I do not doubt . . . you will show the same generosity as you have done before towards a country in which you may count on many and true friends. . . .
>
> Your friend,
> V. Guerrero.

A letter printed in a Mexican periodical probably expressed the national sentiment about Porter more accurately than did Guerrero's tepid thanks; it accused the government of "being a cold spectator to the blunders of Porter, hiding his abuses they gave him cover to commit innumerable arbitrary actions and contributed in a thousand ways to the ruin of the navy." [45]

Off and on for the rest of his life, Porter repaid the Mexicans for the unhappy experiences he had had in their country by writing blistering attacks on them. A few months after he returned home, Senator Robert Y. Hayne of South Carolina, head of the Committee on Naval Affairs, asked him for information about both the Mexican and the Colombian navies, and inquired whether the U.S. service could profit from his information about them. In a fifteen-page tirade, Porter replied that the Mexican Navy was in a "most deplorable state," but what, he asked, could be expected of a country that sentenced criminals to serve in its navy: ". . . a Navy that is merely used as a receptacle for the guilt and filth of a nation" is worse than useless. The Mexicans themselves? He described them as no more than "a nation of assassins," and said they were "devoid of every chivalrous feeling." The Colombians were no better. The U.S. Navy could learn nothing from either, and any attempt to do so would be "to contrast infinity with nonentity."

Branch, Secretary of the Navy; and John Berrian, Attorney General. The only member of the Cabinet not mentioned by Dickerson was Postmaster General William T. Barry.

Porter mellowed on the subject not a whit during his long tour as Chargé d'Affaires and Minister to the Ottoman Empire. While he was so accredited, he wrote a book entitled *Constantinople and Its Environs* . . . and in it he compared and contrasted Turkey and Mexico:

> Like Mexico, every thing is beautiful in the distance; but nothing will bear examination. . . . Enter the villages, the streets are almost impassable from filth, and you meet only a ragged, dirty, squalid population. . . . The few in power, revelling in affluence and splendour, have reduced the mass of the people to a degree of misery which appears insupportable. This is Turkey and this is Mexico . . . but mark the difference in other respects. Here the mass of the people are honest . . . and virtuous too. The Mexicans are a nation of thieves and prostitutes. Murder and robbery here are the rarest occurrences. . . . In Mexico. . . . They murder . . . for the love of blood.

In June 1835, writing from Turkey, he told Farragut: "My sufferings in Mexico, the trials of fortitude I underwent, exceed all belief; but now I am enjoying Elysium, compared to what I then suffered in body and in mind." [46]

Late in September 1829 Porter, thankful to leave Mexico, departed for home, carrying dispatches from Poinsett. As soon as he arrived, in the first week of October, he delivered them in Washington, a service for which he later tried to collect $600 from the government. His main purpose in visiting the capital, however, was to promote his own interests. He called upon President Andrew Jackson, Secretary of State Martin Van Buren, and other officials, and found the new administration much more "business like" than its predecessor.[1]

The Commodore felt that he had every reason for confidence about his immediate future. Senator Mahlon Dickerson of New Jersey had assured him that Jackson would take care of him; relatives were telling one another that the President was sure to "do something handsome" for him; on a visit to the ship in which his son, David Dixon, was serving as a midshipman, the President had greeted the youngster most affably and asked him when he expected "Pa home"; and now Jackson had received him in Washington "with the utmost kindness."[2]

By the middle of October Porter was back with his family in Chester, Pennsylvania. He found them in good health and wrote complacently to Poinsett, "I make them by my presence very happy." On the 22nd, a dinner was given for him and, on that occasion, he presumably gratified his neighbors by telling them that it was good to be home, that he had been everywhere, but of all places, Chester was the finest.

He was in Chester for the best of reasons: he had nowhere else to live. His financial collapse in Mexico had compelled him to surrender Meridian Hill which, despite his boost for Chester, he had earlier told Evalina, was "that most beloved of all spots on the earth." It is difficult to trace either when or under what circumstances Meridian Hill was disposed of. According to David Dixon Porter, his father, while still in Mexico, "was obligated to sacrifice at a forced sale, his place near Washington for one-third of its value." Unquestionably, some sort of a transaction took place, for someone named Richard Smith advertised in the papers that Meridian Hill was for sale.[3]

Yet, part or all of the property must have reverted to Porter's ownership. During January 1829, he leased his mansion to the most unlikely prospect: John Quincy Adams. The lame-duck President wanted a temporary retirement haven in Washington, and Meridian Hill, having been built for two-family occupancy, was ideal for his residential requirements. One wing could be used by the President and his wife, Louisa; the other by son John and his family. On 3 March 1829 John Quincy Adams walked more than a mile from the White House to his new home, thereby avoiding any participation in the raucous ceremonies that inaugurated Andrew Jackson. "At Meridian Hill Adams found himself withdrawn as completely as if he had been a thousand miles from the nation's capital. However painful and mortifying the defeat, he welcomed the relief from responsibility, the quiet of the countryside."

Adams' "relief" was of short duration. In April he wrote to his prodigal son, George Washington Adams, in Massachusetts, requesting him to come help pack for the family's return to Quincy. En route to Washington George, penniless, in debt, and an unmarried father-to-be, committed suicide by jumping off the Providence–New York boat. His parents were almost insane with grief; the ex-President's *Memoirs* are without entry for the next few months. John Quincy and John returned to Massachusetts in June, leaving John's family to take care of Louisa, who was too ill to travel. In July, the Adams family "unexpectedly found the Porter mansion sold over their heads," and a departure date of 1 August imposed.[4]

Porter told President Jackson that he had had to sell his estate in order to pay some of his debts. Six months later the "small amount" of cash that he had realized on the sale was "nearly exhausted." There is nothing in the records to show who became the owner of Meridian Hill in 1829, but in 1830 it passed into the hands of a Richard Landsdale, and the story of the estate closes when the mansion was destroyed by fire in 1863.[5]

During the autumn of 1829 Porter settled down in Chester while he waited for the new administration to fulfill its promise to provide him with a job in government. For the next half-year, frustration almost as great as that which he experienced in Mexico was his handmaid. He was "offered one position after another," but they were either so repugnant to him or so picayune in status and income that he had no choice but to turn them down emphatically.

When the Commodore, "poor as a beggar but proud as an emperor," met Jackson on his return, the President offered to reinstate him in the U.S. Navy. Porter replied that he would "sooner beg my bread from door to door than to link my reputation with men who could pronounce it a punishable offense to do all in my power to sustain the honor and interest of the flag and country." Whereupon, Jackson promptly suggested two other possible assignments: Naval Agent at Gibraltar or U.S. Marshal for the District of Columbia. Porter's outrage at those proposals shines through the forced politeness of his language. To the first, he answered, "I have no knowledge of commerce," and to the second, "I . . . [could not even consider] drawing my support from the misery of others." He was bitterly resentful because he considered that, once again, there was a wide disparity between the treatment meted out to him and that extended, under similar circumstances, to Jackson. In a letter to Senator Dickerson he allowed his resentment to blaze forth: "What would Gen¹ Jackson have said, and what would the people of the U.S. have said, if Mr. Monroe had offered him the Marshalence [?] of the District of Columbia instead of Minister to Mexico?" [6]

It may have been a desire either to emulate Jackson or to satisfy his ache for revenge that led him to suggest that he be given the position for which he considered himself eminently suitable in both talent and experience: he asked the administration to name him Poinsett's successor in Mexico, preferably as minister, but if necessary as chargé d'affaires. Even David Dixon Porter had to admit that such an assignment would have been fraught with disaster: "It must be confessed, that he had a feeling of animosity against the government that had treated him so badly. He desired to triumph over his enemies . . . Fortunately there was no opening for him in that direction. . . ." Indeed, had Porter returned to Mexico as U.S. minister in 1830, the date of the Mexican War's outbreak might have been advanced precisely sixteen years.

The administration, however, continued to offer unattractive jobs. David Dixon tells of his father's refusal to accept "at the highest pay," the post of Governor of the Naval Asylum, a sort of retirement home for officers, because to do so would once again bring him into contact with colleagues who had condemned him. He also turned down the collectorship of any port in the country, on the grounds that such a position would be far inferior to those he had already held.

His confidant, Dickerson, sympathized with his disappointment, assuring him that Jackson's offers had been made in "kindness," and that they were then, and would be until Congress convened in December 1829, the only openings available in government service. Knowing Porter's well-deserved reputation for choleric outbursts and fearing that he might altogether ruin his chances if he did not guard his tongue, Dickerson warned him that any impetuosity would be seized upon by the opposition press, which was always on the lookout for "the least whisper to cause trouble." He added, however, that, so far, the Commodore had couched his refusals in "terms that can give no offense." [7]

As he had done in Mexico, Porter opened his safety valve—self-pity. He lamented that if the administration could or would do nothing for him, he would "set it down as one more disappointment, and a bitter one, for the first awaken[ing] of my hopes was the Election of Gen¹ Jackson." Before he had been home three weeks, he was moaning to Dickerson that, because of the President's assurances, he had "cast myself and family adrift on the world, and am at this moment pennyless and dependent on his own magnanimity, to make or mar my fortunes, to exalt or to further depression." Several weeks passed without any more offers from the administration and his low spirits plummeted when his father-in-law, William Anderson, died on 16 December. This death removed about the only remaining source of support for the Commodore and his family, and Porter begged the long-suffering Dickerson for relief from "the torturing anxiety amounting allmost to hopelessness, which now torments and oppresses me."

At the beginning of the new year, the government dredged up another appointment that Porter considered repulsive: Consul in Tripoli. He scornfully refused to accept it, saying, "it would not afford a support for my family . . . I would not think of taking them to such an exile. I was a prisoner there for near two years and know . . . what it is." He turned to friends for help, and apparently gave some consideration to taking an editorial position. John Skinner, his ally in the cause of José Miguel Carrera, advised him strongly against a career for which he was so totally unprepared, and recommended instead that he "establish a Naval Academy, putting yourself at the head, as Thayer is of the Military Academy." * [8]

With the spring of 1830 came the first attractive offer the administration had made: appointment as Consul-General to the Barbary States. He accepted at once, and sailed for Algiers in the early summer. However, news that awaited him at Port Mahon in the Balearic Islands hinted that his streak of miserable luck which began when he landed on the beach at Fajardo remained unbroken: the French had just occupied Algiers, and since his credentials were addressed to the Dey, he was indeed in "an awkward position." For several months, while awaiting rescue in the form of

---

* West Point, founded in 1802, was being reorganized by Sylvanus Thayer during his long superintendency from 1817 to 1833. The Naval Academy at Annapolis was not established until the early 1840s.

a substitute appointment, he idled about the Mediterranean, calling at Gibraltar, Tunis, Naples, and Leghorn.*

Not until mid-April 1831 was a new post found for him. Secretary of State Van Buren notified Porter that he had been appointed U.S. Chargé d'Affaires to the Ottoman Empire. Congress had recently acted to establish an American Legation in Constantinople. The sum of $36,500 had been appropriated for that purpose, broken down as follows: $4,500 for the salary of the chargé d'affaires; $4,500 for his "outfit"; $2,500 for the salary of a dragoman (interpreter); and $25,000 for "contingent expenses," meaning for the purchase of expensive presents required by the Turkish officials with whom negotiations had to be conducted. Porter's most pressing responsibility in his new assignment was to clear away obstacles to the conclusion of the first commercial treaty between the United States and the Ottoman Empire, and to exchange ratifications.[9]

The history of the American-Turkish treaty stretched back to the late eighteenth century when the newly independent United States was looking toward the eastern Mediterranean for trade opportunities to replace its loss of rich British Empire markets. From the time of the first tentative approaches to the Turks in the 1790s until success was achieved in 1832, American naval officers played prominent parts. Four of Porter's colleagues, Captains William Bainbridge, John Rodgers, William M. Crane, and James Biddle, had a hand in the negotiations. In 1820, Bainbridge, commanding the Mediterranean Squadron, returned to Constantinople under circumstances more auspicious than those which had attended his visit twenty years before when the Dey of Algiers had forced him to carry tribute to the Sultan. Nevertheless, his dispatch of a special envoy to negotiate a treaty with the Turks accomplished nothing. In 1824, following a hint from the Ottoman government that it was desirous of legalizing commercial relations with the United States, Captain John Rodgers was sent to the Sublime Porte. Between 1825 and 1827 he met with Turkish officials on several occasions, but although he was always treated deferentially, he also found it impossible to reach any definite agreement concerning American trading rights and privileges in the Ottoman Empire. In 1828, after another hint from Constantinople, Captain William M. Crane and David Offley, U.S. Consul in Smyrna and the leading American businessman in that part of the world, were appointed joint commissioners to deal with the Turks. Lengthy negotia-

---

* The Porter papers contain little on this period. His only letter extant was written at Port Mahon on 26 November 1830, and dealt with details of the French occupation of Algiers. It contained no news about either his movements or his sentiments.

tions, which occupied the winter of 1828–1829, failed to persuade the Sultan's officials that American trade should be treated on terms of equality with that of the major European powers.

In the spring of 1829 Andrew Jackson became President and he was anxious to achieve the success with Turkey that had been denied to John Quincy Adams. Captain James Biddle was named to replace Crane, and he and Charles Rhind, a New York importer and exporter, were sent as commissioners to assist Offley. In early 1830, Rhind went alone to Constantinople and, despite much vacillation on the part of the Turks, managed to sign a treaty with them on 7 May. The agreement contained nine "public" articles and a "private" one. Most important among the public articles were those that granted the United States most-favored-nation status regarding tariffs, extraterritorial rights, the power to appoint consuls, and trading privileges in the Black Sea equal to those of other countries. The private article granted the Turks some unimportant concessions concerning the building of naval vessels in the United States.

When Biddle and Offley heard the results of Rhind's unilateral work, they were annoyed at his presumption and attacked him for acceding to the insertion of the secret provision. Their objections were echoed in the Senate when it debated acceptance of the Turkish treaty, and although the public articles were overwhelmingly endorsed, so many Senators felt that secrecy was contrary to an honest and open foreign policy that the private article was struck out.[10]

It was at this point in the negotiations that Porter was assigned the Turkish post, and his was the responsibility to assuage Turkish resentment about the Senate's refusal to accept the secret proviso. He threw himself into the task with great enthusiasm, for all along he had felt that implementation of the treaty was the only way in which the sorry state of American trade with Turkey could be remedied. He recorded his reaction when, shortly after arriving in Constantinople, he had looked upon "a long thick line" of masts in the harbor: "There are all the nations under the sun, except American, of which I do not believe there is one! It is astonishing how indifferent our countrymen are to the rich commerce of this great and wonderful empire, as well as that of the Black Sea."

In August 1831 he set about trying to arrange appointments with the two men whose advocacy was essential if ratifications were to be exchanged: Sultan Mahmud II, and the Reis Effendi, an official roughly equivalent to foreign minister. He soon managed to arrange for an informal audience with the Sultan—a mere chargé could not be granted an official audience as could a minister—and got along very well with "the grand seigneur . . . the 'brother of the sun and the moon,' " as one American newspaper called him.

Not until mid-September could Porter convince the Reis Effendi that the Senate's refusal to accept the secret article was meaningless, since existing American laws already permitted the Turks almost every privilege supposedly lost by its deletion. No sooner had this obstacle been removed than another loomed ahead. The Turks discovered that the American translation of the treaty differed slightly from theirs. Here, Porter had to surrender and promise that, should this variance give rise to any disagreement, he would abide by the Turkish version.[11]

On 5 October 1831 Porter and the Reis Effendi took part in ratification ceremonies at the latter's house in Constantinople. They stood facing one another, each with his copy of the ratified treaty held "as high as the head," then exchanged copies. The endorsement read: "This is the Imperial ratification of the treaty between the noble and glorious possessor of the world, and the noble chief of the United States of America."

Martin Van Buren, who had been replaced as Secretary of State and was serving as American Minister to Great Britain, wrote from London to tell Jackson that he had read about the exchange of ratifications: he congratulated the President and mused that the treaty would make "glorious materials for a message." But the best Jackson could do in his annual message presented on 6 December was to say that "some difficulties" had arisen since Porter's arrival, but that he anticipated the treaty would be "speedily effected." Not until 4 February 1832 was the President able to announce that the pact was in force.[12]

Disagreement was not over, however. Almost immediately after ratification, the Turks imposed a 15 per cent tariff on American goods, whereas the tariff on French goods was only 3 per cent. Since the treaty placed the United States on the same basis as France, Porter was instructed to protest, and the following August he was able to report that the unwarranted increase had been removed. Despite the fact that a discriminatory tariff had, for a while, been levied on American goods, U.S. trade with the Ottoman Empire picked up impressively, according to the administration, at least. In his annual message on 4 December 1832, Jackson reported: "Our treaty with the Sublime Porte is producing its expected effects on our commerce. New markets are opening for our commodities. . . . A slight augmentation of the duties on our commerce, inconsistent with the spirit of the treaty, had been imposed, but on representation of our chargé d'affaires, it has been promptly withdrawn."[13]

With his main diplomatic business satisfactorily concluded, Porter settled down in Turkey where, with the exception of a few months spent in the United States during 1838–1839, and an occasional jaunt around the Mediterranean, he stayed for the remainder of his life. At first, he resided in "a modest house" in Pera, a suburb of Constantinople, and summered on the Bosporus. Later, he moved to permanent quarters at San Stefano, seven miles south of the city proper, on the Sea of Marmora, and used the house in Pera for his office.

At San Stefano he lived well in what he called "the Palace." David Dixon Porter, who twice visited him there, says that the house was originally Turkish in design, but his father built and rebuilt it until it became "a very handsome residence, in the modern Greek style, containing all the conveniences that could be desired." It was large enough to be divided into three sections: Porter's own quarters consisted of a reception room, parlor, dining room, library, bedroom, and bath; the second section, which he referred to as "the Harem," was used by his sister, Mrs. Mary Brown, and her family, who joined him in 1834; and the third was reserved for guests. The house was furnished in "Turkish style," and its reception room contained "a rich carpet and a divan covered with Damascus satin. The curtains were of the same material." The extensive grounds included a vineyard, an orchard, and gardens. From these lavish quarters, Porter had a spectacular view across the island-dotted Sea of Marmora to the town of Scutari and, in the distance, he could see "the city of Constantinople, with golden minarets, handsome palaces and private residences ornamented in fanciful style . . . [rising] from the rich frame of the landscape like a great brilliant in a golden setting."

As recounted by David Dixon, Porter's daily routine seems to have been little plagued by toil. Every morning at 8:00 he stepped out onto the veranda to watch three Turkish servants hoist the American flag, "with as much ceremony . . . as if they were on board a ship of war." After breakfast, while he sat in his dressing gown stroking the fur of an Angora cat in his lap, his sister would read to him "for a couple of hours," generally works "of a solid kind, theology, history, travels, and the classics." Thereafter, he would "retire to his room for several hours," during which no one ventured to disturb him. The middle of the day was taken up by dinner, usually of local cuisine, as "his liking for Turkish habits extended even to their cookery." Meals were "served with a great deal of form" by two waiters, one of whom always stood behind Porter's chair and ministered solely to his wants. In the early afternoon, his carriage and horses stood ready to take him into Constantinople to attend to any diplomatic business he might have, or to favorite outdoor spots around the neighborhood.[14] On the whole, it was a pleasant way of life, and must have been especially so to Porter, following his horrid experiences in Mexico.

In spite of this leisurely way of life, his literary output was staggering. During the early years of his tenure in the Ottoman Empire he wrote his second and last book. For three years he sent long, detailed letters about his exotic new environment and its people to James K. Paulding, fellow "Kilkenny Lad" of Washington Irving's coterie in 1807. In 1835, Paulding had the letters published under the title: *Constantinople and Its Environs. In a series of letters exhibiting the actual state of the manners, customs, and habits of the Turks, Armenians, Jews, and Greeks . . . By an American, long resident at Constantinople.* It is a reasonably interesting, thorough, and readable guide book, which his son claims did well, and "the proceeds of its sale were devoted by the Commodore to the education of his eldest daughter [Evalina]."

Besides maintaining regular correspondence with family, friends, and enemies, Porter wrote a spate of letters to the State Department. Four Secretaries were the unhappy recipients of this epistolary torrent, and Daniel Webster's predecessors, Edward Livingston, Louis McLane, and John Forsyth, must have felt as he did in 1841 when his patience finally ran out and he told the Commodore point-blank not to "write so often." [15] Certainly, most of the correspondence flowed only one way between Washington and Constantinople. While Porter addressed several hundred letters to the State Department between 1831 and 1842, the four Secretaries together sent him precisely fifty-eight communiqués, many of which were nothing more than printed circulars. Luckily, Porter's secretaries, especially his nephew George A. Porter, were blessed with legible handwriting, for as the Commodore aged and sickened, his always miserable penmanship became practically indecipherable. The content of Porter's writings boxed the compass, but at least some of his correspondence pertained to his official functions.

Although in one personal letter he spoke of his moving in "the dull and sickening round of diplomacy," he appears to have thoroughly enjoyed his prestige and authority. In 1836 he expressed his "perfect contentment" with his official situation, and three years later, when he was promoted to Minister Resident, he must have liked it better still. He basked in the approval of Sultan Mahmud II, who ruled the Ottoman Empire during most of Porter's tour of duty. According to his son, in the early days of his assignment, the Commodore was visiting the government dockyard and happened to meet the Sultan. Together, they walked around the establishment while Porter, "with great frankness, pointed out all the defects in the Turkish naval system, without offense to his majesty, who told him he would send his naval pasha to consult with him on the subject which he did." [16] This episode resulted in Mahmud making Porter his informal advisor on naval reform.

It was on the Commodore's advice that the Sublime Porte hired Henry Eckford, who had built the *Guerrero* for the Mexican Navy, to be his "chief naval constructor." Eckford died in service in 1832,* but his employee and successor, Foster Rhodes, completed a new frigate for the Turks and, in May 1835, Porter attended her launching ceremonies, to which the whole court, including the Sultan's harem, was invited. Two years later, the Commodore advised the State Department that Mahmud wanted to hire American officers for his Navy, and was told that only retired officers, not those on active service, could be approached.[17]

A common interest in naval matters led to frequent meetings between the Sultan and the Commodore. Whenever Mahmud caught sight of Porter at a favorite picnic spot called "the valley of the Sweet waters," he would invite him to share "pipes and coffee." The Sultan's visits to San Stefano, where Porter had his estate, brought them together for "many interviews which gradually paved the way to a very social and friendly state of affairs."

In 1838 Porter paid a visit to the United States and, when he returned the following year, he found that Mahmud was dead and his son, Abdul Mejid, was sitting on the imperial throne. On 23 May 1840 Porter presented his credentials as Minister Resident to the new Sultan and reported that his "reception was highly flattering." † Nevertheless, the Commodore never achieved with Abdul Mejid the easy informality he had enjoyed with Mahmud. Overlooking the obvious reason for the lack of close harmony between the two, David Dixon Porter ascribes it to the personality of Abdul Mejid who, he says, was "a very different character from his father, the late sultan, never indulging in familiar intercourse with any one. . . ."[18] Abdul Mejid was only sixteen when he succeeded to the throne and could not have been expected to have much in common with a fifty-nine-year-old retired American naval officer.

There was little to roil Turkish-American relations during Porter's thirteen years of service in Constantinople. Once the tariff discrepancy had been settled, only one episode marred the smooth operation of the commercial treaty. In 1839 Great Britain wangled new trade concessions from the Ottoman Empire, and it took the Commodore most of that year to extract similar privileges for his country, as specifically called for in the Turkish-American treaty.

A couple of the minor diplomatic problems that Porter faced deserve comment. He wrote lengthy if infrequent letters approving the activities of American missionaries in the Sultan's domains, and his son described

* David Dixon Porter says that Eckford returned to the United States because of ill health, but a dispatch to the State Department in 1833 proves him wrong.
† David Dixon Porter is in error when he gives 1841 as the year in which his father presented his credentials.

him as taking "a deep interest in the prosperity of the American Board of Foreign Missions." Perhaps, but toward the end of his life, missionaries in Turkey protested that the Resident Minister paid no attention either to their needs or to their advice, and the Department chided him for this omission.

During the spring of 1836, the Sublime Porte made a suggestion which, had it been accepted, would have changed the history of the United States and the Middle East. The American Consul at Salonika notified Porter that Ottoman officials had approached him with an offer to sell the island of Cyprus to the United States. The Commodore advised the Consul to forget that the offer had been made, then fired off to Washington the Consul's letter along with his own advice that America already had enough land and should avoid the "evils" of colony-grabbing.[19] This attitude marked quite a change in the quondam annexer of Nukahiva Island.

A few other examples of a different and more philosophical Porter stand out amid the temper tantrums, hypochondriacal moanings, and delusions of persecution that characterized his final years. Having received a most cordial and complimentary letter from David Glasgow Farragut, he replied to "the grateful heart" of "my dear Glasgow":

> . . . I am getting old, have had many sorrows, much sickness and affliction, and have lasted much longer than men do under such circumstances generally; but I bear all with sufficient fortitude, and, as I have nothing to merit from fortune more than she has done for me, I have nothing to complain of on her account. I have never been elated with prosperity, and ought not, and I hope I am not depressed at the loss of worldly goods. My country has thus far taken care of me, and I hope by good conduct to merit what she has done, by endeavoring to serve her to the utmost of my power. There was a time when there was nothing that I thought too daring to be attempted for her; but those times are past, and appear only as a confused and painful dream. A retrospect of the history of my life seems a highly-coloured romance, which I should be very loth to live over again. . . .

Considering Porter's racist and nationalistic intolerance on occasion —his anti-Semitism, his lifelong anglophobia, and his abhorrence of Mexicans—it is refreshing to read the quite contrary sentiments which he included in his book on Constantinople:

> I have been a traveller all my life, and am personally familiar with the people of every quarter of the globe, white, black, tawny, and copper-colored. . . . If you wish me to sum up the result of all my wanderings, experience, reflections, enjoyments, and sufferings, here it is in a few words. I have found that there is not that vast disparity of wisdom, intelligence and virtue, between the different nations of the earth, which the vanity of every people imagines. . . . I have found every where the faculties of the human mind, and the virtues of the human heart, best adapted to the attainment of

happiness in the situation in which providence hath placed us, and above all, I have discovered that . . . those who set themselves up as the standards of excellence, and as models to all nations in every circumstance and situation, are for the most part supremely ignorant blockheads or arrogant coxcombs.[20]

Unfortunately, one has to conclude that those philosophical observations were mainly window dressing. Porter certainly was not about to use his font of accumulated wisdom for the solution of personal problems which plagued him throughout his long stay in the Ottoman Empire. Nor were the difficulties he had in Turkey new. Change the names of places and people, alter the dates, and his bulging file of letters dispatched from Constantinople could have been written in Veracruz. Running through his correspondence from both places are his almost obsessive anxieties about rank; finances; personal relations, both inside and outside his family; and health.

As to rank, the Porter who kept reaching for the title of either admiral or general in Mexico was not apt to be content for long with his lowly status as chargé d'affaires in Turkey. For more than seven years he hammered away at the State Department to promote him to minister. He started his campaign immediately after ratification of the commercial treaty, suggesting that his chores would have been much eased had he enjoyed ministerial position, for the Turks did not like having to negotiate with a mere chargé. As soon as he had cleared away the disagreement concerning the tariff discrepancy in 1832, he was back again with the argument that only Turkish pressure was making him ask for advancement. From 1833 until the end of 1837, he complained steadily, if infrequently, that it was his lack of status that made it impossible for him to conclude successfully his diplomatic errands.

The one and only trip he made to the United States during his Turkish service was motivated partly by his desire to argue his case for higher rank. He emphasized to Martin Van Buren, who had become President the year before, that the Grand Duchy of Tuscany and the United States were the only two powers represented at the Sublime Porte by chargés d'affaires. So outrageous did he deem this situation that he would, he told the President, accept promotion to minister without any increase in pay, strange talk for a man who was ever financially embarrassed. His long campaign was finally successful. In March 1839 he was appointed "Minister Resident" in the Ottoman Empire at a salary of $6,000 and a contingent fund of $3,500 a year, by the standards of the time, handsome compensation. Thomas Hart Benton said that Congress had responded so generously for Porter's "special benefit" as an act of national gratitude to a naval hero.[21]

He could use all the financial help he could get. Debts quickly contracted in Turkey were piled upon his earlier failing investments, the cost of supporting a large family, the long-standing muddle of his accounts with the Navy Department, and the ruin in Mexico of what little fiscal stability he had previously possessed.

The Commodore's new financial difficulties had started almost immediately upon his arrival in Constantinople when he set about spending the $25,000 the U.S. government had allocated for the purchase of presents for Turkish officials whose favor was essential if the treaty were to be ratified. The way diplomatic business with the Sublime Porte had to be conducted in the 1830s today would be considered criminal. The Turks made no pretense about the bribery involved. The Reis Effendi furnished him with a list of the twenty-one officials concerned, a description of the gift each one should receive, and its cost. Porter appended the Reis' itemization to a letter he sent the State Department announcing ratification of the treaty. The elite share, of course, went to the Sultan, who received a $5,000 fan made of "heron feathers," and a jeweled snuffbox costing $10,000, although Porter had earlier commented to the Secretary of State that His Majesty would be more appreciative of a steam boat "made to resemble a swan." *

In order to get the treaty ratified, Porter spent a total of 533,745 Turkish piasters, or $29,152.50, a sum which exceeded his appropriation and swallowed up his contingency fund for the next year. Showing classic symptoms of a guilty conscience by expressing fear that he would have to face "the charge of rashness which has too frequently been supposed to be a strong trait in my character," he begged the government to approve and refund his expenditures. In the spring of 1832 Congress responded to his pleas and provided an extra appropriation: $6,000 to pay off his obligations, and $10,000 for his use in the future.[22]

Less than a year later, he was back at the public trough. In a ten-page letter, he demanded monetary assistance and, after apologizing for his complaint, had the colossal effrontery to say, "as I believe it is the first time in my life of long public service that I have done so." The Secretary of State answered with the unhelpful observation that he realized chargés d'affaires could not live on their salaries, then pointed out that the President was by law forbidden to take any remedial action, and relief would

---

* "Exchanging" presents with the Turks was a one-way street. All Porter received in return for almost $30,000 worth of gifts were "seven lambs, thirteen chickens, and a Basket of Cherries." In earlier negotiations, Captain John Rodgers gave the Sultan a diamond ring and a diamond snuffbox and, in return, was given "a Turkish pipe, a shawl, two silk gown patterns, two handkerchiefs and a small box of sweetmeats."

have to come from an additional appropriation by Congress. On the first day of 1836, still preoccupied with money, Porter wrote the Secretary a fourteen-page letter, in which he wailed that he had to give his family $2,370 a year, keeping only $2,310 for himself, and that already his contingency fund, supposed to last for the remaining 364 days of the year, stood at under a thousand dollars.*

With new burdens piled upon the old, Porter's accounts with the government reached a stage of such utter confusion that neither he nor anyone else knew exactly where he stood. In 1835 Secretary of State John Forsyth looked into his total indebtedness, saw nothing but chaos, and insisted that Porter straighten out his accounts at once. The Commodore's attempts to comply with the Secretary's wishes were no more successful than similar efforts had been in the past. The degree of his helplessness in keeping his accounts straight is demonstrated by two instances. In the first, he revised upward by $500 the cost of the gifts he had bought for Turkish officials in 1831. At the time the gifts were purchased he had submitted to the Department an itemized bill of $29,152.50 for them. In 1835 he raised that total to $29,652.50, and appended the payment of extra sums amounting to $1,138 for the "Capt° Pasha" and $2,100 for the Reis Effendi. In the second, he sent to Washington two letters carrying the same date during 1836: he was consistent only in the number of cents he owed, for in one, he admitted to a debt of $12,218.71, and in the other to $9,666.71.

The necessity of reaching a settlement with the government was another reason for his returning to the United States in 1838, but absolutely nothing was resolved. After conversations with Treasury auditors, he told Forsyth that his obligation was $1,997.15, a sum so small that it could be repaid by installments deducted from his salary. A week later, his debt had somehow dropped to $997.00. Unfortunately, the Treasury had not arrived at the same optimistic conclusions, and Forsyth had to tell him that the total of his indebtedness stood at $5,427.95, but added that he hoped Congress would enable him to meet this obligation through the appropriation for his "outfit as Minister Resident to Turkey." [24]

The extra income that went along with his ministerial rank helped, but did not cure, his financial ills: nor was it provided soon enough to save him from acute embarrassment. He had to ask Forsyth to advance $2,000 on his salary so that he could pay for his trip from the United States back to Constantinople. The Secretary refused on the grounds that he could not legally comply, and Porter recalled that he departed from

---

* In 1838 Porter told his son that because "of the bills which your Mother has run up," he had been forced to cut her allowance to $1,500 a year. [23]

Washington so "very short of money . . . that I could not pay my passage until I arrived in Smyrna." He was compelled to leave his family so bereft of funds that in September of that year, Evalina had to borrow $500 from a relative, putting up her silver plate as collateral.

Porter was never able to straighten out his debt to the government. He was even confused about how much of his new $6,000 ministerial salary was supposed to be applied against it. He begged Forsyth to reduce from $1,500 to $1,000 the sum he was required to repay annually, stating that he must have the extra money, and the Secretary replied that $1,000 was all that he had ever been asked to repay in any one year. In 1841 Porter estimated that it would still take him "about two years" to wipe out his obligations to the government.[25]

While the Commodore was in Turkey his fertile imagination busied itself with two financial projects: if the U.S. Navy were to grant him a disability pension, his economic ailments might be eased, and if he could collect on his Spanish and Mexican claims, they might be cured. He was already receiving from the Navy a pension of $40 per month, which he allocated for the education of his elder daughter, Evalina, but he decided to capitalize on the wounds and illnesses which he had suffered during his long public service. While at home in 1838, heartened by the support of his good friend James K. Paulding, who had become Secretary of the Navy, he amassed testimonials from colleagues, who constituted an impressive array of naval talent and experience: Isaac Hull, Charles Stewart, Isaac Chauncey, Joshua Blake, Daniel T. Patterson, Charles Goldsborough, John Downes, Samuel Hambleton, and J. Orde Creighton.*

There were conspicuous omissions from the list of supporters. Downes was the sole representative of all those who sat on Porter's court-martial. It is certainly understandable that Porter would not have asked James Barron, James Biddle, or Jesse D. Elliott to speak for him. But the name of the senior officer of the Navy was also missing: Captain John Rodgers' failure to act can only mean that he had not forgiven Porter for what he looked upon as inexcusable behavior in connection with the Kennon court-martial and arrant insubordination during and after the Fajardo incident. Porter was either being obtuse or bluffing when he wrote to Paulding: "The oldest officer of the navy now living, for reasons known only to himself, declines giving any information in my case." [26]

He intended to base his claim upon the wound he suffered on 1 January 1800 at the Bight of Leogane off Haiti, but the Attorney General's office advised that only disabilities suffered after 23 April 1800 could be

---

* Creighton wrote James K. Paulding in support of the Commodore's petition on 10 October 1838, and died the next day.

considered. Hence, most of his backers focused upon the attacks of yellow fever he had suffered in 1823 and 1824 while he commanded the West India Squadron, but a few of them introduced other service-incurred disabilities. Samuel Hambleton talked about an onset of yellow fever that felled Porter when he was head of the New Orleans Station in 1808. Charles Stewart mentioned the aftereffects of his imprisonment in Tripoli from 1803 to 1805, but, for some curious reason, omitted any reference to the wounds Porter suffered while attacking the Bashaw's barges on 3 June 1803. Stewart even dragged in the results of the court-martial, in which Porter had been "persecuted out of that gallant navy," as a form of disability. Other supporters roamed equally far afield with stirring and irrelevant accounts of Porter's heroism in the *Essex* at Valparaiso.

At first, it seemed that the chances for success were good. Secretary Paulding told him that a law passed on 3 March 1837 could be applicable to his case and, if so, he would receive $3,150, based upon $12.50 a month from 1803 to 1825. Unfortunately, Porter's application was only "refered to the Naval Committee of the Senate and never reported on." [27] The efforts of his colleagues had been in vain, and he never received a disability pension.

Porter put most of his effort to recoup his shattered fortunes into resurrecting his claims against Spain and Mexico. In February 1836 he learned that Texas might be annexed by the United States, and he hoped that, if such happened, Washington would assume payment of bona fide debts owed by Mexico to American citizens. Consequently, he wrote Secretary of State John Forsyth begging him to arrange an exchange of his "ten square leagues of land on the river Guasagualpo" in Tehuantepec for tracts along the Sabine River in Texas. Of course, he added, he would also accept money for his Mexican lands. A few weeks later he reverted to the subject in a twenty-page letter to Forsyth which amounted to an encomium of his own services in Mexico. He estimated that Mexico owed him a total of $150,000 in recompense for his abandonment of his claims against the Spanish *Consulado* of Havana and as a reward for his contributions to that republic. He tried to persuade Joel R. Poinsett to intercede in his behalf during 1840,[28] but since the United States did not annex Texas during his lifetime, that door remained closed to him.

Because of these abortive claims, a missing box shadowed Porter's last years and ruined what little rapport still remained between him and most of his immediate family. When he left for the Mediterranean in 1830, he locked in a closet of his house in Chester an old unpainted box of a "much used" appearance. He warned Evalina that it contained the papers upon which his Spanish and Mexican claims were based, and told her to guard it carefully.* When he returned to Chester in 1838 he discovered that the closet was unlocked and the box missing. For the five remaining years of his life, he was haunted by the loss. Disclaiming expectation of personal profit, since he would be dead long before any return could be realized, he emphasized that "to the last moment of my life I shall make inquiries as to the papers on which so much property is depending, which if recovered would be a princely fortune to all my family."

Three of his close relatives fell under his suspicion as perpetrators of the theft: in reverse order of probability, they were his second son David Dixon, his wife Evalina, and his eldest son William David. David Dixon, the only son with whom he remained on affectionate and confiding terms, was considered only briefly. In 1838, before leaving home to return to Constantinople, Porter demanded an explanation from him. David Dixon's reply does not appear to be extant, but he obviously denied indignantly any guilt, whereupon Porter replied that he would accept as "sufficient . . . [your] assurance that you know nothing of the missing papers . . . but your Mother . . . [said] that you had examined all the papers, although she had requested you not to do so. . . ."

Porter's acceptance of the fact that David Dixon was innocent, not only led to the two once more becoming confidants, but permitted the Commodore to enjoy one of the few truly happy occasions of his later life. On 10 March 1839, thirty-one years to the day after his own marriage to Evalina, he attended the wedding of David Dixon and George Ann Patterson in Washington. The marriage had been delayed so that both Porter and Daniel T. Patterson, the bride's father, could be present. The two old naval colleagues, who had been friends since long before the War of 1812, reveled in the festivities that united their families and in their own friendship which, since Patterson luckily had not been required to sit on Porter's court-martial, was still intact. One syrupy comment on the event was that it "would be hard to find a prettier, little domestic drama than this, colored as it was with a tinge of naval romance, cast upon it . . . by the presence of the two Tripoli veterans. . . ."[29]

But his relief from anxiety was quickly over, and for the rest of his

---

* A notice placed in the Sunday Book Review of *The New York Times* led me to Mr. and Mrs. Carroll Van Ness of Owings Mills, Maryland. Mr. Van Ness is a direct descendant of David Porter, and he and his wife permitted me not only to read, but to take for copying, many previously unused letters of both David and David Dixon Porter which were in their possession. Some of these letters are in fragments, but they supply much information on Porter's relations with his family, and particularly about the missing box. I have referred to them as the Van Ness Collection of the David Porter Papers.

days Porter wrote letter after letter to his favorite son, pouring forth his suspicions of Evalina and William. Even before the matter of the purloined box was raised, relations between David and Evalina Porter, the parents of ten children, had deteriorated into mutual hatred. To David Dixon, the Commodore extrapolated Evalina's part in the loss of the box into unflattering commentary about her on a variety of subjects, never calling her "my wife" but always "your Mother." When he first discovered that the papers were missing, he told David Dixon that Evalina might be responsible, because:

> Your Mother destroyed a will that I wrote before I left America [in 1830] which had reference particularly to the papers which are missing. She also, she informed me [,] destroyed many other papers of mine but for what reason I know not—but there is no accounting for many things that are done by her and I am determined to submit to her evils unless they affect my honour.

Not only did Evalina deny any complicity in the theft of the papers, she contended that the box had never existed, except in the deluded memory of her husband. Porter accused her of trying to make "my children believe that I have lost my mind, and that I never had such a box of papers, but she may discover when too late that, on this subject at least, my mind is as fresh and vivid as it ever was. . . ." He glumly added, "if I have not lost my mind, it is not because she has not done enough to drive me crazy. . . ." He argued that it was Evalina, not he, who was insane: in fact, she had been in that state for a long time, and the only reason he had not already committed her was that "she drew from me a promise that I would not place her in a mad house if I should discover that she was crazy." However, he told David Dixon, he would put her away if it became necessary, not only because there was "much method . . . in her madness," but also because of "her sinister designs. . . . It grieves me to think that Evalina [his daughter] should be made the subject of comment and perhaps ridicule by accompanying her mad Mother wherever she chooses to take her, and be obliged to listen to all the slander and malice and calumnies, some of which I fear may have had influence on her pure mind." He concluded his letter: "Your Mother . . . exercises such a baneful influence over Evalina and Henry, that neither of them writes to me." [30]

Considering the pains he had taken to impress upon his wife the importance of the papers, Porter doubted that she could have forgotten about them. Even if she had not destroyed them, as she had other records of his, he judged her responsible. The precious documents had been left with her for safekeeping, and she should never have let "any one have access to the closet where they were deposited." He went so far as to insist that she either sign an affidavit swearing that she would "deliver the papers up," or confess that she had destroyed them, and remarked that the latter would be better than continued doubt for it would, at least, "put to rest the subject forever." Nevertheless, it would be tragic if they really had been destroyed, for "all my troubles and anxieties for a quarter of a Century should be thus thrown away."

Evalina's perhaps understandable reluctance to sign any affidavit allowed her husband to state that "if she refuses to do so the disgrace and odium of sacrificing the interests of her children will rest on her." When, in 1841, she gave in and took an oath that she knew nothing about any such papers, Porter expressed incredulity that "she who never forgets anything has lost her memory about the papers." However, deciding to adopt a course of philosophical tolerance, he told David Dixon: "I forgive her as she has taken her oath of her ignorance of all the facts and must ascribe her conduct to one of those fits of insanity with which she informed me she was once afflicted and to which I attributed much of her conduct."

Amid all his fulminations about the box, Porter evidently did not forget the scandalous behavior that his wife had been accused of a decade before, and commented to his attorney in Pennsylvania, "All Chester knows how she left the town in hot water, just before I returned from Mexico. . . ." Poor David Dixon had to read an even more scurrilous charge against Evalina when his father wrote about "an Irish school master who I found closeted with your Mother in her room under the pretext that she was taken lessons in Greek until I told her how indecorous it appeared, when she asked me for money to pay him off. . . ." * At the same time as Evalina was being subjected to her husband's allegations of misconduct, her son William was making similar, if vague, charges. The latter threatened to tell his father about "certain things," unless she could "prove her innocence" to him. David Dixon, in a coldly wrathful four-page letter to his brother, expressed his contempt for William's outrageous accusation.[31]

Porter's temporary suspicion of David Dixon and his more lasting doubts about his wife were secondary to his prime suspicion, which was against his eldest son, Lieutenant William David Porter, U.S. Navy, the family black sheep. Apparently, the last time there had been any cordiality between father and son was on 28 February 1839 when William, whose first wife had died, married a girl from Norfolk, Virginia, with his

---

* A couple of the fragmentary letters in the Van Ness Collection contain suggestions that this Irish schoolmaster had drawn some "caracatures" of the family, but they are not concrete enough to allow valid conclusions to be drawn.

father in attendance. Not long after that event, the Commodore was writing scathing comments about William: he believed he had irrefutable evidence that his son had perpetrated the theft of the papers. William had been on assignment in the Mediterranean before his father left for home in 1838 and had visited him both at San Stefano and at Tunis. For what other reason, Porter asked, would he call on a father with whom he had long been on bad terms than to sound him out concerning the box, file away the information, and steal the papers when he returned home?

In 1840 Porter accused William directly:

> The suspicion of your having the papers . . . arises from observations which you yourself have made, and which you could not have made, had you not had access to the papers. . . . I now tell you that . . . if you have them, as I am convinced you have, I shall as much as I shall regret it, expose you to the world unless you immediately give them up . . . so that I can make use of them to substantiate my claim on Mexico which is now suspended for the want of them. . . . The inquiry is now going on, and the sooner you stop it by the surrender of the papers, the greater regard you will show for your own character.

After reading this evidence of paternal trust and affection, it is not hard to understand why the son "expressed a wish to sever all family connections" with his father.

William did what he could to clear himself, going so far as to swear before a Justice of the Peace in the District of Columbia, ". . . [the papers] have never been in my possession, that I have not, either directly or indirectly, participated in the disposition of them, and that I have no knowledge whatever in whose hands the said papers now are." He might as well have saved his J.P.'s fee. His father refused to believe him, and filed a deposition stating that if, after his own death, "my son William should have possession of the papers," and gave them up, "he, the said William, is not to enjoy" any part of the proceeds: if, on the other hand, he had them and refused to surrender them, the claims against Spain and Mexico were to be withdrawn permanently so that William could never benefit from his crime.[32]

Porter continued to belabor his eldest son about the missing box and anything else that came to mind:

> William is such an abominable liar there is not a word to be believed that he says, and I expect every day to hear that he has had his nose pulled, and his bottom kicked, for some of his falsehoods. . . . Until he explains to me how he got information about my claims on the Consulado of Havana I cannot believe that he has not had access to my papers . . . were he to swear until he is black in the face.

The Commodore went to the extreme of writing David Glasgow Farragut, whose wife's sister had been William's first wife, about his "well-founded" conviction that his son had stolen the papers. He asked Farragut whether he recalled William ever making any remarks about them, but no reply seems to exist.

Porter also accused his son of borrowing $100 from Commodore John Downes and trying to discharge the debt with a note "which was not good." * Porter's catalogue of William's dark deeds accused him of having stolen clothing "and other effects" from his cousin Lawrence Heap and applied them "to his own use." For some reason—it could not have been delicacy—he never mentioned one disgraceful fact about William which he knew to be true. His son, while married for the second time, had fathered a child by one of his own household servants.[33]

For the rest of his life Porter remained adamant against his eldest child. A codicil to his will cut off "my son William D. Porter" from any share in his estate, with the exception of "one Spanish dollar." In a letter to his wife, he explained that he had done so "on account of his bad conduct." †

No papers supporting Porter's Spanish and Mexican claims were ever recovered, and there is no way of finding out what happened to them. There are several possibilities, however. During the last years of his life, Porter's behavior was, to say the least, erratic, and it is imaginable that his wife was correct when she charged that the entire matter came out of his confused mind. On the other hand, Evalina seems to have been neurotic and, possibly, psychotic; she may have destroyed the papers and later forgotten completely that she had. There is nothing approximating legal proof of the charges leveled against William. Porter's assumption of his son's guilt was based on the latter's intimate knowledge of the facts, but the Commodore must have talked so incessantly about his Spanish and Mexican claims that William could have picked up all he knew from

---

* In borrowing money from Downes, William was following his father's example. In 1838 the Commodore sent Downes $2,000, leaving $1,030 still due in principal and interest on a debt that dated back to 1822. Many years later, David Dixon repaid Downes in full. There is no way of knowing whether Porter's charge that William issued a worthless note was justified or not. What remains of Downes' reply to Porter ends just at the point where it would have confirmed or denied that William had done so.

† During the Civil War, William commanded the ironclad USS *Essex,* and to those who did not know the relationship between him and his father, the name of his ship must have seemed quite appropriate. He was badly scalded in action before Fort McHenry on 6 February 1862, and later fought well against the ironclad CSS *Arkansas* on the Mississippi. He still managed to get in trouble. In 1863, he was "angrily defending himself in a naval court against charges of insubordination preferred by Admirals [C. H.] Davis and Farragut. William had antagonized both of these officers while he had been on the Mississippi. . . ." He died of the aftereffects of wounds and illness on 1 May 1865.[34]

his father's rantings. Even David Dixon, who hated William, believed him innocent of the theft. On 29 August 1842, little more than six months before he died, Porter wrote Evalina that he suspected a servant girl had stolen the box and, when she found the contents valueless to her, burned them to get rid of incriminating evidence.[35] Probably he had at last hit upon the truth.

Although Porter's younger sons, Theodoric, Hambleton, and Henry Ogden, had nothing to do with the missing papers—being either out of the country or too young when the theft took place—their relations with their father were not much better than those of William. Theodoric's troubles were primarily academic. When, having been accepted by the Military Academy at West Point, he failed to graduate, his father was crushed and let him know it. In April 1836 Porter wrote to the Secretary of War, ascribing Theodoric's scholastic difficulties to his own "long and frequent absences," which made it impossible to oversee properly the boy's education. He decided that Theodoric's talents would be well applied in the diplomatic corps, and he promised to start his training in oriental languages. He also asked Captain Daniel T. Patterson to "take care of" Theodoric; David Dixon, he said, was old enough to care for himself. Theodoric did not go into the diplomatic service; had he done so, he might have become a beneficiary of his father's well-developed nepotism, and had a permanent sinecure in the American Legation at Constantinople. Instead, he re-entered the Army in 1838, and, on 18 April 1846, when he was serving as a lieutenant in the Seventh Regiment, was killed in action—the first American officer to die in the Mexican War.[36]

Midshipman Hambleton Porter is seldom mentioned in family correspondence, and the few references to him are uncomplimentary. His trouble-making brother, William, notified Porter that, had the boy stayed much longer in Chester, he would have become "a perfect sot." Hambleton put himself in a bad light by writing a letter to the captain of the USS *Hudson* asking that a lieutenant with whom he had quarreled "wave rank" so that they could duel. In 1841 Porter lamented to David Dixon that he had not heard from Hambleton for many months and was sure that he had "cut my acquaintance," grumbling that he was like his younger brother Henry in being "given too much to pleasure and idleness." *

Relations between Porter and Henry Ogden Porter, his youngest son, were particularly hostile. The Commodore accused his wife of "poison-

---

* As had his brother Thomas almost twenty years before, Hambleton Porter died of yellow fever which he contracted "early in the Mexican War," according to David Dixon Porter, on 10 August 1844, according to the historian of Chester, Pennsylvania.[37]

ing" the boy's mind against him, and evidently she did. Furthermore, Henry's activities kept him enveloped in his father's disapproval. In 1836 he was in the Mediterranean serving as a midshipman under his father's enemy Jesse D. Elliott, who reported that "little Henry . . . [is] a very smart intelligent boy" who requires "a tort rein on him to make a man of him." Henry later returned to school but, much to his father's dismay, left in 1840, and applied on his own to re-enter the Navy. Positive that without further education, his son could never achieve a rank higher than midshipman, Porter refused to recommend him. The boy ignored him, received his commission anyway, and, in the process, became so angry with his father that he broke with him. A year later, a repentant Henry asked for passage money to visit Porter in Constantinople. Citing as evidence the miserably written letter he had just received, the Commodore cast animadversions on his son's educational background, and told him, "of course, I will never send it [money] until I am assured that your conduct . . . is proper." He predicted that Henry would be "sent home as a deserter," and concluded that he hoped to live long enough to see "a change in you for the better." It is to be doubted that his son was placated by the signature: "Your affectionate father." [38]

Henry improved not a bit. Having "contracted the liquor habit," he was court-martialed at Port Mahon during 1842 on the impressive charges of "Intoxication; Quarreling and Fighting; Disobedience of Orders & Contempt of a Superior Officer; Unofficerlike and Insubordinate Conduct; Assault of a Superior Officer." Evidently, by some miracle, he managed to be acquitted of that staggering catalogue of naval felonies and misdemeanors, for in April 1843 the Commodore of the Mediterranean Squadron ordered him to report to a new ship. Two years later, he was writing to his mother from the newly established Naval Academy at Annapolis.*

The Commodore was kindlier and more tolerant towards his two surviving daughters, Evalina and Imogene, than he was to his sons, David Dixon excepted. Evalina was his favorite and her name appears in his correspondence more frequently than that of her younger sister. Porter charged that, by her "evil" and "malicious" statements, his wife had alienated Evalina's affections, but the relationship between father and daughter seems to have been cordial on both sides. To Porter, the "most interesting event" of 1833 was learning that his "little daughter Evalina

---

* At the time of the Civil War, Henry O. Porter was an acting lieutenant and fought in the USS Hatteras against the famed CSS Alabama. He was captured and, according to his brother, "died from the effects of wounds and disabilities" incurred in the battle and during his subsequent imprisonment. If so, he managed to live with them until 22 May 1872.[39]

entertained an evening party of 40 young ladies of her own age and danced until 3 o'clock in the morning . . . it gives me more pleasure than I can express." When, in 1842, she married her cousin, G. Harris Heap, he sent his blessings and his sympathy over the opposition she had met from her mother. Evalina and her husband went to Constantinople and cared for the ailing Commodore until he died.

Porter's younger daughter and youngest child, Imogene, is mentioned hardly at all in the voluminous Porter correspondence. In 1839 he allotted his wife $1,500 a year, out of which she was supposed to provide for Imogene's schooling. About the only other reference to her is a letter Porter wrote to her in 1841, apologizing because his debts to the government made it impossible for him to buy her the horse she requested, and congratulating her for no longer biting her fingernails.[40]

Considering how harshly Porter treated his sons, it is remarkable how diligently and tenderly he watched over his nephews. To be sure, as his boys came of age, he placed them in the armed forces, but aside from criticizing their characters and habits, he paid little attention to them. But throughout his Turkish assignment, he was an open, unabashed, and usually successful nepotist on behalf of his sisters' children. He even told the Department on one occasion that he had been accused of "undue exertions to secure appointment of some members of my family."

He had to find employment for two nephews who showed up in Constantinople in 1832: John Brown, son of his sister Mary, arrived in February, and nine months later was joined by George A. Porter, son of his sister Ann, and brother of David H. Porter, who had been killed in the *Guerrero*.* The presence of these young relatives was partly responsible for Porter's incessant harrying of any Legation employee whose job might be filled by one of his nephews. In fact, most of his personal imbroglios were connected with nepotism.

An exception was the clash he had with Nicholas Navoni, who had informally represented the United States since 1821, and whose head rolled before either of the nephews arrived. Almost as soon as he arrived in Constantinople, Porter feuded with Navoni, fired him, and stopped his pay. He notified the Department that Navoni had been "insolent," and that his "indifference and ill-grounded hostility produced all this delay" in the ratification of the treaty. The erstwhile dragoman fought back with what little ammunition he had: he complained that his superior must have exceeded his authority in dismissing him so summarily, and accused him of cheating the U.S. government by inflating the value of the

---

* George was the sole survivor among Ann Porter's four sons. At about the same time as David H. was killed, Alexander and John died.[41]

presents he bought for Turkish officials. When Navoni finally took his forced departure, he carried off with him the *"takara* of chase," the hunting permit for the entire legation. Although Porter wrote a seventeen-page letter to the Department about the loss of the permit, he did not reveal how it was recovered. Navoni filed his last appeal the following spring, when, in asking for financial aid, he called the Department's attention to the services he had rendered for more than a decade under Offley, Biddle, and Rhind, and begged for "justice." His pleadings were all to no avail: he received no more justice than he did compensation.[42]

According to the Secretary of State, President Jackson regretted that Porter had stopped Navoni's pay without authorization, but acceded to his request for a successor, appointing William B. Hodgson as "Principal Dragoman." This young expert in Arabic and Turkish had been sent to Constantinople to assist Porter in getting the treaty ratified, and had been granted "the authority to negotiate the ratification," in the event the latter should be unable to fulfill that responsibility. In the fight with Navoni, Hodgson backed Porter all the way, probably in the hope of inheriting the appointment as dragoman and its salary of $2,500 a year. He advised the Department that Navoni had expected to be made chargé d'affaires, and burned with resentment and jealousy over Porter's selection: moreover, he had twice previously been discharged as dragoman, once by the British for "falsehood" and once by the Neapolitans for "petty theft." Hodgson also supported his chief by attesting that the stated valuation of the Turkish presents was correct.

Porter chose Hodgson to carry the ratified treaty back to the United States. The new dragoman reached America in mid-January 1832 and, by the following June, was back in Constantinople.[43] He should have stayed in the States, for he incurred the wrath of Porter within a few months of his return to his post. The word "fantastic" is none too strong to describe what happened to him.

Nepotism appears to have been the chief cause of the break between the Commodore and Hodgson. When John Brown and George A. Porter arrived on the scene, Hodgson was quick to recognize what it would mean to have such an excess of Porters infesting the U.S. Legation in Constantinople. On 1 December 1832, he wrote the Secretary that he thought Porter's "favor of his nephews" was unfair, since neither of the youngsters, one of whom was only nineteen, could be useful: they would never be able to learn Turkish, for the simple reason that they did not know Latin, and the Legation's only dictionary was Latin-Turkish. A week later he made his first, but certainly not his last, request for reassignment, declaring that Porter was confiding everything to his nephews and nothing to him.

In March 1833 the Department noted that Porter had made a "vague complaint against Mr. Hodgson," but before long the Commodore's "complaints" were satisfactorily explicit. According to Hodgson, he soon "reprimanded me with the violence of quarter deck authority," and although he was being temporarily retained as dragoman, he had been discharged as Porter's private secretary. In May, he was raked for "disregard of my orders . . . abuse of confidence," and attempting "to embroil this Legation with the Porte." [44]

The Commodore wrote the Secretary that besides the offenses listed above, Hodgson had seized, and even had the effrontery to use, the Legation's seal, and it was only with the greatest difficulty that he had recovered it. Hodgson argued that keeping the seal was the prerogative of the dragoman, and he had had no choice but to use it because Porter knew nothing about which papers required embossment, or about the trade formalities that had to be satisfied; furthermore, he lived so far out of town that American ships would lose a whole day if they had to await Porter's endorsement.

Hodgson counterattacked by charging his superior with criminal action connected with the death of the shipbuilder, Henry Eckford. When the latter died he had in his possession $50,000 worth of Turkish opium and, as executor of the estate, Porter found ships to export it, planning to be reimbursed by Eckford's heirs, once the drugs had been sold abroad. Since the Commodore never emerged from poverty, it is very doubtful that the transaction was ever completed, to say nothing of whether the grave charge was true in the first place. In the same connection Hodgson accused Porter of trying to pad Eckford's accounts so that he and corrupt Turkish officials could split $2,000 of the estate. When he once again asked for another post, "since I have never been so unhappy," [45] little did he know that in comparison with his immediate future, he was in a state of bliss.

In midsummer the enraged Porter notified the Department that he had fired the "vexing and embarrassing" Hodgson from his dragoman's position for trying to usurp his authority. The Commodore's thirst for revenge against the "vain and silly young man" was not slaked by dismissing him, for he even tried to have Hodgson arrested by the U.S. Navy. When he learned that the former dragoman had gone to the flagship *United States,* he asked Commodore Daniel T. Patterson to arrest him and keep him on board ship until Washington decided what punishment should be inflicted. Porter explained to the Secretary of State that "some restraint must be placed on a wild and eccentric mind . . . that knows no bounds to its folly, its vanity, its unwarrantable and silly ambition, and its propensity for mischief." Meanwhile, Patterson replied that since Hodgson was not subject to martial law he had no right to detain him.

In addition, Porter claimed that a horse given to him by the "Pacha of the Dardanelles" had been stolen by his erstwhile subordinate, and for months wrote letter after letter, one of them ten pages long, to the Department about that miserable animal. Almost a year later, he was still supplying the Department with details of the theft. Commodore Patterson also was informed about the horse and was told that Hodgson was "a contemptible poltroon, a pitiful swindler, and an unfit companion for gentlemen." Swearing that the Pasha had given the horse to him, not to Porter, Hodgson protested to Washington about Porter making him the object of "criminal accusations" and attempting to have him imprisoned by the Navy. He ended his tale of woe with the wonderful phrase, "whilst my bosom heaves with grief and indignation." [46]

Before long, the young and bewildered Hodgson had to contend not only with the unrestrained hatred of an aged and vindictive naval hero, backed by two nephews at the legation, but with physical violence at the hands of another Porter. David Dixon Porter was a midshipman in the *United States,* and although his main preoccupation was courting Captain Patterson's daughter, George Ann, he was, as always, able to find time to defend his father. One night in November Hodgson went to dinner on board the flagship, and returned to shore in a barge commanded by David Dixon. Hodgson claims that when they reached the shore, young Porter told him that what was coming was due to "the trouble you have given my father," then made a "violent and ungentlemanly outrage upon my person." He was knocked down by a blow on the side of the head, "kicked and abused," and suffered the extra humiliation and expense of having his new "$35 coat" destroyed. Hodgson could not challenge David Dixon to a duel, because he would be dismissed from the diplomatic corps for such action, and could only report the incident to the State Department in the hope that justice would be done.

The Commodore told the story differently. According to his version, his son, "in consequence to some offensive remarks of Mr. Hodgson respecting me, made in his presence, gave to Mr. Hodgson a rather severe chastisement with a horsewhip. . . ." David Dixon spent $35 on a new coat for his adversary, and the Commodore then considered the incident closed. Although David Dixon devotes many pages of his *Memoir* to his father's assignment in Turkey and mentions Hodgson, he is eloquently silent about his own disgraceful behavior.

Washington refused to get excited about the strange events taking place in its legation at Constantinople. Obviously, one cannot accuse President Jackson of hyperbole when he described the relationship between Porter and Hodgson as a "want of sympathy." Hodgson had been promised reassignment, but he did not get it until June 1834, when he was appointed "confidential agent to Egypt," and quite properly considered himself exonerated from Porter's gross accusations. Of course, the Commodore claimed the victory as his: he had removed an annoying obstacle, put his nephew George A. Porter in its place, and been assured by the Secretary of State that no one in the administration had censured him for his treatment of his former dragoman.[47]

Nevertheless, he continued his sniping. In 1834, he refused to allow Hodgson any back pay, on the grounds that he had done no work for the past two years. In this instance, he was defeated: the government compelled him to send Hodgson $1,274.16 out of his contingency fund for 1836. During 1834 there was a rumor that his adversary had been appointed Consul in Constantinople, and the Commodore admitted that it "occasioned me much surprise." However, he was enough on his good behavior to promise that if Hodgson stayed out of his way, he would return the favor, but the necessity never arose. He could not resist a couple of parting shots: in a letter to Patterson in 1835, he described Hodgson as "incorrigible" and "impertinent," and a year later, in a letter to Mahlon Dickerson, called him a "spy" and a "contemptible creature." The reader who has plowed through Porter's unedifying story of his relations with Hodgson comes to his statement "so much for Mr. Hodgson" with a sigh of relief.[*]

It must not be thought that while the Commodore represented his country at the Sublime Porte, his flair for controversy could be restricted to a single quarrel. While his melee with Hodgson was at its height, he happily plunged into three other feuds. One was with Charles Rhind, architect of the Turkish-American commercial treaty which Porter had eased through ratification. He accused Rhind of misconduct in that, while serving as a commissioner, he had perpetrated a "shameful deception . . . on the Porte" by inserting the secret provision into the treaty, and although the practice of accepting presents from officials of a host country was forbidden by the Constitution of the United States, he had accepted gifts from Turks. The Sultan's government was, he said, irate that Washington had not punished its machiavellian commissioner. He shrugged off Rhind's threat to sue, and told him that he would continue to view him "with contempt."

His second tussle was with William N. Churchill, U.S. Consul at Constantinople, who referred to Navoni, Hodgson, Rhind, some members of the Sultan's household, "and others" as his "fellow-sufferers" from the Commodore's vile disposition. In 1834, Porter admitted to the Department that the Consul had described him as having "a garrelous temper

---

[*] Hodgson remained in the diplomatic service. Among other assignments, he went to Morocco as special agent in 1835, and to Tunis as Consul in 1842.[48]

that nothing more or less than an angel can satisfy," and added that he took "some merit to himself for retaining my good graces for two years." The Commodore's single comment was that Churchill had been "unworthy of . . . [my] good graces" for even so short a period as two years. Some time during the next year, the Commodore relieved Churchill of his consulship and nominated John Brown, thus indicating that nepotism had been a contributing factor in Churchill's dismissal. When Brown turned down the position on the grounds that he could not live on its low salary, and temporarily returned to the United States, the other Porter nephew, George A. Porter, was, of course, nominated.

His third feud was with David Darmon, U.S. Consul at Jerusalem and Jaffa (then under Ottoman jurisdiction). Darmon, a Jew, had written what Porter considered a "scandalous letter," for which he was promptly sacked. In notifying the Department of his action and the reasons for it, Porter emphasized his consul's religion.* [49]

Porter's animosities extended beyond his family and his employees to collide with two officers of the U.S. Navy, namely, Captains James Biddle and Jesse D. Elliott, both antagonists of long standing. He had treated Biddle coldly ever since he had refused to take him along on the first cruise of the *Essex* in 1812, and his dislike was reinforced by Biddle's having served on the court-martial that condemned him in 1825. During 1831, when Biddle was Commodore of the Mediterranean Squadron, the two men had come together again, and Biddle made every effort to heal the breach. When Midshipman David Dixon Porter got into trouble with his commanding officer, Biddle went to his assistance, and when Porter requested transportation to his new post in Constantinople, he promptly furnished him with the brig *John Adams*. His efforts were to no avail; the implacable Porter continued to snub him openly.

If Porter disliked Biddle, he detested Jesse D. Elliott. Ever since Elliott's craven flight from the scene of the duel between Barron and Decatur in 1820, Porter had held him in total contempt, and when Elliott helped convict him for his landing in Puerto Rico, contempt turned to hatred. Under the circumstances, it was inevitable that there would be a clash when, in 1835, Elliott succeeded Biddle as Commodore of the Mediterranean Squadron. Porter fired the first gun by refusing to ask the Turkish government for an official pass that would allow Elliott to visit Constantinople. Nearly eighteen months later when Porter needed transportation in order to carry out a diplomatic errand, Elliott retaliated by

---

* Porter's anti-Semitism was marked. His book *Constantinople and Its Environs* is full of uncomplimentary remarks about the Sultan's Jewish subjects, and he sometimes went so far as to refer to Mexicans as "jews."

informing him that the Navy had none available. He could not, however, maintain his stand and eventually provided a schooner.

In the autumn of that same year, 1837, Porter complained to Washington that his enemy was actively interfering with his duties as chargé. Elliott's biographer says that sometime during the late 1830s relations deteriorated to the point where Porter issued a challenge to a duel, but mutual friends managed to keep the two apart until tempers cooled. Elliott was in the United States in 1838 and 1839, at the same time Porter was there, and he tried to speak to his old antagonist in a Baltimore hotel, but was cut dead. In April of 1839 Porter wrote to Samuel Hambleton that he was tired of Elliott's "cracking his jokes" about him. Although he says nothing about it, there is every reason to believe that Porter, apt recaller of old wrongs, was delighted when Elliott's turbulent behavior finally caught up with him in 1839. For censurable actions while he was commanding the Mediterranean Squadron, he was court-martialed, convicted, and sentenced to a four-year suspension, the first two without pay, a punishment much more severe than that to which Porter had been subjected. By the time Elliott was reinstated in 1843, his enemy was dead.[50]

Towards the end of his life, Porter had four nephews in Constantinople with him,* and it became extremely difficult for him to juggle salaries and positions in order to fulfill his ardent desire to care for all of them. It was because of his efforts to do so that he fell into the last of his imbroglios with the legation staff. His antagonist was one no better identified than as "J. Asker," the "second dragoman," but presumably he is the same person David Dixon Porter refers to as "Mr. Askeroglu, an Armenian," whose job it was "to interpret Mr. Hodgson's interpretations to the interpreter of the grand vizier!" It will be recalled that in 1835 nephew John Brown, having refused to accept the post of consul at Constantinople, returned to the United States. Unable to find suitable employment at home, he returned to Turkey a year later, and his uncle felt obliged to find a place for him. Asker was his obvious target. The Commodore had promised him the position as first dragoman, but he now reneged and gave the assignment to Brown. Understandably resentful, Asker protested to the Department, and the rupture between them became final when Porter learned what he had done.

Asker weathered that storm and continued to serve as second dragoman until another Porter relative became available for appointment. In

---

* Porter's brother-in-law, Dr. Samuel D. Heap, Sr., had three sons, G. Harris, Lawrence, and Samuel D., Jr. G. Harris and Samuel Jr. were involved in one way or another with the legation at Constantinople, along with the Commodore's other two nephews, John Brown and George A. Porter. As mentioned earlier, G. Harris Heap married Porter's elder daughter, Evalina, in 1842.

January 1839, the Commodore wrote the Department that he wanted his nephew, G. Harris Heap, an expert on oriental languages, to replace the second dragoman. Secretary Forsyth answered dourly that, while he would not forbid the substitution of Heap for Asker, some people might object since Heap "is a member of your family." Somehow, the tenacious Asker managed to withstand the threat from Harris Heap, but the following year Porter notified Washington that he had discharged him, and candidly admitted why: Asker's salary could be used to supplement George A. Porter's income.[51]

During 1841, nepotism brought Porter face-to-face with the novel situation of having to choose which of two nephews he would favor. The Department told him that John Brown was being replaced as first dragoman by Samuel D. Heap, Jr., another Porter nephew. Porter hesitated over how he should handle this unexpected development, but eventually sided with Brown and, having made that decision, went all the way to support him. He declared that Brown was indispensable and, when young Heap arrived with his commission, moved to protect Brown from financial embarrassment by bluntly notifying the Department that he would pay Brown's salary of $2,000 a year out of his contingency fund. He reported that Heap was useless as first dragoman since he knew no Turkish, while Brown was not only thoroughly professional in carrying out his duties, but was "a gentlemanly person." In this instance, Porter marked a victory. By the autumn of 1842, Samuel D. Heap either persuaded himself or was persuaded by the Commodore that he was *persona non grata* at the legation, and left Constantinople. A few weeks after the departure of his cousin, Brown thanked the Department for re-appointing him as "Principal Dragoman." He had found himself a real sinecure, staying on at the legation in Constantinople in one capacity or another until his death in 1872.[52]

As Porter's relationships with his family and with others deteriorated, so did his health, although he managed to avoid the bubonic plague which swept through the eastern Mediterranean in 1832 and again in 1834. When he discovered, during the first outbreak, that he had been in contact with someone who was infected at the time, his preventive measures were draconian. He went into complete seclusion for twenty-four hours and tried to seal off his house from the outside world: nothing was allowed in "without undergoing purification. Letters and papers are smoked; other articles when practicable, are passed through water."

When the plague struck again two years later, he put the same routine into operation, and added some other precautions. David Dixon, who was visiting him at the time, says:

> The Palace, as it was called, was fitted with a fumigating closet; carpets, curtains, and everything that could contain the germ of disease were removed, and nothing was left except wooden chairs and bed. A stranger entering the house—after being fumigated—would be given a seat on a wooden chair in the middle of the room. . . .[53]

Nevertheless, the Commodore suffered from a complex variety of other ailments. During the winter of 1833 he brooded, "I am from time to time very sick and good for nothing . . . I feel as if the whole world, and all that is in it, were indifferent to me. This climate will never suit me; I cannot live long here. I abandon myself to my fate . . . I am sometimes exceedingly wretched; perhaps no one in my situation could be more so." In the middle of that year, he was housebound for five months with what he called a "bilious inflammatory fever" that left him "totally inert." He attests that he was saved by the arrival of "Dr. H. [Samuel D. Heap, Sr.], my brother-in-law, my two sisters, and the rest of his family, together with my son Theodoric." Late in the year, he was reinfected with fever and his treatment was, to put it mildly, macabre: "In less than two hours, I was bled copiously three times; and besides in the course of the morning, leeched in both temples, in the abdomen, and cupped in the back of the neck. Besides mustard plasters all over, and prescriptions without number. Nothing less could have saved my life; but it has almost destroyed me."

A few months later, in a letter to Farragut, he described his ailments differently:

> For a year past, I have been . . . on the verge of the grave, and the whole time afflicted with loss of speech; and even now speak with difficulty and pain. At one time it was thought to be a paralisis of the tongue, but this was not, fortunately, the case; however it was bad enough, and perhaps nothing but my removal to this vilage where the air and water are pure and excelent, and living in the most persevering retirement and tranquility, have saved me. I find myself now recovering gradually but slowly, yet find myself very weak. . . .[54]

In 1835 he had his first heart attack, which he called "angina pectora," and five months later was still so stricken that his sister, Mrs. Mary Brown, had to write all his letters for him. He told his wife that he had "been gradually sinking for two years," but that he expected to improve when Dr. Heap visited him again in a few months. Heap arrived as anticipated, and the two took an extended trip through Italy and southern France, then went to Tunis where the Commodore decided that he had "greatly benefited by the journey, and doubtlessly shall return to Constantinople in the spring, much improved, both in body and in mind, which has been greatly injured by my sickness in Turkey. . . ."

He did feel better after the trip, and from 1836 to 1840 his only complaints were minor. He was ill when he arrived in the United States in 1838, but a visit to Virginia Springs "much benefited my health." On the way back to Turkey in 1839, he was laid low with "scurvey," and when he went ashore in Smyrna, he fell off a horse, and "somewhat disfigured my face." [55]

The year after his return to his post, he was again housebound by angina, and late in 1841 he told David Dixon that he had suffered "a very severe attack." A third onset, which struck him in 1842, caused "such inroads upon the Commodore's constitution, that," David Dixon records, "he became very feeble. . . ." Throughout the autumn of that year he was so incapacitated that the signatures on his letters to the Department were illegible.

With proper nineteenth century piety, David Dixon described his father's last days:

> The Commodore's life, during the last two years, had been much embittered by bodily and some mental suffering, and toward the last he endured the most excruciating agony, but he bore it with Christian fortitude. When he could no longer read it himself, he had the sacred book read to him by friends. . . . Suffering and emaciated as he was, his hold upon life was very strong. . . .

On 3 March 1843, after several days of anguish, David Porter died of "perdicarium & pleura," [56] which may be described as the failure of a heart weakened by pleurisy.

While Porter's body awaited transportation to the United States, it was enclosed "in spirits in a leaden coffin," further protected by two outside caskets, and temporarily interred in front of the flagpole by his house. His first funeral was held at San Stefano three days after his death, and was attended by the diplomatic corps, high officials of the Turkish bureaucracy, and his numerous relatives. Sultan Abdul Mejid expressed "sincere pain and regret," and a complimentary obituary in the Ottoman "Tablet of News" referred to Porter as "a great naval warrior. . . . He was a brave man, and his body was covered with wonds [wounds]. He never knew fear." [57]

In America, Secretary of the Navy Abel P. Upshur announced that he still considered Porter an officer in the U.S. Navy because of his "devoted patriotism, his consummate skill, and his indomitable courage. . . . The President [John Tyler] therefore directs that the flags be hoisted at half-mast . . . ," that "thirteen minute guns be fired at navy yards and on ships at noon of the day after receiving this order . . . and that the officers of the navy and marine corps wear crape on the left arm for the space of thirty days."

The brig of war *Truxtun* was sent to carry Porter's remains back to the United States. She arrived in Constantinople in October 1843 and, after disinterment ceremonies that resembled those of his burial, the body was embarked and reached home that December. The Commodore's second funeral, which was held in Philadelphia in January 1844, amounted to an impressive commemoration of his naval career. He was buried on the grounds of the Naval Asylum in that city, but, later, when the directors of Woodlands Cemetery generously offered to bestow a plot and erect a monument to him as a public honor, he was once more moved. The shaft of his monument carries on its east side the single word "PORTER," but the following inscriptions are on the north, west, and south sides, respectively:

Commodore David Porter
One of the Most Heroic Sons of
Pennsylvania
Having long represented his Country
with Fidelity
As Minister Resident at
Constantinople
Died at that City
In the Patriotic Discharge of his Duty,
March 3rd, 1843.

His Early Youth
Was Conspicuous for Skill and
Gallantry
In the Naval Service of
The United States
When the American Arms
Were exercised with Romantic
Chivalry
Before the Battlements of
Tripoli
He was on all occasions
Among the Bravest of the Brave
Zealous in the Performance of
Every Duty
Ardent and Resolute
In the Trying Hour of Calamity
Composed and Steady
In the Blaze of
Victory.

In the War of
1812
His Merits were Exhibited
Not merely as an
Intrepid Commander
But in Exploring New Fields of

Success and Glory
A Career of Brilliant Good Fortune
Was Crowned by an
Engagement
Against Superior Force and
Fearful Advantages
Which History Records
As an Event
Among the Most Remarkable
in
Naval Warfare.

A different sort of a memorial for Porter was held on 27 June 1844 at the Walnut Street Theater in Philadelphia. An eyewitness reported that following a play starring Junius Booth, "an emblematic tableaux to the memory of the gallant Porter" was erected on the stage, "after which was performed 'The Nautical Drama of American Valor! or Yankee Tars on hand!' " [58]

His death cleared up his financial muddle not at all. From the legation in Constantinople, Samuel D. Heap, Jr. wrote Evalina Porter that her husband had left four or five separate wills, and since he was in doubt as to which superseded which, he refused to act as executor: he added the bleak news that the Commodore's debt "still shows a balance due the gov't of near $7,000." A will that Porter had signed on 12 October 1842 proved to be valid, and, according to its terms, he left everything to his wife for the duration of her unmarried natural life: should she remarry, the children were to share equally two-thirds of the estate, and all of it after her death. There were two codicils: the one that cut off William D. Porter with "one Spanish dollar," and another that bequeathed to "my beloved son David D. Porter . . . the whole amount of whatever may be recovered from my claims on Spain and Mexico in the event that the papers appertaining to them, which are now lost, might be forthcoming. . . ."

David Dixon Porter had to even off the ragged ends of his father's life. First, he had to establish himself as head of the family, and the effort to do so involved him in a clash with his elder brother William. In order to reinforce his own claim to that status, William shortened his name from "William David Porter" to "David Porter." All that this accomplished was to confuse the post office so completely that much of his personal mail was delivered to David Dixon, who was delighted: "Some how his plans all come to our knowledge. . . . It would astonish him to know how much of his correspondence I have on file!" Although there is nothing in the records on the subject, it may have been the misdelivered mail that enabled David Dixon to threaten exposure of the many skeletons in

William's closet. In any case, David Dixon ended forever the threat that his elder brother would direct the affairs of the family.

The government did much to assist David Dixon in the settlement of his father's debts, especially those owed to the Navy Department. In June 1844, Evalina Porter was notified that Congress had appropriated $6,000 "for the outfit of your deceased husband at Constantinople." David Dixon later wrote that $4,750 of that sum was supposed to go to Evalina, and $1,250 to reduce the government debt. He boasted that he "finally succeeded (in a way that no one else could have done) in getting the whole six thousand allowed; and the 1250 claims of the Navy Department set aside. . . ." [59]

He also attempted to realize something on his father's claims against Spain and Mexico. His and his mother's hopes soared in 1845 when the United States annexed Texas but, as Evalina had been warned might happen, this heralded the onset of the Mexican War, and actually worked against her interests. David Dixon optimistically estimated that his father's services to the Mexican Republic were worth $100,000 and calculated that the debt owed by the Spanish *Consulado* of Havana amounted to "about $160,000" in principal and interest. In the early 1850s he asked James Gadsden, the American Minister to Mexico, to discuss his claims with "President Santa Ana," but Santa Anna went permanently out of power, Gadsden could not or would not do anything, and the project collapsed.

Simultaneously, David Dixon was busy trying to realize some return on his last hope—his father's land grant in Tehuantepec. He hired A. H. Palmer as his agent to press the claim, and at the end of 1853 Palmer wrote that he anticipated success since Santa Anna was "personally cognizant" that the claim was valid. Six years later, Palmer was forced to report that he had made no progress whatever. Within a few months even more lugubrious news was dispatched by Palmer: the tract of land in Tehuantepec had, over the years, been awarded to five or six others. None of the claims, including Porter's, had, it seemed, any validity.

Two decades later, David Dixon was still trying to get title to the land in Tehuantepec, thereby proving that whatever else might have been lacking in his character, dogged determination was not. In 1879, thirty-six years after his father's death, when the Secretary of State reported that a search through the Tehuantepec archives, ordered by the American Minister to Mexico, had unearthed no scrap of evidence that backed the original Porter claim, David Dixon finally gave up his pursuit. [60] The inability of his son to realize anything from Spain or Mexico wrote finis to the father's lifelong quest for a fortune to leave to his heirs.

Even though David Porter's career was, according to his own standards, a failure, it had considerable impact upon his times. He altered global economics by temporarily annihilating British whaling in the Pacific, thereby helping to give his own country almost a monopoly of that essential industry for the next half-century. His impact on American foreign policy was more than peripheral. He was the first American imperialist: although his annexation of Nukahiva was not accepted, he was the first to incorporate distant, settled lands into the United States. He toiled, if prematurely and abortively, to use the Navy to open Japan to Western influence, and his work was remembered in the planning of Perry's famous expedition.

Porter was most influential in the relations between the United States and Latin America. It is at least possible that his early opposition to General James Wilkinson's nebulous plans to invade Mexico in 1808 averted Spanish-American hostilities. As a leading member of the cabal backing the Carreras in Chile during 1817 and 1818, he helped to confuse the question of U.S. recognition of Latin-American independence at a time when such a policy also might have led to war with Spain. His command of the Mexican Navy from 1826 to 1827 was disastrous to him, but perhaps it spoiled what slight chance Spain still had of recovering Latin America. Conversely, his spur-of-the-moment invasion of Puerto Rico could have had the most dire consequences, for it occurred only eleven months after the President had pledged that, so long as the European powers refrained from territorial expansion in the Western Hemisphere, the United States would not interfere in their internal or external affairs, namely in their existing Americal colonies. It is difficult to imagine a much more direct violation of that pledge than Porter's unauthorized landing at Fajardo, and the United States was lucky to escape unscathed from that potential catastrophe.

To Porter his life was disappointing. He never earned the unsullied personal fame and the great riches for which he strove, and most of his closest personal associations ended dolefully. As with most men, both his victories and his defeats emanated from easily identifiable personal characteristics. His successes resulted from his courage, energy, patriotism, and farsightedness; his failures from his choler, impulsiveness, conceit, self-pity, and vindictiveness. David Porter was far from being an admirable or even a likable man, but his eventful life altered to some degree the world in which he lived and, in so doing, history as well.

ABBREVIATIONS

AHR	*American Historical Review*
DAB	*Dictionary of American Biography*
DDP	David Dixon Porter (papers only)
DFT	Despatches from Turkey (USSD)
DIT	Diplomatic Instructions to Turkey (USSD)
DNB	*Dictionary of National Biography*
DP	David Porter
DPCI	Minutes of the proceedings of a Court of Inquiry directed to investigate the conduct of David Porter (RCGM), (USND)
DPCM	Court-Martial of David Porter (RCGM), (USND)
HAHR	*Hispanic American Historical Review*
HSP	Historical Society of Pennsylvania
LC	Library of Congress
LRC	Letters Received by Secretary of the Navy from Captains (USND)
LRMC	Letters Received by Secretary of the Navy from Masters Commandant (USND)
LS	Letters Sent to Officers by Secretary of the Navy (USND)
MHS	Massachusetts Historical Society
MVHR	*Mississippi Valley Historical Review*
NA	National Archives
NJHS	New Jersey Historical Society
NYHS	New York Historical Society
PRO	Public Record Office (London)
QR	*Quarterly Review* (London)
RGCM	Records of General Courts-Martial and Courts of Inquiry of the Navy Department, 1799–1867 (USND)
USNAM	United States Naval Academy Museum
USND	United States Navy Department
USSD	United States State Department
VNC	Van Ness Collection, David Porter Papers, Owings Mills, Maryland

I

Chapter I narrates details of David Porter's life from his birth in 1780 through 1807. Material is sparse about his family background and early years, and neither David Dixon Porter's eulogy of his father, *Memoir of Commodore David Porter of the United States Navy*, nor Archibald D. Turnbull's *Commodore David Porter, 1780–1843* throws much light on them. Facts presented have come from contemporary newspapers and magazines, naval histories by Allan Westcott et al. and Edgar S. Maclay, and biographies of John Barry.

Porter's early service in the American Navy, from 1799–1802, is better documented. Basic sources are the United States Navy Department (USND), *Naval Documents Related to the Quasi-war between the United States and France* (*France*), 7 volumes, and letters in Container 16 of the David Porter Papers, Library of Congress (DP Papers, LC). Useful secondary works are Gardner W. Allen, *Our Naval War with France,* and Fletcher Pratt, *Preble's Boys: Commodore Preble and the Birth of American Sea Power.*

From 1802–1805, during the war with Tripoli, Porter served in the Mediterranean and spent much of that time as the Bashaw's prisoner. Two official sources are primary here: USND, *Naval Documents Related to the United States Wars with the Barbary Powers* (*Barbary*), 6 volumes; and the microfilmed USND, Letters Sent by Secretary of the Navy to Officers, 1798–1868 (LS). Frequently cited is Glenn Tucker's excellent *Dawn Like Thunder: The Barbary Wars and the Birth of the U.S. Navy.* Additional details are supplied by R. C. Anderson, E. S. Maclay, Fletcher Pratt, and Hamilton Cochran; two works on Tripoli—one by Charles W. Furlong, the other by Henry S. Villard; and biographies of Stephen Decatur and John Rodgers by Charles L. Lewis and Charles O. Paullin, respectively.

In September 1965 I went to Tripoli to look over the terrain and pick up any extra information about Porter and the *Philadelphia* that might be available. An interview with the Kingdom of Libya's Director of Antiquities in the Castle where Porter was imprisoned, as well as a perusal of the scanty materials in the library there, added little to what I already knew.

Information on Porter's Mediterranean service from 1805–1807 comes from the above-cited naval sources on the Barbary Wars (USND, LS), and USND, Letters Received by the Secretary of the Navy from Masters Commandant (LRMC). Container 16 of the DP Papers, LC, casts light on Porter's imbroglio with the British at Malta. Contemporary and later magazines and newspaper articles amplify the official documents in showing Porter's role in the commissioning and delivery of the Tripoli Monument now at Annapolis.

1. A. D. Turnbull, *Commodore David Porter, 1780–1843*, p. 8; *New England Historical and Genealogical Register,* 30 (1876), pp. 460–461; W. B. Clark, *Gallant John Barry, 1745–1803,* p. 161; Allan Westcott et al., *American Sea Power Since 1775,* p. 9; E. S. Maclay, *History of the Navy from 1775 to 1893,* 1, p. 139; David Dixon Porter (DDP), *Memoir of Commodore David Porter*

of the United States Navy, pp. 8–9; E. S. Maclay, *A History of American Privateers,* p. 90.

2. DDP to John S. Barnes, 18 February 1874, DDP Papers, NYHS; W. B. Clark, *op. cit.,* p. 362; Joseph Gurn, *Commodore John Barry . . . ,* p. 252; W. B. Clark, *op. cit.,* p. 408; Albert Gallatin to David Porter, the younger (DP), 30 March 1809, Albert Gallatin Papers.

3. *New England Historical and Genealogical Register,* 30 (1876), pp. 460–461; *ibid.,* 33 (1879), p. 49; *Boston Marriages, 1752–1809,* p. 443; DDP, *Memoir,* pp. 9, 10; *Analectic Magazine,* 5 (September 1814), p. 22.

4. *Federal Gazette* (Baltimore), 12, 21 March 1796; DDP, *Memoir,* p. 11; *Federal Gazette,* 19 March, 9 June 1796; DDP, *Memoir,* pp. 12–13.

5. David Porter the elder to John Barry, 18 April 1798, USND, *Documents Related to the Quasi-war between the United States and France* (USND, *France*), 1, pp. 55–56; *Columbian Centinel* (Boston), 23 March 1799; Fletcher Pratt, *Preble's Boys . . . ,* p. 201; DDP, *Memoir,* pp. 19–20; Fletcher Pratt, *op. cit.,* p. 202; G. W. Allen, *Our Naval War with France,* p. 135; DP, *Constantinople and Its Environs . . . ,* 2, pp. 10–11.

6. Thomas Truxtun, 14 February 1799, *Journal,* in USND, *France,* 2, p. 329; Thomas Truxtun to SecNav, 14 February 1799, *ibid.;* DDP, *Memoir,* p. 21; Justin Winsor, *Narrative and Critical History of America,* 3, p. 367; Thomas Truxtun, 14 February 1799, *Journal,* in USND, *France,* 2, p. 329.

7. Reprinted in Thomas Truxtun, 14 February 1799, *Journal,* in USND, *France,* 2, pp. 327–328; Thomas Truxtun to SecNav, 14 February 1799, *ibid.,* p. 329; John Rodgers to SecNav, n.d., in *The New Hampshire Gazette* (Portsmouth), 27 March 1799; *Federal Gazette,* 12 April 1799.

8. SecNav to Samuel Barron, 23 September 1799, USND, *France,* 4, pp. 217–218; SecNav to DP, 8 October 1799, *ibid.,* p. 266; Fletcher Pratt, *op. cit.,* p. 205.

9. G. W. Allen, *op. cit.,* p. 147; "U.S. Consul General, St. Domingo," to Silas Talbot, 2 January 1800, USSD, *France,* 5, p. 3; DP, Letter Copy Book, 1838–1839, *passim,* Container 16, DP Papers, LC; William Maley, 1 January 1800, *Journal of Experiment,* USND, *France,* 5, p. 4; William Maley to SecNav, 27 August 1800, *ibid.,* 6, p. 295; "Officers of the U.S. Navy . . . ," *ibid.,* 7, p. 338.

10. Fletcher Pratt, *op. cit.,* p. 208, n. 4; Silas Talbot to DP, 3 March 1800, USND, *France,* 6, pp. 263–264; A. D. Turnbull, *Commodore David Porter, 1780–1843,* pp. 33–34; "Prize Agent of the Experiment," to Silas Talbot, 21 August 1800, USND, *France,* 6, p. 274.

11. SecNav to Charles Stewart, 16 July 1800, USND, *France,* 6, p. 156; Governor of Puerto Rico to President Thomas Jefferson, 19 January 1801, *ibid.,* pp. 100–101; Footnote to list of captured French armed vessels, 1798–1801, *ibid.,* p. 312; E. S. Maclay, *History of the Navy from 1775–1893,* 1, p. 207.

12. DP to Samuel Hambleton, 12 February 1812, in DDP, *Memoir,* p. 100; Acting SecNav to Andrew Sterrett, 10 April 1801, USND, *Naval Documents Related to the United States Wars with the Barbary Powers* (USND,

Barbary) , 1, p. 429; Glenn Tucker, *Dawn Like Thunder: The Barbary Wars and the Birth of the U.S. Navy*, p. 142.

13. E. S. Maclay, *op. cit.*, 1, p. 228; Glenn Tucker, *op. cit.*, p. 62; E. S. Maclay, *op. cit.*, 1, pp. 217–218; R. C. Anderson, *Naval Wars in the Levant, 1559–1853*, p. 396; Glenn Tucker, *op. cit.*, p. 22.

14. Glenn Tucker, *op. cit.*, pp. 135–136, 121–122, 138–141; Andrew Sterrett to Richard Dale, 6 August 1801, USND, *Barbary*, 1, p. 537; Glenn Tucker, *op. cit.*, p. 143; Richard Dale to Danish Consul, Tripoli, 8 August 1801, USND, *Barbary*, 1, pp. 537–538; in Glenn Tucker, *op. cit.*, p. 144; E. S. Maclay, *op. cit.*, 1, p. 232; SecNav to Andrew Sterrett, 17 November 1801, USND, Letters Sent by Secretary of the Navy to Officers, 1798–1868 (LS) .

15. SecNav to DP, 18 February 1802, USND, LS; SecNav to "Commanding Officer of the Chesapeake," 27 March 1802, USND, *Barbary*, 2, p. 96; SecNav to DP, 30 March 1802, USND, LS; John D. Kilbourne, Librarian of the Maryland Historical Society, letter to author, 27 January 1965; DDP, *Memoir*, pp. 28–29.

16. U.S. Consul, Gibraltar, to SecState, 31 May 1802, USND, *Barbary*, 2, pp. 162–163; Glenn Tucker, *op. cit.*, pp. 153–154, 160; Alexander Murray to Jacob Jones, 16 October 1802, USND, *Barbary*, 2, p. 299; Henry Wadsworth, 11 February 1803, *Journal, ibid.*, p. 362; Hamilton Cochran, *Noted American Duels. . . .*, pp. 39–40; Henry Wadsworth, 6 April 1803, *Journal*, USND, *Barbary*, 2, p. 388; G. W. Allen, *Our Navy and the Barbary Corsairs*, p. 125.

17. Henry Wadsworth, 2 June 1803, *Journal*, in USND, *Barbary*, 2, p. 436; E. S. Maclay, *op. cit.*, 1, p. 239; Court of Inquiry on Richard V. Morris, in Charles Goldsborough, *The United States Naval Chronicle*, in USND, *Barbary*, 2, pp. 529–531.

18. List of Commission and Warrant Officers, USND, *Barbary*, 3, p. 15; Fletcher Pratt, *Preble's Boys . . .* , p. 212; William Bainbridge to U.S. Consul, Tangier, 29 August 1803, USND, *Barbary*, 3, p. 2; Glenn Tucker, *op. cit.*, pp. 198, 204–208.

19. E. S. Maclay, *op. cit.*, 1, p. 246; Court Inquiring into the Loss of U.S. Frigate Philadelphia, USND, *Barbary*, 3, p. 290; William Bainbridge to SecNav, 1 November 1803, *ibid.*, p. 172; DP to Henry Wadsworth, 5 March 1804, *ibid.*, p. 475; Court Inquiring into the Loss of U.S. Frigate Philadelphia, *ibid.*, p. 194; Edward Preble to SecNav, 10 December 1803, *ibid.*, p. 256.

20. William Knight to Thomas L. Bristol, 1 November 1803, USND, *Barbary*, 3, p. 180; Henry Allen to William Allen, 14 November 1804, *ibid.*, p. 141; Glenn Tucker, *op. cit.*, pp. 217–218; William Knight to Thomas L. Bristol, 1 November 1803, USND, *Barbary*, 3, p. 180.

21. William Bainbridge to Edward Preble, 5 December 1803, USND, *Barbary*, 3, p. 253; *ibid.*, 6, p. 415; William Bainbridge to Susan Bainbridge, 1 November 1803, *ibid.*, 3, p. 178.

22. Washington Irving, *Works*, 3, p. 96; Isaac Bailey, *American Naval Biography*, p. 182; E. S. Maclay, *op. cit.*, 1, p. 251; Glenn Tucker, *op. cit.*, p. 246; DP to Henry Wadsworth, 5 March 1804, USND, *Barbary*, 3, pp. 475–476;

U.S. Chargé d'Affaires, Tunis, to William Bainbridge, 16 July 1804, *ibid.*, 4, p. 272.

23. William Bainbridge to Edward Preble, 5 December 1803, USND, *Barbary*, 3, p. 253; Glenn Tucker, *op. cit.*, p. 261; Robert T. Spence to Mrs. Keith Spence, 12 November 1804, USND, *Barbary*, 4, p. 352; C. W. Furlong, *The Gateway to the Sahara: Observations and Experiences in Tripoli*, pp. 114–119; H. S. Villard, *Libya: the New Arab Kingdom of North Africa*, p. 136.

24. E. S. Maclay, *op. cit.*, 1, p. 269; Nicholas C. Nissen to "His Danish Majesty," 29 February 1804, USND, *Barbary*, 3, p. 421; DDP, *Memoir*, pp. 62, 64–65; Fletcher Pratt, *op. cit.*, p. 213; E. S. Maclay, *op. cit.*, 1, pp. 296–297; William Bainbridge to U.S. Chargé d'Affaires, Tunis, 19 December 1804, USND, *Barbary*, 5, p. 201; Glenn Tucker, *op. cit.*, pp. 288, 314.

25. Report of Surgeon Lewis Heerman, 3 August 1804, USND, *Barbary*, 4, p. 348; C. L. Lewis, "Reuben James or Daniel Frazier?" *Maryland Historical Magazine*, 19, No. 1 (April 1924), pp. 30–36; Edward Preble, 4 August 1804, *Journal*, USND, *Barbary*, 4, p. 338.

26. Glenn Tucker, *op. cit.*, p. 316; Hamilton Cochran, *Noted American Duels . . .* , pp. 37–38; Robert T. Spence to Mrs. Keith Spence, 12 November 1804, USND, *Barbary*, 4, p. 352; John Darby, 3 September 1804, *Journal, ibid.*, p. 506; Charles Morris, Jr., "Late in Septr." (1804), Abstract of Journal, *ibid.*, p. 513; Charles G. Ridgely, "Description," in *Naval Magazine*, 1, pp. 172–175, in *ibid.*, p. 509; Robert T. Spence to Mrs. Keith Spence, 12 November 1804, *ibid.*, p. 353; Glenn Tucker, *op. cit.*, pp. 327–332, 342.

27. Glenn Tucker, *op. cit.*, pp. 371–392, 411; Treaty of Peace and Amity between the United States and Tripoli, USND, *Barbary*, 6, p. 81.

28. Hezekiah Loomis, 4 June 1805, *Journal*, USND, *Barbary*, 6, p. 86; U.S. Consul General, Algiers, to John Rodgers, 4 June 1805, *ibid.*, p. 82; William Bainbridge to SecNav, 10 September 1805, *ibid.*, p. 276; John Rodgers to Thomas Robinson, Jr., 20 August 1805, *ibid.*, p. 238.

29. U.S. Consul, Marseille to President Thomas Jefferson, 5 November 1806, Thomas Jefferson Papers, MHS; C. O. Paullin, *Commodore John Rodgers . . .* , p. 62; DP to John Rodgers, 24 January, 3 February 1806, USND, *Barbary*, 6, pp. 353, 361; SecNav to DP, 28 April 1806, *ibid.*, p. 423; DP to SecNav, 5 August 1806, USND, Letters Received by Secretary of the Navy from Masters Commandant (LRMC).

30. DP to Thomas Truxtun, 12 September 1807, DP, Letter Book, 1807–1808, Container 16, DP Papers, LC; Thomas Truxtun to DP, 23 September 1807, *ibid.*, DP to SecNav, 29 October 1807, *ibid.; The Times* (London), 5 July 1814; Fletcher Pratt, *op. cit.*, pp. 214–215.

31. DP to SecNav, 19 August 1806, USND, LRMC; Hugh Campbell to John H. Dent, 22 August 1806, USND, *Barbary*, 6, p. 477; Glenn Tucker, *op. cit.*, p. 430.

32. DP to SecNav, 21 April 1806, USND, LRMC; DP to Congress, 24 November 1807, USND, *Barbary*, 6, p. 530; Tripoli Monument Inscription, Annapolis;

Analectic Magazine, 6 (December 1815), p. 461; Andrew Tully, *When They Burned the White House,* p. 183.

II

Porter's life between 1807 and 1810 divides into six hectic months in 1807–1808 prior to his departure to command the Naval Station at New Orleans, and his unhappy two years in that office. His friendship with Washington Irving is described by Pierre Irving, George S. Hellman, and Stanley T. Williams. Events leading up to the court-martial of James Barron for the loss of the *Chesapeake* and Porter's part in that trial are narrated in Edwin M. Gaines's unpublished doctoral dissertation, *Outrageous Encounter! The Chesapeake-Leopard Affair of 1807* (University of Virginia, 1960); USND, *Proceedings of the General Court Martial . . . of Commodore James Barron;* Charles L. Lewis, *The Romantic Decatur,* and C. S. Forester's article in *American Heritage* on the Barron-Decatur duel. Details of Porter's personal life, including his marriage and his association with young David Glasgow Farragut, come from his son's *Memoir,* C. L. Lewis' life of Farragut, and Richard S. West, Jr.'s life of David Dixon Porter.

Basic sources on Porter's two years in New Orleans are USND's microfilmed Letters Received by Secretary of the Navy from Masters Commandant (LRMC); Letters Sent by Secretary of the Navy to Officers (LS); and David Porter's letters to his best friend, Samuel Hambleton, in the David Porter Papers, Container 15 and Volumes 1 and 2, Library of Congress. During his command in Louisiana, Porter had an indirect association with Dr. Benjamin Rush, and for information here L. H. Butterfield, *Letters of Benjamin Rush,* 2 volumes, was used. Porter's confrontation with General James Wilkinson was direct, and many details are taken from works by Isaac J. Cox, Royal O. Shreve, Thomas P. Abernethy, Irving Brant, as well as from the General's own three-volume masterpiece of evasion, *Memoirs of My Own Times.* Porter's troubles with William C. C. Claiborne, Orleans Territorial Governor, are narrated in the Governor's *Letter Book, 1801–1810,* and the State Department's *Territorial Papers, Orleans Territory.*

1. G. S. Hellman, *Washington Irving, Esquire . . . ,* p. 82; S. T. Williams, *The Life of Washington Irving,* 1, p. 76; DP to Samuel Hambleton, 26 July 1814, DP Papers, 2, LC; *Analectic Magazine,* 4 (September 1814), pp. 225–243; Pierre Irving, *The Life and Letters of Washington Irving,* 1, p. 306.
2. E. M. Gaines, *Outrageous Encounter! The Chesapeake-Leopard Affair of 1807, passim;* John Stricker to John Rodgers, 31 January 1807, USND, *Barbary,* 6, p. 512; C. L. Lewis, *The Romantic Decatur,* p. 93; USND, *Proceedings of the General Court Martial . . . of Commodore James Barron, passim;* C. S. Forester, "Bloodshed at Dawn," *American Heritage,* 15 (October 1964), p. 43; USND, *Proceedings of the General Court Martial . . . of Commodore James Barron, passim.*

3. DDP, *Memoir*, p. 71; J. H. Martin, *Chester . . . Pennsylvania*, p. 455; Portrait of Evalina Anderson Porter, in R. S. West, Jr., *The Second Admiral: A Life of David Dixon Porter, 1813–1891*, opp. p. 9; C. J. Ingersoll, *History of the Second War . . .* , p. 12; DDP, *Memoir*, p. 72.

4. SecNav to DP, 1 March 1808, USND, Letters Sent by Secretary of the Navy to Officers (LS); DP, Circular to his officers, n.d. (probably mid-March 1808), USND, Letters Received by Secretary of the Navy from Masters Commandant (LRMC), DP to SecNav, 12 May, 25 June 1808, *ibid.*, SecNav to DP, 27 April, 4 June 1808, USND, LS.

5. C. L. Lewis, *David Glasgow Farragut: Admiral in the Making*, pp. 311 (n. 4), 5–7; *La Gazette* (New Orleans), 24 June 1808, in *ibid.*, p. 311 (n. 7); DDP, *Memoir*, p. 78; DP to SecNav, June–December 1808, *passim*, 13 September 1808, USND, LRMC; C. L. Lewis, *op. cit.*, pp. 18–19.

6. C. L. Lewis, *op. cit.*, p. 313 (n. 20); Benjamin Hodgdon to SecNav, 21 August 1800, USND, *France*, 6, p. 274; Joaquin Garcia to Thomas Jefferson, 19 January 1801, *ibid.*, 7, pp. 100–101; C. L. Lewis, *op. cit.*, p. 313 (n. 20).

7. *New England Historical and Genealogical Register*, 17 (1863), p. 20; DDP, *Memoir*, p. 99.

8. SecNav to DP, 10 June 1808, USND, LS; DP to SecNav, 9 July 1808, USND, LRMC; SecNav to DP, 5 July, 13 August 1808, USND, LS; DP to SecNav, 14 August, 7 September 1808, USND, LRMC; DDP, *Memoir*, p. 82; DP to Samuel Hambleton, 19 December 1808, DP Papers, 1, LC.

9. DP to SecNav, 7 August, 14, 18 November 1808, USND, LRMC; SecNav to DP, 7 October 1808, USND, LS.

10. DP to SecNav, 26 June, 24 August, 19 September, 30 November, 17 December, 24 August 1808, 15, 18 February 1809, USND, LRMC.

11. DP to SecNav, 19 February, 16 March, 1 April 1809, USND, LRMC; SecNav to DP, 24 April, 23 May 1809, USND, LS.

12. (Cobbett's) *Rush-Light*, No. 11; *Commercial Advertiser* (New York), 3 March 1800, in L. H. Butterfield, *Letters of Benjamin Rush*, 2, p. 818, Appendix 3 (n. 5), pp. 1213–1218; Benjamin Rush to John Adams, 15 December 1807, *ibid.*, p. 959; DP to SecNav, 7 March 1809, USND, LRMC; Benjamin Rush to John Adams, 26 April 1810, in L. H. Butterfield, *op. cit.*, pp. 1041–1042.

13. I. J. Cox, "James Wilkinson," DAB, 20, pp. 222–224; Irving Brant, *James Madison: Secretary of State, 1800–1809*, p. 203; I. J. Cox, "General Wilkinson and his Later Intrigues with the Spaniards," AHR, 19 (July 1914), pp. 799, 800.

14. I. J. Cox, "James Wilkinson," DAB, 20, p. 225; Irving Brant, *op. cit.*, p. 346; T. P. Abernethy, *The Burr Conspiracy*, p. 274.

15. R. O. Shreve, *The Finished Scoundrel: General James Wilkinson . . .* , pp. 248–249; DP to James Wilkinson, 25 April 1809, USND, LRMC; James Wilkinson to DP, 25 April 1809, Container 15, DP Papers, LC; DP, Notes, n.d., *ibid.*; Samuel Hambleton to DP, 23 April 1809, *ibid.*; DP, Notes, n.d., *ibid.*

16. DP, Notes, n.d., Container 15, DP Papers, LC; DP to SecState, 4 May 1809,

ibid.; SecNav to DP, 14 August 1809 (misdated 1807), USND, LS; DP, Notes, n.d., Container 15, DP Papers, LC.

17. R. O. Shreve, *op. cit.,* pp. 250–252; DP to SecNav, 19 August 1809, USND, LRMC; James Wilkinson, *Memoirs of My Own Times,* 2, Appendix, no. p. number; I. J. Cox, "General Wilkinson and his Later Intrigues with the Spaniards," AHR, 19 (July 1914), p. 812; I. J. Cox, "James Wilkinson," DAB, 20, p. 225; DP to Samuel Hambleton, 12 October 1811, DP Papers, 2, LC.

18. DP to SecNav, 28 June, 6 September 1809, USND, LRMC; DDP, "Ancestry of David Porter," in *New England Historical and Genealogical Register,* 30 (1876), p. 461; DDP, *Memoir,* p. 84; DP to Samuel Hambleton, 1 June 1809, DP Papers, 1, LC; DP to SecNav, 15 October 1809, 4 February 1810, 16 August 1809, 1 March, 7 April 1810, USND, LRMC.

19. DP to SecNav, 1, 14 June, 4 February, 7 April 1810, USND, LRMC; DDP, *Memoir,* p. 79; DP to SecNav, 7 April 1810, USND, LRMC.

20. DP to SecNav, 5, 7 May 1810, USND, LRMC; DP to Samuel Hambleton, 12 October 1811, DP Papers, 2, LC; W. C. C. Claiborne to SecState, 30 March 1810, W. C. C. Claiborne, *Letter Books,* 1801–1810, 5, pp. 24–29.

21. DP to SecNav, 12 May 1810, USND, LRMC; DP to SecState, 21 September 1810, DP Papers, NYHS; DP to SecNav, 1 June 1810, USND, LRMC; SecNav to DP, 29 March, 11 June 1810, USND, LS; SecNav to DP, 11 July 1810, USND, LS; Thomas B. Robertson to SecState, 8 April 1810, USSD, *Territorial Papers,* 9, *Orleans Territory,* p. 881.

22. SecTreas to DP, 3 October 1810, DP Papers, 2, LC; DP to SecNav, 29 December 1810, USND, LRMC; DP to Samuel Hambleton, 30 October 1810, 24 June 1812, DP Papers, 2, LC; *New Hampshire Patriot* (Concord), 26 July 1814; DDP, *Memoir,* pp. 81, 82.

23. DP to Samuel Hambleton, 1 July 1810, 19 March 1811, DP Papers, 1, LC; DP to SecNav, 19 June 1811, USND, LRMC; DP to Samuel Hambleton, 27 September 1810, DP Papers, 2, LC; SecNav to DP, 13 December 1809, USND, LS; DP to Samuel Hambleton, 18 July 1810 (misdated 1809), 24 August 1810, DP Papers, 1, LC.

24. DP to Samuel Hambleton, 18 July 1810 (misdated 1809), DP Papers, 1, LC; Isaac Bailey, *American Naval Biography,* p. 184; DDP, *Memoir,* p. 85; C. L. Lewis, *David Glasgow Farragut. . . . ,* p. 22; DP to Samuel Hambleton, 1 July 1810, DP Papers, 1, LC; C. L. Lewis, *op. cit.,* p. 314 (n. 1); DP to Samuel Hambleton, 3 August 1810, DP Papers, 1, LC.

III

This chapter recounts Porter's activities between his return from New Orleans in 1810 and the conclusion of his first wartime cruise in 1812. Prime sources for his professional duties are USND, Letters from Secretary of the Navy to Officers (LS). USND, Letters Received by Secretary of the Navy from

Masters Commandant (LRMC); and USND, Letters Received by Secretary of the Navy from Captains (LRC). Details and opinions are buttressed by wide use of the David Porter Papers, both those in the Library of Congress and those in the U.S. Naval Academy Museum, and the Samuel Hambleton and John Rodgers Papers. Additional material comes from David Dixon Porter's *Memoir* and Archibald D. Turnbull's *Commodore David Porter, 1780–1843*.

Background on the famous frigate *Essex* is taken from USND, *American Fighting Ships*, Volume 2; articles published by the Essex Institute in Salem, Massachusetts; and maritime and naval histories by Samuel E. Morison and George F. Emmons. For the War of 1812 and Porter's first cruise in the *Essex*, Alfred T. Mahan, C. S. Forester, Fletcher Pratt, Edgar S. Maclay, Irving Brant, Benson J. Lossing, and William James proved useful, as did Farragut's biographers, A. T. Mahan, Loyall Farragut, and especially Charles L. Lewis. *Analectic Magazine* and the press of New York, Boston, Philadelphia, Washington, and Baltimore provide contemporary coverage.

1. DP to Samuel Hambleton, 23 October 1810, 24 August 1810, DP Papers, 2, LC; DP to SecNav, 20, 27, 16 August 1810, USND, LRMC; SecNav to DP, 18 August 1810, USND, LS.

2. DP to SecNav, 7 January 1811, 29 April 1812, USND, LRMC; DP to Samuel Hambleton, 28 February 1812, in DDP, *Memoir,* p. 100; J. G. Van Dusen, "Paul Hamilton," DAB, 8, pp. 189–190; Samuel Hambleton to DP, 7 March 1812, Samuel Hambleton Papers.

3. W. P. Strauss, *Early American Interest and Activity in Polynesia, 1783–1842,* p. 146; DP to SecNav, 7 February 1811, USND, LRMC.

4. SecNav to DP, 28 July, 2 August 1810, 12 July 1811, USND, LS; DP to SecNav, 21 July 1811, USND, LRMC; USND, *American Fighting Ships*, 2, p. 366; C. L. Lewis, *David Glasgow Farragut . . . ,* p. 26; G. L. Streeter, "Historical Sketch of the Building of the Frigate *Essex* . . . ," *Proceedings of the Essex Institute,* 20 (1856), p. 74; *Salem Gazette,* 26 October 1798; G. H. Preble, "The First Cruise of the United States Frigate Essex," *Essex Institute Historical Collections,* 10, part 2, p. 6; USND, *American Fighting Ships*, 2, p. 366.

5. *Independent Chronicle* (Boston), 3 October 1799; S. E. Morison, *The Maritime History of Massachusetts, 1783–1860,* p. 100; USND, *American Fighting Ships*, 2, p. 366; G. H. Preble, *op. cit.,* p. 20; G. F. Emmons, *The Navy of the United States from the Commencement, 1775–1853,* p. 9; A. T. Mahan, *Admiral Farragut,* pp. 16–17.

6. DP to SecNav, 28, 9 August 1811, USND, LRMC; C. L. Lewis, *op. cit.,* pp. 23–24, 26, 38–39.

7. A. D. Turnbull, *Commodore David Porter, 1780–1843,* p. 90; C. L. Lewis, *op. cit.,* p. 316 (n. 6), Fletcher Pratt, *Preble's Boys . . . ,* pp. 165–166; DP to SecNav, 12 October 1811, USND, LRMC; SecNav to DP, 17 October 1811, USND, LS; DP to SecNav, 24 October 1811, USND, LRMC; SecNav to DP, 31 October 1811, USND, LS.

8. C. L. Lewis, *op. cit.,* p. 22; DP to Samuel Hambleton, n.d., in DDP, *Memoir,*

p. 99; DP to Samuel Hambleton, 29 September, 22 October 1810, DP Papers, 2, LC; SecNav to DP, 9 June 1811, Container 15, *ibid.*

9. A. D. Turnbull, *op. cit.*, p. 99; DP, *Journal of a Cruise Made to the Pacific Ocean . . . in the United States Frigate Essex, in the Years 1812, 1813, and 1814 . . .* , 1815 ed., 1, p. 27; DP to P. L. Parton, 31 December 1811, DP Papers, United States Naval Academy Museum; DP to SecNav, 8 June 1812, John Rodgers Papers.

10. E. S. Maclay, *History of the Navy . . .* , 1, p. 319; SecNav to DP, 12 November 1811, USND, LS; Irving Brant, *James Madison: The President, 1809–1812,* p. 36; *Analectic Magazine,* 6 (November 1815), p. 388; DP to SecNav, 29 June 1812, USND, LRMC.

11. *Analectic Magazine,* 6 (November 1815), p. 388; *New-York Herald,* 27 June 1812; Loyall Farragut, *The Life of David Glasgow Farragut,* p. 14; DP to SecNav, 28 June 1812, USND, LRMC; *New-York Herald,* 26, 27 June 1812; SecNav to DP, 30 June, 10 July 1812, USND, LS.

12. *New-York Evening Post, New-York Herald,* 11 July 1812, Sir Augustus John Foster, *Jeffersonian America . . . , passim;* Loyall Farragut, *op. cit.,* p. 15; William James, *The Naval History of Great Britain . . .* , 6, p. 124; *The Times* (London), 12 August 1814.

13. SecNav to DP, 24 June 1812, USND, LS; DP to SecNav, 3 September 1812, USND, Letters Received by Secretary of the Navy from Captains (LRC); C. S. Forester, *Age of Fighting Sail . . .* , p. 7; DP to SecNav, 3 September 1812, USND, LRC.

14. *Analectic Magazine,* 6 (April 1816), p. 305; DP to SecNav, 3 September 1812, USND, LRC; E. S. Maclay, *History of the Navy . . .* , 1, p. 328; *Analectic Magazine,* 7 (April 1816), p. 305.

15. *Niles National Register,* * 19 September, *New-York Spectator,* 12 September, *New-York Herald,* 12 September 1812; William James, *op. cit.,* p. 127; *The Times* (London), 2 October 1812.

16. Loyall Farragut, *op. cit.,* pp. 16–17; C. L. Lewis, *op. cit.,* p. 45; Sir John T. Duckworth to DP, 5 August, to SecNav, 31 August 1812, in DDP, *Memoir,* pp. 95–96; SecNav to DP, 22 September 1812, USND, LS; DP to SecNav, 1 September 1812, USND, LRC; Secretary to Admiralty, ? May 1814, Captains' In-Letters, in A. T. Mahan, *Sea Power in Its Relations to the War of 1812,* 2, p. 134.

17. Edward Baines, *Baines' History of the Late War . . .* , p. iv; *The Times* (London), 28 December 1812, 20 March 1813; *Morning Chronicle* (London), 29 December 1812; *The Times* (London), 12 July 1814.

18. B. J. Lossing, *The Pictorial Field-Book of the War of 1812 . . .* , p. 455; DP to Samuel Hambleton, 7 September 1812, in DDP, *Memoir,* p. 97; DP to SecNav, 3 September 1812, USND, LRC; SecNav to DP, 12 September 1812,

---

* This journal was in existence from 1811 to 1849. It was first known as *The Weekly Register* and, in August 1814, it became *Niles Weekly Register.* The title *Niles National Register* was not used until September 1837 but, for the sake of clarity, it has been used throughout these notes.

USND, LS; *New-York Spectator*, 19 September 1812; DP to SecNav, 14 October 1812, USND, LRC; DP, *Journal of a Cruise Made to the Pacific Ocean . . .* , 1815 ed., 1, p. 1; William James, *op. cit.*, 5, p. 366.
19. *Democratic Press* (Philadelphia), 18 September 1812; B. J. Lossing, *op. cit.*, p. 441; William James, *op. cit.*, 6, p. 125; *Niles National Register*, 20 September 1812; DP to SecNav, 19, 23 September, 14 October 1812, USND, LRC.

IV

Porter's famous voyage to the Pacific, from the time he left the Delaware Capes through his assaults upon British whalers in the Galápagos Islands, 1812–1813, is narrated in this chapter, and three major sources are used: his own description in *Journal of a Cruise Made to the Pacific Ocean, by Captain David Porter, in the United States Frigate Essex, in the Years 1812, 1813, and 1814. . . .* , 2 volumes, Philadelphia, 1815 (DP, *Journal,* 1815) ; the onslaught against Porter made almost immediately after publication of the *Journal* by William Gifford, editor of the British *Quarterly Review*, Volume 13 (July 1815) (QR) ; and Porter's lengthy preface to his second edition with the same title, 2 volumes, New York, 1822 (DP, *Journal,* 1822) , in which he defended himself. Biographical material on Gifford, David Dixon Porter's *Memoir*, and Charles L. Lewis' life of Farragut provide additional details. Felix Riesenberg, *Cape Horn*, and Samuel E. Morison, *The Maritime History of Massachusetts, 1783–1860,* settled points of dispute arising from Porter's description of his travails in passing from the Atlantic to the Pacific.

To cover the time Porter was based at Valparaiso, histories of Chile and of American relations with that nation by Luis Galdames, John C. Pine, James J. Auchmuty, and Henry C. Evans, Jr. have been consulted, as have biographies of Joel R. Poinsett by J. Fred Rippy and Charles J. Stillé, and an unpublished doctoral dissertation on José Miguel Carrera by Joseph F. Straub. Information about whaling in the Pacific is taken from Alexander Starbuck and Edouard H. Stackpole, *The Sea Hunters*. The latter kindly allowed me to read part of the manuscript of his forthcoming book, *Whaling During the War of 1812*, and conversations with him on Nantucket Island were most helpful. For analysis of the effect, both immediate and long-range, of Porter's war on British whalers, I have read the works of James F. Cooper, Barber Badger, Washington Irving, Henry M. Brackenridge, Thomas H. Benton, Theodore Roosevelt, Ralph D. Paine, Alfred T. Mahan, Fletcher Pratt, and C. S. Forester.

1. S. E. Morison, *The Maritime History of Massachusetts, 1783–1860,* p. 203; William James, *An Inquiry into . . . Naval Actions,* p. 79; Pierre Irving, *The Life and Letters of Washington Irving,* 1, p. 341; Sir Leslie Stephens, "William Gifford," DNB, 7, p. 1189; *Quarterly Review,* 13 (July 1815) (QR), p. 353; *Cobbett's Weekly Political Register,* 30, No. 17 (27 April 1816) , pp. 513–514; E. Smith, "William Cobbett," DNB, 4, pp. 598–601.

2. *Analectic Magazine*, 6 (July 1815), p. 57; William Bainbridge to DP, 25 September 1822, William Bainbridge Papers; H. M. Brackenridge, *History of the Late War* . . . , p. 246; James Madison to DP, 7 December 1822, Container 15, DP Papers, LC.

3. DP, *Journal*, 1815, 1, pp. 61, 1; DP to Samuel Hambleton, 19 October 1812, in DDP, *Memoir*, pp. 101–102; DP, *Journal*, 1815, 1, pp. 1–13.

4. DP, *Journal*, 1815, 1, pp. 2–3, 29–30, 1–3, 14, 24, 15–18; C. L. Lewis, *David Glasgow Farragut* . . . , p. 54.

5. DP, *Journal*, 1815, 1, pp. 19, 22 (misnumbered 24), 20, 22–23, 21; QR, p. 353; DP, *Journal*, 1822, 1, p. xi.

6. DP, *Journal*, 1815, 1, pp. 28, 35–38; QR, p. 354; W. A. Roberts, *The U.S. Navy Fights*, p. 83; DP, *Journal*, 1815, 1, pp. 39–40; QR, p. 353; DP, *Journal*, 1822, 1, p. xiii.

7. (Fn.), *Niles National Register*, 11 December 1813; DP, *Journal*, 1815, 1, pp. 45–64.

8. DP, *Journal*, 1815, 1, pp. 60–61; C. S. Forester, *Age of Fighting Sail* . . . , p. 204; J. F. Cooper, *History of the Navy* . . . , 2, p. 121.

9. Felix Riesenberg, *Cape Horn*, pp. 191–195, 197; Sir John K. Laughton, "George Anson," DNB, 1, p. 504; DP, *Journal*, 1815, 1, p. 76; Felix Riesenberg, *op. cit.*, p. 436.

10. DP, *Journal*, 1815, 1, pp. 65–69; QR, p. 355; DP, *Journal*, 1822, 1, p. xvi; *ibid.*, 1815, 1, pp. 69–76; Sir John K. Laughton, *op. cit.*, p. 504.

11. DP, *Journal*, 1815, 1, pp. 76–87; C. L. Lewis, *op. cit.*, p. 62.

12. DP, *Journal*, 1815, 1, pp. 84, 90–92; QR, p. 355; S. E. Morison, *The Maritime History of Massachusetts, 1783–1860*, p. 54; DP, *Journal*, 1822, 1, pp. xvi–xix; William Bligh, *Journal*, n.d., in Irvin Anthony (ed.), *The Saga of the Bounty*, pp. 17–18; Felix Riesenberg, *op. cit.*, pp. 348–349.

13. DP, *Journal*, 1815, 1, pp. 88, 90–93, 128–129; William C. Feltus, *Journal*, 4 April 1813; C. L. Lewis, *op. cit.*, pp. 63 (n. 20), 322 (n. 21); DP, *Journal*, 1815, 1, pp. 92–101; *ibid.*, 1822, 1, pp. 92–93; Loyall Farragut, *The Life of David Glasgow Farragut*, p. 21; C. L. Lewis, *op. cit.*, p. 64.

14. J. F. Straub, *José Miguel Carrera*, pp. 1–76; J. C. Pine, *The Role of United States Special Agents* . . . , p. 154; H. C. Evans, Jr., *Chile and* . . . *the United States*, p. 13; C. J. Stillé, "The Life and Services of Joel R. Poinsett," *The Pennsylvania Magazine of History and Biography*, 12, Nos. 2 and 3 (1888), p. 154.

15. H. C. Evans, Jr., *op. cit.*, p. 15; J. C. Pine, *op. cit.*, pp. 183–185; C. J. Stillé, *op. cit.*, pp. 154–155; E. A. Stackpole, *Whaling during the War of 1812*, pp. 18–19; Alexander Starbuck, "History of the American Whale Fishery . . . ," *Report of the Commissioner for 1875–1876*, U.S. Commission of Fish and Fisheries, pp. 93–94; J. J. Auchmuty, *The United States Government and Latin American Independence, 1810–1830*, p. 126.

16. C. J. Ingersoll, *History of the Second War* . . . , p. 14; J. F. Rippy, *Joel R. Poinsett, Versatile American*, p. 48; DP, *Journal*, 1815, 1, pp. 106, 103, 107–110.

17. DP, *Journal*, 1815, 1, pp. 107–115; QR, pp. 357–358; DP, *Journal*, 1822, 1, pp. xxiii, 99–100, 105–106.
18. E. A. Stackpole, *op. cit.*, ch. 3, p. 4; DP, *Journal*, 1815, 1, pp. 111–112, 117–136.
19. DP, *Journal*, 1815, 1, pp. 137–162.
20. E. A. Stackpole, interview with author, 1 September 1966; DP, *Journal*, 1815, 1, pp. 159–160; C. L. Lewis, *David Glasgow Farragut . . .* , p. 70; QR, pp. 361–362; DP, *Journal*, 1815, 1, pp. 158–164.
21. DDP, *Memoir*, p. 137; DP, *Journal*, 1815, 1. pp. 166–197.
22. DP, *Journal*, 1815, 1, pp. 198–208, 220, 208–214; Fletcher Pratt, *Preble's Boys . . .* , p. 228.
23. C. L. Lewis, *op. cit.*, pp. 77–79; E. A. Stackpole, *Whaling during the War of 1812*, p. 241; DP, *Journal*, 1815, 1, pp. 214–224.
24. DP, *Journal*, 1815, 1, pp. 222–256; R. C. Suggs, *The Hidden Worlds of Polynesia . . .* , p. 50; DP, *Journal*, 1815, 1, pp. 251, 256–259; DP to SecNav, ? August 1824, USND, Letters Received by Secretary of the Navy from Captains (LRC).
25. *Montreal Herald*, 23 July 1814, in *Eastern Argus* (Portland, Maine), 25 August 1814; *The Times* (London), 22 July 1814; C. H. Snider, Jr., *The Glorious "Shannon's" Old Blue Duster . . .* , p. 177; QR, pp. 362–363; DDP, *Memoir*, p. 243; William James, *The Naval History of Great Britain . . .* , 6, p. 420; QR, p. 363.
26. *Niles National Register*, 7 August, 11, 25 September, 30 October, 18 December 1813; Charles Warren (ed.), *Jacobin and Junto . . .* , p. 262; John Brannan, *Official Letters . . . during the War with Great Britain*, pp. 175–179; *Niles National Register*, 15 January 1814; *American Advocate* (Hallowell, Maine), 7, 28 May 1814; Barber Badger, *The Naval Temple . . .* , p. 120.
27. Washington Irving, *Works*, 8, pp. 101–102; H. M. Brackenridge, *History of the Late War . . .* , pp. 168–169; T. H. Benton, *Thirty Years' View . . .* , 2, p. 498; Theodore Roosevelt, *The Naval War of 1812*, p. 165; R. D. Paine, *The Fight for a Free Sea . . .* , p. 154; Fletcher Pratt, *Preble's Boys . . .* , p. 231; C. S. Forester, *Age of Fighting Sail . . .* , pp. 205–206.

V

Porter's sojourn in the Marquesas Islands in 1813 is the topic of this chapter. Besides the two editions of his *Journal of a Cruise. . . .* and the antagonistic commentary of the *Quarterly Review,* the excellent collection on the Pacific at the Peabody Museum in Salem, Massachusetts, has provided material, as have general works on that area by Robert C. Suggs, James M. Callahan, C. Hartley Gratton, Wallace P. Strauss, and J. C. Furnas. I have consulted previously cited naval histories, biographies of David Porter, David

Glasgow Farragut, James Cook, Matthew Fontaine Maury, John Jacob Astor, and James Madison, and have read Herman Melville, *Typee*, and Charles R. Anderson, *Melville in the South Seas*. Two articles, Ralph Linton's "Marquesan Culture" and Harry L. Shapiro's "Les Iles Marquises," are most useful in understanding the culture that was so puzzling to Porter. An interesting glimpse at the imperialistic attitudes of the early twentieth century is provided by Edward L. Beach, who regards Porter as "The Pioneer of America's Pacific Empire." A considerable number of periodicals, British and American, contemporary and more recent, piece together the immediate and the lasting effects of Porter's activities in the Marquesas.

1. R. C. Suggs, *The Hidden Worlds of Polynesia* . . . , pp. 31–32; Arthur Kitson, *Captain James Cook* . . . , pp. 277–279; DP, *Journal*, 1815, 2, pp. 7–8.

2. J. M. Callahan, *American Relations in the Pacific* . . . , p. 19; DP, *Journal*, 1815, 2, p. 9; C. H. Gratton, *The Southwest Pacific to 1900*, p. 90; R. C. Suggs, *op. cit.*, p. 47; Josiah Roberts, letter, 6 November 1795, Massachusetts Historical Collection, Series T (1795) New Bedford Public Library; W. P. Strauss, *Early American Interest and Activity in Polynesia, 1783–1842*, p. 13; R. C. Suggs, *op. cit.*, pp. 49–50.

3. DP, *Journal*, 1815, 2, pp. 3–6, 9–17; Herman Melville, *Typee*, p. 307; DP, *Journal*, 1815, 2, pp. 15–16; QR, p. 364.

4. DP, *Journal*, 1815, 2, pp. 19–20; F. L. Williams, *Matthew Fontaine Maury: Scientist of the Sea*, pp. 23, 25, 30, 72; C. L. Lewis, *David Glasgow Farragut* . . . , p. 324 (n. 5) ; J. F. Cooper, *History of the Navy* . . . , 2 (extra illustrated edition, NYHS), p. 257; DP, *Journal*, 1815, 2, pp. 20–21; *ibid.*, 1822, 2, p. 18.

5. DP, *Journal*, 1815, 2, p. 24; D. W. Knox, *A History of the United States Navy*, p. 101; DP, *Journal*, 1815, 2, pp. 31, 69–70, 132, 66–67.

6. DP, *Journal*, 1815, 2, p. 31; C. L. Lewis, *op. cit.*, pp. 84–85; DP, *Journal*, 1815, 2, pp. 23, 16, 63, 30, 88.

7. James Barnes, *David G. Farragut*, p. 14; *Worcester Yeoman*, n.d., in *Salem Gazette*, 9 August 1825; R. C. Suggs, *op. cit.*, p. 52; DP, *Journal*, 1815, 1, p. 14; *ibid.*, 2, p. 143; QR, p. 371; DP, *Journal*, 1822, 1, pp. xlv–xlvii.

8. DP, *Journal*, 1815, 2, pp. 60–62; QR, p. 368; DP, *Journal*, 1815, 2, pp. 25–26, 29–30, 52–57, 112–113, 122–123, 133.

9. Ralph Linton, "Marquesan Culture," in Abram Kardiner, *The Individual and His Society*, p. 150; DP, *Journal*, 1815, 2, pp. 34, 68–69, 118, 142; Ralph Linton, *op. cit.*, p. 183; DP, *Journal*, 1815, 2, pp. 113–120, 134–135.

10. DP, *Journal*, 1815, 2, pp. 48–49; H. L. Shapiro, "Les Iles Marquises," *Natural History*, 67 (April 1958), p. 212; DP, *Journal*, 1815, 2, pp. 49, 56, 43–44, 54–55, 65–66, 127, 128, 123–124.

11. C. L. Lewis, *op. cit.*, p. 324 (n. 6) ; DP, *Journal*, 1822, 2, pp. 31–32; Ralph Linton, *op. cit.*, p. 155; R. C. Suggs, *op. cit.*, p. 57; H. L. Shapiro, *op. cit.*, p. 313.

12. DP, *Journal*, 1815, 2, pp. 30–32, 22, 33; Ralph Linton, *op. cit.*, pp. 179–180; DP, *Journal*, 1815, 2, pp. 38–41, 58–59, 66–67.

13. DP, *Journal*, 1815, 2, pp. 70–74, 77–79; K. W. Porter, *John Jacob Astor: Business Man*, 1, pp. 224–225, 231–232; Harvey O'Connor, *The Astors*, p. 28; DP, *Journal*, 1815, 2, pp. 79, 80–81.

14. DP, *Journal*, 1815, 2, pp. 82–84; J. C. Furnas, *The Anatomy of Paradise* . . . , p. 246; Irving Brant, *James Madison: Commander in Chief, 1812–1836*, p. 275; DP to James Monroe, 27 February 1815, in E. L. Beach, "The Pioneer of America's Pacific Empire: David Porter," *United States Naval Institute Proceedings*, 34 (June 1908), pp. 561–562.

15. *Independent Chronicle* (Boston), 13 July 1814; *Providence Chronicle*, 23 April 1819; *Niles National Register*, 18 October 1817; DDP, *Memoir*, pp. 194–195; E. L. Beach, *op. cit.*, pp. 552, 560, 562, 563.

16. QR, p. 371; *Columbian Centinel* (Boston), 16 July 1814; *Salem Gazette*, 15, 19 July 1814; H. M. Brackenridge, *History of the Late War* . . . , p. 247; J. C. Furnas, *op. cit.*, p. 246.

17. DP, *Journal*, 1815, 2, pp. 90–97.

18. James Barnes, *David G. Farragut*, p. 16; DP, *Journal*, 1815, 2, pp. 97–108; Wilmon Menard, "A Forgotten South Sea Paradise," *Asia*, 33 (September 1933), p. 454; DP, *Journal*, 1815, 2, pp. 108–110, 102–103, 109–111; Ralph Linton, *op. cit.*, p. 158.

19. C. S. Stewart, *A Visit to the South Seas* . . . , 1, pp. 227, 308; J. M. Callahan, *American Relations in the Pacific* . . . , p. 341 (n. 13); F. L. Williams, *Matthew Fontaine Maury: Scientist of the Sea*, p. 72; H. M. Brackenridge, *op. cit.*, pp. 246–247; QR, pp. 369–371, 383; DP, *Journal*, 1822, 1, lxiv, lxvi–lxvii.

20. *Worcester Yeoman*, n.d., in *Salem Gazette*, 9, August 1825; *Salem Gazette*, 26 August 1826; The Reverend H. Roberts, in *The Friend* (Honolulu), n.d., American Activities in the Central Pacific, Roll 2, "Marquesas," Peabody Museum, Salem, Mass.; Herman Melville, *Typee*, pp. 129–130, 106; C. R. Anderson, *Melville in the South Seas*, p. 98; E. A. Stackpole, *The Sea-Hunters* . . . , pp. 445–446.

21. DP, *Journal*, 1815, 2, pp. 140–142; Loyall Farragut, *The Life of David Glasgow Farragut* . . . , p. 31; C. L. Lewis, *David Glasgow Farragut* . . . , p. 88; DP, *Journal*, 1815, 2, pp. 142–143; *ibid.*, 1822, 2, p. 161; C. L. Lewis, *op. cit.*, pp. 324 (n. 18), 89; DP, *Journal*, 1815, 2, pp. 143–144; *ibid.*, 1822, 2, pp. 180, 184–185.

22. C. H. Snider, Jr., *The Glorious "Shannon's" Old Blue Duster* . . . , p. 175; DP, *Journal*, 1822, 2, pp. 178–192; William Feltus, *Journal*, 6, 13 March 1814; DP, *Journal*, 1822, 2, pp. 193–194; *Boston Commercial Gazette*, 23 October 1817; *Analectic Magazine*, 10 (November 1817), pp. 426–427; *Boston Commercial Gazette*, 23 October 1817; DP, *Journal*, 1822, 2, p. 225.

23. DP, *Journal*, 1822, 2, pp. 194–198, 81; William Feltus, *Journal*, 7 May 1814; DP, *Journal*, 1822, 2, pp. 198–201; William James, *Naval History of Great Britain* . . . , 6, p. 420.

24. DP, *Journal*, 1822, 2, pp. 201–205; Admiralty, *Journal of the Proceedings of His Majesty's Ship Phoebe*, 18 April 1814, Adm. 51/2675, Public Record Office; DP, *Journal*, 1822, 2, pp. 206–231; DP to SecNav, 10 February 1816, U.S. Congress, *American State Papers, Naval Affairs*, 2, pp. 96–97.

25. QR, pp. 371–373; DP, *Journal*, 1822, 2, p. 225; C. S. Stewart, *A Visit to the South Seas . . .* , 1, p. 308.

26. Herman Melville, *Typee*, p. 129; *London Spectator*, n.d., in *National Intelligencer*, 1 February 1843; *Christian Watchman* (Boston), 5 February 1843; *New York Aurora*, n.d., in *Daily Herald* (Newburyport, Mass.), 6 January 1843.

27. J. W. Church, "A Vanishing People of the South Seas," *National Geographic*, 36 (October 1919), pp. 299–303; H. L. Shapiro, "Les Iles Marquises," *Natural History*, 67 (April 1958), p. 214; R. C. Suggs, *The Hidden Worlds of Polynesia . . .* , p. 57; Ralph Linton, "Marquesan Culture," in Abram Kardiner, *The Individual and His Society*, p. 137; R. C. Suggs, *op. cit.*, p. 57; J. W. Coulter, "Marquesas," *The Encyclopaedia Britannica*, 14, p. 937.

VI

The body of this chapter concerns the defeat of the *Essex* by HMS *Phoebe*, under Captain James Hillyar, and HMS *Cherub* in Valparaiso Harbor on 28 March 1814. Porter's letters to the Secretary of the Navy and the 1822 edition of his *Journal of a Cruise. . . .* constitute the major American documentation for the battle; on the British side, that role is played by Hillyar's letters to the Admiralty, his official account of the battle, and the logs or journals of HM ships *Phoebe, Tagus,* and *Briton.* Previously cited American naval histories have been consulted, as have the three works of William James, biased British naval historian, a more modern Canadian account (apparently taken directly from James) by Charles H. Snider, Jr., and John Marshall, *Royal Naval Biography.* . . . Charles L. Lewis and other biographers of Farragut add many details to the description of the battle.

The letters, official reports, and biographies of Joel R. Poinsett, American Special Agent to Chile, and the works of Joseph F. Straub, J. Fred Rippy, Henry C. Evans, Jr., Arthur P. Whitaker, and W. B. Stevenson piece together a mosaic of conditions in Chile and Peru which affected both Porter and Hillyar between the time the battle ended and their departure from South America in mid-1814.

Information on Porter's activities in the Chesapeake area is found in his letters to and from the Secretary of the Navy, his son's *Memoir,* previously mentioned histories of the War of 1812, and newspaper and magazine articles from both sides of the Atlantic. Charles O. Paullin, Frederick Merk, Samuel F. Bemis, Allen B. Cole, and the David Porter Papers are the authorities for Porter's suggested cruise to Japan in 1815.

1. William James, *The Naval History of Great Britain* . . . , 6, p. 457; DP to SecNav, 4 April, 3 July 1814, USND, Letters Received by Secretary of the Navy from Captains (LRC) ; Barber Badger, *The Naval Temple* . . . , p. 121; C. J. Ingersoll, *History of the Second War* . . . , p. 14; DP, *Journal*, 1822, 2, pp. 171, 140; Henry Adams, *History of the United States of America*, 6, p. 177.

2. DP to John Downes, 10 January 1814, DP Papers, USNAM; DP, *Journal*, 1822, 2, pp. 142–143, 161, 162, 143; J. F. Straub, *José Miguel Carrera*, p. 76; DP, *Journal*, 1822, 2, pp. 143–144.

3. *Salem Gazette*, 29 July 1814; John Marshall, *Royal Naval Biography* . . . , 2, Part 2, pp. 853–858; A. T. Mahan, *Sea Power in Its Relations to the War of 1812*, 2, p. 248; DP, *Journal*, 1822, 2, p. 144.

4. K. W. Porter, *John Jacob Astor: Business Man*, p. 230; William James, . . . *Naval Occurrences* . . . , p. 319; DP, *Journal*, 1815, 2, p. 225; Harvey O'Connor, *The Astors*, pp. 26–28; *Independent Chronicle* (Boston) , 11 July 1814; A. T. Mahan, *Admiral Farragut*, p. 32; DP, *Journal*, 1822, 2, p. 157.

5. Journal of the Proceedings of His Majesty's Ship *Phoebe* (hereinafter known as *Phoebe* Journal), 25 March 1813, Adm. 51/2675; William James, . . . *Naval Occurrences* . . . , p. 319; John Marshall, *op. cit.*, pp. 860–861; C. J. Ingersoll, *op. cit.*, p. 15; James Hillyar to Admiralty, 14 October 1813, Captains' In-Letters, Adm. 1/1950.

6. James Hillyar to Admiralty, n.d. (probably early November 1813) , Captains' In-Letters, Adm. 1/1950; *ibid.*, 12 January 1814, Adm. 1/1949; *ibid.*, n.d. (probably early November 1813) , Adm. 1/1950; *Phoebe* Journal, September 1813–8 February 1814, Adm. 51/2675.

7. James Barnes, *David G. Farragut*, pp. 17–18; DP, *Journal*, 1822, 2, pp. 144–145; DP to SecNav, 13 July 1814, USND, LRC; A. T. Mahan, *Admiral Farragut*, p. 36; J. R. Spears, *The History of Our Navy* . . . , 3, p. 27; Loyall Farragut, *The Life of David Glasgow Farragut*, p. 33; DP, *Journal*, 1822, 2, pp. 145–146.

8. C. H. Snider, Jr., *The Glorious "Shannon's" Old Blue Duster* . . . , p. 163; C. S. Forester, *Age of Fighting Sail* . . . , p. 208; DP, *Journal*, 1822, 2, p. 146.

9. DP to SecNav, 4 April 1814, USND, LRC; John Marshall, *op. cit.*, p. 863; DP to SecNav, 4 April 1814, USND, LRC; William James, . . . *Naval Occurrences* . . . , p. 312; John Marshall, *op. cit.*, p. 863.

10. DP, *Journal*, 1822, 2, p. 146; Hillyar's Official Report, in *Morning Chronicle* (London) , 6 July 1814; James Hillyar to Admiralty, 26 June 1814, Captains' In-Letters, Adm. 1/1950.

11. DP, *Journal*, 1822, 2, p. 148; DP to SecNav, 3 July 1814, USND, LRC; James Hillyar to Admiralty, 28 February 1814, Captains' In-Letters, Adm. 1/1950; *Niles National Register*, 20 August 1814.

12. C. L. Lewis, *David Glasgow Farragut* . . . , pp. 94–95; James Hillyar to Admiralty, 26 June 1814, Captains' In-Letters, Adm. 1/1950; DP, *Journal*, 1822, 2, pp. 149–153; James Hillyar to Admiralty, 28 February 1814, Captains' In-Letters, Adm. 1/1950.

13. *Phoebe* Journal, 15 February 1814, Adm. 51/2675; William James, . . . *Naval Occurrences* . . . , p. 314; DP to SecNav, 3 July 1814, USND, LRC; DP, *Journal*, 1822, 2, pp, 147–148; James Hillyar to Admiralty, 28 February 1814, Captains' In-Letters, Adm. 1/1950.

14. James Hillyar to Admiralty, 26 June 1814, Captains' In-Letters, Adm. 1/1950; DP to SecNav, 3 July 1814, USND, LRC; *Phoebe* Journal, 27 February 1814, Adm. 51/2675; C. S. Forester, *Age of Fighting Sail* . . . , p. 209.

15. DP, *Journal*, 1822, 2, pp. 163–164; James Hillyar to Admiralty, 13 April 1814, Captains' In-Letters, Adm. 1/1950; Thomas Staines to Admiralty, 18 October 1814, in Irvin Anthony (ed.) , *The Saga of the Bounty,* pp. 347–349; *Phoebe* Journal, 21 May 1814, Adm. 51/2675.

16. DP to SecNav, 4 April 1814, USND, LRC; Hillyar's Official Report, in *Morning Chronicle* (London) , 6 July 1814; James Hillyar to Admiralty, 26 June 1814, Captains' In-Letters, Adm. 1/1950; DP to SecNav, 4 April 1814, USND, LRC.

17. Joel R. Poinsett to SecState, 2 April 1814, USSD, Special Agents, Poinsett; J. F. Rippy, *Joel R. Poinsett, Versatile American,* p. 54; H. C. Evans, Jr., *Chile and . . . the United States,* p. 19; James Hillyar to Admiralty, 10 February 1814, Captains' In-Letters, Adm. 1/1949; Joel R. Poinsett to SecState, 2 April 1814, USSD, Special Agents, Poinsett, H. M. Brackenridge, *History of the Late War* . . . , p. 253.

18. DP to SecNav, 4 April 1814, USND, LRC; Hillyar's Official Report, *op. cit.;* William James, . . . *Naval Occurrences* . . . , p. 307; DP to SecNav, 4 April 1814, USND, LRC; Hillyar's Official Report, *op. cit.*

19. DP to SecNav, 4 April 1814, USND, LRC; J. F. Cooper, *History of the Navy* . . . , 2, p. 149; DP to SecNav, 4 April 1814, USND, LRC.

20. Barber Badger, *The Naval Temple* . . . , p. 131; Washington Irving, *Works,* 8, p. 111; C. L. Lewis, *op. cit.,* pp. 98–99, 326–327 (n. 18) , 99–100, 101, 102, 327 (n. 20) ; Loyall Farragut, *op. cit.,* p. 31.

21. DP to SecNav, 4 April 1814, USND, LRC; DP, *Journal*, 1822, 2, pp. 233–236; Hillyar's Official Report, *op. cit.;* J. R. Spears, *The History of Our Navy* . . . , 3, p. 45.

22. DP to SecNav, 4 April 1814, USND, LRC; Loyall Farragut, *op. cit.,* p. 39; Hillyar's Official Report, *op. cit.;* DP to SecNav, 4 April 1814, USND, LRC; *Phoebe* Journal, 13 November 1814, Adm. 51/2675; USND, *American Fighting Ships,* 2, p. 366.

23. DP to SecNav, 4 April 1814, USND, LRC; C. L. Lewis, *op. cit.,* pp. 104–105; Hillyar's Official Report, *op. cit.;* James Hillyar to Admiralty, 26 June 1814, Captains' In-Letters, Adm. 1/1950.

24. *The Times* (London) , 22 July 1814; Hillyar's Official Report, *op. cit.;* *Annual Register* . . . *for the Year 1814* (London) , p. 173; in *Analectic Magazine,* 8 (September 1816) , p. 226; John Marshall, *Royal Naval Biography* . . . , 2, Part 2, p. 863; *The Times* (London) , 25 July 1814; QR, p. 372.

25. William James, . . . *Naval Occurrences* . . . , p. 311, C. H. Snider, Jr., *The Glorious "Shannon's" Old Blue Duster* . . . , p. 172; William James, *The Naval History of Great Britain* . . . , 6, p. 418; William James, *An Inquiry*

BIBLIOGRAPHIC NOTES

into . . . Naval Actions . . . , p. 82; William James, *The Naval History of Great Britain . . .* , 6, pp. 421–422.

26. *Niles National Register,* 16 July 1814; *New-York Spectator,* 16 July 1814; *Columbian Centinel* (Boston), 13 July 1814; *Niles National Register,* 23 July 1814; *Independent Chronicle* (Boston), 25, 21 July 1814; *Columbian Centinel,* 9 July 1814.

27. F. L. Pattee, *The Poems of Philip Freneau . . .* , 3, pp. 318–321; in J. D. Richardson (ed.), *. . . Messages . . . of the Presidents,* 1, p. 549; *The Reportory* (Boston), 29 July 1814; *Salem Gazette,* 22, 19 July 1814.

28. H. M. Brackenridge, *History of the Late War . . .* , p. 252; Henry Adams, *History of the United States of America,* 8, pp. 180–181; D. W. Knox, *A History of the United States Navy,* pp. 107–108; Theodore Roosevelt, *The Naval War of 1812,* pp. 294, 301, 305–306; W. A. Roberts, *The U.S. Navy Fights,* p. 91; C. H. Snider, Jr., *op. cit.,* p. 174.

29. DP to SecNav, 4 April 1814, USND, LRC; DP, *Journal,* 1822, 2, p. 173; H. C. Evans, Jr., *Chile and . . . the United States,* p. 20; W. B. Stevenson, *Historical and Descriptive Narrative of . . . South America,* 3, p. 122; J. F. Straub, *José Miguel Carrera,* p. 83; James Hillyar to Admiralty, 20 June 1814, Captains' In-Letters, Adm. 1/1950; DP, *Journal,* 1822, 2, pp. 173–174.

30. J. F. Rippy, *Rivalry of the United States and Great Britain over Latin America,* p. 10; DP to Joel R. Poinsett, 13 April 1814, Joel R. Poinsett Papers; J. F. Rippy, *Joel R. Poinsett, Versatile American,* p. 54; Joel R. Poinsett to SecState, 14 June 1814, USSD, Special Agents, Poinsett; J. F. Rippy, *op. cit.,* p. 56; H. C. Evans, Jr., *op. cit.,* p. 20.

31. DP, *Journal,* 1822, 2, pp. 249–252; James Hillyar to Admiralty, 20 June 1814, Captains' In-Letters, Adm. 1/1950; Thomas Sumter, U.S. Minister to Brazil, to Stephen Decatur, 24 September 1819, in DP, *Journal,* 1822, 2, pp. 252–256; *Phoebe* Journal, 13 November 1814, Adm. 51/2675; C. O. Paullin, *Commodore John Rodgers,* p. 395.

32. DP, *Journal,* 1822, 2, p. 241; A. T. Mahan, *Admiral Farragut,* p. 49; Hillyar's "Passport" to Essex Jr., in DP, *Journal,* 1822, 2, pp. 241–242.

33. A. T. Mahan, *Sea Power in Its Relations to the War of 1812,* 2, p. 398 (n. 2) ; in DP, *Journal,* 1822, 2, pp. 175 (misnumbered 157)–176; C. L. Lewis, *op. cit.,* pp. 109–110; SecNav to DP, 13 July 1814; USND, LS; DP to SecNav, 9 July 1814, USND, LRC; DP, *Journal,* 1822, 2, p. 176.

34. *American Advocate* (Hallowell, Maine), 16 July 1814; *Independent Chronicle* (Boston), 1 August 1814; *Niles National Register,* 23 July 1814; DDP, *Memoir,* p. 254; William Bainbridge to DP, 28 July 1814, Container 15, DP Papers, LC; DP to SecNav, 23 August 1814, USND, LRC.

35. F. F. Beirne, *The War of 1812,* p. 335; A. T. Mahan, *Sea Power in Its Relations to the War of 1812,* 2, pp. 398–406, 94.

36. DDP, *Memoir,* pp. 261, 254; Glenn Tucker, *Poltroons and Patriots . . .* , 2, pp. 552–553; *Annual Register . . . for the Year 1814* (London), p. 185.

37. DP to SecNav, 23 August 1814, USND, LRC; in DDP, *Memoir,* p. 255; Loyall Farragut, *op. cit.,* p. 49; DP to SecNav, 27 August 1814, USND, LRC; C. O. Paullin, *op. cit.,* pp. 285–286.

38. DDP, *Memoir*, p. 256; William James, *The Naval History of Great Britain
. . .* , 6, p. 456; DP to SecNav, 19 July 1814, USND, LRC; *Niles National
Register,* 15 April 1815; William James, *op. cit.,* p. 456; DDP, *Memoir,* pp.
256–257.

39. DP to SecNav, 7 September 1814, USND, LRC; DDP, *Memoir,* pp. 257–260;
J. S. Williams, *History of the Invasion and Capture of Washington . . .* , p.
295; C. O. Paullin, *op. cit.,* p. 287; William James, *op. cit.,* p. 463; F. F.
Beirne, *op. cit.,* p. 311.

40. DP to SecNav, 29 October 1814, USND, LRC; Pierre Irving, *The Life and
Letters of Washington Irving,* 1, p. 231; DP to SecNav, 14 October, 9
December 1814, 8 February 1815, USND, LRC; *Annual Register . . . for the
Year 1814* (London), p. 176.

41. DP to SecNav, 12, 21 February 1815, USND, LRC; S. F. Bemis, *John Quincy
Adams and the Foundations of American Foreign Policy,* p. 489; in *Niles
National Register,* 10 March 1821.

42. Frederick Merk, "The Genesis of the Oregon Question," MVHR, 36 (March
1950) , p. 593; A. S. Mackenzie, *The Life of Commodore Oliver Hazard
Perry,* 2, pp. 101–102; Charles Morris, *Autobiography,* pp. 75–76.

43. DP to Joel R. Poinsett, 20, 28 July 1816, Gilpin Collection; Frederick Merk,
op. cit., p. 593; A. P. Whitaker, *The United States and the Independence of
Latin America, 1800–1830,* p. 194 (n. 11) .

44. *National Intelligencer* (Washington, D.C.) , 25, 26 January 1821; *Niles
National Register,* 10 March 1821; S. F. Bemis, *op. cit.,* pp. 488–489; C. O.
Paullin, *Diplomatic Negotiations of American Naval Officers, 1778–1883,* p.
220; A. B. Cole (ed.) , "Captain David Porter's Proposed Expedition to the
Pacific and Japan, 1815," *Pacific Historical Review,* 9 (1940) , pp. 61–65;
Tyler Dennett, *Americans in Eastern Asia . . .* , p. 243; A. B. Cole (ed.) , *op.
cit.,* pp. 61–65.

VII

Porter's activities between 1815 and 1822 divide into four sections and
Chapter VII covers them as follows: his work as a member of the Board of Navy
Commissioners; his ownership of an estate in Washington and the commence-
ment of financial difficulties from which he never escaped; his part in the
Barron-Decatur duel; and his significant role in connection with the develop-
ment of a Latin-American policy for the United States.

Information about his tenure as a Navy Commissioner comes from Richard
S. West, Jr., *The Second Admiral: A Life of David Dixon Porter, 1813–1891,*
David Dixon Porter, *Memoir,* and naval histories by Allan Westcott et al.,
Harold and Margaret Sprout, Edgar S. Maclay, and Alfred T. Mahan; the best
account is Charles O. Paullin, *Commodore John Rodgers. . . .*

I owe a particular debt to Robert B. Lyle, Executive Director of the
Columbia Historical Society in Washington, who wrote me a lengthy letter on

Porter's estate at Meridian Hill, and directed me to pertinent magazine articles. West and Paullin are also utilized, and, on this subject, even David Dixon Porter's generally unreliable *Memoir* may be read with some confidence. Porter's financial troubles are outlined in letters to and from Samuel Hambleton in the David Porter and Samuel Hambleton Papers.

Three works are basic for the Barron-Decatur duel and Porter's role in it: Hamilton Cochran, *Noted American Duels and Hostile Encounters*, Don C. Seitz, *Famous American Duels*, and, primarily, C. S. Forester's "Bloodshed at Dawn" in *American Heritage*. C. L. Lewis, *The Romantic Decatur*, Alexander S. Mackenzie, *The Life of Commodore Oliver Hazard Perry*, C. O. Paullin, and David Dixon Porter provide additional facts and interpretations.

Two authors were invaluable in comprehending Porter's activities in U.S. Latin-American affairs, especially his support of José Miguel Carrera in Chile. Laura Bornholdt's *Baltimore and Early Pan-Americanism*. . . . is first rate. Joseph F. Straub's unpublished doctoral dissertation, a biography of José Miguel Carrera, leaves much to be desired in literary style, but contains abundant and exclusive material. For Latin-American backgrounds on Chile and Argentina, Luis Galdames and Ricardo Levene, respectively, were consulted. Early American interest in Latin America must surely be one of the most thoroughly covered episodes in American diplomatic history, and I have availed myself of the output of John Quincy Adams, Samuel F. Bemis, Henry C. Evans, Jr., Charles C. Griffin, John C. Pine, William S. Robertson, Graham H. Stuart, and Arthur P. Whitaker. The three volumes of William R. Manning (ed.), *Diplomatic Correspondence of the United States Concerning the Independence of the Latin American Nations*, were extensively utilized.

1. United States Congress, *American State Papers, Naval Affairs*, 1, pp. 356–357; Allan Westcott et al., *American Sea Power Since 1775*, p. 88; C. O. Paullin, *Commodore John Rodgers*, pp. 304–306.

2. Harold and Margaret Sprout, *The Rise of American Naval Power, 1776–1918*, pp. 92, 93; C. O. Paullin, *op. cit.*, pp. 305–309; William Bainbridge to DP, 5 June 1815, William Bainbridge Papers; Irving Brant, *James Madison: Commander in Chief, 1812–1836*, p. 388.

3. G. H. Genzmer, "Benjamin W. Crowninshield," DAB, 4, p. 578; J. Q. Adams, 26 October, 2, 3 December 1818, *Memoirs*, 4, pp. 144, 185.

4. DDP, *Memoir*, p. 268; C. O. Paullin, *op. cit.*, pp. 309–311, 316; SecNav to Langston Cheeves, 2 December 1811, in E. S. Maclay, *History of the Navy* . . . , 1, pp. 319–320; A. T. Mahan, *Sea Power in Its Relations to the War of 1812*, 1, pp. 260–262; E. S. Maclay, *op. cit.*, 1, p. 320; DDP, *Memoir*, p. 268.

5. C. O. Paullin, *op. cit.*, pp. 311, 317, 318, 319–320; DDP, *Memoir*, p. 269; C. O. Paullin, *op. cit.*, pp. 320–322.

6. DDP, *Memoir*, pp. 268–269; *National Intelligencer*, 2 March 1819, in C. O. Paullin, *op. cit.*, pp. 316–317; R. S. West, Jr., *The Second Admiral: a Life of David Dixon Porter, 1813–1891*, pp. 6–7.

7. Land Records of the District of Columbia, Liber AL, folio 166, in R. B. Lyle, letter to author, 11 December 1964; DDP, *Memoir*, p. 265; W. B. Bryan, *A

History of the National Capital, 2, pp. 5–6; F. A. Emery, "Mount Pleasant and Meridian Hill," *Records of the Columbia Historical Society,* 33–34 (1932), p. 197; A. B. Cole (ed.), "Captain David Porter's Proposed Expedition to the Pacific and Japan, 1815," *Pacific Historical Review,* 9 (1940), p. 63.

8. R. B. Lyle, letter to author, 11 December 1964; DP to H. M. Brackenridge, 26 October 1817, H. M. Brackenridge, *Letterbook;* C. O. Paullin, *op. cit.,* p. 362; R. S. West, Jr., *op. cit.,* p. 5.

9. H. A. Kellar, "John Stuart Skinner," DAB, 17, p. 200; DDP, *Memoir,* p. 269; J. K. Paulding, *The Bulls and the Jonathans . . . ,* pp. 363–372; DDP, *Memoir,* pp. 270, 273–277; C. L. Lewis, *David Glasgow Farragut . . . ,* pp. 142–143, 313–314 (n. 21); R. S. West, Jr., *op. cit.,* p. 6.

10. DP to Samuel Hambleton, n.d. (1817), 21 November 1817, Container 15, DP Papers, 2, LC; Laura Bornholdt, *Baltimore and Early Pan-Americanism: A Study in the Background of the Monroe Doctrine,* p. 67; DP to Samuel Hambleton, 12 May, 5 November 1818, Container 15, DP Papers, LC; DP to Samuel Hambleton, 13 November 1818, Samuel Hambleton Papers; DP to Samuel Hambleton, n.d. (1818), 14 July 1819, Container 15, DP Papers, LC.

11. C. O. Paullin, *op. cit.,* p. 302; R. S. West, Jr., *op. cit.,* p. 7; Stephen Decatur to DP, 22 March 1815 (misdated 1814), in C. L. Lewis, *The Romantic Decatur,* p. 154.

12. C. S. Forester, "Bloodshed at Dawn," *American Heritage,* 15 (October 1964), p. 45; D. C. Seitz, *Famous American Duels,* p. 168; Hamilton Cochran, *Noted American Duels . . . ,* p. 68.

13. Hamilton Cochran, *op. cit.,* p. 53; A. S. Mackenzie, *The Life of Commodore Oliver Hazard Perry,* 2, pp. 182–183; C. S. Forester, *op. cit.,* p. 74; William Bainbridge Papers; C. L. Lewis, *The Romantic Decatur,* p. 216; Hamilton Cochran, *op. cit.,* pp. 68, 70.

14. A. S. Mackenzie, *op. cit.,* 1, p. 281, 2, pp. 128–136, 182–183; Glenn Tucker, *Poltroons and Patriots . . . ,* 1, p. 400; Hamilton Cochran, *op. cit.,* p. 65.

15. Hamilton Cochran, *op. cit.,* pp. 72, 74; C. S. Forester, *op. cit.,* p. 76; DDP, *Memoir,* p. 417.

16. Hamilton Cochran, *op. cit.,* pp. 75–77; DDP, *Memoir,* pp. 417–418; D. C. Seitz, *op. cit.,* p. 225; C. L. Lewis, *The Romantic Decatur,* p. 232.

17. DDP, *Memoir,* p. 418; DP to Samuel Hambleton, 20 April 1820, DP Papers, 2, LC; John Rodgers to DP, 7 August 1822, John Rodgers Papers.

18. J. F. Straub, *José Miguel Carrera,* p. 86; W. S. Robertson, *Rise of the Spanish-American Republics . . . ,* p. 186; A. P. Whitaker, *The United States and the Independence of Latin America, 1800–1830,* pp. 199–200; S. F. Bemis, "Early Diplomatic Missions from Buenos Aires to the United States, 1811–1824," *Proceedings of the American Antiquarian Society,* 49 (19 April 1939), p. 39; J. F. Straub, *op. cit.,* p. 117–120.

19. Laura Bornholdt, *Baltimore and Early Pan-Americanism: A Study in the Background of the Monroe Doctrine,* pp. 79, 61–62; J. F. Straub, *op. cit.,* p. 122; DP to James Monroe, 3 January 1819, in S. F. Bemis, *op. cit.,* p. 39; José Miguel Carrera to Luis Carrera, n.d. (February 1816), in G. H. Stuart, *Latin America and the United States,* p. 414; J. E. Straub, *op. cit.,* p. 123.

20. Laura Bornholdt, *op. cit.*, p. 67; J. Q. Adams, 1 February 1820, *Memoirs*, 4, p. 516; J. F. Straub, *op. cit.*, p. 131.

21. Theodorick Bland, 25 May 1818, *Diary*, in Laura Bornholdt, *op. cit.*, p. 62; C. C. Griffin, *The United States and the Disruption of the Spanish Empire, 1810–1822*, p. 128; J. F. Straub, *op. cit.*, pp. 127, 128; J. Q. Adams, 1 February 1820, *Memoirs*, 4, pp. 515–516.

22. J. F. Straub, *op. cit.*, p. 128; Laura Bornholdt, *op. cit.*, pp. 68–69; J. C. Pine, *The Role of United States Special Agents in the Development of a Spanish American Policy, 1810–1822*, p. 461; J. F. Straub, *op. cit.*, p. 130; Laura Bornholdt, *op. cit.*, p. 68.

23. Laura Bornholdt, *op. cit.*, pp. 65, 66–67; J. C. Pine, *op. cit.*, p. 502; J. Q. Adams, *Memoirs*, 5, p. 57, in A. P. Whitaker, *op. cit.*, p. 291 (n. 27); J. Q. Adams, 22 November 1819, *Memoirs*, 4, pp. 444–445.

24. Laura Bornholdt, *op. cit.*, p. 60; J. F. Straub, *op. cit.*, pp. 128, 131; S. F. Bemis, *op. cit.*, p. 40; J. F. Straub, *op. cit.*, pp. 143, 146–150; A. P. Whitaker, *op. cit.*, pp. 233–234.

25. Laura Bornholdt, *op. cit.*, p. 131; DP to Joel R. Poinsett, 19 October 1818, Joel R. Poinsett Papers; *Baltimore Patriot*, 28 March 1818, in Laura Bornholdt, *op. cit.*, p. 107 (n. 55); Luis Galdames, *A History of Chile*, p. 486; J. F. Straub, *op. cit.*, p. 133; DP to Joel R. Poinsett, 19 October 1818, Joel R. Poinsett Papers.

26. "Lautaro, I–VII," *National Intelligencer*, 30 September–8 October 1817; DP to Joel R. Poinsett, 23 October 1817, Joel R. Poinsett Papers.

27. J. C. Pine, *op. cit.*, p. 243; Address of Henry Clay in Congress, 28 March 1818, in J. F. Straub, *op. cit.*, p. 136; Laura Bornholdt, *op. cit.*, p. 79.

28. J. F. Straub, *op. cit.*, p. 138; DP to Joel R. Poinsett, 23 October 1817, Joel R. Poinsett Papers; G. H. Ryden, "Caesar Augustus Rodney," DAB, 16, p. 83; A. C. Gordon, "John Graham," DAB, 7, p. 478; SecState to Caesar A. Rodney and John Graham, 18 July 1817, in W. R. Manning (ed.), *Diplomatic Correspondence of the United States Concerning the Independence of the Latin American Nations*, 1, pp. 42–45.

29. H. M. Brackenridge, *Voyage to South America . . .* , 2, pp. 313–359; A. P. Whitaker, *op. cit.*, p. 249; H. M. Brackenridge, *op. cit., passim;* DP to H. M. Brackenridge, 26 October 1817, H. M. Brackenridge, *Letterbook;* W. F. Keller, *The Nation's Advocate: Henry Marie Brackenridge and Young America*, p. 193; DP to Joel R. Poinsett, 23 October 1817, Joel R. Poinsett Papers.

30. Laura Bornholdt, *op. cit.*, p. 102; SecState to Caesar A. Rodney, John Graham, and Theodorick Bland, 21 November 1817, in W. R. Manning (ed.), *op. cit.*, 1, p. 49; H. C. Evans, Jr., *Chile and . . . the United States*, pp. 23–24.

31. Laura Bornholdt, *op. cit.*, p. 91; H. M. Brackenridge, *op. cit.*, 1, pp. 237–239; Laura Bornholdt, *op. cit.*, p. 104.

32. Luis Galdames, *op. cit.*, p. 197; Ricardo Levene, *A History of Argentina*, pp. 311–312; Luis Galdames, *op. cit.*, pp. 212–215; J. C. Pine, *op. cit.*, pp. 276–278, 283 (n. 131), 282.

33. SecState to Richard Rush, 30 July 1818, in W. R. Manning (ed.), *op. cit.*, 1,

p. 74; J. C. Pine, *op. cit.*, p. 282; Theodorick Bland to SecState, 2 November 1818, in W. R. Manning (ed.), *op. cit.*, 2, pp. 946–1005; Bernardo O'Higgins to John B. Prevost, 30 September 1819, in *ibid.*, p. 554; J. C. Pine, *op. cit.*, pp. 304–306; H. M. Brackenridge, *op. cit.*, 2, p. 33; Baptis Irvine, *Strictures on a Voyage to South America* . . . , p. iii.

34. J. F. Straub, *op. cit.*, pp. 152, 153–156; W. B. Stevenson, *Historical and Descriptive Narrative of Twenty Years Residence in South America*, 3, p. 129.

35. DP to James Monroe, 2 January 1819, James Monroe Papers; Baptis Irvine, *op. cit.*, pp. 40–41, 53; J. F. Straub, *op. cit.*, pp. 175–181; Luis Galdames, *op. cit.*, p. 206.

VIII

This chapter narrates the pivotal events of 1823 and 1824 which wrecked David Porter's career in the U.S. Navy. He accepted command of the West India Squadron, with his primary responsibility the eradication of the pirates who infested those waters. In general, he did well until late in 1824, when he landed with armed American forces at Fajardo in Spanish Puerto Rico to exact from local officials an apology for insults rendered to two of his officers. By that time, he had, for a number of reasons, incurred the hostility of President James Monroe, Secretary of State John Quincy Adams, and Secretary of the Navy Samuel L. Southard.

Basic sources for this chapter are collections of the Navy and State Departments. For the first: USND, Letters Received by Secretary of the Navy from Captains (LRC), and USND, Letters Sent by Secretary of the Navy to Officers (LS). For the second: USSD, Consular Dispatches, San Juan; USSD, Notes from Foreign Legations, Great Britain; and USSD, Dispatches from Special Agents, Thomas Randall. William R. Manning's three-volume *Diplomatic Correspondence of the United States Concerning the Independence of the Latin American Nations* is helpful, and the David Porter Papers are frequently cited. Essential are John Quincy Adams' *Memoirs*, Volumes 6 and 7. Biographies of David Porter, David Dixon Porter, and David Glasgow Farragut are supplemented by previously cited naval histories, Gardner W. Allen, *Our Navy and the West Indian Pirates*, and Francis B. C. Bradlee, *Piracy in the West Indies and Its Suppression*. Explanations and circumstances of Porter's landing at Fajardo are found in the disorganized but invaluable USND, Records of General Courts Martial and Courts of Inquiry of the Navy Department, 1799–1867 (RGCM) for both of Porter's court sessions. The first was "Minutes of the Proceedings of a Court of Inquiry directed to investigate the conduct of David Porter" (DPCI). The second was the "Court Martial of David Porter" (DPCM). Also used was Porter's published pamphlet entitled *An Exposition of the Facts and Circumstances which Justified the Expedition to Foxardo. . . ."*

1. Henry R. Wadsworth to Henry Clay, 10 December 1822, in J. F. Hopkins (ed.), *The Papers of Henry Clay*, 3, p. 337; SecNav to DP, 20 December 1822, USND, LS; *Niles National Register*, 11 January 1823.

2. SecState to MinSpain, 28 April 1823, in W. R. Manning (ed.), *Diplomatic Correspondence of the United States Concerning the Independence of the Latin American Nations*, 1, p. 183; DDP, *Memoir*, p. 271; *Nantucket Inquirer*, 25 June 1822; *Niles National Register*, 19 April 1823.

3. Allan Westcott et al., *American Sea Power Since 1775*, p. 93; A. P. Whitaker, *The United States and the Independence of Latin America, 1800–1830*, p. 273; *Annals of Congress*, 15th Congress, 2nd Session, 2, p. 1418, in *ibid.*, p. 286.

4. DDP, *Memoir*, p. 271; C. L. Lewis, *David Glasgow Farragut . . .* , p. 152; E. S. Maclay, *History of the Navy from 1775 to 1893*, 2, pp. 111–112; DDP, *Memoir*, p. 271; James Biddle to Governor of Cuba, 30 April 1822, in G. W. Allen, *Our Navy and the West Indian Pirates*, p. 28; Governor of Cuba to James Biddle, n.d., in *Niles National Register*, 1 June 1822.

5. J. Q. Adams, 20 July 1818, *Memoirs*, 4, p. 113; H. B. Clarke, *Modern Spain, 1815–1898*, pp. 65–71.

6. SecState to DP, 1 February 1823, USND, LS.

7. DP to SecNav, 5 February 1823, USND, LRC; DP to Evalina Porter, 11 November 1826, DP Papers, 3, LC; C. L. Lewis, *op. cit.*, pp. 154–155; Loyall Farragut, *The Life of David Glasgow Farragut . . .* , p. 92; *Columbian Centinel* (Boston), 22 October 1831.

8. DP to "Commissioners of the Navy," 21 December 1822, in USND, "Minutes of the Proceedings of a Court of Inquiry directed to investigate the conduct of David Porter," Records of General Courts Martial and Courts of Inquiry of the Navy Department, 1799–1867, DPCI, RGCM; DDP, *Memoir*, p. 281; E. S. Maclay, *op. cit.*, 2, p. 112.

9. R. S. West, Jr., *The Second Admiral: a Life of David Dixon Porter, 1813–1891*, p. 11; DP to SecNav, 25 June 1824, USND, LRC; C. L. Lewis, *op. cit.*, p. 153.

10. *St. Thomas Times*, n.d., in A. D. Turnbull, *Commodore David Porter, 1780–1843*, p. 256.

11. G. W. Allen, *op. cit.*, p. 42; C. L. Lewis, *op. cit.*, pp. 156–157; *Niles National Register*, 19 April 1823; DP to Governor of Puerto Rico, n.d., in DDP, *Memoir*, p. 284; Governor of Puerto Rico to DP, n.d., in *ibid.*, p. 285.

12. *Niles National Register*, 19 April 1823; SecState to MinSpain, 28 April 1823, in W. R. Manning (ed.), *op. cit.*, 1, p. 185; MinSpain to Foreign Minister of Spain, 10 January 1824, in *ibid.*; SecState to MinSpain, 28 April 1823, in United States Congress, *American State Papers, Foreign Relations*, 5, p. 408.

13. C. L. Lewis, *op. cit.*, p. 156; D. G. Farragut, *Journal*, n.d., in E. S. Maclay, *op. cit.*, 2, pp. 116–117; G. F. Emmons, *The Navy of the United States . . .* , p. 78, in C. L. Lewis, *op. cit.*, p. 342 (n. 16) ; E. S. Maclay, *op. cit.*, 2, p. 118; C. L. Lewis, *op. cit.*, pp. 161–162; DP to SecNav, 16 April 1823, in USND, LRC.

14. G. F. Emmons, *op. cit.*, p. 78, in C. L. Lewis, *op. cit.*, p. 342 (n. 16) ;

J. Wilkinson to DP, 24 April 1824; USND, LRC; DP to SecNav, 10 August 1824, *ibid.*, Isaac Chauncey to Judge Advocate, 23 May 1825, USND, DPCI, RGCM; C. L. Lewis, *op. cit.*, p. 161.

15. *New-York Evening Post,* 10 April 1823; DP, letter, n.d., in *ibid.*, n.d., in A. D. Turnbull, *op. cit.*, p. 262; *New-York Evening Post,* 23 April 1823, in *Niles National Register,* 17 May 1823.

16. DP, "private letter," n.d., in *Niles National Register,* 19 July 1823; Governor of Cuba to DP, 10 May 1823, DP Papers, 3, LC; DP to Governor of Cuba, 20 January 1825, in *ibid.*, 24 February 1825; SecState to MinSpain, 28 April 1823, in W. R. Manning (ed.), *op. cit.*, 1, p. 184.

17. F. B. C. Bradlee, *Piracy in the West Indies and Its Suppression,* pp. 46–47; DP to SecNav, 10 May 1823, USND, LRC; A. T. Mahan, *Admiral Farragut,* p. 65; DP to SecNav, 10 May 1823, USND, LRC.

18. In A. D. Turnbull, *op. cit.*, p. 263; C. L. Lewis, *op. cit.*, p. 162; Edmund DuBarry to SecNav, 25 September 1838, Container 15, DP Papers, LC; Ralph Voorhees to SecNav, 4 October 1838, *ibid.*, C. L. Lewis, *op. cit.*, p. 163; *Nantucket Inquirer,* 4 November 1823.

19. R. E. Cushman, "Smith Thompson," DAB, 18, pp. 471–473; C. O. Paullin, *Commodore John Rodgers . . . ,* p. 325; Letters signed by Isaac Chauncey, October 1823, USND, DPCI, RGCM; R. G. Albion, "Samuel Lewis Southard," DAB, 17, pp. 411–412; *Nantucket Inquirer,* 2 September 1823; Letters signed by Samuel L. Southard, USND, LS; A. D. Turnbull, *op. cit.*, p. 263; SecNav to DP, 27 September 1823, USND, LS; C. O. Paullin, *op. cit.*, p. 323.

20. SecNav to DP, 28 October 1823, USND, LS; J. D. Richardson (ed.), . . . *Messages . . . of the Presidents,* 2, pp. 213–214; Judah Lord to SecState, 12, 19 November 1823, USSD, Consular Dispatches, San Juan.

21. SecNav to DP, 22 December 1823, USND, LS; DP to SecNav, 24 January 1824, USND, LRC; SecNav to DP, 22 December 1823, USND, LS; DP to SecNav, 16 October 1824, USND, LRC; SecNav to DP, 22 December 1823, USND, LS.

22. DP to SecNav, 18 February 1824, USND, LRC; R. S. West, Jr., *op. cit.*, pp. 11–12; DP to SecNav, 4 May 1824, USND, LRC; R. S. West, Jr., *op. cit.*, pp. 12–13; DP to SecNav, 25 June 1824, USND, LRC; R. S. West, Jr., *op. cit.*, p. 11; ? to ? (fragmentary letter), 24 June 1824, USND, DPCI, RGCM.

23. James Monroe, Deposition in answer to queries of DP's Court-martial, 25 July 1825, USND, DPCI, RGCM; ? to ? (fragmentary letter), 24 June 1824, *ibid.*; SecNav to DP, 21 October 1824, USND, LS.

24. John Lawrence to Sylvester Allen, 4 July, John Lawrence to DP, 5 July, DP to John Lawrence, 23 July, Sir Edward Owen to DP, 28 September 1823, USSD, Notes from Foreign Legations, Great Britain; DP to Sir Edward Owen, 22 November 1823, in DP to SecNav, 25 June 1824, USND, LRC.

25. British Chargé d'Affaires to SecState, 4 May 1824, USSD, Notes from Foreign Legations, Great Britain; J. Q. Adams, 7 May 1824, *Memoirs,* 6, p. 322; SecNav to DP, 31 May 1824, DP Papers, 3, LC; DP to SecNav, 25 June 1824, USND, LRC.

26. SecNav to DP, 31 December 1823, 5 March 1824, USND, LS; DP, Testimony, 2 February 1824, "Court Martial of David Porter," USND, Records of General Courts Martial and Courts of Inquiry of the Navy Department, 1799–1867, DPCM, RGCM; SecNav to DP, 31 December 1823, to Beverly Kennon, 7, 8 January 1824, USND, LS.

27. Beverly Kennon, Defense, Court Martial Decision, 24 February 1824, "Court Martial of Lieutenant Beverly Kennon," USND, RGCM; SecNav to DP, 29 March 1824, USND, LS; DP to SecNav, 5 June 1824, USND, LRC; John Rodgers to DP, 17 January 1824, John Rodgers Papers.

28. DP to SecNav, 18 October 1824, USND, LRC; R. S. West, Jr., *op. cit.*, p. 13; SecNav to DP, 29 July 1824, USND, LS; DP to SecNav, 10, 11 August 1824, USND, LRC.

29. John Mountain, letter, 5 July 1824, in *Niles National Register*, 15 October 1825; Thomas Randall to SecState, 6 September, 31 October 1824, USSD, Special Agents, Randall.

30. DP to SecNav, 12 October 1824, USND, LRC; SecNav to DP, 14 October 1824, USND, LS; R. W. Logan, *The Diplomatic Relations Between the United States and Haiti, 1776–1891*, p. 214.

31. DP to SecNav, 18 October 1824, USND, LRC; SecNav to DP, 21 October 1824, USND, LS; DP to SecNav, 22 October 1824, USND, LRC; DP to President James Monroe, 26 October 1824, *ibid.*, President James Monroe to DP, 12 March 1825, USND, DPCI, RGCM; DP to President James Monroe, 12 March 1825, *ibid.*

32. SecNav to President James Monroe, 1 December 1824, in DDP, *Memoir*, p. 296; J. D. Richardson, *op. cit.*, 2, pp. 258–259; J. Q. Adams, 2 December 1824, *Memoirs*, 6, p. 434.

33. DP to SecNav, 15 November 1824, USND, LRC; Advertisement, "$1,000 Reward," Cabot, Bailey & Co., 25 October 1824, USND, DPCI, RGCM; Charles T. Platt, Report, 11 November 1824, in DP to SecNav, 15 November 1824, USND, LRC.

34. Charles T. Platt, Report, 11 November 1824, in DP to SecNav, 15 November 1824, USND, LRC; Charles T. Platt, Testimony, 8 July 1825, USND, DPCM, RGCM; Robert Ritchie, Testimony, 11 July, *ibid.*, Charles T. Platt, Testimony, 9 July 1825, *ibid.*

35. DP to SecNav, 15 November 1824, USND, LRC; Charles T. Platt, Testimony, 9 July 1825, USND, DPCM, RGCM; DP to SecNav, 15 November 1824, USND, LRC; DP, *An Exposition of the Facts and Circumstances which Justified the Expedition to Foxardo . . . (Exposition)*, n.p. number, in DDP, *Memoir*, p. 329.

IX

This chapter recounts the direct consequences of David Porter's landing at Fajardo in Spanish Puerto Rico late in 1824: namely, his abrupt removal from command of the West India Squadron, the proceedings of the court of inquiry set up to investigate the circumstances of the landing, and the court-martial that followed in 1825. The animus against Porter, easily discernible in the James Monroe administration, was passed along in even more obvious form to the John Quincy Adams administration, which actively worked to condemn Porter. Instead of showing at least some contrition, which might have saved him, Porter fought back with every resource at his command, thereby incurring even greater administrative hostility. His court-martial found him guilty of disobedience and insubordination toward President Adams and Secretary of the Navy Samuel L. Southard. Even though his sentence of suspension for six months at full pay was remarkably lenient, he resigned his commission in the U.S. Navy, in which he had served for twenty-eight years, and prepared for what turned out to be lifelong exile.

To a considerably greater extent than in Chapter VIII, USND, Records of General Courts-Martial and Courts of Inquiry of the Navy Department, 1799–1867 (RGCM) have been used as the basic documentation for both Porter's Court of Inquiry (DPCI) and his Court-Martial (DPCM). The papers of David Porter, James Monroe, and John Rodgers are frequently cited. Especially valuable are the writings of President John Quincy Adams. His published *Memoirs*, Volumes 6 and 7, have been helpful, but they often omit specific dates and appointments. Two collections at the Massachusetts Historical Society, Adams' *Diary* and his "Rubbish III," contain little more than daily listing of appointments: nevertheless, they fill many gaps left by the *Memoirs*. David Porter's special pleading in his published defense, *An Exposition into the Facts and Circumstances which Justified the Expedition to Foxardo . . . ,* is used sparingly. Biographies of David Porter, David Dixon Porter, and John Rodgers, as well as David Dixon Porter's *Memoir,* have been consulted. Thanks to the intense national interest aroused by David Porter's confrontation with two successive administrations, contemporary newspapers have been cited with greater frequency than usual, as have later commentaries on the justice of Porter's conviction by the court-martial.

1. DP to SecNav, 24 January 1825, USND, LRC; SecNav to DP, 27 December 1824, USND, LS. SecNav, n.d., in G. W. Allen, *Our Navy and the West Indian Pirates,* p. 86; SecNav to Lewis Warrington, 27 December 1824, USND, LS.

2. J. Q. Adams, 16, 24 December 1824, *Memoirs,* 6, pp. 445, 453–454; James Monroe, "Rough Notes," 18 July 1825, James Monroe Papers, Series I, 34; James Monroe, Deposition in answer to the queries of DP's court-martial, 25 July 1825, USND, DPCI, RGCM; *Boston Weekly Messenger,* 4 August 1825.

3. J. Q. Adams, 24 December 1824, *Memoirs,* 6, pp. 453–454; J. D. Richardson, *op. cit.,* 2, pp. 276–277.

4. J. R. Soley, *Admiral Porter,* p. 13; *La Gaceta de Puerto Rico,* November 1824–June 1825, *passim;* DP to Governor of Cuba, 20 January, Governor of Cuba to DP, 22 January 1825, in *Niles National Register,* 26 February 1825.

BIBLIOGRAPHIC NOTES

5. DP to Lewis Warrington, 28, 29 January 1825, USND, DPCI, RGCM; Fletcher Pratt, *Preble's Boys* . . . , pp. 292–293; DP to SecNav, 30 January 1825, USND, LRC; SecNav to John Rodgers, 28 February 1825, John Rodgers Papers; J. Q. Adams, 3 January 1825, "Rubbish III"; J. Q. Adams, 25 January 1825, *Memoirs*, 6, p. 479.

6. DP to SecNav, 8 March 1815, USND, LRC; Joel R. Poinsett, Address, 7 February 1825, *Register of Debates . . . Congress*, Gales & Seaton, 1, p. 488; DP to James Monroe, 10 March 1825, USND, DPCI, RGCM; James Monroe to DP, 12 March 1825, *ibid.*, DP to James Monroe, 12 March 1825, *ibid.*

7. J. Q. Adams, 12 March 1825, *Diary;* DP to Samuel Hambleton, 15 March 1825, DP Papers, 3, LC; DP to SecNav, 17 March 1825, USND, LRC; SecNav to DP, 16 March 1825, USND, LS; DP to SecNav, 19 March 1825, USND, LRC.

8. J. Q. Adams, 30 May 1825, *Memoirs, 7*, p. 18; J. Q. Adams, 15 April 1825, *Diary;* J. Q. Adams, 16, 17 April 1825, *Memoirs, 6*, p. 529; Charges and specifications against DP, 7 July 1825, USND, DPCM, RGCM.

9. DP to SecNav, 13 April 1825, USND, LRC, in SecNav to DP, 20 April 1825, USND, LS; SecNav to DP, 20 April 1825, *ibid.*

10. J. Q. Adams, 16 April, 10 May 1825, *Memoirs, 6*, p. 520; Isaac Chauncey, Decision, 5 May 1825, USND, DPCM, RGCM; DP, Testimony, 10 August 1825, *ibid.*, J. Q. Adams, 6 May 1825, "Rubbish III."

11. Isaac Chauncey to Judge Advocate, 25 May 1825, USND, DPCI, RGCM; Court of Inquiry verdict, 9 May 1825, *ibid.*

12. J. Q. Adams, 12 May 1825, *Memoirs, 6*, pp. 544–545; J. Q. Adams, 14 May 1825, "Rubbish III"; SecNav to DP, 28 May, 22 June 1825, USND, LS.

13. J. Q. Adams, 17, 26–28 May 1825, *Diary;* J. Q. Adams, 30 May 1825, *Memoirs, 7*, p. 18; J. Q. Adams, 1, 6 July, 5 August 1825, *Diary.*

14. DP, "Advertisement of Exposition . . . ," 11 May 1825, in *Niles National Register*, 18 June 1825; DP, *Exposition*, n.p. number, in DDP, *Memoir*, pp. 309–311; J. Q. Adams, 2 June 1825, *Memoirs, 7*, p. 22; SecNav to DP, 13 June 1825, Container 15, DP Papers, LC; DP to SecNav, 14 June 1825, USND, LRC.

15. *Niles National Register*, 18 June 1825; G. W. Allen (ed.), *The Papers of Isaac Hull*, pp. 62–63; F. W. Waldo, *Trial of Lieutenant Joel Abbot . . . on Allegations Made Against Him by Captain David Porter, passim.*

16. List of Court-martial judges, 7 July 1825, USND, DPCM, RGCM; B. J. Lossing, *The Pictorial Field-Book of the War of 1812*, p. 724; DP to John Downes, 1 January 1825, DP Papers, Van Ness Collection.

17. DP, Testimony, 10 August 1825, USND, DPCM, RGCM; Charges and specifications against DP, 7 July 1825, *ibid.*

18. DP, Testimony, 7 July 1825, USND, DPCM, RGCM; Judge Advocate's decision, 7 July 1825, *ibid.;* Court-martial decision, 7 July 1825, *ibid.;* A. D. Turnbull, *Commodore David Porter, 1780–1843*, p. 278.

19. Prosecution testimony, 8 July–3 August 1825, USND, DPCM, RGCM: DP, Testimony, 5, 6 August 1825, *ibid.*

20. *Niles National Register,* 16 July 1825; *New-York Spectator,* 5, 13 August 1825; *Boston Patriot,* n.d., in *Salem Gazette,* 19 August 1825; *Salem Gazette,* 19 August 1825; *Worcester Yeoman,* n.d., in *ibid.*

21. J. Q. Adams, 28 July 1825, *Memoirs,* 7, p. 38; George Harrison to John Rodgers, 25 July 1825, John Rodgers Papers; T. H. Benton, *Thirty Years' View . . . ,* 2, p. 498; A. D. Turnbull, *op. cit.,* pp. 266–267.

22. Court-martial verdict, 10 August 1825, *ibid.;* J. Q. Adams, 30 May 1825, *Memoirs,* 7, p. 19; Verdict, Court-martial of Midshipman Alexander Van Dyke, 9 May 1825, USND, RGCM; DP to Joel R. Poinsett, 21 August 1825, Gilpin Collection; Court-martial verdict, 10 August 1825, USND, DPCM, RGCM.

23. Court-martial decisions, 6–13 August 1825, USND, DPCM, RGCM; J. Q. Adams, 13 August 1825, "Rubbish III;" J. Q. Adams, 16 August 1825, *Diary;* J. Q. Adams, 17 August 1825, "Rubbish III."

24. DP to SecNav, 17 August 1825, USND, LRC; J. Q. Adams, 19 August 1825, *Diary,* "Rubbish III."

25. J. B. Nolan, *Lafayette in America Day by Day, passim;* DDP, *Memoir,* p. 312; J. Q. Adams, 3 September 1825, *Diary;* Unsigned letter, n.d., Container 15, DP Papers, LC; J. Q. Adams, 3 September 1825, *Diary; National Intelligencer,* 3 September 1825; Unsigned letter, n.d., Container 15, DP Papers, LC.

26. Charles Morris to John Rodgers, 4 October 1825, John Rodgers Papers; J. Q. Adams, 19 December 1825, *Memoirs,* 7, p. 87.

27. DP, Letter, n.d., in *National Intelligencer,* n.d., in *Eastern Argus* (Portland, Me.) , 30 August 1825; DDP, *Memoir,* p. 343; DP to Evalina Porter, n.d. (probably early 1827) , DP Papers. 4. LC: Evalina Porter to press, n.d., DP Papers, Van Ness Collection; DP to Hezekiah Niles, 19 March 1832, in *Niles National Register,* 25 August 1832.

28. *Franklin* (Pa.) *Gazette,* n.d., in *National Intelligencer,* 30 August 1825; *National Intelligencer,* 18 August 1825; *Niles National Register,* 27 August 1825; *American Annual Register for the Years 1825–1826,* p. 51; *Richmond Enquirer,* n.d., in *New Hampshire Patriot and State Gazette* (Concord) , 5 September 1825.

29. *New-York Spectator,* 22 August 1825; *Portsmouth Journal* (N.H.) , 3 September 1825; *Salem Gazette,* 26 August 1825; *Nantucket Inquirer,* 29 August 1825.

30. T. H. Benton, *Thirty Years' View . . . ,* 2, p. 498; Edward Everett to A. H. Everett, 9 September 1825, Edward Everett Papers; DP, *Trial of Lieutenant Joel Abott . . . , passim;* Niles National Register, 15 October 1825.

31. Samuel Perkins, *Historical Sketches of the United States . . . ,* p. 22; DDP, *Memoir,* pp. 342–343; DDP to John Barnes, 3 May 1875, DDP Papers, NYHS; R. S. West, Jr., *The Second Admiral: A Life of David Dixon Porter,* pp. 16–17.

32. G. W. Allen, *Our Navy and the West Indian Pirates,* p. 71; A. D. Turnbull, *op. cit.,* pp. 279–280; Fletcher Pratt, *Preble's Boys . . . ,* pp. 236–237.

33. J. Q. Adams, 20 July 1818, *Memoirs*, 4, p. 113; J. Q. Adams, 24 December 1824, *ibid.*, 6, pp. 543–454.

X

Porter's calamitous service with the Mexican Navy from 1826 to 1829 is discussed in this chapter. Much of my material is based on Robert L. Bidwell's unpublished doctoral dissertation, *The First Mexican Navy, 1821–1830* (University of Virginia, 1960). His research was thorough and his writing is lucid; I have never read a better dissertation. Other essential sources were the David Dixon Porter Papers, Volumes 3 and 4, and the documents in Container 15 at the Library of Congress; the Van Ness Collection at Owings Mills, Maryland, provided a number of useful letters. Most of Porter's voluminous correspondence with Joel R. Poinsett, American Minister to Mexico, is in the Gilpin Collection at the Historical Society of Pennsylvania; the Poinsett Papers there contain little that is pertinent to my subject. Elmer W. Flaccus' article on Porter and the Mexican Navy is based almost entirely on the Gilpin Collection. Biographies of David Dixon Porter and his *Memoir* furnish details otherwise unobtainable.

For U. S. diplomatic problems with Mexico and Spain arising from Porter's naval war against the latter, I have relied upon the U. S. State Department Despatches from Mexico, and Consular Letters, Havana and Veracruz; William R. Manning (ed.), *Diplomatic Correspondence of the United States Concerning the Independence of the Latin American Nations*, 3 volumes; and John Q. Adams *Memoirs*, Volume 7. Information on Mexican internal affairs during Porter's tenure was supplied by James J. Auchmuty, Arthur P. Whitaker, Hubert H. Bancroft, George L. Rives, James A. Magner, and especially W. R. Manning, *Early Diplomatic Relations between the United States and Mexico*. Helpful were biographical materials on Thomas Cochrane by himself, Christopher Lloyd, and Sir John K. Laughton; on Joel R. Poinsett by J. Fred Rippy and Dorothy M. Parton; on José de San Martín by Margaret H. Harrison; and on Mahlon Dickerson by Josiah C. Pumpelly. Contemporary press opinion was gleaned primarily from *Niles National Register* and the *National Intelligencer*.

1. DP to John Rodgers, 6 March 1825, in R. L. Bidwell, *The First Mexican Navy, 1821–1830*, p. 418; Laura Bornholdt, *Baltimore and Early Pan-Americanism* . . . , p. 62.
2. J. J. Auchmuty, *The United States Government and Latin American Independence, 1810–1830*, p. 133; Christopher Lloyd, *Lord Cochrane: Seaman-Radical-Liberator* . . . , pp. 143 ff; M. H. Harrison, *Captain of the Andes: The Life of Don José de San Martin* . . . , p. 114.
3. Thomas Cochrane to José de San Martín, 6 January 1822, in Thomas Cochrane, *Narration of Services in the Liberation of Chili, Peru, and Brazil* . . . , 1, p. 241; R. L. Bidwell, *op. cit.*, pp. 20–22; Sir John K. Laughton, "Thomas Cochrane," DNB, 4, p. 631.

4. Thomas Cochrane and "all the captains," n.d. (probably 1822), in Thomas Cochrane, *op. cit.*, pp. 214, 282; Christopher Lloyd, *op. cit.*, p. 172.

5. A. P. Whitaker, *The United States and the Independence of Latin America, 1800–1830*, p. 591; DP to Joel R. Poinsett, 21 August 1825, Gilpin Collection; W. R. Manning, *Early Diplomatic Relations between the United States and Mexico*, pp. 29–30; DP to Joel R. Poinsett, 22 August 1825, Gilpin Collection; Pablo Obregón to DP, 24 September 1825, *ibid.;* DP to Pablo Obregón, 25 October 1825, *ibid.;* R. L. Bidwell, *op. cit.*, p. 525.

6. *National Intelligencer*, 24 September 1825; DDP, *Memoir*, p. 348.

7. DP to Joel R. Poinsett, 25 October 1825, Gilpin Collection; DP to Mahlon Dickerson, 18 August 1829, Mahlon Dickerson Papers; J. Q. Adams, 10 February 1826, *Memoirs*, 7, p. 115; SecNav to William B. Finch, 7 February 1826, USND, Letters Sent by Secretary of the Navy to Officers.

8. R. L. Bidwell, *op. cit.*, pp. 401–402; DP to Robert Y. Hayne, "December 1829," Container 15, DP Papers, LC; R. L. Bidwell, *op. cit.*, p. 403; J. R. Soley, *Admiral Porter*, p. 18; R. L. Bidwell, *op. cit.*, pp. 425–426.

9. G. L. Rives, *The United States and Mexico, 1821–1848*, 1, p. 37; R. L. Bidwell, *op. cit.*, pp. 325–344, 367–371, 352; DDP, *Memoir*, p. 351.

10. D. M. Parton, *The Diplomatic Career of Joel Roberts Poinsett*, pp. 98–99; R. L. Bidwell, *op. cit.*, pp. 355–358.

11. DDP, *Memoir*, p. 349; R. L. Bidwell, *op. cit.*, p. 289; DDP, *Memoir*, p. 351; *National Intelligencer*, 20 June 1826; DDP, *Memoir*, pp. 351–352.

12. DP to SecNav, 1 July 1826, DP Papers, 3, LC; Joel R. Poinsett to SecState, 8 July 1826, USSD, Despatches from Mexico.

13. DP to Joel R. Poinsett, 16 May (misdated April), 26 July 1826, Gilpin Collection; G. F. Lyon, *Journal of a Residence and Tour in the Republic of Mexico in the Year 1826*, 2, p. 228; DDP, *Memoir*, pp. 252–253.

14. DP to Robert Y. Hayne, "December 1829," Container 15, DP Papers, LC; R. L. Bidwell, *op. cit.*, p. 248; DDP, *Memoir*, p. 355; E. W. Flaccus, "Commodore David Porter and the Mexican Navy," *Hispanic American Historical Review*, 34, No. 3 (August 1954), p. 368; DDP, *Memoir*, p. 355.

15. DDP, *Memoir*, p. 353; DP to Joel R. Poinsett, 30 September 1826, Gilpin Collection; R. L. Bidwell, *op. cit.*, pp. 428–429; DP to Joel R. Poinsett, 15 August 1826, Gilpin Collection.

16. DDP, *Memoir*, p. 354; DP to Joel R. Poinsett, 6 September 1826, Gilpin Collection; R. L. Bidwell, *op. cit.*, p. 437.

17. *El Astro de la America*, 13 October 1826, in *National Intelligencer*, 30 December 1826; DP to "a warm personal friend," in *Niles National Register*, 12 August 1826; DP to Evalina Porter, 11 November 1826, DP Papers, 4, LC; José Rincón to DP, 6 December 1826, DP Papers, Van Ness Collection.

18. R. S. West, Jr., *The Second Admiral: A Life of David Dixon Porter, 1813–1891*, p. 21; DDP, *Memoir*, p. 352; R. L. Bidwell, *op. cit.*, p. 444; *National Intelligencer*, 27 May 1826, in *ibid.*, p. 445; R. L. Bidwell, *op. cit.*, p. 445.

19. DP to Joel R. Poinsett, 5 December 1826, Gilpin Collection; R. L. Bidwell,

op. cit., pp. 446–447; DP to Joel R. Poinsett, 19–20 January, 3 March 1827, Gilpin Collection; DP to Samuel Hambleton, 20 February 1827, DP Papers, 4, LC; *Niles National Register,* 3 February 1827.

20. DP to Samuel Hambleton, 20 February 1827, DP Papers, 4, LC; DDP, *Memoir,* p. 357; *Niles National Register,* 2 June 1827; DP to Joel R. Poinsett, 3 March 1827, Gilpin Collection.

21. R. L. Bidwell, *op. cit.,* pp. 451–453; DP to Joel R. Poinsett, 19–20 January 1827, Gilpin Collection; DDP, *Memoir,* p. 358; DP to MinWar, 9 November 1827, in R. L. Bidwell, *op. cit.,* p. 471; DP to Joel R. Poinsett, 23 June 1827, Gilpin Collection.

22. "Rodney" to SecState, 29 January 1827, USSD, Consular Letters, Havana, in R. L. Bidwell, *op. cit.,* p. 453; J. Q. Adams, 19 February 1827, *Memoirs,* 7, p. 229; J. Q. Adams, 10 May 1827, *ibid.,* p. 269; *Niles National Register,* 31 March 1827.

23. *Niles National Register,* 2 June 1827, in R. L. Bidwell, *op. cit.,* p. 450; SecState to Pablo Obregón, 21 May 1827, in W. R. Manning (ed.), *Diplomatic Correspondence of the United States Concerning the Independence of the Latin American Nations,* 1, pp. 285–286; Pablo Obregón to SecState, 26 May 1827 in W. R. Manning, *Early Diplomatic Relations between the United States and Mexico,* p. 271; J. Q. Adams, 7 June 1827, *Memoirs,* 7, pp. 289–290; R. L. Bidwell, *op. cit.,* pp. 478, 479.

24. Pablo Obregón to DP, 21 June 1827, in W. R. Manning, *Early Diplomatic Relations between the United States and Mexico,* p. 271; Pablo Obregón to Secretario, 3 August 1827, in *ibid;* Joel R. Poinsett to SecState, 5 October 1827, USSD, Despatches from Mexico; DP to Joel R. Poinsett, 30 October 1827, Gilpin Collection.

25. Charles Ridgely to SecNav, 30 June 1827, in R. L. Bidwell, *op. cit.,* p. 473; William Taylor to SecState, 26 November 1827, USSD, Consular Despatches, Veracruz; Manuel Gonzales Salmón to Alexander H. Everett, "April 1828," in W. R. Manning (ed.), *Diplomatic Correspondence of the United States Concerning the Independence of the Latin American Nations,* 3, pp. 2158–2159; Alexander H. Everett to Manuel Gonzales Salmón, 20 April 1828, in *ibid.,* pp. 2159–2160.

26. R. L. Bidwell, *op. cit.,* pp. 474, 477; DP to ? (fragmentary letter), 24 July 1827, DP Papers, Van Ness Collection; R. L. Bidwell, *op. cit.,* pp. 476–477.

27. DP to Samuel Hambleton, 30 July 1827, DP Papers, 3, LC; R. L. Bidwell, *op. cit.,* pp. 477, 480; DP, unsigned eight-page memorandum, beginning "In November 1826 . . . ," Gilpin Collection.

28. R. L. Bidwell, *op. cit.,* p. 497; H. H. Bancroft, *History of Mexico, Works,* 13, p. 35; R. L. Bidwell, *op. cit.,* pp. 443, 525; H. H. Bancroft, *op. cit.,* pp. 40–41; R. L. Bidwell, *op. cit.,* pp. 458–460, 481–482; William Taylor to SecState, 26 November 1827, USSD, Consular Despatches, Veracruz.

29. DDP, *Memoir,* pp. 364–365; R. L. Bidwell, *op. cit.,* pp. 487–491; DDP, *Memoir,* pp. 369–374.

30. DDP to William H. Rideing, 9 December 1886, in R. L. Bidwell, *op. cit.,* 9,

491; *Niles National Register,* 1 March 1828; E. W. Flaccus, "Commodore David Porter and the Mexican Navy," *Hispanic American Historical Review,* 34, No. 3 (August 1954), p. 370; DDP, *Memoir,* pp. 374–375.

31. *Niles National Register,* 1 March 1829; William Taylor to SecState, 8 March 1828, USSD, Consular Despatches, Veracruz; R. L. Bidwell, *op. cit.,* pp. 498–500, 495.

32. DDP, *Memoir,* p. 351; DP to Evalina Porter, 11 November 1826, DP Papers, 4, LC; DP to Samuel Hambleton, 20 February 1827, *ibid.*

33. DP to Evalina Porter, 16 November 1826, DP Papers, 4, LC; DP to Joel R. Poinsett, 27 February 1828, Gilpin Collection; Pablo Obregón to Evalina Porter, 1 November 1827, DP Papers, 4, LC; W. D. Smith to Evalina Porter, 5 November 1828, *ibid.*

34. DP to Joel R. Poinsett, 12 January, 21 May, 20, 4, 21 July 1828, Gilpin Collection; R. L. Bidwell, *op. cit.,* pp. 503–505.

35. DP to Joel R. Poinsett, 28 February 1828, Gilpin Collection; E. W. Flaccus, *op. cit.,* pp. 371–372; R. L. Bidwell, *op. cit.,* p. 501; DDP, *Memoir,* p. 375; R. L. Bidwell, *op. cit.,* p. 492.

36. DP to Joel R. Poinsett, 3 June, 21 July, 29 October, 25 November 1828, Gilpin Collection.

37. DP to Evalina Porter, 15 December 1828, 14 January 1829, 15 December 1828, DP Papers, 4, LC.

38. H. H. Bancroft, *History of Mexico, Works,* 13, pp. 41–44; DP to MinWar, 29 December 1828, in R. L. Bidwell, *op. cit.,* p. 539; MinWar to DP, 2 January 1829, in *ibid.,* p. 540; DP to Evalina Porter, 14 January 1829, DP Papers, 4, LC; DDP, *Memoir,* pp. 377–379.

39. DDP, *Memoir,* pp. 379–383; DP to SecState, 24 February 1836, USSD, Despatches from Turkey; DDP, *Memoir,* p. 389; R. L. Bidwell, *op. cit.,* p. 542.

40. *Niles National Register,* 18 September 1829; J. A. Magner, *Men of Mexico,* pp. 317–318.

41. *New-York Gazette,* n.d., in *Portsmouth* (N.H.) *Journal and Rockingham Gazette,* 15 August 1829; H. G. Ward, *Mexico,* 1, p. 228; R. L. Bidwell, *op. cit.,* pp. 550–559, 1.

42. DP to Joel R. Poinsett, 9 February 1829, Gilpin Collection; DP to Secretario, 3 July 1829, DP Papers, 4, LC; DDP, *Memoir,* pp. 350, 383–384; R. L. Bidwell, *op. cit.,* p. 543.

43. W. H. Callcott, *Santa Anna: the Story of an Enigma Who Once was Mexico,* p. 62; A. P. Whitaker, *The United States and the Independence of Latin America, 1800–1830,* p. 593; H. B. Parkes, *A History of Mexico,* p. 191; A. P. Whitaker, *op. cit.,* p. 594; D. M. Parton, *The Diplomatic Career of Joel Roberts Poinsett,* p. 145; DP to Joel R. Poinsett, 19 October 1829, Poinsett Papers; DP to Mahlon Dickerson, 9 October 1829, Mahlon Dickerson Papers.

44. J. C. Pumpelly, "Mahlon Dickerson of New Jersey," in *Proceedings of the New Jersey Historical Society,* Second Series, 11 (1890–1891), pp. 133–156; C. R. Erdman, Jr., "Mahlon Dickerson," DAB, 5, pp. 289–290; Mahlon Dickerson to DP, 27 April 1827, Container 15, DP Papers, LC; Mahlon

Dickerson to DP, 30 March 1829, in DDP, *Memoir,* pp. 386–387; DP to Mahlon Dickerson, 13 July 1829, DP Papers, 4, LC.

45. DP to SecState, 24 February 1836, USSD, Despatches from Turkey; *Niles National Register,* 17 October 1829; *El Sol,* 24–25 September 1829, in R. L. Bidwell, *op. cit.,* p. 545.

46. DP to Robert Y. Hayne, "December 1829," Container 15, DP Papers, LC; DP, *Constantinople and Its Environs . . . ,* 1, pp. 223–234; DP to David Glasgow Farragut, 20 June 1835, in C. L. Lewis, *David Glasgow Farragut . . . ,* pp. 204–205.

XI

The final segment of Porter's life, 1829–1843, was occupied in unsuccessful efforts to procure a sinecure with the government until he was appointed Chargé d'Affaires and later Minister to the Ottoman Empire. He held this combined position for the last thirteen years of his life, returning home only once. The Mahlon Dickerson and Joel R. Poinsett Papers, in the New Jersey Historical Society and the Historical Society of Pennsylvania, respectively, are useful for the months of Porter's disappointment. Samuel F. Bemis, *John Quincy Adams and the Union,* J. Q. Adams, *Memoirs,* Volume 8, and a letter from Robert B. Lyle, Executive Director of the Columbia Historical Society in Washington, explain what happened to Porter's Meridian Hill estate during and after its occupancy by John Quincy Adams.

Charles O. Paullin, *Diplomatic Missions of American Naval Officers,* and Henry M. Wriston, *Executive Agents in American Foreign Relations,* furnish U.S. background for the first Turkish-American Treaty; L. S. Stavrianos *The Balkans Since 1453* does the same for the Ottoman Empire. Basic sources for Porter's official activities in Constantinople are the correspondence between Porter and four Secretaries of State in USSD, Despatches from Turkey (DFT) and Diplomatic Instructions to Turkey (DIT). Much additional information is gleaned from three repositories of David Porter Papers: the Library of Congress (Volumes 5 and 6 and Container 15), the U.S. Naval Academy Museum, and especially the previously unused letters in the Van Ness Collection (VNC), now in the custody of Mr. and Mrs. Carroll Van Ness of Owings Mills, Maryland.

The Van Ness Collection is particularly important in delineating the financial, familial, and health troubles which afflicted Porter in Turkey. Additional material in this field comes from David Dixon Porter, *Memoir,* and from biographies of David Dixon Porter and David Glasgow Farragut by Richard S. West, Jr. and Charles L. Lewis, respectively. Specific details about Porter's children are provided by John H. Martin, *Chester . . . Pennsylvania,* the *New England Historical and Genealogical Register,* 30 (1876), David Porter, *Constantinople and Its Environs. . . .* (a published collection of letters written to his old friend James K. Paulding), and the Daniel T. Patterson Papers in the Naval Foundations Collection at the Library of Congress. USSD, Despatches from Turkey, David Dixon Porter, *Memoir,* and the contemporary press describe Porter's death and burial.

1. *American and Commercial Daily Advertiser,* 6 October 1829; DP to Cashier of the Bank of the United States, 7 February 1830, Simon Gratz Autograph Collection; DP to Joel R. Poinsett, 19 October 1829, Joel R. Poinsett Papers.
2. Thomas D. Anderson to William Anderson, 24 May 1829, DP Papers, 4, LC; DDP to Evalina Porter, 23 July 1829, 5, *ibid.,* DP to Mahlon Dickerson, 9 October 1829, Mahlon Dickerson Papers.
3. DP to Joel R. Poinsett, 19 October 1829, Joel R. Poinsett Papers; *Niles National Register,* 7 November 1829, DDP, *Memoir,* p. 368; *National Intelligencer,* 12 October 1828.
4. S. F. Bemis, *John Quincy Adams and the Union,* p. 154; J. Q. Adams, 3 March 1829, *Memoirs,* 8, p. 104; S. F. Bemis, *op. cit.,* pp. 160, 178–182.
5. DP to Mahlon Dickerson, 9 October 1829, Mahlon Dickerson Papers; DP to Joseph Anderson, 10 January 1829, DP Papers, USNAM; R. W. Lyle, letter to author, 11 December 1964.
6. J. R. Soley, *Admiral Porter,* p. 14; DP to Mahlon Dickerson, 9 October 1829, Mahlon Dickerson Papers; DP to SecNav, 10 October 1829, DP Papers, Van Ness Collection (VNC) ; DP to Mahlon Dickerson, 12 October 1829, Mahlon Dickerson Papers.
7. DP to SecNav, 10 October 1829, DP Papers, VNC; DDP, *Memoir,* pp. 395, 393; A. D. Turnbull, *Commodore David Porter, 1780–1843,* p. 305; Mahlon Dickerson to DP, 23 October 1829, DP Papers, USNAM.
8. DP to Mahlon Dickerson, 15, 18 October, 1829, Mahlon Dickerson Papers; Congress of the United States, *Biographical Dictionary of the American Congress, 1774–1961,* p. 481; DP to Mahlon Dickerson, 18 December 1829, Mahlon Dickerson Papers; DP to Joseph Anderson, 10 January 1830, DP Papers; USNAM; John S. Skinner to DP, 2 February 1830, DP Papers, 5, LC.
9. DDP, *Memoir,* p. 395; *Niles National Register,* 18 September 1830; DDP, *Memoir,* pp. 397–399; SecState to DP, 15 April 1831, USSD, Diplomatic Instructions to Turkey (DIT) ; C. O. Paullin, *Diplomatic Negotiations of American Naval Officers,* p. 150; SecState to DP, 15 April 1831, USSD, DIT.
10. C. O. Paullin, *op. cit.,* pp. 133–134, 141–151.
11. DP, *Constantinople and Its Environs . . . ,* 1, p. 198; *Niles National Register,* 19 November 1831; DP to SecState, 13, 23 September 1831, USSD, DFT; C. O. Paullin, *op. cit.,* p. 151.
12. DP, *Constantinople and Its Environs . . . ,* 1, p. 51; Martin Van Buren to President Andrew Jackson, 25 November 1831, in Andrew Jackson, *Correspondence,* 4, p. 378; J. D. Richardson (ed.), *. . . Messages . . . of the Presidents, 1789–1897,* 2, p. 1114; C. O. Paullin, *op. cit.,* p. 153.
13. SecState to DP, 3 April 1832, USSD, DIT; DP to SecState, 15 August 1832, USSD, DFT; J. D. Richardson (ed.) , *op. cit.,* p. 1157.
14. DDP, *Memoir,* pp. 403, 405, 407–408, 410–411.
15. DDP, *Memoir,* p. 420; SecState to DP, 22 September 1841, USSD, DIT.
16. DP to Dr. J. P. DeKay, 12 January 1832, Hubert S. Smith Collection; DP to

Mahlon Dickerson, 23 November 1836; Mahlon Dickerson Papers; DDP, *Memoir*, pp. 403–404.

17. DDP, *Memoir*, p. 413; William B. Hodgson to SecState, 8 May 1833, USSD, DFT; DP to SecState, 19 May 1835, *ibid.;* SecState to DP, 16 May 1837, USSD, DIT.

18. DDP, *Memoir*, pp. 405, 412; DP to SecState, 24 May 1840, USSD, DFT; DDP, *Memoir*, pp. 414, 415.

19. DP to SecState, 20 November 1839, USSD, DFT; DDP, *Memoir*, p. 409; SecState to DP, 2 February 1842, USSD, DIT; DP to SecState, 20 April 1836, USSD, DFT.

20. DP to David Glasgow Farragut, 20 June 1835, in C. L. Lewis, *David Glasgow Farragut* . . . , pp. 204–205; DP to James K. Paulding, 6 January 1834, in DP, *Constantinople and Its Environs,* . . . , 2, p. 322.

21. DP to SecState, 5 October 1831, 11 September 1832, USSD, DFT; DP to SecState, 1833–1837, *ibid. passim;* DP to President Martin Van Buren, 21 January 1839, *ibid.;* SecState to DP, 19 March 1839, USSD, DIT; T. H. Benton, *Thirty Years' View* . . . , 2, p. 498.

22. DP to SecState, 5 October 1831, USSD, DFT; DP, *Constantinople and Its Environs* . . . , 1, p. 49; DP to SecState, 30 September 1831, 30 May 1832, USSD, DFT; C. O. Paullin, *op. cit.,* p. 140; DP to SecState, 5 October 1831, USSD, DFT; SecState to DP, 2 July 1832, USSD, DIT.

23. DP to SecState, 20 January 1833, USND, DFT; SecState to DP, 10 April 1833, USSD, DIT; DP to SecState, 1 January 1833, USSD, DFT; DP to DDP, 3 November 1838, DP Papers, VNC.

24. SecState to DP, 10 September 1835, USSD, DIT; DP to "5th Auditor," 15 May 1835, USSD, DFT; DP to SecState, 1 February 1836, *ibid.;* SecState to DP, 31 July 1837, USSD, DIT; DP to SecState, 19, 26 January 1839, USSD, DFT; SecState to DP, 12 April 1839, DP Papers, 5, LC.

25. DP to SecState, 13 March 1839, USSD, DFT; SecState to DP, 14 March 1839, USSD, DIT; DP to DDP, 21 August 1841, DP Papers, VNC; R. S. West, Jr., *The Second Admiral: A Life of David Dixon Porter, 1813–1891,* p. 36; DP to SecState, 29 October 1840, USSD, DFT; SecState to DP, 17 December 1840, USSD, DIT; DP to Imogene Porter, 20 April 1841, DP Papers, 5, LC.

26. DP to DDP, 3 November 1838, DP Papers, VNC; Note on letter, J. Orde Creighton to SecNav, 10 October 1838, DP Letterbook, Container 15, DP Papers, LC; DP to SecNav, n.d. (probably late October 1838), *ibid.*

27. Felix Grundy to SecNav, 3 September 1838, DP Letterbook, Container 15, DP Papers, LC; Samuel Hambleton to SecNav, 12 October 1838, *ibid.;* Charles Stewart to DP, 27 September 1838, *ibid.;* SecNav to DP, 12 February 1839, 5, *ibid.;* DP, "Letter of Attorney," 27 March 1839; *ibid.*

28. DP to SecState, 1, 24 February 1836, USSD, DFT; DP to Joel R. Poinsett, 17 March 1840, Gilpin Collection.

29. DP to DDP, 21 August 1841, 19 November 1840, 3 November 1838, DP Papers, VNC; R. S. West, Jr., *op. cit.,* p. 35; Daniel T. Patterson to Harmon Patterson, 13 January 1839, DP Papers, 5, LC; J. R. Soley, *Admiral Porter,* p. 44.

30. DP to DDP, 3 November 1838, 18, 13 July 1840, DP Papers, VNC.

31. DP to DDP, 21 August, n.d. (fragmentary letter), 17 June, 18 July 1840, 21 August 1841, DP Papers, VNC; DP to Samuel Edwards, n.d. (fragmentary letter), *ibid.;* DP to DDP, 21 August 1841, *ibid.;* DDP to William D. Porter, 12 July 1841, *ibid.*

32. R. S. West, Jr., *op. cit.,* p. 35; DP to DDP, 19 November 1840, DP Papers, VNC; DP to William D. Porter, 9 April 1840, *ibid.;* DP to DDP, n.d. (fragmentary letter), *ibid.;* William D. Porter, Affidavit, 4 April 1840, *ibid.;* DP, Affidavit, 17 October 1840, *ibid.*

33. DP to DDP, 21 August 1841, DP Papers, VNC; DP to David Glasgow Farragut, 20 March 1840, *ibid.;* DP to John Downes, 20 March 1841, *ibid.;* DP to ? (fragmentary letter), 29 October 1838, *ibid.;* R. S. West, Jr., *op. cit.,* p. 39; John Downes to DP, 7 December 1841, DP Papers, VNC; DP to DDP, 1 December 1841, *ibid.;* R. S. West, Jr., *op. cit.,* p. 36.

34. DP, "Last Will and Testament," 12 October 1842, DP Papers, 5, LC; DP, "Codicil," 13 December 1841, *ibid.;* DP to Evalina Porter, 12 October 1842, *ibid.;* USND, *American Fighting Ships,* 2, pp. 366–367; R. S. West, Jr., *op. cit.,* pp. 242, 265.

35. DDP to William D. Porter, 12 July 1841, DP Papers, VNC; DP to DDP, 21 August 1841, *ibid.;* DP to Evalina Porter, 29 August 1842, DP Papers, 5, LC.

36. DP to Theodoric Porter, 16 April 1836, DP Papers, 5, LC; DP to Lewis Cass, 13 April 1836, Lewis Cass Papers; DP to Daniel T. Patterson, 7 January 1837, Daniel T. Patterson Papers; DP to DDP, 3 November 1838, DP Papers, VNC; J. H. Martin, *Chester . . . Pennsylvania,* p. 86; DDP, *Memoir,* p. 425.

37. Hambleton Porter to Evalina Porter, 26 October 1837, DP Papers, 5, LC; Hambleton Porter to Captain Henry Ogden, 29 May 1839, *ibid.;* DP to DDP, 21 August 1841, DP Papers, VNC; DDP, *Memoir,* p. 426; J. H. Martin, *op. cit.,* p. 86.

38. Jesse D. Elliott to DP, n.d., in DP to SecState, 17 November 1836, USSD, DFT; DP to Henry O. Porter, 18 July 1840, DP Papers, VNC; DP to DDP, 18 July 1840, *ibid.;* DP to Henry O. Porter, 29 October 1841, DP Papers, 5, LC.

39. R. S. West, Jr., *op. cit.,* p. 36; Enclosure in letter, DP to Henry O. Porter, 29 October 1841, DP Papers, 5, LC; Charles W. Morgan to Henry O. Porter, 20 April 1843, 6, *ibid.;* Henry O. Porter to Evalina Porter, 15 November 1845, *ibid.,* DDP, *Memoir,* p. 426; J. H. Martin, *op. cit.,* p. 86.

40. DP to Daniel T. Patterson, 25 November 1833, Daniel T. Patterson Papers; DDP, *Memoir,* p. 420; DP to daughter Evalina Porter, 29 April 1842, DP Papers, 5, LC; DP, "Letter of Attorney," 29 March 1839, Container 15, DP Papers, LC; DP to Imogene Porter, 20 April 1841, DP Papers, 5, LC.

41. DP to SecState, 4 July 1835, 16 February, 11 November 1832, 13 February 1836, USSD, DFT.

42. C. O. Paullin, *Diplomatic Negotiations of American Naval Officers,* p. 134; DP to SecState, 23 September 1831, USSD, DFT; Nicholas Navoni to SecState, 10 October, 10 November 1831, *ibid.;* DP to SecState, 26 December 1831, *ibid.;* Nicholas Navoni to SecState, 10 March 1832, *ibid.*

43. SecState to DP, 28 March 1832, USSD, DIT; H. M. Wriston, *Executive Agents in American Foreign Relations*, p. 556; William B. Hodgson to SecState, 12 September 1831, 29 February, 19 January, 21 June 1832, USSD, DFT.

44. William B. Hodgson to SecState, 1, 7 December 1832, USSD, DFT; DP to SecState, 27 March 1833, *ibid.;* William B. Hodgson to SecState, 28 May 1833, *ibid.;* DP to William B. Hodgson, 11 May 1833, *ibid.*

45. DP to SecState, 18 May 1833, USSD, DFT; William B. Hodgson to SecState, 9, 8, 26, 9 May 1833, *ibid.*

46. DP to SecState, 19 July, 21 September 1833, USSD, DFT; DP to Daniel T. Patterson, 12 October 1833, *ibid.;* DP to SecState, 15 October 1833, *ibid.;* Daniel T. Patterson to DP, 1 November 1833, *ibid.;* DP to SecState, 28 October–22 December 1833, 7 September 1834, *ibid.;* DP to Daniel T. Patterson, 18 November 1833, *ibid.;* William B. Hodgson to SecState, 11 November 1833, *ibid.*

47. William B. Hodgson to SecState, 25 November 1833, USSD, DFT; William B. Hodgson to Daniel T. Patterson, 19 November 1833, *ibid.;* DP to SecState, 13 February 1834, *ibid.;* SecState to DP, 10 October 1833, USSD, DIT; William B. Hodgson to SecState 25 August 1834, USSD, DFT; DP to SecState, 22 August 1834, *ibid.;* SecState to DP, 10 September 1835, USSD, DIT.

48. DP to SecState, 22 August 1834, USSD, DFT; George A. Porter to DP, 2 January 1837, *ibid.;* DP to SecState, 11 November 1834, *ibid.;* DP to Daniel T. Patterson, 25 November 1835, *ibid.;* DP to Mahlon Dickerson, 25 November 1836, Mahlon Dickerson Papers; DP to SecState, 2 November 1835, 2 January 1842, USSD, DFT.

49. DP to Charles Rhind, 15 December 1832, in DP to SecState, 24 April 1834, USSD, DFT; DP to SecState, 4 July, 21 June, 4 July 1835, 21 November 1834, *ibid.*

50. DDP. *Memoir*, pp. 395–396; DP to SecState, 8 December 1835, 16 April, 22 May, 11 October 1837, USSD, DFT; C. O. Paullin, "Jesse Duncan Elliott," DAB, 6, p. 97; DDP, *Memoir*, p. 420; DP to Samuel Hambleton, 12 April 1839, DP Papers, 5, LC; C. O. Paullin, "Jesse Duncan Elliott," DAB, 6, p. 97.

51. DDP, *Memoir*, pp. 420, 400–401; J. Asker to SecState, 27 July 1836, USSD, DFT; DP to George A. Porter, 17 June 1837, *ibid.;* DP to SecState, 20 January 1839, *ibid.;* DDP, *Memoir*, p. 420; SecState to DP, 21 March 1839, USND, DIT; DP to SecState, 16 December 1840, USSD, DFT.

52. SecState to DP, 25 September 1841, USSD, DIT; DP to SecState, 15 January, 27 May, 25 July, 4 October 1842, USSD, DFT; John Brown to SecState, 14 November 1842, *ibid.;* DDP, *Memoir*, p. 406.

53. DP to James K. Paulding, 1 November 1832, in DP, *Constantinople and Its Environs* . . . , 2, p. 31; DP to SecState, 19 September 1834, USSD, DFT; DDP, *Memoir*, pp. 409–410.

54. DP to James K. Paulding, 16 February 1833, in DP, *Constantinople and Its Environs* . . . , 2, p. 111; DP to Daniel T. Patterson, 18 September 1833, Daniel T. Patterson Papers; DP to James K. Paulding, 11 August 1833, in

DP, *op. cit.,* pp. 144–145; DP to James K. Paulding, 5 December 1833 (misdated 5 January), in *ibid.,* p. 294; DP to David Glasgow Farragut, 20 June 1835, in C. L. Lewis, *David Glasgow Farragut . . . ,* p. 204.

55. DP to SecState, 17 September 1835, USSD, DFT; DP to Evalina Porter, 7 February 1833, DP Papers, 5, LC; DP to Mahlon Dickerson, 23 November 1836, Mahlon Dickerson Papers; DP to SecState, 17 July 1838, USSD, DFT; DP to DDP, 3 November 1838, DP Papers, VNC; DP to SecState, 21 June, 2 August 1839, USSD, DFT.

56. DDP, *Memoir,* p. 416; DP to DDP, 1 December 1841, DP Papers, VNC; DDP, *Memoir,* pp. 420, 421; John Brown to SecState, 6 March 1843, USSD, DFT.

57. John Brown to SecState, 6 March 1843, USSD, DFT; *Philadelphia Gazette,* n.d., in *New York Herald,* 23 April 1843; DDP, *Memoir,* p. 422; Turkish Minister of Foreign Affairs to John Brown, 23 March 1843, USSD, DFT; *Teradai Havadis,* n.d., enclosed in John Brown to SecNav, 18 October 1843, USSD, DFT.

58. *Niles National Register,* 24 April 1843; DDP, *Memoir,* pp. 422, 425; J. H. Martin, *Chester . . . Pennsylvania,* p. 85.

59. Samuel D. Heap, Jr. to Evalina Porter, 20 January 1844, DP Papers, 6, LC; DP, "Last Will and Testament," 12 October 1842, 5, *ibid.;* DDP to Evalina Porter, n.d., in R. S. West, Jr., *The Second Admiral: A Life of David Dixon Porter, 1813–1891,* p. 38; Unsigned letter headed "Senate Chamber," to Evalina Porter, 15 June 1844, DP Papers, 6, LC; DDP to Evalina Porter, 5 April 1860, *ibid.*

60. "Mason Jr.," to Evalina Porter, 27 February 1845, DP Papers, 6, LC; DDP to MinMex, 5 December 1853, DP Papers, VNC; A. H. Palmer to DDP, 8 December 1853, 10 June, 12 November 1859, *ibid.;* SecState to DDP, 3 June 1879, *ibid.*

MANUSCRIPTS, INTERVIEWS, AND PERSONAL CORRESPONDENCE

Adams, John Quincy, Diary, 5 August 1809–20 April 1836, Massachusetts Historical Society, Boston, Mass.

———, Letterbook, 10 February 1825–13 March 1829, Massachusetts Historical Society, Boston, Mass.

———, "Rubbish III" (diary and miscellaneous entries), 19 August 1823–31 December 1826, Massachusetts Historical Society, Boston, Mass.

Admiralty, Captains' In-letters, 1813–1815, Public Record Office, London.

———, Journal of the Proceedings of His Majesty's Ship Briton, 1813–1814, Public Record Office, London.

———, Journal of the Proceedings of His Majesty's Ship Phoebe, 1813–1815, Public Record Office, London.

———, Journal of the Proceedings of His Majesty's Ship Tagus, 1813–1814, Public Record Office, London.

———, Secretary's Common Letters to Captains and Lieutenants, 1813–1815, Public Record Office, London.

American Activities in the Central Pacific, 1790–1870, 18 vols., W.P.A. Project, Peabody Museum, Salem, Mass.

Aziz, Abdul, Director of Antiquities, Kingdom of Libya, interview with author, 5 September 1965, "The Castle," Tripoli, Libya.

Bainbridge, William, Mss, New York Historical Society, New York, N.Y.

Brackenridge, Henry M., Letterbook, Darlington Memorial Library, University of Pittsburgh, Pittsburgh, Pa.

Brewington, M. V., interview with author, 25 November 1964, Peabody Museum, Salem, Mass.

Cass, Lewis, Mss, William L. Clements Library, University of Michigan, Ann Arbor, Mich.

Dickerson, Mahlon, Mss, New Jersey Historical Society, New Brunswick, N.J.

Everett, Edward, Mss, Massachusetts Historical Society, Boston, Mass.

Farragut, David G., "Letters covering entire early period of his career," United States Naval Academy Museum, Annapolis, Md.

Feltus, William C., Journal, 1813–1814, Historical Society of Pennsylvania, Philadelphia, Pa.

Gallatin, Albert, Mss, New York Historical Society, New York, N.Y.

Garrett, Wendell, Associate Editor, The Adams Papers, Massachusetts Historical Society, Boston, Mass., letter to author, 23 November 1964.

Glendinning, Mrs. Marguerite Porter (David Porter's great-great-granddaughter), interview with author, 6 February 1965, Annapolis, Md.

Gilpin MSS Collection (Poinsett Section), Historical Society of Pennsylvania, Philadelphia, Pa.

Gratz, Simon, Autograph Collection, Historical Society of Pennsylvania, Philadelphia, Pa.

Hambleton, Samuel, Mss, New York Historical Society, New York, N.Y.

Jefferson, Thomas, Mss, Massachusetts Historical Society, Boston, Mass.

Keller, William F., Letters of David Porter to Henry Marie Brackenridge.

Kilbourne, John D., Librarian, Maryland Historical Society, letter to author, 27 January 1965.

Lawrence, James, Mss, New York Historical Society, New York, N.Y.

Lightbourne, Alberic G. (Postmaster of Fajardo), interview with author, 10 June 1965, Fajardo, Puerto Rico.

Lyle, Robert B., Executive Director, Columbia Historical Society, Washington, D.C., letter to author, 11 December 1964.

Monroe, James, Mss, Library of Congress, Washington, D.C.

Patterson, Daniel T., Mss, Naval Historical Foundations Collection, Library of Congress, Washington, D.C.

Poinsett, Joel R., Mss, Historical Society of Pennsylvania, Philadelphia, Pa.

Porter, David, Mss (filed with David Dixon Porter Mss), vols. 1–6, containers 15–16, Library of Congress, Washington, D.C.

———, Mss, New York Historical Society, New York, N.Y.

———, Mss, United States Naval Academy Museum, Annapolis, Md.

———, Mss, furnished through the courtesy of Mr. and Mrs. Carroll Van Ness, Owings Mills, Md.

Porter, David Dixon, Mss, vols. 6–14, Library of Congress, Washington, D.C.

———, Mss, New York Historical Society, New York, N.Y.

———, Mss, furnished through the courtesy of Mr. and Mrs. Carroll Van Ness, Owings Mills, Md.

Rodgers, John, Mss, Library of Congress, Washington, D.C.

———, Mss, New York Historical Society, New York, N.Y.

Rosa-Silva, Jorge Ivan, Chairman of the History Department, University of Puerto Rico, interview with author, 11 June 1965, San Juan, Puerto Rico.

Smith, Hubert S., Mss Collection, William L. Clements Library, University of Michigan, Ann Arbor, Mich.

Smith, Robert, Mss, New York Historical Society, New York, N.Y.

Southard, Samuel L., Mss, New York Historical Society, New York, N.Y.

Stackpole, Edouard A., interview with author, 1 September 1966, Nantucket, Mass.

Truxtun, Thomas, Mss, United States Naval Academy Museum, Annapolis, Md.

United States Navy Department, Letters Received by Secretary of the Navy from Captains, 1812–1826, National Archives, Washington, D.C.

————, Letters Received by Secretary of the Navy from Masters Commandant, 1806–1812, National Archives, Washington, D.C.

————, Letters Received by Secretary of the Navy from Officers below the rank of Commander, 1802–1806, National Archives, Washington, D.C.

————, Letters Sent by Secretary of the Navy to Officers, 1798–1868, National Archives, Washington, D.C.

————, Records of General Courts Martial and Courts of Inquiry of the Navy Department, 1799–1867, National Archives, Washington, D.C.

United States State Department, Consular Despatches, San Juan, Puerto Rico, 18 June 1821–16 June 1836, National Archives, Washington, D.C.

————, Consular Despatches, Veracruz, Mexico, 8 March 1822–1 December 1831, National Archives, Washington, D.C.

————, Despatches from United States Ministers to Mexico, 17 August 1825–23 April 1829, National Archives, Washington, D.C.

————, Despatches from United States Ministers to Turkey, 1818–1906, National Archives, Washington, D.C.

————, Diplomatic Instructions to Turkey, 2 April 1823–9 July 1859, National Archives, Washington, D.C.

————, Notes from Foreign Legations, Great Britain, 25 June 1823–27 July 1825, National Archives, Washington, D.C.

————, Notes from Foreign Legations, Spain, 6 October 1821–31 March 1826, National Archives, Washington, D.C.

————, Special Agents, vol. 3, folio 25, Poinsett, 20 February 1813–5 November 1818, National Archives, Washington, D.C.

————, Special Agents, vol. 9, Randall, 1824–1825, National Archives, Washington, D.C.

————, Special Agents, vol. 2, folio 20, Shaler, 8 June 1810–5 March 1815, National Archives, Washington, D.C.

Weatherly, Guy, Archivist III, Hall of Records, Annapolis, Md., letter to author, 2 February 1965.

West, Richard S., Jr., former Professor of History, United States Naval Academy, interview with author, 7 February 1965, Annapolis, Md.

Wilkinson, James, Mss, New York Historical Society, New York, N.Y.

SOURCE WORKS

Adams, John Quincy, *Memoirs: Comprising Portions of his Diary from 1795 to 1848.* Edited by Charles Francis Adams. 12 vols. Philadelphia: J. B. Lippincott, 1874–1877.

Allen, Gardner, W., ed., *Papers of Isaac Hull: Commodore, United States Navy.* Boston: The Boston Athenaeum, 1929.

Anthony, Irvin, ed. *The Saga of the Bounty.* New York: Dell Publishing Company, 1961. (Original edition, New York: G. P. Putnam's Sons, 1935.)

Beale, Richard C., ed. *Journal of the United States Frigate Essex on her First Voyage, 1799–1800.* Salem, Mass.: The Essex Institute (photostat copy).

Boston Marriages, 1752–1809. Boston: Municipal Printing Office, 1903.

Brannan, John, *Official Letters of the Military and Naval Officers of the United*

States, during the War with Great Britain in the Years 1812, 13, 14, & 15. With Some Additional Letters and Documents Elucidating the History of That Period. Washington City; Way & Gideon, 1823.

Butler, Frederick, ed. *Memoirs of the Marquis de La Fayette, Major-General in the Revolutionary Army of the United States of America. Together with his Tour through the United States.* Wethersfield, Conn.: Deming & Francis, 1825.

Butterfield, L. H., ed. *Letters of Benjamin Rush.* 2 vols. Princeton, N.J.: Princeton University Press, 1951.

Claiborne, William C. C., *Official Letter Books, 1801–1816.* Edited by Dunbar Rowland. 6 vols. Jackson, Miss.: Mississippi State Department of Archives and History, 1917.

Cole, Allen B., ed. "Captain David Porter's Proposed Expedition to the Pacific and Japan, 1815." *Pacific Historical Review,* 9 (1940).

Colton, Calvin, ed. *Works of Henry Clay.* 7 vols. New York: Henry Clay Publishing Company, 1897.

Congress of the United States, *American State Papers, Foreign Relations.* 6 vols. Washington, D.C.: Gales and Seaton, 1832–1859.

———, *American State Papers, Naval Affairs.* 4 vols. Washington, D.C.: Gales and Seaton, 1834–1861.

Coxe, Richard S., *An Examination into Commodore Porter's Exposition.* Washington, D.C.: privately printed, 1825.

Crowninshield, Benjamin W., *Court Martial of Capt. O. H. Perry.* Exec. Docs., No. 66, 15th Cong., 1st sess., Vol. 4. Report on charges against Capt. O. H. Perry; Minutes of proceedings; Witnesses; Sentence; Letter of Captain Perry and his defence; Testimony.

Ford, Worthington C., ed. "Letters of William Duane." *Proceedings of the Massachusetts Historical Society,* Second Series, 20 (1906, 1907).

Foster, Sir Augustus John, Bart., *Jeffersonian America: Notes on the United States of America Collected in the Years 1805–6–7 and 11–12.* Edited by Richard Beale Davis. San Marino, Cal.: Huntington Library, 1954.

Hopkins, James F., ed. *The Papers of Henry Clay.* 3 vols. Lexington, Ky.: University of Kentucky Press, 1959–1963.

Jackson, Andrew, *Correspondence.* 7 vols. Edited by John Spencer Bassett. Washington, D.C.: Carnegie Institution of Washington, 1935.

Kotzebue, Otto von, *A New Voyage Round the World in the Years 1823–1826,* 2 vols. London: Henry Colburn and Richard Bentley, 1830.

———, *Voyage of Discovery in the South Sea and Beering's Straits for the purpose of exploring a North-East Passage in the Ship Rurick in 1815–1818.* 3 vols. London: Longman, Hurst, Rees, Orme, and Brown, 1821.

Manning, William R., ed. *Diplomatic Correspondence of the United States Concerning the Independence of the Latin American Nations.* 3 vols. New York: Oxford University Press, 1925.

Morris, Charles, *Autobiography.* Boston: A. Williams & Company, 1880.

Porter, David, *An Exposition of the Facts and Circumstances which Justified the Expedition to Foxardo, and the consequences there of. Together with the proceedings of the Court of Inquiry thereon, held by order of the Hon. Secretary of the Navy.* Washington, D.C.: Davis & Force, 1825.

————, *Constantinople and Its Environs: In a Series of Letters Exhibiting the Actual State of the Manners, Customs, and Habits of the Turks, Armenians, Jews, and Greeks—by an American, Long Resident at Constantinople.* 2 vols. New-York: Harper & Brothers, 1835.

————, *Journal of a Cruise Made to the Pacific Ocean by Captain David Porter, in the United States Frigate Essex, in the Years 1812, 1813, and 1814, Containing Descriptions of the Cape de Verd Islands, Coasts of Brazil, Patagonia, Chile and Peru, and of the Gallapagos Islands.* 2 vols. Philadelphia: Bradford and Inskip, etc., etc., 1815.

————, ————, *2nd edition, To which is now added an introduction, in which the charges contained in the Quarterly Review, of the first edition of this Journal, are examined.* 2 vols. New-York: Wiley & Halstead, 1822.

————, *Minutes of the Proceedings of the Courts of Inquiry and Court Martial in Relation to Captain David Porter Convened at Washington, D.C., on Thursday, the seventh day of July,* A.D. *1825.* Printed by authority from the official record. Washington, D.C.: Davis and Force, 1825.

————, *Trial of Lieutenant Joel Abbot by the General Naval Court Martial.* Boston: Russell & Gardner, 1822.

Register of Debates, 18th Congress, 2nd, Session—25th Congress, 1st Session, December 1824–September 1825. Washington, D.C.: Gales & Seaton, 1824–1837.

Reynolds, Jeremiah N., *Voyage of the United States Frigate Potomac, under the command of Commodore John Downes, during the Circumnavigation of the Globe in the Years 1831, 1832, 1833, and 1834.* New-York: Harper & Brothers, 1835.

Richardson, James D., *A Compilation of the Messages and Papers of the Presidents, 1789–1897.* 10 vols. Washington, D.C.: Published by Authority of Congress, 1900.

Ruschenberger, W. S. W., *Three Years in the Pacific, 1831, 1832, 1833, 1834, by an Officer in the United States Navy.* 2 vols. London: Richard Bentley, 1835.

Stewart, Charles S., *A Visit to the South Seas in the U.S. Ship Vincennes during the Years 1829 and 1830 with Scenes in Brazil, Peru, Manilla, the Cape of Good Hope, and St. Helena.* 2 vols. New-York: John P. Haven, 1831.

United States Navy Department, *Naval Documents Related to the Quasi-war Between the United States and France.* 7 vols. Washington, D.C.: United States Government Printing Office, 1935–1938.

————, *Naval Documents Related to the United States Wars with the Barbary Powers.* 6 vols., Washington, D.C.: United States Government Printing Office, 1944.

————, *Proceedings of the General Court Martial Convened for the Trial of Commodore James Barron, Capt. Charles Gordon, Mr. William Hook, and Capt. John Hall of the United States Ship Chesapeake in the Month of January 1808.* Washington, D.C.: Jacob Gideon Junior, 1822.

————, *Trial of Captain John Shaw, by the General Court Martial holden on board the U.S. Ship Independence, at the Navy Yard, Charlestown, Massachusetts, upon charges and specifications preferred against him by Captain Isaac Hull.* Washington, D.C.: Davis and Force, 1822. (Bound in Yale Collection *Naval Courts-Martial,* Yale University Library, New Haven.)

United States State Department, *The Territorial Papers of the United States.* Compiled and edited by Clarence Edwin Carter. Vol. 9, *The Territory of Orleans, 1803–1812.* Washington, D.C.: United States Government Printing Office, 1940.

Walter, Richard, comp., *Anson's Voyage Round the World.* New Edition edited with Prefatory Notes by G. S. Laird Cowes. London: Martin Hopkinson, Ltd.; Boston: Charles E. Lauriat, Co., 1928.

Warren, Charles, ed. *Jacobin and Junto, or, Early American Politics as Viewed in the Diary of Dr. Nathaniel Ames, 1758–1822.* Cambridge, Mass.: Harvard University Press, 1931.

Webster, C. K., *Britain and the Independence of Latin America, 1812–1830: Select Documents from the Foreign Office Archives.* 2 vols. London: Oxford University Press, 1938.

Wilkinson, James, *Memoirs of My Own Times.* 3 vols. Philadelphia: Abraham Small, 1816.

NEWSPAPERS

American Advocate, Hallowell, Maine.
American and Commercial Daily Advertiser, Baltimore, Md.
Boston Commercial Gazette.
Boston Weekly Messenger.
Christian Watchman, Boston, Mass.
Cobbett's Weekly Political Register, London.
Columbian Centinel, Boston, Mass.
Commercial Advertiser, New York.
Daily Chronicle, Philadelphia.
Daily Herald, Newburyport, Mass.
Democratic Press, Philadelphia.
Eastern Argus, Portland, Maine.
Federal Gazette & Baltimore Daily Advertiser.
Friend (The), Honolulu.
Independent Chronicle, Boston, Mass.
La Gaceta de Puerto Rico, San Juan.
Louisiana Gazette, New-Orleans.
Maryland Gazette, Annapolis, Md.
Maryland Journal and Baltimore Advertiser.
Massachusetts Spy, or, Worcester Gazette, Worcester, Mass.
Morning Chronicle, London.
Nantucket Inquirer, Mass.
National Intelligencer, Washington, D.C.
New Hampshire Patriot & State Gazette, Concord.
New Orleans Weekly Picayune.

New-York Evening Post.

New-York Herald.

New York Herald.

New-York Spectator.

Niles National Register, Baltimore, Md.

Portsmouth Journal, N.H.

Poulson's American Daily Advertiser, Philadelphia, Pa.

Providence Chronicle, R.I.

Reportory and Daily Advertiser, Boston, Mass.

Republican, or, Anti-Democrat, Baltimore, Md.

Salem Gazette, Salem, Mass.

The Times (London).

Virginia Argus, Richmond, Va.

SECONDARY WORKS

Abernethy, Thomas P., *The Burr Conspiracy.* New York: Oxford University Press, 1954.

Adams, Henry, *History of the United States of America,* 9 vols. New York: Charles Scribner's Sons, 1891.

Alden, Carroll S., *Lawrence Kearney: Sailor Diplomat.* Princeton, N.J.: Princeton University Press, 1936.

————, and Westcott, Allan, *The United States Navy: A History.* Chicago, Philadelphia, etc.: J. B. Lippincott Company, 1945.

Albion, Robert G., and Pope, Jennie B., *Sea Lanes in Wartime; the American Experience.* New York: W. W. Norton and Company, 1942.

Allen, Gardner W., *Our Naval War with France.* Boston and New York: Houghton Mifflin Company, 1909.

————, *Our Navy and the Barbary Corsairs.* Boston and New York: Houghton Mifflin Company, 1905.

————, *Our Navy and the West Indian Pirates.* Salem, Mass.: The Essex Institute, 1929.

Allman, Charles, "Shores and Sails in the South Seas." *National Geographic,* 97, No. 1 (January 1950).

American Annual Register for the Years 1825–6 or the 50th Year of American Independence. New-York: G. & C. Carvill, 1827.

American Guide Series, Federal Writers' Project, *Washington, City and Capital.* Washington, D.C.: United States Government Printing Office, 1937.

Analectic Magazine. 6 vols. Philadelphia: Moses Thomas, 1813–1815.

Analectic Magazine and Naval Chronicle. Philadelphia: Moses Thomas, 1815–1816.

Anderson, Charles R., *Melville in the South Seas.* New York: Columbia University Press, 1939.

Anderson, R. C., *Naval Wars in the Levant, 1559–1853.* Liverpool: Liverpool University Press.

Annual Register for the Year 1814. London: Baldwin, Cradock, and Joy, 1815.

Anonymous, "Capture of the Essex," broadside. Boston: privately printed, 1814.

————, *History of the War Between the United States and Tripoli, and Other Barbary Powers*. Salem, Mass.: Salem Gazette Office, 1806.

————, *Mexico and Mr. Poinsett: Reply to the British Pamphlet*. Philadelphia: privately printed, 1829.

Anthony, Irvin, *Decatur*. New York: Charles Scribner's Sons, 1931.

Ashmead, Henry G., *History of Delaware County, Pennsylvania*. Philadelphia: L. H. Everts & Company, 1884.

Auchmuty, James J., *The United States Government and Latin American Independence, 1810–1830*. London: P. S. King & Son, 1937.

Badger, Barber, *The Naval Temple: Containing a Complete History of the Battles Fought by the Navy of the United States From its establishment in 1794 to the present time including the wars with France, and with Tripoli, the late war with Great Britain, and with Algiers*. Boston: Barber Badger, 1816.

Bailey, Isaac, *American Naval Biography*. Providence: Isaac Bailey, 1815.

Baines, Edward, *Baines' History of the Late War, between the United States and Great Britain*, with a critical appendix. Edited by Ebenezer Harlow Cummins. Baltimore: Benja. Edes, 1820.

Bancroft, Hubert H., *History of Mexico*. 6 vols. San Francisco: A. L. Bancroft & Company, 1905.

Barnes, James, *David G. Farragut*. London: Kegan Paul, Trench, Tubner & Co., 1899.

————, *Naval Actions of the War of 1812*. New York: Harper & Brothers, 1896.

Bassett, John S., *The Life of Andrew Jackson*. 2 vols. Garden City, N.Y.: Doubleday, Page & Company, 1911.

Beach, Edward L., "The Pioneer of America's Pacific Empire: David Porter." *United States Naval Institute Proceedings*, 34, No. 2 (June 1908).

Beaglehole, J. C., *The Exploration of the Pacific*. London: A. & C. Black, 1934.

Beirne, Francis F., *The War of 1812*. New York: E. P. Dutton & Company, 1949.

Bemis, Samuel F., "Early Diplomatic Missions from Buenos Aires to the United States, 1811–1824." *Proceedings of the American Antiquarian Society*, New Series, 49 (19 April 1939).

————, *John Quincy Adams and the Foundations of American Foreign Policy*. New York: Alfred A. Knopf, 1949.

————, *John Quincy Adams and the Union*. New York: Alfred A. Knopf, 1956.

————, ed. *The American Secretaries of State and Their Diplomacy*. 10 vols. New York: Alfred A. Knopf, 1928.

Benton, Thomas H., *Thirty Years' View; or, a History of the Workings of the American Government for Thirty Years, from 1820 to 1850*. 2 vols. New York: D. Appleton and Company, 1854.

Bidwell, Robert L., "The First Mexican Navy, 1821–1830." Ph.D. dissertation, University of Virginia, 1960.

Bornholdt, Laura, *Baltimore and Early Pan-Americanism: A Study in the Background of the Monroe Doctrine*. Smith College Studies in History, 34. Northampton, Mass.: 1949.

BIBLIOGRAPHY

Bowen, Abel, *The Naval Monument, Containing Official and Other Accounts of All the Battles Fought between the Navies of the United States and Great Britain during the Late War.* Boston: A. Bowen, 1816.

Bowen, Frank, *Men of the Wooden Walls.* London: Staples Press, 1952.

Brackenridge, Henry M., *History of the Late War, between the United States and Great Britain. Containing a Minute Account of the Various Military and Naval Operations,* 4th rev. ed. Baltimore: Cushing & Jewett, 1818.

——, *Voyage to South America, Performed by Order of the American Government, in the Years 1817 and 1818, in the frigate Congress,* 2 vols. Baltimore: published by the author, 1819.

Bradlee, Francis B. C., *Piracy in the West Indies and Its Suppression.* Salem, Mass.: The Essex Institute, 1923.

Brant, Irving, *James Madison: Secretary of State, 1800–1809.* Indianapolis, New York: The Bobbs-Merrill Company, 1953.

——, *James Madison: The President, 1809–1812.* Indianapolis, New York: The Bobbs-Merrill Company, 1956.

——, *James Madison: Commander in Chief, 1812–1836.* Indianapolis, New York: The Bobbs-Merrill Company, 1961.

Brown, John MacMillan, *Peoples and Problems of the Pacific.* 2 vols. London: T. F. Unwin, Ltd., 1927.

Bryan, Wilhelmus B., *A History of the National Capital.* 2 vols. New York: The Macmillan Company, 1914, 1916.

Buck, Sir Peter H. (Te Rangi Hiroa), *Explorers of the Pacific: European and American Discoveries in Polynesia.* Honolulu: The Bernice P. Bishop Museum, 1953.

Callahan, James M., "American Relations in the Pacific and the Far East, 1784–1900." *Johns Hopkins University Studies in Historical and Political Science,* Series 19, Nos. 1–3 (January–March 1901).

Callcott, Wilfrid H., *Santa Anna: The Story of an Enigma Who Once Was Mexico.* Norman, Okla.: University of Oklahoma Press, 1931.

Carr, William H. A., *The du Ponts of Delaware.* New York: Dodd, Mead & Company, 1964.

Caskie, Jaquelin A., *Life and Letters of Matthew Fontaine Maury.* Richmond, Va.: Richmond Press, 1928.

Chadwick, French E., *The American Navy.* Garden City, N.Y.: Doubleday, Page & Company, 1915.

Channing, Edward, *A History of the United States.* 6 vols., New York: The Macmillan Company, 1917.

——, *The Jeffersonian System, 1801–1811.* Vol. 12 of *The American Nation: A History.* New York and London: Harper & Brothers, Publishers, 1906.

Chapelle, Howard I., *The History of American Sailing Ships.* New York: W. W. Norton & Company, 1935.

Chevalier, M. Michel, *Mexico, Ancient and Modern.* Translated by Thomas Alpass. 2 vols. London: John Maxwell and Company, 1864.

Chidsey, Donald B., *The American Privateers.* New York: Dodd, Mead & Company, 1962.

Chesterton, G. K., *William Cobbett*. New York: Dodd, Mead & Company, 1926.

Church, John W., "A Vanishing People of the South Seas," *National Geographic*, 36, No. 4 (October 1919).

Clark, William B., *Gallant John Barry, 1745–1803*. New York: The Macmillan Company, 1938.

Clark, Thomas, *Naval History of the United States, from the Commencement of the Revolutionary War to the Present Time*. 2d ed. 2 vols. Philadelphia: M. Carey, 1814.

Clarke, Henry B., *Modern Spain, 1815–1898*. Cambridge, England: The University Press, 1906.

Cobbett, William, *History of the Regency and Reign of King George the Fourth*. London: William Cobbett, 1830.

————, *The Progress of a Plough-boy to a Seat in Parliament*. Edited by William Reitzel. London: Faber and Faber, 1933.

Cochran, Hamilton, *Noted American Duels and Hostile Encounters*. Philadelphia: Chilton Books, 1963.

Cochrane, Thomas (Earl of Dundonald), *Narration of Services in the Liberation of Chili, Peru, and Brazil, from Spanish and Portuguese Domination*. 2 vols. London: James Ridgway, 1859.

Cole, G. D. H., *The Life of William Cobbett*. London: W. Collins Sons & Co., 1927.

Congress of the United States, *Biographical Dictionary of the American Congress, 1774–1961*. Washington, D.C.: United States Government Printing Office, 1961.

Cooper, James F., *History of the Navy of the United States of America*. 2d ed. 2 vols. Philadelphia: Lee and Blanchard, 1840.

Cowdery, Dr. Jonathan, *American Captives in Tripoli*. Boston: Belcher & Armstrong, 1806.

Cox, Isaac J., "General Wilkinson and His Later Intrigues with the Spaniards." *The American Historical Review*, 19, No. 4 (July 1914).

————, *The West Florida Controversy, 1798–1813*. Baltimore: The Johns Hopkins Press, 1918.

Coxe, Richard S., *Review of the Relations Between the United States and Mexico and the claims of the citizens of the United States against Mexico*. New York: Wilson & Company, 1846.

Cresson, W. P., *James Monroe*. Chapel Hill, N.C.: University of North Carolina Press, 1946.

Cruz Monclova, Lidio, *Historia de Puerto Rico (Siglo 19)*. 6 vols. San Juan: University of Puerto Rico, 1952.

D'Auvergne, Edmund B., *Envoys Extraordinary*. London: George G. Harrap & Company, 1937.

Davison, Gideon M., *Sketches of the War Between the United States and the British Isles, Intended as a Faithful History of all the Material Events from the time of the Declaration in 1812, to and including the Treaty of Peace in 1815*. 2 vols. Rutland, Vt.: Fay and Davison, 1815.

Dearborn, H. A. S., *The Life of William Bainbridge, Esq. of the United States*

Navy (1816). Edited by James Barnes. Princeton, N.J.: Princeton University Press, 1931.

Dennet, Tyler, *Americans in Eastern Asia: A Critical Study of the United States with reference to China, Japan, and Korea in the 19th Century.* New York: Barnes & Noble, 1931.

Dictionary of American Biography. 22 vols. New York: Charles Scribner's Sons, 1928–1944.

Dictionary of National Biography. 22 vols. New York: The Macmillan Company, 1908–1909.

Du Pont, Bessie G., *E. I. du Pont de Nemours and Company: A History, 1802–1902.* Boston and New York: Houghton Mifflin Company, 1920.

Edwards, Samuel, *Barbary General: The Life of William H. Eaton.* Englewood Cliffs, N.J.: Prentice-Hall, Inc., 1968.

Emery, Fred A., "Mount Pleasant and Meridian Hill." *Records of the Columbia Historical Society, 33–34* (1932).

Emmons, George F., *The Navy of the United States, From the Commencement, 1775–1853; with a brief history of each vessel's service and fate comp. by Lieut. George F. Emmons under the authority of the Navy Dept.* Washington, D.C.: Gideon & Company, 1853.

Evans, Henry C. Jr., *Chile and its Relations with the United States.* Durham, N.C.: Duke University Press, 1927.

Fanning, Edmund, *Voyages & Discoveries in the South Seas, 1792–1832.* Salem, Mass.: Marine Research Society, 1924.

Farragut, Loyall, *The Life of David Glasgow Farragut, First Admiral of the United States Navy, Embodying his Journal and Letters.* New York: D. Appleton and Company, 1882.

Flaccus, Elmer W., "Commodore David Porter and the Mexican Navy." *Hispanic American Historical Review, 34,* No. 3 (August 1954).

Folsom, Benjamin, *A Compilation of Biographical Sketches of Distinguished Officers in the American Navy, with other interesting matter.* Newburyport, Mass.: Benjamin Folsom, 1814.

Forester, C. S., *Age of Fighting Sail: The Story of the Naval War of 1812.* Garden City, N.Y.: Doubleday Company, 1956.

———, "Bloodshed at Dawn," *American Heritage, 15,* No. 6 (October 1964).

Frost, John, *The Book of the Navy; Comprising a General History of the American Marine; and particular accounts of all the Most Celebrated Naval Battles, from the Declaration of Independence to the present time.* New York: D. Appleton & Company, 1843.

Furlong, Charles W., *The Gateway to the Sahara: Observations and Experiences in Tripoli.* London: Chapman and Hull, 1909.

Furnas, J. C., *The Anatomy of Paradise: Hawaii and the Islands of the South Seas.* New York: William Sloane Associates, 1948.

Gaines, Edwin M., "Outrageous Encounter! The Chesapeake-Leopard Affair of 1807." Ph.D. dissertation, University of Virginia, 1960.

Galdames, Luis, *A History of Chile.* Translated and edited by Isaac Joslin Cox. Chapel Hill, N.C.: University of North Carolina Press, 1941.

Gayarre, Charles E. A., *History of Louisiana*. 4 vols. New York: Redfield, 1854–1867.

Gerrard, Bassigney, "Agony in the Sunshine: A History of the Marquesas." 2 vols. typed mss., n.d., Peabody Museum, Salem, Mass.

Goldsborough, Charles W., *The United States Naval Chronicle*. Washington, D.C.: J. Wilson, 1824.

Grant, Bruce, *Isaac Hull: Captain of Old Ironsides: The Life and Fighting Times of Isaac Hull and the U.S. Frigate Constitution*. Chicago: Pellegrini and Cudahy, 1947.

Gratton, C. Hartley, *The Southwest Pacific to 1900*. Ann Arbor, Mich.: University of Michigan Press, 1963.

———, *The United States and the Southwest Pacific*. Cambridge, Mass.: Harvard University Press, 1961.

Griffin, Charles C., "Privateering from Baltimore during the Spanish American Wars of Independence." *Maryland Historical Magazine*, 35 (March 1940).

———, *The United States and the Disruption of the Spanish Empire, 1810–1822*. New York: Columbia University Press, 1937.

Griffin, Martin I. J., *Commodore John Barry*. Philadelphia: published by the author, 1903.

Griffis, William E., *Matthew Calbraith Perry: A Typical American Naval Officer*. Boston and New York: Houghton Mifflin Company, 1890.

Gurn, Joseph, *Commodore John Barry: Father of the American Navy*. New York: J. Kenedy & Sons, 1933.

Handy, Willowdean C., *Forever the Land of Men: An account of a visit to the Marquesas Islands*. New York: Dodd, Mead & Co., 1965.

Hanighen, Frank C., *Santa Anna: The Napoleon of the West*. New York: Coward-McCann, 1934.

Harper's New Monthly Magazine, 19, No. 111 (August 1859).

Harrison, Margaret H., *Captain of the Andes: The Life of Don José de San Martín, Liberator of Argentina, Chile, and Peru*. New York: Richard R. Smith, 1943.

Hasbrouck, Alfred, *Foreign Legionaries in the Liberation of Spanish South America*. New York: Columbia University Press, 1928.

Hatfield, Joseph T., "The Public Career of William C. C. Claiborne." Ph.D. dissertation, Emory University, 1962.

Hellman, George S., *Washington Irving Esquire: Ambassador at Large from the New World to the Old*. London: Jonathan Cape, 1925.

Henao, Jesus Maria, and Arrubla, Gerardo, *History of Colombia*. Translated and edited by J. Fred Rippy. Chapel Hill, N.C.: University of North Carolina Press, 1938.

Herold, Amos L., *James Kirke Paulding: Versatile American*. New York: Columbia University Press, 1926.

Hildreth, Richard, *The History of the United States*. 3 vols. Rev. ed. New York: Harper & Brothers, 1863.

Hill, F. Stanhope, *The "Lucky Little Enterprise" and Her Successors in the United States Navy*. Boston: privately printed, 1900.

Hohman, Elmo P., *The American Whaleman: A Study of Life and Labor in the*

BIBLIOGRAPHY

Whaling Industry. New York, London, Toronto: Longmans, Green & Company, 1928.

Horsman, Reginald, *The Causes of the War of 1812.* Philadelphia: University of Pennsylvania Press, 1962.

Hunt, Charles H., *Life of Edward Livingston.* New York: D. Appleton and Company, 1864.

Ingersoll, Charles J., *History of the Second War between the United States of America and Great Britain, declared by Act of Congress, the 18th of June, 1812, and concluded by peace, the 15th of February, 1815.* Philadelphia: Lippincott, Grambo & Company, 1853.

Irvine, Baptis, *Strictures on a Voyage to South America as Indited by the "Secretary to the (Late) Mission to the La Plata." By a Friend of Truth and Sound Policy.* Baltimore: n.p., 1820.

Irving, Pierre, *The Life and Letters of Washington Irving.* 3 vols. New York: G. P. Putnam's Sons, 1869.

Irving, Washington, *The Works of Washington Irving.* 12 vols. New York: G. P. Putnam's Sons, 1883.

Irwin, R. W., *The Diplomatic Relations of the United States with the Barbary Powers, 1776–1816.* Chapel Hill, N.C.: University of North Carolina Press, 1931.

James, Marquis, *Andrew Jackson: The Border Captain.* New York: The Literary Guild, 1933.

———, *Andrew Jackson: Portrait of a President.* Indianapolis, New York: Bobbs-Merrill Company, 1937.

James, William, *A Full and Correct Account of the Chief Naval Occurrences of the Late War between Great Britain and the United States of America.* London: T. Egerton, 1817.

———, *An Inquiry into the Merits of the Principal Naval Actions between Great Britain and the United States.* Halifax: Anthony H. Holland, 1816.

———, *The Naval History of Great Britain, from the Declaration of War by France, in February 1793, to the Accession of George IV, in January 1820.* 6 vols. London: Harding, Lepard, and Company, 1826.

Johnson, Irving, and Johnson, Electa, "Lost World of the Galapagos." *National Geographic,* 115, No. 5 (May 1959).

Kaufmann, William W., *British Policy and the Independence of Latin America, 1804–1828.* New Haven: Yale University Press, 1951.

Keller, William F., *The Nation's Advocate: Henry Marie Brackenridge and Young America.* Pittsburgh: University of Pittsburgh Press, 1956.

Kitson, Arthur, *Captain James Cook, R.N., F.R.S.; "The Navigator."* New York: E. P. Dutton & Company, 1907.

Knox, Dudley W., *A History of the United States Navy.* New York: G. P. Putnam's Sons, 1936, 1948.

Lande, Irvin M., "War by the Pen: Some Intellectual and Propagandistic Aspects of the Chilean Struggle for Independence, 1808–1820." Ph.D. dissertation, Northwestern University, 1956.

Levasseur, A., *Lafayette in America in 1824 and 1825; or, Journal of a Voyage to the United States.* 2 vols. Philadelphia: Carey and Lea, 1829.

Levene, Ricardo, *A History of Argentina*. Translated and edited by William Spence Robertson. Chapel Hill, N.C.: University of North Carolina Press, 1937.

Lewis, Charles L., *Admiral Franklin Buchanan: Fearless Man of Action*. Baltimore: The Norman, Remington Company, 1929.

———, *David Glasgow Farragut: Admiral in the Making*. Annapolis: United States Naval Institute, 1941.

———, "Reuben James or Daniel Frazier." *Maryland Historical Magazine*, 19, No. 1 (March 1924).

———, *The Romantic Decatur*. Philadelphia: University of Pennsylvania Press, 1937.

Lewis, Michael, *A Social History of the Navy, 1793–1815*. London: George Allen & Unwin, 1960.

Leyda, Jay, *The Melville Log: A Documentary Life of Herman Melville, 1819–1891*. 2 vols. New York: Harcourt, Brace and Company, 1951.

Linton, Ralph, "Marquesan Culture," in Kardiner, Abram, *The Individual and His Society*. New York: Columbia University Press, 1939.

Lloyd, Christopher, *Lord Cochrane: Seaman—Radical—Liberator: A Life of Thomas, Lord Cochrane, 10th Earl of Dundonald*. London: Longmans, Green and Company, 1947.

Logan, Rayford W., *The Diplomatic Relations Between the United States and Haiti, 1776–1891*. Chapel Hill, N.C.: University of North Carolina Press, 1941.

London, Jack, *The Cruise of the Snark*. New York: The Macmillan Co., 1918.

Lossing, Benson J., *The Pictorial Field-Book of the War of 1812; or illustrations by pen & pencil, of the history, biography, scenery, relics and traditions of the last war for American independence*. New York: Harper and Brothers, 1869.

Lyon, George F., *Journal of a Residence and Tour in the Republic of Mexico in the Year 1826*. 2 vols. London: John Murray, 1828.

Macdonough, Rodney, *Life of Commodore Thomas Macdonough*. Boston: Fort Sill Press, 1909.

Mackenzie, Alexander S., *The Life of Commodore Oliver Hazard Perry*. 2 vols. New York: Harper and Brothers, 1840.

Maclay, Edgar S., *A History of American Privateers*. New York, London: D. Appleton and Company, 1924.

———, *History of the Navy from 1775 to 1893*. 2 vols. New York: D. Appleton and Company, 1894.

Macy, Obed, *The History of Nantucket; being a Compendious Account of the First Settlement of the Island by the English, together with the Rise and Progress of the Whale Fishery; and other historical Facts Relative to said island and its inhabitants*. 2d ed. Mansfield, Mass.: Macy & Pratt, 1880.

Magner, James A., *Men of Mexico*. Milwaukee: Bruce Publishing Company, 1942.

Mahan, Alfred T., *Admiral Farragut*. New York: D. Appleton and Company, 1898.

BIBLIOGRAPHY

————, *Sea Power in Its Relations to the War of 1812.* 2 vols. Boston: Little, Brown, and Company, 1905.

Malcomb-Smith, E. F., *The Life of Stratford Canning.* London: Ernest Benn, 1933.

Manning, William R., "British Influence in Mexico, 1822–1826," in Henry M. Stephens and Herbert E. Bolton, eds., *The Pacific Ocean in History.* New York: Macmillan Company, 1917.

————, *Early Diplomatic Relations between the United States and Mexico.* Baltimore: The Johns Hopkins Press, 1916.

Marshall, John, *Royal Naval Biography; or Memoirs of the services of all the flag officers, superannuated rear-admirals, retired-captains, post-captains and commanders; whose names appeared on the Admiralty list of Sea Officers at the Commencement of the year 1823, or who have since been promoted.* 12 vols. London: Longman, Hurst, Rees, Orme, Brown, and Green, 1823–1835.

Martin, Francois-Xavier, *The History of Louisiana from the Earliest Period.* 2 vols. New-Orleans: Lyman and Beardslee, 1827.

Martin, John H., *Chester (and its Vicinity) Delaware County in Pennsylvania; with Genealogical Sketches of some old families.* Philadelphia: Wm. H. Pile, 1877.

Martin, Michael R., and Lovett, Gabriel H., *An Encyclopedia of Latin-American History.* New York and London: Abelard-Schuman, 1956.

Mayo, Bernard, *Henry Clay: Spokesman of the New West.* Boston: Houghton Mifflin Company, 1937.

McCaleb, Walter F., *The Aaron Burr Conspiracy.* New York: Dodd, Mead and Company, 1903.

McMaster, James B., *A History of the People of the United States from the Revolution to the Civil War.* 6 vols. New York: D. Appleton and Company, 1895.

Melville, Herman, *Typee, A Peep at Polynesian Life.* New York: Washington Square Press, 1962 ed.

Menard, Wilmon, "A Forgotten South Sea Paradise." *Asia,* 33 (September 1933).

Merk, Frederick, "The Genesis of the Oregon Question." *Mississippi Valley Historical Review,* 36, No. 4 (March 1950).

Moorehead, Alan, *The Fatal Impact: An Account of the Invasion of the South Pacific, 1767–1840.* New York: Harper & Row, 1966.

Morison, Samuel E., *The Maritime History of Massachusetts, 1783–1860.* Sentry Edition. Boston: Houghton Mifflin Company, 1961.

Morrell, W. P., *Britain in the Pacific Islands.* Oxford: Clarendon Press, 1963.

Mugridge, Donald H., "The United States Sanitary Commission in Washington, 1861–1865," *Records of the Columbia Historical Society,* 1960–1962.

Neeser, Robert W., *Statistical and Chronological History of the United States Navy, 1775–1907.* New York: Macmillan Company, 1909.

New England Historical and Genealogical Register. Vols. 17 (1863), 23 (1869), 30 (1876), 33 (1879). Albany, Boston: J. Munsell.

Nicholas, William H., "American Pathfinders in the Pacific." *National Geographic,* 89, No. 5 (May 1946).

Nolan, J. Bennett, *Lafayette in America Day by Day*. Baltimore: The Johns Hopkins Press, 1934.

O'Brien, Frederick, *White Shadows in the South Seas*. New York: Century Company, 1921.

O'Connor, Harvey, *The Astors*. New York: Alfred A. Knopf, 1941.

Paine, Ralph D., *Joshua Barney: A Forgotten Hero of Blue Water*. New York & London: Century Company, 1924.

———, *The Fight for a Free Sea: A Chronicle of the War of 1812*. Vol. 17 of The Chronicles of America Series, Allen Johnson, editor. New Haven: Yale University Press, 1920.

———, *The Ships and Sailors of Old Salem*. Chicago: A. C. McClury & Company, 1912.

Parkes, Henry B., *A History of Mexico*. 3d rev. ed. Boston: Houghton Mifflin Company, 1960.

Parton, Dorothy M., *The Diplomatic Career of Joel Roberts Poinsett*. Washington, D.C.: Catholic University of America, 1934.

Parton, James, *Life of Andrew Jackson*. 3 vols. New York: Mason Brothers, 1860.

Pattee, Fred L., *The Poems of Philip Freneau: Poet of the American Revolution*. 3 vols. Princeton, N.J.: The University Library, 1907.

Paulding, James K., *The Bulls and the Jonathans; comprising John Bull and Brother Jonathan and John Bull in America*. New York: Charles Scribner and Company, 1867.

Paullin, Charles O., *Commodore John Rodgers, Captain, Commodore, and Senior Officer of the American Navy, 1773–1838*. Cleveland: The Arthur H. Clark Company, 1910.

———, *Diplomatic Negotiations of American Naval Officers, 1778–1883*. Baltimore: The Johns Hopkins Press, 1912.

———, "The Father of Admiral Farragut." *The Louisiana Historical Quarterly*, 13, No. 1 (January 1930). In *Naval Pamphlets*, 138, United States Naval Academy Library.

Paxson, Frederick L., *The Independence of the South-American Republics: A Study in Recognition and Foreign Policy*. Philadelphia: Ferris & Leach, 1903.

Perkins, Bradford, *Prologue to War: England and the United States, 1805–1812*. Berkeley and Los Angeles: University of California Press, 1963.

Perkins, Dexter, *The Monroe Doctrine, 1823–1826*. Cambridge, Mass.: Harvard University Press, 1932.

———, *The Monroe Doctrine, 1826–1867*. Baltimore: The Johns Hopkins Press, 1933.

Perkins, Samuel, *Historical Sketches of the United States, from the Peace of 1815 to 1830*. New York: S. Converse, 1830.

Pine, John C., "The Role of United States Special Agents in the Development of a Spanish American Policy, 1810–1822." Ph.D. dissertation, University of Colorado, 1955.

Porter, David Dixon, *Memoir of Commodore David Porter of the United States Navy*. Albany: J. Munsell, 1875.

Porter, Kenneth W., *John Jacob Astor: Business Man*. 2 vols. Cambridge, Mass.: Harvard University Press, 1931.

Pratt, Fletcher, *Preble's Boys: Commodore Preble and the Birth of American Sea Power*. New York: William Sloane Associates, 1950.

Preble, George H., "The First Cruise of the United States Frigate Essex." *Essex Institute Historical Collections*, 10, part 2. Salem, Mass.: Essex Institute Press, 1869.

Prentiss, Charles, *Life of the Late Gen. William Eaton; several years an officer in the United States Army, consul at the Regency of Tunis on the coast of Barbary, and commander of the Christian and other forces that marched from Egypt through the Desert of Barca in 1805, principally collected from his correspondence and other manuscripts*. Brookfield, Mass.: E. Merriam, 1813.

Priestley, Herbert I., *The Mexican Nation, a History*. New York: Macmillan Company, 1923.

Pumpelly, Josiah C., "Mahlon Dickerson of New Jersey." *Proceedings of the New Jersey Historical Society*, Second Series, 11 (1890–1891).

Putnam, Herbert E., *Joel Roberts Poinsett: a Political Biography*. Washington, D.C.: Mimeoform Press, 1935.

Quarterly Review, 13 (July 1815), London.

Ramsay, David, *History of the United States from Their First Settlement as English Colonies in 1607 to the Year 1808*. 3 vols. Philadelphia: M. Carey, 1817.

Riesenberg, Felix, *Cape Horn*. New York: Dodd, Mead & Company, 1939.

Rippy, J. Fred, *Joel R. Poinsett, Versatile American*. Durham, N.C.: Duke University Press, 1935.

———, *Rivalry of the United States and Great Britain over Latin America*. Baltimore: The Johns Hopkins Press, 1929.

Rives, George L., *The United States and Mexico, 1821–1848*. 2 vols. New York: Charles Scribner's Sons, 1913.

Roberts, W. Adolphe, *The U.S. Navy Fights*. Indianapolis, New York: Bobbs-Merrill Company, 1942.

Robertson, James, ed., *Louisiana Under the Rule of Spain, France, and the United States, 1785–1807*. 2 vols. Cleveland: Arthur H. Clark Company, 1911.

Robertson, William S., *Rise of the Spanish-American Republics as Told in the Lives of their Liberators*. New York, London: D. Appleton and Company, 1930.

Robinson, Fayette, *Mexico and Her Military Chieftains, From the Revolution of Hidalgo to the present time. Comprising sketches of the lives of Hidalgo, Morelos, Iturbide, Santa Anna, Gomez, Farias, Bustamente, Paredes, Almonte, Arista, Alaman, Ampudia, Herrera and De la Vega*. Hartford: Silas Andrews & Son, 1848.

Rodd, Francis R., *General William Eaton; the Failure of an Idea*. New York: Milton, Balch and Company, 1932.

Romero, Matias, *Mexico and the United States: A Study of Subjects Affecting their Political, Commercial, and Social Relations, Made with a View to their Promotion.* 2 vols. New York and London: G. P. Putnam's Sons, 1898.

Roosevelt, Theodore, *The Naval War of 1812.* New York: G. P. Putnam's Sons, 1882.

Rydell, Raymond A., *Cape Horn to the Pacific: the Rise and Decline of an Ocean Highway.* Berkeley: University of California Press, 1952.

Scharf, John Thomas, *The Chronicles of Baltimore; being a Complete History of "Baltimore town" and Baltimore city from the earliest period to the Present Time.* Baltimore: Turnbull Brothers, 1874.

Sears, Louis M., *Jefferson and the Embargo.* Durham, N.C.: Duke University Press, 1927.

Seitz, Don C., *Famous American Duels.* New York: Thomas Y. Crowell Company, 1929.

Shapiro, Harry L., "Les Iles Marquises." *Natural History,* Part I ("History of Contact"), 67 (April 1958); Part II ("Prehistory"), 67 (May 1958).

Sheean, George M., "A Study of Polynesian Agriculture: Part One: A Compilation of the Available Information Pertaining to the Marquesas Islands of the South Seas." Mimeographed mss., n.d., Peabody Museum, Salem, Mass.

Sherman, William R., *The Diplomatic and Commercial Relations of the United States and Chile, 1820–1914.* Boston: Richard G. Badger, 1926.

Shevill, Ferdinand, *The History of the Balkan Peninsula.* New York: Harcourt, Brace and Company, 1922.

Shreve, Royal O., *The Finished Scoundrel: General James Wilkinson, Sometime Commander-in-Chief of the United States Army, who made Intrigues a Trade and Treason a Profession.* Indianapolis: Bobbs-Merrill Company, 1933.

Sinclair, Harold, *The Port of New Orleans.* Garden City, N.Y.: Doubleday, Doran, & Company, 1942.

Smith, Justin H., "Poinsett's Career in Mexico." *Proceedings of the American Antiquarian Society,* New Series, 24 (8 April to 21 October 1914).

Snider, Charles H., Jr., *The Glorious "Shannon's" Old Blue Duster and Other Faded Flags of Fadeless Fame.* Toronto: McClelland & Stewart, 1923.

Soley, James R., *Admiral Porter.* New York: D. Appleton and Company, 1903.

Spears, John R., *David G. Farragut.* Philadelphia: George W. Jacobs & Company, 1905.

———, *The History of Our Navy from its Origins to the Present Day, 1775–1895.* 5 vols. New York: Charles Scribner's Sons, 1897–1899.

Sprout, Harold, and Sprout, Margaret, *The Rise of American Naval Power, 1776–1918.* Princeton, N.J.: Princeton University Press, 1939.

Stackpole, Edouard A., *The Sea-Hunters: New England Whalemen during Two Centuries, 1635–1835.* Philadelphia: J. B. Lippincott Company, 1953.

Starbuck, Alexander, "History of the American Whale Fishery from its Earliest Inception to the Year 1876," United States Commission of Fish and Fisheries. *Report of the Commissioner for 1875–1876.* Washington, D.C.: United States Government Printing Office, 1878.

———, *The History of Nantucket: County, Island, and Town.* Boston: C. E. Goodspeed & Company, 1924.

———, unpublished notes on "Nantucket and the War of 1812," Nantucket Whaling Museum Library.

Stavrianos, L. S., *The Balkans Since 1453.* New York: Rinehart & Company, 1958.

Stevenson, W. B., *Historical and Descriptive Narrative of Twenty Years Residence in South America.* 3 vols. London: Longman, Rees, Orme, Brown, and Green, 1829.

Stillé, Charles J., "The Life and Services of Joel R. Poinsett." *The Pennsylvania Magazine of History and Biography,* 12, Nos. 2 and 3 (1888).

Straub, Joseph F., "José Miguel Carrera." Ph.D. dissertation, University of Illinois, 1953.

Strauss, Wallace P., "Early American Interest and Activity in Polynesia, 1783–1842." Ph.D. dissertation, Columbia University, 1958.

Streeter, Gilbert L., "Historical Sketch of the Building of the Frigate Essex of Salem and Her Subsequent Fate." *Proceedings of Essex Institute,* 20, (1856).

Stuart, Graham H., *Latin America and the United States.* 5th ed., New York: Appleton-Century-Crofts Company, 1955.

Suggs, Robert C., *The Hidden Worlds of Polynesia: The Chronicle of an Archaeological Expedition to Nuku Hiva in the Marquesas Islands.* New York: Harcourt, Brace & World, 1962.

Thomson, John L., *Historical Sketches of the Late War between the United States and Great Britain.* 5th ed., *greatly enlarged and improved.* Philadelphia: Thomas DeSilver, 1816.

Tucker, Glenn, *Dawn Like Thunder: The Barbary Wars and the Birth of the U.S. Navy.* Indianapolis: Bobbs-Merrill Company, 1963.

———, *Poltroons and Patriots: A Popular Account of the War of 1812.* 2 vols. Indianapolis and New York: Bobbs-Merrill Company, 1954.

Tully, Andrew, *When They Burned the White House.* New York: Simon and Shuster, 1961.

Turnbull, Archibald D., *Commodore David Porter, 1780–1843.* New York and London: The Century Company, 1929.

United States Navy, Office of the Chief of Naval Operations, Naval History Division, *American Fighting Ships.* 2 vols. Washington, D.C.: United States Government Printing Office, 1963.

Villard, Henry S., *Libya: the New Arab Kingdom of North Africa.* Ithaca, N.Y.: Cornell University Press, 1956.

Wada, Teijuhn, *American Foreign Policy towards Japan during the 19th Century.* Tokyo: The Tokyo Bunko, 1928.

Wandell, Samuel H., and Minnigerode, Meade, *Aaron Burr.* 2 vols. New York and London: G. P. Putnam's Sons, 1925.

Ward, Henry George, *Mexico.* 2d ed., enlarged. 2 vols. London: Henry Colburn, 1829.

Warden, David B., *A Chorographical and Statistical Description of the District of Columbia*. Paris: printed by Smith, 1816.

Watson, Paul B., *The Tragic Career of Commodore James Barron*. New York: Coward-McCann, 1942.

Wayland, John C., *The Pathfinder of the Seas: the Life of Matthew Fontaine Maury*. Richmond, Va.: Garrett & Massie, 1930.

West, Richard S., Jr., *The Second Admiral: a Life of David Dixon Porter, 1813–1891*. New York: Coward-McCann, 1937.

Westcott, Allan; Fredland, J. Roger; Jeffries, William W.; Kirk, Neville T.; McManus, Thomas F.; Potter, Elmer B.; and West, Richard S., Jr., *American Sea Power Since 1775*. Philadelphia: J. B. Lippincott Company, 1947.

Whipple, A. B. C., *Yankee Whalers in the South Seas*. Garden City, N.Y.: Doubleday & Company, 1954.

Whitaker, Arthur P., *The United States and the Independence of Latin America, 1800–1830*. Baltimore: The Johns Hopkins Press, 1941.

Williams, Frances L., *Matthew Fontaine Maury: Scientist of the Sea*. New Brunswick, N.J.: Rutgers University Press, 1963.

Williams, John S., *History of the Invasion and Capture of Washington, and of the Events which Preceded and Followed*. New York: Harper & Brothers, 1857.

Williams, Stanley T., *The Life of Washington Irving*. 2 vols. New York: Oxford University Press, 1935.

Willis, Nathaniel P., *Summer Cruise in the Mediterranean on Board an American Frigate*. Auburn and Rochester, N.Y.: Allen and Beardsley, 1856.

Wilson, Rufus R., *Washington: the Capital City and Its Part in the History of the Nation*. Philadelphia: J. B. Lippincott Company, 1902.

Wilson, Thomas, *The Biography of the Principal American Military and Naval Heroes; Comprehending Details of their achievements during the Revolutionary and Late Wars. Interspersed with Authentic Anecdotes not found in Any Other Work*. 2 vols. New-York: John Low, 1819.

Wiltse, Charles M., *John C. Calhoun: Nationalist, 1782–1828*. Indianapolis and New York: Bobbs-Merrill Company, 1944.

Winkler, John K., *The du Pont Dynasty*. New York: Reynal & Hitchcock, 1935.

Winsor, Justin, *Narrative and Critical History of America*. 8 vols. Boston and New York: Houghton Mifflin Company, 1888.

Wood, John, *The History of the Administration of John Adams, esq. Late President of the United States*. New-York: Naphtali Judah, 1802.

Wood, William, and Gabriel, Ralph H., *The Winning of Freedom*. Vol. 6 of The Pageant of America. New Haven: Yale University Press, 1927.

Wright, C. Q., "The Tripoli Monument." *United States Naval Institute Proceedings*, 48, No. 11 (November 1922).

Wriston, Henry M., *Executive Agents in American Foreign Relations*. Baltimore: The Johns Hopkins Press, 1929.